Health Education
Teaching Ideas:
SECONDARY

Revised Edition

Part I, Richard Loya, Editor

Part II, Loren B. Bensley, Jr., Editor

Sponsored by the
Association for the Advancement
of Health Education

an association of the

American Alliance for
Health, Physical Education,
Recreation and Dance

ISBN 0-88314-529-4

CONTENTS

PART I

Foreword to Part I, *Kathleen Middleton*   x

Focus on Process

1   Stress on Reading, *Elaine Hals*   1
2   Affective Evaluation Techniques in School Health Education,
        Mary S. Sutherland   2
3   Five Cures for Dull Health Curriculums, *Loren B. Bensley, Jr.*   5
4   Vary Your Teaching Methods, *Glen G. Gilbert*   7
5   Films for Effective Affective Teaching, *James R. Mullen*   9
6   Effective Teaching: Variety in the Classroom, *Mary Sutherland and
        William Hemmer*   10
7   Health Science Fairs, *Henry A. Lasch*   14
8   The Open Contract--A Program of Individualized Study, *B.E. Pruitt*   16
9   The Many Faces of Role Playing, *Lynn Teper-Singer*   18
10 Extra Credit--Make It Meaningful, *George F. Carter*   20
11 Promoting Experiential Learning, *Michael Hamrick and Carolyn Stone*   21
12 The Hospital as Motivator for Health Learning, *Saul Ross*   25
13 Field Trips, *James H. Price*   27
14 Health Games   28
15 Health Games, Simulations, and Activities, *David E. Corbin and
        David A. Sleet*   29
16 Learning Games   31
17 Horse Racing in the Classroom, *Phillip Hossler*   33
18 Fantasy Games, *Ralph Bates*   34
19 Choices, *Lynn Teper-Singer*   35
20 Constructing an Educational Game, *Sally L. Easterbrook*   36
21 Health 4 Fun: A Game of Knowledge, *Raymond Nakamura*   37
22 School Health Bee, *Bernard S. Krasnow*   38
23 Not Merely Nostalgia, *Ralph Edwards*   39
24 Health in Concert, *Clay Williams and Judy Scheer*   40
25 Tuning in to Health Education, *Warren L. McNab*   41
26 Ideas for Successful Health Teaching, *Loren B. Bensley, Jr.*   42
27 The Student Interview Technique, *Marc E. Meyer*   44
28 Positive Peer Influence: School-Based Prevention, *Aida K. Davis,
        Joan M. Weener, and Robert E. Shute*   45
29 Ernie, *Lillian D. Fesperman*   49

Focus on Content

Addictive Behaviors

30	Empathizing with Addicts, *Peter Finn*	53
31	How Much Can I Drink? *H. Richard Travis*	55
32	Senator Hogwash, *Michael Young*	58
33	Student-to-Student Teaching About Tobacco Smoking, *Lorraine J. Henke*	57
34	The Smoking Game, *Ian Newman*	59
35	Making Tobacco Education Relevant to the School-Age Child, *John R. Seffrin*	63
36	A Humanistic-Individualized Approach to Drug Education, *Jerry L. Greene and Phillip G. Huntsinger*	68
37	Drug Use Situations, *Bruce A. Uhrich*	69
38	Chemically Dependent--But Only for One Week, *Kathleen Fischer*	70
39	Learning by Teaching, *Elaine Hals*	72

Aging

40	Aging: A Need for Sensitivity, *Kenneth A. Briggs*	73
41	Picnic in the Park: Humanizing an Aging Unit in a Personal Health Class, *Michael J. Gaeta*	75

Consumer Health

42	Health Anagrams, *Kathleen M. Siegwarth*	78
43	Consumer Wellness, One School's Approach, *Jon W. Hisgen*	79
44	A Healthy Consumer Health Class, *Tom McFarland and Ann Rudrauff*	81
45	The Teenage Consumer, *Lee Ann Larson*	82
46	Crisis Hot Line Experience, *Aloysius J. Jangl*	84
47	Health Help Phone Numbers, *Richard C. Hohn*	86
48	Students Can Have a Say, *Joan L. Bergy and Barney Hantunen*	87

Death and Dying

49	A Unit for Independent Study in Death Education, *Joan D. McMahon*	89
50	Put a Little Life in Your Death, *Charles R. O'Brien*	94
51	Death Education: An Integral Part of School Health Education, *Darrel Lang*	95
52	A Teaching Strategy on Tragedy, *Connie Jo Dobbelaere*	97

Environmental Health

53	Health or Hazard? A Post-China Syndrome Game, *Moon S. Chen, Jr.*	99
54	Nuclear Power Debate, *Bruce G. Morton*	100

55 Health and Safety Education from the Trash Can, *J. Clay Williams and Judith K. Scheer* 101
56 Ecology Games, *Ronald W. Hyatt* 103
57 Guidelines for a Recycling Project, *George H. Brooks* 105

Family Life

58 Easy Ways of Getting into Trouble When Teaching Sex Education, *Glen G. Gilbert* 107
59 Three Teaching Strategies, *Florence J. Snarski and Cecilia A. Lynch* 109
60 The Implementation of Contraceptive Education, *Warren L. McNab* 111
61 Pregnancy--A Gaming Technique, *Edward T. Turner* 112
62 Contraception-Abortion Lifeline, *Glenn E. Richardson* 114
63 Teaching Students About Their Future Role as Parents, *Jan Young* 115
64 Ask the Students Themselves, *A. Gordon Bennett* 117
65 Test Tube Considerations, *Deborah A. Dunn* 118
66 Selected Impacts of Contraception on Man and/or Society, *Patrick Kidd Tow* 119

Mental Health

70 On the Level, *Gus T. Dalis* 126
71 Perceptions of Me, *Jerrold S. Greenberg* 129
72 Enhancing Positive Self-Concept Through Creativity in the Classroom, *Barbara Beier* 131
73 Ideas from a Class in Interpersonal Relations, *Caroll Kaiser* 132
74 Role Playing as a Tool in Mental Health Education, *Lynn Teper* 134
75 The Mirror Game, *Rosa Sullivan* 136
76 How to Cope with Stress in the Classroom, *Charles C. Davis* 137
77 Coping with Violence, *Elaine Hals* 139
78 Personality Spokes, *Rosa Sullivan* 140
79 About Yourself, *Ruth C. Engs* 141
80 A Lesson on Stress, *Janet H. Shirreffs* 142
81 Mental Health Auctioning Strategy, *Patrick Kidd Tow* 144
82 People Labeling Strategy, *Patrick K. Tow and Hal Wingard* 145

Nutrition

83 Creative Food Labels: Consumer Health Education, *Moon S. Chen, Jr.* 146
84 Sensible Dieting, *Marilyn Mudgett and Dorothy Culjat* 147

PART II

Foreword to Part II, *Loren B. Bensley*   150

Focus on Process

85   The Writing Process in Health Class, *Vicki Steinberg and Teresa M. Fry*   153

86   Logo-Mania: Creative Health Art, *Frank Calsbeek*   155

87   Overcoming Xenophobia: Learning To Accept Differences,
        Judith A. Baker   157

88   Factors Important in Teaching Controversial Issues, *Ansa Ojanlatva*   159

89   Teaching About Authoring Systems: Instructional Design Tools for
        Health Education, *Paul D. Sarvela and Marilyn J. Karaffa*   161

90   Tic-Tac-Toe, *Mary Lawler*   163

91   Picture Charades: A Health Teaching Device, *Richard T. Mackey*   165

92   Drawing Interpretations of Health, *Vicki L. Cleaver*   166

93   Using Team Games to Teach Health, *Mark A. Croson and RoseAnn Benson*   167

94   The Concept of Health and Techniques of Conceptual Analysis,
        Joseph E. Balog   169

95   The Town Council Meeting: Decision Making Through a Large Group
        Role Play, *James D. Brown*   172

96   The Health Reporter Pool, *David Wiley*   173

97   Health Education Supermarket, *Mary S. Sutherland*   174

98   Health Education to the Third Power (Cubed?), *Susan Cross Lipnickey*   175

99   Junior High School Students as Facilitators of Elementary School Health
        Education Carnivals, *David K. Hosick and Parris R. Watts*   177

100   Thinking and Writing: A Strategy for Teaching Positive Health
        Decision Making, *Paul Villas*   180

101   Personal Health Via Community Health, *Linda Olasov*   181

102   Using College Students as Senior Peer Teachers in Youth-to-Youth
        Health Education, *Anthony G. Adcock*   183

103   Judgments Required from the Residency Coordinator, *William N. Washington*   185

104   A Community Resource Class Assignment, *Ansa Ojanlatva*   188

105   Evaluating Health News, *Michele J. Hawkins*   190

106   The Classics of Epidemiology: A Critical Thinking Approach,
        Wesley E. Hawkins   192

107   Discipline: A Parenting Dilemma, *Patrick K. Tow and Warren L. McNab*   194

108   Counterbalancing Parental Concerns in Health Education,
        Lorraine G. Davis and Shirley Holder Hazlett   197

109   Incorporating Health Education Competencies into a Content Course:
        The Disease Guidebook Project, *Joanna Hayden*   199

110   Politics and Health, *Randall R. Cottrell*   201

Focus on Content

Addiction

111 Inoculating Students Against Using Smokeless Tobacco,
Melody Powers Noland and Richard S. Riggs   205

112 The 12 Puffs of Christmas, *Warren McNab*   208

113 Drive-A-Teen--A Program to Prevent Drinking & Driving, *Susan Willey Spalt*   209

114 Analyzing Cigarette Smoke, *David M. White and Linda H. Rudisill*   211

115 Promoting a Natural High, *Catherine J. Paskert*   213

116 Alcoholics Anonymous: The Utilization of Social Experience in the
Classroom, *Robert G Yasko*   215

117 "Can a Bike Run on Beer," *Melvin H. Ezell, Jr.*   217

118 Once Upon a Synapse: A Drug Education Simulation in Three Acts,
William M. London   219

119 Investigating the Social Aspects of Alcohol Use, *Tom V. Savage*   222

120 Drug Use, Misuse and Abuse as Presented in Movies, *Kerry J. Redican,
Barbara L. Redican, and Charles R. Baffi*   224

121 Learning About Alcohol Drinking Attitudes and Motivations by
Examining the Vocabulary of Drunkenness, *William M. London*   226

Aging

122 Helping College Students Understand the Older Adult, *Margaret J. Pope*   228

123 As Old as Trees, *Glenn E. Richardson and Susan Bicknell*   229

Chronic Diseases

124 Digging for Healthy Hearts: A Simulated Archaeological Dig for the
Prevention of Cardiovascular Disease, *Wesley E. Hawkins*   230

125 Cancer: A Mini-Documentary, *Stephen C. Corey*   233

Consumer Health

126 Consumer Health: Medical Quackery, *Carolyn E. Cooper*   235

Environmental Health

127 Environmental Health Simulations: Island City and Production,
Glenn E. Richardson, Alan Burns, and Janet Falcone   237

Family Life Education

128 Reducing Anxiety About Teaching a Human Sexuality Program,
Louise Rowling   239

129 Are You Ready for Prime Time Birth Control? *Pamela Wild and Linda Berne* 240
130 "Hey! How Did That Baby Live in That Test Tube?" *David A. Birch* 242
131 Actions Teach Better Than Words: Teen Life Theater and Role Play in
         Sex Education, *Peggy Brick* 243
132 Abortion Attitude Scale, *Linda A. Sloan* 247
133 Marriage Yesterday and Today, *Margaret J. Pope* 249
134 Teaching Abstinence to Today's Teens, *Dee Gibbs Smalley* 250
135 Group Discussion on Contraceptive Issues, *Barbara A. Rienzo* 252
136 Developing and Rejuvenating Relationships, *Jane W. Lammers* 254
137 Courtesies and Rights Within Relationships, *Bethann Cinelli and Robert Nye* 256

First Aid and Safety

138 CPR Drilling Revisited, *Mark J. Kittleson* 258
139 The Improvised Manikin--Homemade CPR Equipment, *Mardie E. Burckes* 260
140 Teaching the Four Cs of First Aid, *Mark J. Kittleson* 264
141 Mock Disaster: An Effective Lesson in Preparation for the Real Thing,
         Gary M. English and Cathie G. Stivers 263
142 The Importance of Child Safety Seat Education, *Karen D. Liller* 266

HIV-AIDS

143 AIDS "To Tell the Truth" Gaming Activity, *Jon W. Hisgen* 268
144 AIDS/HIV Teaching Ideas, *Barbara Beier, J. Leslie Oganowski,
         Richard A. Detert, and Kenneth Becker* 271

Mental and Emotional Health

145 Stress Manifestations Among Adolescents, *Charles Regin* 274
146 An Introductory Activity for Adolescent Communication and Intimacy,
         G. Greg Wojtowicz 276
147 Show and Tell: Developing an Appreciation of Diversity, *Kathryn Rolland* 279
148 Teaching Self-Awareness Through Idiosyncrasies, *Patrick K. Tow,
         Beverly Johnson, and Patricia N. Smith* 280

Nutrition

149 Can You Name These Foods? *Eileen L. Daniel* 282
150 "Digesting" Health Information, *Richard A. Crosby* 283
151 Nutrition Is the Name of the Game, *Paula R. Zaccone* 284

Personal Health

152 Sun Smart: A Peer-Led Lesson on the Effects of Tanning and Sunning on
         the Skin, *Mary Elesha-Adams and David M. White* 288
153 A Quick and Easy Check for Foot Problems, *Dianne Boswell O'Brien* 290

PART I

Foreword

Where is *health* taught at the secondary level? In the elementary school it is usually taught by the elementary teacher along with twenty or so other subjects. In the junior and senior high schools it can be found in many places: health classes; science classes; family living classes; social science classes; home economics classes; and drivers' education classes. In the school district where I taught, it was found in one high school in a class entitled "State Requirements." This unique class included all the "loose end" topics that were required by the State of California to be covered before high school graduation.

Wherever health is taught in the schools, the ultimate success with students is not determined by the title of the class or placement within the curriculum. It is largely dependent upon the quality of the teaching. *Health* can be the most exciting, interesting, and meaningful class in the high school curriculum. Dedicated, energetic, caring teachers do make a difference. Talented teachers can motivate and positively affect the lives of the most gifted students as well as the ones with special problems. This book, *Health Education Teaching Ideas: Secondary,* is for those teachers. It includes innovative teaching strategies that are practical and appropriate in the secondary classroom. The original articles appeared in the "Teaching Ideas" column of *Health Education* and were compiled by a high school health teacher. This book should be a useful and exciting addition to the library of any instructor responsible for health education at the junior and senior high school levels.

Kathleen Middleton, *Director*
School Health Programs
National Center for Health Education
and Contributing Editor to
"Teaching Ideas" column of
Health Education

Focus on Process

Stress on Reading

ELAINE HALS is a teacher of health education at South Shore High School, Brooklyn, New York 11236.

In the last few years large cities throughout the United States have begun to put pressure on school districts to stress the "three R's"—more reading, more math, and more writing. In New York City, where I teach, all of the principals have been instructed to increase the number of periods per week devoted to reading and other basics in the elementary schools. The high schools have been instructed that all subject areas give reading and written homework several times weekly, and that course curriculum should stress the basics. Employers have also been pressuring the schools to improve the reading ability of their graduates. The push is now on to raise the basic skills level of today's youth.

How does this push for basics affect us as health educators? Do we regress to predominantly cognitive teaching? Do we return to stressing facts, and only those things that can be read, written, and tested? About ten years ago health educators began to realize the importance of humanistic values and behavior modification that could be accomplished in health teaching. Our field has seen positive changes, and we have shifted our emphasis into the affective domain. Health education has truly become learning for living—examination of values, decision making, and behavioral alternatives. If we help young people become better, healthier, and more aware, but do not help them to read better, are we in line with the educational goals of the country? Should we be? The pendulum has swung back to pre-1960s education. Should we as health educators re-evaluate our goals, and fall in line with other subject areas? Reading and writing are important; I do not mean to demean their significance. Young people entering the job market must have basic skills in order to survive.

Because both affective and cognitive education are valuable, I feel that we as health educators must combine them in our teaching. Following you will find a few suggestions.

1. Help students to explore new and controversial health issues by having them read and evaluate current newspaper and magazine articles on various subjects—laetrile, cloning, test tube babies, food additives, new drugs, disease cures.

2. Have students keep a written log (to be checked by the teacher periodically) of feelings about the class, their daily decisions, new material learned, or anything the teacher feels is relevant to the class and the students.

3. Have students keep their own vocabulary list of new words learned in class or from text, pamphlets or other reading sources.

4. Have students write letters requesting information, pamphlets, interviews.

5. Offer reading lists of novels, magazines, etc. for outside projects or just additional information.

6. Give students controversial problems for homework and have them write answers that can later be discussed in class and even made into role playing situations.

> Your parents catch you and your friends smoking grass in your room, what would you do?
> You are caught cheating on an exam and the teacher wants to see your parents.

You find that you have venereal disease—your boy or girl friend may have it, too—what do you do?
Do the terminally ill have the right to know they are dying?
You know something that could get your best friend in trouble. You feel what this person did was wrong. You are going to be questioned about the situation. What will you do?

7. Use pamphlets and current publications instead of, or in addition to, text books.

8. Divide class into groups. Have each group research and investigate different aspects of a subject and teach the class.

9. Creative projects that combine reading and writing with other disciplines such as art, photography, music.

10. Have class construct interviews or surveys, then have students survey or interview selected individuals and evaluate results.

Cognitive and affective can be made to work well together. We do not have to forsake our humanistic, affective approach to health education in order to help our students read and write better. Instead of changing the educational goals we have for our students, we should just add one more—a better knowledge of the basics and how they can help our students live better, healthier lives.

Affective Evaluation Techniques in School Health Education

Mary S. Sutherland is associate professor in the Department of Human Studies at Florida State University, Tallahassee, Florida 32306.

Affective measures of evaluation attempt to indicate how a person feels about an idea or subject. Krothwohl[1] in designing the affective taxonomy proposed various degrees of internalization of values, ranging through awareness, willingness to receive, controlled attention, acquiescence in responding, willingness to respond, satisfaction in response, acceptance of value, preference for a value, commitment, conceptualization of a value, preference for a value system, a generalized set, and finally characterization of a particular value. The continuum of affective responses is further divided into five main categories of internalization: receiving, responding, valuing, organization, and characterization.

The quote, "You are a product of every moment you have lived until today," will in part determine responses to any affective questions asked of individuals. Considering the varied backgrounds and experiences within any school population, effective measurement and evaluation in the affective domain can be difficult. Many individuals unfamiliar with the affective domain or attitudinal measurement, have opined that the schools are teaching specific teacher held values, instead of the valuing process. These individuals should be introduced to the above information as well as to the decision-making process, such as that popularized by Simon and used by many health educators in the classroom. Numerous methodologies have been proposed for the measurement of attitudes, some valid and reliable, others not. A sample listing follows of possible affective measurement techniques and appropriate examples of their application in health education. The techniques are presented in no particular order.

Thurston Attitude Scales

This is an equal-appearing-interval procedure that represents various strengths of feelings toward a given statement, objective, or situation. Each statement is weighted by judges to reflect degrees of feelings. The design of the instrument, in order to construct a valid and reliable scale, can be a time consuming process.

Directions: X = Disagree   L = Agree
Using these symbols on the exercise below, please indicate how you personally stand on the issues listed.

_____ 1. (1.5) Drug abusers are only hurting themselves.

_____ 2. (2.0) A poor self concept may lead to drug abuse.

_____ 3. (2.5) Inability to make decisions based on the consequences of the desired behavior may lead to drug abuse.

Likert Scale

One of the most widely used techniques is the Likert Scale. Statements are constructed with responses on a five point continuum of strongly agree, agree, undecided, disagree, and strongly disagree. The testee selects the answer that best describes his/her reaction to the situation.

Directions: Please circle your response to the following statements. Strongly agree = SA; Agree = A; Undecided = U; Disagree = D; Strongly disagree = SD.

1. People abuse drugs when they possess a poor self concept.
SA   A   U   D   SD
2. Excessive peer pressure may cause a person to abuse drugs.
SA   A   U   D   SD
3. Some drugs may serve a useful purpose.
SA   A   U   D   SD

Sort

Individuals are given sets of cards containing statements, traits, or pictures. They are then requested to sort these into piles according to their relative applicability, i.e. *most like me* to *least like me*. An example in a health course would be to distribute pictures of teenagers participating in various activities, and then to have the students indicate which are most and least applicable.

Forced Choice

Individuals are encouraged to select one of several given responses as an expression of their attitudes—similar to the interview technique described below, except that individuals are not asked specific questions.

Directions: Please indicate if you would choose the first option presented in the question, or the second.

1	2	Statements
_____	_____	1. I would rather be alone or with my friends.
_____	_____	2. I prefer to work individually or within small groups.
_____	_____	3. I would rather go to a movie or take a drive in the country.

Interview

The interview is a face-to-face encounter, in which the interviewer asks the testee specific questions. Little deviation from the questionnaire is allowed, except to clarify ambiguous answers.

1. Should drug abusers be encouraged to seek treatment or not to seek treatment?
2. Should drug abusers be encouraged to improve their self concepts, or maintain their present self concepts?
3. Should drug abusers improve decision-making processes, or continue present decision-making practices?

Rating Scales

Rating scales are similar to the Likert Scale, except that instead of using a standard set of options, specific adjective/verb describers are utilized:

Directions: Circle your response about drug abuses on the continuum

DRUG ABUSERS	Possess no self concept.	Possess a poor self concept.	Possess a good self concept.
DRUG ABUSERS	Find it very difficult to communicate.	Find it difficult to communicate.	Find it easy to communicate.
DRUG ABUSERS	Find it very difficult to make a decision.	Find it difficult to make a decision.	Find it easy to make a decision.

Rating scales can be developed with three to seven responses, using describers or single adjectives. The final form should depend on the particular purpose for the utilization of the instrument.

Semantic Differential

In this instrument concepts are measured in terms of evaluation (good-bad), potency (weak-strong), and activity (fast-slow). The respondent checks his response on the scale; the evaluation process assists in distinguishing differences between concepts and individual responses.

Directions: Place an X on the scale to indicate your feelings about each statement below.

ABUSING DRUGS IS:

Good	___	___	___	___	___	Bad
Foolish	___	___	___	___	___	Wise
Beneficial	___	___	___	___	___	Harmful

DRUGS CAN BE:

Good	___	___	___	___	___	Bad
Foolish	___	___	___	___	___	Wise
Beneficial	___	___	___	___	___	Harmful

Open-ended Questions

The open-ended question calls for the respondent to answer by writing statements which reflect an attitude, belief, activity or value. It can assist in measuring attitude structure and socialization.

1. Drug abusers should be encouraged to _____ .

2. Drug abuse is _____ .

3. A positive self concept is _____ .

Projected Techniques

Projected techniques are designed to reveal information about a person's deeper levels of feelings, and his reactions to a phenomenon via pictures. Generally given are the beginning, middle, and ending of a situation related to the pictures, from which the testee must be able to write a complete story.

Projected Behavior

Students are placed in a hypothetical situation and are requested to determine how they would behave under those circumstances.

Bob and Dan are friends of long standing. Bob tries to interest Dan in smoking a joint. Dan should:

a. Smoke the joint.
b. Refuse to take the joint.
c. Take the joint and later throw it away.
d. Take the joint and later smoke it in private.

Additional techniques to be utilized include check lists and ranking sheets, classroom teacher observations, anecdotal records (summaries of attitudes/behavior by the school staff), time sampling (what happened when), sociograms, social distance scales, guess-who questionnaires, and autobiographical sketches.

In contrasting and comparing the various methods utilized for attitude assessment, it is most necessary to establish a set and a setting for instrument utilization. Each of the abovementioned instruments can serve a valid and reliable purpose if applied correctly in the situation for which it was designed.

Affective measurement and evaluation techniques could be used for health instruction in many ways.

1. *To determine student behavioral information to assist in the removal of barriers to the efficient/effective functioning of the classroom educational process.* Specifically with the so-called behavioral problem student, cumulative records are useful to reinforce comments from anecdotal records and previous teacher time sample studies. A sociogram exercise conducted within the class determines the problem student's social status within his peer group; but more importantly, teachers and administrators should observe student attitude and behaviors for true indicators of causes of specific problems. In addition, a clue to behavioral problems is gained from a problem checklist and the professional psychological technique of a Q Sort described above. However, in the final analysis, the teacher must usually sit down with the problem student and communicate directly. The proper leading questions should serve to flush out information related to the true causes of the problem—is it lack of interest and motivation, poor self-concept, poor communication skills, uncomfortable environment or what? The causes of poor behavior can usually be determined by using one or a combination of affective techniques. An appropriate plan of action should be developed by the student, to change his behavior to a more acceptable level for the classroom.

2. *Health Instruction.* Many of these attitudinal devices find their best use in the area of classroom instruction. A Thurstone attitude scale takes considerable time to develop and field-test, but indicates most clearly differing degrees of feelings toward a topic or statement. If the health educator has time to computer-score results, the Likert scales are most useful to compare differences in attitudes. A modified version of the

Likert suits small group discussion activities, as do rating scales, ranking scales, checklists, open-ended sentences, projected behavior techniques and closed sentences directed towards specific behavioral objectives. Activities should be deliberately processed, so that principles of communication, self-concept and decision-making may be applied to specific health content areas. The abovementioned techniques are marvelous ways in which the class and teacher can get to know and appreciate each other, as well as marvelous stepping stones to effective teaching/learning. In summary, an affective technique can be a learning activity, a way of reinforcing and applying specific content covered, and lastly, can be one of many techniques to evaluate an effective health education program.

3. *Attitude Measurement.* The methods and techniques described above measure changing attitudes, both short term and long term. Instruments most helpful in measuring attitudes include Thurstone scales, Likert scales, rating scales, behavioral projected techniques, and behavioral practices checklists. Great attention should be paid to fakability, semantics, and criterion inadequacy. Is the student merely feeding to the teacher what the teacher wants to hear? Do the terms of questions and statements mean the same thing to the tester and the testee? Does the test really measure what it is supposed to?

4. *Evaluation of Classroom Learning.* Attitudinal devices such as open-ended sentences serve to indicate both teacher effectiveness or learning effectiveness. Specific open-ended questions might include:

A. Today I learned _____ .

B. Today I relearned _____ .

C. Today, I wish _____ .

In this manner the health educator gains insight into the student's evaluation of what is going on in the classroom.

In the final analysis, the setting as related to health education should determine the type of instrument used to obtain the most valid and reliable information possible for the most efficient/effective use of time and money for all concerned parties and purposes.

---

[1] J. Stanley and K. Hopkins. *Educational and psychological measurement and evaluation.* Englewood Cliffs, New Jersey, 1977, 229.

Five Cures for Dull Health Curriculums

LOREN B. BENSLEY, JR., is professor of health education, Central Michigan University, Mt. Pleasant, Michigan 48858.

The health education philosophies, concepts, and attitudes of the past are present in many of today's curriculums and are breeding irrelevant, dull, meaningless, distasteful classes in health education.

We are in a time of educational revolutions. Students are questioning our systems, curriculums, teacher qualifications, and pedagogy. They find themselves trapped in an educational system intent on turning them into mechanical robots; irrelevant curriculums combined with poor teachers are forced on them. Fortunately, educational systems are trying to change, but much of the change is no more than an attempt to refine the existing machinery, making it ever more efficient in pursuit of obsolete goals. Alvin Toffler, in his book *Future Shock*, suggests that "instead of assuming that every subject taught today is taught for a reason [we] should begin from the reverse premise: nothing should be included in a required curriculum unless it can be strongly justified in terms of the future. If this means scrapping a substantial part of the formal curriculum, so be it." [1]

Today millions of students are forced through health classes and exposed to meaningless experiences which will in no way result in favorable health behavior.

What evidence do we have to show the public that we are accomplishing our objectives? Will a student be a healthier citizen because of a course in health education?

It is time that we in health education produce results, not a collection of meaningless philosophical statements and purposes. In order to produce results two components must be integrated: a relevant curriculum and a creative and committed health educator. When these two components are plugged into each other, there will be generated electricity, excitement, enthusiasm, and vibrations in the student to turn him on to health learning. Only when the curriculum and the teacher are united will there be an illumination of the student. One without the other will result in total darkness. Unfortunately, much of our school health education has not had the proper electrical engineering to illuminate proper health attitudes and behaviors of our students.

Health education may not be as bleak as the author has presented it. Recent years have brought new insights and encouragement to curriculum development in health education. Approximately ten years ago we had a national school health education study. From this was devised a sophisticated curriculum based on the conceptual approach. About four years ago, the state of Connecticut did a comprehensive study on the health needs and interests of school children. Their document titled "Teach Us What We Want To Know" is extremely valuable in the hands of the health educator. Most of us are familiar with the efforts of New York State in designing a curriculum for their public schools. Their most recent adventure in computerized individualized instruction is certainly encouraging. The State of Michigan is presently developing a curriculum K through 14 in health education. From the most recent drug abuse crisis have resulted some excellent curriculums in this specific subject matter.

Health in Three Grades Only

These new efforts are encouraging; however, the relevance of some of the products that have been prepared are questionable. Take, for example, the school health education study curriculum produced by the 3M Company. The curriculum is so sophisticated and so complicated that 90% of our classroom teachers in Michigan are discouraged from using it. It cannot be said that it isn't a good piece of work; it is in fact a product of excellence. Unfortunately, it's not realistic. This author questions how realistic the K-12 concept is without trained health educators or health coordinators. Wouldn't it be better in health education to isolate three grade levels where health could be emphasized? I suggest that possibly health education be taught in the fourth, seventh, and eleventh grades.

I selected these grade levels because these are the ages where we can help our students develop desirable health behaviors. The nine-year-old has a keen interest in his body as well as in health in general. He shows excitement in learning about the function of his total being. The seventh-grader, on the other hand, is at the critical age in developing positive health behaviors. At age 12 he is confronted with decisions about whether or not he should smoke or experiment with alcohol or drugs. At this age secondary sex characteristics develop, which create a variety of physical and mental problems. The eleventh-grade student has reached the age of sophistication and needs information that will guide his behavior as an adult. He is now a health consumer and soon will be faced with health insurance decisions as well as a multitude of other alternatives. We must also realize that within three years at least half of the girls will be married.

New Names Can Be Magic

In a typical health course in the public schools, units have such titles as Mental Health, First Aid, Sex Education, Alcohol, Tobacco, Drugs and Narcotics, etc. The titles of these units themselves are enough to turn the students off to health. We were plagued for years with the term "hygiene" until the 1920s, when Sally Lucas Jean came up with the term "health education," indicating the change from hygiene teaching to behavior modification. I think the time has arrived when we, as health educators, can be more creative and original in making the appearance of our curriculum exciting to the learner. Just a change in titles of the units may turn a student on to health learning rather than turn him off from what he would anticipate as a dreadful experience. For instance, instead of calling a unit First Aid, why not title it Emergency Medical Care? Sex Education could be called Human Sexuality. A discussion of alcohol, tobacco, and drugs could be titled Mood Modifiers, or a mental health unit Psychic Ecology. The title of a unit should arouse the student's curiosity and create interest. A creative and dynamic curriculum begins with exciting topics.

Are there other topics not included in the traditional health curriculum which could make the course more relevant and prepare students to face future experiences that will affect their mental and physical well-being? Could we introduce a unit, for instance, on death education and suicide prevention? Why not include a unit on psychic phenomena, or one called Health in the Year 2000?

Try Micro-Courses

On the other hand, the present curriculum, based on a unit concept, may not be the proper way to teach health. A school using this concept may require a one-unit health education course for graduation. In such a school, ninth-grade students might attend health education classes five days a week for one semester. I would like to propose a student-centered rather than a teacher-centered approach to curriculum offerings. Under this ap-

proach, a variety of micro-courses would be offered in the curriculum. Students could meet the one-semester requirement by selecting any three 6-week micro-courses any time between their freshman and senior years. This approach is based on the belief that we in health education cannot accomplish all of the objectives for our courses in the limited time allotted to us. What we end up with is 100% cognitive learning, with no success in the affective domain or action domain. I agree with Toffler when he states that "children should be permitted far greater choice than at present [in selecting their curriculum]; they should be encouraged to taste a wide variety of short-term courses."[2] Such experiences should be based on present as well as future needs.

Certain courses based totally on behavioral change can be offered in school curriculums. I can conceive of short-term courses on weight control, smoking, abuse, or physical fitness, and action programs pertaining to ecology. Some of these experiences, if used as micro-courses, could be offered in the evening when students could take them with their parents. I can foresee parent-child courses in weight control, nutrition, or physical fitness. It seems that there would be a wealth of potential in this type of curriculum offering.

Get Involved in the Community

Another suggestion is for a practicum course in which students would be actively engaged in a community project pertaining to the improvement of the health of their community. Students should also be given the opportunity to receive health education credit by working in a local hospital as a candy striper, working with patients as a volunteer in a medical care facility, helping with cancer crusades, etc. These learning experiences under the supervision of qualified people, coordinated by the school health ed-

ucator, could be extremely relevant and educational for the student. Another good idea would be to include a course on ecology, or maybe a reading class in health education. In addition, I would like to suggest that an advanced course at the junior or senior level be offered to students on an elective basis to explore in depth a variety of health-related topics. This could be offered during the summer when the instructor could take the class on weekend camping trips and in an outdoor situation informally introduce and discuss ideas pertinent to the health of both themselves and society.

Let Students Do the Teaching

Students can teach a health education course. Students learn in a variety of ways—from teachers, from materials, from experiences, and from other students. Much of what a student learns comes from his peer group; some of the most meaningful learning is from personal experience. It is unfortunate that many curriculums do not offer opportunities for these types of learning experiences. In a course centered around students teaching students, the teacher could identify five or six students who have leadership abilities and work with them individually to lead small groups of their peers. This gives students responsibility and personalizes the instruction. This approach could be especially useful in large classes.

There are a number of opportunities for creativity in health education curriculum design. The ideas presented in this article are intended to stimulate some thinking on the part of the reader. We have only scratched the surface in looking for innovations in health education curriculum development.

[1] Alvin Toffler. *Future Shock.* New York: Bantam Books, 1970. p. 409.
[2] *Ibid.,* p. 412.

Vary Your Teaching Methods

GLEN G. GILBERT is an assistant professor of health education, P.O. Box 751, Portland State University, Portland, Oregon 97207.

Teachers of health education consistently ask two basic questions about the desirability of using innovative teaching methods. These questions have been raised during numerous inservice workshops over the last few years: (1) why should we provide a variety of teaching methods? and (2) how can we provide such a variety of teaching methods? The answers to both questions are extremely important and any competent health educator should be able to answer both questions.

An answer to the first question can be proposed after referring to what the experts in the field have to say about the need for variety in teaching methods. These authorities draw conclusions based on research and personal experience. They agree that providing a variety of teaching methods is important if we are to enhance the learning setting and to overcome any stigma attached to health education as the result of historical sins committed during the presentation of health education information. In addition, the following are important reasons for providing a variety of teaching methods.

1. An interesting methodology prevents many discipline problems. Students who are interested in what they are doing are much less likely to act inappropriately in the classroom. This holds true for adult students as well as younger students.

2. It is a teacher's responsibility to provide an educational environment. This means teachers must do whatever is necessary and within their capabilities to motivate students to favorably alter health behavior; experience indicates that it is not an easy task. If teachers must stand on their heads to reach the students, then they should do it. Certainly we cannot reach every student, but we can reach many. We cannot all be showmen or great orators, but we should do all we can to favorably alter health behavior.

3. The performance of students is one reflection of teaching performance. If students are not performing well then much of the responsibility must be assumed by the teacher involved. Certainly it is a joint responsibility (student and teacher), but a large part of it must lie with the nature of the instruction. Utilizing appropriate methods is likely to increase student performance.

4. You can make anything *worth learning* interesting. If the material you are presenting is truly worth learning then you should be able to develop a strategy whereby the worth becomes evident to your students. Teachers must be willing to face the fact that they may be presenting irrelevant information. If you can't readily demonstrate that the information you are presenting is relevant, you had better take another look at that information and perhaps update or eliminate it.

How do we provide a variety of relevant teaching methods? Numerous texts have been written on the subject in health education, as well as in other fields. One technique found very helpful is to determine objectives to be achieved, then review the following chart of strategies and make a decision as to which might best facilitate the achievement of stated objectives.

This chart was developed by me for use with pre-service and in-service teachers. Each method is rated as to the likelihood of that particular method accomplishing various types of objectives. The ratings listed in three columns to the right of the method are: "MF" meaning most frequently; "O" meaning occasionally; or if blank, it is highly unlikely that it would be used in such a manner.

Objectives written in the cognitive domain generally require recall of information (e.g., the student will be able to list the seven danger signs of cancer). Affective objectives generally require an analysis of feelings or perhaps result in an attitude modification (e.g., the student will indicate her willingness to assume her part of the responsibility for early detection of cancer by reporting any unusual findings to her doctor immediately without waiting for regular checkups or pain). Psychomotor objectives require action (not just writing and thinking) during the activity or result in the student carrying out a physical action (e.g., the student will be able to demonstrate on Resusci-Anne correct mouth-to-mouth resuscitation). Additional information on objectives is readily available in any of the methods books listed in the bibliography.

It is suggested that the reader or student keep clearly in mind the objectives to be achieved by a class or course, then review the list, checking those methods which might achieve stated objectives. Following such an appraisal, consider how each checked method might be implemented and then make a decision based on feasibility and likelihood of successful accomplishment of objectives. Following these guidelines should discourage selection based only on ease of use and will encourage innovation.

Using this system an appropriate technique should be located if the material being covered is useful and important. The reader may notice an overabundance of available cognitive teaching methods. It generally requires more preparation and thought on the part of the teacher in order to utilize techniques which influence attitudes and stimulate action.

This article has presented a rationale for employing a variety of teaching methods and has presented a list of methods to achieve that end. If readers are unfamiliar with any of the teaching methods, they may wish to review some of the sources in the bibliography and/or correspond with the author.

Summary of teaching methods and strategies according to likelihood of meeting objectives in cognitive, affective and psychomotor domains

	Cognitive Knowledge	Affective Attitude	Psychomotor Action
1. Music	MF	O	O
2. Cartoons	MF	MF	
3. Brainstorming & buzz sessions	MF	O	O
4. Stories with fill-in-the blanks	MF	O	
5. Interviews	MF	O	
6. Pantomimes	MF	O	MF
7. Self-appraisal	O	MF	O
8. Panel discussions	MF	O	
9. Visits to agencies	O	O	
10. Field trips	O	O	
11. Bulletin boards, displays, flannel boards	MF	O	
12. Transparencies	MF	O	
13. Review bees	MF		
14. Value clarification	O	MF	O
15. Mystery puzzles	MF		
16. Word-o-games	MF		
17. Anagrams	MF		
18. Crossword puzzles	MF		
19. Games	MF	O	O
20. Simulated situations or critical incidents	MF	MF	MF
21. Problem solutions (a specific technique)		MF	
22. Mock radio and T.V.	MF	MF	O
23. Personal health improvement projects	O	MF	MF
24. Student produced movies, slides, or videotapes	MF	O	O
25. Debates	MF	O	O
26. Skits	MF	O	
27. Plays	MF	O	
28. Role playing	O	MF	
29. Self-tests	MF		
30. Surveys	O	MF	
31. Oral reports (individual or group)	MF	O	O
32. Guest speakers	MF	MF	
33. Computer assisted instruction	MF		
34. Programmed learning	MF		
35. Experiments	MF	O	MF
36. Demonstrations	MF	O	MF
37. Mobiles	MF		
38. Charts, transparencies or graphs	MF		
39. Models	MF		
40. Slides	MF	MF	O
41. Videotapes	MF	O	O
42. Auditory tapes or records	MF	O	O
43. Films and film strips	MF	O	O

MF= Most frequently
O= Occasionally
If blank, it is rarely or never used in this way.

Films for Effective Affective Teaching

JAMES R. MULLEN is a teacher of English at the Lower Cape May County Regional High School, Cape May, New Jersey 08204.

One of the most significant educational trends of the last decade is the movement toward what is generally known as affective or humanistic education. With roots in the humanistic psychology of Abraham Maslow and human-potential growth centers like the Esalen Institute, humanistic and affective education (the terms are virtually interchangeable) deals with the growth of the whole person—the development of sensory awareness, interpersonal relations, and, perhaps most important, self-awareness and self-knowledge. Every board of education in every city and town in the country has some general statement of goals for the development of the whole person (usually couched in terms of encouraging "good citizenship" and "sound mind"). But in most schools, these goals are empty pieties. Often the best a teacher can do is to try to bring students up to grade, to advance students in basic skills, and maintain a semblance of order. Issues such as drug abuse, lack of interest, disruptive behavior, and poor retention are increasing.

The time has come, more and more educational reformers believe, for affective education to assume its rightful place alongside the more traditional curriculum. One of the main obstacles to this kind of change, however, is a dearth of good, proven materials. Teachers in search of a geography book to use in their classes can choose from hundreds, and huge film catalogs are readily available. But if a teacher tries to find a text or film on affective education, he'd better have some inside information.

One illustration of how useful materials on affective education can be when they are available is a program developed by a small firm of psychologists and film makers in New York City. The company, Film Modules Inc., is being funded by the National Institute of Mental Health, the New York State Department of Education, and the New

York State Narcotic Addiction Control Commission under the umbrella title "Drug Abuse Self-Awareness." Four separate programs for school-related use have been made available.

Each program in the self-awareness series is based on a concept of film usage which was developed by producer-therapist Robert Rubin. The concept's first application was a stress training program for police officers. It has been interposed within the training programs of more than 150 police departments throughout the country since its release in 1970.

The basic premise of Rubin's work is that in most cases films do not elicit genuine involvement and feedback, but rather make of the viewer a passive observer who experiences the film vicariously, at best. Starting several years ago, Rubin began to explore ways of mak-

ing film a more directly involving medium. The "film modules," as he calls his films, are structured to demand specific kinds of feedback and interaction. The result is a remarkably efficient, yet gentle generator of mature behavior.

The heart of each program is a series of film modules that focus on situations of tremendous emotional intensity and which suddenly and unexpectedly stop, leaving the viewer so emotionally keyed up that he or she is likely to have an almost physical need for a discussion or a general exchange of feelings and reactions with others. As any teacher who has ever tried to experiment with group dynamics knows, simply saying to students, "Well, what do you feel—tell us about your feelings" is likely to elicit dead silence more than any other response. The film modules, on the other hand, make a verbal response a kind of necessary relief.

One indication of the success of this concept in forcing a genuine and often profound emotional feedback from students was the response to one of the drug abuse self-awareness films for high school students. A 17-minute module entitled "Fear" was tested with a group of high school teenagers selected at random in a rural school. The students were so eager to talk about their own experiences of fear in a variety of situations that the discussion became a kind of confessional. "I felt like I was experiencing it myself," said one boy referring to the module. "My heart was beating harder and I didn't know what to do. And I was breaking out in a sweat right while I was watching it. I had this feeling that everyone was trying to escape and I was left there by myself." "But," added another, "if you show your fear all the time as you feel it inside of you, then you're usually going to get caught. As you go along and you learn to deal with your fear, then it prepares you better for the next time. But if you let your fear run rampant, you go insane." A video tape was made of this discussion and it was obvious from a single viewing that the discussion included not only the recognition that the fear existed, but the more mature awareness that fear need not be a mastering emotion, that being "in touch" with one's emotions helps one to deal in a more realistic and adult way than if one were less aware.

As the title of the series implies, drug abuse is one target of the films. It is only an indirect target, however. Although each of the film modules in this series deals with teenagers using drugs in a peer-group situation, the emphasis is more on the common emotions and experiences of adolescent growth than on the usual sermonizing lecture so typical of drug prevention programs everywhere. If you really know who *you* are, the program says, if you're in touch with yourself and behaving in a mature and sensible way, drugs won't trouble you. It's only when your head gets messed up (as happens at times to the teenagers in the films) that drugs might cause you trouble. The real key to the drug problem, in short, is not lecturing and punishment, but human self-understanding and self-concept.

A great deal of the success of Rubin's film modules and the supportive material must be credited to his talents as a filmmaker. The films have a quality of such complete honesty and spontaneity that it's difficult to believe they were made from written scripts and performed by teenage actors in New Jersey and Long Island—that they aren't real-life documentaries. The scripts and dialogue are based on hundreds of hours of taped group probes with teachers and young people, often the same kids who later performed in the films. It is easy, therefore, for most teenagers in settings varying from urban to semi-rural to identify strongly with the experiences and feelings presented.

Rubin sees his films as merely one component in a total educational program, and there are extensive teacher guides, intended to be used in a package of twelve lessons but adaptable to a number of different formats. The supportive written materials which guide the leader in the use of the films are so explicit that a teacher (or peer leader) who has never had any experience with group dynamics or affective curriculum can follow them easily. In line with the more process-oriented goals of affective education (as contrasted with the product-oriented goals of traditional education), the introduction to the teacher's guide states: "The main task for the leader . . . when using the film modules is to unlearn, or at least temporarily suspend, what you know about teaching. There is no *knowledge* which you can *teach* in this program." The instructions proceed with such suggestions as (in connection with "Fear") "Ask for volunteers to share personal stories with the others about when they were 'conned' into doing something they were afraid to do and did it anyway." Or (in connection with "Humiliation and Anger") "Keep the discussion on target: 'How would it feel if you were turned in?' 'Did anything like that ever happen to you?'." The teacher's guide includes a series of student work sheets which help students apply what they learn about themselves to real life behavior.

Although the film modules are definitely not product-oriented, they do have specific educational objectives. The teacher's guide explicitly states, for example, that it is desirable to establish that "mature behavior involves making a clear distinction between a feeling and an action." The guide also stresses the importance of peer-group pressure in shaping discussions to examine feelings objectively and the necessity of creating an open, honest, and relaxed classroom atmosphere (with helpful suggestions on how to do this). In various experimental sessions with the films, students quickly realized many of these objectives by themselves. "As you go along and learn to deal with your fear," one boy in a high school

in Schenectady said during a discussion of "Fear," "it prepares you better for the next time."

The films also open the way for some benefits not mentioned in the specific lesson plans. When one teacher in a high school on Long Island used the films, the most striking result he noted was that for the first time the students who favored drugs and those who opposed them were talking to each other and communicating. "Before, no matter what I did, they didn't want to communicate with each other," the teacher said. "Many of the drug users said they needed drugs to communicate, but it emerged during the discussion that they were communicating effectively in the discussion without drugs. That really surprised them."

As for other specific results, the teacher couldn't be sure—"It's still in their minds," he commented several weeks after showing the films. "I don't expect it to provoke permanent change, but they keep referring to the films in all kinds of contexts. It seems to have definitely planted seeds. I've used a great deal of audiovisual material, and this is by far the most effective."

"We spent a lot of time talking about feelings and emotions," commented another teacher who has also used the films. "For a large number of them it really hit home. Lots of kids get completely turned off when adults start discussing drugs—for the last four or five years that's all they've heard. There was none of that when we used the film modules; they could identify with the kids completely."

Another unexpected benefit emerged in a mainly black and Puerto Rican school district in New York City. There are few minority-group teenagers in the films—they were intended mainly for a middle-class suburban audience, and the leader of this particular inner-city drug program reports that students who had seen the films in her district were delighted to observe that for a change the poor and the minorities are not depicted as being closely associated with "the drug problem." Seeing drug abuse not as a racial issue helped to calm the defensiveness and hostility displayed toward most drug programs.

In addition to the high school series, the company has also produced a series on drug abuse self-awareness for teachers, another program for parents, and a single film for students in elementary school that clears up many common misconceptions and unreal fears.

Affective Teaching

Many educators quite legitimately question the role of schools in psychological education. Affective gains are difficult, if not impossible, to measure. Therefore, are such materials safe when used by the average teacher? "Maybe affective education isn't much different from a bull session—and shouldn't school be more than bull sessions?"

The film modules programs offer only a brief immersion in intensive techniques for developing self-awareness, and their positive effects, if left unsupported, will dissipate with time. A learning system has been devised as a follow-up, called "role modules." Here the students reenact (using role playing techniques) the situations presented in the role modules. The goal is twofold, first to reinforce the emotional awarenesses they had attained earlier from the films, and second, to present the many options available for mature behavior in real life.

One could argue that the teacher who would readily agree to use the film modules is probably someone already inclined to favor affective education and to encourage a relaxed classroom atmosphere.

Whatever their emotional benefit, the programs are proving to be useful to a growing number of teachers. As one teacher put it, "They served as a perfect trigger for discussion; they helped to create a nonthreatening environment in which the kids felt free to talk about things that they were really concerned about." Rubin's film modules offer a workable alternative to Clifton Fadiman's illustrated lectures of Dickens. As any teacher who has watched his or her classes drift off in a cloud of boredom knows too well, it's the kind of alternative the schools desperately need.

Effective Teaching: Variety in the Classroom

MARY SUTHERLAND is a master of public health student at the University of Tennessee, Knoxville, Tennessee 37916.
WILLIAM HEMMER is an associate professor in the Department of Health Science, State University College-Brockport, Brockport, New York 14420.

In developing an evaluation procedure for assessing student teacher competencies in a competency based teacher education program, checklists of what the student teacher is expected to do using a variety of techniques have been developed by a consortium of teachers, administrators, and college supervisors of the State University College at Brockport school health program. The field testing of this instrument was conducted with approximately 30 supervising teachers and student teachers. The participants provided many suggestions for the improvement of the assessment instrument, adding components and subtracting others.

All the clues to the qualities of a good lesson are provided for the student teacher before the lesson is planned. Since the clues can be built into the lesson plan the lesson will be better than if student teachers are left to their own devices to develop a good lesson. Therefore, the Competency Evaluation Packet helps the student teacher prepare sound, well-planned lessons which will succeed in the classroom.

Supervising teachers found that they were able to benefit by the checklists of expectations developed and found that their teaching improved because they were conscious of the essential ingredients of a particular type of lesson. A checklist of the qualities which the group felt would ensure success for three types of lessons follows with a discussion of the checklist items.

Demonstration Lesson

The teachers should demonstrate successfully, all of the following.
1. Arouse students' interest and attention before starting.
2. Explain the purpose of the demonstration.
3. Demonstrate the steps in logical order.
4. Explain the purpose of the various steps.
5. Provide clarifying material to the students.
6. Hold the attention of the students.
7. Provide sufficient opportunity for student questions.
8. Give clear answers to student questions.
9. Evaluate the success of the demonstration by eliciting student feedback.

As in any lesson, the teacher must begin by catching the imagination of the students so they will begin to pay attention. Students should know why this idea is being demonstrated. Logical order is important so that students can follow the procedure and understand the reason for each step, as well as, what is happening at each state in the demonstration. Thus, an explanation of the purpose of the steps as the demonstration proceeds is helpful as are any clarifying materials. Clarifying materials can be anything from references to things in the students' own textbook to definitions written on the chalkboard.

The teacher should keep things moving along so students' attention does not wander. This requires enthusiasm, showmanship, and ham acting. Another thing that breaks the monotony of the teacher's voice and helps to hold interest is encouraging student questions as the demonstration moves along. There is nothing like clear, concise answers to encourage more questions which means the teacher must be well prepared to field the types of questions which may arise. At the end of the demonstration, the teacher will want to elicit student feedback, probably with a few questions, such as: What do you think has happened here? Why? Do you agree with this explanation? Why do you suppose we did (this) instead of (that)? What might have happened if we had done (this) at (step 1)? Why?

The teacher evaluates the success of the lesson by probing the depths of the students' understanding of what has happened in the demonstration they have just seen.

Dramatization Lesson

Teachers should be able to demonstrate successfully, all of the following.

1. Arouse students' interests and attention before starting.
2. Select a relevant situation for student participation involving one main idea or issue. This could involve personalities related to an individual's beliefs, hopes, and aspirations.
3. Select students who are well informed on the issues and are self-confident in performing before their peers.
4. Prepare the class in what to look for in the dramatization, e.g. behaviors, feelings, etc.
5. Actively involve the students in the dramatization, but maintain orderly direction toward fulfillment of the objectives.
6. Evaluate the dramatization as it relates to the objectives by means of review, discussions or question-answer sessions.

Again the teacher must have a device for getting students' attention before starting. If the situation to be dramatized is familiar and important to the students, if somehow the students can relate to one or more of the characters, interest can be sustained. Usually situations or ideas which relate to their values, beliefs, or hopes are considered relevant topics by students.

In selecting the actors and actresses for a dramatization, whether it be impromptu or prepared ahead of time, it is important to use volunteers who are self-confident in front of their peers. Nothing kills a dramatization like a shy student who mumbles a few words and quickly tries to sit down because he would rather be almost anywhere except in front of the classroom. The participants in the demonstration should also be those who are well informed on the issues presented and who can easily visualize the situation to be dramatized. This is especially true in impromptu role playing.

Students in their seats should be given a charge by the teacher to look for certain behaviors, feelings, or whatever. The audience should be given an important evaluative or observer role so they will not feel like passive observers, but co-participants in a class enterprise.

Objectives should be made clear to students so they will know why they are doing this dramatization. At the end of the lesson, the teacher should evaluate the dramatization in light of the objectives. Again, a five or ten minute discussion of what happened may be crucial in getting the main point of the lesson across to students. The teacher, for example, might ask: Was the dramatization realistic? Why or why not? Do you think (the protagonist) acted realistically? Why? Would you have said (or acted) as (a character) did? Why? If not, how would you have acted in this situation? How could the dramatization have been improved? Did you ever see anything like this happen in real life? Where? How?

Audiovisual Lesson

Teachers should be able to do all of the following.
1. Explain the purpose of using the audiovisual material to the students.
2. Pose questions for students to seek answers to during the presentation.
3. Use questions to get students to think about material during or after the presentation.
4. Select audiovisual material which will increase the students' depth of understanding and learning of the curriculum content.
5. Involve students in the interpretation of the message presented in the media.
6. Relate the media's message to the curriculum objective.
7. Select media which present the message in an effective manner.
8. Select media with appropriate vocabulary level for the students.
9. Help the children conceptualize.
10. Summarize the main instructional purposes of the media.

Whether filmstrip, 16mm film, film loop, slides or large poster pictures, the teacher should first explain to the students why they are being asked to look/listen to it. In other words, the lesson objectives should be made clear. To involve students and support the purpose explained, ask students several questions in advance, keyed into the objective. One or two questions given in advance are generally all that students can keep in mind. An alternative is for the teacher to pose the questions one at a time during the presentation of the audiovisual material.

The important thing is to get the students to think critically or to inquire about the material being presented, both during the presentation process and afterward. Of course, for worthwhile thinking to be stimulated, the audiovisual material must be carefully selected to focus the students' attention on the objective desired and to foster learning of the content of the curriculum.

The questions and the teaching procedures used should be designed to involve the students in interpreting the media's message. This involvement should encourage creative solutions to problems and interpretation of phenomena and events depicted. The opportunity to use creative abilities sparks the interest and enthusiasm of the students in the project at hand. If possible, the teacher must skillfully allow the media's message to be related to the curriculum objective by the student instead of by the teacher.

The media which present the message effectively are usually best for stimulating student interest through the use of open ended questions. A straight factual presentation makes student involvement difficult since the media seems to be saying, "Here it is folks, this is the way it is, there's no argument possible with these facts." Students, not being subject matter experts, are usually in awe of straight factual presentations and are not able to challenge this type of presentation effectively.

If the media has audio or printed components, the teacher must make sure the vocabulary level is appropriate for the students—not too simple or too hard.

The teacher will want to help the children conceptualize the main objective of the lesson, usually by followup questions that help students understand and evaluate what they have just seen. These followup questions will also help to summarize the main instructional purpose of the media presentation.

Conclusion

Teachers who want to do demonstration, dramatizations, or audiovisual lessons for added variety in their classrooms will find these checklists an aid in remembering all the fine points that are essential for making a lesson click with a class of students. The checklists can be applied profitably both before and after the lesson. Before the lesson, they can be used as a guide in planning so that all necessary components are built into the lesson. After the lesson a teacher can use this same checklist as a thoughtful means of evaluating his/her performance in the classroom. In the light of this evaluation technique, apparent weaknesses can be shored up by extra effort in the planning stage the next time a particular type of lesson is attempted.

Health Science Fairs

HENRY A. LASCH is professor of health science, Department of Physical Education, New Mexico State University, Las Cruces, New Mexico 88003.

Science fairs have been a traditional project in many school districts throughout the United States, reaching a peak of interest after the space-age touched off a fervor of activity in the mathematics and science curricula.

We are now on the threshold of a new era in the health sciences. The crises brought on by drug abuse, the venereal disease epidemic, smoking, alcoholism, destruction of the environment, and other problems have increased public awareness in health. Although it is deplorable that most schools and communities waited for crises to develop before they realized the importance of a comprehensive health program, we are on the brink of one of the greatest expansions in health in the history of public education. Every possible means must be employed to convey the message of school health to the public.

The health science fair is one type of activity that will add new dimensions to school health education. It is similar to the traditional science fair except that it is limited to projects and exhibits which portray health as the central theme. Schools that may not want to sponsor separate health science fairs could designate health as the main topic in their regular science fair. Whatever route is taken, the end results should be worthwhile.

In organizing health science fairs it should be recognized that any type of project can be included as long as it pertains to health. It may cover anything ranging from personal and community health affairs to world-wide health problems. Special emphasis should be given to projects related to health and medical research and current, scientific developments affecting man's health and longevity.

Why Sponsor a Health Fair?

The health science fair presents an unrivaled opportunity to promote greater health awareness among students, school personnel, and the community as a whole. Greater understanding of the importance and scope of health in a changing world can be gained from this type of enterprise. Students may discover new interests and meaning in health and unlimited opportunities exist for creativity in all areas of health. Students who exhibit genuine interest and enthusiasm may show promise for careers in one of the many allied health and medical professions. It is quite conceivable that some of the critical health manpower shortage could be reduced if students were provided opportunities to develop their interests and creative talents in the field of health at an earlier age.

As plans take shape for a health science fair, students should become aware of the multitude of topics and programs which comprise school health, public health, and international health. A health science fair permits greater student involvement in current health affairs. It can also serve as a valuable tool to publicize health among all segments of the community. Education must search for better ways to challenge and stimulate the minds of youth in the diversified fields of health.

The health science fair is an effective way to gain respect for the entire discipline as well as a means of securing more public support for health as a separate subject in the secondary schools. Certain projects can focus on health hazards and deficiencies in the community, thus providing students with a challenge to assist in the solution of current health problems.

Guidelines for Projects

1. All projects entered in the fair should center around some area of health. The theme of the project should be clearly defined and described.

2. Students should select their own projects as long as basic rules and guidelines are followed. These should be clearly established by students and faculty.

3. Projects should be designed by the students, who should be expected to do their own construction and assembling.

4. The general plan of the projects should be approved by a committee of students and teachers.

5. Both individual and group projects should be encouraged.

6. Participants in the fair should be limited to one project in order to strengthen the quality of entries.

Organizational Committees

A health science fair will have a greater possibility of success if committee responsibility is clearly defined and overlapping is avoided. The general administration of the fair can be handled by a steering committee. Other suggested committees are: publicity, design and construction, finance, facilities, and judging. Additional committees may be added as deemed necessary.

Final success of a health science fair will depend upon the cooperation of all committees, the enthusiasm of those who participate in the planning, the motivation of student and public interest, time allowed for adequate preparation of projects, selection of a desirable site, and the continuous publicity given the entire project.

THE OPEN CONTRACT—
A PROGRAM OF
INDIVIDUALIZED STUDY

B. E. PRUITT is a staff member at Lewisville High School, Lewisville, Texas 75067

As a multidisciplinary topic, health education can offer an excellent opportunity to make classroom experiences germaine to individual life styles. Unlike many other areas of study, health education is not obligated to concentrate on fragmented tools which may, or may not, be used to affect life quality. Instead, classroom health offers a chance to experience concepts of living—the "big ideas" of responsible personal health.

At Lewisville High School, we have recognized this opportunity and are attempting to offer classroom health to our students to not only provide them with information about healthful living but to do this in a learning environment which emphasizes individual application of health related information. We have developed a program of individual study, the "open contract." The goal of the open contract program is to provide an environment in which each participant successfully identifies topics or problems within specific health-related areas, acquires information about them, and, by analyzing the gathered information, proposes possible means of dealing with such topics or problems. The ambiguity of this goal is necessary if the vast range of individual differences and needs is to be considered.

Participants in the open contract program are employed as student investigators for 18 weeks. During that time they are considered free citizens within the program. They assume three primary responsibilities: selection of topics or problems for study, selection of methods of investigation or investigation categories, and selection of grades.

Selection of Topics

Participants in the open contract program are free to select topics for investigation, but they are restricted in two ways. They must choose topics within the areas of study established at the beginning of the program, generally corresponding to the basic areas recommended in the Texas Education Agency's Bulletin 691, *Secondary School Health Education Curriculum Guide*. The second restriction is that each selection must be appropriately limited to be effectively dealt with through investigation procedures established by the investigation categories. A topic such as "food" is obviously too broad to be effectively investigated, but a topic such as "food fads" is more appropriate. The teacher never decides what topics are to be studied, for in doing so he would risk losing the individual emphasis of the program. Rather, he establishes boundaries within which the student is encouraged to select any topic or problem of personal interest.

Selection of
Investigation Categories

Once a student has chosen a topic for study he must then select a method of investigation from the investigation categories established by the teacher at the beginning of the program. They must vary in degree of difficulty and value so the student has several choices. A more difficult category may be valued as much as 10 points while a simple category is worth only 5 points. When selecting an investigation category the student must consider how much work he wishes to do with the topic, how many points he wishes to earn, and whether the topic and the method of investigation are compatible.

Following are several examples of possible investigation categories, designed for the ninth grade level and currently a part of the program for Health I students at Lewisville High School. (With a more advanced student, more involved investigation procedures would be appropriate.) The six examples will be explained in relation to the open contract design.

Position Paper: Each six-week period includes three opportunities for the student investigator to express opinions on controversial topics. This expression is done in the form of a position paper. Such statements of personal opinion allow a student to receive credit for investigating his own thinking in the areas of study. The position papers are graded according to how well the selected topic relates to the area of study, the topic is covered, the arguments are presented, and its general tidiness. The maximum value for any position paper is five points.

Critique: The critique category is provided so the student investigator can receive credit for analyzing the variety of information found in the health field. Newspaper and magazine articles, books, films, television programs, or personal interviews all provide opportunities for developing critiques. The student is encouraged to produce a piece of creative evaluation of both the information and the information source. Each critique is valued at eight points and is graded according to how the information relates to the area of study, how a summary of the information is presented, how an analysis of the information is carried out, how the source is identified (usually through a bibliographic note) and its neatness.

Correspondence: In each six-week period, students have three opportunities to receive credit for corresponding with various public health agencies or businesses concerning health-related information. This optional investigation category exposes the student to the variety of agencies, businesses, and associations which are concerned with the health of their clientele and helps the student encounter samples of literature provided by such service organizations. Students are provided with a list of appropriate agencies with which they may correspond. Each correspondence is valued at five points, credited when evidence of the correspondence is presented. As long as the information requested relates to the areas of study, full credit is given.

Examination: Three optional examinations worth up to eight points each are provided every six weeks. Questions are usually essay and deal with class activities, suggested readings, or general information to which the student may have been exposed. What might seem to be a misnomer in referring to examinations as one of the investigation categories is not so when examinations are looked upon as individual investigations of personal knowledge. Students are encouraged to write examinations with this in mind.

Individual Project: The category "individual project" gives the student investigator a chance to express his creativity, expand his knowledge in a health-related topic, and receive credit at the same time.

The design and means of development of the project are entirely up to the student. Bulletin boards, book reports, or special notebooks are common projects. Originality, however, is encouraged. Up to ten points credit may be earned each six-week period by the completion of this investigation category.

Committee Project: If three or more student investigators wish to work together on a project, they may choose to complete the category "committee project." The only restrictions are that only one project may be completed during any one six-week period and the selected topic must relate to the area of study. Each member of a committee may receive a maximum of ten points for a project.

Most, but not all, points are earned through investigation procedures. Up to 30 points may be earned each six-week period through class participation. Regular activities are planned which involve group work, role playing, or guest speakers so that information is provided over areas of study. Many activities are designed to help students with their investigations, or for the sole purpose of having fun with health. The credit available encourages students to take advantage of the activities or to make use of the class time provided for investigating chosen topics.

A progress record is used to maintain a running account of the number of points earned by each participant in the open contract program. An official and an unofficial progress record is kept for each of the three six-week periods during the program. The unofficial record is kept up to date by each student investigator so that he is always aware of where he stands. The official record is placed in a file and kept up to date by the teacher. Official credit is recorded at the time individual investigations are placed on file. At the end of each six-week period, the total of all points recorded on the official record is determined, and the resulting number is the six-week grade.

Selection of Grades

If a student investigator chooses to complete an investigation option, he does not automatically receive full credit. But, points are never subtracted from a student's grade. This evident contradiction leads us to one of the most important aspects of the open contract program—the grading technique.

A major criticism of the traditional classroom environment involves the extremely negative approach used in grading. When averaging is used, one poor grade may destroy all incentive. The open

contract program, on the other hand, involves a completely positive approach. When an investigation is graded it is awarded points for things done well; no points are subtracted for mistakes. For example, if a student completes the investigation category "critique I," he may receive up to 8 points. When grading the presentation the teacher notes any areas in which the critique may be improved. If the teacher feels that the paper is well done then a full 8 points may be awarded. If the teacher sees ways for improvement he may award 4 points or 2 points, de-

pending on the amount of improvement necessary. Any time less than the maximum number of points are awarded, the student has the option of accepting the points awarded by placing the paper on file, or of rejecting the points, making the indicated improvements, and resubmitting the paper to be graded again. If a student is not satisfied with this grade the paper may be reworked once again.

Usually when students rework a category, they improve the number of points earned. If, however, a second presentation receives a lower grade than the first, the student may ask that the first be filed and the original points awarded. Once points are recorded they must not be subtracted. The student is encouraged in every way to earn the highest grade possible.

Final grades are determined by the total number of points accumulated during the 18 week session. A student receives a good grade after completing a certain number of investigation categories well. A poor grade is given when the student chooses to complete fewer investigation categories. The option is available to complete no investigations and fail. This too is considered a respectable choice because the student is held responsible for his decisions.

This totally positive grading technique is essential to the success of the open contract program. The student must feel responsible for his own grade and he can feel that way only if he is allowed the option of correcting and improving his work in each category to a point of personal satisfaction.

Most participants in the open contract program have responded positively to this individualized motivational approach. They have become deeply involved in a variety of health-related areas and, in general, have increased understanding of numerous concepts of healthful living. Perhaps more importantly, however, participants have enjoyed their health education experience.

THE MANY FACES OF ROLE PLAYING

LYNN TEPER-SINGER is an assistant professor in the Departments of Health Science, Physical Education, and Guidance and Counseling at Long Island University—The Brooklyn Center, Brooklyn, New York 11201.

Role playing as a classroom technique has provided a marvelous environment for the exploration of health concepts. In the February 1971 issue of *School Health Review* a step by step procedure of the traditional role playing situation was presented in an article entitled, "Role Playing as a Tool in Mental Health Education." Briefly the steps included:

1. *Sensitizing the group*—present a situation where the class discovers that each person perceives a given situation differently based on past experience, assumptions, and expectations

2. *The Warmup*—describe the role playing situation with limited information

3. *The Enactment*—spontaneous dramatization

4. *The Replay*—the same people switching roles

5. *Student Observation*—discussion by the students about their reactions

6. *The Evaluation*—draw conclusions

At this time I would like to present three alternative approaches to role playing. Although any area in mental health can be explored through these procedures, the following are examples for use in drug education.

Example I

Structure: The class is divided into groups of four. Each group sits in a small circle within a large circle that the groups form.

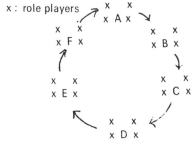

x : role players

Situation: Student arrives home to a family that has discovered a "stash" of drugs hidden away in his/her room.

Roles: Each group will enact the following roles spontaneously without preparation other than deciding on a role. Mother and/or father, brother and/or sister, student.

Procedure: In sequence each group performs their presentation of what they think will happen. (Group A then B then C, etc.) Generally each group has a different approach. The teacher may stop the group and go on to the next group at any point.

Discussion: After all groups have enacted their presentation, the teacher will have several options for proceeding with the discussion depending upon the material presented. Some possibilities include:

1. The class may form new groups based on the behavior displayed by the parents. Students who think their parents would behave as the role was played, would group together with the role players. For example: parent who cries "How could you do this to me"; parent who kicks child out; parent who questions with concern; parent who lectures and does not allow a response, etc.

Discussion questions may include: How do you feel when your parents approach you in this manner when they disapprove of your behavior? For what reasons do you believe your parents respond in this way? How would you approach your child if you were the parent?

2. The class may discuss their reaction to each group's performance.

3. The teacher may present questions for the small groups to discuss based on the diverse material that the teacher has been jotting down during the different presentations. For example:

Describe the ways in which the person caught responded.

For what reason do you believe people would respond in this way?

What information about drugs do you believe was false, which was factual?

What are the penalties for breaking drug laws?

What was your reaction when alcohol was mentioned as alright for the adults but "pot" was put down?

Example II

Structure: Single group performance with stop action directorship by the class. The performing group presents their interpretation of the situation in front of the class (the directors) who are sitting in a semi-circle around the classroom.

x- role players
o- directors

Situation: One student is trying to convince three friends to smoke a joint.

Roles: Person who does the convincing, person who refuses, person who is undecided, person who accepts.

Procedure: The group begins their enactment. At any point any member of the class, as well as the teacher, may stop the action by calling out "Stop Action" and

1. ask a question of a performer about how that performer feels at the moment.

2. assume the role of any of the players with a different approach.

3. ask the present players to switch roles.

Discussion: Questions for discussion may involve aspects dealing with group pressure and the decision-making process.

a. In what ways were the situations realistic or unrealistic?

b. How do you feel when someone tries to convince you to do something that you really don't wish to do?

c. What feelings do you have when you want to convince someone to do something and they refuse?

Example III

Structure: One individual sitting on the edge of the circle who will enact two opposing aspects of himself while the remaining members of the class listen.

x- role player
o- classmates

```
        x o o o
      o         o
    o             o
    o             o
      o         o
        o o o
```

Situation: The forces (feelings and attitudes) within the person that motivate him to use drugs versus those that influence him to refrain from using drugs.

Roles: The role is the dichotomy that exists within us that determines our decisions.

Procedure: The student holds up two hands (puppets may be used if appropriate for the age group). One hand is first used for emphasis "On the one hand why shouldn't I use drugs, everyone is doing it?" The other hand is then used "But on the other hand just because others do it doesn't mean I have to follow their example." The alternation of hands is repeated with each feeling and thought for or against the use of drugs.

Discussion: Questions for discussion may include:

1. In what ways are your feelings similar to and/or different from those presented?

2. What is your response in other situations where a conflict exists between your feelings, thoughts, and attitudes?

When teachers present role playing situations it is most important for them to have a facility for questioning so discussions are meaningful. The teacher's responsibility in role playing is essentially to help students identify and define what they are experiencing, as well as to help them investigate their feelings and reactions. A non-judgmental setting is therefore a must.

Suggestions for questioning:

1. Avoid questions that merely yield a yes or no response or that call for judgments such as good or bad, should or shouldn't.

2. Explore several ramifications of questions:

Clarify a point: If I understand you, you said. . . .

Seek additional information: Would you tell us more about this?

Evaluate: What do you think this might mean? How does the rest of the class feel about this?

Conclude: What happened? Why is this a problem? How could the outcome be altered?

3. Provide an atmosphere where questions arise from and between students as well as from you.

EXTRA CREDIT—
MAKE IT MEANINGFUL

GEORGE F. CARTER is an instructor in the Department of Health and Physical Education, Triton College, River Grove, Illinois 60171.

At one time or another most teachers from the elementary school through the university are confronted by students desiring to do an extra credit paper or project. Many times the student requesting the opportunity has fallen behind his classmates in regular assignments and would like to make amends through extra effort. In other words, the extra credit becomes a make-up which often causes problems for the instructor at or near the close of a term.

During the last nine years, many of my students at Triton College have requested extra credit in Science of Personal Health courses. Reasons for the request vary from the desire to achieve an A rather than a B, to pass rather than fail. Most requests have been made in the last week or two of the semester with little thought given to the learning experience. As a teacher, it is always encouraging to have a student request to do something extra but not under these circumstances. On the other hand, it is undesirable from an instructional viewpoint to deny a student a second opportunity, especially when they have requested the chance.

In the competition for grades, class rank, and as an opportunity to promote learning, the extra credit assignment should be used as a teaching strategy and should be open to all students. The nature of the assignment and appropriate grade compensation should be in keeping with the regular course evaluation procedures. Everything pertaining to extra credit should be carefully explained to the students so that misunderstanding is held to a minimum.

So students understand how they are to be evaluated in health class, students are told the objective criteria used in evaluating their effort. Every effort is made to present the student with the opportunity to earn points toward his eventual grade. All assigned work is given a numerical value and students are made aware of the point value for tests, term projects, abstracts, oral reports, attendance, etc.

Extra credit is not used to replace regular work but to increase opportunities for willing students. The information given to each student enrolled in Science of Personal Health as a handout is shown here. Over the last several years this handout has been revised and it will be continually revised. There is no longer the urgent need for an extra credit project; the extra credit must be carefully planned and contribute to the learning experience of the student.

EXTRA CREDIT OPPORTUNITIES
Science of Personal Health
Dr. George F. Carter, Instructor

Students who are interested in improving their information and skill level are invited to submit extra credit projects. All projects must conform to the established guidelines for compensation. All points earned through extra effort will be added to the previously earned point total. Generally speaking, first come, first served on topics. All work must be in good form to be considered.

1. Students may report information gleaned from reading a newspaper or magazine article which covers the subject being discussed in class. The student must have a copy of the article to present to the instructor and give a brief account of the information to the class. Articles not pertaining to the day's lesson will not count as extra credit. (2 pts.)

2. Students may visit a local, county, or state health agency and make an oral report to the class about the visit. In addition, a one page summary of the visit, person visited, and other pertinent information should be typed and turned in. (5 pts.)

3. Students may visit a local, county, or state health agency for the purpose of explaining the role of the agency. A brief report to the class is required. (3 pts.)

4. Students may visit any health agency or health related agency to get printed material for distribution to the class. (2 pts.)

5. Students may bring a cassette, record, or other audio-visual material to class that pertains to the subject under class discussion. All arrangements for the presentation must be made with the instructor one week prior to the presentation. (4 pts.)

6. Students may review a film, cassette, videotape, or other media production from the Triton College Learning Resource Center collection. The student must make all the arrangements to review the material and submit a one page summary of the material in proper manuscript style. (5 pts.)

7. Students may make arrangements to have a guest speaker come to class to discuss the subject under study. Prior approval must be granted a minimum of one week in advance of the presentation. The student will introduce the speaker. (5 pts.)

8. Students may arrange an interview with some person involved in health care service. A written summary of the interview with appropriate data must be turned in prior to the coverage of the material in class. (5 pts.)

9. Students may make an oral report of an interview with some person involved in the health care delivery industry. This material must be useful to class discussion and approved by the instructor. (3 pts.)

10. A student may submit a proposal for extra credit to the instructor. All proposals must be approved a minimum of two weeks prior to the due date. Point totals will range from 1-5. Suggestions for extra credit are: review a book, movie, play, or meeting; attend a seminar or clinic; critique a popular record or tape, a television program on a health related subject; visit a nursing home, mental hospital; or send for health information which would benefit the class or the person.

The handout has been of immense help in answering questions and assigning extra credit projects. Since my work is at the community college level, these activities attract student involvement. Perhaps you might desire to adapt the guidelines to your school environment but my experience has been an increase of interest in extra credit.

Promoting Experiential Learning

MICHAEL HAMRICK is associate professor and head, Division of Health Science and Safety Education, Memphis State University and CAROLYN STONE is patient education coordinator, City of Memphis Hospital, 860 Madison Avenue, Memphis, Tennessee 38103.

Getting students involved in health education experiences outside the classroom—experiential learning—continues to be a pressing need in health education. The purpose of this article is to promote experiential learning in health education by providing a list of projects to encourage out-of-the-classroom learning. While this list was developed for use in the personal health course, similar lists can easily be developed and implemented in courses where it is important to broaden students' experiences and to facilitate awareness of attitudes, behaviors, and lifestyles that are difficult to accomplish in the classroom.

These projects are designed for the student, not the teacher. Therefore, we suggest that the list be duplicated and distributed to students. These projects should be structured into course requirements so that points or some kind of credit can be earned. Since the projects vary in the amount of time, effort, and involvement required, possible points/credits should also vary. Some projects require several months to finish while others may be completed in a 30 minute interview. Students should be encouraged to pursue areas of personal interest and to take advantage of their talents. Some projects require skill in journalism, photography, movie production, art, research, etc. Students should be encouraged to select only those projects which offer a new experience for them. Finally, guidelines should be developed which specify how and when projects are to be reported.

Experiential Learning Projects

1. Do a film. Compile either an 8mm film or 35mm slides focusing on some topic. This display can be incorporated into a multimedia presentation using audio-tape or any other appropriate media. For example, you might produce a tape-slide show on eating habits of college students, study habits, recreational habits, dating habits, marriage from the woman's point of view, people trying to make conversation, children's ideas about death, etc.

2. Prepare an audio-tape collage. Tape many songs, poems, readings or sounds around a particular theme. The theme might be aging, drugs, self-identity, or sexuality.

3. Select one of the health habits/behaviors that you are concerned about and would like to work on. Develop a plan of action which focuses on the desired behavioral change. Use a behavioral modification plan as described in class. Keep a log on the success/failure of the plan. Follow up with an analysis of the plan and the behavior and what you learned.

4. Pair up with someone else to form a health "therapy" dyad. The purpose of the partnership is to have someone with whom the health habit/behavior can be discussed. Meet with your partner several hours a week. See if you can develop a plan for achieving desired behavioral change. Keep a log of your meetings. Use your partner both as a sounding board and as a monitor to keep you honest.

5. During the semester, keep a log of the behaviors/habits you change or modify. Examine the circumstances of the changes. Can you identify a pattern to the changes made? What did you learn? Report results.

6. Keep a journal. Record reactions to occurrences related to some topic or activity. The journal could chronicle a physical fitness regime or dietary pattern or an encounter group experience running throughout the semester.

7. Prepare and implement a research proposal. Some of you may have ideas for experiments such as the effects of various quantities of alcoholic beverages on reaction time, food tasting experiment, survey of attitudes.

8. Conduct a health demonstration. Some topics may lend themselves to a demonstration—the effects of smoking on heart rate, blood pressure, body temperature or how a medical test such as EEG or EKG works and what it shows.

9. Go to the Health Department, Venereal Disease Clinic as if you were a client seeking help for V.D. You may use a false name if you prefer. Report what you learned. How were you treated? What did you observe in the waiting room, the treatment rooms? How did you feel? What changes would you suggest to make the experience less negative for those who need their services?

10. Interview a person or persons who smoke heavily (yourself if you fit the category). Get a profile on their smoking habits, when they smoke, for how long, how it affects them, why they think they smoke, comments of family and friends about the smoker. Have they ever quit? Why? Why did they resume smoking?

11. Go to a setting unfamiliar to your lifestyle and report your reactions, feelings, etc. Try a walk through an inner city neighborhood, attend church services of a different religious group, go to an adult movie or bookstore, a gay bar, or shop at a small country store.

12. Spend an evening in a local hospital's intensive care waiting room. Listen, observe. If you feel comfortable, talk with the families waiting. Record your reactions, what you learned medically as well as emotionally.

13. Spend a morning making rounds with a public health nurse, food sanitation inspector, rat control investigator, or environmentalist.

14. Go to a community health center and take a seat in line. Examine the attitudes of the staff who work there. Talk to some of the patients. Find out how adequate they think their health care is, what problems they have getting to see a doctor, etc.

15. Conduct a health campaign. Select a health topic and conduct an educational campaign such as anti-smoking, hypertension, sickle cell anemia, cervical cancer detection, population control, human relations.

16. Visit a health foods store and make a list of what you see. Interview personnel who work there about their philosophies on eating. Compare prices of similar foods in grocery stores or pharmacies.

17. Spend one weekend evening sitting in a public hospital's emergency room waiting area. The same evening, spend the same amount of time in a private hospital's E.R. Compare the two physical surroundings, personal attitudes of the staff, the patients you see, their families. How comfortable/uncomfortable would you be if you were a patient?

18. Write a letter to a newspaper or magazine about a current health-related issue that really gets your dander up. Turn in a carbon copy.

19. Visit a health spa. What practices seem valid? What claims are made which seem unrealistic, unhealthy, deceptive, evasive? What do you get for how much money?

20. Go to a free lecture on transcendental meditation. How do you think it works? What are the benefits claimed? What sort of impression did you get from the whole experience?

21. Talk with relatives who have planned a funeral. What were their impressions of the funeral business and the people who assisted them? What details must be attended to when planning a funeral? What legal problems did they run into?

22. Find out resources for contraceptive information. Make a list and include costs, if any, for the services and/or the contraceptive materials. List at least ten resources.

23. Go to the local Unemployment Offices. Sit in the waiting room and listen to the talk around you. Describe the place. Read the notices on the board. Describe any contact with the employees. Wear old clothes. As a variation two people can go together, one dressed in old clothes and one in really good clothes. Describe how individuals differed in their reactions to you.

24. Go to any of the pregnancy counseling resources and ask to have a free pregnancy test. Describe the place, the people, how they treated you. If you are male, you can carry in a urine sample saying it is for your girl friend.

25. On a given night watch TV programs during prime time hours and count the incidents which exploit sex, race, religion, minority groups, occupations, etc.

26. Look in the want ads for jobs which routinely hire only men or women. Call and inquire about the job if you are of the opposite sex. What attitudes did you perceive? Quote any remarks made about sex requirements for the job. Sex discrimination is now against the law in hiring practices. Variaton: Work with a person of the opposite sex Both call and inquire about the job and record the results.

27. Interview a relative or family friend who is retired. Find out how they spend their time, what they like about being retired, what they dislike. What attitudes about being considered "old" do you pick up on?

28. Arrange for the class to "interview" you about a life crisis you have experienced such as divorce, marriage, childbirth, etc. You do not have to answer any question you don't want to. State any limitations before the interview begins.

29. Read an article in a health journal which interests you. Write a two page typed review of the major points of the article. Include your opinion.

30. Survey 5 "lay" magazines (*McCalls, Ladies Home Journal*, etc.) and write a description of the ads which contradict good health practices. You might want to look at magazines such as *Cosmopolitan, Playboy, Oui*, which emphasize attractiveness and appeal. Include a synopsis of the ads' underlying messages.

31. Attend lecture of guest speakers invited to a local university to discuss their views of health related topics. Example: Life after Life lecture, rape prevention demonstration. Summarize the presentation.

32. Attend health education meetings, fairs, programs sponsored by various community agencies. Summarize presentation.

33. Send in health assessment from back of textbook. Summarize what you learned about your health status, risks and behaviors. Takes about 4–6 weeks to get it back.

34. Get a test for diabetes through the Health Department mobile unit, or get a Pap test. Bring the results to class with a written report of how it was done. Ask questions of the personnel as they perform the tests. Try to find out how many people are detected through this system.

35. Write a summary report on the relationship between personality, emotional state, and cancer.

36. Using a very large map of your city, designate the distribution of doctors in the city. Which areas are heavily populated? Which have only a few? Which are undersupplied? You might want to use colored pins to designate different types of physicians. Do the same with dentists. Write your recommendations.

37. Bring an advertisement to class. List its claims. Analyze it for emotional appeal. Are its claims supported by facts? In what ways is the advertisement misleading? Deceiving?

38. From the list of health products investigated by *Consumer Reports* and published in *The Medicine Show*, select one and summarize the findings of *Consumer Reports*. Does the product render any medical or health benefit? What conditions, if any, must be met in its use? What brands are recommended by Consumer Union?

39. Refer to the magazine, *FDA Papers*, a monthly publication of the Food and Drug Administration and identify an example of quackery. What is the claim of the product? What does the FDA say about the product?

40. Tape a radio or TV commercial and bring to class. What kind of propaganda strategy was used? How is it misleading?

41. Conduct a demonstration to test commercial claims of a health product.

42. Write a company for verification of claims made in advertising. Turn in carbon copy of letter and indicate company's response.

43. Write a brief summary report on the published article on chiropractics or a report on any other health related article included in the monthly publication of *Consumer Reports*.

44. Tell about the decisions a heart attack victim or cancer victim makes in going through treatment, surgery, rehabilitation. Comment on length of stay, financial aspects, steps in rehabilitation, changes in lifestyles, etc.

45. Write a summary report on an article published during the past calendar year on a disease. Compare the information with that in the text and comment on the differences.

46. Develop a skit or role playing situation illustrating some attitudinal or behavioral aspect of a disease. For example, simulate the typical reaction of a person observing a diabetic in insulin shock; the reaction of someone to the news that he or she has a chronic disease.

47. Write a position statement on some controversial aspect of various diseases and be prepared to read to class. The position does not necessarily have to be your own.
A. Epileptics should have limited driving privileges.
B. Medical science is going too far with heart transplants.
C. Government restrictions in the form of laws, penalties should be imposed on persons with genetically related diseases.
D. Marijuana should be legalized for use by glaucoma victims.
E. The government is restricting distribution of laetrile because of loss of profits and government grants in research.

48. Interview a person who by nature of his/her job observes death and dying (police officer, mortician, war veteran, physician, nurse).

49. Develop a skit or role playing situation illustrating some aspect of death. For example, how people act at a funeral home, a family making funeral arrangements.

50. Write a position statement on some controversial aspect of death and dying.
A. Too much money is spent on funerals.
B. Young children should be taken to funerals.
C. Being dead is more honorable than being invalid.
D. Burying bodies is a waste of good, productive land.
E. There is too much death in movies and on TV.

51. Visit an Alcoholics Anonymous meeting and report your experience.

52. Write one page position statement expressing an extreme point of view on alcohol. The position does not have to be your own. Read to class, time permitting.

53. Conduct a genetic experiment in class demonstrating dominant-recessive traits. For example, obtain small crystals of phenylthiocarbamide or PTC test papers. Conduct a taste experiment distinguishing between bitter tasters and non-tasters. What are the expected results?

54. Write a case history or biographical sketch on a person with a genetically related disease or condition. Describe the lifestyle of the person and how it differs from "normality." Describe the effects on the family.

55. Find out what kind of genetic services and counseling are available locally, the conditions for service, prerequisites, costs, location, etc. Report to class.

56. Take a copy of the state penal code from the library and extract the basic criminal statutes relating to sex offenses. Note particularly those describing such acts as rape, seduction, carnal abuse, cohabitation, adultery, indecent exposure, loitering, molesting, and vagrancy. Notice, too, laws relating to marriage, (consent, ceremony, verification) contraceptives, pregnancy, abortion, and venereal disease. Report to class.

57. Develop a skit or role playing situation on some aspect of sexuality or sexually related behavior.

58. Select two newspapers (only one from your city), observe and record for one week the newspapers' statistics on marriages, divorces, and annulment. Graph the results. Include in the graph a breakdown on grounds for divorce.

59. Construct a sample marriage contract for yourself with provisions for facets of marital life you consider particularly important. You may want to consider some of the more common features found in marriage contracts today.
A. division of assets held prior to marriage
B. division of income after marriage

C. to have or not have children
D. responsibilities of partners in child care
E. obligations and rights regarding separate careers

60. Conduct a survey on some aspect of sexuality. For example, married couples of different ages could be asked to answer the following questions.
A. What do you see as the purpose of marriage?
B. Who controls the finances in your family?
C. What effect has the women's movement had on marriage today?
D. What are your views on early marriage?

61. Write a story in the "true confession" style that deals with issues of reproduction, birth control, marriage, parenthood, sex roles, etc. The story may be discussed in class.

62. Write a position paper on one of the following statements.
A. A couple should be encouraged to choose the sex of their baby
B. A single person or gay couple should be allowed to raise a child.
C. Men should assume the responsibility of birth control
D. No one should have more than two children
E. Marriage contracts should become the form of marriage law
F. A couple with hereditary disease should not have children
F. Abortion on demand is a basic human right
H. Unlimited availability of contraceptives encourages promiscuity

63. Conduct an experiment/demonstration in class which focuses on the effects of air pollution, water pollution or noise pollution.

64. Draw a cartoon series which illustrates any health-related topic for example:
A. transmission of venereal disease
B. use of contraceptives
C. access to medical care/physician
D. medical terminology or technology
Design it to get a point across to college level students.

65. Demonstrate in class how to test for blood type; how to test for sugar in urine; pregnancy test; T.B. skin test; test for sickle cell anemia. Be sure you understand the whys and hows of what you are testing for and not just the procedure itself.

66. Interview several women who have experienced menopause. What were their attitudes about it before they experienced it? After they experienced it? What myths about menopause were true/untrue for them? How did it affect their families, their marital relationship? Was any medical treatment given? What were the attitudes of their physicians?

67. Attend a meeting of the LaLeche League, the organization that helps women breast-feed their children. Record what you saw, heard, learned.

68. Compare costs of 15 common prescription drugs among several local pharmacies. Include a chain-owned pharmacy, a small neighborhood one, and a hospital-owned pharmacy. Include the attitudes of those you questioned.

69. Compile a list of local psychiatrists. Call and ask for information on: fee scale, training, group or individual therapy, type of therapy (psychoanalysis, primal therapy, gestalt, electroshock, etc.), hospital affiliation.

70. Contact the local organization for wife abuse. What are their findings regarding wife abuse locally, their services, future plans?

71. Interview someone who lives in what would be considered an alternative lifestyle: communal setting, couple who chooses not to have children, unmarried couple living together, homosexual couple living together. Question each person involved.

72. Collect drawings/paintings from young, preschool children depicting their impressions of sexuality. *Check with parents first!* These could include their concept of anatomy, birth, sex roles, etc. Show these to class with your observations and comments made by children. If you have small children you may use their artwork.

73. Write a report on some new medical "gadget," such as mammography, CAT scanners, fetal monitoring. Include any criticism the technique has received as well as its benefits.

74. Interview a couple who has experienced "natural childbirth" (the Lamaze method).

75. Write a self-help guide to common vaginal infections. Include symptoms, treatment, preventive measures, if any. Alternative topic: insomnia, urinary tract infections.

76. Give blood at one of the hospital blood banks. Bring proof of the donation. Include written report of how community blood donation plan works.

77. Visit a Weight Watchers meeting. Record your experiences along with a description of their program. Include a description of "case histories" you might overhear or learn about. How does their plan work?

78. Write an analysis of migraine headaches: what causes them, what happens when they occur, treatment, new ideas of therapy.

23

79. Interview an acupuncturist or an osteopath. Thoroughly document their training programs and the usefulness of their skills.

80. Put together a first aid kit designed for a specific purpose (camping, boat, workroom, etc.). Bring to class and explain whys of the contents you chose.

81. Find out and record 20 people's views on raising the mandatory retirement age to 70. Choose a mixture of ages for your subjects.

82. Design a sensitivity exercise to help a group such as a new class break down initial barriers of discomfort. The aims should be to decrease tension about being in a new, strange group and increasing knowledge about each other. Include factors such as: time needed, materials needed, goals, facilitators' roles and responsibilities.

83. Collect at least five health pamphlets from community sources and critique them as to their usefulness, their appeal. Redesign them to make them more "zingy," more appealing.

84. Review filmstrip/tape on one of three consumer products (shampoo, acne treatments, aspirin) and write a critique of it. Include at least five ads for the product which make misleading statements.

85. Take the results of the health knowledge pretest which was administered in class and complete a profile sheet and validation exercise.

86. Preview health related films available at local libraries and community agencies. Write a summary report.

87. If none of these projects grab you, think of another. Write a plan of action and turn in for approval. Points will be given after reading project description.

The Hospital as Motivator for Health Learning

Saul Ross is assistant professor of physical education, School of Physical Education and Recreation, University of Ottawa, Ottawa, Canada. Previously he was a teacher and physical education department head at Outremont High School in Montreal, Quebec, and instructor of health and physical education at the High School of Commerce in Ottawa, Ontario.

The problem confronting me was written clearly in the faces of the ninth grade boys staring up at me from behind their desks. A number of factors were operating to produce those defiant looks. Some of the boys were repeating grade 9, and almost everyone in the class had repeated one or two school years previously, either in elementary school or in junior high school. The ages of the pupils ranged from 13 years to 17 years. Their attitude also reflected the low status of health education, confirmed by the fact that it was assigned only one period per week. The low opinion they had was also the result of some prosaic standardized teaching approaches to this subject in their previous schooling.

The challenge was obvious. How could we change their attitude to health education? How would we create interest and excitement? What new method could we find that would involve the students directly? What new area of the curriculum could we investigate that would meet the following criteria: not covered before in previous grades, interesting to all the boys, and something to which they could all relate readily?

Before relating how the challenge was met, it is important to describe the school setting. The High School of Commerce is a beautiful new building, constructed as part of an urban renewal project to meet the needs of the people in the immediate area. It is situated in a low-income, inner city area, amid government office buildings, and close to a large area that has been scheduled for urban redevelopment for some time now. Because the curriculum is geared to commercial subjects, over 75% of the student population is female. Few of the students aspire to university; most hope to land a good job after graduating from high school, fairly confident that the commercial education they received will qualify them for many office jobs. The boys aspire to jobs as office clerks, retail salesmen, management trainees, or junior positions in advertising departments; some hope to join the police force.

My first step was to find out what parts of the health education curriculum had been covered. Each boy was invited to tell me and his classmates what areas he had studied or what he could recall from previous years. The topics mentioned were numerous, and the interest in each one varied. considerably. There did not seem to be a clear pattern, nor an exact core of subjects covered, and this assessment applied equally to both my classes.

Pondering the problem, it occurred to me that one area had been omitted completely; it was an area not covered in the textbooks used for health education. The hospital—the largest, most visible health institution—was a topic ignored completely in their health education courses.

My next problem was how to present this topic to really motivate the students. One entire class period was devoted to having each boy relate his experience with a hospital, be it a visit to a friend or relative, a stay in the hospital, or contact with the institution through service in the emergency department or in one of the clinics. The fears, misconceptions, and negative feelings that emerged confirmed my thinking about the importance of delving into this area.

After every pupil had talked, I asked them to write as many questions as they could think up about hospitals. This was something new to them, and after a few protests about not being able to think up any questions, they set to work. Each student was asked to prepare a list of 15 questions for the next lesson. The assignment seemed tough, but the interest was there.

Plans for the next lesson called for dividing the class into small groups of 4 or 5 boys. Each group selected its own chairman and then set about the task of analyzing the lists of questions to consolidate them into one questionnaire. Questions could be combined and, as discussion took place, new questions were added. Each class handed me 5 question sheets, a process that lasted for two lessons. The questionnaires were mimeographed, with adequate space for answers, ready for use well before our trip to the Ottawa Civic Hospital.

I contacted the Ottawa Civic Hospital and arranged for both classes to have a tour of the hospital. Copies of the questionnaires were sent to the Hospital, to help the people there in planning our tour. The Hospital had never had such a large group (25-30 boys) take a tour, and so they planned an itinerary to take into account the large number as well as the interest of the group as indicated by our questionnaire.

Arrangements were made with the school office to free the classes for the afternoon. The cost of transportation was paid by the travel budget of the Physical and Health Education Department.

The tour included visiting the admissions office, records office, emergency department, furnace and boiler rooms, laundry, kitchen, repair rooms, storage room, and underground passageways. Because of the large numbers of boys, laboratories and wards were omitted. The tour ended in a lecture theater where we heard two speakers. The head nurse of radiology explained the use of X-rays and showed one of a clearly visible fracture. The supervisor of orderlies explained the functions of an orderly and detailed the training program he underwent. Each pupil had a questionnaire with him as we toured the hospital and busily wrote answers as they were provided by our guide. At the end of the tour the boys made their own way home from the hospital.

The next few lessons were devoted to following up what we had learned. The discussions that were held pertaining to the various functions of the hospital indicated that students had gained new insights and attitudes. Heart transplants was a subject of current interest and provided us with a natural and logical lead-in to the next topic—study of the heart and circulatory system.

In reviewing this unit in our health education course, I felt the challenge had been well met. The students were involved. They made up a questionnaire, which truly indicated what they wanted to know. By using the small group process to promote interaction, more questions appeared than with a simple compilation of all the original questions. Interest was high and was sustained during the creation of the questionnaire and during the actual visit. There was considerable excitement about visiting the hospital and being guided on a special tour. The interest reflected a real need. The boys explored a new world on the tour of the hospital, a world few people in the community had seen or even thought about.

Two important questions need to be asked. Did students learn? What did they learn? They certainly learned about the operation of a hospital and became aware of parts of the hospital that most people don't know exist. This new knowledge gave them new insight into the complexity of the institution and made them aware of many new employment categories. They were afforded an opportunity to look into a world unto itself, a complex and vital institution in our community. This new knowledge led to understanding which in turn helped to change the negative feelings the boys had to the institution. Career possibilities in the hospital, specifically the position of an orderly, was important new information. Incidentally, the tour also pointed out to the hospital staff the need to embark on an educational and public relations program designed to modify the feelings of people in the community about the hospital.

While attitude is difficult to measure, and certainly no scientific effort was made to assess this area, I sensed a new interest in health education on the part of the students. By using this experience to launch the next topic—heart and circulatory system—the progression was natural and logical as compared to previous years where new subjects were introduced artificially, merely because they were listed next on the course of study.

Did they learn? What did they learn? By forming the questions they learned about the thing they wanted to know, pinpointing the areas they were most interested in. By constructing the questionnaire, they learned to evaluate and discriminate. Perhaps most important, they were directly involved in the entire process.

Field Trips

JAMES H. PRICE is associate professor of Allied Health Sciences at Kent State University, Kent, Ohio 44240.

Even though field trips are "old" teaching techniques, there are thousands of teachers who never leave the classroom. The community is filled with health resources, and all health teachers should make a list of agencies and places to visit which are related to health education.

The major objective of a field trip is to give students firsthand and accurate experiences not obtainable in the classroom. Trips should be taken only when they can contribute to the objectives of the course. The following questions should be answered before the field trip is planned. Will the students be genuinely interested in the trip? Will certain concepts be more clearly understood as a result of the trip? Will the time and trouble be worth the amount of learning produced? Is the trip truly representative of the unit objectives?

Preliminary planning for a field trip takes considerable work and should be scheduled well in advance of the trip. Anytime the class goes exploring in the community there is the possibility of accidents, but careful planning with attention to details can help eliminate many of the hazards of a field trip. Properly supervised field trips, authorized by the appropriate school authorities, usually involve the same legal liability conditions as any classroom activity. Teachers should find out if their state has special restrictions. Both administrative and parental permission will need to be obtained. The parents' permission slip should identify the who, what, when, where, and why of the field trip and clarify who is legally responsible for insurance coverage of the student.

The teacher should visit the site prior to the trip and plan the observations and activities that will best contribute to the unit objectives. Be sure that restrooms, eating accommodations, and first aid stations have been identified. The development of a route map with points of interest marked can help increase learning on the field trip. Arrangements for chaperones, transportation, and finances must be made well in advance of the trip.

Prepare the students for the trip by reviewing the objectives for taking the trip, giving appropriate background information, identifying specific questions

the students should seek answers for, reviewing standards of conduct and safety for traveling and while at the site, identifying any possible allergens or special problems students might encounter (poison ivy, for example). Inform students of special needs, such as clothing, notebooks, expenses, lunch, etc.

Teachers should take along a first aid kit if the trip is going to be all day or if the visitation site does not have first aid supplies. Other items for consideration to take along on the trip include: plastic bags in case someone gets carsick and bags for waste disposal (especially if the students take their lunches).

The group should be kept to a manageable size, by either limiting the number of students who can go or by increasing the number of chaperones and making subgroups. Take along a list of names of all students on the trip and count heads frequently. Other aids are to assign partners for the trip and select a place to meet if a student gets lost. Above all—don't panic! The trip will require a teacher who is enthusiastic, alert, and *flexible*!

Upon arriving at the site, if you are to have a guide, introduce him or her and get the group moving along as quickly as possible. Try to stick to the time schedule while still answering all the students' questions. When leaving, check the class list, thank the guide, and depart promptly. If a problem should arise which will cause the group to be late, telephone the school and let the principal know. This reduces the anxiety in principals and parents who may be waiting for the returning students.

Plan for followup activities after the field trip. Some of the most important learning will come from sharing impressions and discussing events which occurred on the field trip. Further reading, writing, and class projects could grow out of the well-planned field trip. Followup classroom activities will likely reveal to what extent your field trip objectives were met. The class and/or the teacher should follow up and write a thank you letter to the visitation site. A final evaluation of the trip should be formally written and put on file in the main office. Then when other teachers consider visiting the same site, they will have an objective evaluation by one of their colleagues.

HEALTH GAMES

A recent publication presents learning games in several health education content areas.[1] A drug game and an alcohol game from that source are presented here.

What's On My Back

Slang terms for "street drugs" are commonly used. However, the actual drug, its action, its effect, and correct name are often not known. This game will familiarize students with the names, the type, and the effects of drugs. Index cards, felt tip pen and prizes are used. Place a slang term, correct name, and long term effect on separate cards using the list shown here.

Description for Playing: Pin one card on the back of each student without them seeing it.

Instruct the students that they must go to other students and ask for a clue as to

without a doctor's prescription?

Drinking

Alcohol consumption is a widespread practice among all age groups. Alcohol education is one means of correcting the misconceptions many people currently believe and/or practice. This game is designed to help students discriminate between fact and fallacy about drinking.

Description for Playing: One story is given to each student. Intertwined in this story are misconceptions and/or false statements. Each sentence begins with a number. Circle the number of those statements which are *not* true.

Name	Slang Name	Effect
Amphetamines	bennies, dexies, pep pills, uppers, hearts	Alertness, actively paranoid, loss of appetite, delusions, hallucinations.
Barbiturates	barbs, blue devils, downers	Euphoria, physical dependency with dangerous withdrawal symptoms.
Cocaine	coke, snow, snuff	Excitation, sore nose, paranoia, depressive rebound on withdrawal.
Codeine		Euphoria, physical dependence, constipation, loss of appetite.
Heroin	H., horse, scat, junk, smack, hard stuff	Euphoria, physical dependence, constipation, loss of appetite.
LSD	acid, sugar, sunshine	Insightful experiences, distortion of senses, may intensify existing psychosis, panic reactions, "flashbacks."
Marijuana	pot, grass, tea, MJ, weed	Outside stimuli more vivid, relaxation, euphoria, physical dependence.
Methadone	meth	Constipation, loss of appetite.
Morphine	white stuff, morph	Euphoria, physical dependence, constipation, loss of appetite.

"What's on my back" such as an effect, drug name, or slang term.

After a person correctly guesses what his card says he then finds the other students with the rest of the information pertaining to a certain drug. The first group with the correct cards wins a prize.

Discussion Question: 1. What are the immediate effects of each drug?

2. What are stimulants, depressants or hallucinogens?

3. What is the legal, social, physical danger of many of these drugs taken

[1]Woody, age 20, resides with his parents in Mt. Pleasant where he is a sophomore at the university. [2]The females on campus find him very attractive; 6 feet tall, 175 pounds, blond curly hair, and bright, blue eyes. [3]Final exam week has brought about the usual stress, and anxiety many college students experience. [4]In an effort to alleviate the stress, Woody attended a weekend party. [5]It was the usual kind of party he attended with a lot of women, booze and loud music. [6]Many of the females at the party were in constant pursuit of him because his ability to drink

more than anyone else was viewed as a sign of virility. [7]This is partly due to the fact that the alcohol he consumed affected his muscles first. [8]In Woody's case, the alcohol also acted as an aphrodisiac, as alcohol consumption usually does. [9]With these two factors contributing to his virility, one can plainly see why he was pursued.

[10]Woody is a fairly bright guy and has established guidelines for his drinking behavior. [11]First, he always drinks vodka to prevent rapid absorption. [12]Second, he seldom eats any food before he drinks because it fills his stomach and he cannot hold as many drinks. [13]After all, if it's free booze he wants to get all he can. [14]Third, he drinks slowly instead of gulping his drinks to prevent getting intoxicated.

[15]Since he is physically a big guy, he really can drink as much as he wants because he has more body tissue and fluids to dilute the alcohol.

[16]As the evening progressed (3 hours), Woody consumed six mixed drinks (1½ oz. alcohol per drink) and the only observable sign he showed was a slight intensification of his talkative personality.

[17]As the party continued, he talked with friends, danced and asked Joey, an attractive girl clad in jeans, if he could drive her home. [18]Of course, Joey answered yes, and they left the party.

[19]Should Joey have more carefully considered the possible consequences of leaving with Woody? [20]After all, he was only drinking moderately and there are no risks if he drinks moderately. [21]He wasn't acting "funny;" the alcohol he drank stimulated him—that's the primary effect it has on a person. [22]And because both his parents are alcoholics he probably has inherited alcoholism from them. [23]Oh well, why should she worry?

[24]The simple truth of this story is that Joey is the alcoholic and not Woody. [25]Everyone knows that there are more women alcoholics than men.

Questions: Which statements are false? (6, 7, 8, 11, 12, 15, 16, 20, 21, 22, 25).

Important Considerations: The instructor should carefully explain why the above statements are incorrect. This exercise can be used as a pretest prior to discussion or as an evaluative tool after discussion.

[1]Ruth C. Engs, ed., Eugene Barnes, and Molly Wantz, *Health Games Students Play* (Indiana University: Bloomington, Indiana, 1974), pp. 13-23.

Health Games, Simulations, and Activities

DAVID E. CORBIN is in the School of HPER, University of Nebraska, Omaha, Nebraska 68182 and DAVID A. SLEET is director of the Center for Health Games and Simulations, College of Human Services, San Diego State University, San Diego, California 92182.

Games and simulations are widely used as teaching aids by classroom teachers across the country. We think this attests to the potential of simulation and gaming activities in instruction. The Center for Health Games and Simulations at San Diego State University houses the largest single collection of health games and simulations and serves as a resource center for these materials.

During the past five years, we have collected, cataloged, and evaluated games in health for the benefit of consumers. We have found that materials vary enormously in content, complexity, and price—ranging from one-to-one patient education games for under $5.00, to computerized simulators for over $500.00.

The purpose of this article is to give examples of games which can be conducted with little cost or preparation time. After experimenting with these suggestions, you can decide if you want to pursue more formal and expensive commercial products.

Drug Knowledge Game

Print the names of different drugs on index cards, one per student. Be certain to use terms that are appropriate for the grade level you are teaching. See the following examples. Notice that group names, brand names, generic names, and common names are used.

Elementary	Middle School
cough syrup	marijuana
aspirin	nicotine
beer	caffeine
tobacco	glue
coffee	antacids
Tums	Nytol
Rolaids	Sominex
	whiskey
	Anacin
	milk of magnesia

High School	Post High School
heroin	psilocybin
codeine	penicillin
LSD	THC
gin	methadone
Midol	Valium
Ex-lax	Librium
Contact	hallucinogens
hashish	methedrine
wine	peyote
Bufferin	alcohol
cocaine	nitrous oxide
opium	PCP
	morphine
	amphetamines
	mescaline

Next, pin a drug card on the back of each student making sure the student does not know what is written on the card. The object of the game is for students to guess the name of the drug or drug group pinned on their own backs by asking questions of fellow students.

Students should stand up and mingle in a cleared area of the classroom.

The rules are as follows.

1. Ask only yes or no questions.

2. Limit questions to three per person. This forces students to seek information from people other than their friends.

3. Approach the game cooperatively not competitively. Once a person guesses his or her own drug card, pin the card to the lapel. That student continues to mingle answering questions for other students. If time is a problem, set a limit.

Variation: Once the drug is guessed, pin a second card to the student's back for the student to guess.

Use: This game can illustrate how much or how little students know about drugs. Students will find they have been given conflicting information. It will also show some of the problems encountered in the drug culture; for example, buying drugs on the street is not very reliable. A drug may be substituted for another without the buyer's knowledge. Sometimes the seller does not know the difference between drugs. This game can help reinforce the idea that peers are not always reliable sources of information, nor are the sellers of drugs.

This game can also help improve questioning skills and reasoning. If the questions start out general and then become increasingly specific, students will be more successful in guessing their cards. Here are some sample questions—Am I an upper? Am I legal? Am I injected?

Drug Grouping Game

This game is adapted from the game, "Birds, Beasts, and Fowl," by George Enell, Kay Hardman, and Noreen Dresser (1977). It can be used as an offshoot of the drug knowledge game or on its own.

With a drug name card pinned to their lapels, students group themselves according to their cards without talking to each other. The teacher should not tell the students how to group themselves at this point.

After the students have settled into groups, one student from each group leaves the room. The teacher now asks members of different groups what their group is. After they are in agreement, the person outside the room returns and gives his or her perception of the group to see if it is the same as that of the rest of the group.

After this exercise is over you can give more specific instructions for the next segment. For example: Group yourselves into two categories—legal and illegal; or five groups—stimulants, depressants, hallucinogens, narcotics, and others. You can experiment with many possibilities, all of which will help the students learn about drugs and various classifications.

After each grouping exercise, check to make sure all students are in the proper group. If they are not, ask the class if they can find the person or persons who should change groups. Some can fit into more than one group, for example if the groups are legal and illegal then barbiturates could be in either, since they can be prescribed or sold illegally.

Remember, students may not talk while grouping themselves, they must rely on reading the drug cards and "body language" to determine where they belong.

Reproductive System Terms Game

This game is played in exactly the same manner as the drug knowledge game only cards with names of the male and female reproductive system parts are pinned on the backs of the students. This is an excellent activity *for teachers* who will be teaching sex education, since it helps them to talk freely and openly about terms having to do with reproduction. It is not recommended for generalized audiences. Like the drug knowledge game, it helps to illustrate the misinformation that abounds among peers.

Cards can include any of the following

hymen	labia majora
testes	Bartholin's glands
epididymus	urethra
seminal vesicles	glans
fallopian tubes	labia minora
ovaries	Graafian follicle
foreskin	cervix
uterus	clitoris
prostate	seminiferous tubules
vas deferens	vagina
bulbourethral or Cowper's glands	
penis	

Note: "urethra" is part of the male and female anatomy, but, of course, only in the male's reproductive system—this may make it a more difficult term for some.

Food Grouping Game

This game is very similar to the drug grouping game and is also adapted from "Birds, Beasts, and Fowl." Instead of name tags cut out pictures of different foods from magazines. Be certain that you select different foods from all food groups and pseudo-foods such as alcoholic beverages, salt, pepper, condiments. Place all the pictures into a paper bag then have students remove one food cutout without looking and pin it on their lapels. From this point on, the progression is the same as the drug grouping game. Remember, students always group themselves without talking to each other.

Variations: Ask six people to leave the room. Ask the rest of the class to regroup themselves according to their tags this time according to a specific direction, such as foods high in sugar, a balanced meal, high protein foods. When the other students come back into the room they try to guess upon what basis the groups have been formed.

Ask all students to form the four basic food groups (or the basic seven). Make necessary corrections by asking the class as a whole if everyone is in the correct group. If they don't know, help them.

Ask the students to group into foods that are high-risk for dental disease and foods that are low-risk for dental disease.

Ask the students to group into high-risk, neutral, and low-risk for cardiovascular disease.

Experiment with other groupings. After this exercise, students can easily see that there are many different aspects to consider in selecting foods. Just because a food may be low-risk for dental disease, does not mean it is necessarily low-risk for cardiovascular disease. We also like to add foods such as pizza or hamburger which don't fit neatly into any single group.

"Drunk" Synonym Game

There are, reportedly, more synonyms for the word "drunk" than for any other word in the English language. These words say something about how ingrained and accepted alcohol is in our society. To begin this game open the floor to any and all synonyms for the word "drunk." As the students call them out, write them on the blackboard.

Examples:

juiced	inebriated
plastered	pickled
polluted	under the table
zonked	smashed
blasted	loaded
tight	intoxicated

To better see how our society views drunkenness, make another list in categories. This can be done as a class or as an assignment for each individual. The categories could be: technical-medical, funny-happy, tragic-sad, and neutral. Discuss the implications. Invariably the funny-happy category is the largest.

To extend this activity, students can name plays, movies, comic strips, TV shows, and people in which (or whom) alcohol plays an integral part, then categorize them the same way they did the synonyms.

Examples:

Foster Brooks	"Lady Sings the Blues"
Dean Martin	Betty Ford
Andy Capp	Alice Cooper
Ed McMahon	"Streetcar Named Desire"
Hagar	"All in the Family"
Janis Joplin	"Days of Wine and Roses"
W. C. Fields	Wilbur Mills

After trying any of these games, you may wish to try some of the other games on file at the Center for Health Games and Simulations. For more information on the use of games and simulations in health instruction, the reader is encouraged to consult the suggested readings.

Originally presented at Association for Advancement of Health Education Meeting, New Orleans, LA. March 1979.

LEARNING GAMES

Getting To Know One Another

There are several interesting ways for students to get to know one another better. Even though they are in the same class, some students never converse with or know much about many of their classmates. The following exercise provides for a discussion of content within a process designed to expand communication in the classroom; it thereby also increases a sense of trust among class members.

Each pupil is asked to select another pupil with whom to discuss one of several listed topics. The partner selected, however, should be someone whom the selector doesn't know very well. Before discussing the topic, each pair gets to know each other better by discussing their aspirations, feelings about the class, family history, or other matters personal to their lives. After this discussion is completed, the content topic is discussed. Twenty minutes should be allowed for this phase of the exercise.

Possible topics for discussion are:

Foods that I like to eat. (Nutrition)

How to make our homes safe. (Safety education)

How girls are different from boys. (Sex education)

Next, each pair chooses another pair whom they don't know very well, and the process is repeated. This time, however, each pupil introduces his partner to the other pair and a general discussion of pupil's backgrounds, etc. precedes the content-related discussion. The group of four can then be combined with another group of four to make eights and eights can be combined to make sixteens, etc.

Listening Practice

Students are formed into groups of three for the purpose of discussing a question. Questions may range from "How does someone make friends?" to "What's the safest way to ride a bicycle?" During the ensuing discussion, in order for a member of the group to communicate verbally, that member must paraphrase, to the satisfaction of the previous speaker, what was last said. If a paraphrase is attempted but is incorrect, the person who is being paraphrased repeats what he said and the paraphraser again attempts to paraphrase his comments. The purposes of this exercise are:

1. To provide a framework for classmates to talk in small groups and get to know one another.

2. To emphasize that we are often thinking of what we want to say and not listening to what others are saying.

3. To discuss fully the topic at hand in an interesting and effective manner.

4. To underline that communication is often impeded by emotional involvement in the topic, someone who talks for a long period of time, someone who presents a lot of ideas all at once, serious biases, or a poor facility in which to talk and listen. Any of the above can, and often do, create difficulties in hearing accurately what is being communicated and can cause difficulty in paraphrasing.

If this exercise is conducted for a twenty minute period and then discussed fully, pupils will become aware of their listening skills and attempt to sharpen them. A periodic repeat of this exercise will provide feedback on progress in development of listening skills.

Family Drawings

Often children's insights into their family lives are not such that the roles of the family members are readily accessible to them. Perceptions of family life are often repressed and hidden. An activity designed to bring to the surface a child's feelings about his family is one in which he draws a picture of his family in a group activity or some other context. At the conclusion of this activity, drawings are exchanged among all members of the class until each classmate has had the opportunity to review each drawing. Pupils write a one sentence comment, which expresses their reaction, on the back of each drawing they review. Comments should relate to the family as a whole, or to individuals depicted. Next, drawings are returned to the artists with time provided to read the comments of their classmates. A discussion follows of the objectives of this exercise.

Lost on the Moon

This activity helps children to compromise and take part in consensual decision making processes. Each child is supplied with a copy of the following problem:

You are in a space crew originally scheduled to rendezvous with a mother ship on the lighted surface of the moon. Mechanical difficulties, however, have forced your ship to crash land at a spot some 200 miles from the rendezvous point. The rough landing damaged much of the equipment aboard. Since survival depends on reaching the mother ship, the most critical items available must be chosen for the 200-mile trip. The fifteen items left intact after the landing are listed below. Your task is to rank them in terms of their importance to your crew in its attempt to reach the rendezvous point. Place number 1 by the most important item, number 2 by the second most important, and so on through the least important, number 15.

— Box of matches
— Food concentrates
— 50 feet of nylon rope
— Parachute silk
— Portable heating unit
— Two .45 caliber pistols
— One case dehydrated milk
— Two 100-pound tanks of oxygen
— Stellar map of the moon's constellation
— Life raft containing CO₂ bottles
— Magnetic compass
— 5 gallons of water
— Signal flares
— First-aid kit containing injection needles
— Solar-powered FM receiver-transmitter

Below are the correct rankings as determined by National Aeronautics and Space Administration:

15—Box of matches (little or no use on the moon)

4—Food concentrate (supply daily food required)

6—50 Feet of nylon rope (useful in tying injured, help in climbing)

8—Parachute silk (shelter against sun's rays)

13—Portable heating unit (useful only if party landed on dark side)

11—Two .45 caliber pistols (self-propulsion devices could be made for them)

12—One case dehydrated milk (food, mixed with water for drinking)

1—Two 100-pound tanks of oxygen (fills respiration requirement)

3—Stellar map of the moon's constellation (one of the principal means of finding direction)

9—Life raft (CO₂ bottles for self-propulsion across chasms, etc.)

14—Magnetic compass (probably no magnetized poles; thus useless)

2—5 gallons of water (replenishes loss by sweating, etc.)

10—Signal flares (distress call within line of sight)

7—First-aid kit containing injection needles (oral pills or injection medicine valuable)

5—Solar-powered FM receiver-transmitter (distress signal transmitter, possible communication with mother ship).

Each child ranks the fifteen items in terms of importance. Groups of six to eight students are then formed to rank the fifteen items as a group, utilizing consensual decision making rather than voting. No one group member's opinion is allowed to override the group's decision. A comparison of individual and group opinions evidences the advantage of consensual decision making. This analysis is conducted by computing the difference between the NASA rankings and the individual rankings firstly, and the NASA rankings and the group's rankings secondly. The differences for the individual rankings are totaled, as are the differences for the group rankings. The lower the score, the more accurate the rankings.[1]

Cognitive Football

A football field is drawn on the blackboard, and the class is divided into two teams. A content area in health education is selected, for example, nutrition. The teacher has three sets of cards which contain questions pertaining to the content area selected. One set of cards contains relatively easy questions, which when answered correctly, result in a five-yard gain. Another set of questions, somewhat more difficult, result in a ten-yard gain; and the last set of questions is worth 15 yards. The toss of a coin decides which team begins the game with the ball on the fifty-yard line. Team members decide, previous to attempting to answer the question, from which set of cards the question should be selected and thereby how much of a gain will be attempted. Teams alternate answering questions and the team that puts the ball over the opponents' goal line is the winner. Only one team member is allowed to answer the question and may not receive help from his teammates.

Written Conversations

This activity serves to correlate language arts with health instruction and, in particular, family living. The class is separated into pairs, one person assigned the role of child and the other the role of parent. A situation is described, e.g., the child wants to play outdoors with his friends while the parent insists he stay indoors and complete his homework. Each pair then engages in a written conversation recorded on a sheet of paper. No verbalizing is permitted. These paper and pencil conversations should last approximately twenty minutes at which time pairs volunteer to read their conversations to the class. Each conversation read is analyzed with access to "replays" since the conversation has been recorded on paper.

[1] Gene Stanford and Barbara Stanford, *Learning Discussion Skills Through Games* (New York: Citation Press, 1969), pp. 44-47.

HORSE RACING IN THE CLASSROOM

PHILLIP HOSSLER is a teacher of health and physical education and trainer for all sports at the Madison Township High School, Old Bridge, New Jersey 08857.

One of the difficult problems faced by high school educators today is motivating their students, especially in required courses. The problem is convincing students that just because they have to be in the class is no reason why they can't enjoy it and learn something at the same time. Giving stars or lollipops for answering a difficult question or solving a problem is not successful in high school, because older students feel their performance deserves a more beneficial reward, such as the improvement of their grade. In many required courses the students may only do that which is required to pass the course. Clearly what is needed is some sort of activity where the older students are able to feel they are properly reimbursed for their endeavors and still learn something in the process.

I initiated an activity in my health classes wherein the students researched, in class, answers to questions and explanations to the notes that I planned to cover that day. This activity took the form of a horse race. To start class when I use the horse race, I blow a whistle or ring a bell. I have signs in the room saying "Stables," "Race Tips," "Cashier," "Grandstand," etc., and have long strings of colored flags hanging in the room to add authenticity and show the class that I too have enthusiasm and enjoy what I am doing.

Each group of four students is a horse, so there are four jockeys to each horse, and each horse has a name. The first day I put on the overhead projector the drawing of the oval track with the grandstands, flags, and finish line drawn in. In the center of the track I wrote "Hossler's Happy Healthy Horse Sweepstakes." Next I showed on the overhead the ideas I planned to cover that day. For example, when the class starts the study of venereal disease, the notes might look like:

Intro to VD
Venus
skin-to-skin contact
pox, clap
cause
damage to infected

Then I give the class 10-15 minutes to look through the books and pamphlets that I have brought to class or ones they have gotten themselves to discover what I mean by each of these short phrases. Each of the horses is questioned to explain my own notes to me. I speak to a different jockey each time so that everyone is involved at some point.

Each of the phrases is worth a certain point value, usually 1 point. If only one horse gives the correct answer, that horse would get the full point; if two horses give me equally correct answers they would each get one-half point and so forth. The points that each horse receives determine its position around the track. It takes a total of 12 points to run the length of the track.

For example, if horse #1, Sugar Daddy, tells me that skin-to-skin contact is the method of transmission when speaking about venereal disease, he would be correct. If no other horse was able to give me this answer Sugar Daddy would receive the full point. If, however, horse #5, Carmel Corn, told me that skin-to-skin contact was the method of transmitting venereal disease and that coitus was the most common form of skin-to-skin contact for transmitting VD, Carmel Corn would receive three-fourths of a point or he might even steal the full point away from Sugar Daddy since Carmel Corn gave me the more complete answer. The students become involved with the race because of the constant advancing and falling behind on each question. After two or three notes, I write the position of the horses on the track. The jockeys then begin to dig a little deeper the next time for that bit of extra information that will give them the edge over the rest of the pack.

I have also found that researching answers develops teamwork and pride among the jockeys on each horse. They

must research much material in a short period of time, so the notes are delegated to each of the jockeys on the horse so that one might have the answer to a note that the other jockeys didn't have time to find.

After each horse has given me an answer explaining the note, I write the points awarded on the overhead next to their horse's name amid cheers and groans from the jockeys. Then I tell them exactly what I was looking for and give them time to write it in their notebooks before going on to the next note. The order in which the horses respond varies each time so no one horse gains an advantage by being the last to answer each time.

The race continues until all the horses have finished the course. If horse #1 finished first the jockeys cannot sit back and do nothing; they must still answer questions to ensure that another one of the horses doesn't earn more points and "nose them out at the wire."

If there are six horses running, the jockeys on the winning horse each get six points, the second place jockeys each get five points, and so forth. These bonus points are used at the end of the marking period when grades are determined.

This method of teaching requires more time, because the amount of material covered each day may not be as much as with the lecture method. It requires a teacher who is able to instruct and still maintain control of the class amid mild chaos, much laughter, and student enthusiasm. I have found that the grades on the tests after using this method are the highest grades of the marking period.

I personally enjoy using this method of teaching. I don't use it for the entire marking period; instead I tell the class about it in the beginning and then save it until last. This also helps to build enthusiasm toward the activity.

FANTASY GAMES

RALPH BATES is in the Department of Health, Physical Education and Recreation, Ohio State University, Columbus, Ohio 43210.

I have used fantasy games with young children, older children, and adults and have found them to be very successful. Participants become more aware of how they perceive themselves, what they are like as people, their strengths and weaknesses and, most important, they can become aware of emotions and deeper feelings which normally would not be disclosed to individual or group members. I have also found that fantasy is relaxing, helps develop better listening skills, and leads to closer, more meaningful relationships among participants.

In this paper I would like to share several of these games, to use with groups of children as a means of relaxation and to help them learn more about themselves. I will indicate the method I use in presenting these games, and the reader can adapt each one according to individual needs. The books and articles in the bibliography are excellent resources for fantasy games as well as other communication skills for both children and adults.

Make A Person

I have found this game to be effective with children to help you learn what they are like as people.

1. Ask a group of children to think of a person's name and write it on the board.

2. Using the general background of the group as a guide, and the age of the children you are dealing with, establish same criteria for this person. Example: "Billy is 14 and lives at home with his mother, father, brother, and sister."

3. Ask the children the following: With help from each one of you, I would like to find out more about Billy. What is he like as a person? What is he like at home? How does he do in school? What does he like to do? How does he feel about himself? With these general questions as a guide, obtain several responses from each child and write them on the blackboard. If you listen carefully, you will be surprised about how these children feel about themselves, their peers, and their families. Follow this through with a group discussion.

Rosebush and Object Identification

This game is directed more toward older children. You may use the same format for younger children by substituting a flower or animal for the rosebush and object.

1. Ask the participants to close their eyes and get as comfortable as possible. They may sit in their chairs or sit or lie on the floor. Then say the following: I am going to take you on a fantasy trip. I want you to do exactly as I say and be aware of nothing else but my voice.

2. The following questions can be used for the rosebush. You will have to adapt these questions to the other games. What are you like as a rosebush (object)? What are your roots like . . . your stem . . . your leaves . . . your thorns . . . your flowers? What are your surroundings like? What season?

3. Now proceed with the following: In several minutes I will ask you to open your eyes then tell us what you are like as a rosebush. Have each member select a group member after he has described himself to the group. The following questions may be used for discussion.

1. What did you learn about yourself?
2. What did the group learn?
3. How does this relate to disclosure, listening, feedback, communication, and fantasy? (Adapted from Stevens, *Awareness*.)

Ocean Trip

Obtain a record or tape of ocean sounds such as *Environmental Sounds*, or a tape recording from a radio or TV communication center.

1. Have the group relax at their desks or lie on the floor.

2. Tell them the following: I am going to take you on a fantasy ocean trip. I want you to close your eyes, relax, and concentrate on what I say. Imagine yourself approaching a beautiful vacated beach. . . . You begin to walk in the sand. . . . Stop and take off your shoes. As you stand there, feel the sand on the bottom of your feet, the grains of sand sifting through your toes. . . . become aware of that feeling. Begin a stroll toward the water's edge. . . . As you continue your walk, become aware of the sun beating on your face, smell the salty air, hear all the sounds around you. Find a spot ahead of you and sit down in the sand. . . . Hold some sand in your hand. . . . Feel the individual grains of sand sift through your fingers. Stand up and continue your stroll toward the water's edge. . . . Before you reach the water, stand (and sit) in the wet sand. . . . Feel your feet sink into the wet sand. Grab a handful of wet sand. . . . Be aware of the difference between the wet sand and the dry sand. Stand by the water's edge. . . . Feel the water gently flowing under your feet and around your ankles. . . . Stand there and smell the salty air, feel the wind blowing in your face, and be aware of all the sounds around you. . . . (cont'd). . . .

Use your own imagination with this game. After you are through give the group several minutes before they open their eyes and disclose their trip to the group.

The following questions may be used for discussion:

1. How was your fantasy trip?
2. Where were you?
3. What were your surroundings like?
4. What were some of the feelings you experienced?
5. Could you feel the different textures of sand?

Fantasy Dream (This exercise is also directed toward older groups of children.)

Close your eyes and become as relaxed as possible. I am going to take you back to your early childhood to a recurring dream that you used to have then, a dream that you are going to have again.

Don't be afraid. Just concentrate on what I will tell you, and on your experience as my words are spoken. At night, while you are asleep as a small child, the dream would occur over and over again. The dream would begin in the same way. You would get out of bed and walk across the bedroom to the closet. There is now a door behind the closet, a door which you could never find while awake. As you approach the door in your dream it now opens.

As you stand in the door you look down an ancient looking stone staircase. In the dim light you begin to descend the staircase, not at all afraid, down a step at a time. As you approach the bottom of the staircase you stop and hear the gentle sound of water lapping against the rocks below. You approach the water's edge. A small boat is tied to the rocks. Sit in the boat and untie it. Just lie back in the bottom of the boat and let it take you where it wants to go. Sit there, relax, and listen to the water lapping against the boat and rocks, as you gently rock back and forth, back and forth, as the boat drifts down the stream.

As you lie there enjoying your trip you notice a small opening ahead of you. As you approach the opening it becomes larger and larger. You come out of the opening into a new environment which you will now experience. Continue to keep your eyes closed and become aware of the new environment. Where are you? . . . What is it like? . . . What will you do next? . . . What sights, odors, sounds, and movements are you now experiencing? . . . etc. . . . Now open your eyes and disclose your experiences to the group. (Adapted from Masters, *Mind Games*.)

CHOICES

LYNN TEPER-SINGER is an assistant professor in the Department of Health Science, Physical Education, and Guidance and Counseling at Long Island University—the Brooklyn Center, Brooklyn, New York 11201.

One of my beliefs is that the way one feels about oneself is reflected by the choices one makes and the behavior that follows these choices. Therefore, one of the ways I gain an understanding of the individuals within my health classes is by observing their behavior in here and now situations. Then, by exploring the motivations behind their actions, the class takes part in understanding their decisions.

I have found that the following technique arouses strong emotional responses while dealing with making decisions:

Have your class stand in a circle and look around the room at their classmates picking out one person they would like to know better. At a signal from you, their task will be to go over to the person of their choice and nonverbally show that person how they feel. Often no one will move initially. If this occurs you may wait, or you might encourage them further by saying, "You mean no one here wants to know anyone better." This may be met with a display of discomfort or laughter, and at this point it is best to investigate what the students were feeling by discussing their objections to moving. Even if no one in the class responds to the initial experiment, reactions are taking place within each person. Some members may be confused about who they would choose or how they would show their feelings and therefore might not be able to make a decision. They may have thought it over and decided to do nothing. Some people might have hoped that someone would make a decision to come over to them, relieving them of having to initiate the action.

Questions may be raised for classes that will help students tie in their experiences to making choices. The following is one way that this can be explored.

(1) What were your feelings: when I told you what the initial task would be; while you were moving or anticipating someone else's move; after the task was completed?

(2) How did you decide: (a) who you would like to know better; (b) how you would show that person how you feel; (c) whether or not you would act on your feeling?

(3) Outside life experiences in the classroom: (recommended for small groups)

Under what other circumstances have you experienced similar feelings to those you felt here today?

What decisions did you make under those circumstances?

What correlations can you make that will help you understand the patterns of your choices?

What other alternatives do you believe are open to you?

How do you see your ability to make decisions as a reflection of your self image?

During experiences of this sort within classes on both the high school and college level, I have found that it is immaterial whether or not the class moves at your signal. In both cases, students have disclosed feelings about: (1) being rejected—the feeling that the person they choose may not be open to them. (2) Being misunderstood—someone might interpret their action (to the same or opposite sex) as one of sexual interest. (3) Being special—hoping someone would show them their feelings first. (4) Being a risk-taker—in spite of having all the above feelings the person may decide to move.

Some students claim that they like the opportunity to let their feelings be known and are more comfortable showing their feelings than telling someone about them.

This technique is multifaceted. The conflict that takes place within each person often deals with both the feelings the person has about what he wants or doesn't want to do and the feelings about what others want or expect of him. Another area for discussion, therefore, can include what effect other people have on the decision-making process within individuals.

It is my opinion that those teachers who make their own decision to try this technique will find it to be an excellent tool for helping students to discover and understand the decision-making process and their motivations behind the choices they make.

Constructing an Educational Game

SALLY L. EASTERBROOK is an instructor of health education, Department of Health Sciences, Towson State University, Baltimore, Maryland 21204. This article is adapted from a presentation given to the Maryland AAHPER Convention in October 1976, Largo, Maryland.

There are numerous types of games which can be used in a classroom. Among these are the commercially produced game, teacher adapted game, teacher made game, student adapted game, and student made game. The last four are the least expensive. An additional advantage is that they can be constructed to meet specific needs. Steps for developing an educational game for classroom use follow.

1. First, it is essential to know the capabilities of the students who will be using the game—their abilities, attention spans, and reading levels.

2. A prerequisite in game building is to outline clearly the specific purpose of the game. The constructor should know exactly how it will be used in the classroom.

   Games can be used: to introduce new topics, which creates a "set" for the learners; to illustrate an idea; or to review a unit. Some games may be used as pretests and then adapted to serve as a posttest at the end of the unit.

3. Once the purpose of the game has been formulated, the specific content can be outlined.

4. The constructor must then answer some questions concerning the classroom atmosphere during the game.

   How quiet or disruptive should the game be?
   How many students will be directly involved in game play?
If not all students are involved, what can the rest do?
How much competition should be encouraged through use of this particular game?
How much time needs to be set aside for the playing of this game?

5. Next, the constructor needs to decide what type of game to create—a board game, a word game, a team game, or some other format? What types of questions may be open-ended; based on choice, or short answer? Some questions may be opened ended; based on student answers, the players will have to make certain decisions (branching).

6. Actual construction of the game comes next. Parts should be kept to a minimum to prevent the loss and necessary replacement of pieces. If a board game is being constructed, the board should be neat and colorful. All parts should be safe and durable. Covering parts with clear contact paper decreases "wear and tear."

The construction of directions falls into this step also. Directions should be as uncomplicated, clear, and concise as possible. The object of the game should be stated and all possible situations should be included. If questions are asked during the game, an answer booklet providing all acceptable responses should be provided.

7. The last step in game construction is a trial run. A group of students should play the game on their own. From observations made during this session, modifications of time requirements, rules, directions, and wording of questions can be made.

Development, construction, and use of an educational game can be both a fun and profitable way to spend classroom time. Games can be produced for a wide variety of purposes and to meet the particular needs of students. If you haven't yet used this technique, why not give it a try?

Health 4 Fun:
A Game of Knowledge

RAYMOND NAKAMURA teaches in the programs in physical education, School of Education, DePaul University, 1011 W. Belden Avenue, Chicago, Illinois 60614.

From time to time, as a diversion from standard methods, educational games can be excellent tools for learning. "Health 4 Fun" has been a successful game because it requires a lot of knowledge and provides some fun. It can be cooperative or competitive and can be used to develop research skills in dictionaries, encyclopedias, almanacs, textbooks, journals, etc.

The purpose of the game is to fill in the blanks of a play sheet with words or phrases that fit into pre-selected health categories. The filled-in words must begin with certain letters which are chosen at the beginning of the game.

The health categories chosen must suit the level of the class. Each one is written on a separate 3x5 index card. The cards are shuffled and placed face down; four cards are drawn from the pile. As each selection is read, all players write them down in the four category blanks on the play sheet.

Letters are written on another set of index cards, one per card. These are shuffled and four are drawn from the pile. The chosen letters are written in the appropriate blanks on the play sheet.

The Game

Each player tries to think of a word or phrase in each of the 16 blanks on the play sheet that fits the category at the top of the column and begins with the selected letters. An example of a filled-in play sheet follows. To add excitement, a time limit of 2–5 minutes can be put on the game.

The game can be played as a form of solitaire or by the whole class. Teams can be made for more competitive or cooperative games.

At the end of the game, players should research the answers they could not fill in. Discussions often develop when students come up with words or phrases that the others are not familiar with. Answers may be challenged; then they must be verified by research.

In competitive games the play sheets can be scored by adding up the number of correct answers in each column, horizontally and vertically for a maximum score of 32.

Here are some suggested health categories.

1. Body systems, organs, and glands
2. Bones or muscles
3. Fruits and vegetables
4. Meats, nuts or fish
5. Dairy products
6. Ice cream flavors
7. American foods
8. Foreign foods
9. Diets
10. Fitness: names of sports
11. Fresh and saltwater fish
12. Types of transportation
13. Types of fuel
14. Pollutants: cigarette names
15. Pollutants: automobile names
16. Environmental pollutants
17. Germs or bacteria
18. Medical laboratory apparatus
19. Human diseases
20. Communicable diseases
21. Non-communicable diseases
22. Drugs, medicine tradenames
23. Slang for drugs or medicines
24. Over the counter drugs
25. Pollutants: detergents
26. Wines
27. Beer
28. Soft drink tradenames
29. Hospital names
30. Health related journals
31. Health book titles
32. Health authors
33. Famous health people, past
34. Famous health people, present
35. Health organizations or societies
36. Health agencies, offices or departments
37. Health related professions
38. Environment: mountains
39. Environment: extinct animals or birds
40. Environment: endangered species
41. Environment: rivers and lakes
42. Environment: national parks
43. Bakery products
44. Famous restaurants
45. Kitchen utensils
46. Health related household items
47. Things commonly found in the medicine cabinet
48. Health related words over seven letters
49. Breakfast cereals
50. Famous physicians
51. Chemicals found in the body
52. Articles of clothing
53. Plant names
54. Flower names
55. Category of your choice

The degree of difficulty of these categories should be related to the academic level of the class. Many can be refined to offer greater difficulty. For example, a generalized category like prescription drugs can be limited to barbiturates. However, I have found it necessary to include some easy categories to ensure some success.

Category	Human Disease	Bones and Muscles	Auto Trade Names	Medical Apparatus	
D	Diphtheria	Deltoid	Dodge	Dilator	→4
W	Whooping Cough				→1
F	Fabry's Disease	Fibula	Ford	Forceps	→4
L	Leukemia		Lincoln	Lens	→3

Pre-selected Letters

4   2   3   3   24 Total Score

School Health Bee

Bernard S. Krasnow is assistant principal and supervisor of health education at Arturo Toscanini Junior High School in Bronx, New York.

Health education took a dramatic turn last year at Toscanini Junior High School in Bronx, New York. Our school inaugurated its first annual health bee in order to stimulate greater participation and interest in health education and in current health topics.

The project was created out of a desire to change the traditional assembly program so that an atmosphere of excitement would pervade the audience. The health education department held a conference devoted to this idea and it was decided to promote a school-wide health knowledge quiz. This would culminate in a series of grade auditorium programs designed to duplicate the fun and excitement of television quiz programs.

The school's health instructor, Mr. Pluchik, was designated as the teacher-in-charge for the project. He constructed a health knowledge test from our own curriculum which was administered to all the students during their health or science periods. The students who scored highest on this initial survey test were invited to a class winners' run-off. Fifty-five class winners appeared for the run-off test which was held after school. Those with five highest scores in each grade were then designated as finalists and invited to participate in the auditorium quiz programs the following week. They were given extra resources in the form of textbooks, pamphlets, etc., to study from in preparation for the contest.

The auditorium program was modeled after a television panel quiz program. The industrial arts department constructed an electrical response board so that a contestant who knew the answer

was able to press a button to make a light flash in front of him. Mr. Pluchik served as moderator and asked the questions. Three other teachers acted as judges. The questions for the final quiz were selected from among those in the initial survey and the run-off examinations.

There was great anticipation on the part of the contestants and the student body. Publicity had been extensive through public address messages, posters, and class announcements so that most of the students were eagerly awaiting the program. The contests were well received by the audience and seldom has there been more audience enthusiasm. The excitement was, in fact, so great that many times the audience inadvertently shouted out the answer. (We did, in fact, throw the questions to the audience if they were not answered correctly by the contestants.) The scoring was conducted by awarding one point for each question answered correctly. Each contestant had his own personal scoreboard that reflected his current total. This kept the audience posted on the current scores.

Each auditorium program was concluded by awarding a trophy to the health quiz winner of each grade, and the finalists received honor certificates. The school photographer was there to take pictures of all the winners and we plan to display these for publicity purposes.

Our original idea in initiating this project was to focus on health education and current health topics. We are sure that this school-wide program did just that. We are, however, promoting follow-up activities so that our initial efforts are long-lasting. Some of these activities include: establishing a health information reference center in our school library, publicizing the health quiz in the community, establishing a health award for graduation, and promoting health topics to be taught as part of the curriculum in other subjects.

We are also hoping that we can motivate other schools in our district (District 9) to conduct their own Health Bee and, perhaps, even a city-wide contest. We think that it is time to stimulate nationwide excitement for health education. Who knows, a National Health Education Bee may someday stand right alongside our National Spelling Bee.

Not Merely Nostalgia

RALPH EDWARDS is professor of health education and dean of administration and planning, Kingsborough Community College, City University of New York, Brooklyn, New York 11235.

In moods of nostalgia, I am reminded of my elementary school days when we studied health heroes which, if memory serves me, were offered us in pamphlets published by Metropolitan Life Insurance Company. Tales of great exploits by leaders of science and health, including Madame Curie, Louis Pasteur, Florence Nightingale, and Walter Reed, set an example for a generation of youth for concern for human wellbeing and a search for truth, and cannot be minimized or ignored. Studying the life history of famous individuals is a desirable teaching tool and certainly well-known to our academic colleagues. The fact that a famous Hollywood star or an athlete uses a particular deodorant, travels on a particular airline or dresses in a particular garment is valuable where it counts heavily in this society—in the pocketbook. Health educators might seriously consider turning back the clock, for at least part of their instruction, to the Charles Atlas, Babe Zaharias era, to get the attitudinal value and maturation for us in education.

Some may have seen a recent news item concerning Richard M. Eakin, Professor of Zoology at Berkeley. Dr. Eakin, in order to make his subject alive and more interesting, has developed a technique of dressing up in the costume of famous lecturers in areas of zoology. Gregor Mendel, William Beaumont, Charles Darwin, William Harvey, Louis Pasteur are among "guests" that Eakin brings to his students. While teachers cannot be expected to be actors, certainly the impressions made by this instructor and the favorable response of the students suggests a new slant on an old approach to content and impact.

For some time I have introduced courses in health education with a historical perspective. Within these historical perspectives, individuals were sin-

gled out for their contribution to understanding health. Aesculapius and Hippocrates were the heroes of ancient Greece; Celsus and Galen of Greco-Rome; Rhazes, Avicenna, and Moses Maimonides of the Byzantine era; Paracelsus, Vesalius, Pare, Harvey, of the Renaissance; Lind, Hunter, Pinel, Rush, Bright, Braid were the 17th and 18th century heroes of the Enlightenment. The 19th century was full of individual efforts of Europeans as depicted by Claude Bernard, John Snow, Ludwig Ignaz Semmelweis, Rudolf Virchow, Florence Nightingale, Louis Pasteur, Joseph Lister, Richard Kraft-Ebbing, Robert Koch, Paul Ehrlich, Sigmund Freud, and Havelock Ellis. Americans are well placed in the health hall of fame of the 19th century by such luminaries as William Beaumont, Ephraim McDowell, James Marion Sims, William Morton, Clara Barton, William Osler, William Welch, Walter Reed, William Halsted, Simon Flexner, and Walter Cannon.

American contemporaries of the 20th century do not pale when we mention them in comparison to earlier heroes. Howard A. Rusk spent a lifetime treating the physically disabled and educating the public about the importance of rehabilitation; Will and Charles Mayo developed the model for cooperative group medical practice; Paul Dudley White, cardiologist, exercise proponent and physician to a president; Benjamin Spock, baby doctor, child care expert, social critic; Carl and William Menninger, advocates of psychiatric treat-

ment; Karl Landsteiner discoverer of four blood types; Jonas Salk and Albert Sabin, researchers and developers of polio vaccine; C. Walter Lillehi, Arthur DeBakey, Denton Cooley, pioneers in artificial heart devices; Linus Pauling, chemist of molecular structure and advocate of vitamin C; Rachel Carson, who in *Silent Spring* (1962) documented the effects on the environment of synthetic organic insecticides (DDT) and herbicides; John Rock and Gregory Pincus developed a synthetic fertility hormone; Rene Dubos, biochemist and advocate of antibiotic therapy; and, Hans Selye, endocrinologist and exponent of the "stress theory" of disease.

We can add to the list above the yearly Nobel Prize winners in chemistry, medicine, and biology. We do have a large assembly of heroic figures who have spent their professional lives working to keep man healthy and fit. Their accomplishments can be recognized as a teaching device and as a technique for valuable discussion. Their efforts demand applause even in an era which glorifies the anti-hero in fiction, movies, and television. Acknowledging the contribution of real heroes and placing them in a setting of everyday living is an important contribution to the student of health education and to the average citizen.

In bringing the heroes forward, it is not so much a question of what we can contribute to their memory, but rather what remembering them can contribute to us and our teaching.

Health in Concert

This article was submitted by the Senior Health Education Seminar, spring quarter 1976, Bowling Green State University. It was edited by CLAY WILLIAMS, assistant professor of health education, Bowling Green State University, Bowling Green, Ohio 43403 and JUDY SCHEER, assistant professor of health education, University of Toledo, Toledo, Ohio 43606.

What do "Puff the Magic Dragon," "Dead Babies," and "Junkfood Junkie" have in common? These and other such popular songs are a fantastic means of learning about current health issues. A "health concert" is a means of developing health concepts by capitalizing on a popular pastime of today's youth—music.

Music has much appeal for the young and old alike. It can have a calming effect as well as an energizing effect. The topic range is as diverse as the performers themselves. Some approach life with sincerity and heartache while others emphasize humor or entertainment. Listening to music of entertainers like John Denver can create a greater understanding of human emotions, actions, philosophies, and lifestyles. By bringing music into the classroom students and teachers have the tools to elaborate upon the relationship between music and health.

Songs can be used to introduce a unit or to maintain interest during the course of a unit. For example, by using a song like "Junkfood Junkie" as a part of a nutrition unit, a teacher could easily develop several followup activities relating to the theme of the song. This song touches on the social aspects of America's eating habits—the fast food craze, health foods, junk foods, vitamin supplements, and convenience foods.

Using this song to introduce a unit, challenge students to see how many nutrition concepts are in the lyrics. Their lists of concepts could then be used as guidelines to develop an overview of the unit. The song could also serve as a springboard for group activities or individual projects to develop the practical aspects of nutrition. Students may want to survey local fast food chains to obtain data enabling them to compare quantity and nutritional value for the consumer dollar. They could also research nutritional information about foods mentioned in the song. Others may want to construct low calorie meal plans which would provide essential nutrients while allowing occasional indulgence in junk foods without fear of weight gain.

Peter, Paul, and Mary's song "Puff the Magic Dragon," can be focused on marijuana, mental health, value clarification, and understanding one's self and relationship with others, creating an opportunity for lively discussion as students are challenged to search for the numerous interpretations that are provided in the lyrics. Interesting comparisons can be drawn when students are asked to interpret these lyrics both before and after appropriate health units. Students could also be encouraged to express their feelings and knowledge, individually or collectively, in song.

Another application would be to develop a mood chart based on the students' feelings after listening to the song. From this exposure, a discussion could be focused on using alternatives as a means of achieving highs. After such discussions, one could give the students a video camera and allow them to express visually and to share various opportunities for achieving natural highs.

Examples of additional health units and some songs that might be used in each category are as follows:

Drugs
"Mother's Little Helper" Rolling Stones
"The No No Song" Ringo Starr
"Momma Told Me Not to Come" Three Dog Night
"The Needle and the Damage Done" Neil Young
Personal and Social Relations
"At Seventeen" Janis Ian
"Looking for the Right One" Elvis Presley
"Everything I Own" David Gates
Death
"Patches" Clarence Carter
"Ode to Billy Jo"
"Run Johnny Run"

Alcoholism
"What Can A Family Say" America
"Social Disease" Elton John
"Another Try" America
Safety
"Convoy" W. C. McCoy
"Dead Man's Curve" Carpenters
Mental Health
"Sweet Surrender" John Denver
"Twisted" Joni Mitchell
"Leave Me Alone" Helen Reddy
"Brain Damage" Pink Floyd
Environment
"Where Will the Children Play" Cat Stevens
"Big Yellow Taxi" Joni Mitchell
Nutrition
"Junk Food Junkie" Larry Grace
"Savoy Truffle" Beatles
Venereal Disease
"You Left Me Sore" Todd Rungren
Contraception
"Unborn Child" Seals and Croft
"The Pill" Loretta Lynn
Sex Education
"All the Girls Love Alice" Elton John
"Sweet Painted Lady" Elton John
Aging
"When I'm Sixty Four" Beatles
"Old Folks" (from Jacques Brel is alive and well and living in Paris)
"Today is the First Day of the Rest of My Life" John Denver

Suggestions to help make your health concert an effective learning experience are:
1. Use quality audio equipment
2. Screen the songs before they are played to the class
3. Make copies of the lyrics for the students
4. Be open to a variety of interpretations
5. Be aware of misconceptions that may be conveyed in a song
6. Try to use current or well-known songs so the students can identify with them
7. Do not overuse the strategy

Tuning In To Health Education

WARREN L. McNAB is assistant professor of health education, Department of Health and Physical Education, University of Houston, 3801 Cullen Blvd., Houston, Texas 77004.

Music can be used effectively in health teaching because today it incorporates what is taking place in "real life" and stimulates moods in both young and old. Lyrics tell of death, love, life, human relationships, sorrow, happiness, and many other emotional experiences.

In health education these particular topics, as well as several others, are dealt with in the physical, mental/emotional, and social makeup of health. Interpreting music in conjunction with the health education discipline requires students to critically analyze and describe for themselves, based upon their own interpretation of the song and lyrics, what message or mood is being conveyed.

One way in which we used music in health education was to have students interpret a song sung by Melissa Manchester entitled "Midnight Blue." Before playing the record divide the class into groups of four or five and give each student a copy of the lyrics to the song. The groups read along and listen carefully to the lyrics and interpret what is said by applying the song to a specific situation.

The three situations are: (1) A friend is contemplating suicide and is on a ledge ready to jump—you are there trying to persuade this person to stop his/her attempt; (2) there has been a recent death in your immediate family; (3) you and your husband/wife are contemplating, or are on the verge of getting a divorce. Each group is given one of these situations. Based upon their particular situation each group is to relate and interpret what the song's lyrics mean and how it can be tied into the topic of mental health. The song is played and the groups are given ten minutes to decide what the lyrics mean in relation to their assigned topic and how each situation deals with mental/emotional health. These ideas are then shared in a class discussion.

The following lines from Melissa Manchester's song "Midnight Blue" and the students' interpretations serve as an

example of how we applied and interpreted the three situations to the song.

Line 1—*Whatever it is—it'll keep till the morning*
Suicide: Things right now seem unbearable, but perhaps we can iron out the problem tomorrow. Give it one more chance.
Death: If we can just get through today's sadness and grief, tomorrow will be better.

Divorce: Can't our differences be settled tomorrow? Let's sleep on it and we may change our minds.

Line 2—*Haven't we both got better things to do?*
Suicide: You have a purpose in life, you can be somebody, you will hurt others by what you are doing; there is much more in life to experience.
Death: One must go on in life; death is part of living.
Divorce: Can't we try something else besides divorce?

Line 3—*Midnight blue*
Suicide:
Death: Dark, black, fearful, mysterious
Divorce: time of one's life

Line 4—*Even the simple things become rough*
Suicide: Everyone has problems in life. At any one time we may think life is not worth living, but we can adjust to most problems. Suicide won't resolve these problems.
Death: Even though we know death is coming, it is extremely difficult to accept.
Divorce: Every little thing hurts at times like this; there is no simple solution.

This approach to teaching allows students to interpret the message stated in the song and through individual and collective thinking apply their interpretation and feelings to a health related situation. "Midnight Blue" is effective in looking at the different, and yet similar, mental/

emotional problems that are dealt with in a crisis such as suicide, death, or divorce. Followup questions which are brought up can be directly tied into their discussions, for example: How do you *feel* after listening to the song? How do emotions affect one's life? How can emotions be beneficial in one situation and destructive in another? Can music relieve or create stress and tension? What emotions are elicited from you by this song in relation to suicide, death, divorce? How do emotions affect one's behavior? How does one's mental/emotional health affect one's physical and social health?

These are basic questions that are dealt with in the topic of mental health, but the use of music allows students to relate to this information and apply it in a relevant manner. In addition, environmental influences of one's mental health, and how music does indeed affect one's emotional health in both positive and negative aspects of life can be discussed.

Other song possibilities and their related topics are "When I'm Sixty Four" (by John Lennon and Paul McCartney) for aging, "Lighting Bar Blues" (by Arlo Guthrie) for alcohol use, "I Love You" (by Olivia Newton John) for human relationships, "Poems, Prayers and Promises" (by John Denver) for mental health, and "Junkfood Junkie" (by Larry Grace) for nutrition.

Students can also be asked to bring in a record which they feel has a health message or could be applied to a health topic. This particular method of teaching allows for individual thinking, a sharing of ideas, and it stimulates students making health education a fun, relevant and worthwhile experience.

Ideas for Successful Health Teaching*

LOREN B. BENSLEY, JR. is associate professor of health education, Central Michigan University, Mt. Pleasant, Michigan 48858.

As a professor of teaching methods, I am a great believer that how you teach is just as important as what you teach. Many times, we teach the way we were taught, rather than the way we were taught to teach. In order for health teaching to be successful, it is of utmost importance that the methods used be creative and original in every possible way. By doing this, the subject will be more interesting to the students and enhance the opportunities for behavior change. It is important that the material presented to the students be student centered rather than subject centered.

In the past ten years of teaching health education to secondary school and university students, I have discovered four essential points for successful health teaching. First, learning must be enjoyable. If the students find that learning health can be fun, it is then correct to assume that they will enter into the learning experience with a great deal of enthusiasm and excitement. Second, students must become emotionally involved in the learning process. This can be done rather easily in teaching health education; one's health is a personal thing and to become involved emotionally in the subject matter is almost automatic. The third point to consider in teaching health education is that the student should be granted a degree of academic freedom to explore his or her own health needs and interests. By so doing, the student experiences health learning as something which becomes relevant and has a purpose.

*The information in this article is based on material which appeared originally in a column entitled "Ideas for Successful Health Teaching" published in the *Journal* of the Michigan Association for Health, Physical Education, and Recreation. The *MAHPER Journal* editor, Joan Nelson, granted permission for its use.

For this to happen, it is necessary for the teacher to create an atmosphere of freedom without external threats. The fourth essential point in teaching health education is the need for the teacher to know his students. This point cannot be stressed enough. In order for a health teacher to experience success to any degree, it is necessary that he design the course with a full understanding of the students' health needs and interests. The health educator must gather data on the personal health habits, attitudes, and behaviors of those students he is teaching at any one time.

These four points are only a part of successful health teaching; they are mentioned here because oftentimes teachers overlook what might be considered the obvious items in teaching. With these points in mind, it is interesting to explore some different ways to teach health education to secondary school students, such as the following two methods I have found to be successful.

Using Popular Music In Teaching Health

Much of today's popular music has a great deal of meaning behind the strange sounds and muddled voices. By examining some of the music subscribed to by today's youth, the teacher will discover that much is written about drug abuse, human sexuality, environmental conditions, and mental and emotional health. It is suggested that the teacher listen to some of the songs from the very popular and successful rock musical "Hair." The song "Pollution" is concerned with air pollution, whereas the song "Sodomy" refers to human sexuality. This topic is also discussed in the lyrics of music composed by current popular artists such as Mick Jagger and the Rolling Stones, in "Live With Me" or "Let's Spend the Night Together." The group called The Rare Earth also sings about sexuality in their song titled "In Bed." Music about sexuality is extensive, and the health educator can be selective in choosing songs pertaining

to homosexuality, sexual intercourse, or fellatio.

Within the last few years the song "I Never Promised You a Rose Garden" became very popular. This song could be played in class and discussed in relation to mental and emotional health. The discussion could center around the fact that no one promises you everything and you must work for much that you receive in life. For a unit on mental health the author has experienced success with a ninth grade health education class using some of Simon and Garfunkel's work, notably, the songs "Bridge Over Troubled Water," "A Most Peculiar Man," and "Richard Cory." The lat-

ter two are pertinent to the topic of suicide. The students' favorite song pertaining to mental health, however, is "Walk a Mile in My Shoes" by Joe South.

The teacher can also talk about musicians or musical groups and center the discussion around the use of drugs. For example, several years ago two very popular musicians died of an overdose of drugs. The class might discuss the questions why Janis Joplin and Jimmy Hendrix used drugs and eventually took an overdose.

The use of popular music as a medium to teach health has been extremely interesting to me and my students. One reason is because the teacher is using a significant object of the teenagers' life—his music. It is, in effect, a way of reaching students through their own medium.

Using Current and Popular Literature in Teaching Health

Just as effective as using popular music in teaching health education is the use of popular literature. Are there any books you have read in the past year which could be used to teach about health? Often there is a novel, fictional story, biography, or some piece of literature that contains information pertinent to a health education class. When discussing drug abuse, students may read the book *Valley of the Dolls*, a story about barbiturate addiction and the eventual death of the main

character of the story. When discussing the topic of love and personal relationships, the ever popular novel *Love Story* is suggested to the students. This particular story, about two young people who fall in love and marry, is good because of the deep, meaningful feeling the couple have toward each other. It is essential when discussing emotions in regard to human sexuality that mature love be understood. The book *Love Story* brings this out.

There are hundreds of books that could be used for discussion purposes in a health education course. The important things when considering this method are first, that the teacher select a book which is suitable to the subject at hand and, second, that it has appeal to the students. It is both a real challenge and an enjoyable way of teaching.

The Student Interview Technique

MARC E. MEYER is a health education teacher at North Rockland High School, Hammond Road, Thiells, New York 10984.

As health educators we are always looking for ways to encourage class participation. One method seems to work quite well within my health education classes—the "student interview technique."

This technique works well because it has certain qualities which help students in a variety of ways. First, the technique is flexible, each teacher can use the interview for a particular unit or simply for a change of pace in daily routines. Second, it allows each student to communicate his/her ideas to others. It helps develop the ability to communicate and to listen, as well as to stimulate class discussion.

In speaking with my students, a number of them have said that they find the student interview, "interesting," "makes time go faster," "gives us a chance to learn more about our friends," and it is "fun." Of the many activities and options available to my classes, the "student interview technique" allows for a great range of communication and interaction within the classroom.

Below are examples of interviews used at different times throughout the semester. The interview sheet clearly tells each student to interview two individuals within the class. No student is to give more than two interviews. Upon completion, the teacher can simply call on students and the individuals who conducted the interview will tell what they discovered.

I have found that there are a variety of ways one can use this technique. Each teacher should choose that method which best suits his/her situation. The interview can be specific, (drugs, alcohol, sex education, mental health) or general, asking questions as presented here, which explore a variety of ideas and values.

By implementing activities such as the "student interview technique," students come away from class with a better feeling; most were eager to participate and most had a positive learning experience which they will not soon forget.

Interview #1

Instructions:

Interview two individuals in your class. You are not to give more than two interviews.

Questions:
Name?
What was the happiest time of your life?
What do you like to do with your free time?
Favorite musical group?
Things you like best about being in high school?
Brothers and sisters (how many)?
Where do you like to go with your friends?
What is your favorite food?
If you had a million dollars, how would you spend it?
What is your favorite sport?

Interview #2

Instructions:

Interview two individuals in your class. You are not to give more than two interviews.

Questions:
Name?
What three things do you prize most?
If you could visit anywhere in the world, where would it be?
If you could divide $5,000 between two charities, what would they be?
When was the last time you were punished?
Why were you punished?
Do you have many friends?
What do you feel was the best movie you ever saw?
What is important to you?
When was the last time you gave advice to someone?
Did he/she ask for your advice?

Interview #3

Instructions:

Interview two individuals in your class. You are not to give more than two interviews.

Questions:
Name?
What time do you get up each day?
What time do you go to sleep?
Favorite TV program?
When was the last time you gave someone a compliment?
Is it difficult to give compliments?
Is "time" important to you?
What was the most frightening movie you ever saw?
Which was the saddest movie you ever saw?

Positive Peer Influence: School-Based Prevention

AIDA K. DAVIS is a research assistant and JOAN M. WEENER is a project assistant in the Addictions Prevention Laboratory and ROBERT E. SHUTE is assistant professor of health education. They are all at Pennsylvania State University, University Park, Pennsylvania 16802.

Peer pressure is often considered a psychological force—a direct attempt by a group to influence personal behaviors of group members. However, Kiesler and Kiesler[1] have a somewhat broader view which acknowledges unplanned, but nevertheless, highly controlling influences of groups: "All that is required is that the group expect the person to act or believe in a certain way, or that the person think such things are expected of him."

Whether peer influence is defined as psychological forces or group sanctions, the mechanisms and effects are inextricably bound to the operations of social influence, which include teaching, learning, imparting ideas and skills, generating enthusiasm and purpose, and even the application of force. Peer influence and the conformity it engenders is part of a much larger context of cognitive and motivational processes related to social learning.

While any social interaction is potentially influential the greatest power to dispense social rewards and punishments to the individual member is attributed to peer group interactions. It is within the peer group that the effects of social modeling and behavioral shaping tend to be most concentrated. Especially for adolescent and college-aged people, the peer group is often cited as the primary reference group for attitudes, values, and behaviors; it is within the peer group that outside influences (parents, the law, the schools, etc.) are discussed, judged, and mediated. Acquiescence to direct or subtle pressures in peer groups has been linked to some forms of juvenile delinquency, truancy, malicious mischief, sexual experimentation, drug use, and other types of misbehavior directed against self or society.

While the motivation for initiation and continuation of drug use and the conditions under which drug attitudes and behaviors are learned are as varied as the social, religious, educational, occupational, and psychological backgrounds of the user, many writers are now emphasizing the critical role of peer influence as a variable which may override many of these considerations.[2]

Researchers in high schools and colleges have found that the likelihood of personal drug use correlates highly with the drug-using activities of one's peer group. This fact has influenced the development of a variety of school-based peer programs related to student performance and student attitude toward teachers, school, self, and others. The underlying assumption is that if students have a healthy self-concept, a favorable attitude toward their teacher and schools, a number of satisfying and enhancing interpersonal relationships with family and friends, and are comfortable about their values and abilities to make decisions, then they are much less likely to succumb to pressures which encourage self-destructive behaviors.

Several school-based programs have evolved which draw on some of the positive aspects of peer influence. For example, peer and cross-age tutoring and peer counseling, while not specifically oriented toward prevention of drug and alcohol abuse, seek to reduce behavioral problems and bridge the gap between student and teacher (or parents) by providing individualized instruction, personal interactions, and counseling. The school can include exercises which help students discuss and understand the "mechanisms" of peer influence and help them develop skills to deal with influential situations. All of these programs or strategies are meant to develop the individual's sense of personal competence and responsibility. Following are several workable strategies and resources for involving peers in prevention activities in the school setting.

Peer/Cross-age Tutoring

Peer and cross-age tutoring has been included in school programs for a long time as a way of meeting special educational needs. Historically pupils helped or taught other children in order to alleviate the responsibilities and time constraints of the teacher in the one-room schoolhouse. Later, the idea of students helping each other proved to be a promising alternative in traditional schools. The trained tutor was able to establish a personal relationship with other students and could assist them with their school work for both remedial and standard purposes. The learner was able to receive help in a variety of academic areas, while the tutors found that the teaching provided a powerful learning experience for themselves as well.

Tutoring programs vary widely in relationship to the age differences which exist between tutor and pupil. "Peer tutoring" connotes that tutors are the same age or are enrolled in the same course as the learners, whereas older students or students who had completed the course or were not enrolled in it at the same time as the pupils were defined as "cross-tutors."[3]

Tutoring techniques have been promoted as a means of enhancing the learning of both tutor and learner, though some researchers have urged caution in making this claim.[4] Tutoring responsibilities and establishing a close personal relationship with the learner are important affective gains for the student tutor. Opportunities for creating constructive, social, and positive roles, greatly enhance the tutor's school experience.[5] The learner's gains in academic skills and understanding seem to promote self-esteem.

Tutoring as a preventive approach to drug and alcohol abuse relies on the concomitant development of skills which ultimately enhance the student's personal satisfaction with life. These skills include *intra*personal aspects such as improved self-concept, as well as *inter*personal skills—effective communication with others, sharing personal difficulties, etc.

Resources. Many aspects involved in designing and implementing a tutoring program are discussed in a variety of training guides available to schools. The

National Commission on Resources for Youth under the direction of Mary Kohler has developed a tutoring project called "Youth Tutoring Youth." Several hundred programs have been started in schools and by community agencies across the nation. Over 3,500 persons have been trained in the techniques of tutoring through this flexible program which can be adjusted to meet the needs of school or community groups.[6]

The Ontario-Montclair School District in California has developed a cross-age teaching manual designed to help teachers or administrators organize and implement a tutoring program. This manual describes agendas for training seminars and the matching procedure for older and younger students as well as describing scheduling, types of activities, and cost considerations.[7]

A further guide to tutoring is included in volume two of *Balancing Head and Heart: Sensible Ideas for the Prevention of Drug and Alcohol Abuse.*[8] These books were produced for Pennsylvania's Governor's Council on Drug and Alcohol Abuse and contain a general rationale for primary prevention along with descriptions of eleven school-based approaches to prevention of drug abuse, including peer tutoring and peer counseling. Sensible guidelines for implementing strategies and providing resources make this publication a handy reference guide.

Peer Counseling

Another activity, defined by M. G. Sussman, which capitalizes on the positive effects of peer influence, is peer counseling: "a process in which trained and supervised students offer listening, support, and alternatives and other verbal and non-verbal interaction, but little or no advice, to students who refer themselves."[9] Peer counseling programs are usually designed as supportive programs which complement or supplement existing guidance programs in the schools. While including academics, peer counseling programs are generally aimed at clarification of feelings, ideas, and values in order to enhance personal decision-making and resolution. Trained students provide a climate of acceptance for those fellow students who would rather share problems with a peer than with an adult.

Junior and senior high school students are trained in reflective listening skills, problem solving, and providing information or referral if needed, by school counselors, teachers, or psychologists. Training methods consist

primarily of supervised seminars or workshops for selected student volunteers. In some schools the training courses are given for credit, others provide training on an extracurricular basis. A number of programs have established a general "rap room," "drop-in center" or "unwinding room" where students are welcome to come and talk about their concerns. Appointments can also be made for private sessions with one of the peer counselors. This type of program expands available counseling resources and makes it easier for students to discuss problems on a less formal basis. Counselors are trained to recognize and refer students with serious problems to professional counselors.

Resources. A variety of training materials are available for help in implementing peer counseling programs. Samuels and Samuels' book is a thorough review of rationale, needs, organization, and evaluation of peer counseling.[10] The au-

Photo: NEA Communication Services

thors provide a detailed account for interested administrators and participants. The *Balancing Head and Heart* series notes the benefits for both counselors and counselees in communication skills, self-confidence, and self-esteem.

Newsletters such as the one distributed by the National Resources for Youth[11] cover a number of projects in which teenagers counsel their peers. A prevention resource bulletin, "Pyramid," sponsored by the Prevention Branch of the National Institute on Drug Abuse reviews and reports on peer tutoring and counseling prevention programs.[12] A manual entitled *Teen Involvement: A Teen Counselor Training Manual* by Gladys Conroy contains a number of ideas for training teen counselors to work in the area of drug and alcohol abuse prevention.[13]

Integrated Classroom Experiences

More informal, planned interventions in the classrooms, which integrate normal lessons with opportunities for student growth in dealing with situations involving peer and/or social influence, offer attractive, inexpensive starting points for peer prevention programming.

Peer Influence   "Convince Me"   Time: 35 minutes

Purpose: To have students develop an awareness of how they influence and are influenced by their peers.

Materials: One mimeographed sheet for each student in the class. Half of the sheets should have the following written on them:

Role A—You've just left a home basketball game. Your older sister, who's obviously drunk, pulls over and says she wants to show you and your friend how fast her new car can go on a back road near town. You love the feel of speeding and are anxious to accept her offer, so although you think your friend is probably chicken, you try to convince him/her that he/she would be a fool not to go along.

The other half of the sheets should have this written on them:

Role B—You're a fairly shy person and don't want to have anything to do with what your friend suggests.

Procedure
1. Pass Role A out to half the class, Role B to the other half of the class, asking students to keep their role secret.
2. Have each student with a Role A sheet pair up with a student with a Role B sheet. If there is an uneven number, have the extra student watch two others role play.
3. Give students about five minutes to play their roles.
4. Now have students trade roles and again spend about five minutes playing the opposite role.
5. Ask students to return to their seats and have a class discussion about how they felt in each role.
6. Discussion hints:
a. How did you feel in each role?
b. What did your partner do to make you feel that way?
c. What are some pros and cons of trying to get others to do things we want them to do?
d. Under what circumstances would you try to convince a friend to do something?
e. What do you gain when you give in? What do you lose?

Adaptations:
1. Add more roles so that two or three students can try to convince classmates to do something they do not want to do. Have the students rotate roles within the group.
2. Have three students try to convince three other students to do something they do not want to do. The activities can be modified e.g., taking drugs; going swimming in cold water; etc.

Integration Suggestions: Role playing is so versatile and enjoyable that you should find students eager to participate and initiate suggestions. A few possibilities are:

1. Mathematics—Devise roles for students so they may try to convince others of the "best" way to invest $10,000. The setting could be a board of directors meeting for a small business.
2. Art—Devise roles for the artist, the merchant, the buyer, and the skeptic. Have the artist try to convince the merchant to display his creation. Have the merchant try to convince the buyer to buy it. Have the buyer try to convince a skeptical friend that he/she has made a wise purchase. A funny painting or sculpture would be an asset to the exercise. Discuss the motivation of each person in the role-play scene.

Contributed by Liz Kramer and Robert Shute

A number of other peer-related activities such as drop-in centers, alternatives-for-youth programs, vocational skills training, and youth service programs have been developed in both school and community settings. These programs encourage activities which provide meaningful alternatives to drug and alcohol use. Program goals may range from developing clearly defined skills, such as photography, macrame or dancing, to experiencing and sharing insight and ideas with peers and becoming involved in service to others. The concept of service to others as a developmental goal for schools has been acknowledged by Kohler:

> Our schools are no longer filling the needs of our children. A generation ago, living itself provided opportunities for youngsters to be with adults, to grasp the satisfaction of work. Today we stick kids in a world of their own and tell them to stay where they are until we need them. Despite the increased number of "people needs" in our complex society, adolescents aren't given a chance to "help out." We must link the teen-agers into the system—and give them opportunities to help meet human needs.[15]

Alternative projects for peers, along with peer tutoring, peer counseling, and classroom activities, draw strength as prevention activities by using positive peer models rather than focusing on a specific social/or health related problem.

Resources. For those who wish to become more familiar with alternative peer and prevention approaches the following publications are recommended. *Alternative Pursuits for America's 3rd Century: A Resource Book on Alternatives to Drugs* provides a guide to possible projects. The section entitled "Alternatives" in the *Balancing Head and Heart* series offers ideas for teenage projects. *Youth Alternatives,* the monthly newsletter of the National Youth Alternatives Project, offers descriptions of programs as well as funding opportunities and legislative action reports.[16]

The encouraging research and program evaluations point toward the efficiency of using peers as change agents for the prevention of drug and alcohol abuse. Likewise, the translation of the "positive peer influence" concept to other health related or social problems such as contraception behavior, smoking, reckless driving, etc., should be seriously considered when planning school or community prevention programs.

During the past year, a review of the research and existing curricular resources which relate directly to aspects of peer pressure/peer influence was conducted as a task of the Peer Pressure Project (funded by the Addictions Prevention Laboratory and directed by Robert E. Shute). The project staff will have adapted a number of flexible lesson plans from existing resources or will have created new ones when the project is completed.[14] These lesson plans will form one section of a teacher resource package for integrating peer influence lessons into a classroom. A sample lesson with integration suggestions is presented here.

We know of no other compilation of strategies similar to the one being developed for the Peer Pressure Project. Certainly, many excellent ideas for integrating peer influence study can be found in recent texts, curriculum guides, and audiovisual materials on related topics—affective education, humanistic education, developmental education, and confluent education. Several peer-related exercises can be adapted from the wealth of existing materials which schools can use to enhance learning, improve decision-making skills, clarify values, etc., at all educational levels. Generally, these have come to be highly regarded as valid enhancers of the educational experience.

[1]Kiesler, C. and Kiesler, S. *Conformity.* Reading, Mass.: Addison Wesley Publ., 1969.

[2]Dumont, M. "Mainlining America: Why the Young Use Drugs." *Social Policy,* November/December 1971, pp. 36–40.

[3]Deterline, W. A. *Training and Management of Student Tutors.* ERIC Document Reproduction Service, No. ED 048 133, 1970.

[4]Willis, J. and Crowder, J. "Does Tutoring Enhance the Tutor's Academic Learning?" *Psychology in the Schools,* 1974, II(1), pp. 68–70.

[5]Gartner, A.; Kohler, M. C.; and Riessman, F. "Every Child a Teacher," *Childhood Education,* 1971, pp. 12–16.

[6]*Youth Tutoring Youth: A Manual for Trainers.* National Commission on Resources for Youth, 36 West 44th St., New York, 1970.

[7]*A Cross-age Teaching Resource Manual,* Ontario-Montclair School District, 950 West D St., Ontario, Calif., 1971.

[8]*Balancing Head and Heart: Sensible Ideas for the Prevention of Drug and Alcohol Abuse,* Pacific Institute for Research and Evaluation, Suite 201, Quail Ct., Walnut Creek, Calif., 1975.

[9]Samuels, J. and Samuels, D. *The Complete Handbook of Peer Counseling,* Miami, Fla.: Fiesta Publ., 1975, p. 41.

[10]*Ibid.*

[11]*Resources for Youth,* National Commission on Resources for Youth, 36 West 44th St., New York.

[12]*Pyramid,* Pacific Institute for Research and Evaluation, Walnut Creek, Calif.

[13]Conroy, G. *Teen Involvement: A Teen Counselor Training Manual.* New York: Holt, Rinehart and Winston, 1972.

[14]Shute, R. E. *Explorations in Social and Peer Influence: A Resource Manual for Teachers—Grades 7–10,* 1977.

[15]*Alternative Pursuits for America's 3rd Century: A Resource Book on Alternatives To Drugs,* National Institute on Drug Abuse, Washington, D.C., 1974, p. 2.

[16]*Youth Alternatives,* National Youth Alternatives Project, Inc., 1346 Connecticut Ave., NW, Washington, D.C.

Ernie

LILLIAN D. FESPERMAN is a graduate assistant in health and physical education, Miami University, Oxford, Ohio 45056.

Are you tired of teaching digestion, respiration, circulation, the body systems and functions the same way year after year, class after class? Or are you an inexperienced teacher looking for a new approach for old, unchanging yet vital material? In either case, here is a successful, exciting, beneficial solution which can motivate your students.

When I was teaching health at Alexander Graham Junior High School in Charlotte, North Carolina, I was a first year teacher willing to try just about anything that would motivate my students. I had to present a unit on the systems of the body and wanted to try a new, creative approach. After evaluating possibilities, I came up with the idea of constructing a body in class.

Selling my idea to the students was extremely easy and well-received; everyone wanted to "build a body." We first got basic background information on the systems of the body and gathered our ideas and materials for building a body. We included five systems—digestive, skeletal, respiratory, circulatory, and nervous—on our body. Since there were five seventh grade health classes, each class contributed one system to the body.

Information about systems was covered in class by a series of handouts, lectures, discussions, pictures, and films. Students were required to keep a notebook related to the systems which they handed in at the end of the unit. To further instill interest in the students, as we discussed the systems I mentioned ideas and suggestions about the body that we could try. We all knew we were working to gather enough information to construct a life-size body out of a variety of "raw" materials.

After completing the general background information, a system was assigned to each class and that class was responsible for bringing in any materials related to their system. They were also required to read books and study pictures and charts related to their systems. Specific tasks were assigned to small groups, who worked together to make their particular system fit into the body.

The skeletal system included the pelvic bone, upper and lower bones of the arms, finger bones, upper and lower leg bones, the kneecap, the sternum, collarbone, and back vertebrae. The nervous system had the brain and spinal cord, and nerves. Our digestive system was made up of the tongue and esophagus, spleen, liver, stomach, small intestine, large intestine, and the rectum. The nasal cavity, trachea, bronchial tubes, and lungs (one open and one closed) with alveoli were the

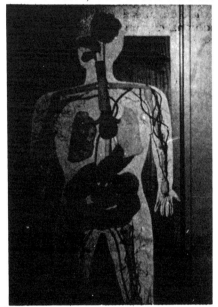

"Ernie", created by seventh grade students.

parts of the respiratory system. The circulatory system consisted of the heart, aorta, large and small veins, and arteries.

We needed a base on which to mount our body parts. After considering the possibilities of cardboard, wood and other hard material, we decided to use a big sheet of plywood so we could attach the organs and have them stay in place. The plywood (about 5' by 3') was supplied by one student's parents. We cut out a body frame from paper, glued it onto the plywood and started assembling organs and parts.

The materials brought in by the classes for use included chicken bones, styrofoam of all sizes and shapes, sponges, thread of assorted colors, wire and plastic-coated wires of various colors and sizes, clay, newspaper, paints, cardboard cylinders, empty thread

spools, balloons, nails, cloth scrap, glue, and toothpicks.

We made some of our bones out of sticks covered with papier maché, and others with styrofoam cut into the shapes of the bones we wanted. The bones were attached to the body frame first along with the trachea, which we made from a cardboard cylinder wrapped in yarn for the cartilage, and the bronchial tubes, which were made from clay. The digestive system was then attached. The tongue was a small, semi-inflated balloon; the esophagus was a small cardboard tube fitted inside the trachea. The stomach and large intestines were papier maché wrapped over blown up balloons. The balloons were then deflated and the papier maché organs cut in half to make a flat surface to mount on the plywood body. The small intestine, liver, and spleen were made out of clay which was dried and painted, then nailed or glued onto the frame. The nasal cavity was cardboard cut into shape, the bronchial tubes were clay, and the lungs were styrofoam. One lung was painted as if it were closed, the other lung was constructed as if it were open. The capillaries were drawn with magic marker and little pieces of sponge glued on it to show the alveoli.

The heart was made by cutting the shape out of a thick sponge, with veins and arteries drawn into it. The pulmonary vein and artery and the aorta were inserted into the sponge with big red and blue wires. From the heart came red and blue arteries and veins made from wire and thread. Veins and arteries not made of wire or thread were drawn on the body with red and blue pens. The nervous system was done with various colored wires for the nerves leading all through the body to the fingers and feet. The spinal cord was made of yellow yarn leading from the brain, which was a piece of plastic cauliflower since the bumps and shape were similar. We cut the cauliflower to make a flat back surface to fit onto the frame. It was definitely an authentic-looking part of the body.

All of the parts were either glued, taped, or nailed into place on the body frame. The bones were mounted first with the trachea, esophagus, and bronchial tubes. Then the lungs, heart, and digestive system was fitted into place. The veins, arteries, and nerves were intertwined into place last, making our body complete. The classes then named our project body "Ernie."

Other suggestions for materials that we did not include in our project that could be added to yours are a mop for hair, or maybe garden hose for intestines. Or how about bottle caps or ping-pong balls for eyes? Other ideas may be to use false teeth or plastic ears to make your body more complete.

The project was stimulating and interesting to the students. The students responsible for making system parts and placing them onto the body also had to explain the operations of the organ or part. They benefited greatly from this project by learning about the human body and working together and had fun doing it. It is an excellent idea to try in your own classroom. Why not create your own "Ernie"?

Focus on Content

Empathizing With Addicts

PETER FINN is senior education and training analyst at ABT Associates, Inc., 55 Wheeler Street, Cambridge, Massachusetts 02138.

Most people who have never experienced a major addiction such as, alcoholism, drug dependence, compulsive eating, or cigarette smoking, have little understanding and often many misconceptions about what it feels like to have a persistent and irresistible craving for a substance or activity. An addiction is defined here as a craving for a substance or activity which a person cannot at the moment resist consistently or for a sustained period of time. In the following learning exercise, students gain insight into the nature of addictions by refraining for an agreed-upon period of time from an activity they have found extremely enjoyable for some time. As a result of this period of "abstinence," students may be better able to appreciate what an addicted person feels like and how they can best help relatives and friends who may have a dependency.

The exercise may also enable some students to realize that they have a strong and perhaps ungovernable urge for a substance or activity and to consider whether their compulsive behavior is healthy and what causes it. The exercise can foster insight into why everyone feels dependent on some activities and provide an inkling of how the students may feel if they are some day deprived of a substance or activity to which they have become accustomed or addicted.

This exercise has been used many times by me at the junior and senior high school level. However, it probably would be successful with elementary school students and adult groups, as well.

Procedure

Have students pick one or two activities which they would find very difficult—perhaps impossible—to stop doing. Then have each student agree in a written contract with the rest of the class to forego the activity for at least a week, but preferably for a month. It might be more enjoyable and educational for students to experiment with a friend or small group, with each person renouncing the same activity. Depending on their "passions," students might:

use no salt or sugar in their food
give up cigarettes
stop seeing or talking with a close friend
not kiss or touch their girlfriend, boyfriend, husband, or wife
not make or answer any telephone calls
get up at 4:00 a.m. every morning (not sleep late)
stop watching television or listening to the radio
give up Coke, coffee, or another favorite beverage
give up a favorite sport or other form of recreation
stop chewing gum

It may be helpful for the students to keep a diary of their behavior and feelings during the experiment to jog their memory when they relate their experiences to the class. Students can also talk into a tape recorder at the end of each day and play back excerpts to the class at the conclusion of the experiment.

Follow-up Discussion

After students have refrained from their activities for at least a week, have the class recount their experiences, then answer the following questions.

1. How many of you succeeded in refraining from your activities for the entire period of time stipulated in your contracts? How soon did those who failed give in? How do those of you who failed give in? How do those of you who failed feel about yourselves—disappointed? angry? indifferent? relieved? How do those of you who succeed feel—superior? sympathetic? resentful? neutral?

2. What did not doing the activity feel like? Did you miss it badly? Did you get angry? frightened? miserable? grouchy? bored? frustrated?

3. Did your relationships with other people change? For example, did you avoid certain people, or people in general, spend more time than usual with certain people, or with people in general, or relate to people differently such as, arguing more than normally?

4. Did talking or being with other students who were refraining from the same activity (or a different activity) help you resist the temptation to give in? Did you ask for, and get, help from other people in your attempts to forego the activity? How did they respond? How would you have liked them to respond?

5. Did other people change their behavior, attitudes, or feelings toward you as a result of your experiment? How did you feel about and react to that?

6. Did you start doing things that you don't usually do, such as forget things, become less observant, overeat, or develop physical symptoms such as headaches, stomach aches, tics, loss of appetite, insomnia, or unusual fatigue?

7. Did your other activities change at all? Did you compensate for the lack of your "forbidden" activity by participating more in some other pursuit? Did the substitute activity help take your mind off the thing you wanted to do? Did your efforts at compensation affect any of the people around you?

8. Were you confronted with an opportunity to "lapse," and did your willpower diminish in the presence of the forbidden activity or object? Were other people considerate in not mentioning the activity or substance, or helpful in suggesting a substitute?

9. Did you go out of your way to avoid the activity or substance, or things that might remind you of it? Did your avoidance behavior help reduce your craving?

10. Did you cheat at all? If so, did you try to engage in your activity just a little and find you couldn't resist resuming it completely? Did you bother to hide your lapses from other people? If so, did anyone catch you cheating? How did they react? How did you feel about being discovered?

11. When you finally did go back to the activity, how did it feel? Did you try to "make up for lost time"?

After the class has explored the issues related to these questions, students can discuss how their actions and feelings might be similar to those of an alcoholic, drug addict, cigarette smoker, compulsive eater, or other addicted person. The group should also consider how its experiences may have been different from those of truly addicted people. For example, the students knew they could resume their activity with impunity at the end of the test period, while an alcoholic, who has stopped drinking or an obese person who has begun dieting knows that to revert to their former behavior is to court disaster.

Students may also erroneously conclude, based on their own success, that addicted people should be able with relative ease to reject their self-destructive practices. The students' experience may have misled them because their own craving was a comparatively mild one and made even more bearable by the realization that it was only temporary.

Finally, focus specifically on how the students feel about addicted people. Do they feel the same way about alcoholics or drug addicts as they felt about themselves during their experiment? Should they? Did they gain any new insights into what it feels like to have an addiction and how addicted people can best be helped to shake off their dependency? Were the students able to identify any compulsive behaviors of their own and gain a better understanding of how to evaluate and cope with them?

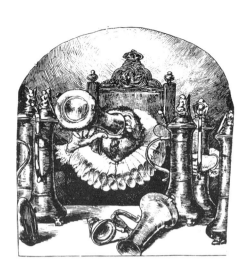

How Much Can I Drink?

H. RICHARD TRAVIS is assistant professor of health science, James Madison University, Harrisonburg, Virginia 22802.

I teach drug education courses and frequently, when discussing alcohol, students will ask how much a person can drink before being considered drunk. I point out that there are many variables that influence the extent to which an individual will be affected by alcohol.

1. Some people are affected more than others because of their biochemical make-up.

2. The attitude or mood of the individual at the time of drinking as well as the environment in which alcohol is drunk influence the effect.

3. Food and liquid in the stomach dilute the alcohol and slow down its absorption.

4. The carbon dioxide in carbonated alcoholic beverages tends to hasten the movement of the alcohol from the stomach through the pylorus to the small intestine where the majority of alcohol is absorbed.

5. The blood alcohol level reached in the body is related to the individual's body weight. A larger person has more body fluids and blood to dilute alcohol than a smaller person. The more alcohol in the blood, the more that can diffuse into the cells of the body. Most states set 0.1% as the blood alcohol level at which a person is considered legally drunk.

A number of charts are available in textbooks or from state divisions of motor vehicles which relate the number of drinks a person consumes to weight

and subsequent blood alcohol level. I use the following chart to have students calculate what their blood alcohol level might be after a certain number of drinks and the number of minutes since they first started drinking. Most students know their body weight, but if not, a scale can be brought into the room for them. They follow these steps to figure their blood alcohol level.

1. Emphasize that this chart is a guide and not a guarantee. Remind the class of the variables that have been listed.

2. If your weight is between two of those shown on the chart, use the lower weight.

3. On the chart, look up the blood alcohol level associated with your weight and the number of drinks that would have been drunk during a certain time period. One drink equals 12 ounces of beer, or 5 ounces of wine, or 1½ ounces of 80–100 proof whiskey.

4. Write down the blood alcohol level from

5. Write down the total number of minutes that would have elapsed between starting to drink and leaving the party, e.g., two hours or 120 minutes.

6. The liver is continuously metabolizing alcohol so we have to make a subtraction from the blood alcohol level from the chart depending upon how long we have been drinking. The correction factor is calculated by first dividing the total number of drinking minutes into 40 minute segments and then multiplying that answer by .01%. This is the correction factor for the alcohol that is metabolized by the liver.

7. Subtract the correction figure from the blood alcohol level that we obtained from the chart in step three. This is the approximate

Addictive Behaviors

blood alcohol level after a certain number of drinks in a certain time period.

8. Refer to the chart to see what the effects of this blood alcohol level might be.

The following example illustrates the steps.

A 180-pound person consumes 4 drinks in two hours.

Steps 3 & 4: .083 blood alcohol level from the chart.

Step 5: 2 hours = 120 minutes.

Step 6: (a) $\dfrac{\text{total \# of drinking minutes}}{40 \text{ minutes}} = a$

$a = \dfrac{120 \text{ minutes}}{40} = 3$

(b) $a \times .01\% =$ correction figure for liver metabolism of alcohol
$3 \times .01\% = .03\%$

Step 7: .083 blood alcohol level from the chart
  − .030 correction for liver metabolism for alcohol
  _____
  .053 estimated blood alcohol level for 180-pound person drinking 4 drinks in 2 hours.

Step 8: The chart indicates that at .05 driving becomes increasingly dangerous.

This activity has been used in the classroom and was also set up as a booth for a campus-wide alcohol awareness day. The students found this a meaningful way to estimate how many drinks they could have and the relationship this would have to their blood alcohol level.

Blood alcohol levels (percentage)

Body Weights	Drinks[a]											
	1	2	3	4	5	6	7	8	9	10	11	12
100 lbs.	.038	.075	.113	.150	.188	.225	.263	.300	.338	.375	.413	.450
120 lbs.	.031	.063	.094	.125	.156	.188	.219	.250	.281	.313	.344	.375
140 lbs.	.027	.054	.080	.107	.134	.161	.188	.214	.241	.268	.295	.321
160 lbs.	.023	.047	.070	.094	.117	.141	.164	.188	.211	.234	.258	.281
180 lbs.	.021	.042	.063	.083	.104	.125	.146	.167	.188	.208	.229	.250
200 lbs.	.019	.038	.056	.075	.094	.113	.131	.150	.169	.188	.206	.225
220 lbs.	.017	.034	.051	.068	.085	.102	.119	.136	.153	.170	.188	.205
240 lbs.	.016	.031	.047	.063	.078	.094	.109	.125	.141	.156	.172	.188

Under .05	.05 to 0.10	.10 to .15	Over .15
Driving is not seriously impaired (although some research indicates fine motor skills may be impaired at .02 or .03 level)	Driving becomes increasingly dangerous .08 is legally drunk in Utah	Driving is dangerous Legally drunk in most states	Driving is very dangerous Legally drunk in any state

[a]One drink equals 1 ounce of 80–100 proof liquor or 12 ounces of beer or 5 ounces of wine.
Reference: New Jersey Department of Law and Public Safety, Division of Motor Vehicles, Trenton, New Jersey.

Senator Hogwash

MICHAEL YOUNG is at Auburn University, Auburn, Alabama 36830.

With a little imagination educational games and activities can be used to promote learning that does get students involved. The objective of one activity may be to introduce factual information while another may promote discussion or enhance decision-making skills. Whatever the overall objective, educational games and learning activities can provide ways to make learning fun. A simulation game designed especially for smoking education is "Senator Hogwash and his tobacco advisory committee."

Simulation games can be used to help clarify values or to introduce factual information along with examining attitudes and/or behaviors about a certain issue. "Senator Hogwash" can bring out not only the health hazards of smoking but can also show that there are many economic, social, and political forces that make quick elimination of cigarette smoking unlikely.

Game Overview

Senator Hogwash is head of the Senate Committee on the Future of Tobacco. To obtain citizen input, and make points with the folks back home, he has appointed a citizen's advisory committee to make recommendations to the Senate Committee. The committee members discuss the issues from the perspective of their assigned roles and prepare a verbal report.

Committee Members

Senator I. M. Hogwash—From Horse Kiss, Kentucky, the Senator serves as an "advisor" to the advisory committee. He has heard ugly rumors of the health hazards of tobacco. He knows that tobacco means money to Kentucky and other tobacco states. He wants to do what is best for all the people he represents but is unclear as to what his position should be.

Medical Doctor—The good doctor once smoked two packs a day but quit smoking about a year ago. He has kicked the habit for good, he hopes. He hates to see anyone smoke because of the craving for a cigarette he still gets whenever he sees someone light up.

Tobacco Company Executive—As vice president of Brown and Jones tobacco company this committee member believes the claims of health hazards due to smoking are unproven. He is not really concerned with health anyway, but with promoting tobacco sales. He believes that government interference in this area would be a blow to the entire free enterprise system of our nation.

Satisfied Smoker—This smoker enjoys his cigarettes and has no desire to quit. He proclaims that smoking is a fundamental right guaranteed by the Constitution and wishes that folks would just let him smoke in peace. He feels that smoking is probably not bad for his health, but even if it is harmful, everyone has to die from something.

Tobacco Farmer—Since tobacco provides this farmer with a major part of his income he is vitally concerned with government plans in this area. He would like to see price supports and other government programs increased. He would hate to see anti-tobacco legislation passed. If that is what the future holds, however, he hopes marijuana will be legalized so he will have another cash crop to take tobacco's place.

Nonsmoker's Rights Advocate—A nonsmoker whose father recently died of lung cancer, this man has led the fight for nonsmoker's rights. He is completely against all forms of smoking and feels some type of government intervention is necessary.

Public Health Educator—This health educator, a specialist in smoking and health, knows the hazards of smoking and is making every effort to turn us into a nation of nonsmokers. He is for higher taxes on cigarettes and feels the funds raised should be earmarked for smoking education and research.

How to Play

The instructor assigns students to play the roles of various committee members. Senator Hogwash, played by the instructor or a student, introduces committee members to each other (players may want to wear name tags) and outlines the committee's task. The committee members discuss the various aspects of the tobacco issue (health hazards, smokers and nonsmokers' rights, economic impact of a possible tobacco prohibition, government's role in tobacco research and promotion, etc.) from the perspective of their assigned roles. Committee members may

compromise when necessary but they try to push through their own ideals whenever possible in order to develop recommendations for the future of tobacco in the United States.

Options

Students not assigned a committee role may be members of the interested public attending the committee meeting. They may wish to ask questions of the Senator and members of the advisory committee. The instructor may wish to appoint more than one advisory committee. These groups could present their recommendations, which may be quite different from group to group. Students who are not members of an advisory committee may be designated Senators and appointed to the Senate Committee on the Future of Tobacco. Advisory committees could present their recommendations to the Senate Committee. Senators could then discuss which recommendations they would like to see incorporated into future legislation.

Students should be introduced to the health aspects of smoking and other issues through lecture material and/or reading assignments. They should not be expected to begin play "cold." Following play, which could run from 30 minutes to one hour or more depending upon the teacher and student interest, a teacher directed discussion period can be of value in providing comments on game play and in restating major issues.

Addictive Behaviors

Student-to-Student Teaching About Tobacco Smoking

Lorraine J. Henke is a health educator at the Eugene Burroughs Junior High School, Accokeek, Maryland.

For the past three years, the decision to smoke or not to smoke has been the subject of formal discussions between eighth grade health education students from Eugene Burroughs Junior High School and elementary students in the fifth and sixth grades in various schools of Prince George's County, Maryland. The project was designed to explore the impact of presenting the smoking aspect of health education between students of close age groups. The assumption was that the fifth and sixth grade students would enthusiastically accept and comprehend the presentation and interchange of health education information with their junior high school student contemporaries. This assumption was proven to be valid.

A typical student-to-student teaching experience consists of a group of seven or eight junior high school health education students visiting a fifth or sixth grade class (frequently a science class). The eighth grade students first present the facts of smoking as a panel, then each of them leads a small group of elementary students in a discussion about the decision to smoke or not to smoke.

During the panel presentation, the junior high school students discuss the effects of tobacco smoking on the body utilizing a machine (constructed by the students) which simulates the effects on the human respiratory system. A filter tip and nonfilter tip cigarette are both "smoked" by the machine. The tar from each of the cigarettes is passed through hollow glass rods representing a person's mouth and throat. The tar that did not adhere to the glass rods then travels to glass test tubes constructed to represent a person's lungs. The presence of tar is always clearly visible, enabling succinct comparisons of tar content to be made between the cigarettes, along with analyses of tar content regardless of the type

of cigarette. Safety precautions to prevent tobacco smoking related fires, why people smoke, and how to quit smoking are presented. The audience is encouraged to join in the discussion and to ask questions of the panel members.

Following the panel presentation, the elementary students are divided into groups and each eighth grader leads a group in discussing the advantages and disadvantages of tobacco smoking. During these discussions, the eighth graders encourage the elementary students to ask questions, to voice honest opinions, and to continue to keep up-to-date regarding the facts about tobacco smoking.

At the conclusion of each instruction program, the visiting junior high school students distribute leaflets stating the facts about tobacco smoking. These leaflets are contributed by the American Cancer Society, the Tuberculosis and Respiratory Disease Association, and the U.S. Department of Health, Education, and Welfare. Also contributed by these organizations for use in the presentations are posters, research data, and other printed materials on tobacco smoking, including the booklet from HEW explaining how to construct the machine which the students used in their presentation.

Several points of interest, noted over the few years of being involved with the student-to-student teaching program, are as follows:

1. Elementary students who plan to attend the junior high school represented by the panel group respond more enthusiastically than do those who are not going to attend that school. Following this revelation, we have encouraged elementary schools to seek the services of the junior high school their students expect to attend.

2. Presentations made to large groups (over 50) of elementary students are not as successful as those given to smaller groups. There appears to be less satisfaction for both

Eighth graders make effective teachers for sixth graders—and especially when they come from the junior high school their audience will attend, when there is a good mix of race, sex, and personality.

the junior high school student teachers and the elementary school students.

3. When the make-up of the panel of junior high students includes a variety of students (in regard to sex, race, personality, and academic achievements), there appears to be a higher audience response (a very good rapport) than if these characteristics were not represented by the junior high school student teachers.

4. Parents of both the elementary and junior high school students involved in the student-to-student teaching program have responded to this form of health education in a very favorable manner.

5. Junior high school students involved in the program have repeatedly stated that their experience in teaching the facts about tobacco smoking has reinforced their decision not to smoke.

6. Repeated requests from the elementary schools have been made to initiate a similar program for other aspects of health education, especially drug education.

Where do we go from here? We are constantly seeking other effective teaching aids like the smoking machine in an attempt to improve our presentations. We are investigating the student-to-student teaching of other aspects of health education. The eighth grade student teachers are invited back each year to relate their experiences regarding tobacco smoking as they progress into the higher school grades. We seek and evaluate the suggestions of the elementary students and their junior high school student teachers. Most important, since the program has been going on for the past few years, we have been able to ask the eighth grade health students (who a few years ago were elementary students attending our student-to-student discussions) what effect the discussions had on their health attitudes and behavior. At this point sufficient data to make a conclusion have not been collected and analyzed. The favorable responses received from those students who had attended the student-to-student discussions, however, please us and spur us on to continue and improve.

Addictive Behaviors

The Smoking Game

Ian Newman is associate professor and chairman, Division of Community Health Education, at the University of Nebraska, Lincoln.

In 1964 a new rationale was published to justify an old ethic. The surgeon general's report on smoking and health reinforced the school's position that it should not allow youngsters to smoke in the school building or on the school grounds. Schools had traditionally forbidden smoking, but now they had new medical evidence to support their nonsmoking stand. Needless to say, smoking did not disappear from the high school, junior high school, or even the elementary school. In an attempt to examine the school's traditional stand on cigarette smoking by its students, a long-term examination was made to document the actual smoking behavior conducted within the school. This paper describes something of the behavior of the young people who smoked in the school and the teachers who attempted to prevent their smoking. Information presented here is based on data gathered over a nine-month period of intensive participant observation.

The General Setting of the Game

The events described in this paper took place in a Midwestern junior high school with 1,800 students. It was assumed that while this school was unique, it did have many aspects in common with other schools across the country and the students were, in fact, typical. The school in question was traditional and authoritarian. Discipline was seen as a necessary requirement of efficient administration.

At the time of the study on which this report is based, an important characteristic that distinguished the act of smoking among junior high

*This material was originally presented to the workshop on educational programs influencing youth at the National Conference on Smoking and Health, September 9, 1970, San Diego, California. The work on which this paper is based was performed pursuant to Contract number PH 108-66-192 of the United States Public Health Service, Department of Health, Education, and Welfare; William H. Creswell, Jr., principal investigator; Warren J. Huffman and Donald B. Stone, research associates.

school pupils from smoking among the adult population was its illegality. As one student put it, "When the teachers can't see the kids, the kids smoke and when the kids can't see the teachers, the teachers smoke." This situation was further complicated by the fact that machines dispensed cigarettes to any consumer, regardless of age. Advertising enhanced the pleasures of smoking through subtle inferences. Adults openly violated No Smoking signs and ordinances. Even members of the Board of Education disregarded the many No Smoking signs posted on the walls of their conference room.

At school the rules against smoking applied only to the students. Faculty members smoked in staff rooms and in the locker room office. The school appeared to be the only place where smoking was prohibited only for minors. Students saw this as a clear contradiction of principle. They pointed out, however, that smoking was not the only item of inconsistence. School regulation applying to the length of hair, the color of girls hair, the length of skirts, and the behavior of athletes all represented inconsistencies of various types clearly noted and described by many of the students. With these conditions existing, any action on the part of the students appeared to them to be justified, and activities related to cigarette smoking took on all the dimensions of a game. Smokers played the game of attempting to outsmart the teachers, who for their part attempted to enforce the school's rules and apprehend the smoking students. Achievement in either role was interpreted as winning.

The Contestants—Students

While smoking patterns differed with each subject, there appeared to be a general configuration which characterized the regular ninth-grade smoker. This is illustrated by the following statement recorded during the course of the study.

> After my dad goes to work I usually have one cigarette, then another one on the way to school. You can usually get one more outside the building before you come in and then after second hour you can get at least half a one if you hurry in the washroom upstairs. At lunch time I usually have one outside and then after fifth hour I have

another one. There's usually a bunch of us who go to the washrooms and there's always someone who's willing to stand watch for the teachers.

The Contestants—Teachers

Smoking was illegal for students. Students were encouraged to be like adults. However, when youngsters smoked—like adults—the heavy hand of the school authority descended on them. It was difficult for students to see why 40% of their adult faculty could smoke and they could not. Teachers, both smokers and nonsmokers, thought it their duty to apprehend students who smoked. Students were better at avoiding the teachers than the teachers were at catching the students. The harder the school authorities tried to catch the smokers, the more fun it was for the smokers, and the higher the status one achieved by foiling the authorities' attempt to apprehend.

This set the ground rules for the game. The risks were challenging. The payoff increased with the teachers' increased efforts to catch the cigarette smokers. The teachers felt great frustration. "If only we could cut down a few trees, they'd have no place to hide and we could catch them," lamented one counselor.

The reward to the students was expressed by one nonsmoker, who said:

> You know, I get a kick out of it every time I see a kid smoke and get away with it. It seems there are still a few things around here that you can do and get away with. It's good to know we can still beat the teachers.

Strategies of the Game

Subjects and other informants reported that smoking occasionally took place in the locker rooms, shower rooms, industrial arts shops, photographic dark room, and even in the classrooms. However, the majority of smoking in this particular school was limited to the washrooms and to a specific location adjacent to the school entrance but hidden from view by four small trees. Because both of these locations were essentially within range of easy scrutiny by the faculty, numerous techniques were utilized to foil detection. Description of one of these will serve to illustrate the process of the game.

The majority of the smoking in the school building was done during the lunch hour and between class periods. At lunch time students went to the cafeteria in three shifts. During lunch they were restricted to an area including the cafeteria and the hallways immediately adjacent to it. This area included boys and girls washrooms, which became the centers for smoking activity. Because this location was heavily traveled by faculty going

to and from lunch, smoking required a well-coordinated team effort. To further complicate the matter for the smokers, two counselors were assigned to patrol this general area.

Those concerned about being caught posted "guards" outside the washroom to warn of approaching faculty members. Methods utilized by the guards to convey their warnings varied with the urgency of the situation. The simplest method was for the guard to go inside and tell the smokers that someone was approaching. However, this endangered the guard as he then ran the risk of being caught in the smoking setting. Another procedure employed by the guard was simply to kick the door with his heel to warn of the approaching faculty member. Still another variation of this procedure was to kick the radiator pipe which passed through the wall. On occasions when a teacher approached too rapidly, or was unnoticed until the last moment, the student on guard would open the door for the teacher and greet him by name in a loud voice so that those inside would get the warning. Nonsmokers often acted as guards, and it was reported that it was safer to have a nonsmoker stand watch. They were less likely to leave their posts for a few puffs with the rest of the group.

Inside the washroom the smokers took additional precautions to avoid being caught. It was a common practice for them to stand close to urinals, sinks, or toilet stools while smoking so that it was an easy matter to get rid of the cigarettes. A wet paper towel was often kept ready to snuff out the cigarette as a last resort to avoid being caught if a teacher entered. Smokers would often stand on the toilet stools which enabled them to exhale smoke close to the air exhaust ducts on the wall. This cleared the smoke from the room. This also provided for easy disposal of cigarette butts by flushing them down the toilet.

While it was not possible to observe the smoking behavior of the girls as closely, informants reported similar practices in their washrooms; however, fewer girls smoked and the necessity for an elaborate warning system was less important. While as many as fifteen boys might congregate to smoke cigarettes at any one time, it was unusual for more than five girls to be present in a smoking situation. Girls were more likely to smoke alone or with one or two classmates. They were more apt to smoke when the washroom was empty or they avoided smoking in school altogether.

Smoking outside the school building, but on the school grounds, was less hazardous. But again students developed sophisticated systems to avoid detection. The most popular location. adjacent to the front entrance of the school and behind a group of small trees, often produced a two-step communication system to foil teachers' attempts to apprehend smokers in the act.

Students found numerous ways to test their skills of concealment against the teachers' skills of detection. Students would smoke in the front rows of the school movie theater on recreation nights. They smoked in the industrial arts shops where numerous odors aided in concealment and in shower and locker rooms which were usually unsupervised. On occasion, when faculty members supervised the loading of school buses, smokers would approach the supervising teacher to see how close they could get without being caught. Smokers and their friends appeared to enjoy the success of such endeavors.

Chances of Changing the Game Plan

Throughout the year the game varied in intensity. At times the faculty would win out, several smokers would be caught and suspended, and smoking would appear to subside. This reinforced the faculty's feeling that discipline did solve the problem. In reality, the smokers had been forced to regroup and utilize their most successful strategies. For awhile they were more careful and worked harder in maintaining the covert nature of their smoking behavior.

As in any game, learning took place. Students decided on new ploys to outsmart teachers and at times they even chose to quit the game completely; they became nonsmokers. However, to change roles and become a nonsmoker was difficult.

Teachers seemed to react to smokers the same way they reacted to students who were failing academically, probably because they had observed that smoking and failing were often associated. Students who were grouped into either of these two categories tended to be treated differently by most teachers. On teachers' evaluations, for example, smokers were rated lower than their nonsmoking colleagues. Teachers expected less of these students and tended to be suspicious of them. As a result, students who were smokers tended to be offered little latitude within the school. By comparison, nonsmokers who functioned successfully within the school were given considerable freedom, which they often abused.

As one individual, a class monitor and football team member, stated:

You know, I can do just about anything I please around here. I get on real good with the teachers. I can walk the halls whenever I want. Teachers let me out of class, monitors never ask me for my

pass; if they do, I just tell them so-and-so sent me on an errand and they never report me for not having a pass—it's rather bad actually.

By contrast, a student who was both a smoker and a poor student related the following incident. He had been given a signed hall pass to visit the office. However, he was apprehended on his way and finally escorted to his office by an assistant principal and a teacher, both of whom questioned the authenticity of his pass. The student's explanation was as follows:

I gave my pass to the teacher and he made some crack about getting out of his class—he's a good guy, however, you know. Then, as I was walking down the hall (this teacher) comes out of his classroom and asks me for my pass. I shows it to him and he makes some wise crack about forging it. He's always sticking his nose where it's not wanted. Then, I goes to the washroom and I came out and (another teacher) asks for my pass. He says the pass was not for the toilet and that I shouldn't waste time. Just as I came in the door, I stopped for a drink of water and she takes my pass and says it don't look like your writing. I gave her a bit of lip and whamo, the assistant principal appears.

These incidents and others suggest that teachers' attitudes toward certain students became inflexible. Consequently, any attempt by these students to modify their own behavioral game plan was met with little recognition and considerable resistance. As one male smoker said:

I decided I was going to go good this year. I even quit smoking. I tried real hard, but they (the teachers) just wouldn't give me a chance. I gave up in the end . . . it seemed that whenever there was trouble they thought I was involved and even when I wasn't they just wouldn't let me be good.

The Observer's Perspective

Having watched the game from the vantage point of a participant observer, trusted by the students and the teachers and not required to take sides in the contest, I noted several points over the duration of the year.

1. Cigarette smoking was not an end in itself. At this age, it wasn't the taste or the association with coffee that encouraged the students to smoke. Smoking was, in fact, just a symptom of the larger problem. The majority of nonsmoking kids thought their friends smoked to ''be big'' or to achieve status. Smokers didn't admit to this, although their actions tended to confirm the motivating forces of status, or at least compensatory behavior.

2. Records showed that young people who smoked at this early age were similar in IQ to

their nonsmoking contemporaries. While the smokers knew what was expected of them, they also knew that they were often not meeting these expectations. School records showed that they were correct in their recognition of low achievement. They were more likely to be failing courses, truant, tardy, and suspended from school than were their nonsmoking contemporaries. They didn't participate in the extracurricular life of the school and their fellow students tended to see them as low social status individuals. They chose friends who were like themselves for support. In other words, they tended to group together as a team—the peer group team.

3. Teachers tended to type individuals who smoked and held lower expectations for them. As a result, teachers tended to resist changes in behavior on the part of the smoker. Smokers had great difficulty in casting off the smoking image of low achievement and poor behavior if they chose to quit smoking.

4. As with all games, one left the scene of contest wondering what would happen if other strategies had been employed by the contestants. It appeared that the smokers had read the wrong signals. While they still attended school, they had already dropped out. The school had provided them with few rewards and they looked other places, in other contests, for more meaningful rewards.

What would have happened if the school had stopped harassing the smokers and admitted to its own hypocrisy, thereby removing the payoff from the game? If at the same time there had been alternative and meaningful activities available to the smokers would they have found less encouragement to smoke?

Would new courses, interesting courses that appealed to these early dropouts, have recaptured their restless spirits to a point where they would have at least become a part of the educational process?

What new methods could be used and what new ways could be made available to these young smokers to find status within the system rather than being forced to compete for status in the smoking game?

How many poorly planned anti-smoking education campaigns actually enhance the status of the smoker by putting him in a position of brave risk taker—willing to stand fast against the statistics, the true games player—willing to gamble against odds and possibly win?

Smoking has to be recognized as something more than a dirty habit. It was a practice, complex and multidimensional in nature, even for the junior high school student. Unfortunately, however, it appeared that the teachers had overlooked this fact and thought they could win out with a single strategy of firm discipline. It was apparent that this single strategy game plan was not successful.

Addictive Behaviors

Making Tobacco Education Relevant

To the School-Age Child

John R. Seffrin, is professor and chairman of Health and Safety Education and director of Operation SmART at Indiana University, Bloomington, IN 47405.

School health education is faced today with a number of challenging opportunities to improve the quality of life through effective instructional programs. Whether it's sexually transmitted diseases, suicide, teenage drinking, illegitimacy or accidental deaths, most health educators feel that our discipline can and should help ameliorate these health problems through sound school health education programs.

Probably no greater challenge exists for school health education today than that of cigarette smoking among youth. Although the per capita consumption of cigarettes has dropped during the last three years, the estimated health-care cost to society because of cigarette-induced illness is fifteen billion dollars annually.[1] What is more important is that at least 340,000 Americans die each year prematurely because they smoke cigarettes.[2] In the words of Joseph A. Califano, former Secretary of Health, Education and Welfare, the unadorned facts clearly show that cigarette smoking is "public health enemy number one."

The cigarette smoking dilemma is a complex cultural problem with many interacting personal and social forces. However, the gross figures suggest strongly that the school curriculum has failed to prevent children and teenagers from beginning to smoke. For example, although the percentage of adults who smoke has gradually declined since 1964, the percentage of children and teenagers who smoke has increased. The rate of increase among teenage girls is particularly alarming.[3] All told, today six million children and teenagers smoke.[4] Past research and experience clearly show that 1) the majority of these youngsters will continue to smoke regularly for life; and, 2) they will be less well and their lives shorter because of their smoking habit.[5,6]

Finally, since the decision to smoke or not to smoke is made very early in life (almost always before age twenty and often by junior high school), the role of school health education, particularly during the primary and middle school years, is of critical importance if health educators are to reach students before they start smoking.[7,8] Until and unless comprehensive efforts are made to provide each school child with meaningful health instruction regarding cigarettes, the carnage in human health and life is likely to continue.

Personal Choice and Responsibility

Effectiveness of instruction is more related to how we teach than to what we teach. In the area of personal lifestyle it is important for the health educator to recognize the pluralism in our society. With the contemporary emphasis placed on personal rights and values, instructional strategies should be tailored accordingly. Therefore, careful planning by the teacher is necessary to provide a balanced as well as scientifically accurate instructional program. For example, in addition to teaching about the health consequences of smoking, instructional time should be used to explore the reasons why some people choose to smoke. In short, the teacher should develop an objective atmosphere in which the pros and cons of smoking can be fully explored.

The theme should be: the student has the ultimate responsibility to decide whether or not to smoke; therefore, the student must be given the pertinent facts in an objective setting. The goal is to provide the student with an opportunity to make a decision based on facts and personal values. Attendant to this approach is the accompanying need for the student to accept responsibility for his or her decision. In an effort to develop an awareness of the full responsibility involved in such a decision, instructional time should be given to explore a number of social issues such as accuracy in advertising, special insurance rates for smokers, and non-smokers' rights.

In the past many working education efforts have been restricted to a narrow, one-sided, health-facts unit which could be accurately described as a "thou shalt not" approach. Besides being a "turn-off" for many students, its greatest weakness was that, in omitting substantive socio-political issues, some of the strong persuasions against taking up smoking were never developed. Thus, millions of children and teenagers have decided to smoke, at least in part, because the only disincentive was an obscure threat to their health decades in the future. To be truly responsive to student needs and to maximize the relevancy and potential impact of our teaching, we must go beyond the statistical correlations associating smoking with age-onset diseases. Morbidity and mortality figures and facts are not enough.

Suggested Facts and Concepts

With the knowledge explosion it is impossible to teach all the facts in any area; thus the professional responsibility of the teacher to select appropriate information to develop valid concepts is critical. Following are selected examples of content and concepts which can be made relevant to students.

Cigarette smoking is our nation's leading preventable health problem. Consensus exists among medical scientists that cigarette smoking is the greatest cause of preventable illness and premature death in the United States.[9,10] This year, for example, over 122,000 people will develop lung cancer in the United States; at least 80% of these cases are due to cigarette smoking.[11] Additionally, thousands more will develop cancers of the throat, oral cavity, pancreas, esophagus and urinary bladder because they smoke.[12,13] Heart diseases, our nation's leading cause of death, will take the lives of smokers at least twice as frequently as non-smokers.[14] Chronic obstructive lung disease, one of our nation's fastest-growing chronic diseases, is largely caused by cigarette smoking.[15] In short, after 30,000 scientific studies over three decades it is apparent that not one measure in preventive medicine could

Photo: National Cancer Institute, *Smoking Programs for Youth*

do more to improve health and to prevent premature death than the control of cigarette smoking.[16]

Cigarette smoking is deleterious to your health now. The association of cigarette smoking to the aforementioned diseases is well established and widely recognized. However, less well known is that cigarette smoking is harmful to the smoker's health immediately. The adverse effects of smoking begin with the first cigarette and get progressively worse as smoking continues.[17] Immediate negative physiological responses to the smoker include increased heart rate, elevated blood pressure, constriction of blood vessels and trachial irritation.[18,19] While permanent, irreversible damage to the lungs does not occur immediately, hyperplasia (overgrowth of cells and overproduction of mucous) begins within weeks of regular cigarette smoking.[20,21] Ciliary action is damaged and trachial-mucosal velocity (TMV) is reduced while one smokes.[22,23] This, in part, explains why smokers are more prone to infectious diseases of the respiratory tract.[24]

In recent years, studies have shown basic pulmonary dysfunction in teenagers who have smoked for only a few years.[25] Although some of the harmful effects of smoking are reversible if a person quits in time (e.g. smokers' lung cancer mortality rates return to non-smoker rates 10 to 15 years after smoking ceases),[26] lung and respiratory tract tissue damage begins with the onset of smoking and becomes worse the longer one smokes.[27] Some scar tissue will re-

sult after only a few months of regular smoking.[28]

There is no such thing as safe smoking. Occasionally reports on smoking suggest that "moderate" or "light" smoking of low tar and nicotine cigarettes may be safe. This implication arises from the well-established fact that smoking's impact on health is a dose/response phenomenon.[29] The number of cigarettes smoked, the frequency of puffing, and the depth of the inhale all relate to increased risks.[30]

The inference, however, that there may be a safe or threshold level below which no harm occurs is unsubstantiated and invalid.[31,32] As already pointed out, adverse effects begin early and grow progressively worse over time.[33] Further, although low tar and nicotine cigarettes are assumed to be less hazardous, no evidence exists which would indicate that they are safe. On the contrary, certain harmful substances, such as carbon monoxide, are in greater concentration in the low tar and low nicotine brands.[34] Scientifically, it is very difficult to make blanket statements about the relative risks of different brands because of individual differences in smoking technique. For example, some smokers who switch to a low tar and nicotine brand may draw harder or inhale deeper and smoke more cigarettes; thus, the relative dosage of nicotine and other substances may be about the same as before.

In conclusion, if a person must smoke, a low tar and nicotine cigarette

may be the least harmful; however, from a health vantage point, any smoking is hazardous to one's health.

Cigarette smoking can be harmful to others, and especially to fetuses. In addition to the well-known irritation factor, which at least 60% of all people experience, there are real health threats from exposure to second-hand smoke.[35,36] The most alarming threat is to persons who are already chronically ill with diseases like coronary artery disease, bronchitis, and chronic obstructive pulmonary disease.[37] For example, people with existing heart disease will develop angina pectoris (chest pain) upon exertion sooner when breathing air polluted with tobacco smoke.[38] Further, animal studies have shown significantly more malignant tumors among those animals breathing second-hand smoke on a daily basis.[39] Finally, children exposed regularly to cigarette smoke have twice the respiratory disease rate of other children.[40] Although the smoker is affected most by smoking, the non-smoker who breathes air polluted with cigarette smoke does experience untoward physiological effects.[41] These unhealthy and immediate effects include elevated blood pressure, increased heart rate, and abnormal carboxyhemaglobin levels (carbon monoxide in the blood).[42] Recent studies confirm that even healthy adults develop marked small-airways dysfunction from breathing secondhand smoke.[43]

The most fearsome impact of second-hand smoke may be on the fetus of the pregnant smoker. Unless the mother stops smoking before the fourth month of pregnancy, some untoward effect can be expected in the baby.[44] Since carbon monoxide crosses the placental bearier, the unborn fetus can be expected to develop carboxyhemoglobin levels comparable to the mother's.[45,46] Since it is known that carbon monoxide displaces oxygen in the blood, it is obvious that the fetus is put at a distinct disadvantage during the most important period of its growth and development. For example, the human fetus' brain is growing at the rate of one to two milligrams per minute at the time of delivery.[47] Thus, any oxygen deprivation is most critical. In addition to having more miscarriages and stillbirths, smoking mothers have babies who weigh less at birth; also their babies are more apt to die during the first year after birth; and, their babies have more respiratory disease during childhood and adolescence.[48,49] One of the most discouraging findings educationally has been the discovery that children whose mothers smoked during pregnancy do poorer on achievement tests in math and reading at ages 7 and 11.[50]

Regular cigarette smoking usually results in a serious dependency problem. Like any drug of abuse, tobacco has the potential of causing serious dependency. Unlike users of other drugs of abuse, however, research indicates that tobacco users will usually become dependent for life—they will be less well and their lives shorter because of their smoking.[51] For example, it is estimated that about 10-15% of the people alive today who ever used heroin are still dependent on it. However, 66% of those still alive who ever smoked cigarettes are currently still dependent on cigarettes and smoke them daily.[52]

While research to elucidate the mechanisms of dependency continues, it is safe to say that cigarette smoking can and usually does result in strong dependency. The psychological factors associated with habit formation and desire to smoke seem to be paramount; but, at least for some smokers, the development of a physical dependence to nicotine may also occur.[53] These stark facts should be included in educational units so that those deciding to smoke are aware, in advance, of the likelihood of future dependency. It is known from national polls that at least 8 in 10 smokers would like to quit if there were an easy way. Such information is particularly critical in view of the recent trend in children experimenting with tobacco at earlier ages. A 1967 British survey of teenagers indicated that among those who smoked more than one cigarette, 80% ultimately became regular smokers.[55]

The advantages of not smoking far outweigh the advantages of smoking. Children and teenagers who choose to smoke do so for certain reasons. Although these reasons may not be clearly elucidated and evaluated, and just as importantly, they may not be understood by the smoker, we must acknowledge that all behavior, healthy as well as unhealthy, is caused. It is a logical assumption that many smokers find their habit enjoyable and somehow, reinforcing. For some youngsters, smoking may provide a way of emulating adults; for others a way of rebelling; and for still others, simply a satisfaction of curiosity.[56,57] Educators should explore with their students these and other possible reasons for smoking. In so doing, educators should avoid a condescending attitude toward reasons advanced in favor of smoking. Since one's values relate intimately to one's rationale for behavior, it is inappropriate to label reasons as right or wrong. The merits and demerits of various reasons should be explored in an atmosphere of respect with an emphasis on value clarification.

However, any comprehensive analysis of the pros and cons associated with smoking leads to one very critical conclusion; that is, the advantages of not smoking far outweigh the advantages of smoking.

Issues for Class Discussion

Since the decision to smoke or not to smoke is an individual one, much of the educational strategy should focus on personalizing lessons. As stated, there should be adequate coverage of the various values and motivations involved in choosing a course of action.

However, to stop at the personal level would be remiss in light of the health care dilemma facing society today. In an effort to explore the responsibility of the individual in society, a careful examination of social policies regarding cigarette smoking is important and relevant. Three examples follow of critical socio-political issues which should be dealt with in the secondary curriculum.

What should be our federal policy toward tobacco? Currently the federal government is inconsistent and contradictory in its policy toward tobacco. Simultaneously, two cabinet-level departments pursue policies which have antithetical objectives. The Department of Agriculture (USDA) continues to support and promote tobacco production. In 1977, for example, the U.S. Department of Agriculture spent approximately 65 million dollars on the various aspects of administering the price-support program for tobacco.[58] Further, the nation's lawmakers included tobacco in Public Law 480, the "Food for Peace" program.[59] Under this program millions of dollars in tobacco have been sent to developing countries around the world.

On the other hand, the U.S. Department of Health and Human Services (DHHS) continues to battle cigarette smoking in many ways. In 1964 the first and landmark *Surgeon General's Report on Smoking* was published. Since then a number of efforts have been instituted at the national level to combat smoking through school and public health education. In 1978, DHEW Secretary Califano established the Office on

Smoking and Health, and money continues to be spent on anti-smoking programs.[60]

Who should pay the smoker's health care bill? The cost of medical care in America continues to rise even faster than the inflation rate. This year, Americans will spend over 245 billion dollars on personal health services, more than any other nation in the

Photo: Operation SmART Decision

world.[61] With the trend toward some form of prepaid, social-health insurance plan for all, greater emphasis needs to be placed on the prevention of disease. For example, it is estimated that 350,000 people will die this year from diseases caused by cigarette smoking.[62] Prior to their death many incurred large medical bills resulting from expensive treatment and lengthy stays in hospitals. Current estimates are that each year at least seven billion dollars are spent on the direct medical costs of treating diseases caused by cigarette smoking. If one adds the lost productivity, the total cost jumps to a staggering 20 billion dollars annually.[63] Presently, the direct health costs are borne primarily by private insurance companies. Eventually, they may all be paid through national health insurance. Regardless of the system, private or governmental, the consumer pays—all the consumers. Should non-smokers pay as much in premiums or taxes as the smoker?

What are the rights of smokers and non-smokers? The spirit of this age is *rights:* rights for the handicapped, rights for Blacks, rights for the aged and rights for children. In all of the above examples, one common denominator exists. Each one of the above represents a minority group. In the case of non-smokers' rights, we are talking about the *majority.* Most children and adults

do not smoke. In spite of this fact, many who are bothered by cigarette smoke feel as though they should not express their discomfort, since it is the smoker's right to smoke.

However, no one is proposing to take away the smoker's right to smoke. On the contrary, all major groups active in the smoking and health controversy maintain that a person has the right to decide whether or not to smoke. However, a distinction needs to be made between a right and a freedom. That is, although one has a right to choose to smoke or not to smoke, one does *not* have the freedom to engage in the practice at will.

Since the beginning of our country, certain limitations have been placed on personal rights. Generally, these limitations are determined by two factors: the health and safety of the public; and the rights that might be abridged by the unrestricted practice of the first right. The adoption of speed limits is an example of protecting public safety. A great jurist once wrote, "My right to swing my fist ends when my fist reaches the end of your nose." Consistent with these principles and precedents, one's right to smoke should not be total and unrestricted. For years, for safety purposes, smoking has been properly disallowed in combustible areas, and, smoking in bed is against the law.

We now know that ambient cigarette smoke can be hazardous to the non-smoker's health, especially to children and persons with chronic illnesses. Since society should promote the public health, a new look at rights for smokers and non-smokers is justified and appropriate.

Summary

Americans consume 615 billion cigarettes annually.[64] Although the per capita consumption for adults has dropped over the past fifteen years, the amount of cigarettes being smoked by children and teenagers has increased. The percent of teenage girls smoking has nearly doubled during the last decade.[65] Because of this trend toward more smoking among the young, and because of smoking's effect on human health and life, educators must redouble their efforts. In spite of the diseases exacted on humans as a result of smoking, cigarette smoking, as such, is not a medical problem; but rather, the real problem lies in educating youngsters prior to the age at which the critical decision to smoke or not to smoke is made.

Through careful planning and professional discretion the school-health team can address this challenge in ways that are meaningful and relevant to students. No longer do we need to threaten the child with dread diseases in the distant future; but rather, instructional strategies can be designed to respect the student's right to choose. However, in choosing, it is imperative that the student grasp the profundity of the decision. Through a comprehensive and balanced instructional effort the student can better understand the personal as well as social ramifications of cigarette smoking. With an emphasis on the role of values and motivations in decision making the student can begin to appreciate the words of Frost:

"Two roads diverged in a wood, and I -
I took the one less traveled by,
And that has made all the difference."[66]

[1]American Cancer Society, Inc. *A national dilemma: cigarette smoking or the health of Americans – report of the National Commission on Smoking and Public Policy to the Board of Directors,* 1978, 4.

[2]U.S. DHEW. Smoking and health, report of the Surgeon General, Washington, DC: USPHS, 1979, ii.

[3]U.S. DHEW. *The smoking digest,* National Cancer Institute, 1977, 13.

[4]Horn, D. How much real progress have we made in the fight against smoking? *Bull Am Lung Assoc,* 1979, *65,* 6–9.

[5]Russell, M. A. H. Smoking problems: an overview, in *Research on smoking behavior, National Institute on Drug Abuse Research Monograph 17,* M. E. Jarvik, J. W. Cullen, E. R. Gritz, T. M. Vogt, and L. J. West, (eds.), (U.S. Department of Health, Education and Welfare. Publication No. (ADM) 78-581). Rockville, MD.: National Institute on Drug Abuse, 1977, 13–33.

[6]U.S. DHEW: *The health consequences of smoking, report of the Surgeon General,* Office

on Smoking and Health, 1978.

[7]American School Health Association. *Introducing tobacco education in the elementary school K-4*, Kent, OH: American School Health Association, 1978, 2.

[8]WHO. *Smoking and its effects on health, report of a WHO Expert Committee*, Geneva, Switzerland: World Health Organization, 1975, 29–33.

[9]Fletcher, C. M., & Horn, D. Smoking and health, *WHO Chronicle*, 1970, *24*, 345–370.

[10]U.S. DHEW. *The health consequences of smoking*, p. 2.

[11]American Cancer Society, Inc.: *Cancer facts and figures 1981*, New York, NY: American Cancer Society, Inc., 1979, 9, 14.

[12]*Ibid.*, p. 19.

[13]U.S. DHEW: *The health consequences of smoking*, ch. 5.

[14]Steinfeld, J. L. Presentation at Opening Plenary Session of the 3rd World Conference on Smoking and Health, in *Proceedings of the 3rd World Conference on Smoking and Health, II*, J. Steinfeld, W. Griffiths, K. Ball, & R. M. Taylor, (eds.), (U.S. Department of Health, Education and Welfare. Publication No. NIH 77-1414). Washington, D.C.: U.S. Government Printing Office, 1976, 21.

[15]U.S. DHEW. *The health consequences of smoking, 1975*, (Publication No. CDC 76-8704). Washington, D.C.: U.S. Government Printing Office, 1975, 61.

[16]Fletcher, C. M., & Horn, D. Smoking and health.

[17]Worick, W. W., and Schaller, W. E. *Alcohol, tobacco, and drugs*, Englewood Cliffs, NJ: Prentice-Hall, Inc., 1977, 77–109.

[18]*Ibid.*

[19]Diehl, H. S. *Tobacco and your health: the smoking controversy*, New York, NY: McGraw-Hill, Inc., 1969, 47–51.

[20]Jay, S. J., Associate Professor of Medicine, Indiana University School of Medicine, Pulmonary Section, interview, February 27, 1979.

[21]*Essentials of life and health*, New York, NY: Random House (CRM Books), 1977, 86–87.

[22]American Lung Association. Chronic smoking lowers rate at which the lungs clear mucus, *Bull Am Lung Assoc.*, July-August, 1977, 15.

[23]Newhouse, M. T. Effect of cigarette smoking on mucociliary clearance, in *Proceedings of the 3rd World Conference on Smoking and Health, II*, op. cit., pp. 131–137.

[24]Diehl, Tobacco and your health, 87–95.

[25]U.S. DHEW, *The health consequences of smoking*, 1978, ch. 6.

[26]U.S. DHEW, *The Smoking Digest*, p. 28.

[27]Royal College of Physicians of London: *Smoking or health – the third report from the Royal College of Physicians of London*, Trent, England: Pitman Medical Publishing Co. LTD, 1977, 76–81.

[28]Jay: op. cit.

[29]U.S. DHEW. *Report of the Surgeon General on smoking and health*, 1964 through 1978.

[30]Diehl, Tobacco and your health, p. 202.

[31]*Ibid.*, 201–206.

[32]Royal College of Physicians of London, *Smoking or health*, pp. 121–122.

[33]Worick and Schaller, *Alcohol, tobacco and drugs*.

[34]U.S. DHEW, *The health consequences of smoking*, 1978, ch. 11.

[35]Speer, F. Tobacco and the nonsmoker, *Arch Environ Health*, 1968, *16*, 443–446.

[36]Burns, D. M. Consequences of smoking – the involuntary smoker, in *Proceedings of the 3rd World Conference on Smoking and Health, II*, 51–58.

[37]Tate, C. F. The effects of tobacco smoke on the non-smoking cardiopulmonary public, in *Proceedings of the 3rd World Conference on Smoking and Health, II*, 329–335.

[38]Aronow, W. S. Carbon monoxide and cardiovascular disease, in *Proceedings of the 3rd World Conference on Smoking and Health, I*, E. L. Wynder, D. Hoffmann, and G. B. Gori, (eds.). (U.S. Department of Health, Education and Welfare Publication No. NIH 76-1221). Washington, D.C.: U.S. Government Printing Office, 1976, 321–328.

[39]U.S. DHEW: *The health consequences of smoking, a report of the Surgeon General: 1972*, (Publication No. HSM 72-7516). Washington, D.C.: U.S. Government Printing Office, 1972, 121–135.

[40]Colley, J. R. T., et al. Influence of passive smoking and parental phlegm on pneumonia and bronchitis in early childhood, *Lancet*, 1974, *II*, 1031–1034.

[41]U.S. DHEW: *The health consequences of smoking, 1975*, 87–106.

[42]White, J.R. & Frobe, H.F. Small-airways dysfunction in non-smokers chronically exposed to tobacco smoke. *New England Journal of Medicine*, 1980, *302*, 720-723.

[43]Burns, D. M. Consequences of smoking.

[44]Goldstein, H. Smoking in pregnancy: the statistical controversy and its resolution, in *Proceedings of the 3rd World Conference on Smoking and Health, II*, 201–210.

[45]Longo, L. D. The biological effects of carbon monoxide on the pregnant woman, fetus, and newborn infant, *Am J Obstet Gynecol*, 1977, *29*, 69–103.

[46]*Ibid.*

[47]Dobbing, J. All flesh is grass, *Kaiser Aluminum News: The World Food Crisis – Man, Mind, Soul*, 1968, *26*, p. 13.

[48]Butler, N. R., et al. Cigarette smoking in pregnancy: its influence on birth weight and prenatal mortality, *Br Med J*, 1972, *2*, 127–130.

[49]Meyer, M. B., & Tonascia, J. A. Maternal smoking, pregnancy complications and prenatal mortality, *Am J Obstet Gynecol*, 1977, *128*, 494–502.

[50]Butler, N. R., & Goldstein, H. Smoking in pregnancy and subsequent child development, *Br Med J*, 1973, *4*, 573–575.

[51]U.S. DHEW: *The health consequences of smoking*, 1978, Preface, p. 5, ch. 1, 2, 3, 4, 6.

[52]Blair, G. Why Dick can't stop smoking – the politics behind our national addiction, *Mother Jones*, January 1979, 31–42.

[53]Royal College of Physicians of London; *Smoking or health*, pp. 43–44.

[54]Olshavsky, R. W. *No more butts – a psychologist's approach to quitting cigarettes*, Bloomington, IN.: Indiana University Press, 1977, 3.

[55]Royal College of Physicians of London, *Smoking or health*, p. 89.

[56]U.S. DHEW: *Teenage smoking – national patterns of cigarette smoking, ages 12 through 18, in 1972 and 1974*. (Publication No. NIH 76-931, Public Health Service) 1976.

[57]Seffrin, J. R. Risks, rewards and values, *Health Values*, September/October 1977, *1*, 197–199.

[58]Eckholm, Cutting tobacco's toll, p. 19.

[59]*Ibid.*, p. 21.

[60]Califano Jr., J. A. A new commitment to wellness, *Bull Am Lung Assoc.*, November 1978, 64, 5–10.

[61]Health Insurance Institute, *Sourcebook of health insurance data, 1979–1980*, Washington, DC: Health Insurance Institute, 1979, 47.

[62]*Cancer facts and figures, 1981*.

[63]*Ibid.*, p. 2.

[64]*Ibid.*, p. 1.

[65]Hill, H. Situational analysis: women and smoking, in *Proceedings of the 3rd World Conference on Smoking and Health, II*, pp. 291–297.

[66]Frost, R. *Complete poems of Robert Frost*, New York, NY: Holt, Rinehart, and Winston, 1967, 131.

Addictive Behaviors

A Humanistic-Individualized Approach to Drug Education

JERRY L. GREENE is an assistant professor and PHILLIP G. HUNTSINGER is an associate professor of health, physical education, and recreation at the University of Kansas, Lawrence, Kansas 66045.

Many teachers individualize instruction to some extent without realizing it by giving special instructions to certain students, by allowing variety in student roles in class, or by allowing work on different skills at different times. This individual attention may be at the expense of the other students because the teacher's plan does not allow for special pacing and involvement. The problem is to create an environment which will let the individual progress through the learning program with a high degree of self-direction and involvement without impeding other students.

The primary objective of the humanistic-individualized approach is to get the students involved in the learning process by doing and thinking with all their capabilities. It is up to the teacher to help students find the most productive way to the student-teacher agreed upon goals. This kind of approach should help students learn the process of self-education in addition to the subject matter.

The following steps should be adhered to for implementing this teaching strategy:

Self-diagnosis: The teacher should develop this part of the instructional unit so that it is conducive to the student's mode of learning. See the diagnosis exercises.

Prescribed activities: The teacher must determine the kind and quantity of input and practice that students must complete before they can meet the desired objectives.

Program of learning experiences: This is the total program of prescribed experiences that the teacher develops for the students. It includes: Input—these experiences allow the students to further develop their competencies in areas shown to be weak by self-diagnosis. Output—these experiences will allow students to demonstrate the skills and knowledge developed in weak areas after strengthening by input experiences.

Evaluation: The students and the teacher can determine if the learning objective has been attained as a result of the input and output experiences by analyzing specific performance objectives developed for the unit.

We used this approach to teach drug education in the sixth grade, but it is easily adaptable to a number of health education topics. In our class of about 30, the children had been exposed to quality health education from grades 1 through 5. The text used throughout the district was the Scott, Foresman series. The four-week unit covered illegal drugs. The legal ones (alcohol, caffeine, nicotine) were studied in other units.

Self-Diagnosis

Directions: Read the questions and mentally answer them. If you believe you know the correct answer put a check in the "yes" column. If you are not sure of the answer or do not know, check the "no" column. If you need to, check the accuracy of your answers by comparing with other students or with the teacher's

notes. If a question was answered incorrectly, change your answer to the appropriate column.

Can you–	YES NO

1. explain what the term "narcotic" means?
2. define the term "hallucinogenic?"
3. explain what the term "depressant" means?
4. identify the meaning associated with a stimulant drug?
5. describe a volatile substance?
6. classify the following drugs: LSD, tranquilizer, heroin, aerosol sprays, "pep pills"?
7. describe how glue sniffing affects the body?
8. describe the difference between the physical effects of stimulants and depressants?
9. explain what effect a narcotic would have on the body?
10. define drug abuse?
11. list ten reasons why people use drugs?
12. identify common household substances that are dangerous to the body?
13. list ten slang terms associated with drugs?

Prescribed Activities

Directions: Determine the number of checks in the "yes" column. Now deter-mine the percentages. To increase your knowledge you may use the suggested program of learning experiences recommended in the Input and Practice columns.

Results	Inputs	Practices
More than 80%	#1, 7, 8	#1, 7
60 to 80%	#1, 3, 7	#1, 5, 6
40 to 60%	#1, 3, 5, 7	#2, 3, 4, 6
Less than 40%	#1, 2, 4, 5, 6, 7	#2, 3, 4, 5, 6

Program of Learning Experiences

Directions: The learner should follow any or all suggestions in this program. All of the experiences are designed to improve ability to motivate students for individualized instruction.

Proposed learning objective: The learner will be able to develop a basic understanding of drugs and drug usage.

Input

1. Read Chapter 6, *Health and Growth: Book 6* (Scott, Foresman series, 1974).
2. Discuss why our culture is called a "pill culture."
3. Read a programmed learning unit on drugs and drug use.
4. Discuss what role age should play in drug use.
5. View the "Inside-Out" film series and discuss.
6. Discuss the scope of the local drug scene.
7. Listen to a speaker from a community organization that specializes in some aspect of drugs.
8. Plan an input of your own.

Practice

1. Write a report on drugs.
2. Collect and post newspaper and magazine stories on drugs.
3. Plan a role playing scene showing how the character Charlie Brown would describe today's drug users.
4. Develop a bulletin board showing dangerous household substances.
5. Make a crossword puzzle using only slang drug terms.
6. Draw something that would exhibit symptoms of the influence of drugs.
7. Develop a study guide on a cassette for the major drug classifications.

Evaluation

Performance Objectives: The learner will:

1. Define the classification of drugs.
2. Understand the different effects of the various drugs.
3. Understand the difference between the use and abuse of drugs.
4. Know what common household substances are dangerous to the body.
5. Know the slang terms most often associated with drugs and drug use.

Drug Use Situations

BRUCE A. UHRICH is a former instructor in the Health Education Division at the University of North Carolina at Greensboro. He is currently a graduate student in the Department of Health Education at Temple University, Philadelphia, Pennsylvania 19122.

Under what conditions should the use of a drug be regarded as acceptable behavior in our society? To deal with this question I have developed, over the past two years, a series of statements which challenge student values and stimulate classroom discussion. I give students a handout with the following statements and these directions: "Read each statement carefully, then respond by rating each as an acceptable or unacceptable situation in which to use drugs. Be prepared to share each of your answers with the class, and to explain why you answered as you did."

Situation

1. Drinking an alcoholic beverage at a party.
2. Drinking an alcoholic beverage after work to relax at home.
3. Drinking an alcoholic beverage be-fore driving several hundred miles.
4. Drinking an alcoholic beverage alone after an argument.
5. Drinking an alcoholic beverage at a football game.
6. Using a narcotic drug in a hospital for relief of pain following an operation.
7. Use of a narcotic drug by the head of a household in a lower socioeconomic area.
8. Use of a narcotic drug by a physician.
9. Use of a narcotic drug by students in an upper class high school.
10. Use of a narcotic drug as a cough suppressant.
11. Smoking tobacco in a high school restroom.
12. Smoking tobacco after dinner.
13. Smoking tobacco when meeting new people at a reception.
14. Smoking tobacco while riding in a car pool.
15. Smoking tobacco in class.
16. Using a sedative/tranquilizer to commit suicide.
17. Use of a sedative/tranquilizer to relax a neurotic personality.
18. Use of a sedative/tranquilizer to en-courage sleep because of a loud roommate.
19. Use of a sedative/tranquilizer pre-scribed by a physician and then drinking heavily.
20. Use of a sedative/tranquilizer to relax before having to make a speech before a large group.
21. Utilizing marijuana at a dorm party.
22. Using marijuana after work to relax at home.
23. Refusing when handed a "joint" by your best friend.
24. Utilizing marijuana on a daily basis.
25. Using marijuana before an in-tramural softball game.
26. Starting each day with a cup of caf-feine, before anything else.
27. Taking a "hit" of some stolen ni-trous oxide.
28. Sniffing glue at a party.
29. Taking aspirin every time you feel any pain.
30. Receiving a painkilling drug from a paramedic for injuries at the scene of the accident.

Because the choices are limited to the extremes of acceptable or unacceptable, most students are highly motivated to verbally qualify their feelings. This situation allows the instructor to act as a true facilitator. For each statement, all students indicate by a show of hands which response they chose. Several students with acceptable and unaccept-able ratings are then asked to explain their choice and supportive feelings. The result is class discussion, exposing all class members to a variety of opinions.

Chemically Dependent—
But Only for One Week

KATHLEEN FISCHER is a health teacher at the Orono Middle School, Long Lake, Minnesota. She is now in her second year of teaching and participated in the program described here last summer.

Hazelden (Center City, Minnesota), located 40 miles northeast of the Twin Cities, is a treatment center for chemically dependent people. This was the setting for an in-service education program for 80 educators this past summer. The program, in cooperation with the Minnesota Department of Education, was funded by a grant from the Hill Family Foundation. Eight educators per week were provided with a "live in" experience, participating in the full rehabilitation program with patients and staff. The purposes of the program were to develop a "gut level" feeling and attitude toward people with a dependency problem, to become more aware of the causes of chemical dependency problems, and to become aware that patients in treatment share the same basic needs with all men.

"God grant me the serenity to accept the things I cannot change, the courage to change the things I can, and the wisdom to know the difference." These words have taken on a much greater significance for me now after having spent a week at Hazelden. They are words which can be found in every room there, either inscribed on a wall plaque or being verbalized in group sessions. They are one part of the rehabilitation program for the chemically dependent person.[1] But what

does this have to do with rehabilitating chemically dependent people? During my "live in" experience I was able to grasp the impact of that simple verse and its meaning to the entire program, and despite the fact that I am not chemically dependent, my experience was realistic in every other sense.

Eight of us, four women and four men, came to Hazelden as patient-observers. Our backgrounds included public school teachers, high school counselors, and psychiatric clinic personnel. Each of us was assigned a different unit as our home for the week, which would be the essence of our experience. No two of us would have the same situation, and yet we all would have grappled with some intense feelings at the end of our stay.

Hazelden is in a picturesque setting. The long driveway has a way of quieting one's mind with a gentle peacefulness that all works for good here. A patient's first contact with the inside is the detoxification unit. Minimum stay in this area is at least one day, and most patients are eager to move to a unit as there is little to do here.

All of the treatment takes place in the units, which are essentially structured in a home-like atmosphere. There are three units for men and two for women. The only time all of the units are together is at meals and lectures, and then no fraternizing is allowed. The reason behind the no fraternization policy is to prevent patients from building up support groups which will set back their own rehabilitation. Our educator group, though, certainly appreciated the special afternoon sessions we had together. It was the first time I had found myself in an environment where I was the minority. And yet as the week progressed we discovered we were more alike than different.

Surprisingly enough, Hazelden is not harboring a group of skid row alcoholics. There is not a stereotype for a chemically dependent person. All of them are everyday real people—many of the women are housewives and mothers. There were young girls, quite a few older women, and two nuns there at that time. The number of older women surprised me, but it was pointed out that today is as good a day as any to start living a better life.

The day is rigidly scheduled for patients; this is to aid in their treatment, for at some point they must again start meeting these kinds of responsibilities. All three meals must be attended; each patient has a work responsibility such as vacuuming, cleaning the unit kitchen, etc.; morning, afternoon, and evening lectures must be attended; and daily group therapy sessions must be participated in. The rest of the day is spent reading assigned materials, meeting with staff, playing solitaire, sitting around the table drinking coffee and smoking cigarettes. (The cigarette consumption increases during a patient's stay at Hazelden. This could be expected since they are attempting to alleviate one problem at a time. The ever-present smoke, however, can be quite overwhelming to non-smokers.) No recreational pursuits are provided for patients. I found this confining for my usually independent nature, but the patient's purpose for being there is not for having a fun time.

The entire program is based on the Alcoholics Anonymous twelve steps. These steps basically require a person to surrender control of his life to a higher power (belief in God per se is not a requirement), to confess to oneself all one's faults and virtues, and to then confess this to another person. When a patient reaches the fifth step in the program he is then free to return

---

[1] Chemically dependent refers here to a person who is dependent either on alcohol or drugs. Alcohol is also considered a drug, and it is considered to be the number one drug problem in this country.

to the outside world. The staff determines when a patient is ready to proceed to the next step, and this can be anxiety-producing for some patients who feel they are further along than the staff thinks.

Upon arrival at Hazelden, patients do not know how long they will be staying there. The normal period of time is approximately three to four weeks, although some patients may go into the extended care unit and remain up to a year. That unknowing fear can be a great stress factor in the rehabilitation. Most of them want to make their confinement as short as possible, but occasionally one will find a patient who has found Hazelden a secure place away from reality and would prefer to stay there. Few patients fully realize the personal depths to which their treatment will take them. Within them are the anxieties, frustrations, worries and resentments which carried them to the chemical escape they so desperately needed. Many of these people for the first time in their lives are having to face feelings they have hidden for years.

Each patient is treated according to his own personal needs. An essential part of recovery is learning to communicate feelings. Informal group therapy sessions aid in this task. In these sessions, patients are forced through questioning by the group to open up about themselves and get their true feelings out. The group can become quite hard on a person, and it is natural for people to avoid making responses that get at their feelings.

Patients do not have a magic formula prescribed for them when they leave so that they will not go back to chemicals. But if treatment has been effective they have much more than magic, for they have gained a self-understanding which can lead to a fuller, happier life. The stresses and difficulties of daily living are always present, and this is where their belief in a higher power must be strong.

The Hazelden experience is extremely worthwhile in a personal and professional sense. All of us should be given the opportunity to look within ourselves. All who are involved in the "helping" professions deal with people every day who are leading themselves to the brink where they only have one other out, and that may be chemicals. Each of us must take responsibility for sharing our own feelings and accepting these feelings as real. In turn, the process of self-acceptance can then go forth to others. This then will become the process we should use in preventing chemical dependency.

Our concern becomes that of the "feeling" life of people. Levi N. Larson, Education Director, North Dakota State Department of Health, says the real hope of drug abuse prevention lies in meeting the emotional needs of people—the need to be loved, to be heard, to be understood, the need to share feelings, the need to have meaningful communication with other people. Responding to these needs is how we get people off drugs. In doing this sooner lies the hope of keeping them from "getting on" drugs.

Learning by Teaching

ELAINE HALS is a teacher of health and physical education at South Shore High School in Brooklyn, New York. She is a new member of the SHR Editorial Board.

Drug education, an area of the health curriculum vital to high school students, is an area that easily turns young people off. They are tired of being preached to, moralized to, and lectured at. My dilemma was how to get the necessary information across, without losing the attention and interest of my health classes. I tried conventional lessons, contract teaching, and other methods, but somehow still lost them.

Last term I decided to let the students teach the unit to each other. I broke each of my classes into three committees and selected three of the most verbal members in each class to act as chairmen of the committees. The committees were selected by me so that there would be an equal number of verbal people in each group.

The three committees were:
1. Why drugs?
2. The facts.
3. Treatments available, including overdoses and emergency first aid.

In each class the committees had one day in class and two days in the library to organize their projects.

The committees had complete latitude in handling their subject, knowing that they had two days for their presentation. In one class for example "the why" committee spent one day on adults and drugs, and one day on young people and drugs. In the other class the committee dealt with drugs in advertising, sports, the school environment, and the home. In both classes the committee members asked questions of the class and involved them as part of the presentation. When it became necessary I was able to add information, ask questions, or guide the committee and the class. The students made up and ran off their own stencils, some brought in music of today that concerns itself with drugs, and one group even made up a role playing situation (and used class members to act it out).

The role playing situation was as follows: (a) parents waiting up for teenager to come home from party — young person comes home stoned; (b) reverse situation: teenage boy or girl waiting for parents to come home from a party—parents come home drunk.

This situation, and the discussion that followed, helped the students look at life for a moment from their parents' point of view, and to help them understand themselves in terms of their tolerance for others. The students listened to each other and were nonjudgmental. No value judgments were made, but the information necessary for the students to make their own value judgments and their own decisions was available. This information was given to them by a source that they were willing to listen to—their classmates.

It was a worthwhile experience for the class, and for me. The students in my classes felt free to express their opinions as well as their knowledge. They had a chance to step into the teacher's role for a short while and to see the class from a different point of view. The students received not only the needed information of the drug unit but experience in working in a group and seeing their project through to completion. The unit was more meaningful than if I had taught it.

After evaluation, the students found some flaws: (a) people came unprepared to give their reports and (b) people read long technical reports not meaningful to the class. In general, they favored this method. As for me, I really got to hear about and understand the drug "problem" from a young people's point of view.

This is an approach that I will use again.

Aging

Aging: A Need for Sensitivity

KENNETH A. BRIGGS is an assistant professor of health education at the State University of New York, College at Cortland, Cortland, New York 13045.

With our culture's shift from revering the old to worshipping youth and the breakdown of the extended family into separate nuclear units which usually exclude the elderly, a whole generation of young people are uneducated and insensitive to the elderly and their needs. Comprehensive school health education, which seeks to improve the quality of life through informed choices, is a good place to educate school age children about aging. It not only makes students more aware and sensitive to the needs of the elderly; it also educates them for their own aging.

Following are some suggestions to help create an awareness and caring for the elderly and their problems. These exercises help show students what it is like to be old in a culture that treats senior citizens the way we do.

Sensory Deprivation Simulation Exercises

The following simulation exercises try to bring to the young and healthy a sensitivity to what it must be like to be old and suffering from common sensory insults reported by the elderly.

Arthritis (reported by 33 out of 100 elderly)

Using cellophane tape, tape students' fingers together in various combinations, e.g., tape thumb and index finger together and the 4th and 5th fingers together. Wrap elastic bandages around the knees to simulate stiff knees. Have students perform simple tasks and then share their experiences of what it might be like to be old and have arthritis.

Visual Handicaps (reported by 15 out of 100 elderly)

Take sunglasses or laboratory protective glasses and smear vaseline on them until you get your desired visual loss. Have students wear the glasses and perform everyday things such as reading a menu or a newspaper, or look up the phone number of a pharmacy that will deliver prescriptions to old people (if there is one). Have students record and share their reactions.

Hearing Loss (reported by 22 out of 100 elderly)

Place a cotton ball in the student's exterior ear canal. For a more pronounced effect, have them also wear headphones or earmuffs. Have students listen to the TV or radio at a low level, or try to carry on a conversation with someone who has no hearing loss and must shout at them to be heard. Again, have students share their feelings.

Loss of Touch

Cover the students' fingers with rubber cement and after it dries, have them try to thread a needle.

Loss of Smell

Have students taste various foods while pinching their nostrils shut.

Multiplicity (polymorbidity)

Certainly many elderly people suffer from many aging insults. They may have a hearing loss, arthritis, and a visual handicap. To help students understand multiplicity and what it might be like, have several students perform tasks with various combinations of the above simulations. For example, one student can simulate finger arthritis, visual loss, and loss of touch and smell then go to the cafeteria and buy a carton of milk. Upon returning, have the student share some of his feelings during the experience as an older person with sensory deprivation. Be sure to exercise necessary safety precautions when students perform such simulations.

Songs and the Elderly

A lot of popular songs have been written recently that do a good job of developing a caring sensitivity and awareness of the elderly in listeners. Following are some examples of such songs and their artists.

"Old Man"—Neil Young
"Old Friends" "Voices of Old People"—Simon and Garfunkel
"When I'm Sixty-Four" "Eleanor Rigby"—The Beatles
"Two Lonely Old People"—Wings
"Hello Old Friend"—Eric Clapton
"Lonely People"—America
"Good Company"—Queen
"Hello in There"—Bette Midler
"I Never Thought I'd Live to be 100"
"Travelin' Eternity Road"—Moody Blues
"Let Time Go Lightly"—Harry Chapin
"Father and Son" "But I Might Die Tonight"—Cat Stevens

A nice touch to make aging education come alive in the classroom is to add slides of old people to the music. It can be quite powerful in creating sensitivity to aging.

Activities for Application and Discussion

Have students share some of their fears about growing old.

Have students draw pictures of themselves showing what they will be like when they are 100 years old. What losses do they show?

Have students think of or photograph things in a grocery store that demonstrate our insensitivity to the aged such as, unit pricing numbers and prices that are too small to read, bulk packaging, no carry out service.

Have someone in class carry on a conversation with another person in class who has simulated speech problems that follow a stroke by placing a ping pong ball in his/her mouth.

Use the following opinionnaire to generate discussion about the elderly.

Indicate to the right of each statement whether you agree or disagree.

1. Old people are better off living with other old people.
2. Old people need rehabilitation.
3. Rehabilitation is done best in a nursing home.
4. Sixty-five is a good age at which to retire.
5. Old people live happier lives away from the young, competitive world.
6. Old people should be kept active.
7. Old people suffer a sense of loss when their children leave home.
8. Our society encourages old people to be productive and useful.
9. Old people should stay in their own homes, if possible.
10. Old people should be discouraged from dependent relationships with agency personnel.
11. Most older people are ready to rest and don't want to be involved in "doing things."
12. Old people cannot learn as well as young people because of deterioration of the brain associated with aging.

Take two pictures of, for example, a street corner or the entrance steps to a bus. One picture of your chosen scene should be in focus and the other should purposely be out of focus. This will dramatically demonstrate the problems encountered by those elderly who have a serious vision loss and the insensitivity we have to these people by having such things as "Do Not Walk" signs that are too small to read.

We cannot overlook the most obvious and valuable resource of all—the elderly themselves. Bring the elderly to the students or take the students to the elderly. Allow them to ask questions of each other, spend time together, and most important of all, try to understand each other.

Because of the nature of our modern society and quite often the insensitivity it carries with it for the elderly, health education about and for aging that tries to reintroduce the elderly to those who may be out of touch and insensitive to them is imperative. Such education can be valuable for the aged as well for all those who may better understand the exigencies of the years to come.

Picnic in the Park

Humanizing an Aging Unit in a Personal Health Class

MICHAEL J. GAETA is a doctoral candidate and graduate teaching assistant in the Department of Health Education, Oregon State University, Corvallis, Oregon 97330.

Students in my Personal Health class had a picnic in the park with 54 elderly residents from Heart of the Valley Retirement Center and Nursing Home Complex in Corvallis, Oregon as the culmination of a unit on aging. In planning the aging unit I decided to design a program that would provide the students with an accurate knowledge base of the biological, psychological, and sociological aspects of aging; and even more important, provide them with experiences that would sensitize them to the realities of aging. All of this was to be terminated in a picnic, a celebration of life bringing the young together with the old.

"Ageism" is prejudice and discrimination leveled by one age group against another.[1] It is just as volatile and injust as other forms of bigotry such as racism and sexism. It is founded upon ignorance, myth, stereotypes, and fear. It results in alienation, despair, deprivation, powerlessness, and even hostility. The only way to combat this prejudice is to meet it head on with accurate information and experiences that will demonstrate to people of all ages how cruel it is to think of our elders as inhuman.

A total of six class periods were devoted to the aging unit. We started the first class with Palmore's "Facts on Aging" quiz,[2] which covers basic facts and misconceptions about aging. The quiz takes approximately 10 minutes to administer, but stimulates much discussion about basic physical, mental, and social facts and the most frequent misconceptions about aging. The quiz contains factual information documented by empirical data. This tool is an excellent resource that provides the students with a relevant vehicle for more clearly understanding the multidimensional topic of aging.

The second class was devoted to a cursory examination of the more common and current biological theories of aging. The primary objective was to familiarize the students with the present theory of the etiology of senescence. An excellent comprehensive review of the biological theories of aging is found in the *Handbook of the Biology of Aging*. It provides an excellent framework.[3]

In the third class session students had the opportunity to discuss aging with a 69-year-old senior activist. Several days before the class students were instructed to write down any questions they had about any aspect of aging. The guest speaker was given the questions a few days ahead of her scheduled talk so that she could more accurately ascertain the needs and concerns of the students.

Sitting in a large circle with the class, the speaker answered questions and related her philosophy of life so eloquently that the entire class was caught up in her bubbling enthusiasm for life. She shared her feelings on everything from sexuality to death. After a standing ovation, the students without coercion lined up and one by one proceeded to hug and kiss her as they left the class. It was obvious that those students went away with a more positive and beautiful perspective on aging.

The fourth class period consisted of aging simulation games. With the help and expertise of a gerontology professor, the students were divided into groups of five. Shoe boxes filled with paraphernalia to simulate impairments brought on by the aging process were passed out to each group. Arthritic, visual, hearing, aphasic, and stroke impairments were simulated as part of the exercise. Each "impaired individual" was given a task to do alone. This was followed up by a group task. These simulations enabled the students to more realistically understand the impairments and restrictions that many aged people live with each day. For an excellent review of aging simulation games see *Health Education* September/October 1977.[4]

In class five a gerontological counselor addressed the area of psychosocial needs of the elderly. The counselor emphasized that we are all creatures of need—to be fed, kept warm and dry, to grow and develop at our own pace, to be held, caressed, recognized, loved and stimulated. While most people recognize the importance of practicing and subscribing to these tenets in the early years of human development, many of us forget that these needs must be met from cradle to grave if we are to reach

Laurence Garner, left, talks with student Mark Rabichaud.

On Friday, June 2 1978, the **Gazette-Times** of Corvallis, Oregon ran this picture story about the class described by Gaeta in this article. The photographs on this page were taken by Tom Warren.

Lunch in the park

The 40 students in Michael Gaeta's Personal Health class at Oregon State had a special final examination—a box lunch in Chintimini Park with 40 residents of Heart of the Valley Center.

Jeanette Stoner, Rosemary Wick, Barbara Quinn and Cindy Miller entertained by singing to the senior citizens.

Jeannette, who is a freshman pre-veterinarian student from Hood River, said students brought their own lunches and exchanged them with a senior.

"It was the neatest final I've ever taken," she said. "I used to be afraid of growing old, but I learned from the seniors that they have a lot of fun, have hobbies and really get around the community." She said she's also learned how they cope with arthritis, hearing and seeing problems.

Youngsters and oldsters soak up the sunshine.

Danita Ruzic, chats with Cora Warner, holding cup, at the picnic in Chintimini Park. Danita has been spending each morning at Heart of the Valley Center and produced a term paper on her experiences.

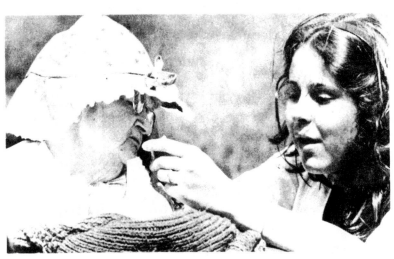

Kimberly Koehler, left, helps Marian Taylor with her picnic lunch.

optimum growth and development. This last session put the finishing touches on preparing the students for the picnic with the elderly.

Working in conjunction with the activities director from Heart of the Valley Retirement Center and Nursing Home the groundwork was laid for the picnic. The picnic called for the exchange of box lunches with the elderly. The students were asked to prepare a lunch complete with treats not usually found in an institution. Arrangements were made through the administrator for the Center cafeteria to provide box lunches for the students plus lemonade and coffee for the entire group.

The activities director took care of publicizing the event at the Center. Signs were placed in the elevator and on the bulletin boards notifying the residents of the picnic. A list of potential participants from the nursing section was compiled and these patients were contacted and asked if they would like to attend the event.

The park chosen for the picnic was one block away from the Center so no bus transportation was necessary. However, since our group would have to cross a busy street to get to the park, the Corvallis police were contacted and they agreed to provide traffic direction and assistance.

The local newspaper was contacted and told of the picnic in the park. It was thought that the publicity would be good for both the Heart of the Valley Center and the health education department.

The day of the picnic was beautiful. The sky was blue, the sun was shining and the temperature was pleasant. I arrived at the Center at 11:30 and found patients lined up in the lobby eagerly waiting to depart. The police arrived shortly thereafter and were given instructions as to when we would depart and what route we would traverse to reach the park. Within a matter of minutes students started to arrive and we began hooking them up with residents from the Center. As I looked out of the main doors, the group of elders and students reminded me of a beautiful parade. A meeting of the young and the old. People with canes, some in wheelchairs, all being escorted by students. Human beings that had been separated by walls, not walls of wood or stone, but walls of ignorance and fear, were sharing love, food, talk, and companionship. As I moved about the group taking pictures, I was amazed at the rate and quality of interaction that was happening all around me.

Students with musical talents played harmonica, guitar and sang to entertain the group. Song sheets of old time favorites printed in large block type were distributed and the whole group joined in the merriment by singing songs, clapping hands, tapping feet, and laughing.

After sharing lunch in the warm sun, gifts were handed out to the elderly by the students. With the extra gifts students suggested that we have a contest and hand out gifts in descending order from oldest to youngest. A 94-year-old grandmother won first prize.

Time seemed to fly by and before we knew it the time had come to leave the park. On the way back to the Center traffic was blocked up both ways on Harrison Boulevard, as students and residents moved in a procession that stretched from the park to the Center. Residents and staff from the Center were in the windows waving to our group as we arrived.

The reactions from students and elders alike was unequivocally positive. No sooner did we get back to the Center than one elderly woman asked when the next picnic was to be scheduled.

Without any question, it was obvious that many of the fears, myths, and stereotypes of aging were bashed down that day. With a little bit of imagination, coordination, planning, and cooperation, a picnic in the park on a sunny day in May gave a group of personal health students the opportunity to learn first hand that aging is not all negative and that old people are no different from young people.

[1]Butler, Robert N. "Ageism: Another Form of Bigotry." *Gerontologist*, 1969, Vol. 9: 243–46.

[2]Palmore, Erdman. "Facts on Aging—A Short Quiz." *Gerontologist*, 1977, Vol. 17, No 4.: pp. 315–20.

[3]Finch, Caleb E. and Leonard Hayflide (eds.) *Handbook of the Biology of Aging*, Van Nostrand Reinhold Co., New York, 1977.

[4]Briggs, Kenneth. "Aging: A Need for Sensitivity." *Health Education*, Sept./Oct. 1977, pp. 37–38.

HEALTH ANAGRAMS

KATHLEEN M. SIEGWARTH is instructor, Department of Health and Physical Education, Bowling Green State University, Bowling Green, Ohio 43403.

Health educators realize that the techniques used in teaching can serve as catalysts to the material being presented. One way to help students learn about health care specialists in the community health unit of the health education curriculum is with anagrams. The procedure consists of using handouts containing anagrams, which when properly unscrambled spell out occupations in the health care profession. They are constructed to read as names. Under the caption "My Name Is" the anagrams are listed in columns and opposite is a column headed by "My Occupation Is" with appropriate blanks. Periods are not to be considered in translation, but all letters must be used.

Example:

My Name Is	My Occupation Is
1. Stu Coil	1. _____

·The correct answer is oculist.

Here are several ways this idea might be used in class.

1. Distribute the sheet one week prior to the scheduled lesson day. Make it an individual contest whereby the student with the most correct answers would receive recognition as determined by the teacher. In case of a tie, a "playoff" would be held in class. New words would be put forth and a time limit set. When time expires the one with the most correct answers is the winner. Have the other students work the same problems. They then can offer any answers missed by the contestants and rate their own accomplishment.

2. Divide the class into two teams. Have each group elect a captain who is responsible for recording the solution for each anagram and serves as their spokesman. Allow 30 minutes for each team to work. Validate the answers between the two teams at the end of the time limit. The team with the most correct answers is the winner. Should a tie occur a playoff is held immediately, with a five minute time limit.

3. Group anagrams into similar categories. For example, psychiatrist, psy-

chologist, and analyst. This enables the teacher to distribute them during the unit in which they are pertinent.

4. Release the anagrams in groups of five or ten daily over a one to two week period. Answers to the problems may be turned in the next day and new ones distributed. A winner is declared after all answers have been submitted.

Following is a list of 45 anagrams with the appropriate answers.

	My Name Is	My Occupation Is
1.	Heston Satisgole	Anesthesiologist
2.	Les G. Trail	Allergist
3.	Lenore Vut	Volunteer
4.	Sandie Sure	Nurse's Aide
5.	Togol I. Scadir	Cardiologist
6.	Hope Toast	Osteopath
7.	Lori N. Stouge	Neurologist
8.	Tobias T. Nicer	Obstetrician
9.	Phil O. Mostogoth	Ophthomologist
10.	Patti Goolsh	Pathologist
11.	Nate I. Picidar	Pediatrician
12.	Chris T. Stipay	Psychiatrist
13.	Sol Goitur	Urologist
14.	Gail T. Sodoir	Radiologist
15.	Gib O. Loist	Biologist
16.	Tania M. Torrids	Administrator
17.	Tad I. Porsit	Podiatrist
18.	Seth Doorpit	Orthopedist
19.	G. O. Nurse	Surgeon
20.	Rod Ryle	Orderly
21.	Ted Tins	Dentist
22.	Thor Stondoit	Orthodontist
23.	Ricator Porch	Chiropractor
24.	Gipsy T. School	Psychologist
25.	T. S. Chime	Chemist
26.	Tod Roc	Doctor
27.	Unis T. Tortini	Nutritionist
28.	Patricia Pylsthesh	Physical Therapist
29.	Nyle G. Gostico	Gynecologist
30.	Thom Toilgoes	Hemotologist
31.	Scott Goily	Cytologist
32.	Nat I. Eidic	Dietician
33.	Stanlie Chet Comlodig	Medical Technologist
34.	Caine Y. Xanchirt	X-ray Technician
35.	Peter Lance Grantitoir	General Practitioner
36.	Toni Priceset	Receptionist
37.	Mort G. Sealdito	Dermatologist
38.	Mic A. Prade	Paramedic
39.	Sy A. Lant	Analyst
40.	I. N. Rent	Intern
41.	I. C. Shypain	Physician
42.	R. E. Sun	Nurse
43.	Pam C. H. Stair	Pharmacist
44.	Morie T. Topst	Optometrist
45.	Cher E. Raser	Researcher

Consumer Wellness, One School's Approach

JON W. HISGEN is a health instructor in Pewaukee Public Schools, 210 Main Street, Pewaukee, Wisconsin 53072 and an instructor of consumer health for the University of Wisconsin, Milwaukee.

Every year I instruct my consumer health units at the seventh and ninth grade levels I am made acutely aware of people's trusting nature. In this "credit card culture" where we exist, instant pleasures are a signature away. There is no better example of this approach to consumer decisions than in the world of health products and services. We blindly use hit or miss tactics in everything from wiping out those unsightly blemishes with steam to strengthening our rectus abdominus muscle with electric belts.

The condition of wellness is a combination of many interacting forces, including the individuals' environment, their reaction to it, associations, psychological background, and ability to accept attitudinal change. Today's health consumer is more likely to face these forces after his/her health has been threatened in some way. Consumer wellness is not an easily acquired status but must be learned.

My initial seventh grade consumer health activity is to sell each student a bottle of Dr. Lemke's Stomachic Drops using a stereotypical medicine man approach. The following is an example of the pitch I use to convince the class the product works.

1. I tell students about a college assignment to recreate a medicine from an old medical text.
2. I chose Dr. Lemke's drops because of its advertised ability to cure both acne problems and split ends (7th grade concerns).
3. The mysterious ingredient is capsicum that must be imported from Africa and grown hydroponically.
4. I finished making the product in two months and successfully field tested it on my friends and myself.
5. I unsuccessfully asked for support from the AMA and Bristol Meyers.
6. I decided to market the product through magazines after receiving a patent on the product.
7. I bought a factory to grow capsicum and produce Dr. Lemke's drops.

8. Sales have increased each year for the last three years.
9. Famous people have endorsed the product (the Osmonds, the Jackson Five).
10. A local newspaper is coming to take advertising pictures of students holding the product.
11. If the students bring the money next time we meet, I'll give them a special offer of two bottles for the price of one.

Over the past five years around 91% of the students have agreed to bring the cost of the product the next day while in fact 70% actually did. When I tell the students that a cruel hoax was played upon them the following responses can be heard: "I'll never trust you again." "We thought you were above that." "Well, you certainly made me look foolish." "I was just playing along with your little game."

The alarmingly high number of gullible consumers pointed out the need for

some direction in our consumer health program. Out of this we instituted a consumer health program entitled WISE MAN.

W ise
I independent   M otivate
S afe/effective   A ware
E valuate   N otable

Each of the letters represented a competency we wanted our students to have by the time they left our health program.

1. The student will be able to make *wise* and careful decisions about the consumer products and services he/she uses (consumer health protection).
2. The student will be able to make decisions *independent* of outside influences (e.g. advertising, pseudo-science, etc.).
3. The student will be able to choose products and services that are both *safe* and *effective.*

Photos by Jon W. Hisgen

4. The student will be able to *evaluate* new and existing health products and services (the work of government agencies, insurance programs, alternative medical practices, etc.).
5. The students will be able to *motivate* others in their present or future family to make wise consumer health decisions (well-thought out family medicine chests and first aid kits).
6. The student will be *aware* of pitfalls facing the consumer of health products and services (quackery, superstitions, fads, and fallacies).
7. The students will be able to make *notable* savings in their consumer health budget and notable improvement in their overall wellness.

Our school's consumer health program is based on these competencies. A copy of our consumer health curriculum and methods guide can be obtained by writing the author.

Consumer Health

A Healthy Consumer Health Class

TOM McFARLAND is a consumer education specialist at the Family Life Education Center, Toledo Public Schools, Toledo, Ohio 43604. ANN RUDRAUFF is educative services specialist for WGTE-TV, Channel 30, in Toledo.

Our experience has shown that the most successful way to teach consumer health is to throw out traditional classes and have students learn by doing, using the community as a classroom. Most of the learning experiences we describe are oriented toward high school or college level but adaptations can be made to suit various school aged or community groups.

Advertising

Thorough understanding of how advertising works is necessary for the consumer health student. Some suggested activities are:

Ad substantiation campaign. Survey local media for advertisements of health and beauty products. Printed ads can be brought to class; radio and TV ads can be taped for discussion. Many ad agencies and TV and radio stations throw away their tapes and layouts and are happy to see someone get some use from them.

Claims made in the ads are scrutinized and some are selected for analysis. Students write company presidents and ask for factual substantiation of the advertisement. This is examined to see if the claim is justified. The information gathered can be shared with classmates and can be made public.

Counter-ads. Since advertising is obviously biased, consumers deserve to hear the other side of the story. Students prepare counter-ads such as, "aspirin is all the same, it may cause internal bleeding." A visit to an ad agency or asking an advertising man in as guest instructor can help students prepare their ads. Students should then try to get local media to use their counter-ads as public service spots.

Fraudulent charities. Most of the fraudulent groups are centered around research in disease prevention and cure, and they have bilked consumers out of millions of dollars. In this project to ex-

pose such operations, students paint and label empty coffee cans with "American Cancer Center," "National School for Epileptics" or some other phony health agency name. Working in pairs, the students take money and write down pledges. After counting the money, it is returned to donors with an explanation. This activity should be widely publicized so that they can learn without being unnecessarily embarrassed. More people will know they should check before giving.

Health Insurance

Health insurance is a crucial issue about which few consumers have a working knowledge. One way to identify and probe health insurance issues is by values clarification techniques.

Voting on pertinent questions. How many of you have health insurance? How many are covered under a family policy? How many are covered under a group policy? How many have Blue Cross-Blue Shield? How many can list the exclusions in their policy?

Forced choice questions. These help students decide which alternative they prefer: private medicine or socialized medicine; unnecessary luxury or necessity? Students can vote by moving to either side of the room, then find someone there to discuss the reasons for their decision. The teacher can design questions to bring out important points to be discussed.

Values continuums. Use to encourage participation in discussion of current issues related to health insurance. Health costs are: too high—just right—too low. Medicine should be: socialized—totally private. Health insurance is: a waste—all right—crucial. I usually block out the center of the continuum to discourage students who find it too easy to be indifferent.

Rank order. (1) List major exclusions found in insurance policies. Rank in order of danger to consumers. (2) List ways to learn about health insurance and rank in order of preference. Teachers can use this list in planning classes. (3) List types of health insurance coverage, and rank in order of importance to the consumer or in order of expense, such as: basic hospital, major medical, dental rider, maternity benefits. Students can share their rationales for rankings in groups of three.

Price Comparison Research

These research results can shed much light on future buying practices. A certain type of product is selected for study by

groups of students. Types of health products good for study include: prescription drugs, over-the-counter drugs, perishable foods, cosmetics, or food sold in a health food store.

After groups are formed, students plan to visit a variety of stores such as a chain food store, small pharmacy, and discount store. Prices may vary depending on location of the store, so encourage students to visit suburban, rural, and urban areas, if possible. Items to be price-checked should be standardized by brand, size, weight, count, or whatever, so results will be comparable and accurate.

Groups can make charts to depict their results, analysis of data, and conclusions. Presentations to the whole class should be made.

Health Practitioner Interviews

The teacher can assign job classifications or let students select the one they are most interested in, to go out and interview someone in that area. Several possible candidates are listed under "guest speaker" later in the article.

Make sure students are aware of how to contact people, set up interviews, and ask pertinent, interesting questions. Role playing in the classroom before the interview will give confidence to carry out the project successfully.

Follow up activities include: oral reports, role play, group comparisons of categories, mock debates with students playing the role of the person interviewed, and so on.

General

Guest speakers. A wealth of information can be provided to students by outside experts. This is especially helpful if field trips are not within the budget. Teachers can call on a wide selection of community people including:

Health practitioners—doctors, pharmacists, paramedics, nurses, public health officials, nutritionists.

Governmental or voluntary agencies—Better Business Bureau, Consumer Protection Agency, Post Office, local health departments, civic groups.

Educators—university health staff, consumer specialists, other teachers from the school.

Business—insurance agents, food packers, advertising agencies, credit bureaus, health food store owners, cosmetologists, lawyers.

If a speaker's time is limited, tape the presentation for the rest of the classes. Invite several guest speakers at once to form a panel or have a debate on a given topic. Preparing the speakers and students ahead of time and following up makes this more effective.

Pretest. This is a good way to assess the group's knowledge, misconceptions, background, values, and behavior. It can be used to learn what the students want to know or as a springboard for discussion. If the test includes content-based information covering the entire course, it can be used as a posttest.

Some sample questions are:
1. Content-based items (true or false)— Toothpastes are necessary for good dental health; the best relief of arthritis pain is prescription drugs; gargles or mouthwashes are not effective treatment for sore throats. 2. Attitude and behavior-based items—I see a doctor and a dentist at least once a year; I am adequately covered by medical insurance; I have a good credit rating. 3. Unfinished sentences—I spend money foolishly on_____; I really shop around for _____.

Experiment with some of the activities described here; adapt and apply them to your own teaching situation. Remember, an involved class is a "healthy" class.

Consumer Health

The Teenage Consumer

LEE ANN LARSON is a 7th and 8th grade health teacher at the Dexter McCarty Middle School, Gresham, Oregon.

The marketplace is wide open to today's teenage consumer. As the target of constant bombardment by advertisers, the teenager with access to money is in the position of making decisions with very little information. Health products, in particular, appeal to the teenager with their promises to beautify. Although information for the student in this vital area is hard to find, I teach a unit with seventh and eighth graders to develop awareness of consumer health education.

To understand any new body of knowledge familiarity with the terms that relate to that area is necessary. The students' first task is to find definitions of appropriate words. We use health books rather than dictionaries to give students specific subject definitions rather than general definitions which they may have trouble applying to topical situations. This list of words introduces the unit:

bait and switch	media
code-dating system	nostrum
comparison shopping	patent medicine
consumer	product
cosmetic	proprietary compound
dentifrice	quack
fraud	trademark
indirect lie	

The students next investigate some facts about their role as consumers. What is the history of health products and services? What about the "medicine man" of the old west and his cure-all drugs? How are his claims different from or the same as advertising that we might hear or see today? Students investigate how advertising affects the consumer and just how much advertising is directed at their age group and why. They take a look at how Americans spend their health dollar, and of total income how many of their dollars are spent for health products and services.

Middle-school students are still secure with the thought that if they get sick or hurt their parents or some other adult will make sure they are taken care of properly. This unit's lessons present them with situations and factual histories in which they must make some decisions of their own. What if their doctor tells them that they have a disease which cannot be cured, but they read about a doctor who can cure the disease? What if they are told they have cancer of the leg and it must be amputated, but someone knows of a doctor who has a cure for cancer? The possibilities are endless and the

cases do not even have to be so dramatic. This leads to an investigation of quackery and a realization that they are one of the prime target groups because of their susceptibility. Mail-order quackery traps them with its glamour and seeming privacy of the postal system. They get involved with researching training, signs, and results of quackery.

Students can become pretty outraged about what quacks are "getting away with." At this point, students investigate some of the organizations working in some way to protect the consumer from fraud. They study the Food and Drug Administration, Federal Trade Commission, U.S. Postal Service, American Medical Association, Consumer's Union, and Better Business Bureau. Throughout the discussions, students are reminded that these organizations are handicapped by their dependence on consumer complaints to act. If the consumer is too ashamed, too afraid, or too lazy to report an incident or complaint, other unsuspecting consumers will be subjected to the same treatment by a fraudulant person or company.

Even if students have some information on quacks and the groups which protect the consumer, they are still left with the problem of what to look for in good medical services. Investigation continues with some of the guidelines to follow in selecting a physician followed by a review of specialists (pediatrician, general practitioner, internist, surgeon, psychiatrist, etc.). Students need to look for the physician best able to handle their needs at various stages in life. An increasingly important aspect of medical service is that provided by hospitals. Students try to find out what kinds of hospitals exist and what questions should be answered before choosing a hospital.

The next project gets students involved in investigating a product. With school funds, I purchased three brands of several products from a discount store, adding another price to the label from a regular grocery store or drug store. The products used were aspirin, toothpaste, shampoo, deodorant, vitamin tablets, ready-to-eat cereal, and acne preparations. Knowing seventh and eighth grade students, I emptied all of the containers before using them in the classroom. The class arranged itself in groups to provide an equal number to work on each product. To make it somewhat fair, each group drew a number to indicate its turn at choosing a product. Once the preliminaries were settled, each group received a form on which to write the information to present to the class. The questions include:

1. What is the history of the product? (Where did it come from? Who found it and how? How long has it been around?)

2. What are the ingredients as they are listed on the label of the product?

3. What are the uses for the product as listed on the label?

4. Can this product cause any harm? (Not only the particular brands they are investigating, but any other brand of the same product. In most cases this information is not on the label so they will have to do further reading.)

5. Is any brand of this product better than others? Where did you find that information? (Students have a tendency to rely on advertising, written or word-of-mouth, to make this decision. Encourage them to use resource materials to see if they can find reliable information.)

6. What is the price comparison for the product? (Comparing the same brand at two different stores, different brands at the same store, and different sizes of the same brand. I purchased the products, as much as possible in the same size, but students sometimes take it upon themselves to check on other sizes.

7. What is the latest information about this product? (I collected all the information I could—magazine and newspaper articles—about a product and let the students decide what is significant enough to report to the rest of the class.)

8. What do advertisements for this product look or sound like? (Students can cut ads from magazines to show or report ones they have heard on the radio or from friends, or seen on television.)

The reports to the class can produce more questions and further research plus a wealth of basic information.

One of the common concerns to come from this investigation is the inadequate information found on the labeling standards and new ones currently under consideration. Included in the unit are not only the products investigated, but any product which may in some way relate to health and safety, such as baby cribs and toys. This is also an excellent time to get into nutrition labeling. A fun exercise is for students to design a label for a product, including all of the information they think is important for the consumer.

Another way to get students thinking about health products and selections is to have them collect advertisements about many different brands of some product.

After students decide which brand of the product is best, using only the advertisements, each will tell how confident he feels in his decision. The students will also indicate other information they would like to have to make an even better choice.

Crisis Hot Line Experience

ALOYSIUS J. JANGL is health education instructor and subject area coordinator at Ardsley Middle School, Ardsley, New York 10502.

The emergence and impact of two relatively new mental health concerns, death and suicide education, can be viewed as outgrowths of the education system attempting to ensure healthy personality development. Nevertheless, mental health areas within the health education curriculum are often neglected or poorly presented. Why? Perhaps the curriculum is largely fact-oriented with little accommodation for the bulk of affective content involved in mental health. The wealth of emotions and attitudes combined with inexperience and/or fear of affective teaching may make some health educators apprehensive about such vital health areas.

With statistics climbing, suicide is now the third leading cause of death among young people between the ages of 15 and 19, and it ranks first or second on college campuses. The area of suicide and its prevention should be of vital concern to the health educator. Suicidology, the scientific study of suicide, investigates the many complex causes leading individuals to self-destructive behavior. Research has shown that suicides are not spontaneous. There are clues that foreshadow this behavior to which both educator and student alike can become sensitized. Armed with this awareness and sensitivity, preventive and reinforcing steps can be taken to help the individual. It is erroneous to assume that handling suicidal behavior or any "abnormal" behavior is the psychiatrist's or psychologist's province alone. Suicide prevention is not exclusively a medical or psychiatric problem. Health educators can operate within certain limits in teaching and counseling. Moreover, they can help shoulder their mental health responsibility by presenting the essential facts concerning crisis behavior in a meaningful way to their students.

The following is an example of an instructional strategy that has been used in a middle school mental health unit dealing with crisis prevention and intervention. It may encourage other health educators toward more effective affective teaching and the rewarding experience of humanistic health education.

Behavioral Objectives for Students

1. Cite particular situations which have the potential for critical or self-destructive behavior.

2. Devise a reference list of persons, groups, or agencies that deal with suicide or attempted suicide.
3. Identify clues in the individual's behavior that suggest a need for consultation with a professional specialist or a need for other forms of immediate help.
4. Identify and suggest various constructive alternatives and psychological first aid advice.

Instructional Materials

1. Battery operated walkie-talkie; 50 ft. extension.
2. Record player with microphone and speaker jacks; speaker with 50 ft. extension jack cord; microphone jack cord.
3. Thirty or more dittos of Crisis Hot Line Evaluation Sheet.

CRISIS HOT LINE EVALUATION SHEET

Instructions
Place the name of the student who is the crisis hot line operator in the numbered box atop each column. While listening carefully to the conversation, check off, in the vertical column under each operator's name, the psychological first aid advice he suggests.

	NAME OF OPERATOR				
PSYCHOLOGICAL First Aid	1.	2.	3.	4.	5.
Listens attentively					
Takes complaints seriously					
Evaluates seriousness of intention					
Examines intensity of emotional disturbance					
Assesses resources available					
Does something tangible					
Affirmative, yet supportive					
Asks directly about suicidal thoughts and intent					
Not misled by passing second thoughts					
Suggests personal or professional assistance					

This evaluation sheet has been formulated from the article "Ecological Aspects of Self-Destruction: Some Legal, Legislative and Behavioral Implications," by Calvin Frederick in *Health and Human Values* by Allure Jefcoat (John Wiley & Sons, Inc., New York, 1972) pp. 172-80.

Instructional Activity

Instruct each student in the class to write out a critical situation which would warrant a call to a local crisis hot line center. Next, distribute a Crisis Hot Line Evaluation Sheet to each student. Select one student who wishes to be the crisis hot line caller and another student to be the crisis hot line operator. The hot line caller will be stationed outside the classroom speaking into the microphone, thus relating the incident to the entire class within the room via the extension speaker. Only the selected crisis hot line operator will be able to respond with questions, advice, or "psychological first aid" via the walkie talkie, while the other class members listen and evaluate the operator's performance on their sheets. Five to seven minutes of dialogue is usually sufficient.

Follow-Up Activity

After the hot line dialogue, the performances of both students are discussed by class members through their evaluations and any additional comments by the teacher. Two different students are selected and the activity is repeated. At the end of the period, the assignment for the next class is given: (1) to list all the persons, groups or agencies mentioned, dealing with suicide or attempted suicide (2) to list any verbal or behavioral clues that indicated or implied any self-destructive behavior on the part of the crisis hot line caller.

TEACHING IDEAS

Health Help Phone Numbers

RICHARD C. HOHN is an associate professor in the College of Health and Physical Education, University of South Carolina, Columbia, South Carolina 29208.

"I'm pregnant!" What a way to start a conversation. The young lady sitting across from me was young, pretty and just about the age of my own daughter. I knew her from my health class but was totally unprepared for such a statement from her. I looked more closely. Her eyes were red and a little wild looking, something like a cornered animal. She wasn't kidding! She had come to me for help. Why me? I'm just a health teacher.

Is it possible that this story could be your story? Are you a teacher, parent, counselor or just a friend to individuals with problems?

The story above is fictional but the situation is not. With that in mind I set out to identify sources which could provide information for health related problems. The sources had to be immediately available, free, and accessible to anyone, anywhere.

After listening to many persons in the helping professions bemoan the lack of immediately available, free information, a search was undertaken to identify as many toll free health related telephone numbers as possible. Outlying health professionals should especially benefit from this information. It is fine to be in a major metropolitan area or near a large university, but it is another matter altogether to be in the middle of nowhere and need immediate up-to-date information. When there is a problem, information is needed immediately, not days or weeks later.

The information in this article can be utilized by students, faculty, parents, and others free of charge. It would seem only reasonable that these numbers be posted in conspicuous places in the school and given to faculty and parents for their use. If you have a question or concern—call!

Being aware of these numbers and recording new ones in the spaces marked "other" will be helpful. Periodicals and newspapers will have new numbers as they become available.

NATIONAL HOTLINES

Compiled by
Richard Miller, George Mason University
Mary Hundley, AAHE Program Assistant

Alcohol Hotline	800-ALCOHOL
American Academy of Allergy	800-822-ASMA
Amercan College of Obstetricians and Gynocologists	800-INTENDS
American Council on Transplantation	800-ACTGIVE
Association of Heart Patients	800-241-6993
Auto Safety Hotline	800-424-9393
Bulimic and Anorexia Self-Help	800-762-3334
Consumer Information Hotline	800-772-9100
Drug Abuse Prevention Hotline	800-638-2045
Hazardous Waste Hotline	800-424-9346
National Asthma Center Lung Line	800-222-LUNG
National AIDS Hotline	800-342-AIDS
National Cocaine Hotline	800-COCAINE
National Child Abuse Hotline	800-422-4453
National Down Syndrome Society Hotline	800-221-4602
National Gay and Lesbian Crisis Line--AIDS	800-221-7044
National Hearing Aid Helpline	800-521-2610
National Pregnancy Hotline	800-238-4269
National Runaway Switchboard	800-621-4000
National STD (Sexually Transmitted Diseases) Hotline	800-982-5883
Office of Cancer Communications	800-4-CANCER
Organ Donor Hotline	800-24-DONOR
Right-To-Know Hotline	800-535-0202
Shrink Link Hotline	800-336-6333
Toughlove	800-333-1069
Toxic Substances Control Act Hotline	800-424-1404
U.S. Public Health Service AIDS Hotline	800-221-7044
VD National Hotline	800-227-8922
Other	

_____

_____

_____

Updated March 1992

Consumer Health

Students Can Have a Say

JOAN L. BERGY, *formerly a consumer specialist with the U.S. Food and Drug Administration in Seattle, Washington, became on September 4, 1973 the director of the Seattle Area Office of the U.S. Consumer Product Safety Commission. BARNEY HANTUNEN is the regional public information officer, Public Health Service, Department of Health, Education, and Welfare, Region X, Seattle.*

A student voice in government rule-making? A consumer voice in government rule-making? Impossible, you say?

Not really, if you look into a little known publication—the *Federal Register*. Students—consumers—can have an impact on, for example, the selection of the route for the proposed Pacific Crest National Trail, the labeling of cosmetics, and a whole host of planned federal actions which affect all aspects of our daily lives, if they learn about this publication and are willing to take action.

The *Federal Register* is a legal document published Monday through Friday by the Office of the Federal Register, National Archives and Records Service, GSA, Washington, D.C. 20402.

The *Federal Register* provides a uniform system for making available to the general public regulations and legal notices issued by the Executive Branch of the federal government. Also included are Presidential proclamations and Executive Orders as well as various federal documents required to be published by Act of Congress.

The format used to present regulations in the *Federal Register* includes:

. . . A preamble which reviews the background of the proposal

. . . A statement of the proposal

. . . Information on the procedure for submitting comments

. . . Where comments should be forwarded

. . . The deadline date for receipt of comments

Following the expiration date the federal agency considers all comments and takes action. The action may be in the form of a "final order" printed in the *Federal Register,* including the effective date for the regulation.

A new requirement now makes it mandatory that every "final order" is to include a summary of the types of comments received and whether the "final order" includes, rejects, or modifies comments received. In any case the "final order" must include the information on which the decision was based.

The process of rule-making begins after Congress passes a law and the President signs it into law. Then, it is the responsibility of the federal agency charged with carrying out the law to prepare appropriate regulations to implement the law. Preparation of regulations is a complex and time-consuming task. However, once that job is done, the regulations are printed in the *Federal Register*.

This is the critical point. Usually 60 days are allowed for comment. This is the time when the student—the consumer—will have the opportunity for reacting to and commenting on the proposed set of regulations. It is also possible to change current regulations by the rule-making process. An individual or any group may petition a federal agency to propose a change in regulations.

The system falls short, however, when consumers do not participate. More often than not the number of comments received in response to *Federal Register* proposals is very limited.

In March 1973, as an example, FDA published in the *Federal Register* a proposed change in regulations that would require cosmetic ingredients to be listed in descending order of predominance on labels attached to each cosmetic product. The proposal specified details about the label design, language to be used, size of print, as well as fragrances, coloring, and flavoring used in the product. As of May 1973, the sources of comments were as follows:

. . . Cosmetic industry and associations—19

. . . Professional organizations—1

. . . Universities—3

. . . Other federal agencies—1

. . . Organizations—5

. . . Individual consumers—267

A second example is the proposal to require a warning statement on the labeling of aerosol containers, which was published in the *Federal Register* during March 1973. One of the several proposed warning statements was: "Warning: Do not inhale directly; deliberate inhalation of contents can cause death." As of May 1973, the following summarizes comments received:

. . . Aerosol industry and associations—21

. . . Organizations—2

. . . Universities—5

. . . Consumers—1

It should be pointed out that the *Federal Register* is not the easiest document for the student or the consumer to locate. It is available from the Superintendent of Documents, Government Printing Office, Washington, D.C. 20202 at a cost of $340.00 per year; single copies cost $1.50 each. Most libraries stock the publication. It is also generally available through libraries maintained by federal agencies in the Regional Office cities of Boston, New York, Philadelphia, Atlanta, Chicago, Dallas, Kansas City, Denver, San Francisco, and Seattle.

From time to time proposals published in the *Federal Register* are included as news items in local daily newspapers. However, more often than not very little information is included to guide the student or consumer in submitting timely comments to the appropriate place.

So how can students become involved? How can they gain access to the "system" of federal rule-making? How can they gain a perception of the process which will stand them in good stead as they move from academic community into the community at large?

A prerequisite, of course, is availability of the *Federal Register* in the classroom or the school library. A committee of students might review the *Federal Register* for a period of time in order to select a proposal for class consideration.

Once the proposal is selected, the committee might develop information and perhaps a demonstration project to illustrate to the class what the present regulations are and what changes are contemplated in the proposal. In addition, the students might analyze proposed changes in the regulations and their effect upon industry, the consumers, and others concerned with the subject under consideration.

Upon reaching a consensus and having reconciled various points of view, the comments could be submitted to the agency, as indicated in the *Federal Register,* which has responsibility for preparing the "final order."

The students would then need to develop a follow-up plan to assure continuity in their efforts to observe the final outcome of the process. When the "final order" does appear in the *Federal Register* the students will be in the unique position of comparing their own experience and accumulated materials to the final outcome.

Most important of all, they would have seen, and shared in, the rule-making process. They would, hopefully, have developed a heightened concept of their rights and responsibilities in the American rule-making process.

49

A Unit for Independent Study in Death Education

JOAN D. McMAHON is a health education teacher at Thomas Johnson Junior High School in Lanham, Maryland.

The subject of death and dying is most often rejected by the conscious mind of the American people. Our society is one aimed at the preservation and enhancement of life; denying death and reducing its harshness have helped to cushion the American people's fear of their eventual end.

In coming to grips with the dying process and death, a person may have a better understanding of his own feelings and those of others who are actually experiencing dying and death. Death, for most people who are touched by it, presents a crisis state out of which coping with a new life-style becomes extraordinarily difficult. Too many people die suddenly and leave their families totally unprepared to rearrange their living patterns. Learning how to cope with a crisis, then, would appear to aid an individual in his adjustment to such a change as death brings.

A unit for independent study in death education has been prepared; this is an educational method that allows progress at an individual learning rate. It is the primary objective of the unit to help people come to grips with their own feelings and attitudes toward death and the dying process so that life will be more rewarding and enjoyable and death will become less feared.

The unit was compiled for advanced high school or college students or those professionals interested in improving their knowledge of the dying process and death. It was originally developed from suggested course outlines by Daniel Leviton of the University of Maryland, who is cur-

rently teaching a course on death education to over 300 students a semester. In an article in the *Journal of the American College Health Association,* Leviton outlined his topics and speakers for the course.[1] Some of the same general topics are included in this unit. It consists of behavioral objectives, questions to be answered, activities to be performed, and assessment tasks.

UNIT IN DEATH EDUCATION

Prerequisites: Any combination of the following: practicum in counseling; work in crisis intervention centers or on hot lines; course utilizing techniques; course in the psychology of adjustment.

Course Content:

Subunit A: The Taboo of Death
Subunit B: Definitions of Death: Biological, Social, and Psychological
Subunit C: The Crises of Man
Subunit D: Views on Death and Dying
Subunit E: Understanding the Dying Patient or Relative
Subunit F: The Funeral, Burial, and Bereavement: Psychological Implications
Subunit G: Understanding Suicide and Self-destructive Behaviors

Directions: Perform in the following order:

1. Read the behavioral objective
2. Read the required readings
3. Answer the questions listed
4. Perform the activities
5. Perform the assessment tasks

[1] Leviton, Daniel, "A Course on Death Education and Suicide Prevention: Implications for Health Education," *Journal of the American College Health Association,* April 1971, pp. 217-20.

Before beginning the course: Answer the following questionnaire and save your responses.

QUESTIONNAIRE [2]

1. When you were a child, how was death talked about in your family?
   a. Openly.
   b. With some sense of discomfort.
   c. Only when necessary and then with an attempt to exclude the children.
   d. As though it were a taboo subject.
   e. Never recall any discussion.

2. To what extent do you believe that psychological factors can influence (or even cause) death?
   a. I firmly believe that they can.
   b. I tend to believe that they can.
   c. I am undecided or don't know.
   d. I doubt that they can.

3. What is your belief about the causes of *most* deaths?
   a. Most deaths result directly from the conscious efforts by the persons who die.
   b. Most deaths have strong components of conscious or unconscious participation by the persons who die.
   c. Most deaths just happen; they are caused by events over which individuals have no control.
   d. Other.

4. Who died in your first personal involvement with **death**?
   a. Grandparents or great-grandparents.
   b. Parents.
   c. Brother or sister.
   d. Other family member.
   e. Friend or acquaintance.
   f. Stranger.
   g. Public figure.
   h. Animal.

5. To the best of your memory, at what age were you first aware of death?
   a. Under three.
   b. Three to five.
   c. Five to ten.
   d. Ten or older.

6. How religious do you consider yourself to be?
   a. Very religious.
   b. Somewhat religious.
   c. Slightly religious.
   d. Not at all religious.
   e. Antireligious.

7. Which of the following best describes your childhood conceptions of death?
   a. Heaven-and-hell concept.
   b. After-life.
   c. Death as sleep.
   d. Cessation of all physical and mental activity.
   e. Mysterious and unknowable.
   f. Other than the above.
   g. No conception.
   h. Can't remember.

8. To what extent do you believe in a life after death?
   a. Strongly believe in it.
   b. Tend to believe in it.
   c. Uncertain.
   d. Tend to doubt it.
   e. Convinced it does not exist.

9. Regardless of your belief about life after death, what is your wish about it?
   a. I strongly wish there were a life after death.
   b. I am indifferent.
   c. I definitely prefer that there not be a life after death.

10. If it were entirely up to you, how would you like to have your body disposed of after you have died?
    a. Burial.
    b. Cremation.
    c. Donation to medical school.
    d. I am indifferent.

11. How much of a role has religion played in the development of your attitude toward death?
    a. A very significant role.
    b. A rather significant role.
    c. Somewhat influential, but not a major role.
    d. A relatively minor role.
    e. No role at all.

12. Which of the following most influenced your present attitudes toward death?
    a. Death of someone close.
    b. Specific readings.
    c. Religious upbringing.
    d. Introspection and meditation.
    e. Ritual (e.g., funerals).
    f. TV, radio, or motion pictures.
    g. Longevity of my family.
    h. My health or physical condition.
    i. Other.

13. Which of the following has influenced your present attitudes toward your own death the most?
    a. Pollution of the environment.
    b. Domestic violence.
    c. Television.
    d. Wars.
    e. The possibility of nuclear war.
    f. Poverty.
    g. Existential philosophy.
    h. Changes in health conditions and mortality statistics.
    i. Other.

14. To what extent has the possibility of massive human destruction by nuclear war influenced your present attitudes toward death or life?
    a. Enormously.
    b. To a fairly large extent.
    c. Moderately.
    d. Somewhat.
    e. Very little.
    f. Not at all.

15. Have your attitudes toward death ever been affected by narcotic or hallucinogenic drugs?
    a. Yes.
    b. I have taken drugs but my attitudes toward death have never been affected by them.
    c. I have never taken drugs.

[2] These questions are taken from the "Death Questionnaire" by Edwin S. Schneidman in *Psychology Today* magazine, © Communications/Research/Machines, Inc.

16. What does death mean to you?
    a. The end; the final process of life.
    b. The beginning of a life after death; a transition; a new beginning.
    c. A joining of the spirit with a universal cosmic consciousness.
    d. A kind of endless sleep; rest and peace.
    e. Termination of this life but with survival of the spirit.
    f. Don't know.
    g. Other.

17. What aspect of your own death is the most distasteful to you?
    a. I could no longer have any experiences.
    b. I am afraid of what might happen to my body after death.
    c. I am uncertain as to what might happen to me if there is a life after death.
    d. I could no longer provide for my dependents.
    e. It would cause grief to my relatives and friends.
    f. All my plans and projects would come to an end.
    g. The process of dying might be painful.
    h. Other.

18. How often do you think about your own death?
    a. Very frequently (at least once a day).
    b. Frequently.
    c. Occasionally.
    d. Rarely (no more than once a year).
    e. Very rarely or never.

19. When you think of your own death (or when circumstances make you realize your own mortality), how do you feel?
    a. Fearful.
    b. Discouraged.
    c. Depressed.
    d. Purposeless.
    e. Resolved, in relation to life.
    f. Pleasure, in being alive.
    g. Other.

20. In your opinion, at what age are people most afraid of death?
    a. Up to 12 years.
    b. Thirteen to 19 years.
    c. Twenty to 29 years.
    d. Thirty to 39 years.
    e. Forty to 49 years.
    f. Fifty to 59 years.
    g. Sixty to 69 years.
    h. Seventy years and over.

21. If you could choose, when would you die?
    a. In youth.
    b. In the middle prime of life.
    c. Just after the prime of life.
    d. In old age.

22. When do you believe that, in fact, you will die?
    a. In youth.
    b. In the middle prime of life.
    c. Just after the prime of life.
    d. In old age.

23. If you had a choice, what kind of death would you prefer?
    a. Tragic, violent death.
    b. Sudden, but not violent death.
    c. Quiet, dignified death.
    d. Death in the line of duty.

    e. Death after a great achievement.
    f. Suicide.
    g. Homicidal victim.
    h. There is no "appropriate" kind of death.
    i. Other.

24. For whom or what might you be willing to sacrifice your life?
    a. For a loved one.
    b. For an idea or a moral principle.
    c. In combat or a grave emergency where a life could be saved.
    d. Not for any reason.

25. What is your primary reason for the answer to question 24?
    a. To spare my spouse loneliness.
    b. To avoid loneliness for myself.
    c. To spare my spouse grief.
    d. To avoid grief for myself.
    e. Because the surviving spouse could cope better with grief or loneliness.
    f. To live as long as possible.
    g. None of the above.
    h. Other.

26. Has there been a time in your life when you wanted to die?
    a. Yes, mainly because of great physical pain.
    b. Yes, mainly because of great emotional upset.
    c. Yes, mainly to escape an intolerable social or interpersonal situation.
    d. Yes, mainly because of great embarrassment.
    e. Yes, for a reason other than above.
    f. No.

27. Suppose that you were to commit suicide, what reason would most motivate you to do it?
    a. To get even or hurt someone.
    b. Fear of insanity.
    c. Physical illness or pain.
    d. Failure or disgrace.
    e. Loneliness or abandonment.
    f. Death or loss of a loved one.
    g. Family strife.
    h. Atomic war.
    i. Other.

28. Suppose you were to commit suicide, what method would you be most likely to use?
    a. Barbiturates.
    b. Gunshot.
    c. Hanging.
    d. Drowning.
    e. Jumping.
    f. Cutting or stabbing.
    g. Carbon monoxide.
    h. Other.

Subunit A: The Taboo of Death

Behavioral Objective: The student will be able to freely discuss and come to terms with his own feeling concerning death.

Answer the following questions:

1. Why do language barriers exist on the subject of death and dying?
2. How do you perceive death?
3. What euphemisms can you think of to describe death and dying?
4. Do all persons have a negative attitude toward dying?

Activities:

Interview a person about his feeling toward death.

Assessment Tasks:

1. Either talk with someone about your ideas on death or tape record your ideas and replay them.
2. Save the responses that you made to the Schneidman questionnaire.

Subunit B: Definitions of Death: Biological, Social, and Psychological

Behavioral Objective: The student will be able to differentiate between the biological, social, and psychological definitions of death.

Answer the following questions:

1. What is the biological definition of death?
2. What constitutes social death?
3. What constitutes psychological death?
4. How do these definitions interrelate?

Activities:

Upon reading all required readings for this subunit, make a chart depicting the interaction and separation of each definition of death.

Assessment Tasks:

1. Define biological, social, and psychological death as described by the various authors listed in the required readings.
2. Cite three case histories (can be hypothetical) that depict each type of death.

Subunit C: The Crises of Man

Behavioral Objective: Upon identification of the different stages of adjustment to a crisis, the student will apply these stages to death and dying.

Answer the following questions:

1. What are Fink's stages to the adjustment of a crisis?
2. What are Bowlby's stages to the adjustment of a crisis?
3. What are Kubler-Ross's stages of adjustment to a crisis?
4. Do the terminally ill adjust to death and dying according to the stages above?

Activities:

1. Write a story about a terminally ill person who must cope with his own immediate death in terms of Bowlby's model (2 pages).
2. Examine a crisis in your life and determine which model or combination of models approximates your crisis state.

Assessment Tasks:

1. Correlate five patients in Kubler-Ross's book to Bowlby's model as to the stages of adjustment they went through during a crisis.
2. Read one of the following and write a two page explanation of how a character goes through any of the stages mentioned by Fink:
   Death Be Not Proud, John Gunther
   A biography of Eleanor Roosevelt, any author

Subunit D: Views of Death and Dying

Behavioral Objective: Upon examining the required readings on the views of death and dying, the student will be able to briefly explain how death and dying are perceived from the viewpoint of children, adolescents and young adults, the middle aged, the elderly, and the terminally ill.

Answer the following questions:

1. What are the developmental stages in childhood that lead to a mature concept of death?
2. Name three adjustment mechanisms that affect the elderly's attitudes toward death.
3. Name four factors which influence the terminally ill's adaptation or adjustment to their impending death.
4. Do college students perceive death as threatening? Support or refute.
5. How do you feel the middle aged population feels about dying in their prime?

Activities:

1. Create a hypothetical situation concerning a child's reaction to the loss of a pet.
2. Predict how you would react if a person in your family was diagnosed as terminally ill. How do you think they would want you to react?
3. Identify your feelings if you were suddenly faced with the realization that you had a terminal illness.

Assessment Task:

Plan a chart illustrating the various age groups, variables affecting their death attitudes, the behavior that should or should not manifest itself on experiencing a situation involving death, and the views held by each age group on the subject of death and dying.

Subunit E: Understanding the Dying Patient or Relative

Behavioral Objective: Upon learning of the impending death of an individual, the student will be supportive and perceptive of their feelings and needs. The student will also be able to develop strategies for helping the dying patient or relative to cope with death, dying, and bereavement.

Answer the following questions:

1. What emotional and psychological needs should a relative have fulfilled in order to cope with the impending death of a relative?
2. What emotional and psychological needs should the patient have fulfilled in order to cope with his own impending death?
3. Explain the reactions and emotions of those who confront dying daily, e.g., police officers, the mili-

tary, morticians, clergymen, physicians, nurses, etc.
4. How would you feel in the presence of a dying person?
5. Should a patient be permitted to return home to die? Why or why not?
6. Whose responsibility is it to tell a person he is going to die?

Activities:

1. Interview any two of the following concerning their reactions and emotions in observing death and the dying process: police officer, mortician, war veteran, physician, nurse.
2. Identify those factors which cause relatives to desert a dying patient. Do these apply to yourself?

Assessment Task:

Eric is a 14 year old Negro with sickle cell anemia. His family has kept from him all mention of the disease, its symptoms, and its fatal outcome. He has been sleeping a great deal lately and his general condition has been weakening. His teacher has been discussing biology and disease causing organisms with him. He has been asking questions as to whether he has a disease. Eric has noticed that he has little energy and thinks he may have a serious disease but his family has not told him anything. You can perceive that he may ask you what disease he has and what it will do to him.
What needs and feeling do you suppose Eric has? Develop a strategy to cope with Eric's dying with him and his family on your visits.

Subunit F: The Funeral, Burial, and Bereavement: Psychological Implications

Behavioral Objective: This student will be able to evaluate the American grief process and formulate constructive plans for his or a relative's death.

Answer the following questions:

1. Who should make the arrangements for the funeral? Who should be responsible for the final decisions on place of burial, method of body disposal (cremation, burial, etc.)?
2. What constitutes a normal bereavement reaction? What constitutes an abnormal one?
3. What are the religious implications for burial? What are the psychological implications for burial?
4. What grief reactions can be expected upon learning of the death of a child, a teenager or college student, a middle aged individual, or an elderly person?
5. What happens to the family or persons who continue to live after a close friend or relative has died?

Activities: Choose two

1. Consult a funeral director and/or visit his "lab."
2. Decide what your role would be in the death or dying process of mother or father; brother or sister; husband or wife; young child; close friend; acquaintance; and pet.
3. Write your will and go over the legal implications with a lawyer.

4. Plan a financial statement that would include mortgage, insurance policies, children's education, and funeral expenses.

Assessment Task:

Prepare a detailed and operable plan to be used in the event of your death. Include who should be notified of the death, expenses, settlement of the estate, disposal of personal possessions, etc. What is the rationale for your plans and did you account for the needs of the family who would be left?

Subunit G: Understanding Suicide and Self-destructive Behaviors

Behavioral Objective: The student will be able to devise a reference list of persons, groups, or agencies that deal with suicide. He will also be able to identify clues in the individual's behavior that suggest a need for consultation with a professional specialist or a need for other forms of immediate help.

Answer the following questions:

1. Why do children commit suicide?
2. Why do college students commit suicide?
3. What are clues that a person may want to kill himself in the near future?
4. What is crisis intervention and how can it be used in suicide prevention programs?
5. What can you do as a professional or nonprofessional to help an individual cope with his problem?
6. When should you recognize the necessity for professional psychological therapy for the individual? What persons or agencies are available for such referrals?
7. Does a person have the right to take his own life?

Activities:

1. Visit a suicide prevention center or a crisis intervention center that deals with suicide intervention.
2. Contact the Center for Studies of Suicide Prevention, National Institute of Mental Health, Rockville, Maryland 20852.
3. Interview two specialists on campus or in the community who would be in contact with suicide problems: health educator; clergy; sociologist; psychologist; counselor; or health service personnel.

Assessment Tasks:

1. Make a list for your immediate reference of persons, groups, or agencies that you could contact if you face a suicide case.
2. Identify those clues to suicide behavior that constitute immediate help, psychiatric help, or other professional services.
3. Retake the Schneidman questionnaire and compare your responses from your first attempt.

REQUIRED READINGS

Readings from outside published sources are an important part of the unit. Students should be encouraged to make use of computerized on-line databases to locate appropriate materials.

Put a Little Life in Your Death

CHARLES R. O'BRIEN is a graduate student in the Department of Health and Physical Education at Bowling Green State University, Bowling Green, Ohio 43403.

During the past years in health instruction, there has been a major drive by educators to include the topic of death and dying in the curriculum of their institutions. One of the many reasons for this impulse is because of the changes in society. With these changes, death has been taken out of the family structure and been replaced by "outsiders."

Years ago death was a significant aspect in the foundation of the family. An individual was born, lived, and died at the same location. Death at this time was an experience which was cherished by the family, friends, and individual religious beliefs. At the present time however, people tend to hide their children from the reality of death and pay others to take the burden off their hands. Recently this factor has presented numerous mental problems for a number of Americans. Some of these problems have resulted in child runaways, suicide, breakdown of religious beliefs, and have forced changes in individual life patterns. Because of these and other reasons, the public and the education profession think it is necessary for the topic of death to be included within the educational structure.

Since death education is beginning to be included in many school systems, it has created problems such as: what content areas should be included in a death unit and how are the content areas to be taught? Some major personal questions should be examined before you attempt to construct your unit on death. The first question should be: do you know *your* philosophy on death?

Research indicates that there are two basic philosophies dealing with death. In both of these philosophies the primary concern is awareness. The reason for this is that by being *aware* of death the individual may be able to see the full life cycle and make the proper choice of philosophies to complement the individual's behavioral needs.

Philosophy 1 is death fear. In this philosophy people have such a fear of death that they change certain patterns in their life to accommodate this fear. By doing this they minimize the risk of death and also many of life's pleasures.

Philosophy 2 is death acceptance. In this philosophy individuals understand and accept the reality of death. Through acceptance of death within themselves, they lead their lives in whatever way they wish, and accept the final outcome of these actions.

The second personal question one should ask is: Do you fear death? If the answer to this question is yes, take another look at this fear, determine if you fear death or if you fear dying. These are two terms which sometimes are used synonymously, but are they really? Death means *the end of life* whereas dying is *the process of death*. There are many ways of dying such as through disease, aging, and accidents. With an individual there is only one death. This death may come in two speeds: slow as in disease, old age, and pollution; fast as in accidents, suicide, war, and domestic violence.

Once you have gone through this self-realization process, you should be able to see one of the basic reasons for teaching about death—the students' wellbeing. Death education could be an important aspect of every individual's life. Death as we know it now is something which happens to everyone, but is something we have little control over. Individually we may be able to put off death through exercise, diets, and good health practices, but death itself remains the same.

Now that you are aware of your views on death you can start examining topics which will be included in the death unit. The following topics can be included.

1. Religious beliefs
2. Rituals
3. Stages of dying
4. Types of funerals
5. Insurance
6. Attitudes toward death and dying
7. Heaven-hell concept
8. Death philosophies
9. Euthanasia (direct-indirect)
10. Types of dying (physical-mental-social)

Once you have your topics planned, find the teaching activities to complement your lesson. Here are just a few.

1. Visit a cemetery
2. Visit a funeral home
3. Invite guest speakers (coroners, doctors, lawyers)
4. Make poems
5. Make up tombstones and epitaphs
6. Write an obituary
7. Write out wills
8. Make up a life inventory
9. Role play
10. Interview students
11. Look up laws on death (state and taxes)
12. Crossword puzzles

To help with the classroom activities, teaching techniques like small group discussions, debates, and problem-solving seem to be enhanced by the use of recordings. Below is a list of records which pertain to death education and help stimulate student participation.

1. "Ohio"-Neil Young
2. "Life in the Bloodstream"-The Guess Who
3. "Unborn Child"-Seals and Crofts
4. "Imagine"-John Lennon
5. "Talisman"-The Guess Who
6. "Fiddle in the Sky"-Seals and Crofts
7. "Changes IV"-Cat Stevens
8. "Follow Me"-Seals and Crofts
9. "Better off Dead"-Elton John
10. "Heaven Only Moved Once Yesterday"-The Guess Who

In today's society we find it morbid to discuss and think of our own death. By not discussing death, we place it in the closet hoping it will not become a reality we will have to face. A unit on death would make possible a needed discussion to help eliminate the problems discussed earlier. It would also help students understand the full meaning of life and bring out the necessity of understanding death.

Death and Dying

DEATH EDUCATION:
An Integral Part of School Health Education

Darrel Lang is health coordinator for the Turkey Valley Community Schools, Jackson Junction, Iowa, and a member of Iowa's task force for comprehensive school health education.

School health education is a continuous process which enables the student to assume individual responsibility for developing and maintaining personal behaviors which promote total wellness.[1] If this goal is to ever be achieved, death education needs to be integrated into the school's health curriculum.

Six years ago a death occurred in my family and this was my first close contact with death. I felt totally inadequate and concluded that many of my students probably fit into this same model. To counter this inadequacy, I integrated a death education unit into our mental health strand for the secondary level.

Before I could develop a proper unit that would adequately serve the majority of my students, it was necessary to conduct a ten-question attitude/information inventory. From this inventory, I was better able to understand my students' feelings about death.

The inventory is self-explanatory and gave me a fairly good perspective on the approach I should take with my students towards death education. The following is a copy of the unit in death education that I feel has adequately served my students.

Death Education Unit—Outline

Day 1 —Introduction to death education.
Survey on death.
Drawing: Visual Impression of Death.

Day 2 —Vocabulary of death.
Funeral customs around the world.

Day 3 —Protestant-Catholic View of death.
(Minister & priest guest lecturers).
Other religious views of death.

Day 4 —Class collage on life and death.

Attitude/Information Inventory

1. To what extent do you believe in a life after death?[2]

	Male	Female

   A. Strongly believe in it.
   B. Tend to believe in it.
   C. Uncertain.
   D. Tend to doubt it.
   E. Convinced it does not exist.

2. To what extent do you belive in reincarnation?

	Male	Female

   A. Strongly believe in it.
   B. Tend to believe in it.
   C. Uncertain.
   D. Tend to doubt it.
   E. Convinced it cannot occur.

3. How often do you think about your own death?

	Male	Female

   A. Very frequently (at least once a day).
   B. Frequently.
   C. Occasionally.
   D. Rarely (no more than once a year).
   E. Very rarely or never.

4. What does death mean to you?

	Male	Female

   A. The end; the final process of life.
   B. The beginning of a life after death; a transition, a new beginning.
   C. A joining of the spirit with a universal cosmic consciousness.
   D. A kind of endless sleep; rest and peace.
   E. Termination of this life but with survival of the spirit.
   F. Don't know.

5. What aspect of your own death is the most distasteful to you?

	Male	Female

   A. I could no longer have any experiences.
   B. I am afraid of what might happen to my body after death.
   C. I am uncertain as to what might happen to me if there is a life after death.
   D. It would cause grief to my relatives and friends.
   E. All my plans and projects would come to an end.
   F. The process of dying might be painful.

OPTIMI
CONSILIARII
MORTUI

OPTIMI
CONSILIARII
MORTUI

6. When you think of your own death (or when circumstances make you realize your own mortality), how do you feel?

                                                         Male   Female

  A. Fearful.
  B. Discouraged.
  C. Depressed.
  D. Purposeless.
  E. Resolved in relation to life.
  F. Pleasure in being alive.

7. If you had a choice, what kind of death would you prefer?

                                                         Male   Female

  A. Tragic, violent death.
  B. Sudden but not violent death.
  C. Quiet, dignified death.
  D. Death in a line of duty.
  E. Death after a great achievement.
  F. Suicide.
  G. Homicidal victim.
  H. There is no "appropriate" kind of death.

8. What are your thoughts about leaving a will?

                                                         Male   Female

  A. I have already made one.
  B. I have not made a will, but intend to do so some day.
  C. I am uncertain or undecided.
  D. I probably will not make one.
  E. I definitely won't leave a will.

9. To what extent do you belive in life insurance to benefit your survivors?

                                                         Male   Female

  A. Strongly believe in it; have insurance.
  B. Tend to believe in it; have or plan to get insurance.
  C. Undecided.
  D. Tend not to believe in it.
  E. Definitely do not believe in it.

10. What are your thoughts about funerals?

                                                         Male   Female

  A. Feel they are very important for the bereaved.
  B. Tend to feel they are valuable.
  C. I am uncertain or undecided.
  D. Definitely do not believe in them.

Day 5 —Filmstrip, *Living with Dying*,[3] on how America lives with death.

Day 6 —Five stages of death, grief and bereavement.

Day 7 —Film: *"What Man Shall Live and Yet See Death*[4], Part I.

Day 8 —Film: *What Man Shall Live and Yet See Death*[4], Part II. Drawing students' own tombstone and writing epitaphs.

Day 9 —Pictorial report on epitaphs taken from cemeteries. Death-related music.

Day 10—Group reports on death
  1) Life insurance
  2) Military view on death
  3) Medical examiner
  4) People who have been brought back to life.

Day 11—Fantasy exercise on death.[5]

Day 12—Field trip to funeral home.

Day 13—Positive-negative euthanasia.

Day 14—Explaining death to children.

Death has been a fascinating subject that people have always questioned. Through a thorough unit on death education, many questions and thoughts about death may be answered. It is hoped this approach would better educate our youth and eventually our society. We all should have a better understanding of death, for we *ALL* will face it some day.

1. *Definition of Comprehensive School Health Education,* Iowa's Task Force on Comprehensive School Health Education.

2. *Perspectives on Death Student Activity Book,* David W. Berg, George G. Daugherty, 1972., p. 2-4, Arlington Press, 201 Eighth Ave. S., Nashville, Tenn. 37207.

3. Sunburst Communications, Pleasantville, N.Y. 10570.

4. Area Educational Agency, Film's, Inc., 1972.

5. *Psychology of Death & Dying,* John C. Morgan, Richard L. Morgan, Westinghouse Learning Press, Sunnyville, CA.

Death and Dying

A Teaching Strategy on Tragedy

CONNIE JO DOBBELAERE *is a graduate assistant at Bowling Green State University, Department of Health and Physical Education, Bowling Green, Ohio 43402.*

"Mary's life seemed to be at a perfect point! She was 16 years old, pretty, intelligent, enthusiastic, a varsity cheerleader, and had just been elected homecoming queen for her high school. She had a happy home life, with two brothers, four sisters, two parents, and a dog named Brownie. Mary loved life and had everything to live for. On a clear night in March, she was driving home from work, just getting ready to make the left hand turn off of Highway 617 into her driveway—when from nowhere a semi-truck started to pass her on the left. Mary died on March 23, 1976."

A similar tragedy may happen at any time in your community or school system. The question is, how do we prepare our students to handle the death of a friend or loved one properly? Is there ever a proper way to handle this situation?" Death 40 to 50 years ago was accepted as a natural culmination of life. However, today Americans try to cover it up and pretend that when death does occur they will be able to accept it. This idea has not proven to be valid in recent years. There appears to be an inescapable need to furnish our youth with a more comprehensive view of what death really means, how they can cope with a death when it occurs, and why it is important for them to carry on and live a more fulfilled life.

A death education unit taught in a health class needs to be implemented for the benefit of each student. If death is accepted as a natural part of life, an inevitable event in all existence, then we will be able to stress the importance of living life to the utmost for *today!* The main objective, it seems evident, is for the death unit to emphasize the need to develop in each individual a crisp zest for every undertaking, day-to-day, that one can. Life is rich in varied opportunities and the mission is to find and perceive each and every advantage that

arises. We teach death in order to better live and understand the total process of life!

A Tragedy Strategy

Once the need for a unit on death education has been established, the next problem a teacher faces is just exactly how to introduce the unit into the classroom. One teaching strategy, which proved to be very functional in past health instruction and upon which this article is based, used a questionnaire entitled "You and Death," by Edwin Shneidman.[1] It contains approximately 72 questions which were condensed to 40 for class purposes. In essence, it entails answering the questions in an attempt to identify and clarify students' feelings and conceptions on death. The questionnaire proved to be a thought provoking and discussion stimulating technique to introduce the death unit.

For a more complete and interesting discussion of the questionnaire, the students were instructed to mark a star by the most thought provoking questions; an "S" by those which most surprised them; a "T" beside the questions about which they would really like to talk with someone; and an "MI" in front of those questions they would like more information on as they went through the test. These marks pinpointed the areas of most interest for the ensuing discussion. They also symbolized to the

students where their ideals and values needed to be researched and clarified further.

Four of the 40 questions that were clarified at some length in the classroom are discussed here. They exemplify the type of discussion that was carried on as a result of the questionnaire.

The first question seemed to influence the way in which the students answered the rest of the questionnaire: to what extent do you believe in a life after death? a. strongly believe in it; b. tend to believe in it; c. uncertain; d. tend to doubt it; e. convinced it does not exist.

Some students were confused about their feelings on the subject and therefore seemed to have a great deal of trouble completing the test. However, others answering the question either completely affirmatively or completely negatively had little trouble with the test. By discussing the question in greater detail it appeared that most of the students felt more at peace with their own feelings towards the subject and felt more open about their convictions because they found out that they were not the only ones who had trouble with the subject.

A second question prompting interest tried to clarify situations in which one would give up one's own life: For whom or what might you be willing to sacrifice your life? a. a loved one; b. an idea or moral principle; c. in combat or a grave emergency where a life could be saved; d. not for any reason.

Most of the students had a great deal of difficulty imagining sacrificing their lives for anyone or anything. Most of the members enjoyed their present lives. However, they all agreed that they would probably change their minds if they were confronted with a real life situation involving one of these choices.

Another thought provoking question had to do with the actual date of one's death: if it were possible, would you want to know the exact date on which you are going to die?

The catalyst of this discussion was supplied by one student's statement that "if I were told that I was going to live to be at least 40 years old, I would live life to its fullest and try to experience all that life affords and not wait for old age to do the things I've always dreamed of doing." Others responded that they would definitely not like to know when they were to die because it was a fearful subject for them and they would rather not think about it. Still another response was shared with the class by a student stating that it really doesn't matter to him whether or not he knew because his religious faith was so strong and he was so satisfied with his present life that anytime death came he would be ready.

Conclusions made from this question helped students to answer and discuss a fourth question: What effect has this questionnaire had on you? a. it has made me somewhat anxious or upset; b. it has made me think about my death; c. it has reminded me how fragile and precious life is; d. no effect at all; e. other effects (specify).

Most of the students responded to the question by either marking "b" or "e." The questionnaire did make them think about their own death but it also made them deliberate about their feelings on suicide. It also brought suppressed feelings out into the open and helped them to be more content with their ideas on death and dying.

As we discussed the whole topic of death once more in the summary, they felt also that they could have responded "c" as well. The discussion of death did remind them of the pricelessness of a fulfilled life and forced them to reevaluate their personal lives at the present time.

Strategy Evaluation

As a final evaluation of this experience, the students filled out a sheet of open-ended statements. These evaluations proved even more valuable than the discussion. It helped students to be more understanding of each other's personal feelings and views on death and the pricelessness of a fulfilled life.

The students were given no directions on the proper way to complete the statements and thus were forced to answer them with their own unique perceptions of the total experience. In sharing some of their answers it is my hope that each reader will see how successful the strategy proved to be for each participant. Some of the answers from the students follow.

I learned that . . .
—life, though often taken for granted is temporary, and protection of same, even promotion of same is of number one priority.
—"death education" can be an interesting topic if taught with the objective of living life better for now.
—I am able to stand firmly convicted to the belief in life after death—not fearing death as we know it here on earth.
—I am satisfied with my life and death concept.

I want to . . .
—find out more information about the stages of life when one's attitudes toward death change.
—live what life is afforded me to its fullest, but regretfully must adjust to constraints (some of which may be unnecessarily self-imposed).
—live my life to the fullest and when death comes, I hope to accept it gracefully and it accept me the same way.
—live daily with the attitude that today is my only opportunity to tell others why I don't fear death.

I hope that I . . .
—can live life productively, yet joyously— and never stray from the sense of perspective that enables me to "always smell the flowers . . ."
—can develop sharper opinions on some of the questions I was unsure of.
—if I discover I am scheduled to die soon, I can lead exciting final days and not spend my last days pouting and cursing my destiny.
—live to be a ripe old age!!

I was surprised to see that . . .
—some people didn't want to give their lives for others.
—when confronted with the possibility that even I might consider suicide, I really could not think of the way in which I would take my life.
—I don't have very many strong convictions about my attitude toward death.
—some refuse to seek the full life.

I was glad to see that . . .
—my religious faith is strong enough to answer most of these questions with ease.
—I was consistent in my thoughts on death.
—I did have to think as a result of this questionnaire about my feelings on death.

—others believe in God and put their trust in His promise for eternal life.
—Many treasure *living*—not as solely based on survival ethics, but on a *fulfilling* basis . . . "I want all from life that is good and beautiful."

I want to remember that . . .
—today may be my last—I need to keep a smile on my face and a rainbow in my heart!
—no matter what else I learn through my educational career I am sure to remember *today!*
—whatever I do with my life—the only important thing is to die with Jesus controlling my heart.
—death is not the end!
—life has order, peace, love and total appreciation of nature."

Death education can be a mind-expanding unit if taught with the objective of getting the students to learn to accept and understand death and to think of it as an inevitable end to life, as we know it here on earth. When they can accept this phenomenon, they can develop a more meaningful opinion about the necessity to *live* life to the utmost and to instill in themselves a zeal for a more fulfilled life.

It is vitally important that one learns that one does not have to wait for tragedy before confronting the fundamental and ineluctable questions related to death and dying with which one may be confronted. The requirement here is for one to be willing to participate and learn to understand and accept death as a natural part of all life.

[1]Edwin Shneidman, Center for Advanced Study in the Behavioral Sciences, in consultation with Edwin Parker and G. R. Funkhouser of Stanford University, "You and Death," *Psychology Today*, Communications Research Machines, Inc.; Del Mar, CA, August 1970, pp. 67–72.

Environmental Health

Health or Hazard? A Post-China Syndrome Game

Moon S. Chen, Jr. is an assistant professor of health education at Ohio State University, 215 Pomerene Hall, 1760 Niel Avenue, Columbus, Ohio 43210.

How important is it to teach about ionizing radiation or noise protection or industrial safety? For most students, these three topics seem remote and removed from the classroom. However, the movie, *The China Syndrome*, made the Three Mile Island incident and the hazards of radiation hauntingly realistic. Students and teachers in the Harrisonburg area were undoubtedly affected and students elsewhere certainly felt curiosity and a need to know more facts. What better place to bring together the topics of radiation and health hazards of the working environment than in an environmental health course or in a unit on environmental health? And how better to make learning more fun than with a game?

Fun and success with such a game, called "Health or Hazard?", are attributed to proper orientation and to student involvement and discovery. Orientation to the game consists of a cognitive introduction to the basic forms of radiation (e.g., ionizing—alpha, beta, gamma rays, and non-ionizing—microwaves) and how to use time, distance, and shielding for protection. A cognitive introduction to health hazards of the working environment should cover the detrimental effects on humans of noise, dust, gases, and toxic liquids. Protection measures would include environmental manipulation, medical surveillance, management decisions, and personal protection. Students should be taught to adapt such principles to specific hazards (that is where much of the learning occurs).

Following cognitive input, the teacher should divide the class into three equal-sized and intellectually-matched groups. One group will be student referees with responsibility for awarding points and making decisions regarding disagreements between sides. Their preparation will consist of correctly matching hazards with proper health protection methods.

The two other groups will be competing teams. Each team should prepare itself independently. Based on the cognitive information given in class, each team should prepare an array of "offensive" hazards and an arsenal of "defensive" health protection measures. Each hazard and each health protection measure should be written on a separate index card large enough so that it can be read across a classroom.

The spirit of competition between the two sides fosters a spirit of cooperation on each side. Team members naturally help each other in learning the associations between hazards and the proper health protection.

Competition begins after about fifteen minutes of preparation. Each side alternately chooses a player from the opposite team to "challenge." Each challenge is considered a "round." Each team alternately assumes an offensive and defensive position.

During the round the offensive player chooses a hazard with which to "attack" the defensive player. The hazard is hidden from view until the offensive and defensive players face each other in the front of the classroom. The defensive player brings his arsenal of methods. On a signal from the judge, the offensive player flashes his hazard. The defensive

player has fifteen seconds to respond by showing the card with the correct health protection measure against that hazard. If the correct health protection measure is not on one of the defensive player's cards, the defensive player has the same fifteen second time limit to write the proper health protection on a separate index card. No coaching from teammates is allowed.

A score results when either side wins a "round." Decisions regarding which side wins will be made by the student judge for that particular round. The student judge must decide whether the defensive player's response is correct and made within the fifteen-second limit. (The time should be kept by another judge.) If the defensive player displays the correct response within the time limit, the defensive side scores a point. If not, the offensive side wins a point. The first team to win a predetermined number of points wins.

For greater variety and excitement, more than one hazard can be introduced at one time, forcing the defensive players to respond more quickly. This game can be played at the pace of the students. It is fun, exciting, and a harmless way to learn health protection measures against radiation and hazards of the working environment.

Nuclear Power Debate

Bruce G. Morton is an assistant professor of health education, at Temple University, Philadelphia, PA 19122.

The nation is entering its second decade of crisis over energy resources and energy consumption. Gasoline has more than doubled in price in the past two years. The rising price of home heating oil threatens the health and welfare of poor people who are unable to pay their bills. Congress is considering a proposal to relax environmental standards for strip mining and air pollution emissions from coal-burning power plants. Rampant inflation, partly caused by skyrocketing energy costs, threatens public health as government slashes social programs to balance the budget.

Concurrently, the long term commitment of the nation to the nuclear pathway to energy independence is being reconsidered. The major accident at Three Mile Island, together with the less publicized but nonetheless serious incidents at Browns Ferry, Chalk River, Rocky Flats, and Idaho Falls, have thrown a pallor over the once rosy future of nuclear power. At this writing only one state in the country (Tennessee) is now willing to accept radioactive wastes for storage and disposal. Among the general public, concerns about radiation, the potential for sabotage and the contribution of nuclear power technology to nuclear arms development, have grown dramatically in recent years. Among those who define themselves as environmentalists, opposition to nuclear fission power is virtually unanimous.

But there are two sides to each of these questions. Proponents point to the impressive safety record of nuclear plants. They argue that without nuclear power, electricity would be much more expensive than it is now and the air would be more polluted from coal-fired power plants. They contend that there are benefits and risks to every energy alternative and nuclear benefits far outweigh the risks.

In a course I teach on health and the environment I attempted to broach the problem of presenting the conflicting information which clouds the nuclear question, by organizing a debate in which the students assumed the roles of various interested persons as described below. The purpose of the exercise was to provide the students with the opportunity to try on various viewpoints regarding nuclear power in a simulated real life situation. First I provided the students with readings from a range of perspectives; then I presented the pros and cons of each of the relevant issues in as unbiased a manner as possible. A general discussion ensued. Emphasis throughout was placed on determining the credibility of the information and on the subsequent identification by students of the issues, facts and feelings salient to their attitudes and values toward nuclear power. I found a plethora of biased materials written for the lay public from the local electric company and from one of the local anti-nuclear groups active in my community. I augmented this with academically credible sources. (A list of references is available on written request).

The procedures for the debate that I have found to be most valuable are as follows:

1. During the class session prior to the scheduled debate, present or discuss the issues with reference to the articles which the students should already have read. Next, break the students into groups as per the directions below.

2. At the beginning of the second class, just before the debate, give each group 10-15 minutes to compare notes and ideas, and select one person to serve on the panel.

3. Solicit a volunteer or assign someone to be moderator. Charge this person with the responsibility for limiting the time for each presentation and facilitating the democratic opportunity for everyone who wants to speak at least once.

4. Ask those not on the panel to assume the roles of concerned citizens who have the right, and who will be given the opportunity, to ask questions or make statements.

5. Plan 30-40 minutes for the debate including questions and comments from concerned citizens not on the panel.

6. After the debate, open up the class to general discussion and give people the opportunity through discussion and voting to identify the issues, concerns and feelings most important to them, and to clarify and affirm their personal values with respect to nuclear power.

Directions to Role Players

You are a participant in a discussion among local residents and interested persons concerning the proposal by the electric company's directors to build a nuclear power plant in your neighborhood. Each of you may select one of the following roles but there must be at least one person for every role. For the purpose of the exercise attempt to assume the arguments of the role assigned as you perceive they would be. Each person on the panel will have a maximum of five minutes for an initial statement after which there will be time for rebuttal and open discussion.

Participants

Sal/Sally Slick is the electric company's spokesperson. She/he is an outstanding proponent of nuclear power whose special talent is putting the levels of risk posed by nuclear power into perspective with other risks from automobiles, coal mining, natural disasters, cigarette smoking, etc.

Bert/Bertha Booster is the Chamber of Commerce public relations person. Although this character may be either for or against nuclear power, she/he is indefatigable in boostering local business.

Conrad/Connie Concerned is a local resident who is the parent of two children who go to school in the vicinity of the proposed power plant.

Alan/Alice Academic is the local university scientist who is concerned with the balanced presentation of the facts. She/he will often bring out the other side of the argument so that everybody will be apprised of all the facts. She/he likes to put things in the perspective of risks and benefits.

Ed/Edna Ecology is a local environmental activist who is deeply concerned about the ecology of the river on which the plant is proposed to be built as well as a number of other environmental problems.

Be conscientious about limiting the time for each panel member to present and rebut. The purpose of the exercise is to get a range of viewpoints out in the open, not to resolve the issues or to judge the presenters. The 10-15 minutes in groups before the debate assures that each panelist will have a few good points to make, and is itself a good exercise in information sharing. However, you may want to provide the moderator with a few leading questions just to get the discussion going should it come to a standstill. Usually, the reverse occurs— it is hard to limit the debate. The role playing seems to provide many students with a comfortable vehicle for interaction, and the instructor with a method for examining a controversial health concern.

Environmental Health

Health and Safety Education from the Trash Can

I. CLAY WILLIAMS is an associate professor of health education at Bowling Green State University, Bowling Green, Ohio 43402. JUDITH K. SCHEER is assistant professor of health education at the University of Toledo, Toledo, Ohio 43606.

As educators, we constantly dream of ways to obtain effective visual aids to help us develop concepts; however, the difficulty of getting school monies appropriated for visual aids to enhance classroom presentations too often confronts us. I am going to share a secret of how to cope with, even *enjoy*, two problems of our everyday existence— teaching on a shoestring budget and taking out the trash! The trash can offers unlimited potential for collecting an abundance of effective teaching aids. My recent practice of accumulating discarded items provides a wealth of invaluable materials for the classroom that we can use effectively to develop important health and safety concepts.

In my collection is a necktie which is ripped and tattered. It makes me think back to early spring, several years ago. I was itching to get my boat in the water so, on returning home from church, I announced that anyone who wanted to go to the lake should be ready to leave in five minutes. My wife objected saying that I had promised to build some kitchen shelves for her and that I was not leaving the house until the job was done. Needless to say, I was in no mood to build kitchen shelves! Rushing like a madman, I started to cut a board with the circular saw and the next thing I knew, my tie was tangled in the saw blade which was rapidly approaching

my throat! Looking at the mutilated tie and thinking about the close call, I suddenly realized what a perfect visual aid this would make in teaching about hazard potential of various items of clothing. I saved the tie and it became the first of many items in my "trash can collection."

A plastic cup brings to mind a personal example of how an accidental poisoning might occur. I wanted to make a smoking machine out of a liquid detergent bottle so I went into our kitchen, grabbed the soap bottle, and poured its contents into a plastic cup, placed the plastic cup on the window sill and began making the smoking machine.

About a week later, Tom was making lemonade for the twins and found only one clean glass in the cupboard. Looking around, he spied the plastic cup on the window sill and filled it with lemonade for Robby. Robby took a big drink and started to cough and choke tearfully. His mother came running in and said, "What's the matter? Is your lemonade too sour?" She took the glass from him and sampled it herself to see what was wrong, and she's been blowing bubbles ever since! This is an excellent example of how poisonings occur in the home! We are fortunate that the glass didn't contain drain cleaner, automatic dishwasher detergent, or other

toxic substances which would have caused extensive tissue damage. By this example, we can learn quite a lesson about proper storage.

Other trash that can be used to teach about poisons is abundant. A paint can with a "lead-free" label is an appropriate visual aid when teaching about lead poisoning. A rusty, swollen or dented food can might be the focus of questions designed to stimulate an awareness of food poisoning.

Once your trash collection becomes well known, others will bring you items and stories to add.

"I'd like to donate this to your trash collection," said one of my students as he handed me an old extension cord. The cord was peeling and cracked and dried out with wires exposed. He had used this under the carpet for several years. Instead of just telling students not to run extension cords under rugs, this cord can show how friction will break down the insulation. When students were asked to suggest ways that the cord might have become so abused, they told of pets which had chewed through extension cords and about times when heavy duty appliances were used on light duty extension cords causing the cord to deteriorate. One of the values of utilizing items from the trash can is that they act as discussion stimulators providing students with opportunities to share personal experiences.

One such experience involved a handmade sweater which our twins decided to use as a replacement for their lampshade when redecorating their room. The light bulb encrusted with charred wool and the tiny sweater with a hole the size of a grapefruit tell the rest of the story. Luckily, it was a wool sweater! Had it been made with synthetic yarn, it could have caused a fire instead of smoldering as it did. With the sweater and light bulb or other wearing apparel the concept of flammability in clothing could be explored.

The topic of home fires is rich with bizarre stories. This past summer, I heard a lot of commotion in the kitchen, so I came running in from the back yard and saw flames shooting out from behind the refrigerator. The coils on the back of the refrigerator had come into contact with the plug; over a period of time, vibrations had caused the coils to cut through the insulation. The melted plug is a good reminder that we should regularly check our electrical appliances.

In my trash collection I have a dish towel that touched the lower heating element in the oven. A section of it burned away when it was being used as a pot holder and the unsuspecting cook had a fire.

As a child, you probably enjoyed playing with tape measures. Jeff was no exception. While watching TV, he was reeling out a tape measure and watching it spring back. As he reeled it out, the end dropped between a chair and the far wall; Jeff flew out of his chair, eyes like saucers and hair standing on end. The metal tape had come into contact with the prong of a lamp plug which was not all the way into the receptacle. The other end hit the aluminum frame around the sliding glass patio door. At the contact points, the tape melted and charred. Jeff's tape clearly illustrates how seemingly harmless activities can be dangerous if the right conditions exist.

The average person can do little to prevent the unexpected; however, a safety conscious individual can take measures to guard against common hazards. When purchasing electrical

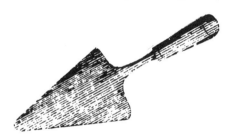

appliances how careful are you to look for the Underwriters Laboratory (U.L.) label? When I found a battery charger at an unbelievably low price I looked on the display card and found the U.L. label. It wasn't until sometime later that I realized the U.L. approval applied only to the cord and plug—not the battery charger. How often we have been led into a false sense of security by not reading the fine print!

Items like the extension cord, sweater, refrigerator plug, tape measure, and U.L. labels are discarded daily. Alert your friends and students to save these types of items for you. It has been our experience that students are much more willing to listen, share, and remember examples of home hazards than they are to memorize lecture notes of do's and don'ts.

Hundreds of suffocations occur in homes each year. Students become directly involved when I introduce the subject of suffocation by placing a plastic bag over my head. I demonstrate when plastic bags are and are not dangerous. A plastic bag, tied in knots, will illustrate the proper method for its disposal.

My mother-in-law receives shirts from the cleaners in plastic bags which

she uses for jobs around the house. When the twins were three, they discovered those bags in Grandmother's kitchen. They were just the right size to get over their heads. I happened to walk in just as Robyn pulled one down over her eyes and nose. Had she been more successful, she would have been in

great danger of suffocation. A larger plastic bag in my collection was on a crib mattress at a hotel which could have tragic consequences if tired parents don't take time to check for such hazards.

Many other household helpers can be hazards. We all know that power tools should be handled with great respect, but often there is a tendency to abuse or be careless with "everyday" tools. You probably have a screwdriver with a blade that chipped because the tool was used as a chisel, a crowbar, or something else for which it wasn't designed. When there is finally an opportunity to tighten a screw, there's not enough blade. As you apply pressure, trying to turn the screw there is danger of per-

sonal injury as pressure causes the broken blade to slip from the screw head.

Another example is my 98¢ bargain hammer which was designed for light use such as driving tacks or small nails. When the kids decided to build a fort in the back yard, they used my hammer to drive spikes. Half the spikes went in crooked so they tried to pull them out. All of a sudden the claw broke, and there was a flying missile that might have put out an eye. **These would-be-architects also damaged my hammer so that the head would no longer fit. To avoid upsetting me, they left it on the workbench just as they had found it, saying wrong. A week later, as I was working on a project the hammer head flew off and sailed**

through the garage window onto the hood of my car. Are you saving your plastic bags, broken screwdrivers and hammers as aids in developing concepts relating to hand tools and home safety?

Annually, hundreds of youngsters are fatally injured as a result of home firearm accidents. Many of these accidents occur because youngsters don't understand the danger of firearms. It is not uncommon for children to consider .22 caliber guns as toys because of the small size of the cartridge. In an attempt to make students appreciate the destructive capabilities of a small bore gun, I showed them a soft drink can which was shot with a .22 hollow point.

This mutilated metal creates a lasting impression when used to illustrate the damage a .22 caliber bullet could inflict on a human body. Gunshot wounds can also be explored with x-rays obtained from a radiologist. My x-ray of a skull that has been penetrated by BB clearly illustrates the importance of safe gun handling.

These items are examples of numerous objects that can be recycled from the trash to the classroom. As educators know, the more we can do to allow students to identify with our subject matter the more we can enhance the learning process. By using common items of junk as a focal point for discussing real life situations, teachers can help students develop important concepts concerning their own health and safety. Tight school budgets and rising inflation might be just the motivating factors to encourage rummaging through the trash for classroom stimulators.

Environmental Health

Ecology Games

RONALD W. HYATT is assistant professor, Department of Physical Education, University of North Carolina, Chapel Hill, North Carolina 27519.

Ecology is currently a "hot" topic in health education courses in colleges and high schools. The topic is relevant, the subject matter is current, abundant resource material is available, the mass media are active on the topic, public and private agencies are concerned, and the students are involved in chang-

ing attitudes and legal approaches toward ecological matters. Still, the competent health education teacher, with all of this support, seeks fresh ideas in teaching ecology. Your department editor has experimented with a learning approach in ecology which is current, innovative, educationally sound, economical, appropriate to several school levels and allows for student creativity. This method is the game simulation technique, which allows students to create their own ecology games with ecology problems and solutions presented in the games.

The rationale for using this instructional technique is, to some extent, based on the games theory which was developed in the 1960s at Johns Hopkins University and other institutions. The games simulation theory, which has been used extensively in social studies, political science, and consumer education, uses reproduced materials,

documents, historical events, and historical persons in a game setting with the rules and regulations for the game based on the possibilities found within that game. Rules and regulations are based on the many combinations which have or could occur in the interplay of people, places, and events. Learning opportunities for the student are many, varied, and allied in theme. Creative situations are different for each student and each group. In brief, the game simulation method produces an excellent learning situation. Granted, this approach is rather a simple one, but it can be modified for use on the college and high school levels and, perhaps, the junior high school level merely by making local classroom adaptations.

It is noted that several commercial games are marketed in the area of ecology. *SMOG, Litterbug,* and *Cleanup* are good examples of these. *Pollution,* a commerical product using game simulation, is suitable for use with junior high school students through adults. The learning experiences described here are different from the commercial games in several respects. Some of these differences are as follows:

1. The students provide the input and knowledge necessary to develop their own game.

2. The game conditions are current.

3. The game situation can be scaled to local problems.

4. The creative aspect is present.

5. Small group work is educational and fun.

6. Decisions must be made by the players which are relevant to their needs of the moment.

Materials Needed

Few materials are needed, and they are inexpensive. Six or eight pieces of cardboard, scissors, felt tip pens or crayons, glue, and scrap paper are sufficient. (Recycling is practicing what you teach!)

Class Organization

Group leaders are appointed, and six to eight students are grouped in the areas of population, water, air, noise, and others as class size warrants. An extensive bibliography is handed out several classes prior to this experience. Students are oriented as to the purpose

of the class: to develop a game related to their area of interest. This game must contain rules and regulations, include choices and chances, and involve a decision-making process. Some of the rules may be preplanned, or they may be developed on the spot. The model of monopoly may be used where dice are rolled or number cards may be developed as a means for the students to travel around the board, encounter the different situations, and experience learning opportunities. Chance cards are placed at appropriate areas, and students have to decide on a course of action. (For example: A student draws a

card and has the choice of additional waste controls in the company in which he owns stock, or he has an increased dividend of two dollars. What will he/she take?) Who wins the game and how winners are declared are parts of the game which the group must establish in their rules and regulations.

Starter Ideas

In case your students need kick off ideas, here is an approach one class used.

NOISE POLLUTION: A player starts out with normal hearing. He moves and lands on a square of rock music (3 decibels hearing loss), construction (−5 decibels), or sonic boom (+ nervousness to your physical condition). Chance cards might be safety legislation, adding carpets and drapes in house, etc.

The teacher can use starter ideas to get the groups rolling, but normally a good introduction to the problem is sufficient.

Desired Outcomes

The following teaching points are among those that should be made forcefully and vividly while ecology games are being used.

1. The "random chance approach" to ecology matters, as expressed by the dice or cards, is insufficient in real life. Cooperative planning must take place if we are to win the ecology game of life.

2. There is a total involvement needed of legal methods, legislative processes, citizenship practices and concepts, industrial concerns, religious beliefs and practices, and genuine concern about people and our environment.

3. An understanding of the interrelationships of ecology systems and subsystems is a prerequisite to effective action.

4. Careful selection in the means of correcting the different ecology problems, so as not to produce additional problems of ecology, is important.

5. There should be a greater concern and knowledge about ecology with its problems and promises.

The kind of game simulation and game development outlined briefly here has worked for this teacher on the college level. The students like it, and its use creates an effective learning situation. Other health teachers on different levels in other locales might well use this approach to help their students learn more about ecology.

Guidelines for a Recycling Project

George H. Brooks is assistant to the dean of the University of Northern Colorado Graduate School and chairman of the Greeley Committee on Environment.

Health educators and their students may become involved in local environmental action by helping to establish a community newspaper recycling program. One such program has been successfully operated since July 1971 by the Greeley (Colorado) Committee on Environment. The committee, appointed by the city council in 1969, originally consisted of about a dozen members—businessmen, housewives, teachers, and faculty members. Other members have been added, including a staff member of the local newspaper—a recent journalism graduate, keenly interested in the committee's work, whose added publicity efforts have greatly helped the success of the project.

The committee decided to undertake a newspaper recycling project after learning that 50% or more of the volume of municipal solid waste is made up of paper and paper products, and that about half of that volume consists of newspapers and magazines. They contacted a paper salvage company in Denver, which assured the committee that they would purchase the paper they collected.

A subcommittee was appointed to find a building to serve as a central collection center. In a long, unfruitful search they found building owners reluctant to permit storage of newspapers because of the potential fire hazard, or desiring to secure a long-term tenant. They investigated the possibility of securing a railroad car on a convenient siding, but learned that a car couldn't be spared. A local trucking firm, learning of the project, offered to spot a semi-trailer in a local shopping center parking lot on collection day, then haul the trailer to the paper salvage company in Denver. Permission was gotten to use the parking lot area —far enough away from the main parking lot traffic pattern, yet permitting smooth in-and-out traffic flow along both sides of the trailer. Arrangements were made with the local police department for traffic control and with the city street department for portable barricades to channel traffic flow along both sides of the trailer.

The second Saturday of the month was selected and publicized as collection day. The Committee on Environment loaded the trailer that first Saturday, while a subcommittee sought volunteer groups to furnish labor for loading in subsequent months. The first day's collection yielded 27 tons. Seeing what the collection could amount to, the committee decided to share the monetary return from the sale of paper with the groups which offered to help —one-third to the committee, one-third to the morning volunteer group, and one-third to the afternoon group. The news media carried the story of the committee's plans for continuing the paper collection on the

second Saturday of each month. Volunteer groups, wanting to earn money for their projects, were soon put on a waiting list as groups were assigned collection days several months in advance.

A telephone answering service agreed to receive calls from aged persons and others unable to bring their papers to the collection center. Trucks and station wagons, furnished by members of the groups working at the collection center, collected papers from callers. Most people who wanted pick-up service made their calls ahead of the 10 a.m. deadline on collection day. There was little cause for concern over abuse of the service.

The Committee·on Environment hopes that Greeley will soon combine its trash collection with recycling on a city-wide basis. However, though the technology is available for such an undertaking, the market for recycled materials needs to be expanded. Even paper collection alone is not yet feasible on a city-wide basis; the paper salvage company says it would be unable to handle all of Greeley's paper along with all the other paper delivered to its docks.

Greeley's Committee on Environment can boast of a great deal of first-hand experience with what has become a widely accepted but not always practiced dictum: man must live with his environment, not despoil it. People will cooperate, if properly informed and motivated with sound, well-planned projects.

Here are some suggestions for those who want to start their own recycling project.

A market for the materials to be recycled is a must. The company accepting secondary ma-

terials must be notified in advance of the start of your project.

Have adequate transportation available. Greeley's first Saturday collection filled a 40-foot van type semi-trailer. Every Saturday since, two trailers have been needed; in March 1972 a third truck was partially filled.

Advise city officials and the police department of your project.

Publicize each collection day, taking into account the different deadlines of daily and weekly newspapers and radio and television stations. Announce and adhere to opening and closing hours; remind people not to leave materials at any other time. Include phone numbers of key committee members and answering service, if any. Give clear instructions on how materials are to be tied, bundled, or boxed.

Liability insurance is a must.

Have adequate workers on hand —a minimum of 10 or 12— during all collection hours. At times even that may not be enough, though at other times it may be too many. Workers may need gloves for handling paper bundles. Lifting bundles by the heavy cord soon wears blisters on tender hands.

Someone should be responsible for receiving the checks by mail from the company purchasing the papers or other materials. A home address or Post Office box may be used. The same person should be authorized to write checks to the volunteer groups who furnish labor for your project, and should keep records of names and mailing addresses.

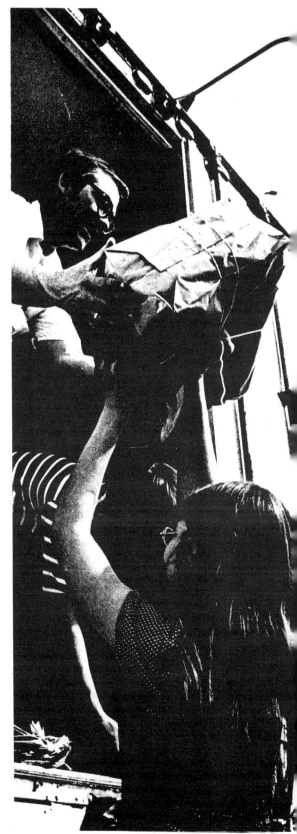

Family Life

Easy Ways of Getting into Trouble When Teaching Sex Education

GLEN G. GILBERT is associate professor of health education, Portland State University, School of Health and Physical Education, P.O. Box 751, Portland, Oregon 97207.

During my career as a health educator I have observed or have had related to me numerous stories of problems teachers have encountered while teaching sex education. Without exception these teachers have been well meaning and have had the best interest of their students at heart. Poor judgment on their part, however, has often resulted in placing their sex education programs in jeopardy; many supporters of sex education have become nonsupporters because of incidents involving poor judgment. It is the hope of this article that such error can be minimized by calling them to the attention of present and future teachers of sex education. The list offered here is by no means complete as teachers are constantly finding new ways to get into trouble. Here are a few easy ways of getting into trouble teaching sex education.

1. *Teaching sex education with inadequate background.* Sex education is one of the few areas where teachers are actually held accountable for what they teach. Teachers of almost any other subject area can have some poor days of teaching and as long as they maintain order it is unlikely they will ever be chastised for their teaching. Let teachers of sex education make an error and you can bet they will hear of it. It isn't that they shouldn't be held accountable, because they certainly should, but that such accountability is rare in education and a major challenge for sex educators. There are few non-dedicated teachers teaching sex education for long, as it is a great deal of hard work. It requires a thorough background in the subject matter—university courses, seminars, and/or a great deal of solid reading. Making content errors in this subject will quickly result in lack of credibility with students, parents, colleagues, adminis-

trators, and will certainly draw the fire of the anti-sex education group.

2. *Keeping your principal or administrator in the dark.* It is imperative that your principals and administrators be apprised of what is happening in your classroom. If you really wish to get into trouble with administrators put them through a couple of late night phone calls from irate parents concerning sex education material or projects which they know nothing about. It is highly likely you will also be blessed with a call from that administrator. Keeping the appropriate administrator up to date, for some, will mean just a statement that you are now studying sex education. For others it will mean detailed lesson plans from which you are not to deviate.

3. *Giving "secret" lessons.* Another surefire way to get into trouble is to have secret lessons with your students. Just make a statement such as "Today's lesson is just between you and me—it is our little secret" and you can be certain many parents will hear of it. You have no business teaching material that you cannot defend.

4. *Violating district or school policy.* This is clearly a violation of your responsibility as a teacher. Curriculum guides are set up to give you parameters to work in, and in a general sense reflect the wishes of the community. You should stay within those parameters no matter what "you know is good" for your students. If you don't agree with the curriculum you should certainly work to change it, and a great many curricula need improvement. Until you get it changed, however, you are legitimately bound by contract to reflect the existing curriculum.

5. *Using poorly constructed home made materials.* Parents especially do not find a poorly constructed penis model or free hand drawings of genitalia amusing. Remember that you are dealing with their children. Giving a homework assignment of freehand drawings of the male and female genitalia may seem innocuous, but many a parent has noted that their daughter drew an erect penis and wondered where she got her model

image. Using anatomical drawings is certainly a legitimate exercise, but have them duplicated for your students.

6. *Using questionable language.* Slang terminology is often all students know of reproductive anatomy and physiology. Students should not be reprimanded for using such terminology unless they use it on purpose to create a disturbance, but they should be tactfully taught the correct terminology. Teachers who feel they must use such terms generally to "get on their level" may soon be on their level equally unemployed.

7. *Not previewing films or materials.* There should be a district committee to approve films, and you are courting disaster if you use films not on the approved list. It is always wise to preview films, but in sex education it is essential. I will never forget an acquaintance of mine who was not teaching health education by choice, and consequently used a large number of films. He ordered the district approved-for-high-school film, "The Story of Eric" (an excellent film on Lamaze childbirth), for his class. As the film progressed he was not prepared for the scene of actual childbirth. He jumped in front of the projector, and his class witnessed a childbirth in vivid color on his white shirt! He had not previewed his film and was not trained or willing to discuss childbirth.

8. *Not being prepared for opposition.* Most programs that are properly established suffer little opposition, as the vast majority of Americans support sex education, but numerous programs have been attacked. All teachers should be able to verbalize the need for sex education when called upon and should anticipate such encounters. Do not respond with hostility or contempt. Parents will have honest questions and they deserve sincere well-documented answers.

9. *Teaching by the joke.* Several instructors have gotten into trouble by telling or allowing students to tell "off color" jokes in the classroom. Teachers telling inappropriate jokes can give the sex education classroom an improper

atmosphere for such an important subject. One local high school teacher got into trouble by leaving his classroom for a long distance phone call. In his absence a student leader was left in charge, who allowed jokes to be told. It was an all male class and the jokes soon got off color and deeper in raw sexual expressiveness. One male not accustomed to hearing women discussed in such terms left the room in tears.

10. *Setting unrealistic goals.* Many programs have been set up with goals and objectives to eliminate VD, divorce, etc. Such programs are doomed to failure. A good example of this is when a program sets out to lower the VD rate. When a good sex education program is established, the VD rate often goes up! The reason for this increase is that people recognize signs and symptoms and go in for treatment. At a later date the rate may go down.

11. *Forcing teachers to teach sex education.* Mandating that all teachers should teach sex education is ludicrous. Forcing teachers to teach in any area they don't wish to teach is unwise. Such action frequently leads to poor quality education, and in sex education that can lead to disaster. Many teachers will never be comfortable teaching sex education. Such unwilling or embarassed teachers can easily be turned to an anti-sex education position by such forced compliance.

12. *Letting personal bias overly influence teaching.* Everyone knows what normal sexual behavior is—it is the way *they* behave. This erroneous belief of major consequence is often carried into the classroom and can be devastating. The advocate of open marriage, marriage at all costs, or any other particular lifestyle has no business preaching it in the classroom. We are all biased. Recognize that bias and be careful not to try to convert your students.

13. *Using inappropriate guest speakers.* The selection of guest speakers must be done with great care. Inviting right-to-life groups to class with brutal pictures can be a traumatic experience for students. Certainly the anti-abortion groups should have the right to express their point of view, but you as a teacher have the right and the responsibility to screen how it is done. Inviting homosexuals to a junior high or high school class is another example of an easy way to get into trouble. Certainly they should have the right to express their opinion, but the problem thus created might jeopardize a total program.

14. *Citing personal sexual experience.* It seems hard to believe that teachers need to be reminded that this is not okay, but it still occurs. Do not let students push you into revealing your personal life. It simply has no place in the classroom.

15. *Using nonapproved questionnaires of students' sexual experiences or attitudes.* It may seem to you that finding out what is actually going on with your students is a good place to start your program, but your principal or administrator is likely to think differently. Remember that such questionnaires may be construed as a reflection of the performance of the school or district as a whole. Be certain to clear all such questionnaires beforehand. They may provide useful information, but be careful they don't cost you your job or hurt the reputation of your school.

16. *Leaving nonapproved reading matter out for public view.* It is of course appropriate for you as a teacher to read anything you wish, but remember that the district has approved materials for use with students. Do not leave nonapproved matter out where a student might pick it up or where an outsider might view it. There is an excellent paperback on birth control and STDs (sexually transmitted diseases) entitled *Intercourse Without Getting Screwed* which is a valuable resource. Many parents, however, may not find the title amusing if they happen to walk by and view it on your desk.

Please ask yourself if you are unnecessarily endangering your sex education program. Sex education is far too important to be eliminated or watered down because of mistakes in judgment. Remember, sex education is one of the few areas of education where teachers are truly held accountable for their teaching. Making errors in teaching history, English, or any other subject seldom results in chastisement, but make an error in teaching sex education and you may be looking for a new line of work.

Readers are advised to review the NEA publication *Suggestions for Defense Against Extremist Attack: Sex Education in the Public Schools,* by the Commission on Professional Rights and Responsibilities, Washington, D. C. Readers might also wish to consult with local universities, the American Association of Sex Educators, Counselors and Therapists (AASECT) and the Sex Information and Education Council of the U.S. (SIECUS) for appropriate courses in sex education in their locale.

Three Teaching Strategies

A soap opera, a silent walk, and a puzzle help present the facts about sexuality in a way that is comfortable for both teacher and students

FLORENCE J. SNARSKI and CECELIA A. LYNCH are health educators teaching sex education courses at Scotch Plains-Fanwood High School, Scotch Plains, New Jersey.

Prior to using any teaching method, the instructor must carefully examine the philosophy of his/her course as well as the role of the teacher in the classroom. Our basic philosophy is that sex education is the study of me-you-us. Sexuality cannot be separated as a discrete, identifiable part of us. It permeates every aspect of our behavior. Therefore, as sex education teachers, our role is to help our students learn more about themselves and others. In our classroom, we consider three general areas of self: physical-psychological-societal. We do agree there is more to the total person than these aspects; however, time and situation limit content offerings.

As health educators, we have a part in the growth of our students in an area that is extremely interesting to them and most humans. It could be so easy to slip into the same techniques for all our classes. Therefore, we strive to use different techniques to meet the needs of each student and the different personalities of each class. Effective teaching strategies can be as important in sex education as solid factual information.

In determining teaching strategies, we feel there are basic questions to ask yourself:

What do my students want to learn?

What do I want my students to learn at this time?

How can I involve my students in this learning? How am I most comfortable dealing with this? Do I have limitations in this area?

Once these questions have been considered, the instructor can institute techniques that will deal with the three areas mentioned: physical-psychological-societal.

YOUR OWN SOAP OPERA

Purpose: In sex education there is a need to explore societal expectations versus individual values.

Objectives

To explore varied life styles.

To become aware of society's expectations for behavior.

To explore alternate modes of responses to life situations.

To stimulate creative thinking.

To illustrate the dynamics of day-to-day living experiences as they influence our choice of behavior.

Procedure: Divide class into groups of four, providing for male/female input in each group, if possible.

Each group is instructed to create a couple, giving biographical structure to the couple, such as age, education, jobs, familial relationships, status of couple's relationship, socioeconomic position, how did they enter each other's life, etc.

After the groups are given about 20 minutes the fictitious couples are presented to the class with a discussion of each couple as they relate to variabilities that may influence their relationship, the future of the relationship, the permanency, and what kinds of needs this relationship meets for each partner.

AWARENESS WALK

Purpose: A relevant task of the sex education teacher is to provide for exploration of differing values among the students. An underlying factor in developing these attitudes stems from previous learning experiences. Though we share some commonalities, we behave individually.

Objectives

To illustrate individual, divergent perceptions in reaction to identical environments.

To stimulate an understanding of one's own learning processes.

To provide insight into one's own responses or lack of responses.

To provide communication channels relevant to different attitudes about sexual behavior.

Materials

Paper/pencils

Ditto slips reading: "We are on a classroom experiment. We are not allowed to talk to you. Please check with my teacher (Name) for further information. We are timed so please do not delay us. Thank you."

Procedure: Divide class into groups of four. Instruct students they are to be nonverbal until further notice.

Each group is to take a walk in and around school environs deciding nonverbally where they are to go and planning to return to the classroom in 10 minutes. One member of the group will take a ditto explanation should anyone confront them in the halls. They are instructed to open their senses to everything around them on the walk.

Start the groups a minute or two apart so that one group moves out of sight before another begins.

Upon returning to the classroom, each student (still nonverbal) is asked to write down all the things they became aware of on their walk.

When all groups have finished writing, allow five minutes for each group to share perceptions among the group and then form a large circle to discuss the differences in perceptions and translate the responses to variances in behavior.

Conclusions: You will find yourself referring to this exercise many times in subsequent classes to explain differences in behavior. This exercise provides a subtle learning experience which requires teacher skill for translation into application.

LIFE PUZZLE

Purpose: A crucial building block for open communication in sex education is the establishment of a "working vocabulary." An innovative review of anatomy and physiology of the male and female reproductive systems is through the LIFE puzzle.

Objectives:

To display knowledge of terms and definitions of reproductive systems—male and female.

To provide student participation in general review.

To determine areas requiring further clarification.

Materials:

Large box
LIFE puzzle

To prepare LIFE puzzle:

1. Cut four letters—L I F E—out of large pieces of construction paper (24 x 36). For coding purposes and ease of instruction, a different color is used for each.

2. Divide each large letter into segments, with each segment containing two pieces which have been cut into interlocking irregular pieces. The number of total segments of all letters is determined by usual class size so each student has at least one puzzle part. Also to be considered are total number of terms and definitions for review.

3. On one half of the segment the anatomical term is written and on its interlocking half is placed the definition.

4. Make a master layout designating what terms are on the appropriate large letter for instructor's reference.

5. Place all puzzle parts into one large box.

Procedure: Students select puzzle parts containing a term or definition pertaining to the reproductive systems. Each student must find partner with corresponding term or definition. Partners present term/definition to the class and then place their portion on the floor to put puzzle together, eventually spelling out the large word LIFE.

Note: Depending upon class size and time schedule, this activity may require more than one class period to complete.

Conclusion: At the end of the lesson, the students have defined their terms. But this can also be used to illustrate the balance of life, that all these terms together "spell" life creating as well as sustaining.

The Implementation of Contraceptive Education

WARREN L. McNAB is an assistant professor of health education at the University of Houston, 3801 Cullen Blvd., Houston, Texas 77004.

Eleven million teenagers in the United States today are sexually active;[1] 20% use contraceptives on a regular basis.[2] The unfortunate result of this behavior is indicated by one million unwanted pregnancies, higher fetal and maternal death risk, increased number of female school dropouts with a greater risk of unemployment, forced marriages, and a higher suicide rate among expectant teenage mothers. These statements certainly indicate the need for contraceptive education as a primary means of prevention.

Contraceptive education is not only providing information and services to prevent teenage pregnancy. It is also education for young men and women who later in life may want a family and will need to select a method of birth control that will allow them to plan for a wanted pregnancy. In addition, contraceptive education teaches those who do not want children to select a method which will allow them the nonparent life style they wish to live. It is imperative that we, as educators of sexuality, reinforce our cognitive objectives and principles through relevant learning activities which will enhance the total sexuality and decision making skills of today's young people. With these concepts in mind the following learning activities are structured for three different target groups—the junior high school

student, the senior high student, and the parent.

**Don't Clown,
Burst Misconceptions—Grades 7–9**

This activity is effective as a *culmination* to a basic introduction of birth control methods, functions, and knowledge dispelling misconceptions. In front of the class is a large, colored drawing of a clown. From his hands, strings project to different colored balloons. Above his head is the caption: Don't Clown, Burst Misconceptions! Inside each inflated balloon is a misconception about contraception; underneath each balloon on construction paper the same size as the balloon is the reason why the statement in the balloon is a misconception.

The activity is started when the teacher asks students of different teams to correctly spell words related to contraception. Examples are diaphragm, endometrium, intrauterine, lactation, gynecology, ovulation, etc. If the student spells the term correctly his team receives two points. If the student misspells the word he must come to the clown drawing, burst a balloon, and explain why the statement in the balloon is false. A correct answer is worth two points. If the student cannot explain why the statement is a misconception, he opens the construction paper balloon and reads the correct answer to the class. An example of a misconception is: A woman cannot become pregnant while lactating. The answer disproving this misconception is: 20% of nursing women who do not use a birth control method become pregnant, and ovulation precedes menstruation. Reaching a certain point total can be the end of the game.

**Projected Future—
Grades 10–12**

Individually students are given the following hypothetical situation: If you and your husband/wife have decided not to have children for a while, or have decided upon a nonparent lifestyle, what contraceptive method would you use to prevent pregnancy? Justify your choice based upon the physical, mental/emotional, and social implications of the contraceptive on your health. For this exercise list the following headings in separate columns: problem; alternatives; consequences; decision.

The problem is selecting a contraceptive. Individually the students fill in the categories based upon knowledge re-

ceived in class and their own feelings about the different methods. There are several contraceptive choices or *alternatives,* and there are many different physical, mental/emotional and social *consequences* that will ultimately affect an individual's decision. After individual selection, groups of four or five students can share their contraceptive choices and justify their selection with others in the group. The teacher and class can then identify similarities and differences of contraceptive preference based upon the physical, emotional, and social factors influencing or prohibiting one's contraceptive choice.

Dear World—Parents

This activity is to help facilitate communication between parents and their sons and daughters. Parents individually and/or collectively decide how they would answer the following letter:

> Dear World:
> I'm a parent with two beautiful teenage children. Tom is sixteen and Christine is fifteen, and both are dating regularly. While I certainly respect and trust them, I want to talk to them about the "facts of life," contraception, and responsible behavior. I know I am much too late, but they seemed to grow up so fast! How can I go about talking to them and what should I say?
>
> Signed Tongue Tied Parent

Following the parents' individual responses they can collectively talk of the problem, what their response would be, and how they would go about talking to a son or daughter. From this involvement parents can share ideas and discuss other ways to open family communication channels about human sexuality.

During our lives we are continually making important decisions based upon what we as individuals feel is best for our own sexuality. Learning activities involving the cognitive and affective domains which help students make decisions based on their own perception of a given situation, reinforces individual responsibility which is paramount to contraceptive education and preventive health.

Bibliography

Guttmacher Institute, *11 Million Teenagers,* Planned Parenthood Federation of America, New York, 1976.

Byrne, Donn. "A Pregnant Pause in the Sexual Revolution," *Psychology Today* 11:2 (July, 1977) pp. 67–78.

Pregnancy—A Gaming Technique

EDWARD T. TURNER is professor and the coordinator of graduate studies, Health, Physical Education and Recreation; and teacher of human sexuality, Appalachian State University, Boone, North Carolina 28608.

Gaming techniques are becoming more and more a part of our educational classroom teaching methods. With the greater use of games numerous companies have been manufacturing simulations and games for use in the classroom. These games are very good but they have two drawbacks: they are expensive; and they may not meet the specific needs of a given teacher's class situation. Games and simulations can be easily thought out and constructed by any interested teacher in order to meet his/her own individual classroom needs. Pregnancy is one such game which was designed for use in a senior graduate college class on human sexuality. The game has been quite successful in that it has greatly enhanced learning through competition in a fun sense. The largest problem in constructing any game of this type is getting your thoughts together on just what you wish the game to encompass. The following construction steps are helpful hints for putting together a board game, such as Pregnancy.

1. Select your topic or area.
2. Collect ideas which you feel should be included on the topic.
3. Select appropriate format for the physical layout of the game.
4. Place the needed information in the appropriate places on your board.
5. Construct your boards with colored tag board or poster board and cover them with clear contact paper in order to increase their longevity.
6. Select equipment including markers, dice, spinner, and decide on the number of players.
7. Select rules and interpretations—play the game a number of times, revise your rules as needed.
8. Mimeograph enough copies of the game and rules so that each member of the class has an individual copy.
9. Revise rules and procedures and adjust game as necessary.

Pregnancy Game—The Layout (See sample drawing and cards)

The Doctor Draw and Conception cards are cut out of heavy paper, and stacked on the board face down. On the back of each card is printed Doctor or Conception.

Pregnancy Rules

Players—2 to 5 players per board. Coed group preferred.
Equipment — board, markers and one die.
1. Decide who is to go first.
2. Each player rolls the die and moves his/her marker, beginning on Start Fin.
3. When a player lands on a space he/she must read aloud the message written on that space. Discussion among group members ensues. This is an important part of the learning concept of the game.
4. If a player lands on Conception or Doctor Draw he/she selects the top card, reads it aloud, and makes the move. The group discusses it.
5. Each player follows the same procedure.
6. The first person to reach the newborn happy face is the winner. The exact number must be rolled on the die in order to reach Baby Happy Face. If another number is rolled the player must wait until the next turn to complete the game.
7. Other players continue until all have reached the end with the total group, including those already finished, still responding in the discussion.

This is just one type of board game that a teacher can construct at a minimum cost. Any other health topic or any other area can lend itself to a similar game. The time and effort in formalizing the idea is well worth the positive learning which ensues.

CONCEPTION CARDS

Abdomen begins to enlarge during the third month—buy loose fitting clothes—Take an EXTRA TURN.

Morning sickness—nausea during the morning hours from 6th to 14th weeks. MISS ONE TURN.

More frequent urination. Uterus is pushing against bladder—MISS ONE TURN in order to buy extra toilet tissue.

GO BACK 4 SPACES

DOCTOR DRAW CARDS

Egg not implanted in uterus properly—go back to nearest conception.

Miscarriage—Natural abortion up until 6th month of pregnancy —go to emergency room—miss one turn then go to StartFin.

Cesarean birth—incision in wall of abdomen in order to deliver baby—stay still and miss three turns.

Artificially induced labor— oxytocin—take two extra turns.

EMERGENCY—Go To Emergency Room and miss two turns

End of 1st month Embryo is ¼″ long, heart beating 65/B/pm, eye, ears, & nose begin to form, & (Doctor's office)

End of 2nd month Embryo is 1″ long. Large head, nervous system functioning, embryo starts to move this point on embryo known as fetus

Rest— Doctor's Office

Emergency Room

CONCEPTION CARD

4th week—Food passing from mother to embryo

2nd week—2 membranes form around embryo—an inner and outer. Fluid between them is amniotic fluid—structure is known as bag of waters.

DOCTOR DRAW

Implantation of zygote in uterus wall—6th to 9th day

Float Trip in uterus for several days

Rapid Cell Division and Zygote Becomes similar to small hollow ball

Three day trip down the tube

Newly fertilized cell is called zygote

Doctor's Office

Doctor Draw

One Sperm of 2-400

PREGNANCY

CONCEPTION

DOCTOR DRAW

Labor Stage 3— immediately after delivery for 10 min. vigorously ends with passing of placenta (afterbirth)

Breathing begins within one minute, feet grasps and baby

DOCTOR DRAW

End of 3rd lunar mth— Fetus is 3″ long, teeth forming under gums, fingers and toes, bare thin nails and sex is distinguishable.

End of 4th lunar mth— Fetus is 6¼″ long, body covered with downy hair, skeleton is hardened, and mother may feel fetus movement.

CONCEPTION CARD

End of 5th lunar mth— Fetus is 9½″ long, more movement, heartbeat can be heard with stethoscope

End of 6th lunar mth— Fetus is 12″ long, large head, skin is very wrinkled, eyelids open and close

End of 7th lunar mth— Fetus is 14″ long, thin and scrawny, reddish skin, if born poor chance of survival

End of 8th lunar mth— Fetus is 16″ long, hair on head more abundant, thin and wrinkled, if born there is a good chance of survival

DOCTOR'S OFFICE

End of 9th lunar mth— Fetus is 18″ long, fat develops underskin giving plumper look, if born excellent chance of survival

10 lunar mth—Fetus is 20″ long, fullterm 5½ to 11 lbs. average wt.

Contraception-Abortion Lifeline

Glenn E. Richardson is in the department of health and physical education at Texas A&M University, College Station, Texas 77843.

When using values clarification techniques, health educators often tend to overlook valuable teaching opportunities within the structure of the value clarifying experience. The valuing experience helps keep students' attention while incorporating facts in an interesting manner. A technique that deals with the sensitive issues of abortion and contraception and yet integrates both teaching and valuing is what I call the contraception-abortion life line. The technique can be adapted to a 20-minute period or continued for several hours of discussion depending on age group, objectives of the unit, and facilitator skills.

Method

On the chalk board or on a large piece of paper, the instructor first draws a life-line with some key points labeled.

A values question is then asked,

"When does life begin?" Students respond independently until all who want to respond, do. An "L" for life is placed on the continuum for each voluntary response.

Once the students have privately or openly contemplated where life begins, a cognitive discussion of contraception and abortion methods can ensue. For each method of contraception discussed, put a mark on the continuum above the life line. The decision of where to place the contraceptive method depends on the action of the contraceptive method.

For example, the condom, foams, jellies, and diaphragm could be placed at a point between 2 and 3 because they prevent the sperm from reaching the egg. The IUD would be placed between 4 and 5 because the IUD prevents implantation of the fertilized egg. Vasectomies would be placed between 1 and 2 since the sperm is never deposited. This allows for an interesting discussion of the contraceptive techniques and can be explained in conjunction with the use of contraceptive kits.

Following the discussion of contraceptive techniques, abortion techniques can be discussed and the periods of most appropriate use be placed on the lifeline. For example, D & C and

suction techniques cover points 5 through 10. Induced labor with saline solution could cover points 10 through 12.

After the cognitive portion of the technique is finished, then the valuing questions begin. Questions such as the following can be used:

1. Which, if any, of the contraceptive methods is acceptable to you intellectually? Spiritually? Emotionally? Socially? For what reasons?

2. Which, if any, of the abortion methods is acceptable to you intellectually? Spiritually? Emotionally? Socially? For what reasons?

The final question in the technique is one that will reinforce personal values or promote the examination of personal values in a way that personal affective and cognitive value dissonance will be avoided or clarified. The question is: Is the mark where you believe life begins on the right or left of your personally accepted contraceptive or abortive methods? If the life mark is on the right of the acceptable contraceptive and abortive techniques, then the preventive action of the methods occurs before life begins and no dissonance related to terminating life should be experienced. But if the life mark is on the left of the methods, then in the perception of the individual, the method takes action after life has begun and potentially could be the source of mental and emotional guilt feelings if the methods are used.

The final question can lead to a discussion of how to find peace of mind when using contraceptive methods, that is, using appropriate methods (if any) which conform to one's own values. If students are unsure when life begins, as many are, then the technique will probably stimulate some pondering. It can also lead to a discussion of the ease of modifying behaviors (use or non-use of contraceptive methods) versus the facility of changing values.

Other questions can be developed to relate the lifeline to other values, e.g., questions regarding spontaneous abortion and life, therapeutic abortion and values, and decisions to abort, keep the child, or give it up for adoption.

The abortion-contraception lifeline, a confluent education technique, places a traditional discussion of contraception and abortion methods within a valuing framework. The technique has been used many times in university classes and has provided a stimulating, clarifying, and valuable experience for teacher and students.

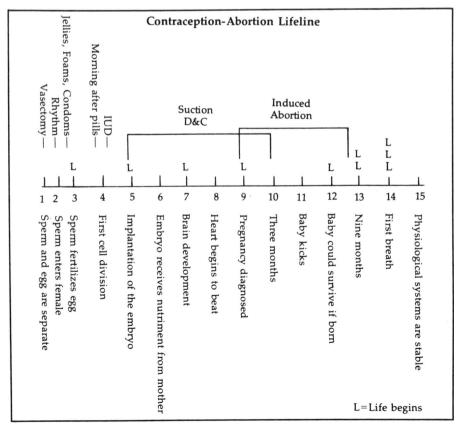

Contraception-Abortion Lifeline

Family Life

Teaching Students About Their Future Role as Parents

JAN YOUNG is a health issues instructor in the Mankato Public Schools, Mankato, Minnesota 56001.

Isn't it interesting, when we think of all of the time and effort that is spent in curriculum development and curricular changes, to realize that we have frequently made a complete circle to find ourselves back where we started? This appears to be more and more evident in the trend to go back to the "open school," to nongraded classrooms, and to teachers working with students of different grades and certainly different interests and talents.

In our attempts to concentrate on technical and scientific advances in knowledge, and our efforts to ensure the proper sequential development of certain basic knowledge and skills, is it possible that sometimes we overlook that which is the most obvious? Are we so concerned about what *we* think the student should know that we tend to overlook what they so desperately need for *their* future mental and social happiness?

In my 11th grade health classes, whenever I pose the question or design an activity relating to future goals, at least three-quarters of every class indicates that some day in their future they plan on being a parent. We give them instruction in many other areas and subjects, but educators neglect to spend much time on the subject of "how to be a better parent."

It is the "in thing" for many students in high school today to talk about how their parents "just don't understand" and are really not "hip" or "in tune" with what is going on. We who work with students every day see much evidence of parent-teen conflicts.

Talk about "learning opportunities"! Let's start taking advantage of these "teachable moments" in our health classes! For a perfect starter, the next time you hear any of your students make a negative remark about their parents, you can come back with the statement, "Well, I suppose they have had little or no training in how to be a parent and so perhaps it would be nice to allow them to make a few mistakes." This, or some similar statement, can get you off the ground into some very interesting "parent training" concepts.

Another interest getter is to write in large letters across the blackboard—TODAY'S LESSON: HOW TO WIN AN ARGUMENT WITH YOUR PARENTS. I can guarantee you their undivided attention!

Recently, I was among the guest speakers at a conference on "interpersonal relationships" at a local high school. A variety of topics were offered simultaneously throughout the day and students chose the five they were most interested in. My assigned topic was "human sexuality and transactional analysis," and for the first session not one student stopped by. They were attracted to the more obviously intriguing rooms labeled "vagabonding Europe," "why you shouldn't get married," and "medical aspects of abortion." Before the second session began, I put a new sign on the door that read: "How to win an argument with your parents!" For that and the remaining sessions, I had a full house, with enthusiastic students. I covered the same material that I had intended to cover, but took a different approach. We discussed many of the concepts from the book by Thomas Gordon, *Parent Effectiveness Training,* and Thomas Harris's book, *I'm OK—You're OK.* By putting myself in their place and approaching parent-teen conflicts from their view, the motivation was there—and the learning outcomes were evidenced by their comments and participation in role playing.

Many basic concepts included in a health class also relate to basic content areas in parenting.
1. *Growth and Development:* A parent who understands growth and development will be better prepared to adjust to changes in offspring.
2. *Attitudes and Habits:* A parent who is knowledgeable about the influence of the home in fostering healthy versus unhealthy attitudes will be more apt to convey positive health attitudes and habits.
3. *Communicative Skills:* A parent who is aware of common communication blocks and adept at using positive communicating skills will have a better chance of fostering and maintaining good family communication.
4. *Decision Making Skills:* Parents who allow their children to make some choices will probably have teenagers and adults who will be more responsible in making decisions that affect their health and welfare.
5. *Coping with Crisis:* Parents who understand that children learn how to cope with crisis situations will be more likely to set a better example for the children in how they as a parent meet a crisis in their family.
6. Parents' concern for their own development of maximum quality of physical, social, and mental health will hopefully develop a similar concern in their offspring.

These concepts are included in many health education programs, but those concerned with communicative skills and decision-making skills are often overlooked. Therefore the remaining part of this article will deal with methods to use these skills in teaching about parenting in a classroom.

The three main skills in parent effectiveness training that I find myself using over and over again in my health classes are:
1. *Active Listening:* this is the ability to understand what the person is "feeling" as well as saying.
2. *Use of "I Messages":* An "I message" consists of three parts:

(1) how you feel, (2) the situation or problem, and (3) the effect or reason.

3. *Who Owns the Problem:* Sometimes a conflict resolves itself when we decide whether it is really *our* problem or something we are *making* our problem. If the problem is *owned* by both parties involved, often a compromise is necessary.

Some examples of the three techniques and how they might be used by a parent, a teacher, or a teenager are given below:

SITUATION: A parent is totally frustrated by her daughter's disregard for house hours or policies established for school nights, weekends, etc.

Positive Parent Responses:
1. "You really seemed upset when I questioned you after you came home late." (active listening response)
2. "I feel bad that you came in so late since I thought we had made an agreement on weekday hours." (I message.)
3. They both own the problem. It is definitely a problem for the mother, because of her concern for daughter's ability to keep up in school. It is a problem for the daughter so long as she is a member of the family living in the same household.

By using either active listening or an "I message" or both, the parent is taking some of the pressure off and may avoid a more serious confrontation than using typical parent responses, which immediately put the person on the defensive, such as: "What is the matter with you anyway?" "When I was your age, if I came in that late I would have been campused for a month." "How do you ever expect to amount to anything? You will never be able to keep a job if you can't obey some orders."

Classroom Strategies
1. Role play family-teenage conflicts in groups or partners.
2. Practice using "I messages" in response to certain situations with a partner.
3. Conduct small group discussions about common teenage-parent conflicts and how to handle them using active listening, "I messages" and transactional analysis positions.

In role playing involving common conflicts, suggest role playing using typical responses in contrast to responses using active listening and "I messages" or problem ownership.

SITUATION I: Jim and Father have frequent arguments over use of the car. Jim feels he should be able to use the car for his dates and his father feels that he should get a job and buy his own car because he thinks Jim does not take good care of the car—leaves it in a mess and uses too much gas.

SITUATION II: Mary, an 11th grader, has a continual hassle at home over her messy room. It has created a lot of friction among the entire family and many heated arguments between Mary and her mother. Who owns this problem—Mary or her mother?

SITUATION III: Jackie has a constant battle every time she dates Jerome. She likes him and feels her parents are unfair and prejudiced because he has long hair and works in a service station. Jackie's parents want her to go to college and feel that her steady dating with Jerome will squelch this as Jerome is planning on taking a one-year mechanics course at a vocational school.

Health teachers can gain an understanding of how to use the main methods which are explained in Gordon's book on parent effectiveness training (PET). There are other general communication strategies which can and should be used, such as paraphrasing and receptive listening. Courses are offered in communications and human relations. The PET classes which are offered in many cities by certified instructors are an excellent way to better understand the principles involved. Practice helps and is really necessary to use the skills effectively and naturally in the classroom.

A common complaint of teenagers today revolves around conflicts with their parents. PET offers what is considered to be a no-lose method of solving conflicts. If you introduce these concepts to your high school students, they start to look at their own personal conflicts with their parents and by putting themselves in their parents' place they often gain much insight into how complicated the job of being a parent can be. They could, as a result of some parent training, become more responsible parents in the future.

Family Life

Ask the Students Themselves

A. GORDON BENNETT is supervisor of health, physical education, and recreation in the Elyria City Schools, Elyria, Ohio 44035.

In spite of a new liberation, including children, we are still Victorian in talking with our youngsters about intimate personal hygiene matters. Yet, they watch us act freely and without restraint; we drink to excess, smoke too much, take too many tranquillizers, eat too much of the wrong things, exercise too little and let our children get hung-up on drugs. Adults are still overly concerned about "hush-hush" and "hidden" subjects, and when anyone mentions sex education in the public schools, everyone panics.

Despite the antiquated fears of parents and the general public about the concept, Elyria High School students overwhelmingly confirmed that they want and need such a program in their city schools.

Students do not talk to their parents about the problem of venereal disease, for instance, but they are very much aware of it. Venereal disease is a small part of the total health education program, yet the statistics in this area of the total subject show us the weakness of our programs in the public schools.

Elyria High School, Elyria, Ohio has an enrollment of 2,734 students, tenth through twelfth grades. In November, 1,767 students went to the gym to see the film "Quarter Million Teenagers," participated in discussion, and were given names and addresses where they could be tested for VD by a health department official.

The next day, about three fourths of the student body were given some form of education on venereal disease. The facts presented were furnished by the State Board of Health and the State Board of Education. Examples of the stark and dismaying statistics furnished follow:

1. The U.S. is involved in the worst epidemic of venereal disease in history.
2. VD is second only to the common cold in the communicable disease field.
3. In Elyria alone the reported cases jumped from 20 to 60 in one year.
4. In Lorain County, Ohio—the twelfth most affected in Ohio— there was an increase of over 25%.
5. In the state of Ohio, reported cases increased over 20%.
6. Cleveland, Ohio had 73,880 new cases and is ranked 8th in the nation in venereal disease increase.
7. Ohio had 218,356 cases of gonorrhea reported.
8. In the U.S. there were *over five million* new cases of venereal disease in one year.
9. It is estimated by leading health authorities that *only 1 out of 8 cases of venereal disease is ever reported.*

After being exposed to those statistics, the Elyria High School students participated in a county-wide VD Awareness Week. They made posters, spent hours manning a booth for the Lorain City Health Department at the Midway Mall, and distributed literature contributed by the State Boards of Health and Education.

In an effort to determine. the attitude of students to health education in general, and to the inclusion of such topics as venereal disease in health education, we asked about 85% of the student body to respond anonymously to questions such as the following:

Do you think health education should be put into our course of study? If so, when?

When did you first become interested and adventurous in sex?
Do you think venereal disease education should be included in a course in health education?

All the students responding felt that health should be taught K-12; the majority favored a formalized health education program beginning sometime between the fifth and ninth grade. None suggested beginning such a program as late as the eleventh or twelfth grade. As one student remarked during the discussion, "If we don't know it by then, it will be too late!" The students wanted health education to cover such topics as personal hygiene, grooming, VD, disease prevention, and dating.

In the area of VD education, our students felt free to acknowledge their need and lack of information. Adults are afraid to talk to their children about intimate physical subjects, but many refuse to allow knowledgeable professionals to do so. What kind of climate is it that will be all for permissiveness at home and in the school, but be almost obsessively opposed to giving young people necessary facts to protect them from the results of this much touted premissiveness?

With the kind of positive response of high school students demonstrated in the brief survey conducted at our high school, it appears imperative· that communities begin to listen to young people and help them get the health education program they feel they want and need.

Test Tube Considerations

DEBORAH A. DUNN is assistant professor and health specialist in the Department of Physical Education for Women, Washington State University, Pullman, Washington 99164.

The July 25, 1978 birth of Louise Brown, the first so-called test-tube baby, intensified an international debate over the ethical, legal, and societal implications of in vitro fertilization (IVF) as a means of human reproduction. With talk of cloning, surrogate motherhood, and parthenogenesis, it's possible that in the years to come, society's reproductive options may be increased, thus placing additional decision making demands on individuals.

Through health education experiences, students can be aided in coming to grips with moral issues which may arise as a result of scientific advances in human reproduction. The following activity was designed to help college students identify a wide range of possible implications of IVF. The same format could be used to elicit consideration of other issues with far-reaching possibilities.

After a review of the actual procedure involved in IVF, the students were asked to recall the reactions of various individuals and groups to the announcement of the first successful IVF. How did prominent scientists and theologians react? How was it handled by the press? What did your family, friends, or acquaintances have to say about it? How did you react to the news?

Keeping these reactions to IVF in mind, the students were asked to silently list some of the questions that had been raised and some of the implications that had been identified. What legal questions have surfaced? How might it affect the family? What could it mean to science?

Students then shared their ideas with the class. Each question or implication offered by the students was written on the board for the entire class to see. (An overhead projector could be used.) Our list contained 26 items including questions or implications such as the following.

Gives new hope to couples who have been childless due to tubal problems.

May help in the discovery of new contraceptive methods.

If the child is not "normal," who is responsible?

Could reveal new information on the first hours and days of life.

One more step toward manipulation of life processes.

Could increase the population.

Women with tubal ligations who changed their minds and wanted to have a child may be able to become pregnant.

Opens door to surrogate mothers.

If several fertilized eggs die with IVF, is this abortion?

May help scientists find ways to prevent some genetic diseases.

When all questions or implications were on the board, students wrote out the three they thought carried that most importance in the debate over this form of reproduction. Then, they placed the number 3 next to the most important question or implication, a 2 by the second most important, and a 1 next to the third most important. The papers were collected and the scores were tallied. The most commonly identified concerns were the question of responsibility should the child be deformed, the new hope given to couples who could not conceive, the fear of manipulation of life processes, and the possibility of the procedure leading to new contraceptive methods.

The followup to the exercise consisted of a discussion of why the questions and implications that were most often raised by the students were worthy of such careful thought and consideration.

Family Life

Selected Impacts of Contraception on Man and/or Society

PATRICK KIDD TOW is a graduate assistant in the Department of Health Education at Southern Illinois University, Carbondale, Illinois 62901.

This teaching strategy was designed primarily for college health survey classes, however, it could also be applied to students in the senior high school setting. This activity could follow after a unit on population growth, human sexuality, or birth control education. It involves dividing a class into separate groups to brainstorm a list of all possible impacts from the usage of contraceptive methods. The topic can be examined in view of the impact upon the individual or society as a whole. Fifteen minutes are usually allotted for this portion.

After this step has been accomplished, their next announced objective would be assigning symbols to each derived impact. These symbols (=, −, or ?) would represent respectively, whether they felt the concerned impact is desirable, undesirable, or questionable. Value judgments must be made as a group. There will be some items that are obviously controversial, therefore, it would be advisable for the classroom teacher to circulate and help facilitate the discussions when necessary. This portion of the activity usually involves about 15 minutes.

Bringing the groups back together as a class, the teacher calls upon a member from each group to share the findings on the emotional impacts of contraceptive usage. On the second round, a different member in each group presents the environmental outcomes. This process continues until all six areas of concern are brought out for classroom discussion and everyone has an opportunity to present their group consensus. This final part should take approximately 20 minutes.

Symbol Designations
+ = positive or desirable
− = negative or undesirable
? = questionable

Emotional Impacts
1. eases fear of pregnancy out of a loving relationship (+)
2.
3.

Physical Impacts
1. contraceptive devices may cause cancer (−)
2.
3.

Social Impacts
1. inlaws frown upon childless couple (−)
2.
3.

Environmental Impacts
1. human race may become extinct (?)
2.
3.

Economic Impacts
1. parents are afforded more time and money to plan family (+)
2.
3.

Religious Impacts
1. considered a violation of religious beliefs by ministers (−)
2.
3.

First Aid and Safety

A Working Model for Simulation Techniques

GLEN G. GILBERT is instructor of health education, University of North Carolina at Greensboro, Greensboro, North Carolina 27412. Much of the material for this article is from the ongoing research by the author for his doctoral dissertation at Ohio State University.

Instructors of emergency care are faced with the challenge of educating personnel to deal with complex situations that require prompt and efficient treatment. The instructor, largely because of time limitations, is often forced to rely on "one shot" coverage of the individual skills involved. Commonly such coverage is followed by a paper and pencil test in an attempt to evaluate the students' ability to apply specific skills.

This article presents an alternative method of teaching and evaluating those skills dealt with in emergency health care classes. It promotes confidence in the students' ability to employ the newly acquired skills in real life situations, presenting a variety of situations that require the application of a multiplicity of first aid skills.

The use of simulated emergency care situations is not a new idea, but this article presents several new variations on simulation design and provides a working model for those persons unfamiliar with simulation techniques.

Simulated situations can be an asset to any emergency care program for the following reasons:

1. They provide examples of real life emergency care situations.

2. They provide practical applications of skills covered in the classroom.

3. They provide practice in the analysis and evaluation of emergency situations without possible injury resulting from judgment errors.

4. They provide an alternate teaching strategy for the instructor.

5. They provide a possible evaluation technique for instructors.

6. They provide students with practice in performing skills under stress and thereby should increase self-confidence.

Simulations can become an integral part of an emergency care instructional program from the onset. They can be used in a variety of ways, some of which are outlined below:

1. They can be used as a direct communication strategy by presenting the situation and the correct performance of first aid procedures by the instructor or the student.

2. They can serve as an instructor-student interaction strategy by presenting the situation and jointly (instructor and class) analyzing the proper course of action and reasoning.

3. They can be a group activity with several people working out a course of action and then undertaking it. This might be better in more complicated situations.

4. They can function as an independent student activity by setting up an area where students come in and perform skills in varied situations.

You may wish to devise your own simulation situations or ask your students to make them up for you, in which case each student should design one situation complete with symptoms and procedures. A file of such student situations can be collected and made available to students for review.

The Simulation Model: Scenario

The student selected to perform as a first aider selects a card, reads the number, and leaves the room.[1] While he is out of the room the situation numbered is set up. Other students are employed as victims with symptom tags, medical alert tags, or whatever is appropriate for the situation, placed on their person. These tags are put at the site of the simulated injury or symptom. The materials which are available to the first aider are placed in the area designated as the situation area.

The student re-enters the room upon notification and reads the card out loud to the class (he is allowed to keep it during the situation). He then examines the situation, makes a judgment based upon the symptom tags, and other information provided, and then performs the proper first aid procedures. The instructor rates the student's performance using a predesigned form.

The more realistic a situation, the better it is as a learning device. There are simulation kits available that include simulated injuries and simulated bleeding which can be used, but they require a much larger amount of time and the cost is often high. The major

---

[1] Selection of situation cards should be accomplished by shuffling and the taking of the top card each time or some other method at the discretion of the instructor. However, it is advised that a random device be employed so that students will not feel their situation was predetermined at the will of the instructor.

advantage of the system described here is that it is relatively fast and inexpensive while providing a good deal of realism.

You may wish to add certain realistic touches such as turning out the lights to simulate night time, adding more props, or even having victims chew cookies and simulate vomiting. The extent to which you carry this is limited only by your imagination.

Critique

Following the completion of situations it is recommended that a critique be held, explaining the proper procedures and clearing up any questions. This can be done after each situation, at the close of each session, or at the end of all the situations depending on the instructor's time schedule and wishes. Copies of the rating form may be distributed and used by fellow students during the performance, for comparison and to reinforce learning. They can also be collected by the instructor to aid him in his rating.

Another technique is to employ overhead projections (showing correct procedures) during the situation, but in such a manner that the participating first aider cannot see them. Flashing the projection immediately after completion of a situation is a technique which also saves class time that normally would be taken reviewing each different situation at a later time.

In the majority of situations several alternate first aid procedures are possible and appropriate. The design of evaluation forms should take this into consideration. Evaluation should be based only on the results of the first aid and not the appearance of any special bandage the instructor had in mind. The intention is to help save lives, not win a neatness contest. However, effective bandages are most often neatly applied.

Preparation for the Instructor

The instructor should develop and review the situations to be sure he understands the correct procedures and has all the proper materials necessary. Tags and other materials should be kept in separate envelopes and numbered for easy access. Masking tape can serve to hold tags in place. Assistants should be recruited and trained to ensure that the situations will be set up rapidly.

The instructor should review all instructions with participants and should present a sample situation.

The makeup of each class determines the situations. First aid for housewives should emphasize more household accidents and first aid for firemen should emphasize burns, smoke inhalation, and so on.

Careful selection of victims is necessary. Some situations require little acting ability (e.g. an unconscious victim), but others require a great deal of showmanship to be effective (e.g., drug freakout). Try to involve everyone at least once as a victim or bystander. You may wish to employ "professional" victims to ensure that the simulations will be well done.

SAMPLE EVALUATION FORM
TRANSFER-BREATHING-BLEEDING

Circle the appropriate number and total at the bottom. Values should be assigned according to the importance of each skill.

	YES Well Done	YES Adequate	NO
1. Was the victim examined quickly for all possible injuries?	3-2	1	0
2. Was the victim quickly removed from imminent danger by an appropriate method?	6-5-4	3-2-1	0
*Note—lack of speed would be a deduction here.			
3. Was victim given proper mouth-to-mouth artificial respiration until victim revives?	5-4	3-2-1	0

    A. Clear Obstructions (1)
    B. Proper head tilt (2)
    C. Timing (1)
    D. Dealing with difficulties (1)
    *Note—in some cases mouth-to-nose, mouth-to-stoma or a manual method may be required.

	YES Well Done	YES Adequate	NO
4. Was victim given proper care for mild bleeding?	3-2	1	0

    A. Direct pressure and elevation (1)
    B. Proper bandage (2)

	YES Well Done	YES Adequate	NO
5. Was victim given verbal encouragement?	2	1	0

    *Note—just saying you will be OK isn't very good verbal encouragement.

	YES Well Done	YES Adequate	NO
6. Was victim treated for shock?	2	1	0

    *Note—remember shock treatment varies.

	YES Well Done	YES Adequate	NO
7. Was proper additional/professional aid called for?	2	1	0

Add _____+2_____
Deductions _____
Total_____
Possible___25_____

Comments:
—Additions can be used to equalize situations so they all have the same point values.
—Deductions include improper order such as treating a fracture before life threatening bleeding.

SAMPLE SITUATION

Situation:
Your brother is playing in the garage when you hear an explosion. There is smoke in the air and the roof appears in danger of collapsing.
Where:
Your home.
Miscellaneous Information:
No one else is home.

Above is the card that is given to the first aider. The information below is not seen by the first aider. It gives the directions for the conduct of the simulation.
Position of victim:
Face down.
Special Instructions for Victim:
Remain unconscious until signaled by instructor.
Special Instructions for bystanders:
No bystanders present.
Supplied Materials:
1. Home materials box (a box containing those first aid supplies generally found in the home.)
Tags:
1. No air going in or out (1) chest
2. Blue skin (1) face
3. Mild bleeding (1) right forearm

PARTICIPANTS INSTRUCTIONS

1. You must treat this *like a real life situation*. Nothing will be assumed—you must do all that you would in a real life situation. To receive credit for any procedure it must be accomplished completely. The only exception to this is procedures that cannot be done in the classroom such as making a phone call.

2. You may use only material *provided* in the testing area.
3. You may *not* use any notes or cards other than those provided.
4. For assistance you may use only those people provided and *you must give* explicit directions for any aid they administer. No undirected assistance or information is to be given by other students or victims.
5. *Time will be an important factor in life threatening situations.* A reasonable time will be allowed for less severe injuries, but do not waste time. (After having used a situation several times an instructor will have an idea of how long it should take to complete and may wish to set a time limit.)

SIMULATION TAGS

Simulation tags which have symptoms written on them are constructed for each situation and attached to victims by masking tape. They are coded by color—red for bleeding, blue for breathing difficulties and cold, green and yellow for miscellaneous symptoms.

Their size is appropriate for the symptom. This means that symptoms that would be obvious such as severe bleeding, have a large tag and clear fluid from the ear, are relatively small. No attempt is made to hide tags any more than in real situations. The objective is not to trick anyone, but rather to ensure a thorough examination.

Burns are listed by degrees for easy identification of proper first aid treatment. Bleeding tags are marked mild, moderate, or severe.

In appropriate situations medical alert tags and cards plus medications are supplied to further aid the first aider in diagnosis. Medications are given in several cases to ensure understanding of the Red Cross position on providing or giving medication. Names on medications and cards should be uni-sex (i.e., Pat) so that male or female victims fit into all situations.

Breaking the Accident Chain

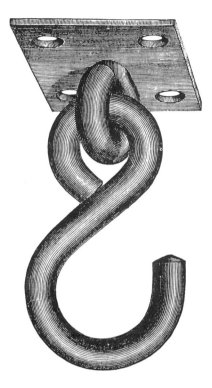

Richard T. Mackey is in the Department of Health and Physical Education at Miami University, Oxford, Ohio 45056.

"Accidents don't just happen, they are caused." It's a simple straightforward statement, but how tough it is to convince people of its validity.

An "accident chain" is an effective instructional device for helping individuals analyze the causes of many types of accidents. It can be used in school health instruction or in an industrial setting. Here's how it works.

The "accident chain" consists of a 2 ×4 length of wood with six, 2 ×2 inch pieces resting on one-half inch dowels cut lengthwise. The dowels are glued to the 2 × 4s. Grooves are cut in the 2 × 2s so they rest on the dowels. The six upright pieces contain chain words and are placed six inches apart so that when any one is removed the chain action will be interrupted when the pieces are toppled. The removal of one word represents the removal of one factor which leads to an accident. Thus the accident chain will not be activated and symbolically the accident will not have occurred.

The first upright represents environmental factors such as: crowding, doors, drinking fountain, floors, lighting, no handrails or weather. The second represents human factors such as: active game, fatigue, horseplay, lack of training or experience, running, violation of rules. Next comes the agent which includes: animal or insect, electricity, fire, gases, liquids, recreational equipment, pencil, student, or vehicle. The trigger is the actual incident which results in the accident. The slipping of the car tires on the pavement, the bat flying out of the student's hands, the toe of the person's foot catching on the stairstep, the rug slipping on the floor, are all examples of the trigger. There are conditions when all the elements leading to an accident are present but nothing triggers it. There must be a trigger for an accident to occur, but if the other factors are changed or eliminated the trigger will not be activated.

In analyzing the accidents ask your students questions such as: What were the environmental factors? How could the conditions been changed to prevent the accident? What was the agent? What was the trigger? How could the situation been changed to avoid activating the trigger?

All accidents can be analyzed with the accident chain model. Why not add it to your instructional devices. Figures 1 and 2 show the accident chain before and after being activated.

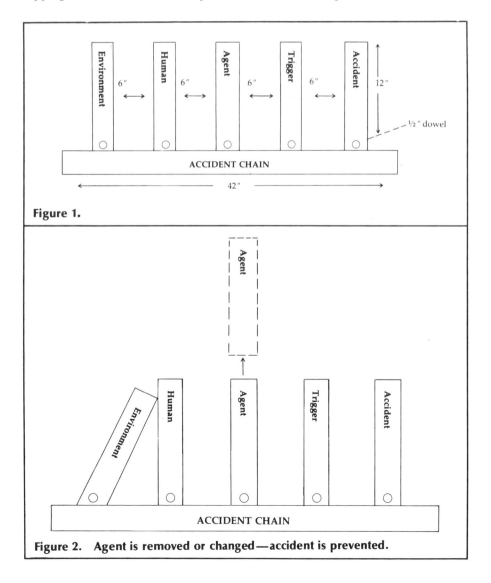

Figure 1.

Figure 2. Agent is removed or changed—accident is prevented.

CPR Drilling

MARK KITTLESON is an instructor in the Health Education Department at Youngstown State University, Youngstown, Ohio 44503. He is currently certified as an instructor-trainer in CPR by the American Heart Association.

Cardiopulmonary resuscitation (CPR) has been making a lot of headlines lately. Several states have now mandated CPR instruction to all high school students before they are allowed to graduate. Many people are turning to the health educator to provide this CPR training. Through the help of the American Heart Association many health educators are receiving this training to teach such courses. Unfortunately, most schools cannot provide the necessary equipment to effectively teach a CPR course. This article discusses problems the CPR instructor will encounter and possible solutions to them.

Problems

There are several problems that health educators face when teaching CPR in almost every learning situation—high school, community college, university, community.

1. Size of Class—It is common to have a great number of students enrolled in first aid or CPR classes, which makes learning difficult. Many institutions, such as the University of Maine at Farmington, limit class size. A large group limits individual help and many students may feel neglected. Other universities, such as Mankato State University, have access to paramedic students who are also instructors. This does alleviate the problem somewhat.

2. Time—Invariably, a few students cannot achieve the certification because the manikins must be returned at a certain date. If you are in a high school or college that does not own its own manikins, you must reserve them from institutions (e.g. American Heart Association, Red Cross, hospitals, ambulance crews) and it might take several weeks before they are available.

Much time is wasted during the actual class period. Only two people can work on a manikin at a time, thus several students must sit around and wait. Telling students to work with one another in-

dependently on a procedure usually does not work. Most students need more structured instruction.

3. Lack of Manikins—Many schools and universities cannot afford manikins. For those who can, few have the proper number to effectively teach CPR (a 6–1 ratio is recommended by the American Heart Association).

4. Areas of Certification—The American Heart Association requires that students master four areas before they are certified—obstructed airway, infant resuscitation, single and two person rescue. It seems almost impossible for one instructor to teach all those areas to a large group of students, but it can be done. All it takes is a little imagination, a little "army regimentation," and a strong voice.

5. Limitations of Manikins—Although the recording manikins are well constructed, they do lack the human touch in several areas. It is important that students work on the following areas on a real human.

(1) The nostrils on the doll need to be tough to stand the wear and tear, which makes them more difficult to pinch than a human nose.

(2) The doll's neck is more rigid than a human's, so students need to practice opening the airway on a real human. By doing so they find the head tilts much easier.

(3) Palpating the pulse is one of the most important techniques. CPR done on a person with a beating heart could result in serious damage. The instructor must emphasize the importance of taking at least 10 seconds to find the pulse. Students should practice taking a pulse on a live person to know what that pulse feels like, where to find it, and how hard to press.

(4) Finding the xiphoid on the manikins is not as effective. Everybody has a different placement for the xiphoid, thus it is important that the students have the opportunity to find xiphoids on several other humans. This is an area of concern because if the xiphoid is pressed on, it will break off and cause internal bleeding.

(5) When you are working on a human, you need to be gentle. When working with a manikin, this gentleness seems to diminish after a few hours. The shake and shout procedure, which is the first step in CPR, can be misinterpreted as a "slugfest" with the victim. Rescuers get a feeling of how hard to shake if they work on a real human. Students learn to gently open the airway when working with a real subject. It is possible when working with a manikin to throw the airway open abruptly, which could be hazardous to the victim.

Class Management

A large class can be successfully managed. First concentrate on procedure; manikins are not needed. Once the procedure is in student memory, learning proper compression depth and ventilation will come fairly quickly with practice on a manikin.

The following procedure works best for me. Other instructors must adapt it to their needs.

Line students up in the hallway in groups of threes. The victims lie on the floor or on several blankets with their heads in the same direction. One student is the observer and stands at the head of the victim. Because of the large number of students it is difficult for the instructor to observe every student. The observer can spot any major mistakes. The third student is the rescuer. All rescuers should kneel on the same side of the victim to prevent confusion when giving instructions; when you say right hand you mean everybody's right hand.

Start with the shake and shout and then opening the airway. Go through the entire procedure until you feel the students have mastered the skill. Make sure students switch around to experience all three roles.

There are several major areas that need repeated work.

1. Moving from chest to mouth and back to the chest in five seconds. This teaches the student to move quickly to the mouth and get back to the chest to find proper hand position. You can drill students—"Find hand position, go to mouth and ventilate; find landmark and hand position, go to mouth and ventilate, etc." Give the students five seconds to ventilate before instructing them to find the landmarks. Drilling for only two minutes can give them the feel for moving quickly.

2. Counting properly for efficient output. Have the student put hands in position on the chest and *without* compression, count at the right rate, then move to the head and ventilate, and go back to the chest. Students can count together or individually. Use a stop watch to see if the students are counting at the proper rate.

3. Switching with a second rescuer. The major problem in the two person rescue is the switch. Locate one rescuer at the head and the second at the chest. The instructor should do the counting and tell the rescuers when to switch. You can see any mixups, which there will be the first few times. Keep this procedure going until you feel the students have mastered this procedure.

4. Finding the xiphoid. A simple drilling technique is to have the students find the landmark (xiphoid), then take their hands off the chest. Keep drilling the students by giving only two seconds to find the landmark and then having them drop their hands.

These drills allow the instructor to teach the students the basic procedure before they even have a chance to get on the manikin. This will reduce needless work on the manikins and reduce idle time; every person is involved. The observer notes whether or not the rescuer is doing the procedure properly, and the victim can inform the rescuer if the hand position is incorrect. Doing this procedure for two hours will drill the proper procedure into the students. Students can concentrate on perfecting the proper compression depth and ventilation rate when they get on the manikin, instead of wasting time learning the procedure on the manikins.

Alternatives to Manikins

If you have a large class and lack enough manikins, you can still give students a simulated compression and ventilation activity. Collect liquid soap bottles and rinse them out. Fill the bottles about three-quarters full with water and reseal the caps. Students should use proper hand position on the bottle and compress. This gives a pretty good idea of compression. Be prepared for occasional leaks.

For ventilation simulation, collect old fabric softener or similar bottles and rinse them out thoroughly. Attach a large balloon to the opening. With a knife, make a small slice in the middle of the bottle and insert the opening of a small balloon in it. Make a larger hole (to stimulate a mouth) below the small balloon. What you have basically is a head and lung. Blowing into the mouth will inflate both balloons; however, in CPR you pinch the nostrils, and thus in this simulation you pinch the smaller balloon. This gives a pretty good idea of how much effort is needed to ventilate a real human. Naturally, these two simulations cannot match a manikin or a human, but they are simple, cheap techniques to teach the general principles of CPR.

Mental Health

On The Level
A New TV Series for and about Teenagers

Gus T. Dalis is a consultant in health education and teaching strategies in the office of the Los Angeles County Superintendent of Schools.

The concluding scene is the high school yearbook office. Alice's boyfriend, Jerry enters . . .

Alice, I should have known you'd be here. Back at the scene of the crime . . . Listen, do you know what's going on?

'Course I know, did you think I didn't see Gail before I left the table?

So go and deal with her, will ya?

Leave me alone, Jerry!

But you started the whole blasted war!

It's none of your business. Why don't you just get out of here!

Hey, look who's getting mad. Go shout like that at Gail!

Don't you tell me what to do! And get something straight, I don't like to fight with people, I can't stand up to anybody and I'm tired of you rubbing my face into it all of the time!

Alice is startled by the sudden opening of the door. It's Gail . . .

Uh, hi Alice.

Gail! What do you want?

I wanted to talk to you . . . can I come in? Come on . . . let me in.

Alright . . . come on in . . . we have a lot to talk about.

The door closes, the screen goes black and the credits appear. The end? Not really. It is really a beginning. By using a group setting and surrounding it with relevant discussion questions and activities, teachers can use dramatizations such as this one about conflict to get at some of the gut-level issues affecting teenagers.

On The Level Series

The above scene is from a program in *On The Level*, a classroom video series for fourteen-to-seventeen year olds that is being broadcast during the school day by many PBS stations. This series consists of twelve 15-minute programs, each of which dramatizes a problem in the lives of this age group. Program topics include: Developing self-concept, accepting feelings, facing conflict, thinking,

The problem here is that Sam doesn't want to be a baker, even though he's taken over the family bakery for his ailing father. The scene is from On the Level, *a new classroom video series for teenagers that focuses on personal and social growth.*

Tyrone, a would-be jazz artist, searches for his identity in "Who Am I?" a program about self-concept that is part of On the Level.

changing family relationships, alone vs. lonely, friendship, coping with stress, career aspirations, peer group membership, prejudice, and love.

Through program viewing along with pre- and post-viewing discussion and activity, students are provided the opportunity to explore the series topics. It is intended that this exploration will yield certain personal and social growth outcomes for students. These outcomes include increased:

- Awareness of the interaction of emotional and physical health;

- Skill in identifying and analyzing the interplay between feelings and outward behavior;

- Understanding of causes of emotional stress and ability to cope constructively with such stress;

- Understanding of their relations with peers, non-parental adults, parents, and younger children.

Accompanying the video series is a Leader's/Teacher's Guide. Included in this guide for each of the 12 video dramatizations is a program summary, background information about the program topic, student outcomes, before-and-after-viewing-the-program questions and activities, and reproducible activity sheets. Each *On The Level* video program has been adapted in an audio format. Unlike the video programs which are open-ended, each audio program gives several alternate endings. Creative use of this audio component should help adolescents discover that there are a variety of different ways to deal with a given issue. A student activity book is also available. It serves as a personal guide to help teenagers explore the life issues dealt with in *On The Level*. The guide includes self quizzes, readings on the topics, and activities to encourage thinking, writing and doing. Students can use the guide for independent study or for an accompaniment to the *On The Level* video or audio series.

Series Development

The *On The Level* series was produced by the Agency for Instructional Television (AIT), a nonprofit American-Canadian agency, in conjunction with a consortium of 32 state and provincial education agencies. Additional funding support came from the Corporation for Public Broadcasting, Exxon Corporation, General Mills, the George Gund Foundation and Union Carbide.

The series is designed to promote the personal and social growth of youngsters fourteen-to-seventeen years old. The series developers define personal and social growth as *a process that fosters possession of skills, information, and attributes needed to shape life events and make constructive and maturing responses in those events. In this context, life events are changes in physical make-up, intellectual development, personal feelings, or changes in relations with others or with the physical environment.*[1]

Planning for the series began in 1977. Using a prospectus published in 1978, AIT staff and consortium representatives sharply defined the series goals in 1979. The project design team developed, in the fall of that year, twelve program topics, each considered relevant to the personal and social growth of high school age youngsters.

In order to validate the program topics and student outcomes, secondary school teachers and other professionals likely to use the series were interviewed in groups and asked to complete a take-home questionnaire. They found the topics in personal and social growth to be familiar and important. There was a general feeling that many of these topics are now included in a variety of curriculum areas, that the intensity and manner in which they are covered varies, and that some topics are distinctly more difficult to teach than others. In addition, the teachers thought that the series would be an important tool for engaging teachers and students in discussions of these relevant issues.

From here the series was put into production. Extensive evaluation was conducted with 4,000 teenagers and their teachers during production. The programs provided the catalyst for teenagers to discuss issues of importance to them. Teenagers reacted sometimes strongly, sometimes timidly, but almost always with the acknowledgement that they were concerned about the issues and appreciated the opportunity to talk about them.

On the basis of student as well as teacher reactions many changes were made in the treatment and scripts. Revisions included: character and plot alterations to make the characters and situations more realistic and relevant to teenagers; and dialogue changes to enhance the program's message and make the programs more comprehensible.

Vehicle for Affective Education

Through experience AIT has found that video programming, when properly shaped, can be useful in enhancing the affective curriculum in school settings. Such series as *Ripples* and *Inside/Out* for the elementary school level and *Self Incorporated* for the junior high level represent efforts to assist teachers in dealing with affective issues in the area of personal growth and development. With the completion of the *On The Level* series AIT has achieved a K–12 affective education program in the area of health education.

The programs for all these AIT series are particularly helpful in facilitating affective learnings. That is, when properly used they are useful in helping students explore their own beliefs, opinions, and likes and dislikes.

Effective Use of the Series

Essentially, proper use of the *On The Level* series involves (1) selection of appropriate questions and activities to precede and follow the program, and (2) the establishment of psychological freedom in the classroom or group setting.

The Leader's/Teacher's Guide contains a pool of questions and activities useful in "squeezing health education affective juice" out of the series. For example, in using the program "Face to Face," which centers around the conflict between Alice and Gail, one of the teachers participating in evaluation of that program selected the following from the Guide:

Before the Program
- Get a group agreement on the definition of conflict. Discuss some of the factors that help to determine the severity of conflict.
- In small groups, make a list of the positive things that can result from conflict. The negative things.

After the Program
- Ask students to respond to the following questions: What were the conflicts in Alice's life? Did any of these conflicts have an effect on Alice's physical and emotional health? If so, how?
- Have each person write an ending to the program's story line. (What happened when Gail and Alice confronted each other?) Discuss the different endings.
- Complete the reproducible activity "How Do You Handle Conflict?" located in the back of the guidebook (this is an instrument useful in determining ways people handle conflict).
- Invite students to discuss the following question: How do you feel about facing conflict?

The most critical element in the successful use of *On The Level* is the teacher. That is, what the teacher does and does not do as he or she *interacts* with teenagers will determine the degree of success or failure in using the series. In addition to utilizing relevant questions and activities, the teacher needs to create a classroom environment that allows free, open and responsible discussion. Such a psychologically free environment should allow diversity without the fear

of recriminations from classmates or the teacher.

To establish such an environment it is helpful for the teacher to set discussion ground rules.[2] For example, "In our discussion today let's have one person speak at a time. Remember it's OK to disagree but don't be disagreeable when you do so. Also, no put downs." As the discussion unfolds the teacher's role is to maintain the ground rules and to refrain from judging students' ideas directly or indirectly.

It was through such a teacher-established classroom environment after viewing the program on conflict that one student reported that she did not feel alone. The student communicated relief in not being "weird" because through discussion she discovered she was not the only one afraid of dealing with conflict. Somehow there seems to be a sense of security in knowing that one's peers have similar anxieties, fears, and joys. This sense of security can come to thousands of high school students if appropriate affective teaching materials as well as teaching behaviors are carefully utilized.

Perhaps the power of the *On The Level* series became most apparent when students responded with disappointment and frustration at the lack of "real" program endings. After viewing the programs students often responded with *What happened to the rest of it? When is the rest of it going to be on TV? I want to see what happens.*

Yet it was this frustration which seemed to be a viable starting point for the exploration of ideas and opinions relative to growth and development. And that is what this series is all about—providing a catalyst for the exploration of life issues relevant to high school students.

[1]Agency for Instructional Television. *Education for personal and social growth of secondary school students.* Bloomington, Indiana: Agency for Instructional Television, 1978.

[2]Agency for Instructional Television. *Research Report 70—Secondary health project: concepts review.* Bloomington, Indiana: Agency for Instructional Television, 1980.

[3]Dalis, Gus T. and Strasser, Ben. B. *Teaching strategies for values awareness and decision making in health education.* Thorofare, New Jersey: Charles B. Slack, Inc., 1977.

Anyone wishing further information about local availability of "On the Level" may contact: AIT, Box A, Bloomington, Indiana 47402, (812) 339-2203.

Mental Health

Perceptions of Me

JERROLD S. GREENBERG is coordinator of health education, State University of New York at Buffalo, Buffalo, New York 14214. He serves as contributing editor for this SHR department, which is designed to be of particular usefulness to the classroom teacher at all levels.

Though realizing the degree of immodesty of which I can be accused, let me risk stating that the most interesting topic to me is me. Further, the most interesting topic to you is probably you. That's nothing startling. We all are interested in ourselves. Realizing this phenomenon, educators recommend that learnings in school be related to the life experiences of the learner. It then seems to follow that with the learner himself the topic of study, the efficiency and effectiveness of the learning process would be maximized.

The question of the appropriateness of oneself as a topic for study within a school setting, however, remains. Since one behaves on how one perceives reality rather than upon reality itself, one's perceptions of oneself will determine many health related behaviors. For example, one possessing a positive self-concept might be expected to walk tall (upright) while one with a negative self-concept might walk slumped over to physically indicate "lowliness"; or one with a positive sense of sexual self-esteem might be outgoing and pleasant, whereas one with a negative feeling about oneself sexually might behave in a shy, withdrawn manner.

Based upon the importance of perceptions of oneself, and, in addition, how others perceive one (since they will behave toward others based upon their perceptions of them) activities should be developed and conducted with students to help them to:

1. More realistically perceive themselves and others.
2. Explore the relationship between their perceptions and how they act.
3. Make whatever adjustments they deem necessary to become what they want to be. Presented in this article are examples of such learning activities.

Sentence Completions

Unfinished sentences which require the student to react by completing them, allow for self-inquiry of a kind to which people are not accustomed. Examples of such questions indicate the breadth of possibilities and range of topics which can be explored with this instructional strategy.

1. I often _____
2. I seldom _____
3. I'm bored when _____
4. I love to _____
5. Other children _____
6. I will _____
7. I must _____
8. I am very _____
9. I wish I could _____
10. My friends are _____
11. My parents _____
12. I wish _____
13. I feel _____
14. I'm happy when _____
15. My body _____

Whereas the completion of these sentences requires the student to think about himself, processing the responses in small groups allows students to explore other childrens' perceptions of themselves. It is hoped that surprises about certain responses will help children be more accepting of others and better understand themselves. If the class trusts the teacher sufficiently, the reading of the responses by the teacher might also aid the teacher to better plan instruction which pertains to the needs of the students.

Discussion Questions

Using questions to stimulate group discussions is not a recent educational innovation, but the types of questions suggested for use here differ from those employed elsewhere.

1. What is the one thing that scares you the most?
2. When are you most hurt?
3. What is the very first thing that you remember?
4. What is the saddest thing that has ever happened to you?
5. What is the best thing that has ever happened to you?
6. What do you dislike most about school?
7. What don't you like about yourself?
8. What do you like most about yourself?
9. What would you rather have: wealth, intelligence, or physical attractiveness?
10. Who is the most influential person in your life?
11. What do you wish?
12. How can you be happy?
13. What do you love to do the most?
14. What was the strongest feeling you had last week (anger, joy, grief, etc. . . .) and what caused that feeling?
15. What is something you can tell us now that you wouldn't have felt comfortable telling us before?

Each group should be reminded that there are no right or wrong answers to such questions and, therefore, they should expect each person to respond differently. The group members' role should be to ask questions of the respondent which will help the group to better understand the response, rather than to attempt to get the group to agree on what would be the "best" answer. As a result of this exercise, it is anticipated that each student will have a more accurate picture of both himself and his classmates than prior to the exercise.

Question Sociogram

An activity which can be used to aid students to see themselves as others see them is the Question Sociogram. Unlike a regular sociogram which asks children to list a number of people they would like to attend a movie with, etc., the Question Sociogram asks children to place the name of the person in the class *most likely* to fit the description implicit in the question. Examples of questions which can be used will help to clarify this technique:

_____ 1) Who most likely is afraid of mice?
_____ 2) Who most likely cannot resist eating a donut?
_____ 3) Who wakes up often with nightmares?
_____ 4) Who loves cowboy movies?
_____ 5) Who loves romantic movies?
_____ 6) Who most wants a lot of money?
_____ 7) Who watches a lot of television?
_____ 8) Who most likely will be a scientist?
_____ 9) Who will be a politician?
_____10) Who will make the best mother or father?
_____11) Who will never get married?
_____12) Who will never use drugs?
_____13) Who is most likely to cheat on an exam?
_____14) Who will be the most thoughtful lover?
_____15) Who will be a talking liberal who won't do anything?
_____16) Who will insist on a small wedding?
_____17) Who would be the best teacher?
_____18) Who is apt to do anonymous favors for people?
_____19) Who will always be physically attractive?
_____20) Who would make the best friend?

To the left of each number, students are required to place the name of one student in their group or class. Only one name can be written on the blank line and each blank line *must* have a name on it. After the responses have been made each child can ask each other child which descriptions he most fits, thereby acquiring others' perceptions of himself. To better know oneself is the first step in improving oneself.

Intimacy Questions

Once trust has been developed in a class or group of children, questions of a more intimate nature can be explored. Best discussed in pairs to provide a close relationship, some of the following questions can be employed by a teacher willing to take risks to provide meaningful educational experiences:

1. What do you feel most ashamed of in your past?
2. What have you deliberately lied about? Why?
3. When do you hurt people?
4. What turns you on the most?
5. Do you have any health problems? What are they?
6. What are your least attractive features?
7. Do you believe in God? Organized religion?
8. Are your parents happily married? Why? Why not?
9. How do you feel when you love?
10. What makes you swear?
11. What do you think about homosexuals?
12. Do you like yourself? Why? Why not?
13. What was your greatest failure? Greatest success?

14. Who would you be if you could be anyone else that you wanted?

These questions develop greater closeness between two people who are honest and trusting to begin with, and likewise can develop greater distance between two people who feel threatened by such openness. It is important, therefore, to employ this activity only with a group that has matured and can take advantage of such an opportunity to mature further.

Enhancing Positive Self-Concept Through Creativity in the Classroom

Barbara Beier is on the academic staff in the health education department at the University of Wisconsin, La Crosse, 54601.

I am convinced that one of the major challenges to teachers and other group leaders is the creation of a self-enhancing learning environment. Some special people seem to do this quite naturally out of their own authentic being and their commitment to others. Most of us, however, benefit from suggestions or training in allowing our creative potentials to enhance a positive, humanistic environment in the classroom.

A workshop, "Creative Teaching Methods in Health," offered by the University of Wisconsin - La Crosse Division of University Outreach, allowed the creative process to surface in me. As a young health director I was quite concerned with dispensing cognitive material to my students, but I have begun to understand that young people need more than subject matter. I like to think, now, that I teach the students, not just the subject.

Creative methods for teaching health education can be written, published in books, and distributed nationwide, but these ideas are only tools. Their use depends on you. Your use of ideas to foster positive selfconcept will depend upon your own selfesteem. As John Vasconcellos states,

"Only if you are truly into your own being, possess and value yourself, feel comfortable with and good about yourself, believe in and live your right to be yourself—will you truly enhance selfesteem in those young human beings whose selfesteem, whose lives, are touched by you." [1]

Research literature is filled with reports indicating that cognitive learning increases when selfconcept increases.[2] Following is a series of creative teaching methods compiled to foster a positive selfconcept in students of health education.

Activity #1: Sharing Bags

Grade level: 10th grade

Materials needed: any size paper bag for each student, pictures, fabric, decorative findings, scissors, paste

Background information: In many classes students never have an opportunity to get acquainted with their classmates. All of us share a need for meaningful interpersonal relationships. However, many times creating a classroom environment conducive to positive interaction is awkward and difficult for teachers. This activity could be a good starting point for teachers who seek to facilitate growth in students' potential for interpersonal relationships.

Objective: The student will have the opportunity to recognize meaningful information about themselves which can be shared with classmates.
Procedure:
1. Distribute paper bags, one to each student.
2. Instruct students to select from the fabric, pictures, and decorations.
3. Illustrate on the outside of the bag how they think *other people* see them.
4. On the inside of the bag, have students illustrate how they *see themselves*—how they really are.
5. Upon completion, the bags may be shared with the entire class, with a small group or with a partner.

Follow-up questions:
1. How did you feel when sharing your creation?
2. What are some of the ways you are different from the way others see you?
3. How accurately do you think you preceive yourself?
4. Do you feel good about the way others perceive you, about the way you perceive yourself?
Activity #2: Who's Who of the Week
Grade level: 5th grade

Materials needed: background information on students in class, construction paper, paste.

Background information: An emerging task in education today is to define self-esteem and to discover the process by which it is nurtured. The ultimate in selfesteem is found in the full possession of one's total being - the intellect and the emotions and (especially) the body - in other words, in the self.

Objective: To enhance student selfconcept using personal data and positive reinforcement of accomplishments.

Procedures:
1. Compile a "Who's Who Bulletin Board."
2. Data can be gathered about achievements, hobbies, pets, future goals, family members, etc.

3. Phone calls to students' homes may uncover information special to students while promoting health education to the parents.
4. When data is collected and written up, duplicate and distribute to all students in the class.
5. Pictures may accompany written information for a personal touch.
6. Designate one student per week to be recognized as "Who's Who Student of the Week."
7. Present bulletin board materials to honored student at end of the week.
Activity #3: Who Am I?

Grade level: 3rd grade

Materials needed: 3x5 notecards, pencils.

Background information: Every person needs recognition. It is expressed cogently by the lad who says, "Mother, let's play darts. I'll throw the darts and you say 'Wonderful.' "[3]

To enhance student selfconcept using students' own thoughts and ideas. To give the student recognition from teacher and classmates.

Procedure:
1. Have students write out biographical information. Include such things as talents, family happenings, hobbies, favorite places, activities, etc.
2. Collect the cards.
3. On occasion, read the cards at the beginning or end of class.
4. Include a teacher description also.

As health educators, promoting positive selfconcept in the classroom can be challenging but quite rewarding. By creatively letting loose, involving the students, giving students' recognition, and by allowing the student to *feel* in the classroom setting, a teacher can creatively enhance positive selfconcepts. As a kindergarten student put it, "When you ask me how I feel, I'm the only one who can tell you! And I like that!"[4]

[1]Vasconcellos, J., Chairman of the Joint Legislative Committee on Educational Goals and Evaluation, Member of the California Legislature.
[2]Purkey, W. W. *Self-concept and school achievement.* Englewood Cliffs, New Jersey: Prentice-Hall, Inc., 1970.
[3]Baughman, M. D. *Educator's handbook of stories, quotes, and humor.*
[4]Canfield, J., & Wells, H. C. *100 ways to enhance self-concept in the classroom.* Englewood Cliffs, New Jersey: Prentice-Hall, Inc., 1976, p. 207.

Ideas from a Class in Inter-personal Relations

CAROLL KAISER teaches health education at Minnetonka Senior High School, Excelsior, Minnesota. Her interpersonal relations classes, composed of sophomores, juniors, and seniors, are the most popular of the ten health classes offered for credit.

Interpersonal relations stresses the importance of self-image and self-acceptance in the development of personality. Without a secure self-image and a healthy self-acceptance, a person cannot risk the emotional investment necessary to relate to another individual. With a secure self-image and healthy self-acceptance, a person can risk the necessary emotional investment, and he gradually acquires a repertoire of successful behavior. Building this repertoire of successful behavior is a process of becoming and individuation. Thus, a cyclical evolvement takes place: self-image and self-acceptance determine the quality of interpersonal behavior; the quality of the interpersonal behavior determines the growth of personality; the growth of personality determines self-image and self-acceptance.

Some of the techniques I use in the interpersonal relations classes attempt to improve self-image and self-acceptance in order to develop a repertoire of successful interpersonal behavior. One device is what I call "Laws of the Robot." In this experiment I try to show students that the human condition is coped with, understandably and even justifiably, on a nonrational, even emotional, basis, and that this is not bad. In the Laws of the Robot, I pose hypothetical situations which students must try to solve using a purely computerized type of logic. My direction to students is that they are to consider themselves as robots. Before they are allowed to enter human society, they must take a test to determine whether the "three laws" which are built into their robot being are functioning properly. The laws are a functional part of the circuitry and I further emphasize that all circuits are logical and cannot be altered in any way without serious damage, and that as robots they cannot violate the three laws either through action or through inaction. The laws are rigid, almost mechanical:

1. A robot may not injure a human or through inaction allow a human to come to harm.
2. A robot must obey orders given it by a human except where such an order might conflict with the first law.
3. A robot must protect its own existence as long as such protection does not conflict with the first or second law.

Before the exercise is over the students become bogged down and almost disfunctional in solving the hypothetical situations. To their great frustration, logic is not enough for a solution because nonlogical ramifications of the problem must be taken into account.

Another device I use for teaching self-awareness and self-acceptance is what I call the "Protoplasmic Blobs." These are a series of drawings or blobs faintly resembling humans, which elicit student interpretations of what the blobs are feeling. Since it is relatively easy to catalog gestures that people use to intensify statements, I felt that I could use protoplasmic blobs to illustrate the subtlety of gestures, the idea being that if a student could perceive the gestures in this experiment, he might more readily perceive them in his everyday living. Interpreting these characters is similar in a sense to the process people go through to interpret the Rorschach Ink Blot Test. This particular exercise is used in conjunction with a unit on body language. The exercise consists of 26 blob illustrations on a paper. At the bottom of the page are listed 26 comments. The students match each comment with the blob character it best expresses. For example, a student may interpret two characters as "quarreling," and he would supply a comment most appropriate for that depiction which might be, "please forgive me just one more time." Students can work individually or in a group where students compare their different interpretations. Incidentally, this exercise can lead to some interesting and effective role playing.

The "Environmental Box" idea is used toward the end of the unit on self-awareness as a final project. It is especially effective and rewarding for those students who are not adept verbally. The students are asked to portray or depict in visible form a concept or feeling they possess. They are to "remove" this feeling from environmental competition by "placing" it in a shoe box, fix the cover on the box, and then cut a hole in one end for the observer. Peering into the box and observing these visual manifestations of a student's inner life in complete isolation from an outside environ-

mental force is a most cogent experience. The strength of this project lies in the fact that the completed assignment ranges from the most simple illustration to the most complex and intricate ones, involving, in some cases, mirrors, electric lights, and small models to create illusory effects.

Since communication is an integral part of interpersonal relations, I have used as an additional technique a short unit on the sign language of the deaf. Often, in the verbal language we use in everyday conversation, parallel conversations are conducted in which one person is not really listening to the other. Ultimately, after much parallel conversation, the art of real listening is lost. Teaching students basic sign language makes them

aware for the first time of the intensity and the miracle of human communication. One is forced to look at and study the person who is doing the communicating. One sees all the nuances and connotations of what is said and felt. One of the high spots in this unit is a lecture given in sign language by a deaf lecturer. The intensity and concentration observed at this point is worth a whole year of teaching. I might add that teaching this skill is not difficult or time-consuming, and the hand alphabet can be learned in 15 or 20 minutes. Since there are hand gestures that make up entire words rather than spelling out each letter in the word, I also introduce five or ten hand gestures every day until each student develops quite an extensive vocabulary.

Role Playing as a Tool in Mental Health Education

Lynn Teper is assistant professor of health education at Long Island University, Brooklyn Center, Brooklyn, New York. She was formerly an instructor at Kingsborough Community College in Brooklyn.

Teachers of health education must transmit to students the concept that physical and mental health are interrelated. Each is an aspect of the total individual; each is dependent on the other for optimal functioning. Formerly the mental component of health was overshadowed by health educators in their attempt to educate the student about bodily functions, but gradually, mental health has gained importance and is now a significant aspect of many health education curriculums. Through units in mental health, it is hoped that students will learn to meet with some adequacy their personal, interpersonal, and social conflicts and thus will function more completely as young adults.

One of the tools available for promoting healthy behavioral patterns is known as "sociodrama." Sociodrama is a spontaneous, impromptu expression dramatizing intergroup relations and collective ideologies. The students who play a role in a sociodrama do not recite from a script. A situation is presented to the class and without prior preparation students are chosen or volunteer to act out the particular situation.

Man is a role player, in a sense, every day of his life. An adolescent girl, for example, can be a daughter, a friend, a student, a member of a club, etc. Each individual is characterized by a certain range of roles which dominates his or her behavior. The role player in a sociodrama is aware that he is acting out a role, even though he may be unaware that the role, as he enacts it, reveals many of the conflicts that confront him and others.

The process of sociodrama unfolds as follows:

Step 1—Sensitizing the group

It is important for the participants to recognize that people perceive and interpret situations and stimuli differently. As a result of their particular interpretation, attitudes are developed by each individual which result in different responses. This understanding can be gained by having several students view and report on a given situation. The result will usually yield a variety of opinions as to what took place, as when witnesses are asked to report on an accident or crime. This will reveal to some degree the lack of reliability between observers due to a predisposition to select different aspects of the situation for notation. In addition, it will help students to see that their way of seeing and interpreting situations is not the only way.

Step 2—The Warm Up

This step involves setting up the situation for the sociodrama to take place. Topics for enactment can include conflict with the family, peer group relationships, attitudes involved with topics included in sex education or the use of narcotics. The instructor states the situation somewhat abstractly. Roles are described and volunteers are selected or chosen. For example: A girl is troubled by the fact that she is given little freedom from her parents. At this point someone is chosen for the role of the girl, another for the role of the mother; father and possibly a sister or brother can enter the scene.

Step 3—The Enactment

At this point, without any additional preparation the role players act out what they believe would happen when the family was together.

Step 4—Helping the audience observe intelligently

Much of the value of sociodrama depends on the discussion with the class following the spontaneous dramatization. Some of the questions could be:

1. Do you feel that the enactment was realistic?

2. As future parents, what do you believe the role of the parent should be?

3. How do you think parents and their children can come to better understand one another?

In other situations as well as this one the prime concern should be to discuss causes of behavior and appropriate ways of behaving and to encourage self-appraisal.

Step 5—Replaying the situation

It is helpful for students to see how the situation looks from different angles by switching roles. The daughter may become the parent or volunteers may replace those who have already participated. This will bring additional insights into the situation.

Step 6—The Evaluation

In the evaluation it is important to emphasize that with positive flexible attitudes individual growth takes place. Students need to discover for themselves that anxiety, fears, and immobility are not inherent in an object, event, or person, but are within themselves. The individual needs a positive attitude toward change. To say "I'll try" means motivation for growth is present.

If real learning is to take place, problems studied in school should deal with crucial situations in the lives of the student no matter what the subject area may be. The use of sociodrama in health education classes is one way to implement this approach since it allows students to explore some appropriate ways of dealing with others as well as with themselves. It is a process whereby one can look at familiar conflicts seen through the eyes of others. Subsequently, recognition that one is not alone in some of his confrontations may result in lessening anxiety. A three way process is established.

1. The teacher relates with the students through interest and involvement.
2. The students relate with one another by participating, observing, and commenting on the sociodrama.
3. The students relate to the teacher by referring to the teacher for guidance and structure.

Moralizing by the teacher is curbed and condemnation and judgment by an adult figure are eliminated.

Involvement is a key to understanding for students. Whether the student is a role player or part of the discussion group that evaluates the sociodrama, involvement is a significant outcome. Conflicts often will be left unresolved, but hopefully the students will have witnessed or have been a part of acting out and discussing a variety of ways for promoting healthy interactions involving the individual in his environment.

Mental Health

THE MIRROR GAME[1]

ROSA SULLIVAN is a health education teacher at Herbert Hoover Junior High, Lackawanna, New York 14218.

It is so extremely important for individuals to be able to look back on themselves in order to be evaluative of their personality traits. Many times people cannot detect their negative faults or, in contrast, tend only to find negative traits. A mentally healthy individual should be able to search on both sides and progress to working out "bad" traits. The following activity is one way to work toward this.

Objectives
1. To have a better understanding of who you are as you see yourself.
2. To have a better understanding of how others see you.
3. To recognize and understand that others always do not see you as you see yourself.
4. To appreciate the fact that you have negative points and evaluate how to change them if you wish to.
5. To evaluate how others see you and decide if that is your true image.

The Game
Duplicate a list of 20-30 personality traits suitable to the students' age group. (The group I used this game with was 14 years of age and enrolled at a junior high school.) Set them up in columns with room for graduated ratings of self and partner. (See example.)

Procedure
1. Have each student pick a partner with whom they are familiar.
2. After passing out the list, stress that they are not to talk while they are evaluating themselves or their partner.
3. The groups have 10-15 minutes to make their judgments.

4. They then compare what they marked about themselves and each other. This should reveal a number of differences between their self-impressions and how they are perceived by others. This may take as long as 15-20 minutes.
5. During the last 5 minutes in class and continued as a home assignment, students should write on the back of their papers three things they learned about themselves that they did not know before. They should also explain what these three things mean to them.

Follow up
(15-20 minutes of another class or as a home assignment)
1. With your class go over the list and mark each word as either positive or negative (example: if you marked always or sometimes for sensitive then it is positive; if you marked seldom or never for sensitive then it is negative).
2. A sheet containing the following questions is then passed out and the teacher requests the student to be as truthful as possible in responding since no one will see their answers without their expressed permission.

   What image did you project to your partner?

   What are some of the traits you feel you possess but others do not feel you possess?

   Why do your perceptions differ from others' perceptions?

   Do you have a strong self-image? (Do you like yourself or if you weren't you, would you like you?)

   Do you have more negative or **positive traits? Why?**

   Everyone has traits they do not like. Think about two of your negative ones and explain how you can go about changing them.

[1] Adapted from *Go To Health* (New York: Dell Publishing Co., Inc., 1972), p. 98.

TRAITS		SELF				PARTNER			
		Never	Seldom	Sometimes	Always	Never	Seldom	Sometimes	Always
1. Sensitive	+								
2. Arrogant	−								
3. Silly	−								
4. Trusting	+								
5. Tender	+								
6. Two-faced	−								

How to Cope with Stress in the Classroom

CHARLES C. DAVIS is coordinator for health/physical education instructional programs, State University College at Oswego, Oswego, New York 13126.

Learning alternatives for handling stressful situations and then giving students an experience in handling stress and developing coping ability is something often left out of the classroom. As educators we often find it difficult to place students in situations where they can learn practically how to handle various stressors. Much of what we say is abstract or theoretical until the student is forced to confront stress. The following stress sheet is designed as a practical way for students to identify stress and then analyze how they cope with various stressful situations. A deeper discussion of stress and the learning of alternative situations to various life problems can be better understood. The stress sheet is adaptable for many age groups and grade levels.

Step 1: Content

The students are taught the intricate details of life and stress in their class. The following aspects are reviewed.
1. The stress concept—what is stress? discussion of Hans Selyé's theory of stress.
2. Stress as it affects our lives—stress is not inherently good or evil, it is dependent on the consequences of our reactions to stressors.
3. Coping with stress—General Adaptation Syndrome (GAS), the physiological response to stress; flight/flee response or coping behavior (general alternatives).
4. Learning ways to cope with stress—protecting the ego ideal under stressful situations; defense mechanisms; Maslow's hierarchy of human needs.
5. Adapting to stress—suggestions for learning to cope with stress in a constructive manner; positive and negative consequences of deviations.

Step 2: Learning to Cope with Stress Constructively

Students are given a stress sheet to relate classroom theory to actual confrontations with stressful situations. The students are asked to take the following stress sheet home and fill it out after undergoing stress.

Stress Sheet

This sheet is designed to stimulate interest in and an understanding of how you react to and cope with stress. It is also hoped that completion of this sheet will cause you to do some reflective thinking on how to handle the "wear and tear of life" or stress.
1. Identify: A stressful situation; the stressor(s), internal and/or external primary stimulus causing the stress.

2. Which of the following behavioral responses did you use to cope with the stress? Place an x next to how you responded.
   Fight   Freeze   Flight
   Compromise
   Briefly describe the consequences of your response: it did _____ did not _____ alleviate the stressful situation.
3. Check any defense mechanisms that you used to deviate from the stressor.
   _____ avoidance _____ regression
   _____ deny reality
   _____ fixation
   _____ repression _____ sublimation
   _____ projection
   _____ other (specify)
   _____ rationalization
4. Draw a line to indicate how you expended energy as you progressed through the Adaptation Syndrome.

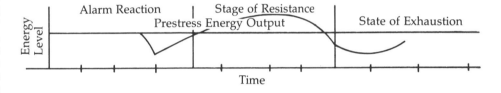

5. Sources of help. Did talking with anyone help you cope with or adapt to the stressor?

no _____ yes _____

specify whom _____

6. What deviations did you use to equalize the effect of the stress on the body? (for example sports, reading, etc., please specify). Briefly describe how your deviations relieved the stress.

7. Did any psychologically induced pain cause a physical reaction?

no _____ yes _____

specify _____ e.g., prolonged tension leads to upset stomach.

Step 3: Behavioral Outcomes

After taking home a predetermined number of stress sheets the students should have some stress-relieving skills, such as the following.

1. Analyze some of the stressors common to the experiences of students, such as competition or failure.

2. Understand the meaning of the terms stress, stressors, stressful situations.

3. Analyze the individual use of defense mechanisms in stressful situations used to minimize conscious anxiety.

4. Understand that humans are affected by and respond to stressors as total organisms.

5. Understand the general categories of behavioral responses to stress: flight, fight or compromise.

6. Understand the consequences of conversion reactions such as psychologically induced pain manifesting physical reactions when stressors are not successfully adapted to or deviated from.

7. Investigate how individual coping behaviors (sports, dancing, etc.) successfully allow an individual to alleviate stressors.

Step 4: Classroom Adaptability

1. Students can be asked to do several stress sheets over an extended period, then analyze how they cope with and adapt to stress.

2. Break students into small discussion groups, give each group the job of depicting: what is stress? or what is mental health? or what is the relationship between stress and mental health?

Give each group about 20 minutes to come up with their pictorial descriptions. No words can be used in any of the three assignments. When the allotted time has ended, the instructor holds up the finished product from one group and the class responds to what they see depicted. The same is done for the other groups. The instructor phrases the questions in a way which will extract the relationship between stress and mental health.

The outcome of the stress sheets exercise encompasses the interrelationship of the theory of stress and how it relates to mental health by personalizing stress through the stress sheets and visually depicting the wide interpretations of what stress is.

Coping With Violence

ELAINE HALS teaches at the South Shore High School in Brooklyn, New York 11236.

What can we as health educators do to reverse or at least slow down the chain of violence with which our students live? Our objectives should be: (1) to have students consider *all* life as positive, (2) to guide students in establishing constructive goals for the future, (3) to help students explore their values and priorities, (4) to help students explore the impact of violence on our society, and (5) to assist students in finding nonviolent methods of handling potentially explosive situations.

These are difficult objectives to reach. How do we achieve them? One way is to plan for the mental health segment of the required health course (or any other appropriate segment, e.g., urban problems, crime, values and goals) to include discussion topics and activities such as the following.

Topics

1. Prejudice—its causes and relationship to violence
2. Respect for the views of others
3. Respect for the property of others
4. Peer pressure; gang involvement
5. Values formation (clarification); priorities
6. Constructive methods of problem solving and dealing with stress
7. Setting realistic goals for the future
8. The impact of violence on our society
    Fear of involvement
    Fear of going out alone
    Tendency to overreact
    Crimes committed in self-defense
    People arming themselves
    Acceptance of violent deaths as statistics
9. Need for feelings of self-esteem
    Being recognized by others as worthwhile
10. Constructively compensating for weaknesses
11. Handling emotions—learning to think before acting
12. Working towards a healthier society
    How?
    Role of the individual
13. Value of life—own and others
    Everyone is important to someone

Activities

1. Role playing
    Mock court case
    Student caught cheating
    Racial or ethnic role reversals
2. Values activity
    Have students rate the following as acceptable or unacceptable for themselves. Discuss reasons for each student's choice.
    a. breaking laws they don't believe in
    b. law enforcement agencies
    c. smoking marijuana
    d. our government
    e. cheating
    f. demonstrations against the establishment
    g. compare students' values with those of their parents
    h. capital punishment
    i. plea bargaining
3. *Search for Values* (Pfaum/Standard, Cincinnati, Ohio 1974). Read section on Time, Lesson 3: "Examining Personal Goals"
4. Simon, Sidney B., Howe, L. W., Kirschenbaum, Howard, *Values Clarification: A Handbook of Practical Strategies for Teachers and Students* (Hart Pub. Co., New York, 1974). Play the Bomb Shelter Game (prejudice) and the Transplant Game.
5. Am I Worthwhile Task
    Have each student talk about self for two minutes saying *only* good things. Do this activity in groups. Have the group members help the individual speaking whenever necessary. The purpose of this activity is to help each student see that he or she is worthwhile.
6. Values Auction from *Auction Game* by Richard Cohen in his graduate course, "Health Education in the Secondary Schools," at Brooklyn College.
    Give each student an imaginary $1,000 to bid with, give them a values list, and hold an auction. If several students are willing to bid the entire $1,000, have each give his or her reason for wanting the item and then allow the class to vote. After the auction evaluate student priorities.

Items To Be Auctioned

1. Invitations to all the most exciting parties (any place with anyone in the whole world) every single night.
2. To possess perfect health and a strong, flexible, beautiful, graceful body.
3. A lifetime without "hassling." No one will tell you what to do or how or when to do it.
4. A daily "storm" of new ideas; original poems, songs, books, movies running through your head; visions of paintings to paint, pots to mold, buildings to design and build.
5. To be the richest person in the world.
6. The opportunity to direct the workings of the whole world . . . to control individuals, businesses, monies, whole nations.
7. No "hang-ups" whatsoever; to possess self-knowledge.
8. A chance to spend a year with the greatest religious figure of your faith—past, present, future.
9. To live forever without growing old.
10. The opportunity to stick up for and protect the person or thing to which you feel the greatest allegiance (like sticking with a friend through a crisis or fighting for your country, etc.).
11. To have the perfect romance/or the perfect love relationship (s) with the person (s) of your choice.
12. To have a computer-bank of facts and information in your head; to be able to answer any questions and solve any problems which present themselves to you.
13. To have the strength always to do what you believe to be right. To be a person of integrity.
14. To have the skills, know-how, and time to really help others and serve humanity.
15. To have a real sense of what is fair and just; to deal with others as honestly and fairly as possible.
16. To be at peace with yourself and know the purpose of life.
17. To become a professional athlete of your choice.

Health educators will not be able to eliminate violence, but we can encourage our students to examine the causes and end results of violence. We can show them more constructive outlets for their anger and their frustrations, as well as how to set and reach positive goals for the future.

Personality Spokes

ROSA SULLIVAN is a health educa-tion teacher at Herbert Hoover Jun-ior High School, Lackawanna, New York 14218.

Man has qualities about himself that are of great value to him in reference to future ambitions. He also has faults and because of these he sometimes is incapable of ac-complishing goals. It is a necessary objective of life to be able to recog-nize both faults and positive attri-butes which can hinder or enhance man in his quest of the future.

At what age should a person be-gin to examine his own personality to establish priorities in life and plans to achieve in these areas? The answer is it is never too soon to initiate at home or in the classroom, activities to stimulate thinking in these areas. Personality Spokes is one activity to achieve this end.

Objectives

For students to—

1. Recognize assets in their per-sonalities.

2. Recognize faults in their per-sonalities.

3. Delve into themselves and be able to establish short and long-term goals.

4. Evaluate what faults and as-sets will help them to achieve or fail to reach their goals.

5. Communicate with others what they find out about themselves.

Procedure

1. Have each student pick a part-ner.

2. Each student is to draw three half dollar size circles: two at

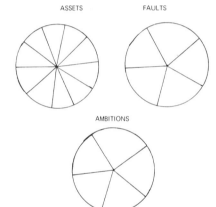

ASSETS FAULTS

AMBITIONS

the top and one at the bot-tom of a piece of paper (see example). Next he is to draw spokes as if these circles were wheels. One top circle has 10 spokes and is labeled per-sonality assets. The other top circle has 5 spokes and is labeled faults. The bottom wheel has 5 spokes and is labeled ambitions.

3. Each student is to fill in the spokes accordingly, examine what they wrote and then draw lines from the assets to the ambitions these assets will help satisfy. Then the student is to draw lines from the faults to the ambitions that these faults will prevent from satis-fying.

4. The students should then ex-change and examine each other's papers.

5. Each student next explains to partner why these assets and faults will help or hinder his ambitions. They also should talk about *how* important these ambitions are to them, and *why* they are so impor-tant.

TEACHING IDEAS

About Yourself

RUTH C. ENGS is assistant professor, Department of Health and Safety Education, Indiana University, Bloomington, Indiana 47401.

A "mentally healthy" person is often characterized as having an accurate perception of reality, able to maintain close interpersonal relationships, able to communicate openly and honestly with others, and aware of personal goals, values, abilities, and behavior.[1] Because of the variety of environmental stresses and our individual backgrounds, we all have different problems of living. The extent to which we learn to successfully cope with these stresses often determines how mentally healthy we are.

One of the primary objectives of mental health education in the classroom is to help the student become aware of himself, his communication techniques, and his behavior as an aid in learning to cope successfully with life. The following warm up can help the student become acquainted with himself, with others, and

with the class as a whole. It can help to create an atmosphere for fostering open communication and self-knowledge leading to better mental health.

These instructions should be related to the class by the instructor:

We are now going to do some get acquainted exercises. We first will do a relaxation exercise to tune in to ourselves. Then we will do several exercises to get to know others in the class. This may be a new experience for some of you, however, most people find it fun. If for some reason you find you do not wish to continue, you can stop at any time. However, I'm sure you will find it enjoyable.

Relaxation (10 minutes)

1. First put your head on your desk and get comfortable in your chair or lie down on the floor and get comfortable.
2. Close your eyes, relax, and become aware of the sounds in the room.
3. Next, I want you to pay attention to your breathing. Feel the air go in and out.
4. Now I want you to take a deep breath, feel the air going in your lips, down into your lungs; feel air go out. (Repeat this two times.)
5. You should feel relaxed; in fact, it is probably the first time you have relaxed today.
6. Now become aware of your feet, feel them against the floor, in your shoes. Now tighten your feet as long as you can. Now relax.
7. Become aware of your calf, (continue with thighs, whole leg, shoulder and buttocks, chest, fist, neck, face, whole body).
8. You will feel relaxed; become aware of parts of your body, touching the chair (floor).
9. Now relax. And take a deep breath.

Body Trip[2]—The Magic Golden Ball (10 minutes)

To be used after people are in a relaxed state.

Imagine that you see a warm golden ball in front of you.

As you watch it, it slowly begins to shrink becoming smaller and smaller.

When it is the size of a dime it moves toward you.

It gets closer and closer and finally attaches to your forehead.

Then it turns into a magic warm golden paint.

It flows over your forehead, nose. Smell it, taste it.

As it flows it feels warm and glowing.

When it reaches your neck the magical paint takes on different colors and still flows over your body—shoulders, upper arms, lower arms, fingers, chest,

stomach, genetalia, thighs, legs, feet, toes.

You are now surrounded in a warm bath of colors and feel good. I will count backward from 10 to 1. While I am counting, start opening your eyes. At the count of 1 you will be wide awake and feel good.

I now want you to turn to the person next to you and discuss what you experienced.

Getting Acquainted[3]

1. Go up to someone you do not know but think you might have something in common with and would like to know better. One person talks for two minutes while the other just listens. Then reverse the role. Now, the two of you find another pair you do not know. Introduce your partner to the other pair.
2. Go up to someone you think you have nothing in common with. Sit back to back and talk. Join another pair and discuss things you learned about communication by sitting back to back.
3. Go up to another person you do not know. Look each other in the eyes. Do not talk. Follow each other's hands around as if you were looking in a mirror. Join another pair and discuss what you learned about yourself and the other person by doing this.

Debriefing

1. Get back into a big circle. What did you experience with the fantasy trip?
2. How does it feel to go up to a stranger and talk?
3. How much did you find you had in common with the person you thought you had nothing in common with?
4. What problems did you have in communicating back to back?
5. What did you learn about nonverbal communication or about your own communication skills from sitting back to back?
6. Who led in the hand mirroring? Why? What did you learn about yourself in this exercise, about the other person?

[1]Maslow, Abraham H., *Toward A Psychology of Being*, 2nd edition, Van Nostrand-Reinholt Co., Toronto, 1968.

[2]Adopted from Dick Price's "Gestalt Workshop," Esalen Institute, Big Sur, California.

[3]Pfeiffer, J., and Jones, J., *A Handbook of Structured Experiences for Human Relations Training*, Vol. I-IV, University Associates, Iowa City, Iowa.

TEACHING IDEAS

Mental Health

A Lesson on Stress

JANET H. SHIRREFFS is in the Department of Physiology and Health Science, Ball State University, Muncie, Indiana 47306.

A generally accepted educational principle is that students learn best in an environment in which certain moderate to high expectations are made clear to students but is only minimally or moderately stressful. Excessive stress may be so incapacitating that no effort on the part of the individual can alleviate it. It is impossible for learning to take place in an overly stressful environment in which the adaptive potential of students is exceeded. Of course, individuals differ in both perceptions of stress and in their ability to cope with stress and conflict in their daily lives and these differences are important considerations for the educator in discussing stress and emotional health.

Although health educators cannot teach mental health *per se*, it is possible to provide classroom experiences dealing with mental health and the solution of every day problems which can help students tune-in to real life situations, feel the emotions they evoke, and analyze actions and behaviors which

they can use to alleviate these emotional crises in constructive, appropriate ways. This is the case in the following classroom technique:

Goal: (1) Learn what stress is
(2) Learn what anxiety and/or anger feels like as the result of encountering a stressful experience
(3) Learn how stress can best be handled in positive and constructive ways to resolve problems and reduce feelings of being "overwhelmed" by appropriate individual action.

Level: This classroom experience has been used effectively at the college level during a unit on mental health. The learning experience would also be applicable at the senior and junior high school level with some modification.

Method: (1) Students should be fairly comfortable with teacher and vice-versa.
(2) Class environment should be humanistic and typically low-stress prior to the experience.
(3) Teacher should have made evaluation requirements of the class very specific, including an announcement that no unannounced quizzes would be given during the semester.

Following introductory class periods devoted to personality development and enhancement of mental health, the instructor should enter class with a test or quiz which has been prepared from materials the students were supposed to have read and additional questions which are not from the assigned readings. Below is an example of a test of this type.

HES 100 Personal Health
Quiz 1
Emotional Health

1. List Erikson's Eight States of Personality Development. (8 points)
2. In defining and describing the psychotic personality disorders, the text speaks of organic and functional causes. Describe each. (4 points)
3. Give three examples of character disorders. (3 points)
4. According to the text, what is anxiety? (5 points)

Keeping very serious, announce: "You will be having a test now, please remove all materials from your desks." You will notice abrupt changes in facial expression, body movements etc., ranging from panic to anger which can provide a basis for a discussion of bodily manifestations of anxiety.

Pass out tests. Allow the students about three minutes to look over the test and announce: "Write your feelings at this moment on the bottom of the test paper." A number of reactions actual students have reported during this activity are: complete confusion; helpless; I would like to throw my chair at you for springing this on me; anger; complete nothingness; a burst of adrenalin shot through my system; disgust and frustration; my heart fell, anxiety, shocked, confused; feeling of total lack of control; insecure; I am feeling completely lost and kind of scared.

Announce immediately after you have asked the students to record their feelings on the bottom of the test page: "This is not a real test, but an experience to get each of you to realize right now what stressful situations can make you feel like inside. (You will hear sighs of relief, laughter, and comments such as "I didn't think you'd do anything like this to us, whew!")

STRESS MODEL

	Stress		
Anxiety	*Frustration*	*Anger*	**Emotional Responses**

Endocrine functioning as a consequence of parasympathetic system's reactions to stress

	Stress	
Adrenalin	*Non-adrenalin*	**Physiological Response**

Increase in blood pressure, heart rate, sweating, dilation of pupils, etc.

Flight	*Fight*	*Internalization with no release*	**Behavioral Adaptation**

Individual differences in alleviating stress

Potentially constructive	*Potentially destructive*
Deal with anxiety and anger as they occur in small pieces.	Let anger and anxiety build up by not recognizing internal feelings and/or by not acting on them.
Be assertive, honest, and real when situations involving people create feelings of anxiety or anger.	Be aggressive and outwardly hostile or submissive when situations involving people create feelings of anxiety or anger.
Select and use appropriate physical outlets for venting anger and anxiety (running, cycling, playing tennis, or playing piano).	Attempt to hold in and repress feelings of anger and anxiety and try to forget the situations that caused them.
Appropriate use of defense mechanisms.	Inappropriate overuse of defense mechanisms.

Discussion: General questions which relate to this experience include: What is stress? What situations are stressful to you? How can stress resulting in anger or anxiety be handled constructively and destructively? What do you do with anger when you feel it? What are some constructive outlets for anger and anxiety? What do you think are the dangers of repressed anger and anxiety?

Lecture: The model presented on the next page can serve as a framework for a lecture on stress, including its emotional, physiological, and behavioral parameters. Health-generating resolution of stress should be emphasized.

Health educators cannot eliminate the many stresses their students will encounter in their daily lives. They can, however, help students to examine the types of situations which evoke individual stress reactions and can discuss alternative ways of coping with stress, so that young people will be able to incorporate health-generating behaviors into stress-provoking situations in their lifestyles.

81

Mental Health Auctioning Strategy

PATRICK KIDD TOW is an assistant professor in the Department of Health and Physical Education at Old Dominion University, Norfolk, Virginia 23508.

This teaching strategy is appropriate for secondary school or college level health classes. I have used it at the end of a mental health or drug education unit, but it might also be applicable to any health unit which uses value clarification.

Each participant begins with a set sum of money—let us say $25,000, and is entrusted to keep a running tally of how much they have spent and what was bought. Members of the class bid on certain aspirations, loves, or wishes in an auction. The items for auction could pertain to physical, emotional, social, or even spiritual health.

The instructor plays the part of an auctioneer. Only he or she should know what items are up for auction and should try to keep the bids as high as possible. Fervor and interest will grow as the soaring bids become more competitive. The auctioneer should deal with each item one at a time by announcing and writing it on the board. After the final bid is accepted, the selling price is written next to the item.

The objective of this strategy is to evoke introspection on what values the individual cherishes. At the same time, students can see which behaviors and values are held in high esteem by their peers. The impulsive and eccentric nature of some participants may also become apparent. After completing the exercise, there will soon be an influx of comments and questions from the results.

The following items have been auctioned off in a mental health class.

1. Guarantee to die a peaceful and painless death when the time comes
2. Ability to prevent World War III
3. Ten extra years added on to your life
4. Never have to work and still be paid
5. Ability to save the life of one person
6. Phenomenal love for children
7. Ability to play any musical instrument desired
8. Be boss and sole owner of a company
9. Own the only solar-powered sports car
10. Travel back or forward in time and change history
11. Be considered a fantastic lover
12. Be the most loved and popular politician in the country
13. Never have a sick day in your life
14. Possess unrivaled intelligence or genius
15. Eat as much as you want and never get fat
16. Be the author of the world's best-selling book
17. Be considered a successful financial wizard
18. Be exceptionally skilled in any sports one desires
19. Phenomenal love for animals
20. Never have an enemy in the world, be loved by all
21. Die with a clean conscience, no debts, and no sins left behind
22. Guarantee to never become addicted to any drugs
23. Climb the highest mountain and survive
24. Be granted more handsomeness or beauty
25. Reincarnation into anything or anyone desired

Additional objectives may be achieved by modifying this auctioning strategy. Following are some suggestions.

Reduce or increase the number of items to suit a specific health topic being covered.

Distribute a list of items for auction so they may be arranged according to individual preferences.

Allow small groups to submit public bids as a consensus.

Permit borrowing or lending of money among participants to see how many overextend themselves.

People Labeling Strategy

PATRICK K. TOW and HAL WINGARD are assistant professors in the Department of Health and Physical Education at Old Dominion University, Norfolk, Virginia 23508.

Labels	parent	teacher	neighbor	TV star	stranger	Total
Alcoholic						
Mentally Disturbed						
Homosexual						
Drug Addict						
Divorcee						
Total						

CATEGORIES OF PEOPLE

Many people are in the habit of labeling or stereotyping other members of society. Some of these "tagged victims" may be acquaintances of those doing the labeling. While peer group coercion has been able to provide the necessary motivation for constructive changes in our lives, it can also be destructive in nature. The insidious manner in which labels and stories can spread help blow the picture far out of proportion. Perhaps someday we may come to realize such practices tend to do more harm than good.

An innocent person defamed by a circulating, malicious slander may feel the intense social and emotional impacts. Public denial of such labels may be interpreted as frantic attempts to conceal guilt. There is always that tragic alternative of the stigmatized acting in accordance with the label bestowed upon him. On the other hand, there is also the possibility that a label accurately depicts a person's past or present. Nevertheless, such unscrupulous denotations expressed out of spite or ignorance tend to diminish the faith and trust one has in one's fellow man.

Stigmatization is only one part of the concern. The other is one which many of us fall prey to on a number of occasions. Our fear surfaces when listening ears begin to believe and treat a person according to that real or unreal stigma. Such occurrences may appear to be a concerted effort to prevent an individual from joining the mainstream of American society. Perhaps some people believe whatever actions are associated with a given label warrant public denouncement ad infinitum. The resulting social and emotional damages could be avoided if we were sensitized to the ramifications of our persistent "pigeonholing" behavior.

This teaching strategy is intended to draw out various prejudices, biases, and fears governing our lives. It will become obvious in discussions among high school or college students that some concerns are groundless and based upon sheer ignorance. However, there will be some thoughts expressed which were based on feelings derived from personal experiences which might not necessarily be refuted. Therefore, it becomes absolutely essential for teachers and students alike to pay heed to what is being said.

The teaching instrument to be used is shown as a table. The rows represent five types of labels apt to be used as brands for certain undesirables. The columns represent five categories of people that are hypothetically given the labels. Students are directed to correlate each label with every category of people and assign a score to indicate the degree of tolerability they have toward these individuals. The range of scores is: 4–will always be able to tolerate; 3–will frequently be able to tolerate; 2–will sometimes be able to tolerate; 1–will seldom be able to tolerate; 0–will never be able to tolerate.

Examples of the process involved should be provided for the students. For example, a student examines the hypothetical situation that one of his parents is an alcoholic. He may find that fact absolutely intolerable and assigns a score of zero. On the other hand, he may be quite willing most of the time to accept the fact that his favorite TV star turned out to be an alcoholic. If this is the case, the student would assign a score of three. In another example, a student may be willing to tolerate his homosexual teacher most of the time and scores a three. However, he may seldom feel tolerant enough to associate with a homosexual stranger and assigns a score of two.

A sum of totals from each row and column reflect that label or category of people deserving the most and least degree of tolerance. For example, the highest row total found associated with divorcee would suggest that student is more tolerant of divorcees than any of the other given labels. By the same token, the highest column total, which is associated with stranger, may indicate that student is more tolerant of their improprieties than the other category of people. The lowest row or column totals may indicate that label or category of people least tolerated by the student.

Other variables besides what given in the table can be used in substitution. Any of the following can be added to people categories: brother/sister, politician, cousin, boy/girlfriend, or minister. Any of the following labels can be used, too: transsexual, shoplifter, murderer, marijuana smoker, hit-run driver, suicide attempter, child abuser, or bisexual. Of course, there are also other possible alternatives that can be conjured up by the teacher.

In the ensuing discussions, students should begin to realize people with such labels used in this strategy need more empathy than sympathy from other people. Most anyone can provide pity, but understanding is a step beyond what the stigmatized may expect. It is fortunate that changing times and people in today's world beckon us to relent and modify our opinions about others now deemed out of place in our society.

Nutrition

Creative Food Labels: Consumer Health Education

MOON S. CHEN, JR. is visiting assistant professor, Department of Health, Physical Education, and Recreation, Box 4070, Texas Tech University, Lubbock, Texas 79409.

Any unit or course in consumer health should include a section on what to expect on food labels. Described in the following outline is one way to facilitate student learning in food labels.

Teacher Preparation

1. Read the handout, "A Consumer's Guide to Food Labels," by Margaret Morrison from the June 1977 *FDA Consumer.*
2. Prepare enough copies of the handout for distribution to each student.
3. Write the names of approximately five to seven fresh fruits on strips of paper so that there are enough for each class member and each fruit is more or less equally represented.

Place these strips of paper in a bag. Students will draw these strips for their assignment.

Behavioral Expectations for the Student

As a result of this exercise, the student will be able to:

1. Make a food label and in doing so will be familiar with the various components of food labeling.
2. Make judgments on the quality of various food labels.
3. Experience, discuss, and categorize the decision-making processes of many consumers.

Procedure

Day One

1. Introduce the topic of food labeling with emphasis on reasons for labeling

food, FDA requirements for food labels, explanations of the various components of the nutrition information label.
2. Introduce the idea of a contest to be conducted the next class day on food labels. Each class member draws from a paper bag a choice of a fresh fruit. These choices are not to be revealed to other members of the class. For the next class assign students to read the handout, "A Consumer's Guide to Food Labels," and make a label for the choice they drew from the paper bag that would conform to FDA

guidelines. Any information that is not available, such as net weight, may be estimated or made up.

3. Announce that there will be prizes (first prize and runner-up) awarded to the most original label, the most popular label, the most attractive label.

Day Two

1. Have all those with the same fruits place their labels in one area of the classroom. The objective is to place labels in such a way that they will "sell" themselves. Have students put a price on their items.
2. Once labels are in place, distribute three pieces of paper to each student for ballots.
3. Instruct students to write their choices for the best label on their ballots. Students may distribute their voting on these ballots in any fashion they wish—all three ballots for their choice of best label, two ballots for one choice and one ballot for another, or one ballot for three different choices.

4. Invite volunteers to tally the ballots.
5. After the ballots have been tallied, announce the winning labels and award the prizes for the best label and runner-up. The teacher may decide what to do in case there are ties.
6. Prizes could be books or fruits.
7. The teacher should then follow up this exercise with a discussion on consumer decision-making in the marketplace and ask class to share their experiences and their decision-making.

Sensible Dieting

1. Investigate commercial health spas and community recreational facilities. Compare cost, services offered, equipment available, and reputation. Investigate commercial diet clinics comparing type and length of "treatment," promises made, food plan, consideration for changing food habits, and success rate.

MARILYN MUDGETT is associated with the Health Education Department, Group Health Cooperative. DOROTHY CULJAT is presently evaluating the weight control program of Group Health Cooperative, 200 15th Avenue East, Seattle, Washington 98112.

2. Make a study of doctors who specialize in weight control. Examine professional qualifications, length of treatment, types of treatments (pre-packaged foods, pills, shots, hypnosis, etc.), success rate, and possible health dangers.

Dieting is an obsession for many Americans. Money readily spent on fad diets, exercise devices, over-the-counter weight loss aids; miracle foods, and national self-help organizations all add up to a billion dollar weight reduction industry. Physical activity has been taken out of the realm of the natural and is under the domain of big business—health spas, athletic clubs.

The search to be thin can be confusing and costly to the consumer. Students need accurate, unbiased information to make decisions about weight control and learn how to protect their pocketbooks at the same time. The following assignments are methods of educating the potential consumer.

3. Visit the local drugstore and make a list of the over-the-counter reducing aids available or visit a library or bookstore and note the number and titles of books on dieting.

4. Compile magazine and newspaper advertisements on diets, diet aids, and slimming devices. Evaluate the reliability of these advertisements analyzing the use of objective facts, pseudoscientific words such as "cellulite" and "diuretic," or claims to do something for nothing such as, "lose ugly fat while you eat the foods you love."

5. Write to adolescent summer weight camps and adult "fat farms" for brochures. Figuring length of stay and desired weight to be lost, determine how much each pound of weight loss would cost.

6. Make a survey of family and friends to determine if they ever dieted, types of diets, aids, products and/or facilities used, success rate, and cost.

Two excellent resources for consumer education and weight control are *Thin From Within* by Jack Osman and *A Diet for Living* by Jean Mayer.

PART II

Foreword

Health Teaching Ideas - Secondary was first published in 1983. The publication has been very popular and has experienced a consistent demand from those interested in improving the delivery of health education. Since 1983, the *Journal of Health Education* has continued to print teaching strategies under the heading of "Teaching Ideas." Practically all of these are included in the revised edition of this publication. In addition, other teaching strategies have been included that will eventually be printed in the *Journal*.

Although the title states "secondary," teaching strategies have been included here that would be applicable for middle school through the college level. Users of this volume have the flexibility of adapting the teaching strategies to the grade level that is most appropriate for them.

The Association for the Advancement of Health Education believes that Part II will add to the value of the earlier materials and make this expanded volume an excellent reference for all those seeking workable ideas in teaching and delivering health education programs.

As editor, I wish to thank the authors for sharing their creativity and successes with the profession. Without their willingness to make this professional contribution, the new edition could not have become a reality.

Within the covers of this book are a multitude of ideas to make health education relevant and exciting for the student -- and enjoyable and rewarding for the teacher. I invite the reader to explore the innovative and successful experiences presented here.

Loren B. Bensley, Jr., *Editor*
Professor of Health Education
Central Michigan University
Mount Pleasant, Michigan

Focus on Process

The Writing Process in Health Class

Vicki Steinberg and Teresa M. Fry

In Exeter Township's Health III class, a health quarter course required for graduation, teacher Terry Fry involves students in the learning process using various writing techniques. Previously, Mrs. Fry used teacher generated lectures, quizzes, tests, and a few learning centers to give students a basic understanding of human sexuality. For four years, Mrs. Fry used traditional methods, but she was bored with the finished assignments, particularly since she teaches four similar classes in one quarter; therefore, a test meant 120 students turned in dull true/false or matching answers. Also, Mrs. Fry was concerned that students were not really involved in their own learning process.

Although many of the tests remain the same, through the writing process there is more interaction between students and between the students and the teacher. At first, Mrs. Fry tried a simple assignment. She began by telling the class about her birds and the bees' talk with her mom and her misconceptions about sex. Class members then wrote in class their recollections of a similar talk with their parents. Those students who did not recall a talk or were sure they had never been involved in such a discussion wrote what they will tell their children. Since some of the information is quite revealing, students who do not share but do turn in the rough draft and each class member receives credit for the assignment. Using this simple writing, Mrs. Fry breaks the ice, showing that everyone has the same thoughts and experiences. Students who have written in order to learn about themselves realize how nervous both they and their parents were.

This early success encouraged Mrs. Fry to give extra credit to students who interview their mothers about their own

Vicki Steinberg is a teacher in the English Department of Exeter Township School District in Reading, PA 19606. Teresa M. Fry is a teacher in the Physical Education/Health Department of Exeter Township School District.

births. Obviously, some students do not live with, or even know, their birth mothers. These students have a sheet of ten options from which to choose, such as to interview three different people or express their own views concerning sex education in the schools. This interview gives the student an insight into the times of his birth and brings parents and teenagers together. One boy discovered he had been born on the day that Bobby Kennedy was shot and was named after Kennedy, while many kids found their dads had been in Viet Nam at the time of their births and had not even known their baby's sex. This assignment makes students talk to their parents pleasantly and brings them closer for a moment or two because it gives students insight into their personal history.

For a full week, about half way through the course when class members are comfortable with each other, the Flour Baby Project begins. Here each student must make a baby from a five pound sack of flour and carry him/her everywhere for seven days. During the week, in order to achieve more than an average grade, students may do two different interviews about the Flour Baby Project, one to obtain the parental view of the project and any suggestions for improvement and one interviewing a parent other than the student's own concerning being a parent. Other topics include checking the finances associated with having a baby and writing about the information.

As a culminating exercise, students complete sentences such as "I learned that..," "I now know that..," and "I hated that . . . " At the end of the questions, students may give opinions about the project and how they would change the project. After papers are turned in, the class orally reviews the ideas.

As classwork, students split up into groups of three or four to write dialogues about the birthing process. After rough drafts are completed, students read their dialogues aloud to the class. Typical encounters include scenes about

the start of labor, getting to the hospital on time, or the labor process—the physical and psychological aspects of birthing. Students don't feel a need for a grade; they enjoy themselves and reveal knowledge at the same time.

As Mrs. Fry continues to use the writing process, she finds more uses for it. A recent addition to her course is a chronological description of the steps of the menstrual cycle. After the lecture, students write their understanding in paragraphs to clarify any mistaken concepts in timing and to solve problems before the same question appears on a test.

Previously, each Health III class wrote research papers on various topics from rape to child abuse to in vitro fertilization, but the papers were repetitive and copied word for word from the source material. This problem ended when Mrs. Fry presented the class with a list of different ways to tackle writing the researched material. Instead of simply copying the material, students could write a diary of a child abuser, a Phil Donahue interview with a surrogate mother, a dialogue between a lawyer and a rape victim, or anything similar. These options made the teacher's and the students' jobs more enjoyable and therefore a better learning experience. Even those students who wrote a traditional research paper had to add a personal final paragraph to humanize the text.

The most recent writing started in class but was finished outside class. First, the class brainstormed reasons, pro and con, for a teenager having a sexual relationship. A recorder kept track of the ideas and the class received a copy the following day. Working individually, class members drafted a discussion of four ideas from the list. Mrs. Fry had magazine articles available to help back up responses. For extra credit, students could have their parents read and sign the paragraphs, again opening discussion at home through writing.

Because of the added written assignments, students learn more about themselves, other people, and their families. Tests and quizzes do not allow the close feelings among class members or students teaching themselves to see their feelings.

The teacher also learns more about what members of the class know and can adapt future work to problem spots. Through end of the quarter evaluations, she can also discover what needs to be taught differently, faster or slower, or in more detail. Fortunately, none of the extra writing is a large burden in time because students have found their voices and are interesting as well as knowledgeable.

Because the English faculty at Exeter has been encouraging all teachers to use writing in their classes and providing ideas to make it possible in each unique situation, the health curriculum has become an exciting and enjoyable educational experience for both students and teachers.

Logo-Mania: Creative Health Art

Frank Calsbeek

The logo or trademark is a powerful communication tool in the hands of a creative health teacher. It is useful for getting students to examine the "humanizing" messages that health agencies develop and project for themselves. Artistic symbols are used to craft a likeness or identity for the organization's mission and philosophy. These images are planned and developed with intent and purpose. Each is significantly different and is a projection of the unique qualities that an institution or agency wishes to convey about itself

The idea of a logo or trademark is very old. Marks have been found on early Chinese porcelain, on pottery jars from ancient Greece and Rome, and on goods from India dating back to about 1300 BC (Morgan, 1986).

Set the Stage

Students can be motivated to become involved in logo-mania by calling their attention to a logo that many have seen, but few may understand. The caduceus, with its two snakes entwined in opposite directions around a wand made of olive wood and gold, always arouses their curiosity. Point out the fact that both snakes are "eyeballing" each other and that they are surmounted by two wings. Students generally recognize that the wings are symbolic of speed; they are sometimes affixed to a track shoe and given as an award to the school's track star. These wings belonged to

Frank Calsbeek is in the Health Education Division of Southwest Texas State University, San Marcos, TX 78666.

Hermes, the speedy messenger of the gods in Greek mythology. The wand was a gift from Apollo and had the power to unite all beings divided by hate. Hermes discovered the unifying power of the wand when he threw it between two fighting snakes who promptly wound themselves around it in friendly association. The wand also possessed magical powers over dreams, waking, sleep, and even death.

Later, a single snake wrapped around the staff came to be a symbol for Aesculapius, the god of medicine. Today it is the symbol of the medical profession.

Health Logos Today

Health agencies are very sensitive to the public's perception of their image. Their logos take form as a symbol, set apart by unique design, with distinctive coloring, lettering, or any combination of these. The purpose is to give a powerful identity to the health agency or

group. Usually the logo is field-tested to see if it accurately reflects the image that the organization has of itself. It must also mold this image in a positive way. Images can be misinterpreted, amplified, or ignored.

A healthy image will exhibit or elicit some, if not all, of the following characteristics or responses: 1) strong emotional response, 2) appearance of power, 3) sense of experience, confidence, and tradition, and 4) slow process resulting from consistent repetition (Napoles, 1988).

Discovering a Logo's Image

Five current health logos are provided on the following page to use for reproduction as an overhead transparency. They represent professional, voluntary, and official (tax-supported) health organizations and agencies. Some may be well known and easily recognizable. Others may be unfamiliar to your class. An identification key is given at the end of this article.

Project these logos on a screen and have students examine each one individually. Ask probing questions that focus on the following:

1. What objects do you recognize in each logo?

2. What symbolic meaning does each object have?

3. To which agency/organization does this logo belong?

4. What do you know about the mission of the agency?

5. What impression do *you* have about the identity and image of each agency/organization?

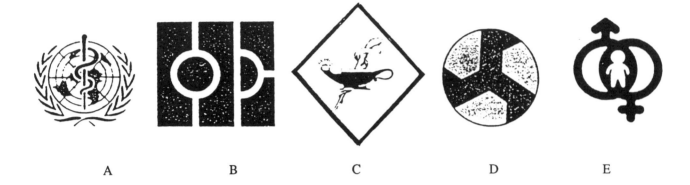

| A | B | C | D | E |

Creative Logo Design

Have students form six design teams of three to five students. Ask each team to creatively design a logo that projects an image and identity for one of the following school-based groups:

Team 1. A local SADD chapter
Team 2. Your cafeteria program
Team 3. The nurses' health center
Team 4. Crossing guard program
Team 5. Custodial/janitorial service
Team 6. Smoking cessation group
for teens

Art materials such as paper, rulers, compasses, color markers, and other items should be supplied. Students may be apprehensive at first, claiming they have little or no art ability. Reassure them that the design concept is central and that perfection could be carried out later by an art professional. What is needed is the basic idea.

Encourage students to creatively translate the image and identity of each school service group (or others, if they apply) into the logo design. It may be necessary to inquire from each service group how it views itself and its mission. Suggest that each logo should utilize popular colors that would make it attractive for a T-shirt or coat emblem.

After all teams have completed their design task, culminate the activity by having each group share its creation with the other design teams. Prominently display all six logo designs and invite school service group members to view the logos and verify if their mission and identity were accurately projected.

Logo-mania is fun. It encourages students to participate in a contemporary art form while creating an awareness and appreciation for different health service groups at their school.

Key to Logos

A. World Health Organization
B. Association for the Advancement of Health Education
C. American School Health Association
D. American Public Health Association
E. March of Dimes - Birth Defects Foundation

Morgan, H. (1986) *Symbols of America.* New York: Viking Penguin, Inc., p. 7.

Napoles, V. (1988). *Corporate identity design.* New York: Van Nostrand Reinhold Company, Inc., p. 11-26.

Overcoming Xenophobia:
Learning To Accept Differences

Judith A. Baker

Health educators are often called upon to interact with special population groups. Some of the special populations health educators serve are the medically indigent, the homeless, the elderly, the obese, gays, the disabled, racial minorities, and alcoholics. Unfortunately, most health educators and their clients have been raised in a society which tends to view people with these characteristics in a negative and stereotypical manner (Snyder, 1986). When these societal views are internalized, xenophobia limits the ability of health educators to provide quality service to all clients. Xenophobia is a term used here to identify the fear of strangers or anyone viewed as different from the norm.

The disasterous impact of xenophobia on the practice of health education is apparent in the case of internalized ageism of elderly clients. Obstacles to early detection of breast cancer among elderly women listed by Frank-Stromborg (1986) are myths about older people, viewing pain as an inevitable part of aging, and attributing symptoms to aging rather than illness. Internalized ageism and its associated fatalism may lead to diminished perceptions about the serious consequences of developing diseases which might otherwise be prevented. And, elderly adults who have internalized ageist beliefs that older people are clumsy, ineffectual, fearful, dependent, and slow (Shaie & Shaie, 1977) prevent themselves from

enjoying the opportunity to improve quality of life in later years with physical activity.

Strategies exist to help health educators overcome negative and professionally destructive attitudes toward clients. As part of a community health education class at a midwestern university, students were encouraged to overcome xenophobia in themselves and others. To prepare for teaching the unit on special populations, the instructor first examined her own xenophobic reactions and participated in each of the learning strategies. The only materials necessary were a brief xenophobic assessment questionnaire, a list of 10 successful people from the special population of choice, a list of books and movies about the special population, and a written description of student assignments. Three class sessions were allotted for the learning unit. Each of the strategies presented can be adapted for use in a variety of health education classes including those dealing with human sexuality, aging, alcohol abuse, and weight management.

In the first class session, self-awareness is addressed. The first and last names of all students enrolled in the class are written on name tags. Students are asked to select one name tag other than their own and place the name tag on someone in the room to whom they believe the name belongs. Additionally, students are asked to give a fabricated introduction based solely on appearances to the class about the people they selected. Following the introductions, class discussion is generated about the stereotypes used during the name tag activity. Next, students are asked to recognize how they feel about each

of the client groups listed previously on a brief questionnaire. Reactions to working closely with clients possessing each of the listed characteristics are ranked by each student following the question: "Would you feel uncomfortable or ill-at-ease when working with any of these clients?" Many prejudice attitude questionnaires or instruments have been developed which also can be used to measure xenophobic reactions (Wingard, 1981; Smith, 1973). The first session enables the instructor to identify one or two special population groups for which most of the students in the class express the greatest xenophobic reaction.

In the second session, the instructor helps students to identify all the myths commonly heard about the special population group of choice. Students are asked to collect factual knowledge about the characteristic or the group of people from materials provided in class. Misunderstandings and myths are corrected in class by the students.

Next, students are asked to consider how society oppresses people with the characteristic. What labels are commonly used to describe people with the characteristic? How does the label serve to perpetuate stereotyping and oppression? Are the connotations of the labels helpful to strengthening the self-esteem of people with the characteristic?

Repeated and positive personal exposure with people who possess the characteristic may help to alleviate xenophobic reactions. Outside classroom assignments include the suggestion that students get to know these people socially or at least outside a professional setting. Students could attend a self-help group com-

Judith A. Baker is an assistant professor in the Department of Health Education, Texas Woman's University, Denton, TX 76204.

prised of these people. Students are provided with a list of movies and books depicting the special population in a positive manner. Students compete by trying to identify the greatest number of famous and successful people from the special population.

Other ways to reduce xenophobia in addition to increased self-awareness, knowledge, and personal exposure are simulations, role plays, and role reversal. A simulation is conducted by having students verbally express their immediate reaction to each of the following situations: (1) you had to listen to an obese speaker in class talk about Overeaters Anonymous, (2) the specialist to whom you have been referred for a medical problem is obese, (3) your best friend from childhood who came to visit is obese, (4) you discover that you are obese.

Examples of role plays and role reversals are essay assignments about what life would be like if 90 percent of the U.S. population were gay or if the student woke up tomorrow weighing 50 extra pounds. In the third session, dialogues based on the essays are created and acted out by students in class. In addition, students report on their experiences in completing the outside classroom assignments.

The use of these strategies in a community health education class aided students in comprehension of a complex issue. Students were able to generate their own examples of ways xenophobia acts as a barrier to the practice of community health education.

Once students work through all the strategies for reducing their xenophobia, they will be better able to work with a greater variety of clients. Even if they cannot identify xenophobia in themselves, they have responsibilities as health educators to recognize the problems encountered by their clients. Clients themselves can benefit from experiencing these strategies to help overcome their internalized xenophobia. Quality health education requires that health educators engage in the professional and personal development necessary to overcoming xenophobia.

Frank-Stromborg, M. (1986). The role of the nurse in early detection of cancer: Populations sixty-six years of age and older. *Oncology Nursing Forum, 13*(3), 66–74.

Schaie, L. W., & Schaie, J. P. (1977). Clinical assessment and aging. In J. E. Birren and K. W. Schaie (eds.), *Handbook of the psychology of aging.* New York: Van Nostrand Reinhold.

Smith, K. (1973). The homophobic scale. In G. Weinberg, *Society and the healthy homosexual.* New York: Anchor.

Snyder, M. (1986). Self-fulfilling stereotypes. In D. Goleman and D. Heller (eds.), *The pleasures of psychology.* New York: New American Library.

Wingard, J. (1981). Measures of attitudes toward the elderly. *Experimental Aging Research, 6,* 229–313.

Factors Important in Teaching Controversial Issues

Ansa Ojanlatva

A few years ago one of my assigned courses was a required methods course for those intending to teach health education at the secondary school level. Most of the students in these courses were physical education majors and as often is the case, they were studying health education as their second teaching field. Unfortunately, in these circumstances, students often expect health education to be an easy field of study, and therefore, by the time of their senior year, many still are unaware of the knowledge, skills, and sensitivity needed to teach controversial health issues.

Additionally, Merki[1] found evidence in 1976 that there is a plethora of instruction about physical fitness; but life-related topics such as human sexuality, mental health, and consumer issues, frequently requested by students, are often lacking completely in the curriculum. This has prompted my search for activities which might increase student awareness of the qualifications to teach controversial issues.

I developed the following teaching/learning activity with the above stated objective in mind. Specifically, the activity concentrated on drawing out information about the following:

1. the instructor: his/her characteristics and professional background;
2. the subject matter: the cognitive substance and the continuity of it in relation to other subjects;
3. the method of teaching: the planning of instructional activity, the instructional methods, and the possible evaluative procedures.

Before this session students engaged in values clarification activities and they were aware that they would not be forced to participate. However, as future teachers of health education, they were encouraged to participate in the activity. In this class no one refused.

The students were told to:

1. pick a topic "from the hat" (all were

Ansa Ojanlatva is in the department of Health Science and Human Ecology, School of Natural Sciences, California State College, San Bernardino, CA 92407. Her article was accepted for publication in June 1980.

questions commonly asked by high school students about sexuality), and

2. take five minutes to write down:
   (a) how they would answer the question (subject matter);
   (b) how they would teach about it (method of teaching);
   (c) what qualifications a teacher should possess to present the materials in an effective manner.

The students worked on the topics without discussing them with each other. Time did not allow for all topics to be discussed, but after the five-minute period several questions were selected to be answered:

1. What is a wet dream?
2. Do women have wet dreams?
3. What is masturbation?
4. What is a normal penis size?
5. Can the sperm supply be used up?
6. What is homosexuality?

The material* presented during this session included:

1. The instructor's role.
   (a) knowledge required,
   (b) sensitivity needed for discussing the topic or issue, e.g.:
      (1) sensing other people,
      (2) feeling comfortable with one's own sexuality.
2. Subject matter.
   (a) facts,
   (b) continuity.
3. Methods of teaching.
   (a) planning a program including elements such as:
      (1) support from needed community groups and from parents,
      (2) personal involvement from students,
      (3) adequate time for learning, feedback, and evaluation,
      (4) meetings with students and their parents.
   (b) using methods of instruction elaborating on:
      (1) positive vs. negative approaches,

*The students used the following book as a resource: Read, Donald A., and Greene, Walter H. *Creative teaching in health.* New York: MacMillan Publishing Co. Inc., 1975.

   (2) values clarification,
   (3) positive climate,
   (4) openness to any relevant questions.
   (c) planning evaluative procedures.

The evaluation revealed that in most cases the activity accomplished what it was meant to accomplish. Twelve students participated in this class experience, and each turned in an evaluation. Following is a synopsis of their reactions to the questions on the evaluation sheet.

1. *Did you find out anything about yourself as a teacher?*

Four students indicated it was hard to talk about sex; three of them suggested careful preparation was essential for the outcome; and five felt comfortable in talking about sex with the class, who posed as high school students. There was indication of not having the needed information to teach the subject, and of having found out what to teach and what not to teach.

2. *Did you learn anything about the requirements of the subject matter?*

The answers ranged from "no" (two students) to "different things" (one student). Some of the particular requirements were:

(a) getting your points across.
(b) using teaching aids effectively.
(c) preparing up-to-date material.
(d) needing more preparation than previously expected.
(e) needing so much factual information, knowledge of attitudes and behaviors, plus ability to talk and listen.
(f) needing information from related subjects such as psychology, anatomy, etc.

3. *Did you learn anything about the factors needed to plan a controversial teaching unit?*

The variety of responses makes a summary somewhat difficult. Some of the responses cautioned:

• not to ask students to reveal personal information they may not wish to reveal;
• to think more about how the subject matter may affect the student;
• to prepare for extreme feedback. (The responses seemed to refer to

possible need for counseling after study of controversial issues—e.g., a student's bursting into tears during discussion of death and dying issues.)

Further, the answers revealed that the students realized the importance of the following:

- the need for a comfortable attitude in the teacher to make students feel comfortable.
- the necessity of an organized picture of the various factors in sex education and the particular steps to consider.
- the need for a lot of planning before a teaching unit can be implemented.
- the consideration of class makeup: social background, experience.
- the need of the other related subjects in planning a unit (anatomy, psychology, sociology, human sexuality related topics).

4. *How did you feel when you had to teach the topic?*

Two students indicated they felt nervous because they did not know how the class was going to react. Five students indicated the opposite: they felt comfortable in talking about the issue raised. Three students indicated embarrassment or hesitance in the beginning. And two students said they felt inadequate in terms of factual knowledge.

5. *Any other comments?*

The answers to this last question indicated overall feelings:

- objection to an activity involving homosexuality.
- "The class today was great. . . . I thought it was one of the most unusual classes I have been to."
- interesting exercise (two students).
- "I think teaching on sexuality should fall within the limits of the approved curriculum if you want to keep your job as a secondary school teacher."

This activity was meant to make students aware of the information, skills, and sensitivity needed to teach controversial subjects. The topics were chosen based upon issues discussed in class, which happened to be on sexuality. In the same manner, one might raise questions about use and abuse of drugs, or any other subject for which there is no one solution.

---

[1]Merki, Donald. *Personal communication,* January 1980.

[2]Read, Donald A., and Greene, Walter H. *Creative teaching in health.* New York: MacMillan Publishing Co., Inc., 1975.

Teaching About Authoring Systems: Instructional Design Tools for Health Education

Paul D. Sarvela and Marilyn J. Karaffa

Microcomputers have become increasingly important as educational tools in the health education program (Petosa & Gillespie, 1984). Adoption of microcomputer technology has occurred not only for hardware systems, but also for software systems. Even though there has been an increase in the quantity and variety of software for health education, one of the biggest problems facing health educators who try to use computer-assisted instruction (CAI) is the shortage of high quality educational software (McDermott & Belcastro, 1983; Sarvela, Ritzel, Karaffa, & Naseri, 1989). Therefore, health educators sometimes find it desirable to develop CAI to meet a specific need. Since many health educators do not have computer programming skills at the level necessary to create high quality software, authoring systems can serve as an excellent alternative. Authoring systems are software packages that are designed to create CAI through a process of mediation between the author and a high-level computer programming language (Whiteside & Whiteside, 1987/1988).

The purpose of this paper is to present and describe the methods of a teaching technique which aims to introduce and develop proficiency in applying one of the authoring sys-

Paul D. Sarvela is an associate professor in the Department of Health Education, College of Education, Southern Illinois University at Carbondale, Carbondale, IL 62901. Marilyn J. Karaffa is an assistant professor in the Department of Health and Physical Education, College of Arts and Sciences, Youngstown State University, Youngstown, OH 44555.

tems currently available for health educators, Apple SuperPILOT. (SuperPILOT is an authoring package which enables instructors to develop CAI in an efficient and effective manner. Features include a comprehensive tutorial, an excellent set of documentation materials, and four editors: lesson text, graphics, sound effects, and character set.) This technique was designed for students enrolled in a basic microcomputer applications course at Southern Illinois University at Carbondale. With minor adaptions, this approach would be excellent for in-service workshops and training programs for health educators working in a variety of settings (i.e., schools, hospitals, community agencies, and worksites).

Preparation

In private industry, computer software design and development is usually dictated by a set of specifications. We have found this strategy to be an effective way to teach design and development of health education CAI as well. Figure 1 shows an example of a specification that we have prepared for use in our CAI classes.

For the project, the instructor should organize students into groups. It has been our experience that groups of three or four students usually are best. Next, documentation and programs created by students (or instructors) in previous sessions should be made available to the students. These materials are extremely helpful to students as they study the best ways to design and develop their authoring packages.

Implementation and Time Frame

The lessons and activities are implemented in the following sequence:
(1) Introduce CAI (1 hr).
(2) Review Instructional Systems Design (ISD) model of curriculum development (1 hr).
(3) Discuss special curriculum development issues related to CAI (1 hr).
(4) Introduce basic SuperPILOT commands (1 hr).
(5) Demonstrate previously developed student or instructor-generated programs (1 hr).
(6) Student review of SuperPILOT tutorial (3 hrs).
(7) Student design and development of CAI materials (8 hrs).
(8) Pilot testing and revision of CAI materials (3 hrs).
(9) Student demonstration of their projects to class (1 hr).
In our classes, 20 hours have been allotted to the process of teaching how to use the SuperPILOT authoring package.

Necessary Materials

The following materials are needed to implement this teaching technique: one Apple 2e computer with two disk drives and monitor per group; one SuperPILOT authoring system per group; one blank disk per group; checklists for pilot testing the CAI materials (i.e., Horne & Gold, 1983); student background readings on CAI and ISD (i.e., Bork, 1984; Sarvela & Noonan, 1988; Damarin & White, 1986); and resources on the health education topic for the CAI selected by the group (students gather these materials).

Integration with Other Topics

This project is part of a course taught at SIUC entitled "Computer Applications in Health Education." While the focus of this project is on skills relative to the development of computer software, students also integrate and apply current information from a variety of health education content areas (nutrition, drugs, stress) through the selection of their topic for the CAI and subsequent development of the program. Furthermore, this project could be integrated with a health education curriculum and instruction class, when the class is studying various instructional delivery systems.

Previous Results

We have used this method of teaching for the past three years. It has proven to be an effective approach, as demonstrated by the innovative, high quality health education programs that have been designed and developed by our students. For the past two years, we have demonstrated several of our student projects and teaching techniques at computer sessions at annual meetings of AAPHERD. For example, in 1988, we conducted a workshop on how to develop and teach a course on computer applications in health education. At the 1989 meeting, we demonstrated several programs developed by our students. CAI program topics included: exercise, functions of the heart, caffeine, cocaine, alcohol, and dietary fiber.

Bork, A. (1984). Computers in education today—and some possible futures. *Phi Delta Kappa, 66*(4), 239–248.

Damarin, S. K. & White, C. M. (1986). Examining a model for courseware development. *Journal of Computers in Mathematics and Science Teaching, 6*(1), 38–43.

Horne, D. A. & Gold, R. S. (1983). Guidelines for developing health education software. *Health Education, 14*(6), 85–86.

McDermott, R. J. & Belcastro, P. A. (1983). The microcomputer bandwagon is here—but watch your step! *Health Education, 14*(6), 76–79.

Petosa, R. & Gillespie, T. (1984). Microcomputers in health education: Characteristics of quality instructional software. *Journal of School Health, 54*(10), 394–396.

Sarvela, P. D. & Noonan, J. V. (1988). Testing and computer-based instruction: Psychometric considerations. *Educational Technology, 28*(5), 17–20.

Sarvela, P. D., Ritzel, D. O., Karaffa, M. J. & Naseri, M. K. (1989). Applications software packages in the school health program. *Health Education, 20*(2), 43–49.

Whiteside, M. F. & Whiteside, J. A. (1987/1988). Microcomputer authoring systems: Valuable tools for health educators. *Health Education, 18*(6), 4–6.

Figure 1. CAI Authoring Package Specification

Objective: The objective of this assignment is to demonstrate the ability to use the SuperPILOT authoring package. This assignment is a group effort. Each group will submit one set of project deliverables.

Points: The assignment will be worth 35 points.

Task Description: Each group will submit a CAI tutorial lesson and relevant documentation designed and developed by the group. The topic of the tutorial shall be a health issue (e.g., teenage pregnancy, cocaine, or aerobic exercise) of the group's choice.

Deliverables: The CAI tutorial will be comprised of the following deliverables:

1) tutorial documentation
   - objectives of tutorial
   - target audience
   - equipment requirements
   - design strategy
   - operator directions
   - listing of tutorial program
   - pilot test results

2) tutorial
   - introduction and objectives
   - description of how to use system
   - interactive with the learner
   - use of the following commands:
     - T:
     - A:
     - M:
     - TY:
     - TN:
     - J:
     - W:
   - content valid
   - about a 7–10 minute program
   - include a test section with response analysis
   - closing message for further health information on topic

3) disk of tutorial

162

TIC-TAC-TOE

Mary Lawler

Want to get your students interested, involved, and excited? Need something different to motivate everyone from the brightest to the least gifted in your classes? Strike it rich with something as simple as tic-tac-toe.

In tic-tac-toe students pair up and administer their own game by being master/mistress of ceremonies, judge, and contestant at the same time. Students love to compete and cannot be passive while playing this game. It's based on the timeless game everyone knows how to play, so attention can be placed on learning or reviewing the material at hand.

First, I wrote questions and answers on our current unit. Questions were then judged as easy, medium, or difficult. Difficult questions should not be true/false, in order to eliminate guesswork. The number of questions can be adjusted to your material or time restraints. Table 1 lists a sample of questions used in our substance abuse edition.

I began with 25 easy and medium questions and 6 difficult questions. Fewer difficult questions are needed because they earn fewer squares within the tic-tac-toe grid. The questions are typed with the acceptable answers following. For example: Chewing tobacco causes a white patch in the mouth called ————. (leukoplakia)

Mary Lawler is a teacher at Greenfield-Central High School, Greenfield, IN 46140.

One copy of each question is needed for each two students in the class. I used several different methods for preparing the necessary questions. They can be typed on colored paper, coded for the degree of difficulty. Another way is to type all questions on white paper and code them for difficulty by marking the end of the sheets with the appropriate color. One copy of each question is then placed in an envelope; the envelope is sealed and slit at one end to expose the color coded end of the questions (questions can thus be selected without being read). Another method is to print the questions on cardstock, of three different colors; these are more durable but take more time to prepare.

The class is divided into partners to begin the game. Once a player selects a difficulty level, their opponent reads the appropriate level question from the cardstock stack or envelope. The first player answers and if correct, places their symbol, X or O, in the tic-tac-toe grid. Xs or Os earned with correct responses to easy questions can only be placed in the four corners, medium questions in the mid-box, and difficult questions in the center of the grid, as shown in Figure 1 (see next page).

Missed questions are returned to the stack or envelope and remain in play until answered correctly. It is possible the question may recycle to be asked of the player who previously played it. However, it is entirely by chance and students are rewarded for remembering. Only the difficulty of the question is in the control of a player, not the actual question selected.

Players continue taking turns until the game is won or a draw is declared. Players then draw a new tic-tac-toe grid and continue playing until all questions have been answered correctly and taken out of play. Progress throughout the game varies with ability of the students. Students in my health classes (grades 9 and 10) play the entire packet in 30 to 45 minutes.

Students benefit by working at a self-paced, directed activity at a difficulty level of their own choosing. They are involved on task with reading, answering, judging answers, and planning strategy. The teacher's role should be only as final judge for accuracy and fairness.

The game is easily adaptable to any subject material and grade level. It has been a fun, exciting activity that left my students involved, interested, and excited over health class.

Questions and Answers for the Substance Abuse Unit

Easy Questions

1. Name a drug in the narcotic category. (heroin, codeine, methadone, morphine, opium)
2. What are the narcotics used for in medicine? (stop pain, stop a cough, stop diarrhea)
3. What is the natural source for narcotics? (opium, poppy plant)

4. Where is all cocaine grown? (South America)

5. Free-basing is a method of using which drug? (cocaine)

6. Is caffeine a stimulant? (yes)

7. Can you overdose on caffeine? (yes, but it takes a lot)

8. What effect does a barbiturate have on a person? (can calm or put you to sleep)

9. Do anti-depressants make people high? (no)

10. What group of drugs make a person see things which aren't really there? (hallucinogens)

11. —————————is anything which causes a change in your body physically, mentally, or emotionally. (drug)

12. Stopping drug use and getting sick because the addiction isn't fed is called ——————. (withdrawal)

13. ————— - dependence involves both tolerance and withdrawal. (physical)

14. ————— - dependence means you think you need the drug. (psychological)

15. Name one cancer besides lung cancer caused by tobacco use. (oral, kidney, throat)

16. In 1972 cigarette ads were banned on —————. (TV and radio)

17. ————— is a disease caused by smoking and is both incurable and progressive. (emphysema)

18. Name three things you cannot do while smoking. (answers will vary but may include swim, kiss, live)

19. What type of alcohol is found in alcoholic beverages? (ethyl)

20. What is the only organ in the body which can break down alcohol? (liver)

21. If someone had four mixed drinks, how long would it take to break down all of the alcohol in their body? (four hours)

22. Which produces a stronger beverage: fermentation or distillation? (distillation)

23. What usually happens when the BAC level reaches 10%? (death)

24. Which happens first with al-cohol use: relaxation or loss of balance? (relaxation)

25. Name the organization which works with teen-agers who live with an alcoholic. (alateen)

Medium Questions

1. What is the disease in which fat replaces normal cells due to the damage done by alcohol? (cirrhosis)

2. What is the best way to quit smoking? (cold turkey)

3. What narcotic is often found in cough medicine and pain relievers? (codeine)

4. Name a medical use for amphetamines. (narcolepsy or hyperactivity)

5. What is the most commonly used drug in America? (alcohol)

6. Approximately — % of all fatal auto accidents involve alcohol. (50)

7. Which drug is the most addictive in the world? (cocaine)

8. What is the term for needing increasing doses of a drug to get the same effect? (tolerance)

9. ————— in tobacco makes it addictive. (nicotine)

10. ————— in tobacco causes cancer. (tar)

11. What group is the only American group to increase its tobacco use? (teenage girls)

12. Which gets into your system faster: a smoked cigarette or chewing tobacco? (smoke)

13. Which has more tar, ammonia, carbon monoxide, and hydrogen cyanide: mainstream or sidestream smoke? (sidestream smoke)

14. Proof is equal to —— times the percent of alcohol. (two)

15. —————is when an alcoholic cannot remember. (black-out or alcohol amnesia)

16. ————— oz. of beer has an equal amount of alcohol as ——oz. of wine. (12:5)

17. Five ounces of ————— has as much alcohol as a shot of —. (wine: hard liquor)

18. 1 1/2 oz. of whiskey has —— oz. of ethanol. (1/2)

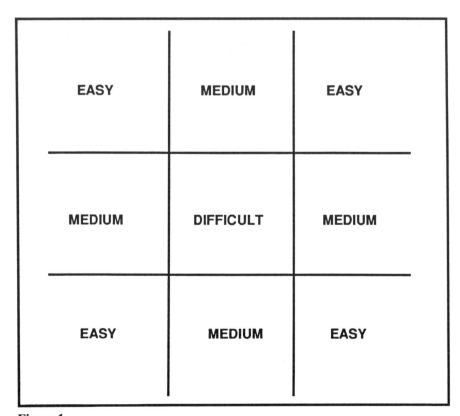

EASY	MEDIUM	EASY
MEDIUM	DIFFICULT	MEDIUM
EASY	MEDIUM	EASY

Figure 1.

19. What is the active ingredient in marijuana? (THC or delta-9 tetrahydro-cannabinol)

20. One marijuana joint has the same ability to cause cancer as - ——— of cigarettes. (one)

21. Name the hallucinogen which causes violent hallucinations and was once used as an anesthetic for animals. (PCP)

22. Most names for prescription depressants end in ———. (-al)

23. When legal penalties have been decreased for drug use or possession it has been ———. (decriminalized)

24. ——— are abused to build muscles and may lead to cancer and other health problems. (steroids)

25. Glue, butyl nitrate, and gasoline belong to the group of drugs known as ———. (inhalants)

Difficult Questions

1. Chewing tobacco causes a pre-cancerous white patch in the mouth called ———. (leukoplakia)

2. Lung cancer is ———% fatal. (95%)

3. The lit end of a cigarette reaches what temperature? (900-1200 degrees F)

4. What would be the effect of 60 milligrams of nicotine taken all at once? (death)

5. What's the difference between a problem drinker and an alcoholic? (alcoholic is addicted, problem drinker's drinking leads to problems but they may not be addicted)

6. ——— is a drug used for aversion therapy in treating alcoholism. (antabuse)

Picture Charades:

A Health Teaching Device
Richard T. Mackey

Looking for a classroom activity that your health students will find exciting and fun-filled? Try picture charades. It's enjoyable, promotes learning effectively, and is particularly good in helping students clarify vocabulary words you include in your health instruction.

The rules for pictures charades are quite simple. They are really the same as for regular charades, but instead of acting out the words, participants must draw a picture of the word, phrase, etc.

Here are the rules: Divide the class into teams of four to six members. All teams can compete against each other at the same time, or you can arrange other forms of competition. The important thing is to keep all teams actively participating.

You, the teacher, can act as the leader, or you can appoint a student leader and you become an observer. The leader has a list of four or five terms, phrases, or perhaps definitions pertaining to the health topics the class has been studying. At the start of the game, a captain from each team goes to the leader and gets the secret word. The captain hurries to his or her team and draws a picture of the term. The captains may, in addtion to drawing the picture, sketch a dashed line indicating the number of words or syllables in the phrase or word. They may answer only yes or no to questions from teammates. The team member who discovers the correct term becomes the new captain, rushes to the leader to verify the correctness of the term, and then gets a new one. The first team to identify all the terms is, of course, the winner.

You can supply the health vocabulary words or terms or invite your students to develop a list. A list pertaining to dental health, for example, could include the following: fluoridation, soft bristles, unwaxed floss, bicuspid, brush and floss once in every 24 hours, toothpaste, junk food, and gingivitis.

If you students enjoy a challenge and you want to add some zest to your health class, picture charades are for you. After you see them play the game, you'll probably find a way to become a participant yourself. The author did!

Richard T. Mackey is in the Department of Health, Physical Education and Recreation at Miami University, Oxford, Ohio.

Drawing Interpretations of Health
Vicki L. Cleaver

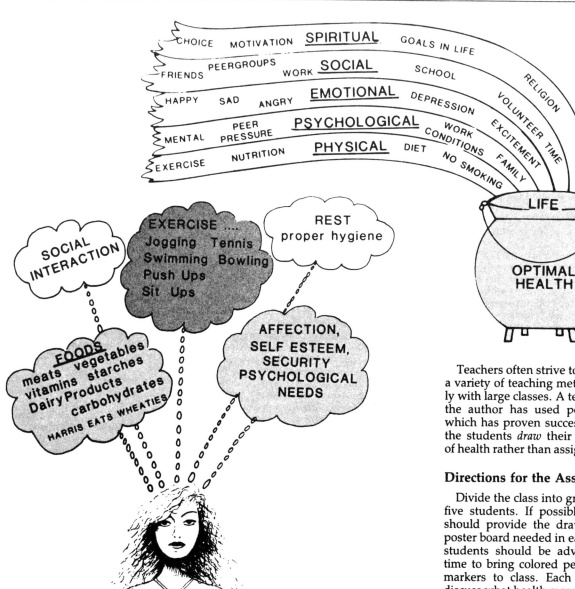

MISS PHYSICALLY FIT

Teachers often strive to effectively use a variety of teaching methods, especially with large classes. A technique which the author has used periodically and which has proven successful is to have the students *draw* their interpretations of health rather than assigning an essay.

Directions for the Assignment

Divide the class into groups of four to five students. If possible, the teacher should provide the drawing paper or poster board needed in each group. The students should be advised ahead of time to bring colored pens, pencils, or markers to class. Each group should discuss what health means, then draw a picture representing their interpretation. Give each group approximately 45 minutes to discuss and complete the drawing. Have each group hang their picture in the room. If time allows, have a representative from each group explain the group's drawing.

On this page are samples of creations by former students.

Vicki L. Cleaver is assistant professor in the Health, Physical Education, and Recreation Department, 119 Huston Huffman Center, University of Oklahoma, Norman, OK 73019.

Using Team Games to Teach Health

Mark A. Croson

RoseAnn Benson

Correct health information is an important part of a growing student's life. However, the health educator must be able to get the student's attention in order to clarify what is fact or myth, healthy or unhealthy. A lasting impression that will involve students in a stimulating learning experience in the classroom will aid retention of material. Learning by doing will result in greater retention because learners who are required to be active in the learning process must be attentive.

Purposeful activities that are based on a student's interests include teaching strategies involving problem solving and active student participation, as in group games. Well-known team games such as volleyball, football, and baseball are natural vehicles to interest all students in learning.

Three examples are described here. Student objectives could include but are not limited to recalling or explaining key terms, definitions, and ideas. Each game is appropriate for introducing material with which the students are already familiar, or reviewing for an exam. These games are exciting activities that will get everyone out of his/her seat and involved in the action.

Mark A. Croson and RoseAnn Benson are in the Department of Health, Sport and Leisure Studies at George Mason University, Fairfax, VA 22030-4444.

VERBAL VOLLEYBALL

Classroom Organization

Organize classroom chairs into three rows per team, facing each other.

Questions

The questions should be organized into three levels of difficulty. Level one, the easiest questions, go to the passers. Level two, more difficult questions, go to the setters. Level three, the most difficult questions, go to the spikers. Regardless of question difficulty, students must have a set time in which to respond. A typical time limit would be 15 seconds.

Rules

The students are organized into two teams and a coin is flipped to determine which is the offensive team. The team serving the ball is the offense and the team receiving the ball is the defense. The individual in the offensive serving position draws and reads a level one question to the passers. If they answer correctly, the server draws and reads a level two question to the setters. If they answer correctly, the server draws and reads a level three question to the spikers. If they answer correctly, the referee draws and reads questions in the same order to the offensive team. The question series continues until one team misses. If the defense misses, a point is awarded to the offense. If the offense misses, a side out is awarded to the defense and team members rotate. By rotating, each

student has the opportunity to respond to questions at all three levels of difficulty. Points can be scored only by the offensive team.

Penalties

Penalties are assessed by the referee for answering out of turn, or any inappropriate classroom behavior. For defensive team penalties, a point is awarded to the offensive team. For offensive team penalties, side out is awarded to the defensive team.

Equipment

Three hats from which to draw each level of question are needed.

Variations

The game may be focused on individuals, small groups, or the entire team depending on how the teacher wants to direct who may respond to the questions.

FOOTBALL FOLLIES

Questions

The questions should be organized into three levels of difficulty. Level one questions, the easiest, are worth 5 yards. Level two questions, more difficult, are worth 10 yards. Level three questions, the most difficult, are worth 15 yards. Regardless of question difficulty, students must have a set time in which to respond. A typical time limit would be 15 seconds.

Rules

A diagram of a football field including yard markers is made on the chalkboard. The students are organized into teams and choose the order in which they are to respond to a question. A coin is flipped to determine which is the offensive team. The offensive team student whose turn it is to answer a question, chooses the difficulty level/yardage. The referee draws and reads the question. If the question is answered correctly the yards are awarded. The offensive team has four chances to make a first down or 10 yards. If they succeed, they continue with four more chances. If they fail, the defensive team is awarded the ball and has four opportunities to make a first down.

Penalties

Penalties are assessed by the referee for answering out of turn or for any inappropriate classroom behavior. The penalty cards are shuffled and one is drawn and assessed against the guilty team.

Equipment and Materials

Three football helmets are needed to hold the three levels of questions. A white penalty flag is needed for the referee to drop when a penalty is to be assessed. Penalty cards consisting of 5, 10, and 15 yard losses should be made on 5 x 8 cards. If the penalty is against the offensive team an additional card, "fumble," should be added. A paper football marked with an arrow placed on the playing field marks direction and progress toward a touchdown (7 points).

BASEBALL BOOGALOO

Classroom Organization

The classroom should be organized into a diamond shape with chairs for bases and player positions.

Questions

The questions should be organized into four levels of difficulty. Level one questions, the easiest, are worth a single. Level two questions, more difficult, are worth a double. Level three questions, even more difficult, are worth a triple. Level four questions, the most difficult, are worth a home run. Regardless of question difficulty, students must have a set time in which to respond. A typical time limit would be 15 seconds.

Rules

The students are organized into two teams and choose their batting order and field position. A roster must be submitted to the umpire. A coin is flipped to determine which team is at bat. The offensive team student whose turn it is to answer a question chooses the difficulty level/number of bases. The umpire draws and reads one question. The individual at bat has only one strike to correctly answer a question. If the question is incorrectly answered an out is assessed and the next batter is up, and so on until three outs. If the question is correctly answered the team in the field has the opportunity to throw the batter out by answering a question of equal difficulty. Single and double questions are answered by the infield (as a group). Triple and home run questions are answered by the outfielders (as a group).

If two base runners reach base safely, the defense may attempt to answer two additional double questions in order to make a double play. If they miss one question, the lead runner advances one base. If they miss both questions, one runner scores and the other advances one base. Players advance bases as forced by the hitters following them.

Penalties

Penalties are assessed by the umpire for answering out of turn or for other inappropriate classroom behavior. If an offensive player breaks a rule, an out is then assessed. If a defensive player breaks a rule, a walk is given to the player at bat.

The Concept of Health and Techniques of Conceptual Analysis

Joseph E. Balog

To take what there is, and use it, without waiting forever in vain for the preconceived - to dig deep into the actual and get something out of that - this doubtless is the right way to live.

-Henry James

The ancient Greeks viewed health as one of the greatest goods. In fact the cult of Hygeia claimed that health was the foremost good and "the most desirable thing" (Temkin, 1977). However, other cults cautioned against the glorification of health. The Stoic philosophers did not view health as an absolute value, but they did emphasize the idea that health was necessary for the practice of virtue (Temkin, 1967, 1977). Regardless of where the ancient Greeks and modern day health educators rank the value of health, this concept is still at the core of the profession's role and existence in society. As a consequence, it is imperative for health educators to help their students and future professionals in their understanding of what it means to be healthy.

This is perhaps one of the most difficult intellectual tasks which confronts health educators. The reasons for this are many and have been discussed elsewhere (Balog, 1981, 1982, 1985). In general, though, studying the concept of health remains elusive for two very important reasons. First, the

Joseph E. Balog is with the Department of Health Science, State University of New York, College at Brockport, Brockport, NY 14420.

concept of health is not an empirical fact or a directly observable and objective phenomenon. Rather, health is a human construct that is defined in accordance with our cultural values, social norms, and presuppositions about its existence. Second, the profession of health education has traditionally devoted little and formal study to analyzing concepts in its curriculum.

The task of defining health is difficult, but the fact still remains, an understanding of health is a most essential and fundamental ingredient for being a health educator. Thus, health educators should ask of themselves, and of their students, "What does health mean?" even if for no other reason than simply that someone may have an answer or provide a clearer and more insightful way of viewing health.

The following activity is presented to help health educators in facilitating a discussion on the concept of health while providing some basic techniques for conducting conceptual analysis. A more detailed and thorough description, which contains additional examples and dialogue, can be found in *Conceptual Questions in Health Education and Philosophical Inquiry* or in Eta Sigma Gamma's monograph, *Ethics and the Field of Health Education* (Balog, 1982, 1985).

Conceptual Analysis Activity

The overall goal of this activity is to help students in constructing their own view of health. More specifically, the main objective of this exercise is to

develop, record, and refine two lists as common features which your students use in describing why they think someone should be considered healthy or ill. Note that including the examination on illness helps students in developing their views on health.

Begin this exercise by handing out a sheet of paper which asks two questions about a list of people. The questions and list may look as follows:

Conceptual Analysis Activity

Are the following people healthy? Explain.

Are the following people ill? Explain.

- A person with bronchogenic carcinoma (lung cancer).
- A person with hypertension and anginal pain.
- A student-athlete who is a top middle distance runner.
- An aerobic physical fitness instructor.
- A person with dyschromatic spirochetosis (discolorization of the skin caused by a spirochete).
- A person with myopia (near-sightedness).
- A person who is a paraplegic.

As the instructor, you may wish to develop your own list. However, if you do use alternative examples, make sure the items on your list reflect the following ideas and techniques of conceptual analysis.

Hand out the list and have your students take it home as an assignment. The students' task is to answer the two questions by writing out a brief explanation on why they think the people on the list are healthy or ill. When the students return during the next class period, the instructor's main tasks are: (1) to facilitate a dialogue and (2) to record on the board, two lists (one for health and one for illness) of common terms, phrases, and/or features which students use in explaining whether the individuals on the handout are healthy or ill. Developing two lists and contrasting the ingredients for defining health and illness should help the class in seeing how they view these two concepts.

Classroom Discussion and Model Cases

Begin the discussion by using a model case example on illness. For your purpose, a model case example is a person from the list who would be typically seen as being ill in our society. Choose the example of a person with brochogenic carcinoma.

Identify and list the common features of an illness which your students use in their explanations. For example, they may offer descriptions such as an abnormal growth is present, the condition can cause death, or this person's body is not functioning properly.

Next, select another model case such as the person with hypertension and anginal pain. Once again, list common descriptions which the students present in explaining why this person is ill. Compare and merge the list by adding or subtracting items which the students believe are essential criteria in determining what is an illness.

Contrary Cases

The next step in your analysis is to use a contrary case example. A contrary case is similar to a model case except the interest lies in inquiring into examples which people typically believe are the opposite of an illness or disease. The idea is to consider cases which people would say "Whatever an illness or disease is, this case certainly isn't an example of it."

Choose the example of a student-athlete who is a top middle distance runner. The objectives are (1) to compile a list of features which the students use in describing health and (2) to compare and contrast this list to the above list on illness.

Next, use the example of the aerobic fitness instructor, and as above, compare, contrast, and merge into one list of features which students offer in talking about health. You may find students wanting to disagree with the items on the health list. Welcome the arguments, but also try to draw out and identify items which can be placed on the list.

Counterexamples

Counterexamples are cases where a premise might be true, but the conclusions are false. A person with dyschromatic spirochetosis is a good example to use with this technique. For instance, this condition is a discolorization of the skin caused by a spirochete. Most people, including your students, would argue that this physical state is abnormal and represents an improper or unnatural body functioning. However, point out that a famous medical sociologist, David Mechanic, discovered that in a South American tribe this condition was so common, "Indians who did not have (it) were regarded as abnormal and were even excluded from marriage" (Mechanic, 1968).

This is a good place to propose to the class that some conditions which might seem abnormal, improper, and considered ill by some people can also be judged as healthy by others. Thus, this example raises the question of whether a person can be healthy even if an abnormality or an improper physical functioning exists. After you discuss this point, see if you need to add or subtract any items on your list of health and illness.

Related Cases

As the example of dyschromatic spirochetosis points out, when students discuss the concepts of health and illness it isn't long before they need to start examining related concepts like normality, natural body designs, or proper physical functioning. Thus, the purpose of using related cases in conceptual analysis is to discuss concepts which are similar, connected, or related to the concepts of health and illness.

The examples of a person with myopia or a person who is a paraplegic are good cases for beginning this dialogue. In both cases, students might be quick to agree there is present an improper functioning, an unnatural functioning, or an abnormal functioning, but slow to conclude that these individuals are unhealthy. As a result, students are led to question whether these criteria should be on their list of common feature for health or illness.

These examples also beg a discussion on whether a person can be physically abnormal, or have an improper physical functioning, yet at the same time be considered healthy. Students will want to say, for example, "Yes a physical limitation of improper functioning is present, but this does not mean these people are unhealthy." Try to pin point the criteria they use in arguing and justifying their positions and add or subtract these items to your lists.

Summary

At this point, you should have recorded on the board two lists of common features which your students developed in describing health and illness. The class, however, may still be unsure and confused about the concepts they have been discussing. Thus, the instructor must tie together the activity and offer a summary. In general, your summary should include the following three points.

First, you should note that a variety of views were offered, because health and illness are concepts which individuals define relative to their cultural values and presuppositions about these two concepts. Second, point out that ideas of health and illness usually group into three different themes or categories. The first theme centers on the idea that health and illness are opposites. The absence of one establishes the presence of the other, i.e. health is the absence of disease or illness. A second theme views health and illness in regard to how well an individual adapts, adjusts, of functions daily. For instance, an individual who can not carry out his or her daily tasks would be considered ill. On the other hand, an individual who functions well in life would be viewed as being healthy. Finally, a third popular way of viewing health and illness is simply by a person's own self-assessment. In this case, all that really counts is how an individual perceived his or her own level of health and illness.

Next, review your list on health and determine into which category the student's view of health falls. Then, move on to constructing a definition of health which evolves from the student's list of health criteria.

Finally, bring the discussion full circle. Go back to Henry James' quote and note that in defining health and illness, there are no absolute answers. The answers people create, however, are very real and greatly influence: (1) people's attitudes toward achieving health; (2) which professions are responsible for dealing with health; and (3) which patterns of dealing with health are appropriate concerns of the health professions. Thus, the challenge facing students of health is to develop answers to the perplexing conceptual questions about health and illness and argue why one is better than another. Challenge your students not to accept preconceived answers, but "...to dig deep into the actual and get something out of that - this doubtless is the right way to live."

Balog, J. E. (1981). The concept of health and the role of health education. *Journal of School Health, Sept.,* 461–464.

Balog, J. E. (1982). The concept of health and disease: A relativistic perspective. *Health Values: Achieving High Level Wellness, 6(5),* 7–13.

Balog, J. E. (1982). Conceptual questions in health education and philosophical inquiry. *Journal of School Health, 52(4),* 201–204.

Balog, J. E., J. H. Shirreffs, R. D. Gutierrez, & L. F. Balog (1985). Ethics and the field of health education. Eta Sigma Gamma, *Monograph Series, 4(1),* 63–110.

Mechanic, D. (1968). *Medical sociology: A selective view.* New York: The Free Press.

Temkin, O. (1977). *The double face of Janus: And other essays in the history of medicine.* Baltimore: The Johns Hopkins University Press.

Temkin, O. & L. C. Temkin, eds. (1967). *Ancient medicine: Selected papers of Ludwig Edelstein.* Baltimore: The Johns Hopkins University Press.

The Town Council Meeting: Decision Making Through a Large Group Role Play

James D. Brown

Health educators are often challenged to develop a strategy concerning a controversial issue that includes decision making, maximum participation, and a balance between information giving and discussion. Because the *Town Council Meeting* can be adapted to many group settings, many educators may enjoy an activity that provides detailed information, dramatizations, heated debates, judgments, and fun.

Directions

The specific directions for this activity are:

1. *Role assignments.* Establish the council meeting date and assign the various roles a few days in advance to allow for adequate preparation. The roles include: the mayor (1); council members (6–10); presenters for the pro side of the issue (4–6); presenters for the con side of the issue (4–6); media representatives (1–4); and concerned citizens (3–10). Choose the role players carefully. Usually it is best to use volunteers or individuals known to enjoy being in front. The presenters are the key to a successful program because their role demands effort and ingenuity. For example, they may want to "plant" a few concerned citizens. Since our local council meetings are televised, our role players recently had a wonderful time mimicking the mannerisms of our civic leaders.

2. *Information gathering.* The teacher can have most of the materials available and should allow a few days for students to gather additional resources. This could include interviews with civic leaders and the members of the council, surveys, visiting agencies, etc. All class members should take part in the information gathering.

3. *Choice of topic.* The most appropriate topics are controversial issues that are currently before our state and local governments. A review of your town council's agenda may find such issues. For example, our class chose an ordinance under consideration by the local council banning smoking in public buildings and public transportation. Other issues

could be: D.W.I. legislation, drinking age, flouridation, metal can ban, nuclear power, pollution controls, fire arms, seat belts, mandatory retirement for civic and school employees, and many others.

4. *Time frame and the council meeting agenda.* By taking class time to give the assignment carefully, hold strategy meetings, complete the council meeting and develop some appropriate follow-up activities approximately three full class meetings can be used. The council meeting needs an agenda and time schedule. A number of options can be equally effective. For example, the presenters could have each member make a timed presentation or elect one or two members to role play expert testimony. Time should also be set aside to have council members question the presenters and to have the concerned citizens respond. Once the testimony is completed the members of the council vote on the issue. Prior to submitting their news copy to the class the following day, the members of the media should interview the participants.

5. *Follow-up.* During the following meeting have the members of the media present their coverage of the proceedings. This could be in the form of a newspaper article or presented as a radio or TV spot. Follow the media presentation with a class discussion. Some of the key questions for the class discussion might include: (1) How accurate were the members of the media? (2) Who changed their position on the issue during the council meeting and why? (3) What were the major points developed on the pro and con sides of the issue? (4) For those who might be interested, what activities could group members take part in to support their side of the issue at the local or state levels?

The Teacher's Role

The teacher's role in any controversial issue is to guide, motivate, clarify, and help gather reliable sources. The teacher must remain unbiased; more specifically, the teacher's role encompasses the following services: to help define the problems, to evaluate student progress,

to help collect and analyze data, to guide students through the problem solving process, to ensure decision making, to develop follow-up activities, to ensure participation and to take a stand on the issue, if asked, after students have expressed their decisions.

James D. Brown is with the Department of Health and Physical Education, 20 Rothwell, University of Missouri, Columbia, Missouri 65211.

The Health Reporter Pool

David Wiley

Students, who are often viewed as "receptacles" in which to deposit health-related information, should be more actively involved in the learning process. A primary problem with mass-produced teacher guides and curriculum manuals in health education is that they tend to focus more on subject matter than on student participation. The field of health education, however, presents many opportunities to actively involve the student in the learning process. The goals of health education differ from other subjects, such as mathematics, geography, or history, where knowledge is factual and cumulative. In health education, knowledge should be combined with efforts to influence positive health attitudes, effective decision-making skills, and promotion of positive health behavior.

The Health Reporter Pool is an activity that can combine a variety of student-centered activities into a single lesson format. The central idea of the Health Reporter Pool activity is that a student is selected to role play a particular health-related "character." The choices for characters are limitless, for example, a bacterium, a carbohydrate, a drug abuser, a positive self-esteem, a good decision, or the human immunodeficiency virus (HIV). Based on class size, a number of other students are selected to be reporters "assigned" to cover a press conference, in the presence of the

David Wiley teaches at Southwest Texas State University, San Marcos, TX 78666.

class, with each health-related character.

Several days prior to the press conference, the character and the reporters conduct research to discover facts and other health-related issues pertaining to the character. Reporters must formulate relevant questions such as: "What is it like to be a bacterium?"; "What good do you do anyone?"; or "If you are supposed to help humans, why do you constantly have to be controlled?" The teacher can limit or expand the types and number of questions based on availability of time and resources.

An exchange between the reporters (R) and the character (C) might go as follows:

R1: "So tell me, what makes you, a bacterium, so important?"
C: "Well, I am very important in helping the body conduct a variety of functions."
R2: "Would you be so kind as to elaborate on two or three of these functions?"
C: "First of all, I assist the intestinal tract in the digestion of food. In addition, I can help ward off certain infectious organisms."
R3: "Please describe your relationship with antibiotic drugs."
C: "As you may be aware, I've never really enjoyed being around antibiotics, and I'll tell you why. . . ."

The Heath Reporter Pool can be used with a variety of grade levels (7-12) and diverse ability groups. In addition, this activity is structured with maximum flexibility to allow the teacher to fit it

into specific time frames and availability of resources. For example, the activity can be used as a 10-minute introduction to a new unit or as an entire class session on a particular topic. Also, the teacher can design questions for the participants to research or rely on the students to generate their own set of questions and responses. Most importantly, no special materials are needed for this activity, although students should be encouraged to use appropriate props to represent their specific character.

Advantages of using the Health Reporter Pool are numerous. First, it actively involves students in the learning process. Health class then becomes "something to do," rather than "something to attend." Students become involved in researching a particular subject for something besides a research paper or other written report. Second, topics that many students might consider boring (e.g., nutrition, infectious disease, personal health) can be made exciting and fun. In addition, controversial topics (e.g., AIDS, sexuality, substance abuse) can be approached from an impersonal perspective that could serve to reduce the inherent volatility of many of these issues. Third, the activity can be used with special populations. For example, classes comprised of a predominantly minority population can examine health care issues from the perspective of that particular group and even carry on the interview in a language other than English.

Fourth, the Health Reporter Pool can be used to integrate health with other content areas. As an example, the problem of AIDS can be examined from a sociological perspective, with the health educator and sociology teacher using the Pool to serve as an introductory activity in a coordinated effort to provide a focus on the topic. Thus the activity provides a medium to spread the health education curriculum across related content areas within a school. Fifth, students must learn beyond rote memorization and advance to higher level thinking and interaction skills. With the Health Reporter Pool, students learn to answer a range of questions focused on advancing discussion beyond basic facts.

Finally, students have the opportunity to develop public speaking skills. For many students, speaking before a group is a very uncomfortable experience. By structuring the activity carefully, the teacher can provide students with the opportunity to practice speaking in a controlled environment. For those students who speak comfortably in front of a group, the Pool provides an opportunity to ad lib and have fun creating an interesting interview.

The Health Reporter Pool idea has the potential for use in a variety of ways. Teachers have the discretion to use the activity in a strictly controlled manner or to allow students to construct their own interviewing activity. As this activity is used throughout the school year, the more comfortable and creative students can become in its use.

Its most important characteristic is that it directly involves students in the process of learning. The Health Reporter Pool provides teachers with a creative and challenging activity in which students may develop new skills while refining skills that already exist.

Health Education Supermarket

Mary S. Sutherland

This learning strategy is appropriate for a secondary health education classroom or a college personal and community health course. The strategy has been used successfully in selected health content areas such as mental health, drug education, family health, or diseases and is applicable to any health education content unit which uses value clarification and/or decision making techniques.

The participants are grouped as an imaginary family unit for a wellness shopping trip, where they can purchase items to attain a more healthful lifestyle. Family members might consist of a loving father and mother, each about forty-five years old. The parents are typical hardworking individuals, both employed full-time, who want the best for their family and desire to love as well as be loved. All family members are affectionate. Children may display the following characteristics:

A. A single eighteen-year old son, who displays a fondness for alcohol and a need to be loved.

B. A sixteen-year old daughter who is extremely popular with boys. However, her morals are suspect.

Each family unit member will then visit the health supermarket and purchase appropriate wellness items. The shopping aisles may be divided as follows:

Aisle one—Mental Health
Aisle two—Alcohol
Aisle three—Family Health
Aisle four—Venereal Disease
Five items from each aisle may be purchased by every family member, based upon family health needs. Upon completion of the shopping trip, each family unit member will share reasons for his or her selected purchases and how the purchases will help the family improve its level of wellness.

Following is a sample list of available items in each aisle. Only the items mentioned are to be purchased:

Aisle one items: (1) package of food, water, air; (2) package of sleep, dreams, and warmth; (3) mental illness candy; (4) shelter; (5) pill for self-love; (6) pill for parental love; (7) pill for sibling love; (8) pill for love of parents; (9) independence syrup; (10) person's favorite music; (11) changing values mix; (12) behavior; (13) happiness; (14) emotional snacks; (15) maturity.

Aisle two items: (1) religious drink; (2) social drink; (3) machine for changing drinking habits; (4) tape of teenage drinking habits; (5) reality-escaping drink; (6) excitement drink; (7) six pack of peer pressure drinks; (8) bottle of alcohol and driving attitudes; (9) pint of effects of alcohol; (10) gallon of alcohol and accidents; (11) a heavy drinker mix; (12) pill to become an alcoholic; (13) pamphlets on number of alcoholics in U.S.; (14) receipt from alcohol cost; (15) understanding; (16) helping hand.

Aisle three items: (1) societal pressure; (2) choice of schools; (3) communication package; (4) responsibility cans; (5) cultural mix; (6) bag of unity; (7) can of security; (8) jar of affection; (9) pound of family pride; (10) sale on ethics.

Aisle four items: (1) bag of truth; (2) penicillin tablets; (3) appointment for the doctors; (4) appointment to a public health clinic; (5) jar of symptoms; (6) ounce of fear; (7) package of ignorance; (8) a pill for courage to tell parents; (9) change of sex practice pill; (10) slice of its going away.

Mary S. Sutherland is at Florida State University, Department of Human Services and Studies, 215 Stone Building, Tallahassee, FL 32306.

Health Education to the Third Power (Cubed?)

Susan Cross Lipnickey

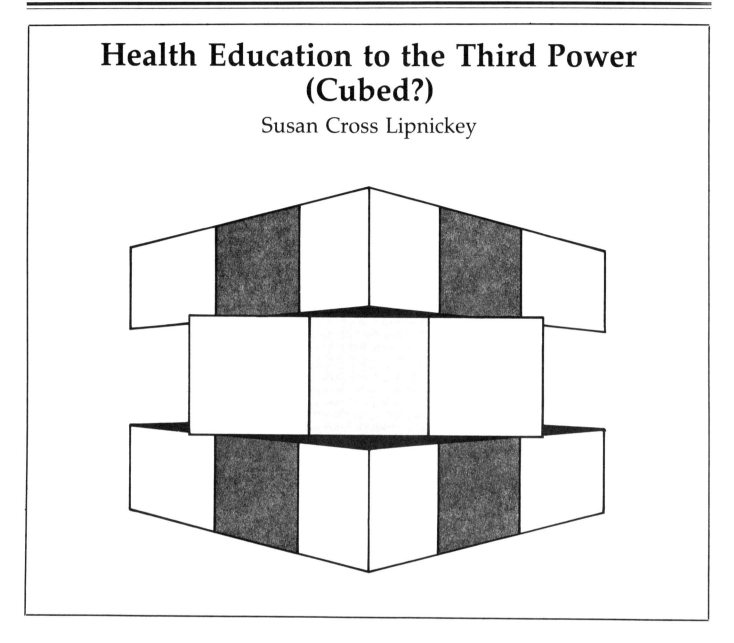

They seem to be everywhere. Grandparents have them. Parents have them. Children of all ages can be seen with them at school, at airports, in front of the television, and when they are supposed to be in bed sleeping. What is this ubiquitous object? Why, it is none other than Rubik's Cube (a trademark of Ideal Toy Corporation).

Rubik's Cube is a six-sided, six-colored manipulative object. Each side has nine smaller squares. The object is to get each side to contain nine squares of all one color so that there is one side which is all orange; one which is all green; and

Susan Cross Lipnickey is an instructor in Miami University's HPER Department, Oxford, Ohio.

so forth. This manipulative puzzle works beautifully to help explain the concept of school health education.

There are six 'sides' to school health education: for the learner there is the side of health knowledges, the side of health attitudes, and the side of health behaviors and practices; the health 'program' also has three sides, or facets. These are the healthy school environment, the health instruction which occurs within the school, and the school health services.

Health knowledges, in this case, refer to what the student actually knows, that is the skills or information she/he has gathered along the way: the long term benefits of frequent aerobic exercise; how to perform CPR; the advantages of

wearing a seatbelt; and the need for positive coping skills, to name a few. One could easily assign nine health knowledges to each of the nine squares on the health knowledges side of the 'cube.'

Health attitudes include how one feels about one's own health as well as how one feels toward the health knowledges she/he has gained and which are reflected in one's health practices. Does the student have the attitude that "it will never happen to me" and smoke cigarettes because she/he enjoys it now?

Health behaviors and practices are what one actually *does*. These practices may be positively or negatively influenced by the health knowledges and attitudes previously noted: brushing and flossing one's teeth in combination with regular dental check-ups; driving at a rate no greater than the speed limit; or asking for an explanation from the physician when one doesn't understand something. Each health behavior exhibited by the student could be assigned a block on the health behaviors/practices side of the 'cube.'

The healthy school environment, one of the three sides of the 'School Health Program' portion of Rubik's Cube is comprised of such 'blocks' as good lighting for the students; the opportunities for peer interaction within the school setting; and an adequate amount of time for physical exercise and eating, as well as intellectual stimulation and challenge. The health instruction side of the 'School Health Education' cube has blocks such as a field trip to a water purification plant; the viewing of health films or discussion of current events related to health; a guest speaker from an organization such as the American Heart Association; or the teacher delivering a lecture on a current health topic. School health services, the sixth side of our cube which is neither more nor less important than the preceding five sides, is composed of such blocks as vision and scoliosis screening; the treatment of health emergencies within the school setting; and the administration of tuberculin tests for faculty and staff members. There are numerous other examples which could occupy the blocks which comprise each of the six sides; the aforementioned are only a few.

School Health Education is more than the sum of these facets; it is the interrelation of these dimensions. When one of these six facets of school health education is incomplete, then at least one other dimension is affected. Just as is the case with Rubik's Cube, there is no way to have only one of the sides incomplete. At no one time can just one of the dimensions be incomplete due to the high degree of interrelatedness among them. What we as health educators must do is to realize and appreciate the fact that school health services are not only tied very closely to and are dependent upon health instruction and a healthy school environment, but they affect very closely and are dependent upon the health knowledges, attitudes, and actions of the learner. It is also important for us to understand that there is a reciprocal relationship with the learner affecting the program as much as the program affects the learner.

Going back to our Rubik's Cube of School Health Education, three of the sides may each consist solely of one color, but the side representing attitudes, the side representing behaviors (as affected by Tom's attitude that accidents only happen to others), and the side representing healthy school environment are a mixture of colors. It is quite possible then that only three, or half, of the sides are composed of blocks of all one color: health knowledges, health instruction and school health services.

On the other hand, positive relationships can exist between the learner and the program. The following illustrates just such a relationship with the facets of the program affecting the learner . . .

Julie is a fourth grader at Lane Elementary School. She, as with most fourth graders, was not an overly health conscious person. Two weeks ago, during recess, she fell and suffered a severe laceration of her lower left leg. The school nurse was able to stop the leg from bleeding, take the "sting" out of the wound, and reassure her that everything would be okay. She explained to Julie, while they were waiting for her mother to come, the importance of keeping the wound clean and giving it a chance to heal. The school nurse showed Julie how to change the dressing so she could explain it to her mother and help in the process. Her wound healed beautifully.

In this example there is primary interaction among five of the six facets . . . *Health Knowledges:* Julie learned how to change the dressing and why it was important to keep the laceration clean; *Health Attitudes:* we can assume she felt it was important because she followed the directions, resulting in the complete healing of the wound; *Health Behaviors:* Julie followed the advice of keeping it clean and changed the dressing to aid in the healing process; *School Health Services:* the school nurse was there to provide emergency treatment as was needed; *School Health Instruction:* the school nurse not only provided information in the form of why it was essential to keep the wound clean, but she also taught Julie the skill of changing a dressing. The only side of the cube not primarily involved in this illustration was that of the healthy school environment. The school health services and health instruction were responsible for influencing the knowledges, attitudes and behaviors of the learner; thus five of the six sides of our cube became one-colored sides and therefore so did the sixth.

Utilizing Rubik's Cube as a conceptual model for the School Health Education Program allows us to incorporate the dimensions of 'the learner' with the dimensions of 'the program.' Since neither can exist without the other, it is vital for us to combine the two in one model and not look at 'the learner' as an entity in and of itself, or 'the program' as divorced from 'the learner.' Health instruction directly affects the health knowledges of the learner—if something is not taught, the learner will not have the opportunity to learn it. If it is taught effectively, hopefully the student will have that knowledge to add on to as time goes on and new information is learned, as well as to draw upon when that particular body of knowledge provides relevant information. But the knowledge of the learner can be affected by the healthy school environment as well: if the room is too cold or too hot the student may be unable to concentrate and, therefore, miss essential concepts; if the classroom environment is one in which the student is frightened or intimidated by the teacher, how much knowledge will she/he gain? School health services, as demonstrated in the example of Julie the fourth grader, also has the potential to influence the learner's body of knowledge. Health attitudes and practices can also be influenced by the program—role models of health behavior, reinforcement of positive health practices by the teacher, and encouragement in acquiring positive health behaviors not previously demonstrated by the student.

In addition, the student can influence the three program parts—what the student knows or doesn't know may influence what is taught; the student's attitude may influence the rules for safety in the school; the student's practices may influence the type of school health services required. It should also be noted that the three segments within 'the program' portion affect each other and the same is true for the three segments which comprise 'the learner' segment. The model of Rubik's Cube also affords us the advantage of looking at each of the components within the learner as multidimensional. For example, knowledge is not just one item but encompasses a myriad of pieces of information and skills gathered from as many sources.

So, Rubik's Cube, the toy so popular among today's children of all ages, provides us with a unique approach to looking at School Health Education as a multidisciplinary and diverse entity.

Junior High School Students as Facilitators of Elementary School Health Education Carnivals

David K. Hosick and Parris R. Watts

During the early 1980s, Watts and Stinson (1981) began to advocate "health education carnivals" for elementary school students. These carnivals are similar to traditional health education fairs which have been popular for years (Daughtrey, 1976; Lafferty, Guyton & Pratt, 1976; McKenzie, Scheer & Williams, 1981). The most obvious similarity of the carnivals and fairs is that they both employ many of the same instructional strategies and materials. However, where a typical health fair includes screening tests, the health education carnival does not. The latter actually is comprised of a wide variety of health education activities, incorporated into a festive, carnival-like setting; hence, the reason for its name. Although health professionals still are involved in the carnivals, physicians, dentists and nurses replace their usual work apparel with costumes that are more appropriately related to the activity areas of which they are a part.

Watts and Stinson initially developed the health education carnival concept to expose undergraduate elementary education majors to the

Parris R. Watts is an associate professor of health education at the University of Missouri-Columbia, Columbia, MO 65211. David K. Hosick is the former eighth grade science and health teacher in the Phelps County Missouri School District. He currently is a ninth grade science and health instructor at Blue Springs Junior High School, Blue Springs, MO 64015.

natural learning patterns of children prior to a formal student teaching experience. From the beginning, objectives of the health education carnival have been the promotion of (1) personal interaction between the facilitators and children, (2) meaningful health education experiences for the children, (3) cooperative involvement among the facilitators as they plan and implement the activities, and (4) positive public relations within the school and throughout the community. The authors of this article simply have extended those expected outcomes into a new dimension by replacing the elementary education majors with junior high school students. In using junior high school students as facilitators of an elementary school health education carnival, all four of the previously stated objectives were achieved for the elementary students,

their school, and the community. Involvement of junior high school students in facilitative roles enabled them to better appreciate their own health within a context of a broader based experience. In addition, they were able to develop a sense of teamwork by joining together in a common cause. Also, the junior high school students were given a great deal of responsibility for providing a quality health education learning opportunity for elementary school students, and they felt much personal pride when their efforts were successful.

Organizing Junior High School Students as Facilitators

The carnival idea was presented to eighth grade students of the Phelps County Missouri School District as a

Photo: David Hosick

part of their junior high school science and health education course. Video tapes of other carnivals were shown and synopses of certain journal articles were distributed for review (Watts & Stinson, 1981; Petty & Pratt, 1982; Bays, 1986; Wolf, 1986). After students informally discussed the idea among themselves and considered it as a group, they decided to conduct the carnival. It should be noted that the health education carnival was not the only learning activity within the course. A health textbook was utilized and traditional health education class sessions were held throughout the semester. In preparation for the health education carnival, the class was divided into five different groups. After the groups were organized, each was given the opportunity to choose from among five health conceptual areas included in the carnival. Those instructional areas were (1) smoking, alcohol, and other drugs, (2) physical fitness, (3) nutrition, (4) dental health, and (5) first aid. Figure 1 outlines tasks completed by students and by the teacher of the course during the nine weeks devoted to preparation for and staging of the health education carnival event.

Overview of Activity Areas

Following are brief descriptions of the five conceptual areas included in the health education carnival.

Smoking, Alcohol, and Other Drugs — Employed a smoking machine to demonstrate the effects of cigarette smoke on the lungs along with the encouragement not to smoke. Brief descriptions of what happens within the human body when people drink alcohol or use other drugs. Playing of a smoking, alcohol and other drugs game which included basic questions about those substances, with emphasis placed on advantages of not using them. Distribution of coloring books, iron-on and stick-on patches and informational pamphlets pertaining to this activity area.

Physical Fitness — Display of a model of the human heart and identifying and explaining its various anatomical parts. Use of a stethoscope for students to listen to their heartbeats

and to participate in a physical activity and then listen to determine how much faster their hearts beat in response to exercise. Playing of a game which emphasized the sequence of blood flow through the chambers of the heart and reviewed how the heart works. Distribution of pamphlets and other resource materials on blood circulation and the benefits of maintaining physical fitness throughout the elementary school years and beyond.

Nutrition — Introduction of the four basic food groups and an explanation of the importance of each. Discussion of "junk foods" and provision of actual substitute foods for the children to eat selected from among the four basic food groups. Playing of a nutrition game wherein students reached into a sack of groceries and placed the food item withdrawn into its proper basic food group.

Dental Health — Presentation of a skit involving the elementary students themselves where they were introduced to dental caries and given a graham cracker to eat. Plaque revealed on their teeth and cleansed away by using carrot and celery sticks to demonstrate how foods can help clean

the teeth. Proper brushing of the teeth included in the skit, along with other dental hygiene practices.

First Aid — Introduction to the three degrees of burns and a demonstration on how to properly treat each. The correct way to bandage burn injuries in order to help relieve pain and prevent infection stressed. Printed resource materials dealing with burns distributed.

Conducting the Carnival

During the week of the health education carnival, regularly scheduled daily class periods for the eighth grade science and health course on Tuesday, Wednesday, and Friday were used for the carnival. On each of those days, the 56-minute scheduled class time was used to set up, conduct the carnival, and disassemble the activity areas. The first ten minutes of the class period were used to assemble and organize the five activity areas. Then on each day, a different class (second grade on Tuesday, third grade on Wednesday, and fourth Grade on Friday) participated in the carnival, held in the

Figure 1. Student Task Assignments and Teacher Checklist	
Weeks	**Student Task Assignments**
1–2	Develop the activity/conceptual area, including the selection of a carnival theme and send for and/or locally secure information and resource materials.
3–5	Organize information received and materials secured for use in the carnival activity areas.
6–7	Work on banners, posters, handouts, and costuming for the activity areas.
8	Complete all preparatory work and rehearse presentations to be made within each activity area during the carnival.
9	Conduct the health education carnival for the elementary school students.
Weeks	**Teacher Checklist**
1–3	Motivate the junior high school students and offer ideas which will, in turn, generate additional ones.
4	Start to promote the carnival among the administration, faculty, and staff of the school and keep students on task.
5	Secure volunteers from among school personnel to help publicize the carnival within the elementary school and throughout the community (to promote parental and family involvement) and continue to keep the students progressing in their work.
6–7	Encourage carnival facilitators (students) to finalize work on their activity areas.
8	Preside over the rehearsal sessions; select student facilitators to visit the elementary school classes to promote the carnival event, and make certain that media coverage is arranged.
9	Coordinate the efforts of the student facilitators during the carnival.

178

school gymnasium. Students in each class were divided into five separate groups and assigned to begin at a different learning center. They were then rotated through all five activity areas so that every student was exposed to each set of learning experiences.

All five groups of junior high school facilitators were given seven minutes to conduct their activity area session. The seven minute time period typically consisted of one minute to introduce to the conceptual material, two minutes of information sharing, two to three minutes of games or other hands-on activities for the children, and one minute to synthesize and conclude the learning experience. During the weeks of preparation for the carnival, the junior high school student facilitators where instructed to design the activity areas so that they would (1) be child-centered, (2) provide basic information at the proper grade level, and (3) promote learning and fun throughout the experience. All three goals were effectively achieved, best evidenced in the attentive behavior and enthusiastic response of the elementary school children.

After all groups had rotated through each station, plenty of time at the end of the class period remained for disassembly of activity areas and clearing out of the gymnasium. With everyone working together, there was no need for junior high school students to miss any additional class time outside the regularly assigned science and health class period.

Carnival Follow-Up

After the health education carnival was over, the primary author of this article, who also was instructor of the eighth grade health class, visited elementary school classes involved in the experience. He found students studying, completing the worksheets, and using the pamphlets and other printed resource materials provided for them during the carnival. Elementary school students clearly seemed to be more conscious of their health and expressed considerable interest in following good health habits they had learned during the carnival. Two ex-

amples of the lasting impact of the carnival on their lives were noted by the junior high school science and health teacher. Members of the third grade class confessed they had no idea that milk was so good for the body and they proclaimed that they would continue to drink more of it. Members of the second grade class organized a "Smoke Busters" club and promised to wear their "Don't Smoke " emblems to further demonstrate their commitment. The teacher observed that the second grade students remained true to their promise.

Additional follow-up was also done by teachers in each of the three classes involved in the health education carnival. During the next few class meetings, they processed the health related information and materials given to their students. Elementary school teachers expressed sincere appreciation for the outstanding, active learning opportunity made available to their students during the health education carnival. Teachers were surprised that the junior high school students could be so well organized, motivated, and capable of providing such a high quality learning experience for their students.

What was possibly even more amazing is that we never doubted for a moment that they could do it. Junior high school students are "naturals" as facilitators of elementary school health education carnivals. Give them the chance and you will be glad that you did!

Bays, C. T. (1986). The elementary school health fair: A process involving the whole school in health education. *Journal of School Health, 56,* 292–293.

Daughtrey, G. (1976). The Norfolk public schools health fair. *Health Education, 7(4),* 36–37.

Lafferty, J., Guyton, R. & Pratt, L. E. (1976). The University of Arkansas health fair as professional preparation. *Health Education, 7(4),* 24–25.

McKenzie, J. F., Scheer, J. & Williams, I. C. (1981). The health and safety fair: A cookbook approach. *Health Education, 12(1),* 27–29.

Petty, R. & Pratt C. (1983). Student staffed health fairs for older adults. *Health Education, 14(2),* 40–42.

Watts, P. R. & Stinson, W. J. (1981). The health education carnival: Giving the old health fair a face-lift. *Health Education, 12(6),* 23–25.

Wolf, Z. R. (1986). A health fair for school-age children presented by registered nurses. *Journal of School Health, 56,* 192–193.

Thinking and Writing
A Strategy for Teaching Positive Health Decision Making
Paul Villas

When an undesirable or unpleasant event occurs, people are often reminded that it did not have to happen. The advice is that if a different route were taken, the unpleasant occurrence would not have to come to fruition. A television commercial explains this concept perfectly by emphasizing a particular car's braking ability. The commercial promotes the notion that vehicles do not have to be crashed to prove they are safe—vehicles can be safe if you can stop them before they crash. The point is made that the best way to survive an accident is never to have one. This commercial's theme becomes the strategy for this teaching idea—something can be done before the point of no return is reached.

Criticism directed toward education today claims that students cannot think critically. Another area of concern is the inability of students to express themselves in writing. Thinking and writing skills can both be enhanced in health education courses by employing a time-line teaching activity, which allows students the opportunity to make positive health decisions at the same time.

The time-line teaching activity is designed with three goals in mind: promote writing skills, enhance critical thinking, and equip and direct students toward healthful decision making. The main objective is to help students understand the consequences of poor health decisions and realize that lack of awareness makes them select poor health choices. Writing and thinking skills are the tools used to achieve the main objective.

Paul Villas is with the Department of Health Science, New Mexico State University, Las Cruces, NM 88003.

The Activity

The assignment begins by providing each student a sheet of paper divided into four columns as shown in Figure 1 with an explanation of the meaning of each area.

Article or Event: This is the heart of the assignment. The students are asked to select a newspaper article, news story, or an event they are familiar with that had negative consequences because of poor health decision making. Examples such as suicide, vehicle accidents, teen pregnancy, anorexia nervosa, etc., could be used. From these articles or events, students creatively but realistically figure out why poor health decisions are made.

Trigger: Under this heading, the student speculates about what could have happened to trigger the particular event in the minutes, hours, or days preceding it. If the event deals with a suicide or attempted suicide, the trigger could have been an argument with parents or a breakup with a boyfriend/girlfriend. If the event was a car accident, the trigger might have been driving under the influence of alcohol in combination with lack of sleep.

History: This column enables the student to discuss situations or conditions that have taken place in a person's life that may make him/her prone to make certain decisions. Poor self-esteem or an inability to make any close friends in the formative years may program a person toward a destructive lifestyle.

Post Event: The lesson or lessons learned from the event go in this column. The lesson could apply both to those who survived or are the main players in the event as well as to those who knew or learned about it. It is important to understand that there are consequences resulting from poor health decisions. The teaching aim is to lead students to resolve not to repeat the events they are reporting on and learn that background information leading to poor health choices can be overcome to promote positive health behaviors.

Final Note

The writing assignment could be as intensive as a teacher desires. The assignment could be done on the sheet of paper provided, or that sheet could be used as a working paper for a more formal writing assignment. Hopefully, by providing opportunities for students to figure out why poor health decisions are made and to understand their consequences, they will not get themselves in the same predicament.

History (Days, Years)	Trigger (Days, Hours, Minutes)	Articles or Event	Post Event

Figure 1. Time-Line Teaching Form

Personal Health Via Community Health

Linda Olasov

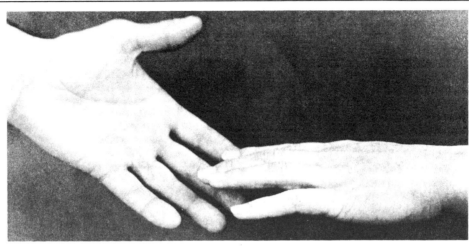

Traditionally, students in personal health classes at universities are asked to complete a variety of assignments. Among them, the most traditional of all is the term paper. Usually it is a two way communication between the student and teacher with few others sharing the information. However, it is possible for a teacher to offer an alternative to the formal term paper, to offer an opportunity to the student to interact in a community health facility through a sharing of information, different perspectives, and skills.

This new partnership between students in a health education class and a community mental health facility has great potential. It provides an opportunity for health students, some of whom may be in teacher education, to have contact with exceptional people and to teach individuals with emotional/behavioral disturbances. It is hoped that contact with these people will result in positive attitudes for health education students. And, the partnership could benefit the patients by infusing some stimulation through learning in an otherwise boring daily existence at a psychiatric facility.

The author, in preparation for this paper, could find no literature dealing directly with the use of mental health facilities or hospitals as placements for students in personal health classes or

Linda Olasov is an assistant professor of education in the Education Department, Northern Kentucky University, Highland Heights, KY 41076.

for any education students. This article will describe the field placement experience for four students in a personal health class who chose to work with exceptional students in a community mental health facility rather than to write a formal term paper.

In the Beginning

The basis for this program was established two years ago by a health educator at Northern Kentucky University who asked a clinical psychologist from Rollman Psychiatric Institute in Cincinnati, Ohio to speak to several classes about mental health. Several groups of students volunteered for a practicum at Rollman in which they helped with patient recreation.

Experience with those students provided incentive for the more ambitious program discussed in this paper. A social worker at Rollman suggested an academic program for patients, and this became the basis for the placement of students in a personal health class.

Objectives

From the viewpoint of the university, there were three objectives for this collaboration: (1) provide an additional preservice teaching option; (2) develop more constructive attitudes through direct contact with emotionally disturbed people; and (3) provide service to the community, one of the university's missions.

From the perspective of the hospital,

this project had four primary objectives: (1) help alleviate the boredom and inactivity which many patients experience in the hospital; (2) enhance the self-sufficiency of patients by teaching them practical skills; (3) provide an opportunity for interested, qualified patients to begin preparing for the General Educational Development (GED) examination while hospitalized, which could continue following discharge; and, (4) educate, through direct experience with a community mental health facility, people whose chosen profession will make them influential in the community regarding attitudes toward mental illness. Objective three was arranged through a second faculty member.

Information About the Hospital

Rollman Psychiatric Institute is a 146 bed state-funded psychiatric receiving hospital. It provides short-term acute care for adults between ages 18 to 65. The mean length of stay at the time of this project was 29 days. The majority of the patients have psychotic episodes and have been probated. Practically all are on psychotropic medication in the hospital for symptom relief. Most patients have a variety of serious behavioral, economic, educational, and interpersonal problems which have resulted in one or more previous hospitalizations. The problems are typically complex and multidetermined. In most cases the goal of hospitalization is to return the patient to the level of functioning he or she had in the community before hospitalization was required.

Arrangements

Four students from the personal health class volunteered for placement at Rollman. Patients were also volunteers and participated in the activities students offered. All students were at least at the junior level. Except for one who was not an education major, the others had previous classroom experience through the practicum component of their Introduction to Education course (120-135 hours).

Students were supervised both by faculty members at the university and by hospital staff. A psychologist served as program coordinator and liaison between the two institutions and was present for all sessions. All students were required to keep and submit to their teachers a written account of their reactions to each session.

Of the students in the personal health class, four out of 29 chose to make presentations to patients on a hospital ward in two sessions, one week apart. The alternative was to hand in a formal term paper. Three of these students were physical education majors with a minor in health education; the fourth was a business major.

Health Presentations

The students were able to choose any topic related to health and to present information about it. Length of the sessions varied in order to accommodate the needs of the presenter and patients. Of the four students who participated, two taught individually and two as a team. They scheduled their sessions with the psychologist about two weeks in advance. One week before they were to present, they submitted to their instructor a topic, bibliographical references, a brief outline of what they intended to do, and how they intended to do it.

The health students presented a total of six programs on a ward for men during a time when the patients were ordinarily restricted to the ward for shift change. Each program lasted from 30 to 90 minutes. No individual or team presented on consecutive weeks because of individual scheduling problems. The following topics listed by presenter were offered: (1) stretching exercises, basic first aid; (2) calisthenics, bandaging; and (3) starting conversations, comedy movie. The overlap of topics was not a problem due to a rapid patient turnover in the hospital, and presenters of the topic were different. There was, however, little sense of continuity or

development of topics because of scheduling problems and each health student presenting two programs unrelated to each other in content.

Student Reaction

Almost all the students expressed some degree of anxiety or fear about going to a psychiatric facility. However, by the end of their experience, all students reacted with positive comments, a sense of learning, growing, and self worth.

The following statements from journals kept by students express their responses to their experiences:

"I learned how lucky I am to have a family, job, and an education." "The experience was one-of-a-kind." "I learned what another side of the world is like." "I really liked it, and enjoyed myself." "Thanks for the opportunity you have given me to view a situation like this. It was a first for me, and I feel I have learned a lot." "Mental illness seemed spooky to me before. Since my visit to Rollman's, I can see that these people just need help, care, and understanding." "Being at Rollman's gave me a real feeling of self worth, that someone really needed me. My spirits were lifted greatly when the patients thanked me for coming to spend time with them and truly wanted me to return."

Evaluation of the Project

From the veiwpoints of both the university and the psychiatric hospital, the major objectives of this cooperative venture were acheived. Collaboration provided future teachers with an inside glimpse of a psychiatric facility. As a pilot project in a novel situation, it challenged their flexibility and creativity. Programs were seen as successful and worth continuing by all involved, including preservice teachers, university faculty, patients, and hospital staff. The programs given by personal health students reached many patients. The university instructor viewed the programs with Rollman as a viable method for providing students with contact with exceptional people and for providing a unique alternative to the traditional term paper.

Student journals reflected a change in attitude toward institutionalized psychiatric patients. Students generally became more confident in their interactions. All the students expressed enjoyment and learning as a result of their experience and urged continuance of this program as a future option for students.

A community mental health facility can provide a mutually beneficial expe-

rience both for patients who serve as students and for their tutors, the university students enrolled in health education courses. The program gives students an opportunity to practice teaching and gives patients an opportunity to participate actively, learn, broaden their experiences, and relieve the boredom of institutional life. The real world and the ivory tower can meet halfway.

Recommendations for Future Collaborations

Several suggestions can be made to those attempting to carry out programs such as that described above:

(1) An individual on the hospital staff must see the need for interaction with the university and be committed to expanding services to the patient population. There are many difficult logistics to work out, e.g., identification of appropriate patients, location, times, and availability of university students. University personnel cannot carry out such a program without inhouse commitment and assistance.

(2) A hospital staff member should be present or readily available at all sessions in order to alleviate student apprehension and to handle any emergencies.

(3) Preservice teachers should have prior classroom experiences. One participant without this prior experience had difficulty with his presentation and interaction with patients. Such students should only be involved if they could team teach with a more qualified student.

(4) All students should come to the hospital the first time with someone they know, someone who can provide feedback and support. Initial teaching could be a team effort; solo teaching could follow when indicated.

(5) Careful coordination and scheduling of topics is needed for students, providing only two sessions of instruction.

(6) Educational activities either at the university or the hospital which might alleviate anxiety and dissipate myths about psychiatric patients would be helpful. Ideally, opportunities for training students in interviewing and psychopathology, both approached from a practical "how to" point of view, could be made available. These subjects are quite relevant for student volunteers both in functioning at the psychiatric facility and in careers as classroom teachers.

Using College Students as Senior Peer Teachers in Youth-to-Youth Health Education

Anthony G. Adcock

A problem often encountered in college health strategy classes is how to make the learning meaningful to students. The conscientious instructor is often frustrated because time constraints limit student practical experience in the education process. One innovative way to develop an effective hands-on experience for prospective teachers is to have them serve as senior peer teachers in youth-to-youth peer teaching programs in the public schools. Considerable evidence exists that peer teaching programs are an effective way of providing health education (National Institutes of Health, 1980).

At Freed-Hardeman College the first peer teaching model was developed in 1981 (Adcock, Chambers, Wilson, 1981). It was prompted by local concern about the extent of smoking in the public schools. Several members of the school board made an effort to ban the use of all tobacco products on school property. One result of the publicity was recognition of the need to develop a program which would help prevent young people from developing the smoking habit. It was believed that a program which would train high school students to teach anti-smoking content to elementary age youth could be effective in achieving this goal. Cooperation of the school board, school principals, and health teachers was assured.

Procedure

Two outstanding students who were willing to work with the high school students were selected from the college strategies class. The college students held planning meetings with the district executive director of the Tennessee Division of the American Cancer Society who suggested printed materials which the Society provided. The students also

Anthony G. Adcock is an associate professor of health education at Troy State University, Troy, AL 36082

met with the high school principal and the health teachers to discuss the youth-to-youth anti-smoking program.

The high school health teachers selected 15 students to participate in the program. The bases for their selection were ability to be positive non-smoking role models and interest in the project. The high school students were in the tenth grade and were 15 or 16 years old. The sixth grade was selected as the focus for the program because few students were already regular smokers, but would soon be entering junior high school where peer pressure to smoke would likely increase.

The college students conducted four training sessions with the high school students. The length of the sessions ranged from 60 to 90 minutes. At the first session, the high school students were divided into five groups of three students each. The purpose and specific objectives of the program were identified. At the second session, specific topics and activities were assigned to each group. Each group was responsible for one presentation of approximately 45 minutes. The remaining sessions were used to develop and refine each presentation.

Films and printed materials from the

American Cancer Society were used by the student groups. The college students also developed materials, and several of the high school students had ideas for materials which were incorporated into the presentations.

Five sixth grade classrooms of students participated in the program, consisting of five presentations during a two-week period. Each group gave the same presentation each session, only to a different classroom of sixth graders. During the presentations, senior peer teachers observed the high school students as they taught and met with them afterwards to discuss the experience and to offer suggestions for future sessions.

In 1982 all students in the college health strategies class were required to participate in the youth-to-youth program. The program was organized in much the same way except that the college students were divided into five teams consisting of two members each. Each team worked with five high school students to develop one module in the program.

Since 1981, additional youth-to-youth teaching modules have been developed for drug abuse and for the prevention of drinking and driving. One year, the youth-to-youth program was included in a state grant for a community-wide drinking and driving program, and the college students were paid a small stipend for their work as senior peer teachers.

Summary

Several benefits accrue from the use of college students in a youth-to-youth teaching program. Undergraduate students who are planning to become health educators gain hands-on experience in program planning and in teaching high school students. Since the high school students immediately apply what they have learned, the college students can see the outcomes of their teaching in a short period of time. In addition, both the high school and the elementary students become enthusiastic about the program.

Senior peer teachers returning to the college classroom engage in mutual problem solving, and class meetings are times for sharing and helping. The college instructor serves as the resource person but otherwise is as much a student as everyone else in the classroom.

Experience has shown that a youth-to-youth program must be carefully planned to be effective. The program must be closely supervised by the college instructor, and adequate time must be given to preparation before presentations. Selection of the high school students is also important to the success of the program. They must be good role models who are self-confident enough to present information to a group of younger students.

Much effort is required to successfully conduct a youth-to-youth program using college students as senior peer teachers, but the interest and excitement it creates are well worth the effort.

Adcock, A. G., Chambers, V., & Wilson, J. (1981). A youth to youth smoking education program for sixth grade students. *Tennessee Journal of Health, Physical Education, and Recreation, 20*(1), 18-19.

National Institutes of Health. (1980, June). *Smoking programs for youth.* Washington, DC: US Public Health Service, NIH 80-2156.

Judgments Required from the Residency Coordinator

William N. Washington

The word *residency* is discussed here can be considered synonymous with field work, internship, and field training. Residency is a time when the student can practice the various processes and responsibilities of a vocation under the supervision of a professional in the field. Such opportunities are generally found in the curriculum of university professional schools such as public health, public administration, education, medicine, social work, and certain departments in other universities.

The *residency coordinator,* an employee, develops a communication link between the university and the community, locates residency sites, places students in residency, counsels students in respect to their residency experience, and in general coordinates all business relating to the residency program. The residency coordinator coordinates all

William N. Washington is an associate professor, the School of Applied Arts and Sciences, Department of Health Science, San Jose State University, San Jose, CA 95092

the activities resulting from the relationship between the university, the student, and the agency.

Residency coordinators may be asked to perform in a specialized or general area. For example, within the school of public health there could be several specialized areas such as health education, nutrition, health services administration, and population planning. In this specialized situation, a residency coordinator would relate only to one program, such as health education. A coordinator who functions as a generalist would relate to two or more specialized areas. A generalist may function as the coordinator for all programs on the professional level.

Functioning as a residency coordinator requires making many judgments that effect the relationship between the university, the student, and the agency in which the student is placed. The coordinator's judgment could affect the reputation of the professional school

and university as reflected by the community's perception of the quality of the university's staff, faculty, students, and programs. The value of the residency experience for the student and the accomplishment of an agency's objective by using a student are all affected by the coordinator's judgments.

The residency program may be conceptualized as having at least four components: (1) preplanning and program selection, (2) residency selection and placement, (3) residency experience, and (4) program evaluation. Preplanning and program selection include those procedures and activities necessary to obtain needed information from students, finding potential health-related agencies willing to act as preceptors, and selecting the appropriate type of program. Residency selection and placement involve using information pertinent to the particular experience desired by a student and then making arrangements for the student to work at an appropriate facility. Field work describes the actual job experience. Program evaluation analyzes all stages of the process relative to the successes, failures, and suggestions for improvement and consideration.

Judgments required from the residency coordinator are discussed in terms of the four conceptualized components of a residency program. Preplanning and program selection is discussed in reference to gathering information from students and making contacts with health agencies; residency selection and placement is discussed in relation to information given to students about agencies willing to act as preceptors; residency is discussed in relation to on-the-job experience; and program evaluation is related to those judgments necessary to determine whether the program meets its objectives.

Preplanning and Program Selection

Information from Students

As much relevant information as possible should be obtained from the student to help the coordinator choose which students should have residency experience. In professional schools, there is a good chance that some students have already had practical career experience equivalent to the responsibilities and tasks performed by graduates of the school, or equivalent to the responsibilities and tasks a student is expected to perform during a residency experience. Depending on the student's desire or financial status, the student may be working while attending school and, therefore may have difficulty fitting in a residency experience. In addition, the university's program may or may not require a residency experience for all its students. Taking all these situations into account, the coordinator must judge which students need a residency.

Students who enter a professional school have various backgrounds and experiences. They differ not only in work experience, but in academic preparation. Some students are interested in doing a residency soon after admission into the school. The coordinator must consider these factors and judge the appropriateness of residency for students. For example, the coordinator may want to ensure that the student will perform competently in the residency. To increase this potential assurance, the coordinator may require the student to complete certain academic courses and/or spend a certain time (for example, one year) in the academic pro-

gram before being considered for residency.

The coordinator counsels the student with respect to the best type of residency. This judgment could be made after reflecting upon the background and career interest of the student. For example, if a student interested in health education has had extensive community health education experiences and proved competent, the coordinator may recommend a residency experience in a hospital setting. This new setting should concentrate on skills that need development, such as skills in administration. Working in administration may provide a more detailed introduction to fiscal matters, personnel, and decision making relative to programs with which the student had no previous experience.

Contacts with Health Agencies

After the coordinator decides which agencies to contact, and after contact has been made, the coordinator must determine which agency is willing to take a student. The agency's willingness goes beyond its agreement to place a student. In this case, willingness infers a sincere desire to provide the students with learning experiences and environments in which they will be accepted and supported. In certain circumstances, an agreement to place a student does not include support and acceptance. The coordinator must judge the willingness of the agency, and make placement accordingly.

Competent Staff and Facilities

Students should be placed in agencies with good facilities and competent staff who have been adequately trained to do the expected quality and quantity of work. The agency staff should be more skilled than the student. Inadequate facilities may mean that the student would be unable to observe all the processes involved in his assignment from its beginning to completion. In such cases, some assignments may be attempted with insufficient input or tests, completed at another agency, or simply not completed.

Agencies are anxious to provide placement for students for a variety of reasons. Some agencies want students for cheap labor, status, or to do work none of the agency's staff wants. Many agencies, however, have positive reasons for wanting students. The coordinator must judge the reasons for placement agreement and the appropriateness of the experiences in relation to the university's program. The experience

must relate to program objectives. The placement decision should be based on what is best for the student, the university, and the agency.

What about the reputation of the agency? The coordinator should examine statements made about and beliefs held toward a potential preceptor and analyze all interactions with the agency to support or refute statements or beliefs. The reputation of an agency is important because the agency's reputation could be transferred to the professional school due to association alone, and association with a highly respected agency could help the community think highly of the professional school. Based on these considerations, the coordinator must make a judgment about the importance of an agency's reputation in residency placement.

The coordinator should establish standards that must be met by an agency being considered for preceptorship. These standards should be of quality that in no way compromises the general standard for excellence of the entire university. Of all the agencies indicating a willingness to act as preceptors, the coordinator should choose those that have met or have agreed to meet the requirements.

Inform Students About Agencies

Several decisions should be made before informing students about agencies willing to act as preceptors. The first is to determine which students to recommend to specific agencies by taking into consideration the experience wanted by each student and the additional types of agencies discussed by the coordinator and the student. The coordinator should give the student an opportunity to interview with any agency. However, the coordinator must also provide guidance to students concerning on which agency they should concentrate their energies, based on interests, background, and abilities. For example, some students may be interested in working at a particular agency because of its prestige, rumors from other students and friends, permanent employment opportunity, and/or staff composition, but they may give little thought to whether the agency can provide the necessary experience. The coordinator should work with the students to clarify potential positive and negative consequences.

The number of students available for placement varies from year to year and from semester to semester. The coordinator should try to have more placement site opportunities than students to ensure placement for all. If the coordinator has the philosophy that each student should have interviews with several agencies and that each agency should be given the opportunity to interview several students for each position, the coordinator should decide how many interviews each student should have and which students should be sent for interviews. To deal with this problem, the coordinator could contact the agencies, tell them how many students are available for interviews, and ask how many students each agency would like to interview. The coordinator can then check the files to determine which students are interested in the position available at each agency. Without showing favoritism, the coordinator should inform all interested students about available positions and, using the first-come, first-served method, refer the predetermined number of students to agencies for interviews. The first-come, first-served rule might be relinquished if, after several interviews, the same students are consistently first and, as a result, obtain an excessive number of interviews. An attempt should be made to achieve a good balance in number of interviews.

Sometimes after several interviews, several students may be selected for placement by more than one agency, and several may be selected by none. A student who has been selected by more than one agency should not be scheduled for additional interviews. If more than one agency wants a particular student, this student should be asked to choose an agency. The coordinator

should continue to arrange interviews for those students who have not been selected. If, after several unsuccessful interviews, a student seems discouraged and disappointed, the coordinator should offer counseling, encouragement, and special attention by arranging an interview after establishing that the student has an excellent opportunity to be selected by that agency. The potential for this student to be selected could be increased through the absence of competition; i.e., the coordinator would send only this student to the agency for an interview.

In order the selection process to operate smoothly, no student should go to an agency for an interview without prior approval by the coordinator.

Residency Experience

In most cases, the residency experience is an unfamiliar situation for students. They are in a new relationship with the residency coordinator and their agencies. The coordinator will need to use keen senses to judge whether a student is having a successful residency and should maintain constant communication with the student to determine whether the student is doing those tasks agreed upon by the preceptor and coordinator. All key actors will be aware of changes in the program they maintain good communication.

The coordinator should ask the student directly whether the residency is successful. The answer, whether yes or no, should be followed by an explanation. In addition, the coordinator should look for both verbal and nonverbal messages. For example, students may say one thing but mean another or say little or nothing about their experience. To understand nonverbal messages the coordinator should obtain additional information about the work situation from the preceptor or other persons with whom the student works. An indepth, personal, and private discussion with the student may disclose the true success of the residency.

If a problem exists, the coordinator should first determine whether it relates to tasks being performed, interactions with the preceptor, interactions with other employees, or a combination of these. Then, the coordinator must solve the problem. One possible solution would be counseling the student and/or the preceptor. Another solution would be to transfer the student to another department within the same agency or transfer the student to a new agency. If the problem relates to the task, the

coordinator could provide some technical assistance or recommend assistance resources. If the problem relates to the interaction between the student and preceptor, the coordinator should act as an intermediary. If neither solution works, the student should be transferred based on the desire of the student and/or the preceptor.

Evaluation

To determine the success of a program it must be evaluated. The degree of evaluation will depend on the evaluation technique's sophistication with success determined on the basis of evaluations from the student and preceptor. The coordinator should make a comparative analysis of both evaluations, whether such evaluations are open-ended, objective, or a combination. The preceptor's evaluation should be compared to the student's to determine the similarities and disparities. By comparative analysis the coordinator can determine the validity and significance of evaluation. For example, if both student and preceptor are given guidelines for writing an open-ended evaluation, but the coordinator receives and this was followed inappropriate and misrepresentative evaluations, questions would exist about the evaluation's validity or significance.

From the evaluations should come several recommendations for changes and new ideas for consideration. Students may suggest (1) courses or work experience that should act as prerequisites to the residency, (2) no future placement at that agency, (3) no future placement under a particular supervisor, or (4) continuation of the past method of selection and placement. The preceptor may also give ideas to use in future placement selection. The coordinator must decide which suggestions should be used in the future to help the program continue to evolve into a better residency program.

187

A Community Resource Class Assignment

Ansa Ojanlatva, Ph.D.

Ansa Ojanlatva is coordinator of the Department of Health Science, Louisiana State University, School of HPERD, Baton Rouge, LA 70803.

Community Health Education classes may effectively be used to introduce students to development of tools for community action. An undergraduate seminar, Health Behavior and Community Health Education, at California State College/San Bernardino includes from four advisement areas: health administration and planning, environmental health and safety, health science generalist, and community health education. For many of them this is the first course on community health education, and for some of them it is the only such course in the present curriculum. The college is on a quarter system which—to some extent—limits the quantity of work to be accomplished at one time, and action programs to be completed by students will have to be reasonable. At the same time, the academic requirements of these students include more homework than normally found in many other institutions (1 unit of 5 or ½ of 2.5 units per quarter), providing ½ to 1 unit more credit per quarter. Therefore, out-of-class assignments are not only desirable but required. The setting is outstanding for health education process.

Often community activities require that individuals team up for action. Few of us can alone accomplish significant tasks demanding interaction with people. This concept is brought to the classroom, and the following is an assignment students have to complete as partial fulfillment of the above stated course.

The assignment itself has gone through many transformations in different types of classes, but it appears to work best here where its purpose is clear, where the time element is appropriate, and where the students are serious enough to complete a started project. After this experience, most students move on to fieldwork and may utilize the newly acquired materials.

During the first week of class, the students are given a syllabus, and along with it they are asked to think about a topic of major interest which eventually could be developed into a community resource. Approximately half of the students do truly come up with topics which are realistic possibilities for a project. These alternatives are listed on the black board during the following session, the instructor adds few, and some of the students suggest additional ones as a result of brainstorming. Two dozen or more suggestions may be listed.

Once all possibilities are discussed, each student is asked to make a commitment and to initial one of them. Two or more students are normally assigned to one project. The rest of the session is used to formulate conclusions of the project ahead. This translates to defining purpose, setting of goals and objectives, and finally division of tasks to be accomplished.

For about five weeks the students work on their assignments, consulting with the instructor when necessary. A report is prepared, it is shared in class, and evaluated by the peers (Form A) and the instructor. Since these projects are designed and completed by the students, the final outcome and format vary from one to another. However, some cover letter information is often shared and includes name, address and phone number(s) of the service(s), contact person(s), time(s) and day(s) of service(s), kinds of service(s) offered, fee(s), population(s) served, type of care (primary, secondary, tertiary), and whether the service can be reached by physically disabled clients.

Although the project is a reasonable task for most students, about one in 15 fails to comply with the requests. With the process of defining roles and assigning tasks, most of the difficulties are worked out early. It seems that the students failing to complete the project have personal problems which seriously interfere with school work.

Another difficulty seems to arise when business establishments are compared with each other. This may be due to the competitive nature of such establishments. Certain information simply will not be available for comparison purposes.

Many of the students in this location come back to school, because they want to do something different in their lives. Often these projects function as a mode to turn negative experiences into positive ones. Sometimes the activity works as a vehicle to learn something completely different from the defined goals and objectives of the assignment. And a few students have used the activity to either define future fieldwork experiences or to provide better tools for the existing ones. Some of the projects have been forwarded for use by the various community groups.

Examples of resources from the most recent classes include:

1. Child Abuse listing for San Bernardino and Riverside Counties;

2. Teenage Alcohol and Drug Abuse Services and Resources in San Bernardino County and Surrounding Metropolitan Areas; (These two re-

source guides were forwarded for use by an area school district.)

3. Veterans Resource Guide (VRG), Alcohol and Drug Abuse Program Services in San Bernardino County, California, 1982; (The guide was compiled by a veteran together with another interested student and it is available for counseling purposes.)

4. Counseling and Support Groups for Families with Terminally Ill Children;

5. ABC's/Alternative Birthing Centers Resource Listing for Southern California;

6. Guide to Ostomy Services, San Bernardino/Riverside Metropolitan Area;

7. Ulcerative Colitis: Alternatives to Surgery (including resources); and

8. Services to the Newly Blind.

Form A

Group activity _____

Consider the group as a whole. Each group had defined objectives related to the purpose of the project. In relationship to these objectives, please, evaluate the presentation you just heard:
5 excellent
4 good
3 fair
2 poor
1 not clear

1. How well did the group meet the stated objectives?
   _____ Comments

2. Based on the stated objectives and considering the time available for this presentation, did the group succeed in presenting enough of the existing problem and were the possible solutions discussed?
   _____ Comments

3. Was the presentation clear? (task division, methods, etc.)
   _____ Comments

4. Any comments about a particular group member?

Evaluating Health News

Michele J. Hawkins

Proliferation of health information in the popular press is increasing at dramatic levels (Broad, 1982; Culliton, 1987). Media sources that provide this health information also have proliferated. One needs only to pick up a newspaper or magazine to find that health receives heavy attention in today's press. Further, while the amount of health news grows, the content is ever changing. What is healthy today, may be found to be unhealthy tomorrow. Levin (1987) states the approximate half-life of a so-called health fact is four years. Hence, formal education can no longer teach health facts that will remain intact during the course of one's life span. Levin further states that changing information regarding health leads to substantial public confusion about what and who to believe, thus progressively diminishing effectiveness of health messages. Compounding the problem is the difficulty the lay person has in understanding the information being disseminated (Yeaton, Smith, & Rogers, 1990).

In response to this proliferation of health information, the public must be able to analyze the accuracy and relevance of information it receives. Being able to analyze this information is even more critical since the public gains most of its health information outside the context of formal education (Miller, Sliepcevich, & Vitello, 1981). Therefore, teaching skills used to analyze health messages critically becomes vital. The following teaching exercise is designed to teach these skills.

Michele J. Hawkins is with the University of Oregon, Department of School and Community Health, Eugene, OR 97403.

Purpose

The purpose of this educational method is to teach critical thinking skills for analyzing health news to high school and college students. In particular, students will be able to use criteria provided to critically evaluate news stories.

Overview of the Teaching Technique

Evaluating Health News takes two class periods (50 minutes each) to complete. The first class period consists of lecture information regarding guidelines used to evaluate the health news. The second class period is used to allow students to evaluate health articles.

On day one, photocopy news stories related to health (the local newspaper is often most relevant to students). On day two, give several magazines that contain health news to students. (Students enjoy analyzing a wide variety of magazines and tabloids. I recommend including several that have sensational stories, such as the *Enquirer*.)

The lecture covers the following points: (1) Discuss importance of analyzing health news today (see introduction and provide relevant examples). (2) Discuss importance of understanding basic research when evaluating health news. The following points may be pertinent:

- Health research involves testing (studies). Studies usually are done one at a time, providing educated guesses (hypotheses) about how living beings function. Since human beings are complex, one experiment or study rarely produces complete results; therefore,

many experiments or studies are needed to understand phenomena under study. When studies are reported in the news, we are presented with one piece of a puzzle. Only after several studies does a more complete picture begin to emerge.

- Research yields new knowledge, but uncovers new questions. When conflicting results occur, it often is because the study may be slightly different from those previously conducted, with a different population (men rather than women, teens rather than elderly).

- When examining health news, specific criteria should be considered.

On day two, provide several magazines and newspapers and have students evaluate articles in class in small groups. During the last 20 minutes of class, let students report on their findings.

Guidelines for Evaluating Health News

Credibility of the Source

Who is reporting the health information? Is it a publication known for printing sensational stories? Or is it a publication that must check its sources for accuracy? Who conducted the research? Was it a research group under auspices of a university or was it a private organization? Who paid for the study? Does the group have a "stake" in the findings, such as a drug company evaluating its own product?

Study Design

What type of study was done - test

tube, animals, humans? Test tube and animal studies usually are done at the beginning of research testing effects of something (drugs, exercise) on humans. While these studies yield important information, the test done with human beings yields the most information. How many subjects are in the study? This is important because many studies that make headlines have few people in the study. The larger the study, the stronger the findings.

What are the characteristics of subjects? Are they women, teens, elderly? One must be careful when generalizing results obtained from one group to another group. For instance, many studies of cholesterol involve men and women who do not know the levels of cholesterol that pose a threat for women. Was there a control group? Having a control group means that one group did not receive the treatment (drug, exercise, diet). At the end of the study, the group is examined to see how it differs from the group that received the experimental procedure. If the experimental group differs from the control group, the change may be attributed to the procedure.

How were subjects selected to be in the study? The strongest studies use a random sampling technique. A good example is using one's school. If you only asked students in one class questions regarding drug use, would you be able to generalize or say that this percentage of students in the

school uses drugs? To be able to generalize about the school, everyone in the school should have an equal chance of being selected to be in the study. Drawing names from a hat or taking every tenth name from an alphabetical listing are examples that approximate random selections.

Has the study been repeated? The more times the study is repeated with similar results, the stronger the findings.

Look for qualifying words such as "in animals" or "in some subjects." Are the results reported as facts or someone's opinions? Does the article include what needs to be examined in future research? What questions remain? Does the article suggest that people change their behavior because of these results?

Broad, W. G. (1982). Science Magazines: The second wave rolls in. *Science, 215,* 272-273.

Culliton, B. J. (1987). Science sections in U.S. newspapers increased dramatically in the past two years. *Science, 235,* p.429.

Levin, L. (1987). Every silver lining has a cloud: The limits of health promotion. *Social policy,* summer, 57-60.

Miller, A.E., Sliepcevich, E. M., & Vitello, E. M. (1981). Health-related articles in the six leading women's magazines: Content, coverage and readership profile. *Health Values, 5,* 257-264.

Yeaton, W. H., Smith, D., & Rogers, K. (1990). Evaluating understanding of popular press reports of health research. *Health Education Quarterly, 17*(2), 223-234.

The Classics of Epidemiology: A Critical Thinking Approach

Wesley E. Hawkins

In a recent article in the *New England Journal of Medicine*, Fraser (1987) suggests that the essential characteristics of a liberal arts education are "those fields that help free students from the limitations of prior beliefs and experiences and that teach important modes of thinking so as to prepare them to ask and answer new questions" (p. 309). Fraser further argues that epidemiology is an example of a discipline that should be—but rarely is—included in a liberal arts education:

Epidemiology has features that resemble those of the traditional liberal arts . . . it (epidemiology) emphasizes method rather than arcane knowledge and illustrates the approaches to problems and the kinds of thinking that a liberal education should cultivate: the scientific method, analogic thinking, deductive reasoning, problem-solving within constraints, and concern for aesthetic values. (p. 30)

Given the pedagogical promise of epidemiology in the liberal arts, it seems appropriate to suggest teaching methods that allow health educators to use the epidemiologic model. One such application is the Classic Studies Inquiry Simulation using actual data and simulating the actual

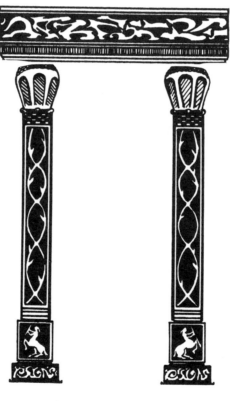

events of classic epidemiologic studies. This type of teaching strategy not only teaches specific skills in epidemiology but also captures the

excitement of reliving simulated historical events—a special brand of excitement incurred by solving the mystery of disease occurrence in populations.

Description of Method

Many aspects of epidemiology may be taught through the Classic Studies Inquiry Simulation. This technique will be demonstrated for teaching major research designs and major rates used in epidemiology. The Classic Studies and respective research designs and rates are illustrated in Table 1.

Objectives. The epidemiological content and general process/critical thinking objectives are: given actual data and historical simulation of events for selected Classic Studies, the learner will (1) select and apply the appropriate epidemiological research design, (2) apply and calculate major epidemiological rates for testing hypotheses, (3) determine information needed to test a hypothesis, (4) reorganize and synthesize data for testing a hypothesis, and (5) draw logical inferences and appro-

Wesley E. Hawkins is an assistant professor, School and Community Health, University of Oregon, Eugene, OR 97403.

Table 1. Classic Studies, Research Designs, and Rates		
Classic Studies	**Epidemiological Research Designs**	**Rates**
Toxic Shock Syndrome Study	Case-Control/Retrospective	Odds-Ratio
Framingham Heart Study	Longitudinal/Prospective	Relative Risk
Kingston/Newburg Fluoridation Study	Randomized Control Trials	Relative Risk/ Attributable Risk

priate conclusions after testing a hypothesis.

Teaching Sequence. This teaching strategy takes three to four class periods and involves three major steps: (1) A background lecture is conducted describing the major research designs and major rates used in epidemiology. Two class periods are required for this step. (2) In the next class session, the Classic Studies Inquiry Simulations (Figure 1) are presented to students in a worksheet or computer software format. The simulations include historical narrative describing the origin, events, and purpose of the Classic Study and actual data presented from the Classic Study with required student tasks that meet content and inquiry objectives of the lesson. (3) The final class session requires students to present inferences drawn after testing hypotheses based on data from the Classic Studies. Students then are required to present this information in an oral presentation and a class discussion format.

Conclusion

Educational techniques such as the Class Studies Inquiry Simulation are needed for teaching critical thinking skills. John Dewey's educational philosophy of emphasizing "how to think" rather than "what to think" seems even more relevant given the increased demands on individuals for critical thinking in our more complex information age.

Ast. D., & Schlesinger, E. (1956). The conclusion of a ten-year study of water fluoridation. *American Journal of Public Health, 46,* 265–271.

Centers for Disease Control. (1980). Annual summary 1980: Reported morbidity and mortality in the United States. *Morbidity and Mortality Weekly Report, 1977* (26), p. 293.

Dawber, T., Kannel, W., & Lyell, L. (1963). An approach to longitudinal studies in the community: The Framingham Study. *Annals of the New York Academy of Sciences, 107,* 593–599.

Fraser, D. (1987). Epidemiology as a liberal art. *New England Journal of Medicine, 316* (6), 309–314.

Figure 1. Classic Studies Inquiry Simulations.

Classic Study #1: Toxic Shock Syndrome Study (Centers for Disease Control, 1980)

Historical Narrative. In 1980, the Centers for Disease Control (CDC) had received reports from Wisconsin and Minnesota of women who had contracted a mysterious illness after the start of their menstrual period. The illness included symptoms such as confusion, aggression, and shock with very low systolic blood pressure. Physicians diagnosed this condition as an earlier identified children's disease: Toxic Shock Syndrome (TSS).

As reports increased, the CDC began to investigate TSS. Their first report on TSS identified 55 cases, 52 of whom were women. Soon afterward CDC researchers conducted a quick telephone survey in which they contacted 52 women who had suffered toxic shock syndrome and an equal number of their friends who had not. The women were questioned about their marital status, frequency of sexual intercourse, intercourse during menstruation, birth control practices, history of herpes or other vaginal infections, use of douches or sprays during menstruation, and use of tampons and sanitary napkins.

Student Simulation for TSS Study. You have been employed recently as an epidemiologist at CDC. You are asked to examine all the factors listed above to determine if any are related to TSS. None of the variables show any relationship except for the factor "use of tampons or sanitary napkins." Your data show that of the 52 women who had suffered Toxic Shock Syndrome, 40 had used tampons, while only 10 of the controls (friends who had not contracted Toxic Shock) had used tampons. What type of research design was conducted in the telephone survey? _____ Test the hypothesis that use of tampons is related to TSS by calculating relative odds or odds ratio. Show calculations of relative odds: _____. For your homework assignment for the next class period, be prepared to discuss inferences you have drawn from testing the effect of tampon use on TSS. Be prepared to discuss how large the odds ratio will have to be to say that tampon use has an effect on TSS.

Classic Study #2: The Framingham Heart Study (Dawber et al, 1963)

Historical Narrative. In the 1940s, there had been much speculation by health officials on the causes of heart disease. In 1948 the U.S. Public Health Service and researchers at the Harvard School of Public Health initiated a study in Framingham, Massachusetts to determine risk factors related to heart disease.

Student Simulation. The year is 1948 and you have been employed recently by the U.S. Public Health Service as an epidemiologist to study risk factors related to heart disease. Your task is to follow subjects from Framingham for a ten-year period and obtain annual measures of serum cholesterol (the variable you are studying) and heart disease. You are asked to compute relative and attributable risk for your 10-year findings that found the incidence for heart disease for males ages 30–49 with serum cholesterol levels above 260 mg% as 186 per 100,000 while for males with cholesterol levels below 190 mg percent the incidence was 50 per 100,000. Test the hypothesis that serum cholesterol is a risk factor for heart disease by calculating relative risk. Show calculations. _____ In addition, what type of research design did you just conduct? _____ For your homework assignment, be prepared to discuss inferences you have drawn from testing the hypothesis that serum cholesterol affects heart disease. Also be prepared to discuss the size of relative risk.

Classic Study #3: Kingston-Newburg Dental Fluoridation Study (Ast, 1956)

Historical Narrative. A classic two-community (Kingston and Newburg, New York) experimental trial was the study of water fluoridation designed by David Ast (Ast & Schlesinger, 1956), who first believed that fluoride had no effect on dental caries. Newburgh would serve as the experimental community (water supplemented with fluoride to 1.1 and 1.2 parts per million (ppm). The non-supplemented control community of Kingston would have its fluoride level unchanged at .1 ppm. The number of dental caries would be compared then to see if fluoride level had an effect.

Student Simulation. You are an epidemiologist assisting David Ast in this dental fluoridation study. You examine preliminary results and find that six to nine year-old children from the control community (Kingston) reported 23.1 decayed, missing, or filled (DMF) permanent teeth per 100 erupted permanent teeth while children from the experimental community (Newburg) exhibited 10 DMF teeth per 100 permanent teeth. Test the hypothesis that fluoride levels are related to tooth decay by calculating relative and attributable risk. Show calculations: _____. Next, what type of research design was employed in this study? For the next class session, be prepared to discuss the inferences you have drawn from testing the hypothesis that fluoride levels are linked to tooth decay. In addition, be prepared to discuss the size of relative risk.

Discipline: A Parenting Dilemma

Patrick K. Tow and Warren L. McNab

The philosophical continuum of parental discipline ranges from "child abuse" on one extreme to "passive acceptance of the child's unmanagable behavior" on the other. Repercussion to disciplinary actions are both positive and negative and affect both child and parental health.

Attempting to apply specific disciplinary measures to correct a child's unacceptable behavior can often be a matter of trial and error. For each couple experiencing parenthood, there will be frustration and aggravation as well as love and delight.

Parents admittedly make mistakes in their administration of discipline. Today the effectiveness of the traditional method of corporal punishment is much in doubt. It is through this method that children quickly learn "might means right." Since

Patrick K. Tow is associate professor of Health Education, Department of Health, Physical Education and Recreation, Old Dominion University, Norfolk, VA 23508. Warren L. McNab is associate professor of Health Education, School of Health, Physical Education, Recreation and Dance, University of Nevada, Las Vegas, Las Vegas, NV 89154.

there are seldom any academic classes addressing the problems of parenting, we are often left with past disciplinary experiences as our only legacy of such skills.

The selection of behavioral management techniques by a parent depends on the child's overt behavior which is interfering with parental rules or guidelines.

Behavioral management is basically a set of procedures that, when appropriately applied, usually decrease undesirable behavior and hopefully increase desirable behavior. These parental procedures require experience and practice to be successful. Punishment is defined as administering an aversive consequence or withdrawing positive reinforcement in order to reduce the possibility of the recurrence of a task or demonstration of a maladaptive behavior (Azrin & Holz, 1966).

Discipline is a state of order based upon rules and regulations. In its simplest terms, it is teaching people to follow specific rules.

There is a major difference between punishment and discipline, however. In punishment, pain follows an act that someone else disapproves of, and the

someone else usually provides the pain. With discipline, the pain is a natural and realistic consequence of a person's behavior. Unlike punishment, discipline is rarely arbitrary; it asks that a child evaluate his behavior and commit himself to a better course of action (Glasser, 1965).

Preventive behavioral management is the best approach to parenting. Management guidelines need to be established early and explained in detail, along with possible consequences as a result of violating these guidelines.

The importance of parent-child communication is paramount in the prevention-behavior management continuum. Being able to discuss fully problems, potential crises, and the providing of parental support, can perhaps reduce the probability of future behavioral problems.

Health problems pertaining to mental health, sexuality, mood modifiers, nutrition, and other related areas often center around a poor self-concept or self-esteem. If potential parents realize the importance of the development of their child's self-concept and facilitate open, two-way communication, discipline techniques will be more easily understood and tolerated.

The positive or negative development of the child depends on the parental attitudes, values, and discipline philosophy which many times emulates the positive or negative relationship they experienced with their own parents.

Glasser (1965) suggests parents take the following steps in addressing behavioral problems:

1. Ask the child if what he/she did was against your parental rules.
2. Ask the child to evaluate himself as to the reason behind his/her actions or behavior.
3. Collectively the parent(s) and child should devise a plan and commitment to do better.
4. As a parent, explain you will not accept anything but a change in behavior.
5. Otherwise, specific consequences of breaking the rules will be enforced.
In following these steps, parents should build on the positive strengths of their children, control emotions, and facilitate positive communication.

The Role of Health Education

Educational methodologies which allow parents or prospective parents hypothetically to recognize potential problem areas, establish guidelines in disciplining children, and practice the communication techniques which enhance the behavioral management procedure, certainly would be beneficial. Prospective parents are not prepared, nor do they realize what parental responsibilities encompass. Education for parenthood segments of health education courses should involve a variety of methodologies geared toward the prevention, management, and communication skills needed to cope with specific behavior problems.

In professional preparation programs, health educators should provide numerous methodologies to students involving disciplinary measures. Following is a procedure that has been successful in providing students in health education with parental behavioral management experience.

Step 1. Identify Discipline Alternatives

Chances are that students in your class have had first-hand experience with a variety of disciplinary measures employed by their own parents. Tap into this valuable resource at your disposal. Depend upon their past encounters to help shape the preliminary portion of the strategy by encouraging them to identify a list of these measures.

After the brainstorming session, carry out a class tally of the number of students having experience in each of the measures listed. This will help students realize there is a commonality, though no absolute uniformity, in discipline practices among parents. It also allows students the opportunity to see there are many different and perhaps more effective ways to handle disciplinary problems. This list usually includes the following disciplinary alternatives:
1. Corporal punishment (i.e., use of physical force).
2. Total loss of privileges (e.g., no TV, music, or parties).
3. Home detention (i.e, grounded at home for a period of time; room confinement).
4. Fines (i.e., suspension or reduced allowance; pay a penalty).
5. Assignment of extra household duties (i.e., additional chores on top of regular duties).
6. Verbal put-downs (i.e., belittle or scold).
7. Curbing of privileges (e.g., earlier curfew, restrictions).
8. Ignoring the problem (i.e., pay little or no attention to the child).
No doubt there are proponents and opponents to one or more of these disciplinary techniques. Part of this step requires students to provide advantages and disadvantages for each of the measures cited.

Step 2. Examine Potential Disciplinary Problems

After identifying specific disciplinary alternatives, the types of problems confronted by new parents over the years should be identified. After all, our society would like to believe its members designate appropriate "punishment" tailored to the nature of the "crime" committed. Presumably the same logic would apply to the disciplinary problems created by children in a family. This second step requires students to list problems frequently encountered at home for which disciplinary measures may be applied. Examples of some potential disciplinary problems would probably include:
1. Talking back or "sassing"
2. Excessive TV watching
3. Use of profanity
4. Staying out late without checking in
5. Lying
6. Shoplifting
7. Fighting with peers
8. Playing with matches
9. Crossing streets without adult supervision
10. Smoking cigarettes
11. Coming home drunk
12. Stealing money from parents
13. Crying or refusing to leave toy or candy section of store
14. Horseplay leading to property damage
15. Cheating at school
16. Accepting treats from strangers
17. Neglecting household chores
18. Looking through pornographic materials
19. Playing hooky from school
20. Running away from home
21. Eating snacks before meals
22. Drunk while driving
23. Crying or refusing to visit doctor's or dentist's office
24. Smoking marijuana
25. Repeat traffic law offender
26. Premarital pregnancy experienced by daughter or caused by son
27. Violation of curfew on weekday or weekend
28. Hitting the parent in anger
29. Hanging around with bad company
30. Failing academically at school
As one can easily surmise from this partial listing of disciplinary problems, some are major concerns while others do not need redress of any kind. Yet many parents have a way of misconstruing a wide assortment of concerns as being a personal matter deserving punitive action. One also sees that some concerns can be handled differently with a young child than with a teenager.

Step 3. Examine Specific Circumstances and Determine a Reasonable Course of Disciplinary Action

This step requires students in the class to be paired off in couples simulating two parents.

Ask the prospective parents to examine each of the situations listed and determine whether it truly constitutes a bonafide disciplinary problem. The parents are then to determine the proper disciplinary action, if any, to be applied to each of the problems listed earlier. It must be stressed to these pseudo-parents that concurrence should exist between them on the final decision. This exercise can also be done individually to symbolize the single parent family.

Step 4. Evaluation and Discussion of the Disciplinary Decision

The last step of this strategy involves convening the class to listen collectively to and discuss similar or different ways these prospective parents would handle such disciplinary problems in their own families. The opportunity to discuss the reasons for variations in approaching the same disciplinary problems should be provided.

Summary

The positive familial relationship can be an extremely rewarding and enjoyable experience. The key, perhaps, is understanding the magnitude of the responsibility of parenthood, the preparation of the predictable, and coping with the unpredictable behavioral management difficulties that one may encounter as a parent.

Even before anticipating a pregnancy, prospective parents should evaluate the needs and goals they hope to satisfy by having children. Every child should be a wanted child. In having children, parents should feel a sense of creative accomplishment in guiding and helping a child grow into a well-functioning adult. The parent is the most important teacher the child will ever have. Helping their children through behavior management in developing positive physical, mental, intellectual, and social adjustments in life can be a wonderfully rewarding experience for parents. Even the best parents make mistakes, but with proper knowledge, planning, and discipline experience, they can overcome many of the difficulties of child-rearing. Good parents will evaluate the discipline situation and respect the child as an individual, satisfy the psychological and behavioral needs of the child, and provide the child with emotional security, sympathy, and understanding.

In the majority of school systems, parenting and behavioral management skills are not included in the health curriculum. There is a definite need for cognitive and effective teachings regarding the behavioral management of children. The objective is to provide as many relevant and realistic experiences as possible to inform students, as potential parents, of the responsibilities in preparing for parenthood.

There is a need to dispel the unrealistic notion that as future parents they will rear perfectly obedient children. Disciplinary measures come in many forms—held in disdain by some and strongly endorsed by others. Effective experimental behavioral management techniques encourage effective parent-child communication skills through listening, critical thinking, and assertiveness.

Health programs which include parental discipline techniques can provide assistance to young people to prepare for parenthood, reduce certain predictable health problems, and hopefully enhance the overall health of the child and parent in the process.

Azrin, N. H., & Holz, O. C. (1966). Punishment, in W. K. Honig (ed). *Operant behavior areas of research and application*. New York: Appleton-Century-Crofts.

Glasser, W. (1965). *Reality therapy*. New York: Harper & Row.

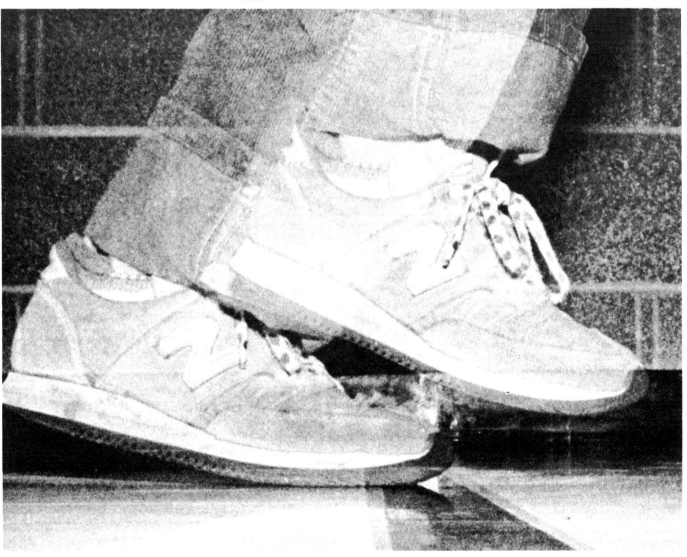

Counterbalancing Parental Concerns in Health Education

Lorraine G. Davis
Shirley Holder Hazlett

Across all parts of the United States, comprehensive health education programs have been implemented, developed, discussed, or at least considered. Because the primary purpose of school health education is to reinforce health attitudes and practices being taught in the home, full support from parents and community members is always a goal of health education coordinators and curriculum specialists.

Parental support is dynamic and ongoing; ways of obtaining the desired support should be considered. The following statements may serve to establish support for the school's role in assisting with the development or responsible health attitudes and behaviors in children.

1. The first five years of life are the most critical with regard to the development of proper attitudes and behaviors.

During the early years, the family unit serves as the basic reference group from which a child's attitudes and behaviors are formed (Glover, 1978, March). Parental love, warmth, and caring support are the foundation for future decision-making (Gordon, 1981, April). Early concepts become rather permanent. During these crucial development years, the public school has not yet entered into a position of influence.

Lorraine G. Davis is an associate professor of health in the Department of Health Education, University of Oregon, Eugene, OR 97403. Shirley Holder Hazlett is project director of the School Health Program, California State Department of Education, 721 Capitol Mall, 3rd Floor, Sacramento, CA 95814.

2. Families with established regular patterns of interactions have the highest rate of transfer of attitudes, values, and behaviors.

Familial beliefs are transferred to children through a process of imitation or modeling (Glover, 1978, March). As a result of verbal and nonverbal interactions, the child emulates attitude and behavior patterns of the parents (Liontos & Liontos, 1981, October 11). Parents who take an active role in communicating with their children are more effective in the transferring of traits. The criticism of a child's family practices is not under scrutiny. Rather, the important of familial interaction is emphasized as the primary determinant of character development.

3. The bond between parent and child is the strongest of bonds; it will survive—but the child needs freedom to explore new directions. Parents need to provide advice and support during this process.

Fortified with familiar guidance, the child must interact with society. He or she must exercise and expand the skill of responsible decision-making. Feelings of capability and self-worth must be carefully nurtured. Parents serve a primary role (Gordon, 1981, April) in this effort, but support makes the process complete. The reinforcement of self-esteem and personal worth provide consistency needed for the child's optimal moral and social development.

4. Neither reading about it nor wishing for it gives a person a skill; skills are acquired through practice.

The child learns responsible decision-making by practicing it at home and at school. Parents teach concepts such as honesty, fairness, and self-respect which are reinforced in the school setting. These concepts contribute to the development of a lifelong skill of responsible decision-

making (Musom, 1979, February). Decision-making must be learned, applied, and the results continuously evaluated. Health education has a goal to assist in the provision of such skills.

5. Telling a child about something does not guarantee participation. Not telling a child about something does not mean he/she won't participate.

If children are to become adults who make responsible decisions about areas such as drug usage and sexuality, they must be knowledgeable and informed. The *less* a young person knows about sex, the *earlier* he/she is likely to engage in sexual activity (Gordon, 1981, April). Adolescents informed about sexuality are more likely to *delay* sexual relations (Liontos, 1981).

Knowledge in and of itself, void of an understanding of consequences of application, is not enough. The information combined with an examination of short- and long-term consequences of behavior is crucial in the decision-making process. Responsible decision-making is included in comprehensive health education.

6. Individuals who feel good about themselves aren't as vulnerable for exploitation and are less likely to exploit others (Gordon, 1981, April).

Self-esteem provides an essential motivational component in responsible decision-making. Children who feel good about themselves are not as easily victimized as people who feel inferior. Women who have self-worth are more likely to resist sexual advances (Kirby & Alter, 1980, November) and less likely to promote undesirable situations. Individuals who are loved and know it are less likely to participate in behaviors solely as attention-getting mechanisms. The home and school can combine efforts to enhance necessary feelings of self-worth.

7. *Parents should charge the school with exposing children to the widest range of views possible, for their decisions will be made in an increasingly complex world. Ignorance will not make decisions simpler—only more dangerous.*

Tomorrow's adults must adapt to a world fraught with obsolescence of skills and continuous expansion and revision of information (Thomas, 1978, September). Children cannot merely be armed with nutrition facts of the '80s for the current "truths" may be revised in the '90s. Parents and schools must assist children in learning to assess accurately and cope constructively with change. Basic survival skills in an ever-changing society include the ability to continue to make responsible decisions in light of new insights.

8. *Education is aimed at teaching people how to think and decide, not what to think and decide.*

School health education enforces positive health behaviors developed early in life. Enhancement of a capacity for responsible moral reasoning rather than the inculcation of a specific set of values is the goal (Muson, 1979, February). The above considerations are neither rigid nor exhaustive. Their purpose is to maintain an avenue of communication between concerned parents and health educators. An understanding of the concepts the statements represent may help to alleviate some of the fears about the role of the school in preparing people for life, particularly in those areas sometimes thought to be in the sole educational domain of the home. The interchange of ideas related to these thoughts may facilitate support for health education and assist families and schools in preparing children for the future.

Glover, A. D. (1978, March). Modeling—a powerful change agent. *The Journal of School Health*, 48: 175–176.

Gordon, S. (1981, April). The case for a moral sex education in the schools. *The Journal of School Health*, 51: 214–218.

Liontos, L. B., & Liontos, D. (1981, October 11). Discussion helps ease sex education hangups. *Eugene Register-Guard*.

Muson, H. (1979, February). Moral thinking—can it be taught? *Psychology Today*, 12: 48–68, 92.

Kirby, D., & Alter, T. (1980, November). The experts rate important features and outcomes of sex education programs. *The Journal of School Health*, 50: 497–502.

Thomas, M. (1978, September). Back to basics—do we want to go? *The Journal of School Health*, 48: 446.

Incorporating Health Education Competencies Into a Content Course: The Disease Guidebook Project

Joanna Hayden

With competencies necessary for practice as a health educator identified (National Task Force, 1985), it is the responsibility of those in professional preparation programs to provide experiences for students that will enable them to acquire these skills. Courses focusing on program planning, teaching, or research methods, by their very nature, provide these experiences. However, even a course such as human disease, which is content heavy, can incorporate activities that encourage acquisition of competencies.

The Disease Guide Book is a project that incorporates health education competencies into a content course. Competencies addressed through this project include: utilization of computerized sources of health related information, matching an information need with an appropriate retrieval system, accessing principle online and other data based health information, and applying various processes in acquisition of resource materials (National Task Force, 1985).

The initial step in the Disease Guide Book Project is student selection of

Joanna Hayden is with William Paterson College in the Department of Health Sciences, Wayne, NJ 07470.

disease topics. All topics to be covered during the semester are written on individual pieces of paper, folded, and placed in a bag. Each student in turn picks a topic out of the bag. This process precludes more than one student from chosing the same topic. It also encourages student investigation of a disease entity that may not have been a personal choice.

The Disease Guide Book Project is divided into two parts, a traditional term paper and a guide sheet. The term paper includes an introduction to the disease topic or historical information, description of the population affected and those at risk, etiology, signs and symptoms, diagnosis, treatment, and prevention strategies, current research, community resources, and bibliography. Since it is difficult to locate textbooks that contain all the information, this limits, to some extent, use of textbooks and encourages investigation into periodic literature and various methods of data retrieval. Investigation of reference sources other than textbooks is encouraged further by requiring that references be current, no more than five years old.

To assist students in acquiring competencies needed for retrieval of current periodic literature, an introduction to library resources is scheduled. This class session is conducted in the library by a reference librarian. It includes instruction on the use of online databases as well as paper indexes and other health related resources. Use of indexes specific to the health professions is emphasized since students tend to use the more general indexes.

The second part of the Disease Guide Book Project is a guide sheet. This is a one to two page summary of some of the information presented in the term paper. The guide sheets eventually will be compiled to form the Disease Guide Book. The guide sheets include: definition of the topic, population at risk, etiology, signs and symptoms, diagnosis, treatment, risk factors, and community resources with addresses and telephone numbers (Figure 1). For consistency, the guide sheet is set up in the same manner by all students. It is required that students contact local, state, and national organizations and agencies related to their topic in order to request print materials. Obtaining materials in sufficient quantity for class distribution is encouraged, if materials are available available free of charge.

Parts I and II of the Disease Guide Book Project are submitted together to the instructor for grading. Part I is graded as a traditional term paper. Part II, the guide sheet, is corrected for errors and omissions and returned for rewrite. The rewritten guide sheet and the bibliography from the term paper then are returned to the instructor. The instructor, or a student volunteer, compiles the guide sheets alphabetically along with the bibliographies, numbers the pages, and prepares a table of contents. The Disease Guide Book is now ready to be copied in sufficient quantity for class distribution. Addition of a cover in a heavier gauge color paper gives a more finished appearance. Spiral binding is suggested.

Content and length of the Disease Guide Book will differ each semester based on the number of students in the class and topics chosen. The Disease Guide Book has ranged from as few as 28 pages covering 14 diseases to as many as 73 pages covering 35 diseases.

Since a substantial amount of time is needed to correct, rewrite, compile, and copy the completed Guide Book, initial submission of materials must take place at least six weeks prior to the end of the semester with deadlines strictly adhered to. It is the instructor's responsibility to correct the guide sheets quickly in order to allow sufficient time for rewriting and resubmission. A deadline in one week for resubmission of the guide sheet is sufficient. If students do not meet the deadline, their topics are omitted from the final Guide Book. Their grades for the project can be reflective of this.

Although the Disease Guide Book project requires ongoing involvement of the instructor, student feedback on its usefulness makes it worthwhile. Along with providing practice for data retrieval skills, this project requires students to summarize information, meet deadlines, and identify and request information from community resources. Students complete the human disease course not only having gained knowledge, but skills and a useful resource tool as well.

National Task Force on the Preparation and Practice of Health Educators. (1985). *A Framework for the Development of Competency-Based Curricula for Entry Level Health Educators*. New York: Author.

Figure 1. Influenza

Definition/Description

Influenza is a contagious respiratory disease.

Incidence/Population at Risk

The highest incidence is seen in children between the ages of 5 to 14. Adults over 65 years of age and those with chronic pulmonary and cardiac disease are more likely to be seriously affected.

Etiology

Influenza is caused by a variety of viral strains. It spreads through direct contact with infected person, or indicted contact through droplet infection.

Signs/Symptoms

Abrupt onset of fever, muscle pains, headache, cough, chills, and weakness.

Diagnosis

Diagnosis is made based on the presence of symptoms.

Treatment/Prevention

Bedrest, oral hydration, and non-aspirin analgesics are used to relieve discomfort.

Yearly vaccination is suggested to prevent infection in the following people:
—persons over 65 years of age
—persons with chronic pulmonary, cardiac disease, and or metabolic diseases; children and teenagers receiving continuous aspirin therapy; residents of chronic care facilities.

Community Resources

National Institute of Allergy and Infectious
    Diseases Office of Communications
Building 31, Room 7A32
Bethesda, Maryland 20892
(310) 496-5717

Centers for Disease Control
1600 Clifton Road
Atlanta, Georgia 30329
(404) 329-3311

American Lung Association—Local chapter

Politics and Health

Randall R. Cottrell

During Spring term, 1988, a course titled "Health Issues" was taught at the University of Cincinnati. A combination of both graduate and undergraduate students enrolled in the class which was scheduled to meet once a week for two and one half hours. Since it was a presidential election year and the Ohio primary would take place during the term, politics and health was one issue included in the course. A learning activity was developed to examine presidential candidates' positions on a variety of health issues. A description of that learning activity follows.

Initial objectives of the project were: (1) upon completion of the assignment, students would be able to explain each presidential candidate's position on selected health issues and (2) upon completion of the assignment, students would be able to discuss how politics impact health policies and decisions. Specific health issues examined were to be selected by students and answers were to be obtained via correspondence and/or phone conversations with each candidate's local or national campaign headquarters.

Procedures

On the first night of class, students were divided into groups of three and each group was randomly assigned a presidential candidate, one who was still in the primary race, to research. All groups were given addresses and

Randall R. Cottrell is an associate professor in Health and Nutrition Sciences at the University of Cincinnati, Cincinnati, OH 45221.

phone numbers for their candidate's local (if available) and national campaign headquarters. This information had been obtained by the instructor prior to class from the local chapter of The League of Women Voters. To identify health issues on which to question candidates, a modified nominal group process method was used and involved questioning students about what they considered to be the most important health issues of today. Votes were used to establish the ten highest priority issues. A description of this technique can be found in the book *Community Health Planning* (Green et al., 1980).

The process of identifying issues was in itself a valuable learning activity. Students were forced first to identify issues, then to prioritize them. In addition they were not only looking at issues from a health perspective, but also from a political perspective. Some of the issues identified involved AIDS funding, abortion, family planning, programs for the elderly, and access to health care.

All groups were told to obtain the most detailed information available regarding their candidate's position on each issue. Students were encouraged to start this project immediately and to be persistent since it might take several weeks and repeated attempts to obtain the information. To help keep students on task, the instructor obtained weekly verbal progress reports on efforts groups had made to obtain information and how successful they had been. Five weeks were allotted for information gathering — the minimum time period to use for this assignment. Even with the five week time frame, a

couple of students did not receive all the information needed until the day reports were due.

Student Reports and Information Processing

Each group was required to prepare and submit a written report of information obtained. In addition, they were required to submit a diary documenting efforts to obtain information for the project. The diary was to include copies of letters sent and responses received and all phone conversations documented with the name of the person contacted, date, and time. Further, each group was to present orally their findings to the entire class. Compiling, processing, and discussing the information gathered from oral presentations took one complete class period. The name of each candidate was placed across the top of the blackboard and issues were listed along the side. One issue was examined at a time with each group reporting their candidate's position on that issue. It was stressed that students were not to "campaign" for their assigned candidate, but just to report the facts. The class as a whole then evaluated each candidate's position on each issue and assigned one of four rankings. A " + " was assigned when it was decided that the candidate's position was favorable toward the health issue, a " − " was assigned if the candidate's position was not favorable toward the health issue, a "G" was assigned when the information available was so general that an evaluation could not be made, and a "?" was assigned when no information could be obtained regarding that candidate's position on the health issue in question.

Results

Overall, the ranking system revealed many more "G" and "?" ratings than "+" or "−" ratings. In general, most students were disappointed in the quality of the answers they were able to obtain and the amount of effort it took to get the information. Local campaign offices were able to supply literature, but staff members and volunteers were not able to answer specific questions. Calling national campaign headquarters revealed a general willingness to send literature, but once again little specific information regarding health issues. Two groups were told by national campaign headquarters to send the specific questions and they would respond in writing. In one case no response was received, and in the other case the same general campaign literature was sent a second time.

So in light of the quality of information obtained, was the learning ac-

tivity a failure? Absolutely not! This activity got students to examine the politics of health. During the discussion of presidential candidates, other important issues surfaced. Students realized that it is difficult to obtain specific information necessary to determine a candidate's position on important health issues. Some students questioned how we as Americans could be informed voters when we cannot obtain more than general platitudes from our political candidates. As a class we considered how important politics are to health issues, how politics can affect funding of health programs, and how health priorities can be altered with a change in administrations. We also discussed how politics plays a role in the hiring of health personnel from the federal level on down.

Recommendations

This activity was successful in getting students to critique the political process, to become more informed on the presidential candidate's positions

on a variety of issues (not necessarily health issues), and to examine the role of politics in health. The following recommendations are made with regard to future use of this activity:

- This activity was developed for use in a course designed primarily for health education majors, but it might also be of interest in basic personal, community, or public health classes.
- This activity should be tried with mature junior and senior level high school students. Since the activity has implications related to our political system, citizenship, and becoming an informed voter, the activity could be used as a joint health/political science project.
- The activity should be tried with other political campaigns. It might be easier to obtain information from candidates involved in local or regional races.

Green, L. W., Kreuter, M. W., Deeds, S. G., & Partridge, K. B. (1980). *Health education planning: a diagnostic approach*. Palo Alto, CA: Mayfield Publishing Company.

Focus on Content

Inoculating Students Against Using Smokeless Tobacco

Melody Powers Noland and Richard S. Riggs

Photo: *Jim Kirby*

According to a recent report by the Surgeon General of the United States, use of smokeless tobacco has increased dramatically over the past 10 years (Department of Health and Human Services, 1986). Researchers just now are beginning to investigate approaches that might be most effec-

Melody Powers Noland and Richard S. Riggs are associate professors of health education in the Health, Physical Education and Recreation Department at the University of Kentucky, Lexington, KY 40506-0219.

tive in preventing use of smokeless tobacco. A number of approaches, however, have been shown to be effective in prevention of smoking behaviors. Effective approaches include:

- Emphasis on immediate physiological effects (such as increased heart rate and blood pressure) (Evans et al., 1978)
- Use of peer models to deliver interventions (Evans et al., 1978; McAlister, Perry, & Maccoby, 1979; Hurd et al., 1980; Seffrin & Bailey, 1985)
- Solicitation of public commitment not to smoke (McAlister

et al., 1979; Seffrin & Bailey, 1985)
- Development of social skills needed to resist the temptation to begin smoking. This has been referred to as "inoculation," "immunization," and "resistance training" (Evans, 1984).

"Inoculation" has been used in smoking and alcohol prevention (Evans et al, 1978; McAlister et al., 1979; Hurd et al., 1980; Evans, 1984; Duryea, 1984.) This approach exposes young people to persuasive arguments or threatening messages to use alcohol or to smoke that they are likely to encounter in the future. By familiarizing students with the arguments before they actually hear them in life situations, students are better able to resist use of substances such as tobacco or alcohol. The name "inoculation" comes from the concept of inoculating individuals with "germs" (social pressure to use substances) in order to facilitate development of "antibodies" (skills for resisting pressure to adopt unhealthy behaviors) (McAlister et al., 1979).

A brief explanation of concepts involved in understanding the inoculation method may be necessary for students. Once the framework of the method has been learned, application to other content areas such as sexuality, consumer issues, nutrition, and other substance abuse areas is more efficient. Since the inoculation approach has been used effectively in smoking and alcohol use prevention, it is appealing that the same approach also might be effective when used with smokeless tobacco.

The subsequent teaching technique outlines a method which is intended to develop skills among junior and senior high school youth to resist pressure to use smokeless tobacco. This method would be introduced subsequent to class instruction on effects of smokeless and smoking tobacco. In this method, students are learning content of persuasive arguments, practicing refutations to persuasive arguments, and receiving feedback on responses. We recommend this method's use as a component of a more comprehensive program that incorporates other effective approaches previously discussed (i.e., emphasizing immediate physiological effects, peer models to deliver interventions, and solicitation of public commitments).

This method has been used successfully in a junior high school class by a peer educator that we trained. The peer educator received the method as detailed below, reviewed the method with us, and spent personal time reviewing materials. Evaluations of the method indicate that it was effective in meeting the lesson's objective. The classroom teacher or a trained peer educator can teach this method in one class session.

Student Objective

The student will deliver effective verbal counterarguments to specific peer statements that encourage use of smokeless tobacco.

Method

The teacher or a trained peer educator will divide the class into groups of four or five, making sure there are a few males in each group. Groups will be instructed to select one person in each group whom they will try hypothetically to talk into using smokeless tobacco. The person from each group is told what students remaining in the room will be doing, then asked to step outside in the hall. Small groups will brainstorm and write down eight to 10 comments they would make to the student to try to talk him into using smokeless tobacco. Those students who are out in the hall will be asked to return to the room and rejoin their groups. The groups then will proceed to try to talk their student into using smokeless tobacco.

Individuals within each group begin stating their persuasions for the student to try smokeless tobacco, then he or she responds to each comment. Allow this process to continue for a few minutes (approximately five to 10), then stop the activity. Ask someone from each group to read a persuasive argument used to persuade the student to try smokeless tobacco. The teacher or peer educator should write arguments on the board, then ask class members what they thought would be a good student response in refusing the smokeless tobacco. Students in class will not have difficulty identifying persuasions to use the smokeless tobacco since these will be similar to persuasions students probably have heard from others in real life experiences. Usually students will not have any difficulty in commenting on persuasions to try smokeless tobacco.

The most important part of the lesson focuses on responses to persuasions and not on the persuasions themselves. The teacher/peer educator should emphasize that criteria for an effective response

should be (1) that the response disputes the accuracy of the argument's main point or (2) whether the response indicates that the main point of the argument was irrelevant to the central issue. These criteria should be described to class members, then class members helped to select or devise effective responses for various persuasions they have used or heard used. Write at least six or seven of these on the board and include both the persuasion and a counterargument that meets at least one of the criteria identified above. If students have a notebook or take notes, ask them to write both the persuasive argument and the effective counterargument in their notes.

Figure 1 shows examples of possible persuasive arguments that peers might use to convince someone to use smokeless tobacco and suggestions for effective counterargument responses. There may be other equally effective counterarguments. Examples are offered as a beginning point for this instructional strategy.

Duryea, E. J. (1984). An application of inoculation theory to preventive alcohol education. *Health Education* 15(1), 4–7.

Evans, R. I. (1978). A social inoculation strategy to deter smoking in adolescents. In J. D. Matarazzo, J. A. Herd, N. E. Miller & S. H. Weiss, (Eds.), *Behavioral health: A handbook of health enhancement and disease prevention.* New York: John Wiley, 765–774.

Evans, R. I., Rozelle, R. M., Mittelmark, M. B., Hansen, W. B., Bane, A. L. & Havis, J. (1978). Determining the onset of smoking in children: Knowledge of immediate physiological effects and coping with peer pressure, media pressure and parent modeling. *Journal of Applied Social Psychology,* 8(2), 126–135.

Hurd, P. D., Johnson, C. A., Pechacek, T., Bast, L. P., Jacobs, D. R. & Luepker, R. V. (1980). Prevention of cigarette smoking in seventh grade students. *Journal of Behavioral Medicine,* 3(1), 15–28.

McAlister, A. L., Perry, C. & Maccoby, N. (1979). Adolescent smoking: Onset and prevention. *Pediatrics,* 63(4), 15–28.

National Institutes of Health. (1986). *The health consequences of using smokeless tobacco.* (DHHS Publication No. 86–2874). Bethesda, MD: U.S. Government Printing Office.

Seffrin, J. R. & Bailey, W. J. (1985). Approaches to adolescents smoking cessation and education. *Special services in the schools,* 1(3), 25–38.

Figure 1. Arguments and Counterarguments

Persuasion: "It's not as bad for you as smoking."
Response: It's really hard to compare smoking with the use of smokeless tobacco. Both products contain nicotine which is bad for your heart and both contain cancer-causing agents. Smokeless tobacco increases your risk for mouth cancer and cigarettes increase your risk for lung cancer. If you can get cancer from both products, neither one is safe.

Persuasion: "All the guys are doing it."
Response: That's not true. Only about 16 percent of males between the ages of 12 and 25 use smokeless tobacco.

Persuasion: "It's cool—it makes you look tough."
Response: I don't see anything tough or cool looking about having that dirty stuff all over your teeth. Tobacco has nothing to do with being cool. Anyway, if I have to do that to be cool, I would rather not be cool.

Persuasion: "All the coaches and athletes chew or dip."
Response: All coaches and athletes do not chew or dip. While coaches and athletes may use smokeless tobacco more than others, the majority of them do not use it.

Persuasion: "It doesn't smell bad like cigarette smoke."
Response: Maybe you need to smell your own breath to see how bad it smells.

Persuasion: "It gives you a buzz."
Response: From what I have heard, it does give you a buzz (high), but that doesn't last very long and then you find yourself wanting another buzz, so you use more tobacco. The result over time could be a drug dependency on tobacco. I'd rather be drug free.

Persuasion: "It helps you relax."
Response: Smokeless tobacco contains nicotine which is a stimulant. Stimulants speed up the heart rate and can increase your blood pressure. I don't call that relaxing.

Persuasion: "You are a chicken if you don't try it."
Response: I really would be a chicken if I tried it just because you told me to. I think it is smart not to use tobacco.

Persuasion: "Plenty of people have used it for years without having any problems."
Response: Not all people who use snuff or chewing tobacco have health problems, but using smokeless tobacco increases your chances for having a number of health problems such as mouth cancers and gum diseases. I'd rather not take a chance.

Persuasion: "My grandmother uses snuff. You mean you're afraid to use something that doesn't bother my grandmother."
Response: Just because your grandmother uses it doesn't make it safe or right. That was your grandmother's choice and not mine. I want to choose for myself and I choose not to try smokeless tobacco.

Persuasion: "Chewing and dipping are not habit-forming like smoking cigarettes."
Response: That's not true. Smokeless tobacco contains nicotine, and you can become dependent on nicotine. Just ask people who use tobacco regularly how hard it is to for them to stop.

Addiction

The 12 Puffs of Christmas

Warren McNab

Grade Level: 7-12

Time Frame: 30 minutes

Materials: Transparencies, overhead projector, and a marking pen

Preparation and Implementation: Cigarette smoking is the largest single preventable cause of illness and premature death in the United States. A smoker's risk of death is much greater because of the direct relationship smoking has to coronary disease, lung cancer, emphysema, and chronic bronchitis.

There are many mental, social, and physical reasons for not smoking. An important concept to emphasize to students is that they always have a choice as to whether to begin to smoke (or continue to smoke).

One creative method to help young people comprehend and remember previously identified reasons for not smoking is to combine these reasons with the melody of "The Twelve Days of Christmas" song. Upon completion of the unit on smoking, the class is broken into groups of five and instructed to brainstorm at least 12 reasons why people

---

Warren McNab is professor of health education, School of Health, Physical Education, and Recreation, University of Nevada, Las Vegas, NV 89154.

should not smoke. Students can use class notes and their textbook if they cannot recall enough mental, social, or physical reasons for not smoking.

The groups of students are then asked to combine these hazards/reasons with "The Twelve Days of Christmas" melody. The first sentence should begin, "On the first day of Christmas, my cigarettes gave to me"—followed by one of the reasons they identified for not smoking. The procedure is followed for the 12 days. Students can be creative and put the reasons in any order.

The fifth reason listed should be spelled out phonetically, to indicate this part of the song is emphasized differently and sung like "five golden rings" in the original song. Groups can also create their own title for their version.

Each group then puts its list on a transparency, which is eventually projected onto a screen. The class collectively sings the 12 reasons given in the songs the groups have written, or certain selected songs may be sung if time is limited.

An alternative to this method is to have the class brainstorm reasons not to smoke, and a recorder writes the reasons given on the board. Class members then select the 12 they would like to use as lyrics to "The Twelve Days of Christmas."

The following is an example of this completed task:

The Twelve Puffs of Christmas

On the first day of Christmas, my

cigarettes gave to me

A whole lot of agony

2nd day - Lots of stinky clothes

3rd day - Yellow teeth and fingers

4th day - Two lungs with cancer

5th day - Leu Ko Pla Kia

6th day - Ashtray-tasting kisses

7th day - Stressful nonstop air flights

8th day - Chronic emphysema

9th day - Coughing family members

19th day - Richer thoracic surgeons

11th day - Terminal carcinoma

12th day - Mourners singing softly

This activity provides an avenue to review material through group participation that emphasizes the negative aspects of smoking and reinforces the positive reasons one should not begin to smoke. Discussions on how to verbally say no to people offering cigarettes may follow this activity.

Drive-A-Teen—A Program to Prevent Drinking and Driving

Susan Willey Spalt

Drive-A-Teen would never have evolved had it not been for a group of dedicated and competent high school students who were willing to devote a great deal of time and energy to the program. Many of the student volunteers had lost close friends in alcohol-related accidents and were anxious to participate in a constructive way to solve a difficult problem. Many of them were extremely concerned about the extent of the drinking behavior in the teenage community, and they were very much aware of their impact on the younger students. Students also expressed concern about the polarization of friendships surrounding alcohol use and the prevalent attitude that drinking is an essential component of a good time. It is significant to note that there are some students who by age 16 or 17 have substantially modified their drinking behavior; for them, the years of early adolescence involved the heaviest alcohol use.

Drive-A-Teen activities are coordinated by three school faculty members who act as program advisors: a project director who coordinates all aspects of the program, a student activities coordinator who is responsible for developing and implementing student activities,

Susan Willey Spalt is health coordinator and Drive-A-Teen Project director, Chapel Hill—Carrboro City Schools, Chapel Hill, NC 27514.

and a high school guidance counselor who acts as a liaison between students and Drive-A-Teen staff. The faculty advisors have been impressed by the mature views of the students, yet concerned by the excessive nature of some of the alcohol related experiences they described. Students who all had had experiences related to alcohol, drinkers and nondrinkers alike, shared a concern for their community and a strong commitment to finding solutions to problems caused by alcohol.

Early student activities centered around launching the transportation

The problem of teenage drinking and driving is only partly reflected by available statistics, namely, that 60 percent of alcohol related highway fatalities are among young people. Alcohol-related accidents are responsible for serious injury and permanent disability. It is well known that teenagers are overrepresented in the number of arrests made for driving under the influence each year. The problem of teenage drinking and driving is exacerbated by their inexperience with both driving and drinking. The problem may also be measured by the anxiety felt by parents as they worry about their teens, waiting for that most dreaded of all phone calls. Drive-A-Teen grew out of a community's anguish following a number of tragic accidents and represents a community's determination not only to end such accidents but to foster responsible attitudes toward alcohol use.

Drive-A-Teen began with a simple

question. Could accidents be prevented if teenagers had an alternative way to get home from social events that they would trust and use? The answer to this question lead to the development of the Drive-A-Teen transportation service. The service involves the use of parents, who volunteer to drive students home when they are stranded, usually because of their own or their friends' drinking. Drive-A-Teen calls are fielded by the local crisis telephone hotline. The telephone counselors help the caller to assess the situation and to consider other transportation alternatives. If necessary, the counselor calls the Drive-A-Teen parent volunteer to relay information about the caller. The parents pick up the students and take them home. No names are ever used.

The transportation system works to prevent accidents in several ways. First, rides are offered to teens who are unsafe to drive or whose friends are unsafe to drive. Second, teenagers can say to each other, "If you don't let me drive, I'm going to call Drive-A-Teen." Third, the very existence of Drive-A-Teen has raised the consciousness of the entire community. Students often refrain from drinking before driving. Adult volunteers have become more aware of the problems involved. The message conveyed to students is that drinking and driving is such a serious problem that Drive-A-Teen is willing to do almost anything to prevent it. The service thus reinforces the existing alcohol education curriculum.

Students were involved in parent volunteer orientation sessions, they helped to develop the system by which Drive-A-Teen phone calls are fielded by the crisis phone service, and they spoke to their peers, personally and through the media. Most important, perhaps, they demonstrated by their interest and enthusiasm that the service was needed and that it would be used.

It was their efforts that provided the initial impetus for expanding the Drive-A-Teen program to address problems of teenage alcohol use in other ways. The need to keep the student body as a whole well informed about the service, coupled with the potential benefits of involving students more actively in the alcohol education program, encouraged the staff to initiate a pilot peer education program. The student peer educators participated in the training program which involved factual information about alcohol, decision-making skills, clarification of values pertaining to alcohol, elements of group facilitation, and a discussion of problem situations common to teenagers. While the scope and extent of the peer education program was limited by time and funds, it demonstrated the potential of peer education to augment both the transportation service and the existing alcohol education program. The students involved learned to better understand and discuss their own attitudes and problems

with alcohol. The experience of leading discussion groups with slightly younger students gave them a greater appreciation for the problems associated with alcohol, and they had the experience of helping to develop a new program in their community.

The interest Drive-A-Teen has generated in the community has sparked an expansion of activities into other areas related to alcohol use. A committee of student volunteers has organized to meet with community officials to develop recreation alternatives acceptable to both teenagers and parents. Students also plan to meet with representatives from the district attorney's office to discuss the feasibility of developing sentencing alternatives for young people arrested on alcohol-related charges.

The evaluation of Drive-A-Teen will reflect the diversity of its activities. The transportation service provided over 100 rides during its first year of operation. There is no way to accurately measure how many students avoided drinking before driving or encouraged their friends to avoid drinking before driving because of Drive-A-Teen; however, informal discussions with students, parents, and teachers suggest that students did in fact become more responsible regarding drinking and driving. The staff will continue to gather information concerning relevant attitudes and behavior through the use of question-

naires, interviews, and informal discussions. Parents and students will both be included. Records will also be kept for evaluation purposes on all Drive-A-Teen student committee functions. The peer education component will be assessed with pre- and posttests. This rather formidable task will be carried out with assistance from the Highway Safety Research Center, University of North Carolina at Chapel Hill.

Drive-A-Teen has brought together people of different ages, backgrounds, and interests to address the problem of drinking and driving. Drive-A-Teen began in a southeastern university town with a total population of about 50,000 and a secondary student population of 2,500. It seems likely, however, that this program could be adapted to fit many communities.

Any such programs must begin with students and with adults whom they trust. It is important to involve both the student "partiers" and the student "leaders." The need for parent volunteers is readily apparent. Parents must be willing to drive at odd hours with students whom they may or may not know. They must be committed to confidentiality, and they must be prepared for those times when the students may be taking advantage of the service. An already existing telephone service is probably necessary. The telephone counselors must be carefully informed about the purpose of the service, and they must be willing to help an often confused, sometimes scared young teenager figure out if he or she really needs Drive-A-Teen.

Drive-A-Teen probably would not have been effective without an already existing alcohol education program. Students had already been exposed to the problems surrounding alcohol use. The active support of community leaders is crucial. Sound and available legal advice is essential to provide legal parameters within which volunteers can function and to address questions as they arise.

It is gratifying to see many teenagers, so long considered only as part of the problem, becoming part of the solution as well. Teenagers and adults have found in Drive-A-Teen a forum where ideas and problems can be openly discussed. The problems of drinking and driving are not going to be solved easily or quickly, yet Drive-A-Teen has given the citizens of one community the opportunity to take joint responsibility for problems and to work toward a solution.

Analyzing Cigarette Smoke
David M. White and Linda H. Rudisill

The results of a ten year study (1975–1984) indicate a clear relationship between teenagers' perceptions of the harmfulness of cigarette smoking and their smoking behavior. As the percent of high school students who think cigarette smokers harm themselves (physically or in other ways) has increased from 26.8 percent to 64 percent, the percentage reporting daily use has decreased from 26.8 percent to 18.7 percent (U.S.D.H.H.S., 1985). This evidence supports what most health educators have believed for years—instruction about health risks of smoking is crucial, especially in the elementary and middle school grades.

The following describes a lesson about the health risks of smoking that has proven to be interesting and effective. This lesson places the student in the unusual position of analyzing tobacco smoke by "sampling" some of the ingredients separately. It not only emphasizes the health risks of smoking, but also encourages the student to be a more intelligent consumer by providing an experience in product analysis.

Teachers who enjoy using "props" should like this one. Though materials required may present some difficulty if they must be transported from room to room, they are easily assembled and critical to the impact of the instructional activity. Materials needed include the following: four balloons, a small glass jar of flour, a small glass of chocolate syrup (about one cup), and a small glass jar of clear syrup, such as Karo syrup.

The following is an example of a "script" of this lesson that has been used with junior high age students. The instructor should adjust the vocabulary for other age groups.

David M. White is an assistant professor of Health Education at East Carolina University, Greenville, NC 27858. Linda Harrill Rudisill is a teacher of health and physical education at Ashley Jr. High School in Gastonia, NC and adjunct-professor of health maintenance at Gardner-Webb College in Boiling Springs, NC.

Focus

How many of you have ever received products in the mail to sample, such as soap, shampoo, or toothpaste? The makers provide a small amount for us to try and then we decide if we want to purchase the product. Suppose we could sample one of these products by breaking it down and trying the main ingredients, that is, by analyzing it. (Teacher may want to discuss the meaning of *analyze*). We might know much more about a product if we could analyze it rather than simply trying a small sample. The purpose of this lesson is to help you analyze a product that is used by millions of people in the United States. Its popularity, however, has been declining for several years. (Emphasize here that it is important not to comment on what the product is until instruction is complete. Have students write the name of the product on a sheet of paper when they think they have guessed correctly.)

Teacher Input

I will *not* ask you to sample these items as I describe them. When I have completed the discussion, you can then decide if you want to try them. Remember, if you do not want to try it, your grade will *not* be affected.

Point to balloons

The product that we are analyzing is associated with over 500 gases and several thousand chemicals. Since I would have to go to a lot of trouble to bring you over 500 gases, I just brought two of them in balloons. This balloon contains some *carbon monoxide*. Joe, after I describe the other chemicals, would you please inhale the gas in this balloon? This gas is odorless, colorless, and, although this amount should not hurt you, this gas is deadly. When you use this product, your blood transports five to ten times more carbon monoxide than normal. This is because carbon monoxide binds to hemoglobin about 240 times more strongly than oxygen does.

Now, Joe, I know what you are thinking. Why should only a guy try this. Sue, I would like you to choose a balloon and try it, too. Remember, if you use the average amount of this product daily, you will lose six to eight percent of your body's oxygen carrying capacity.

Point to other balloons

I have put another of the gases from this product in these balloons. This gas is *hydrogen cyanide*. Hydrogen cyanide is a gas that has been used in the gas chamber. When you use the product we are analyzing the hydrogen cyanide paralyzes your cilia (teacher may need to explain the functions of the cilia here) for 20 to 30 seconds. Now, Carl, would you and Judy sample this ingredient by breathing the gas in these balloons? I'm fairly sure that the amount I have in here will not hurt you; however, remember that this gas paralyzes, or freezes, your cilia for 20 to 30 seconds each time you use the product.

Hold up the jar of flour

In this jar I have a little arsenic. Kathy, would you sample this for us later? I have clean spoons for both you and Tom. Arsenic is a silvery-white, tasteless, poisonous chemical used in making insecticides. It looks like flour and that is what it is mixed with in this jar. Arsenic is associated with the product we are analyzing.

Hold up glass jar (about one cup) of chocolate syrup

In this jar I have a brown sticky substance. If you use the average amount of the product we're analyzing, your body will collect about a cup of this brown, sticky substance a year. Tom, would you put your finger in this jar and then lick your finger? Susan, I know you will help Tom with this.

Refer students to jar of clear syrup

This substance is a poison. It can kill instantly in its pure form, but I have mixed it so that it will not kill you. It looks like clear syrup, so that is what it is mixed with. This poison is habit-forming. It speeds the heart rate an extra 15 to 25 beats per minute, or as many as 10,000 extra beats a day. Also, it constricts the blood vessels and quickens breathing. George, would you sample this for us? Remember, a one drop injection of this substance would cause death! Jean, you are so cooperative in class, and I think George would feel better if someone else were doing this. Another thing, when you use this product, this poison reaches your brain in only seven seconds. If it were not for this ingredient, people would probably not be interested in long term use of this product.

Now, are you all ready to sample a few of the ingredients in this product? Before you answer, I guess I should tell you more. (The following list of facts may be discussed or the teacher may want to add others and delete some from this list.)

● If you start using this product now and continue, you should expect to lose six and one half years of your life.

● If you use it a lot, your chances of dying between the ages of 25 and 65 are about twice as great as for those who do not use this product.

● Over 100,000 physicians have quit using this product.

● Before this day is over, approximately 4,500 young people will have tried or started using this product. By the time they graduate from high school, half the nation's teenagers will have used this product, 18 percent on a daily basis.

● About one and one half billion of these products are used by 54 million Americans for an average of about 27 each day. The substances in this product are the primary cause of 360,000 known deaths a year, an average of 1,000 deaths a day.

● Using this product is one of the largest self-inflicted risks a person can take. It is responsible for more premature deaths and disability than any other known agent.

● More people die from using this product than seven times our annual death toll from highway accidents.

● A pregnant woman who uses this product may be affecting the health of her unborn child. Comparing users with nonusers, users have a higher percentage of stillbirths, a greater number of spontaneous abortions and premature births, and more of the infants die a few weeks after birth. The child's long-term physical and intellectual development may be adversely affected.

● This product will stain your teeth, and users often have bad breath.

You might say, "Surely a person can stop using this product whenever he wants to." My reply is "not necessarily." Remember the habit-forming substance we mentioned. Withdrawal symptoms for using this drug often include tension, irritability, restlessness, depression, anxiety, difficulty in concentrating, overeating, constipation, diarrhea, insomnia, and an intense craving for the product.

A few things that I have not mentioned are:

● If you use this product, you are 1,000 percent more likely to die from lung cancer than those who do not use it.

● You are 500 percent more likely to die of chronic bronchitis and emphysema if you use it.

● Average users of this product are 70 percent more likely to die of coronary artery disease. They also tend to suffer from more respiratory infections, such as colds, than nonusers do.

● Finally, this product is so dangerous that four rotating warning labels are required by law to be on the package.

If you were sent this product in the mail to sample, would you be likely to try it? If you received a box in the mail and on the outside these facts were printed, would you try it?

Have students name the product.

End the lesson with a statement about the importance of making wise decisions which influence your life in positive ways. For example, the teacher might say, "*You* have the power to influence your future in vital ways. The choice is up to *you*. No one can keep you from smoking, and it definitely will affect your entire life, however short or long it may be. Why start and get hooked? But, if you want to smoke, go ahead, it's your life, but it's the only one you will ever get. The only safe cigarette is an unlit cigarette."

U.S. Dept. of Health and Human Services: *Use of Licit and Illicit Drugs by America's High School Students, 1975–1984* (1985). Washington, DC: U.S. Government Printing Office. U.S. Dept. of Health Human Services publication no. (ADM) 85-1394.

212

Addiction

Promoting a Natural High
Catherine J. Paskert

Ever since the mid-seventies when the National Institute on Drug Abuse reported that informational drug education programs were often ineffective in deterring youthful substance abuse, there has been a shift to more broad-based curricula. The evidence that cognitive approaches were sometimes counterproductive and may have influenced some youngsters to experiment with drugs signaled a need for change. Trial balloons were launched to find teaching methods better suited to drug education. Many educators responded by developing and trying different techniques, and the literature was soon flooded with ideas. None claimed to be magic bullets, but affective approaches and especially valuing activities were regarded as having a potential for influencing young people to adopt a drug free lifestyle. Consequently, drug education programs today are mostly multidimensional. Important cognitive features such as basic information about alcohol and drugs remain, but there is an overall greater emphasis on a wide variety of affective and experiential learning activities which aim to help students develop coping skills that have application to everyday living.

One of the most effective and enduring valuing strategies is the "Love List" or "Twenty Things That You Love To Do" (Simon, Howe and Kirschenbaum, 1972). This learning activity, "Feeling Good," is a variation of the "Love List" and is based on the theory that people have an innate need to temporarily alter consciousness or "get high" which they will satisfy chemically if they fail to achieve it in more natural ways, e.g., sports, movies, music, dance, travel, art. This activity also recognizes that drugs are used and abused for many reasons, but the desire to feel good or get high is what actually may be at the

Credit: Debbie Bissonnette (Prism)

Catherine J. Paskert is an associate professor in the Department of Health Professions at Montclair State College, Upper Montclair, NJ 07043.

root of drug taking (Weil, 1972; Weil and Rosen, 1983).

The purpose of "Feeling Good" is two-fold. It aims to demonstrate that alcohol and other drugs are used and abused for a variety of reasons and that the very pleasures which are often attributed to chemical highs can be achieved naturally; that is to say, through health-promoting activities. "Feeling Good" helps students arrive at the important conclusion that the pleasures which drug users associate with their chemicals of choice are also experienced by people engaged in legal or socially sanctioned activities. This is an appropriate activity for students in junior high school through college and also is suited for use with educators, parents, and community groups concerned with the prevention of youthful substance abuse.

Description

1. Ask students to list five or more of their favorite things to do. Make it clear that this is their private list and that they will not be required to share its contents.

2. Instruct students to match each activity on their list with an adjective that best describes their feelings during or after participating in the activity.

3. Compile a listing of adjectives on the chalkboard. To expedite the process and increase student involvement, ask several students to come to the chalkboard and alternate taking turns recording adjectives when volunteered by classmates. When all adjectives including their own have been noted on the chalkboard, instruct recorders to sit down.

4. Ask students if any activity on their list of favorite things to do is illegal or socially unacceptable. If so, ask if they will share only the word that is paired with the illegal activity and circle adjectives that are so identified.

5. Clarity at this point is especially important. The teacher might begin by saying, "these adjectives, with possibly a few exceptions (circled words) describe how you say you feel when engaged in your favorite socially acceptable activities. Think about this: do these words, including those circled, also describe how persons using drugs might possibly say they feel?" "Do some, most, or all of them apply?" "Could you elimi-

nate any of these adjectives?" *Note:* Some students will recognize that the pleasurable physical and psychological effects derived from participation in legal or socially sanctioned activities are not unlike the pleasure seeking effects often associated with substance abuse. The initial reaction of others may be that surely none or very few of the adjectives are related to drug use. When such variations in student responses occur, and they often do, it may be partly a function of experience. Tessler (1980) reports that there are important differences in the opinions of junior and senior high school drug users and nonusers about why kids use drugs. The *nonuser* groups in the Tessler study identified *peer pressure* and *escape* as important motivating factors, whereas the user groups discounted the influence of these and a third factor—experimentation. The majority of users (53.47 percent) claimed that "feeling good" was the principal reason for using drugs.

6. Continue by asking students why they think people do drugs. Ask them to identify reasons that are typically given to explain drug taking and list the responses on the chalkboard. Among the factors that will likely be suggested are: peer pressure, curiosity, availability, to escape, cope, rebel, and get high.

7. Conclude by discussing the idea that although people take drugs for a variety of reasons, getting high is a key factor, and for many this may be the most critical element. At this point a case can be made for getting turned on to something else that is fun but, unlike drugs, is neither physically nor psychologically damaging. Or, put another way, doesn't hurt so much and in so many ways, i.e., shattered personal relationships, poor grades, declining health, and possible drug charges. Most of the reported benefits of drug use can be achieved in more accepted and natural ways. Remind students that this was illustrated by the fact that virtually all the adjectives which they used to describe feelings associated with socially accepted activities were also descriptive of drug taking. Doing drugs is, demonstrably, not the only game in town.

Discussion

The groundwork for acceptance of recreational drug use was set in the 1960s at a time when drug taking was frequently a political statement. Drug use today is more casual. Among adolescents in particular it is often viewed in the same context as going to a movie or an athletic event, and its social acceptability at parties is widespread. Moreover, the problem is both complex and deeply rooted; young people continue to use and abuse drugs in unprecedented numbers.

Educational approaches that appeal to the thrill and glamour of life on a natural high, instead of scare tactics, can be effective vehicles for reaching young people at all levels of drug experience. Most student populations include some youths who are drug free and determined to keep it that way, many who are undecided, and others who will use/abuse drugs no matter what. This learning activity can provide important and much needed reinforcement for those who are drug free as well as those who are undecided, and could also be instructive to the drug users by sending the message that "feeling good" is not an exclusive feature of drug taking. All young people need to be reminded that, yes, there are alternatives to drinking and drugging, and these natural high alternatives appear to be gaining momentum. This is evidenced by the occasional media coverage of school community sponsored events such as mini-marathons which encourage student participation with slogans that exhort, "don't get high on drugs, get a natural high."

There is widespread agreement that getting turned on to themselves is the single most important high for young people today; it is prerequisite to a drug free lifestyle, one that is focused on achieving pleasure via natural rather than chemical means. The challenge is clear: we must convince them that "doing drugs" is neither the best nor the only ticket to "feeling good."

Simon, S. B., Howe, L. W. & Kirchenbaum, H. (1972). *Values clarification (a handbook for teachers and students)*. New York: Hart Publishing Company, Inc.

Tessler, D. J. (1980). *Drugs, kids and schools*. Santa Monica: Goodyear Publishing Company, Inc.

Weil, A. (1972). *The Natural Mind*. Boston: Houghton Mifflin.

Weil, A. & Rosen, W. (1983). *Chocolate to morphine: Understanding mind-active drugs*. Boston: Houghton Mifflin Company.

Addiction

Alcoholics Anonymous: The Utilization of Social Experience in the Classroom

Robert G. Yasko

Alcohol abuse is America's number one drug problem. Nearly 105 million Americans (18 years of age and older) are considered to be drinkers, i.e., they have had at least one drink of beverage alcohol during the past year (Carroll, 1985). Among American high school students, 93 percent have tried drinking, and 71 percent drink at least once a month (Schlaadt & Shannon, 1986). It is estimated that there are 3.3 million problem drinkers among youth in the 14–17 age range—19 percent of the 17 million of this age group (Hafen & Brog, 1983). Approximately 90 percent of college students report drinking during their academic career. Furthermore, it is conservatively estimated that there are at least 10 million alcoholics in the United States (Johnson, 1980).

For five decades, Alcoholics Anonymous (A.A.) has been working successfully for men and women from every kind of background. Virtually all persons in our society have been exposed to alcoholism in some form or other, and it has caused us great consternation and confusion. Alcoholism affects every aspect of society and it has been estimated that 36 million Americans are affected by living with the alcoholic or by having close contact with one (Maxwell, 1976). Beverage alcohol abuse leads to more problems for individuals, families, and society as a whole than any other drug in the United States.

The Objective of Alcoholics Anonymous as a Learning Experience

St. Pierre and Miller (1986) encourage awareness as a priceless educational tool for providing insights which trigger cognition and synthesis of information. Alcohol educators should not be lured

Robert G. Yasko is an instructor in health education at The Pennsylvania State University, McKeesport Campus, McKeesport, PA 15132.

away from including awareness-raising activities because of accountability of issues.

One of the most effective learning experiences is having students attend an "open" A.A. meeting after the factual knowledge of alcoholism has been presented—which must be the foundation of any prevention effort. This meeting is open to non-A.A. persons as well as members. These meetings are the most accessible and vary in format, but usually they are of the speaker type; generally a leader and two or three speakers who relate their stories—how it was with them, what happened, and how it is now (Maxwell, 1984). I have found that first-hand attendance at A.A. meetings accomplishes something a book can never do—awareness (by seeing, hearing, and listening) of what becoming alcoholic is like. Thus, the objective is not just understanding alcoholism, but awareness—which is an invaluable educational experience. Furthermore, A.A. is one of the most effective methods of attaining and maintaining sobriety and this program not only is helpful to the alcoholic, but can also be an excellent program for personality development of all persons, alcoholic or nonalcoholic, drinkers or nondrinkers (Twerski, 1984).

Implementation of Alcoholics Anonymous in the Classroom

Throughout the United States and Canada, A.A. is found in most towns and cities. A.A. can be located through the local telephone directory, newspaper office, police stations, hospitals, or by contacting local priests or ministers. At the beginning of the semester, students are provided with a course syllabus outlining evaluation procedures. During the same class period, the A.A. project assignment is given. The assignment is discussed in detail. Each student will submit a written critique of his or her experience two weeks prior to the end of the semester in order to allow

time for grading. A special case occurs when students cannot complete the A.A. project for reasons beyond their control. The instructor usually is willing to renegotiate the project with a different activity (e.g., article critique or film review).

The following guidelines are discussed in class prior to attending A.A.:

1. Students are permitted to go in small groups (two or three) with classmates, friends, or relatives.

2. Students are not permitted to take any classroom material (pencils, or papers).

3. If students attend an A.A. meeting in their local community, they should not be surprised to see someone there they know.

4. The A.A. meeting is approximately 60 minutes long.

5. Students may be asked by an A.A. member why they are in attendance. Their response should be: "My name is ―――――. I am a student at――― and was asked to observe an 'open' A.A. meeting for a health education class."

6. Students also should be prepared for a "cigarette smoke environment," although A.A. is beginning to hold nonsmoking meetings.

The instructor can add to the cognitive domain by asking questions that stimulate discussion in the affective domain. Affective instruction (which is based on the rationale that behavior is personal) can assist individuals to acknowledge control over and responsibility for their own behavior. As a result, attitudes about beverage alcohol are identified, discussed, modified, and conformed (Dennison et al., 1980). The instructor can utilize the following questions to stimulate discussion in the affective domain when the written critique is due in class:

1. What were your thoughts before attending the A.A. meeting?

2. What were your thoughts during the A.A. meeting?

3. What were your thoughts while leaving the A.A. meeting?

4. Does A.A. benefit our society?

5. Explain the basic nature and operational process of A.A.

6. Did you have any misconception of what becoming alcoholic was like?

7. How large was the A.A. meeting you attended?

8. Are there any differences between female and male alcoholics?

9. How do you now feel about drinking?

10. What is irresponsible and inappropriate beverage alcohol use?

11. What characterizes responsible and appropriate use of beverage alcohol?

12. Would you recommend the A.A. meeting as a learning experience for a future health class?

Conclusion

The author has utilized the A.A. experience not only at the college level, but with high school teachers, coaches, nurses, as well as with adults who enroll in a drug or alcohol awareness class. The open meetings of A.A. offer a wealth of data to the interested learner. This resource has been grossly under-utilized, and valuable as learning from a book may be, it cannot compare with the wisdom of experience. The feedback is overwhelmingly positive, and though this awareness experience is difficult to assess, the value and contribution it makes to student growth warrants its use.

Carroll, C.R. (1985). *Drugs in modern society.* Dubuque, IA: Wm. C. Brown Publishers, p. 5.

Dennison, D., Prevet, T., & Affleck, M. (1980). *Alcohol and behavior: An activated education approach.* St. Louis: C.V. Mosby, 77–78.

Hafen, B.Q. & Brog, M.J. (1983). *Alcohol,* (2nd ed.). St. Paul: West Publishing Co. p. 102.

Johnson, V. E. (1980). *I'll quit tomorrow: A practical guide to alcoholism treatment.* New York: Harper & Row Publishers, p. 1.

Maxwell, M.A. (1984). *The A.A. experience: A close-up view for professionals.* New York: McGraw-Hill Book Company, p. 9.

Maxwell, R. (1976). *The booze battle.* New York: Ballantine Books, p. 6.

Schlaadt, R.G. & Shannon, P.T. (1986). *Drugs of choice: Current perspectives on drug use* (2nd ed.). Englewood Cliffs, NJ: Prentice-Hall, Inc., 146–147.

St. Pierre, R. & Miller, D.N. (1985–86). Future directions for school based alcohol education. *Health Education, 16,*(6).

Twerski, A.J. (1984). *Self-discovery in recovery.* Center City, MN: Hazelden Educational Materials.

National Institute on Alcohol Abuse and Alcoholism

"Can A Bike Run On Beer"   *Addiction*

Melvin H. Ezell, Jr.

Each year approximately 50,000 people lose their lives on our nation's highways and at least 50 percent of these deaths involve a person under the influence of alcohol (*CPWT Report*, 1982). Such accidents are usually attributed to a combination of physical and behavioral impairments involving visual response and acuity, reaction time, concentration, and overall judgment (Edlin, 1982). Furthermore, as shown in Figure 1, the probability of being responsible for an automobile accident involving a fatality increases significantly as blood-alcohol concentration increases (Perrine, 1971).

Purpose

The purpose of the event, "Can A Bike Run On Beer," was to dramatically and objectively demonstrate the relationship between blood-alcohol concentration and the performance of a gross motor skill. The selected skill contained many of the same elements involved in driving an automobile. Therefore, the participants and spectators were encouraged to generalize the results which discouraged driving under the influence of alcohol.

Procedure

Eight male subjects, each a moderate to occasional drinker, were selected from the Corps of Cadets of The Citadel, The Military College of South Carolina, to participate in the demonstration. Each subject was required to read and sign an informed consent statement which described the nature and purpose of the demonstration and indicated that some risks of injury were present in the task.

The subjects were then randomly assigned to one of two groups: Group I "The Sippers," or Group II "The Chuggers." Each group was named for the

Melvin H. Ezell, Jr. is a professor in the Department of Physical Education, The Citadel, The Military College of South Carolina, Charleston, SC 29409.

manner of drinking employed. The subjects next selected a bicycle and were encouraged to practice riding through the test course. The test course itself was approximately two hundred yards in length laid out on a smooth grass surface, free of obstacles, and reasonably safe (Figure 2).

Once subjects felt comfortable with the task, they were required to traverse the course until each one attained baseline scores of at least ninety. Scores were determined by subtracting five points for each error, defined as touching either boundary line with the front wheel, from an arbitrary perfect score of one hundred.

Next, the subjects were served beer at the rate of three ounces per fifteen-minute interval for Group I and "as requested" for Group II. Breathalyzer tests were administered by members of the South Carolina Highway Patrol to all subjects at thirty minute intervals. Following the breathalyzer test each subject was again required to complete the bicycle course as previously described.

Results

Baseline scores established prior to the ingestion of beer indicated that all subjects could successfully complete the test course at or above the selected level of competency (ninety or above or not more than two errors).

Subsequent scores for subjects in Group I were all ninety or above while scores for subjects in Group II declined

as a function of increasing blood alcohol concentration. Final scores for the subjects in Group I were all one hundreds while those in Group II ranged from forty to sixty-five. Blood alcohol concentrations for Group I remained below 0.01 while subjects in Group II recorded blood alcohol concentrations of .12–.16. All subjects in Group II were, therefore, classified as legally "drunk" according to the laws of South Carolina.

Discussion

The results produced through the demonstration "Can A Bike Run On Beer" were expected and provided the dramatic, objective illustration of the relationship between blood alcohol concentration and the ability to perform a gross motor skill. Furthermore, participants and spectators readily generalized the results to the skill required to operate a motor vehicle. The generalization was encouraged by the presence of police officers, breathalyzer equipment, traffic accident displays, and brochures. Participants and spectators were asked numerous questions and made comments regarding the amount of alcohol they typically consumed followed by driving, swimming, and skiing. Through the demonstration, questions, and comments, it appeared to the writer and to others that a meaningful bit of education was taking place. The ultimate results of such education are speculative. However, if only one DUI was averted, the demonstration was worthwhile.

Recommendations

The following recommendations are offered to those who might wish to conduct a similar demonstration:

Establish a meaningful philosophy for conducting such a demonstration and secure administrative support.

Obtain assistance from local and state law enforcement agencies.

Publicize the event on campus and beyond to include appropriate high school and college groups. Notify newspaper publishers and TV stations, making certain that they are properly educated regarding the nature and purpose of a demonstration. This should be accomplished through a written statement prepared by those conducting the demonstration.

Select an area similar to the one previously described. Intramural athletic fields and football stadiums are most appropriate if adequate spectator areas are available.

Subjects should be "drinkers" and, of course, of legal age to consume alcoholic beverages. An informed consent statement should be read and signed by each subject and a witness.

Beers should be purchased by those conducting the demonstration and served to the subjects in cups. Avoid assistance from beer distributors.

Bicycles should be provided in a variety of sizes, all appropriate for riding on a grass surface.

Faculty and student assistance should be recruited to perform the following tasks:

Scorekeeper to record amount of beer consumed, blood-alcohol concentration, and task performance score.

"Barkeeps" (two) to serve beer to the subjects as instructed and to report such information to the scorekeeper.

Head referee to count the number of errors and report the score to the scorekeeper.

Assistant referees (four) to throw "flags," indicating errors, and reporting to the head referee.

Police officers (four) to operate breathalyzers and report results to the scorekeeper, explain procedures, provide displays, and literature.

Announcer to keep spectators informed regarding results as posted on the scoreboard as well as to provide occasional comments. (i.e. "reaction time worsens by 50 percent as BAC reaches 0.10").

"Can A Bike Run On Beer" was co-sponsored by The Citadel's Department of Physical Education and the Collegewide Committee on Alcohol Awareness. The writer wishes to express appreciation for assistance to Dr. Debbie Miller who conducted a similar demonstration at The College of Charleston.

Edlin, G. & Golanty, E. (1982). *Health and wellness.* Boston, MA. Science Books International, p.281.

Perrine, M. W., Waller, J. A. & Harris, L. S. (1971). Alcohol and highway safety: Behavioral and Medical Aspects. U.S. Department of Transportation.

Report from the Committee on Public Works and Transportation to the 97th Congress, 2nd Session (1982, Sept. 23). Report No. 97-867, p.7

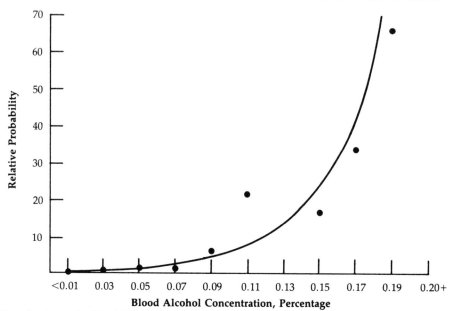

Figure 1. Relative Probability of Being Responsible for a Fatal Crash as a Function of Blood-alcohol Concentration.

(From Perrine et al., "Alcohol and Highway Safety: Behavioral and Medical Aspects." NHTSA Tech. Report, DOT HS-800-599, 1971.)

Figure 2. Bicycle Test Course
(Eleven inches × approximately two hundred yards)

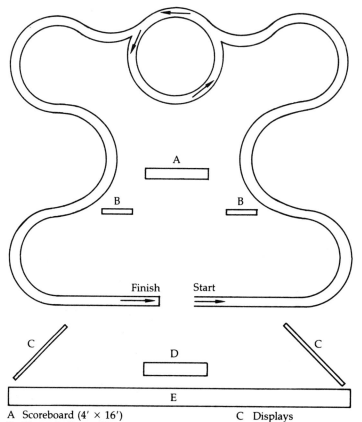

A   Scoreboard (4' × 16')   C   Displays
B   Group I, Group II   D   PA and Breathalyzer
                                   E   Spectator Area

Addiction

Once Upon a Synapse: A Drug Education Simulation in Three Acts

William M. London

In order to facilitate rational, critical thinking about psychoactive drugs as they relate to personal health and political controversies, instruction about basic pharmacological principles is important. Just as instruction about sexual physiology can reduce "magical thinking" about sexual relations (e.g., pregnancy cannot result from one's first coital experience), instruction about pharmacology can reduce thinking about drugs as if they were magical potions.

The main problem in teaching about pharmacology is the complexity of the topic. Instructional activities are needed that can make difficult pharmacological concepts as real, relevant, interesting, and comprehensible for students as possible. The purpose of this article is to describe such an activity that can be conducted in college level health science classes and, possibly, at the secondary level as well. The activity, "Once Upon a Synapse," can be completed in about 45 minutes. The behavioral objective is to enable students to describe various mechanisms by which psychoactive drugs have been theorized to alter normal neuronal functioning and thereby produce psychological effects.

At a minimum, about 10 students are needed to effectively illustrate the mechanisms. A class of 20 to 40 students makes the simulation clearer and more entertaining.

William M. London is an assistant professor in the health education program at Kent State University, Kent, OH 44242.

Materials

"Once Upon A Synapse" is a simulation which is to be performed as a three-act play. The only instructional material needed for the actual simulation is a chart placed at the front of the room on which is listed the dramatis personae (see Figure 1). The chart should be large enough to be readable by the entire class. The ridiculous names of the characters listed on the chart invariably generate laughter throughout the activity thereby making the technical nature of the topic less intimidating.

The simulation should be proceeded by a brief lecture on drugs and the nervous system. Recommended materials for this preliminary lecture include overhead transparencies that illustrate: (1) the structure of neurons; (2) the movement of sodium and potassium ions across the nerve cell membrane (which in the essence of the nerve impulse); (3) the movement of neurotransmitter molecules from presynaptic vesicles to postsynaptic vesicles; and (4) the reuptake of the neurotransmitters by the presynaptic neuron.

An overhead transparency that lists various mechanisms (including those illustrated by the simulation) by which drugs are believed to affect neuronal communication should be presented to conclude the lesson. Such mechanisms include: (1) altering membrane permeability; (2) mimicking neurotransmitters; (3) blocking neurotransmitters from binding to receptors; (4) altering synthesis of neurotransmitters; (5) blocking reuptake of neurotransmitters; (6) altering release of neurotransmitters; (7) altering deactivation of neurotransmitters; and (8) altering storage of neurotransmitters in vesicles (Ray & Ksir, 1987).

Procedure

Students are seated facing the center of the room in a U-shaped formation with a gap of about five feet at the midpoint region of the curve. The seating arrangement is used to represent two nerve cells (neurons) in the brain and the synapse between them. The seating arrangement with the initial positioning of the characters is diagrammed in Figure 2.

Following a brief lecture on neurotransmission, the activity proceeds in three "acts". In Act I, nor-

---

Figure 1. Dramatis Personae

Ethel (or, technically, Ethyl) Alcohol a depressant drug
Coco Cocaine a stimulant drug
Neil Neuron a nerve cell
Nellie Neuron a nerve cell that receives input from Neil Neuron
Norman Neurotransmitter a chemical messenger sent by Neil Neuron
Vic (or Vicki Vesicle) a storage bin for chemical messengers from Neil Neuron
Rita Receptor a receiver of chemical messages sent to Nellie Neuron

mal transmission of an electrical message across an excitatory synapse is simulated. (Normal transmission in an inhibitory synapse can also be simulated in a second run through Act I.) Act II illustrates how alcohol affects normal transmission. Act III illustrates how cocaine affects normal transmission.

The teacher begins by requesting volunteers for the "lead" roles in the play: Rita Receptor, Norman Neurotransmitter, Ethel (or, technically, Ethyl) Alcohol, and Coco Cocaine. To help students to relate to the lock-and-key relationship between receptors and neurotransmitters, it is advisable to choose a female to play Rita and a male to play Nor-

man. (This may also generate some playful humor!) If in the teacher's judgment, there is a big enough group, the reality of the simulation may be enhanced by designating more than one participant to play each lead role. Each participant not assigned to a lead role is designated as part of Neil Neuron, Nellie Neuron, or Vic (Vicki, if preferred) Vesicle depending upon seating position (see Figure 2).

The teacher directs the action as follows:

Act 1: Normal Neurotransmission at an Excitatory Synapse
Step 1: The nerve impulse begins with the participant seated at the dendritic end of Neil Neuron (point A of Figure 2).

The participant raises his or her arms and then places them back down. This signals the next participant over to do the same and continues down the line Neil Neuron participants to point 2. The arm raising and lowering procedure is likely to be familiar to students as "the wave": a popular pastime in recent years for spectators at sporting events. Each student's arm raising and lowering represents the movement of sodium and potassium ions across the cell membrane at each point along the neuron.
Step 2: Vic(ki) Vesicle (point B) opens up and releases Norman Neurotransmitter into the synapse.
Step 3: Norman Neurotransmitter binds to Rita Receptor (point C). (A hug or even a handshake will do.)
Step 4: A wave begins at point C and proceeds along Nellie Neuron to point D).
Step 5: Rita Receptor releases Norman Neurotransmitter.
Step 6: Norman Neurotransmitter is pumped back into Vic(ki) Vesicle. (This process, known as reuptake, replenishes the supply of neurotransmitter molecules). Participants are asked to be creative and improvise how reuptake should look.

If the teacher decides to simulate an inhibitory synapse, I recommend having a wave continually repeating in Nellie Neuron that stops repeating upon the binding of Norman Neurotransmitter to Rita Receptor.

The teacher can process Act I by asking the class to brainstorm how a drug that reaches the brain could conceivably disrupt the normal neurotransmission process simulated by the class. Students who have ideas on this matter should be instructed to "become" the drug and act out the ideas that they brainstorm.

In Act II and in Act III, the teacher can direct the class to simulate hypothesized actions of two commonly abused drugs: alcohol and cocaine. The teacher may decide to pass up Act II and Act III if students respond well during the processing of Act I.

Act II: Alcohol is Imbibed
Step 1: A wave begins at point A.
Step 2: Ethel Alcohol interferes with the propagation of the wave. Ethel might want to hold some participants' hands down.

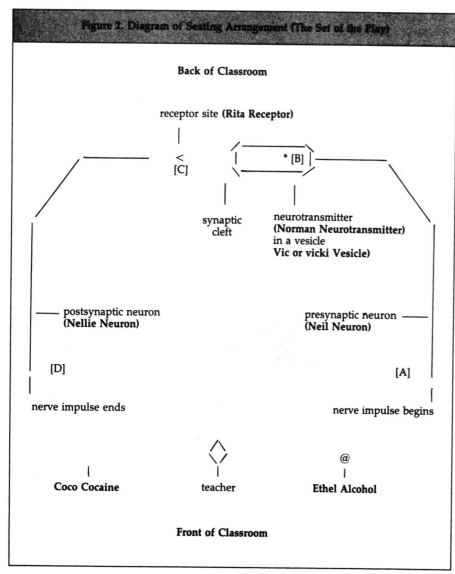

Figure 2. Diagram of Seating Arrangement (The Set of the Play)

Back of Classroom

receptor site **(Rita Receptor)**

< [C]   * [B]

synaptic cleft

neurotransmitter **(Norman Neurotransmitter)** in a vesicle **Vic or vicki Vesicle)**

postsynaptic neuron **(Nellie Neuron)**

presynaptic neuron **(Neil Neuron)**

[D]

[A]

nerve impulse ends

nerve impulse begins

@

Coco Cocaine   teacher   **Ethel Alcohol**

Front of Classroom

Step 3: No release of Norman Neurotransmitter. No wave begins in Nellie Neuron.

Teachers can explain that many scientists have lost confidence in the hypothesized mechanism illustrated in Act II which suggests that alcohol interferes with membrane excitability. Many now believe that, like other central nervous system depressant drugs, alcohol may mimic the neurotransmitter, gamma-aminobutyric acid, which has inhibitory effects when it binds to its receptor site (Ray & Ksir, 1987).

Act III: Cocaine is Administered
Step 1: A wave begins at point A.
Step 2: Vic(ki) Vesicle (point B) opens up and releases Norman Neurotransmitter into the synapse.
Step 3: Norman Neurotransmitter binds to Rita Receptor (point C).
Step 4: A wave begins at point C and proceeds along Nellie Neuron to point D.
Step 5: Coco Cocaine stops Rita Receptor from releasing Norman Neurotransmitter. (Cocaine interferes with the reuptake process).
Step 6: Waves continually repeat from point C to point D. Students can easily relate this to the intensified experiences produced by cocaine administration.

Step 7: The teacher explains that the interference with reuptake along with binding of cocaine to special (unsimulated) receptor sites may explain the stimulation effects of cocaine. Some researchers also believe that the severe depression experienced by some chronic cocaine users may result from failure to replenish the supply of neurotransmitter (Gregler & Mark, 1987).

Much more than after Act I, after the demonstrations of Acts II and III, students are likely to have ideas on other ways that drugs can act at the neuronal level. Thus, at this point, the teacher should repeat the brainstorming session. The teacher can then compare the students' brainstormed list of mechanisms with the teacher's own list on overhead transparency (as described above under "Materials"). Teachers should ask students to imagine the psychological effects resulting from each proposed mechanism of drug activity.

It is not so important for students to be able to recite the names of various neurotransmitters or to explain the *specific* hypothesized actions of *specific* drugs. Emphasis of the discussion should be on general concepts of neurotransmission and drug actions, and how these relate to drug effects.

Conclusion

The actions of psychoactive drugs at the neuronal level can be a daunting topic of study. "Once Upon a Synapse" makes the topic real, relevant, interesting, enjoyable, and comprehensible for students by facilitating group interaction.

Indeed, the simulation can be used primarily as a group energizer for drug education programs that emphasize social support and skill building strategies.

Facilitators should be prepared for outbursts of laughter and friendly teasing of the students in the lead roles. The classroom environment will appear chaotic but will actually be carefully choreographed. Students tend to want to "get it right" and thus will tend to cooperate with a facilitator who is well-prepared.

Gregler, H.L. & Mark, H. (1987). Medical complications of cocaine abuse. *New England Journal of Medicine, 315,* 1495–1500.
Ray, O. & Ksir, C. (1987). *Drugs, Society, and Human Behavior (4th edition).* St. Louis: Times Mirror/Mosby College Publishing.

According to recent surveys parents are now considering alcohol abuse a serious problem that the schools should address. This is a change from recent years when "drug abuse" was the major concern. In fact, parents were often relieved to discover that youngsters were "only drinking" and not using other substances. This reawakening of popular interest in the prevention of alcohol abuse provides an opportunity for program development. So the problem faced by health educators is not one of gaining support for a program but, rather, one of responding in ways likely to have an impact on the lives of students.

One does not have to visit many classrooms to note that there seems to be a great deal of confusion about what ought to be included in an effective alcohol education program. At least four different types of programs are in use. While there is generally some overlap of the different types of programs, it is useful to identify each type so that strengths and weaknesses can be noted.

One predominant type is the biological emphasis. Teachers using this approach emphasize the impact of alcohol on the body. Students are acquainted with the properties of alcohol and how it functions in the body. While the knowledge of alcohol effects on the body is an important aspect of any problem, it is not sufficient. First of all, the factors that influence individual decision-making and the choice to drink or not to drink are not given consideration. In addition, many of these programs have a negative emphasis. It seems to be assumed that if students are made aware of all of the terrible things that alcohol does to the body, then students will not drink.

A second type of a program in the schools tends to confuse alcohol and alcoholism education. The major thrust here is on alcoholism and the dangers of becoming an alcoholic. In fact, this emphasis has become so popular that the author is usually inundated in alcohol education courses with questions about alcoholism and how one can tell if he or she is an alcoholic. Once again, while some of this information is useful, alcohol abuse should not be confused with alcoholism. Any individual may abuse

Investigating the Social Aspects of Alcohol Use

Addiction

Tom V. Savage

Tom V. Savage is an associate professor in the Department of Curriculum and Instruction, Texas A&M University, College Station, TX 77843.

alcohol at any time. In addition, this approach fails to emphasize decision-making and tends to have a negative flavor.

A third approach, more common than we would like to admit, is the "evils of alcohol" approach. These programs emphasize moralizing and preaching to students about why they should not drink and how evil it is. Such programs tend to use scare tactics that emphasize the horrible consequences of drinking. The usual results of these classes are knowing glances passed among students, communicating that they know better than the teacher and that the teacher is out of touch with reality. Students often assume an adversarial position of defending drinking and attempt to refute the moralistic arguments of the teacher. More than one of these types of classes have been brought to an embarrassing conclusion when a student asks the teacher, "Do you drink?".

A fourth approach may be labeled the "resource blitz." These programs feature a daily procession of resource people and

material. Police officers, reformed alcoholics, counselors from alcoholism rehabilitation programs, films, and field trips are the major ingredients of this approach. While many of these resources might be worthwhile, most of these programs lack focus.

And though there are elements of these four approaches that might be useful in designing an alcohol education program, they all lack some critical elements.

The first step in developing an alcohol education program involves clarification of the goals and purposes of the program. This helps guide both the content selected for study and the activities students will experience.

What should be the goals and purposes of a sound alcohol education program? Perhaps the major goal should be to help students make responsible and intelligent decisions about their drinking behavior. It must be recognized at this point that complex factors are involved in the decision to drink. An alcohol education program must address these complex factors. Learning about alcohol is only one part of this process. Students need to address the sources of attitudes and behavioral expectations that influence individuals to drink to the extent that they abuse alcohol. Above all, the program must have a realistic focus and one that avoids adversarial relationships between teacher and student.

Another component that should be addressed in alcohol education programs is that of the social context of alcohol use. The social environment and social reinforcements or sanctions have a strong impact on the attitudes and behaviors of individuals. There are many aspects of the social environment that send messages to individuals regarding appropriate drinking behaviors.

One way of beginning a study of the social aspects of alcohol use is to pose the following questions: Why do people drink? What satisfactions do they get from drinking? How do individuals influence their drinking behavior and patterns? What drinking behaviors and patterns are taught in our culture?

Several interesting projects can involve students in the search for answers to these types of questions. Students should be allowed to gather data, state their findings, and analyze the impact that social reinforcement has on their attitudes and behavior. The role of the teacher should be one of suggesting questions and sources of information and prompting students to evaluate the meaning of the data.

Societal attitudes are influenced in both obvious and subtle ways. Some of the more obvious means might be through advertisements that promote various forms of beverage alcohol. Other, more subtle, means might be found by analyzing the content of cartoons, television programs, and movies.

Analysis of advertisements is a project many teachers have utilized. The first step involves collection of advertisements, usually from various popular magazines. When undertaking this project, it is useful to have students identify the magazine where the advertisement was found. This is helpful when identifying the audience for which the advertisement was intended. It should be noted that television commercials could also be included in the investigation. As advertisements are collected, the following questions can be posed:

1. What does the advertisement show?

2. Why do you think these elements were selected for inclusion in the advertisement?

3. What is the message of the advertisement?

4. What attitudes and behaviors does the advertisement seem to be reinforcing?

5. What impact do advertisements have on the attitudes and behaviors of people?

6. What information is not included in these advertisements that is important to know?

As a follow-up, the advertisements could be grouped, and a summary made of the common elements and messages they seem to convey. For example, does the fact that nearly all advertisements portray alcohol use in settings that are exciting, sexy, and fun have any impact on our views of when alcohol should be used?

A rather subtle source of information about alcohol use, one that is often overlooked, is the cartoon. Cartoons relating to alcohol use are plentiful. They appear regularly in newspapers and magazines. Just the fact that cartoons with alcohol-related themes are so plentiful is a useful bit of information to discuss. As cartoons are collected, they could be grouped according to common themes. Cartoons can be found illustrating nearly every reason that could be given for drinking. The following questions could be asked:

1. What is the message of the cartoon?

2. Why do you think drinking behavior is portrayed as humorous?

3. What reasons are given for drinking in this cartoon?

4. How valid are those reasons?

5. Why do you think the cartoonist chose this topic?

6. What influence do jokes and cartoons have in shaping attitudes and behaviors of people?

A second method to use with cartoons is what is called a task card, which is a way of individualizing student involvement. A task card might consist of a cartoon related to drinking behavior, along with a series of questions or tasks to be completed by the student. For example, a cartoon might be presented that relates to drunkenness. The following questions and tasks could be included:

1. How is drunkenness portrayed in this cartoon?

2. Why do many people think drunkenness is funny?

3. Why is getting drunk the goal of many people when they drink?

4. Poll your classmates. How many of them think getting drunk is desirable? Why do they feel that way?

5. Construct a blood alcohol level chart that shows the probable changes in behavior associated with different changes in the blood alcohol level.

The project of different students and their task card projects should be shared with the class and discussed. At this point, it might be helpful to address some of the common myths surrounding alcohol use.

Another rather subtle source of information about alcohol use is the content of television programs and movies. While some types of beverage alcohol may not be advertised, there is a considerable amount of drinking behavior portrayed during the programs.

One interesting approach is to divide the class into the teams and have them conduct a television survey. Simple survey forms can be developed and different students assigned a particular viewing time and program. They should be asked to identify the program, the number of times alcohol was mentioned or used, the context of the drinking, the purposes for which alcohol was used, the consequences of the usage, and the number of times any other beverage was mentioned or used.

Students are often surprised to discover that other beverages are mentioned only rarely during the context of any given program. It is almost as if no other beverages were available.

After a period of time, perhaps a week, the results can be tabulated and presented to the class. They might pay special attention to the context of alcohol usage. How many times was it used to enhance sexuality, to relieve tension or stress, to escape an unpleasant situation? Once again the students should be asked to state the types of messages that are being sent about the use of beverage alcohol.

A sound alcohol education program must include several components. It has been the purpose of this paper to suggest ways of investigating one of the components that is often overlooked, that of the social aspects of alcohol use. An understanding of how these complex forces influence attitudes and behaviors can help move students toward the goal of responsible decision-making.

Drug Use, Misuse and Abuse as Presented in Movies

Kerry J. Redican, Barbara L. Redican and Charles R. Baffi

Movies represent a form of the mass media and are an important instrument of communication. Analysis of the effects that movies have on people has produced much debate among professionals from a variety of disciplines. Regardless of the stand a person takes, however, the potential influence of movies on people's knowledge, attitudes and behavior cannot and should not be underestimated.

Health behaviors presented in movies often can be interpreted as "norms" to viewers. To the health educator, these implied "norms" may not be the ones most conducive to healthy lifestyles or reduction of risk taking behaviors. Examples of implied "norms" might be the way drug use is presented in movies. Many movies imply that people use substances to better enable them to cope or for recreation and imply that these reasons make it all right to use drugs.

In an effort to have students evaluate how movies present drug use, the following learning activity was developed. This activity has been used in junior and senior high school classes, as well as health education workshops for teachers and other health professionals. The activity has been well received by these groups.

Kerry J. Redican is an associate professor of health education at Virginia Tech, Blacksburg, VA 24061. Barbara L. Redican is a registered nurse in Blacksburg, VA. Charles R. Baffi is an associate professor at Virginia Tech.

This learning opportunity is designed to stimulate student discussion regarding how movies present drug use. Since movies do represent an ad form and since people interpret movies in different ways, this learning opportunity should not be considered to be a definitive way to analyze how drug use is presented in movies.

Structure of the Learning Opportunity

As part of a course assignment in health education, students can be

Directions: For the film being observed, respond to the following statements by *circling one* of the following choices located beside each statement.

SA = Strongly Agree
A = Agree
U = Undecided
D = Disagree
SD = Strongly Disagree
NA = Not Applicable (drug-related scenes not in film)

Note: Information regarding scoring can be found under the Scoring and Interpretation Section.

Number of drug use scenes in the film _____ .
Generally the scene in the film or movie:

(1) Encourages or condones the use of mood modifying substances.	SA	A	U	D	SD	NA
(2) Does not show the negative effects of using mood modifying substances.	SA	A	U	D	SD	NA
(3) Promotes use of mood modifying substances as a solution to boredom.	SA	A	U	D	SD	NA
(4) Associates the use of mood modifying substances with fun or pleasure.	SA	A	U	D	SD	NA
(5) Encourages the use of mood modifying substances as a problem-solving behavior.	SA	A	U	D	SD	NA
(6) Suggests that use of mood modifying substances ia a "norm" (in other words "everyone is doing it!").	SA	A	U	D	SD	NA
(7) Portrays people who abstain from using mood modifying substances as immature, not adult, or "nerds."	SA	A	U	D	SD	NA
(8) Shows an easy solution to the results of misuse or abuse of mood modifying substances.	SA	A	U	D	SD	NA
(9) Portrays the hero or heroine as one who uses mood modifying substances.	SA	A	U	D	SD	NA
(10) Portrays the use of mood modifying substances as a means of enhancing performance (intellectual, physical, spiritual, etc.).	SA	A	U	D	SD	NA

asked to pick out a certain film and use the instrument in Figure 1 in evaluating how drug use is presented.

In order to maximize the discussion on movies, it is best to observe the following points.

- Don't let students review movies that are considered outrageous in terms of their drug content. For example, movies such as *Animal House* or Cheech and Chong films portray unrealistic drug-taking behaviors.

- In any given analysis, be sure to have students determine if any closure was reached regarding the negative side of drug use. For example, some films may glorify drug use initially, but as the movie proceeds, it is easily seen that drug use is interfering in the person's life.

Summary

Once again, the purpose of the learning opportunity is to stimulate classroom discussion. Hopefully, as an end result, the student and teacher will watch movies with a keener eye and an insight as to how drug use is being presented.

Scoring and Interpretation

Step I: *Scoring:* Use the following method of scoring your responses:

[SA]	Strongly Agree	= 5 points
[A]	Agree	= 4 points
[U]	Undecided	= 3 points
[D]	Disagree	= 2 points
[SD]	Strongly Disagree	= 1 point
[NA]	Not Applicable	= 0 points

Step II: *Add your points as follows:*

Statement 1:	_____ Points
+	
Statement 2:	_____ Points
+	
Statement 3:	_____ Points
+	
Statement 4:	_____ Points
+	
Statement 5:	_____ Points
+	
Statement 6:	_____ Points
+	
Statement 7:	_____ Points
+	
Statement 8:	_____ Points
+	
Statement 9:	_____ Points
+	
Statement 10:	_____ Points
Total Points:	_____ Points

Step III: After you have added up the total points, place an "X" on the appropriate point on the following line that best represents your total points. Once you've placed the "X" that represents the total points, you can easily see the film's position regarding drug use.

"Anti" Drug Use Position   "Pro Drug Use" Position

<   -------------|----------------|----------------|----------------   >
10   20   30   40   50

Step IV: Comments regarding analysis of movie (e.g. what kind of closure was reached?)

Learning About Alcohol Drinking Attitudes and Motivations by Examining the Vocabulary of Drunkenness

William M. London   *Addiction*

According to editors of the *Dictionary of American Slang*, "the concept having the most slang synonyms is drunk" (Wentworth & Flexner, 1975). The dictionary listed 353 of these synonyms (Levine, 1981) and 323 synonyms in its appendix. Spears (1986) listed over 1,870 synonyms, while Abel (1985) listed over 1,620 slang terms defined as intoxicated," "drunk," or various degrees of drunkenness.

Reasons for the vastness and richness of our vocabulary of drunkenness are not clear (Abel, 1985). However, semanticists have suggested that how we use language to name things affects how we perceive things (Postman & Weingartner, 1969). Thus, our vocabulary of drunkenness reflects our culture's attitudes, values, and thoughts about the use of alcohol (Abel, 1985).

An important role of alcohol educators is to facilitate open discussion about attitudes and motivations related to drinking and drunkenness. The purpose of this article is to describe how that can be accomplished by using our vocabulary of drunkenness to provide insights about alcohol in American society.

The activity is recommended as part of alcohol education for students in secondary schools, colleges, and universities. It also has been used successfully as part of inservice training for school personnel. The activity can take from as little as 45 minutes to as long as 90

minutes depending upon what (if anything) the teacher decides to omit from the method described below, the dynamics of the group, and the size of the group. (The activity can be carried out with any class size.)

Method

The teacher asks each student to draw a line down the middle of a piece of paper. Students are given a minute to list on the left side of the page, as many words (including slang words) meaning *snow* as they possibly can. This is followed by a brainstorming session so the teacher can write all words generated by the students on the chalkboard. The task is intended to confound students, and most groups will struggle to generate 10 words. The teacher must be careful not to give students too much latitude because some especially sophisticated groups may come up with many more words if allowed to use words that refer to types of snow.

Students then are given a minute to list on the right side of the page as many words (including slang words) meaning *drunk* as they can. This, again, is followed by a brainstorming session in which the teacher records student responses. Students tend to know enough synonyms to enjoy the challenge of filling the board with brainstormed responses. This brainstorming tends to be accompanied by frequent outbursts of laughter in response to many of the words, including those words typically regarded as profane.

(To discourage students from calling out profane words may defeat

part of the purpose of the activity by, in effect, discouraging them from discussing what the use of such words to mean drunk implies about common attitudes of Americans toward drunkenness. However, at the secondary school level, the teacher may need to compromise out of respect for community standards.) Brainstorming continues until there are about 30 seconds during which no new responses are made. From a prepared list of synonyms for drunk (which can be assembled from Abel, 1985; Levine, 1981; Spears, 1981; Spears, 1986; and Wentworth & Flexner, 1975) with synonyms having the same first letter clustered together, the teacher reads aloud.

In processing the activity, the teacher asks the class why it was so much easier to generate words for drunk than words for snow. After a brief discussion, the teacher explains that Eskimos have 30 different words for snow, including one for falling snow, one for "snow on the ground," one for "drifting snow," and one for "blowing snow." The large number of words reflects the importance of perceiving various aspects of nature central to Eskimo culture (Cross, 1979). The teacher facilitates discussion about what the vast number of synonyms for drunk implies about attitudes toward drunkenness in popular American culture.

In groups of four to six, students are asked to discuss what the nature of synonyms for drunkenness implies about common motivations for drinking in America. Students generally note that most of the words connote violence or destruction (e.g., stoned, bombed) or silliness (e.g., blotto, schnoggered), al-

---

William M. London is an assistant professor in the health education program at Kent State University, Kent, OH 44242.

though a few have more mild connotations (e.g., tipsy, high). The teacher reconvenes a meeting of the entire class and asks for volunteers to share what they concluded in their groups.

During the ensuing discussion the teacher may wish to present relevant viewpoints of scholars for students to critique. For example, Levine (1981) suggested that violent words are directed at what "might be thought of as ordinary or everyday consciousness" and thus the appeal of getting drunk "is the anticipation of a break with ordinary consciousness."

Synonyms such as "woofled" connote a degree of self-handicapping. Tucker, Vuchinich, & Sobell (1981) provided experimental evidence that sometimes people drink alcohol as a self-handicapping strategy. Berglas & Jones (1978, p. 406) defined a self-handicapping strategy as "any action or choice of performance setting that enhances the opportunity to externalize (or excuse) failure and to internalize (reasonably accept credit for) success." They suggested that, for those who are uncertain about their competence, to fail at a task due to the self-handicapping of drunkenness normally is preferable to failure that clearly indicates stupidity or incompetence. Thus, self-handicapping might be part of the motivation for some people to "woofle" themselves before such challenges as test-taking, proposing a first date, and getting up to dance at a party.

Since students are asked to discuss the lesson in their small groups, the activity can make some students noticeably uncomfortable (perhaps, especially, those students who tend to deny their own alcohol abuse or those who have significant others who abuse alcohol). The small groups provide students an opportunity to express their feelings and to receive social support. The teacher should be available and responsive to students who wish to discuss further their reactions to the activity. Some students may be encouraged to seek help and the teacher must be prepared to offer appropriate referrals.

Abel, E. L. (1985). *Dictionary of alcohol use and abuse: Slang, terms, and terminology*. Westport, CT: Greenwood Press.

Berglas, S., & Jones, E. E. (1978). Drug choice as a self-handicapping strategy in response to noncontingent success. *Journal of Personality and Social Psychology, 36,* 405–417.

Cross, D. W. (1979). *Word abuse: How the words we use use us*. New York: Coward, McCann & Geoghegan.

Levine, H. G. (1981). The vocabulary of drunkenness. *Journal of Studies on Alcohol, 42,* 1038–1051.

Postman, N., & Weingartner, C. (1969). *Teaching as a subversive activity*. New York: Dell.

Spears, R. A. (1981). *Slang and euphemism*. Middle Village, New York: Jonathan David Publishers.

Spears, R. A. (1986). *The slang and jargon of drugs and drink*. Metuchen, NJ: Scarecrow Press.

Tucker, J. A., Vuchinich, R. E., & Sobell, M. B. (1981). Alcohol consumption as a self-handicapping strategy. *Journal of Abnormal Psychology, 90,* 220–230.

Wentworth, H., & Flexner, S. B. (Comps. & Eds.). (1975). *Dictionary of American Slang, 2nd edition*. New York: Crowell.

Helping College Students Understand the Older Adult

Margaret J. Pope

Our society has seen a tremendous increase in the number of people over the age of 65 and in the past decade, an awareness of their problems and some possible solutions have surfaced. Doctors, gerontologists, social workers, therapeutic recreators, hospital and nursing home administrators, and psychologists recognize the problems of this growing population, and many health educators are aware of the gap that exists between the older adult and the college student.

Teaching a unit on aging in a health education class at the university level made this author aware of the many possibilities for older adults and college-age students to communicate. There is a definite need for inter-generational communication, and the opportunity for mutual understanding of problems should be afforded the health class and the older adult.

As an introduction to the unit, the students were administered a test, "Facts on Aging—A Short Quiz" (Palmore, 1977). This test contains only 25 items, takes only a few minutes to complete, is easily scored, and gives a good indication of misconceptions about aging. The scores on this short quiz showed that the students possessed little accurate knowledge about the older adult. Some of their misconceptions were: The majority of old people are senile with defective memories; old people are all alike; old people are unable to learn anything new; physically they feel bad all the time and are totally incapable of any type of exercise; and they are mentally withdrawn with little contact

with the world outside their limited environment.

The approach taken to try and alleviate these misconceptions was to invite five adults from the Retired Seniors Volunteer Program to class. All were over 65 years of age and they were still active members of the community.

In preparation for these visitors, the class was divided into groups with a discussion leader. The following broad topics were chosen as discussions areas: (1) social life, (2) income and retirement, (3) exercise and keeping fit, (4) transportation, and (5) safety and crime. The students developed questions pertinent to each area. These were collected by the discussion leader to use as points of discussion with the older adults.

Following are some of the questions that the students asked the older adults:

What do you do for entertainment?
Do you feel isolated and lonely?
Do you find it hard to live on a fixed income?
Do you exercise regularly?
If so, what type of exercise?
Do you feel bad?
Do you feel safe in your environment?
Have you fallen or had a personal accident in the last five years?
Has a crime of any kind been committed against you or your partner in the past five years?
Do you ever think of death?
Do you have a lot of medical bills that are brought about by your personal health problems?
What method of transportation do you use?
Do you feel safe using it?
Would you want to live in a nursing home?
Would you want to live with your children?
What is your biggest problem in day-to-day life?

On the days the older adults came, the classroom was arranged with the desks in a circle. This allowed the older adults to sit among the students and to feel more relaxed and at ease. Each older adult was given an opportunity to relate personal information to the students, including living arrangements, if married how long, the number of children, and social interests. The older adults visited the classroom for three days and during this time, good rapport developed between them and the students. Some of the students became so interested in the adults that they planned to visit them in their homes. The experience seemed to be invaluable to both generations.

At the conclusion of the class on the last day the older adults visited, the students wrote individual evaluations, guided by the following questions:

Did you think this was a good learning experience?
Did it change any of your thoughts about older adults?
Would you like to see this practice continued in this class?

The evaluations revealed that the students previously had a number of misconceptions about the older adult. Many were surprised how actively involved these people were in community and social activities. Most of them had assumed that older adults were in nursing homes or health care facilities. They were also amazed at the amount of mental clarity older adults possessed. This encounter seemed to change the students' stereotyped opinion of the older adult as a senile member of an institution. They became aware that the older adult can still be a viable and contributing member of society.

Margaret J. Pope is professor, Health, Physical Education and Recreation Department, Jacksonville State University, Jacksonville, AL 36265.

Palmore, E. (1977) Facts on Aging—A Short Quiz. Gerontology, 17 (4).

As Old as Trees

Aging

Glenn E. Richardson and Susan Bicknell

Ageism, a form of discrimination based on old age, is a powerful, socially reinforced prejudice existing in our society. One method to combat ageism in the educational setting is experiencing the following activity, As Old as Trees.

The class is given a blank sheet of paper and asked to draw a symbol that represents their perception of old people. They are given time to complete this task, and a few are asked to share their drawings and give explanations. Generally, symbols such as rocking chairs, wheelchairs, nursing homes, and canes emerge from the participants in this activity.

Leaving the drawings and the classroom, the group (in good weather) is taken outside near a group of trees.

Glenn E. Richardson is coordinator of Allied Health Studies, Department of Health and Physical Education, Texas A&M University, College Station, TX 77843. Susan Bicknell is a Health Education Major in the Department of Health and Physical Education, Texas A&M University, College Station, TX 77843.

Dyads are formed with one member of the dyad blindfolding (blindfolds are provided by the instructor) the other student. The blindfolded students are turned around two or three times to lose their sense of direction and then informed by the instructor that their partners will lead them to a tree within a reasonable radius. They are instructed to get to know the tree so that when they return without a blindfold, they will be able to identify the tree. The dyads go out, each to their own tree, and the students, mostly by touch, become acquainted with the root systems, the texture of the tree surface, the knots and branches if within reach, and other distinctive features. The student, when satisfied that he/she knows the tree, is led back to the instructor at a central place, turned around two or three times and then the blindfold is taken off.

When all have returned, the students who were blindfolded attempt to locate their trees. Generally, students are successful in this endeavor; then the other member of the dyad is blindfolded and the activity repeated. Following the ac-

tivity, discussion questions can be raised to highlight the analogy between getting to know a tree with its unique qualities and getting to know older people as individuals rather than as stereotypes. For example:

1. For those of you who were able to find your tree, how were you able to find it?

2. What were distinctive features with each of your trees?

3. Did you feel environmental wear on your tree?

4. You may have identified your tree with a rough exterior, but how would you judge the interior of your tree? Do you think it still produces life-maintaining fluids to its branches and leaves? Can you tell that by looking just at the outside of the tree?

5. How can you tell that your tree is still alive? Is there any evidence? (leaves, fruit, etc.)

6. How many seasons do you think your old tree has seen? Can you imagine the story this tree could tell if it could relate what it may have seen over the years?

7. How can you relate getting to know a tree with getting to know an older person?

The discussion can lead students at this point to realize the effort to identify a tree from the rough, wrinkled exterior, and how much easier it might be to identify individuality in older people. The analogy can be drawn that as the old, rough exterior of the tree houses its life processes, so older people, though aged, still have within the throb of vitality. And sometimes we don't see the interior where there is so much warmth, excitement, and love.

At this point a discussion of the aged as a source of wisdom, spiritual strength, comfort, and other integral sources of living would be treated. For a more detailed description of these thoughts, see the article "Ageism: Need We Discriminate."[1]

After the discussion the students are returned to the class, given another piece of paper, and asked to draw a symbol of "old age." Drawings of wine bottles, books of life, owls, trees, and other symbols representing the concept of improving with age and sources of wisdom emerge from the students. A look at their first picture and a comparison with the second picture lead to an interesting discussion of change.

[1]Jose, N. L., and Richardson, G. E. Ageism: need we discriminate. *Journal of School Health,* Vol. 50, No. 12 (September, 1980), pp. 419-421.

Digging for Healthy Hearts: A Simulated Archaeological Dig for the Prevention of Cardiovascular Disease

Wesley E. Hawkins

In recent years, health professionals increasingly have targeted younger audiences such as high school and college students for education on risk factors related to cardiovascular disease. Various teaching methods have been implemented in providing learning experiences about the prevention of cardiovascular disease. Teaching techniques have ranged from the direct lecture method to more experiential teaching methods such as inquiry problem solving techniques, the latter being the focus of the present article.

The inquiry technique emphasizes problem solving and discovery rather than direct transferral of information from teacher to student in the traditional lecture class. As Kime, Schlaadt, and Tritsch (1977) who advocate the use of inquiry in health education noted, "the teacher's basic task is to provide data to assist students in their search for relevant data. The teacher is a primary motivator (extrinsic) in the approach to learning as a task of discovering something rather than learning about it" (p. 142). More specifically, the inquiry technique is a problem solving process that first requires the student to gather, analyze, and categorize data for concept formation, and then formulate generalizations about the data gathered (Northwest Regional Educational Laboratory, 1972).

The teaching technique described below, named "Digging for Healthy Hearts," uses an inquiry approach to assist young persons in examining the relationship between personal cardiovascular disease risk and lifestyle habits. Specifically, the inquiry approach that will be described in this article is a simulated archaeological dig that depicts a hypothetical high risk and low risk civilization for cardiovascular disease.

Purpose

The major purpose of the Digging for Healthy Hearts Teaching Technique is to utilize an inquiry and problem solving approach in educating high school and college students about risk factors and preventive health behaviors related to cardiovascular disease.

Overview of the Teaching Technique

The Digging for Healthy Hearts technique requires three 50 minute class periods for completion. The first class period is the simulated archaeological dig and requires students to use an inquiry problem solving approach examining the relationships of personal cardiovascular disease risk and lifestyle habits. Simulating an actual archaeological dig, artifacts are buried representing health behaviors of hypothetical civilizations that would be high risk and low risk for cardiovascular disease. For example, based on risk factors identified in past research on cardiovascular disease (e. g., smoking identified from the Framingham study), artifacts such as old cigarette lighters would be buried to represent the high risk behavior of smoking. For the low risk civilization, artifacts such as old cans of low fat foods (e.g., tuna fish cans) would be buried.

Students are told to pretend they are archaeologists and to start digging for artifacts in their assigned areas. Students are asked first to hypothesize which artifacts represent a low risk or a high risk civilization. During the second class period, student stories of the civilizations are presented. At the third and final class meeting, research findings on risk factors related to cardiovascular disease are presented. After presentation of risk factors by the instructor, students are asked to compare and contrast health behaviors of our present American civilization with their own fictional civilizations derived from the archaeological dig.

Behavioral Objectives

(1) After visual inspection of artifacts from the simulated archaeological dig, the student will categorize artifacts as representative of health behaviors as either at-risk or preven-

Wes Hawkins is an assistant professor in the Department of School and Community Health, University of Oregon, Eugene, OR 97403.

tive in relation to cardiovascular disease.

(2) After visual inspection of artifacts from the simulated archaeological dig, the student will write a minimum three paragraph fictional story describing health behaviors for cardiovascular disease for the hypothetical civilization and a minimum three paragraph fictional story describing health behaviors of the high risk civilization.

(3) The student will list a minimum of four major risk factors related to cardiovascular disease based on findings from the Framingham study and Type A behavior research.

(4) The students verbally will compare and contrast, in class discussion, the health behaviors of their fictional civilizations with those of behaviors of modern United States individuals in terms of cardiovascular health and disease.

Specific Procedures for Implementation

Specific procedures will be discussed within the context of the three class periods required for completion of the Digging for Healthy Hearts teaching technique. In addition, the lesson plan for this technique is presented as Figure 1.

First Class Period: Simulated Archaeological Dig Utilizing Inquiry Approach.

The first task of the instructor is the establishment of an outdoor dig site where artifacts can be buried easily. Dig sites can be located on school grounds or close to the school. Unused gardens, wooded areas, stream or creek beds, sand beach areas, or sawdust piles can simulate an archaeological dig site.

Next, the instructor buries artifacts that are representative of (1) a low risk civilization and (2) a high risk civilization related to cardiovascular disease. Artifacts for the high risk civilization include such items as old cigarette packages, cigarette lighters, containers of high-fat food products such as canned meats, an old blood pressure cuff, and a genealogical diary showing

---

Figure 1. Lesson Plan	
Unit Title: Prevention of Chronic Disease Unit	Date: _____
Conceptual statement: Knowledge of preventative health behaviors will reduce the risk of cardiovascular disease.	Time: _____
	Grade: _____
Objectives: 1. After visual inspection of artifacts from the stimulated archaeological dig, the student will categorize artifacts as representative of health behaviors as either at-risk or preventive in relation to cardiovascular disease.	Teacher: _____ Teaching points: _____

Objectives:
1. After visual inspection of artifacts from the stimulated archaeological dig, the student will categorize artifacts as representative of health behaviors as either at-risk or preventive in relation to cardiovascular disease.
2. After visual inspection of artifacts from the simulated archaeological dig, the student will write a minimum three paragraph fictional story describing the health behaviors for the hypothetical low risk civilization for cardiovascular disease and a minimum three paragraph fictional story describing the health behaviors of the high risk civilization.
3. The student will list four risk factors related to cardiovascular disease based on findings from the Framingham Heart Disease Study and from Type A behavior research.
4. The student will verbally compare and contrast in a class discussion the health behaviors of their fictional civilizations with the present day United States in terms of cardiovascular health and disease.

Content (progression)	Learning activities	Evaluation for activities

I. The Framingham Study
   a. Purpose
     1. Study conduct in Framingham, Mass. to determine factors related to cardiovascular disease.
   b. Methodology
     1. Longitudinal study—follows persons over time and then examine which factors related to cardiovascular disease.
 II. Findings from Framingham Study (risk factors identified).
   a. Smoking
   b. Diet
   c. Obesity
   d. Family History of Cardiovascular Disease
 III. Findings from Rosenman and Friedman linking Type A behavior to coronary heart disease.
	1. Stimulated archaeological dig in outdoor setting. Bury artifacts that depict a high risk and a low risk civilization for cardiovascular disease (e.g., LOW RISK—running shoes, low fat food containers; HIGH RISK—cigarette lighters). Have groups designate whether artifacts belong to high risk or low risk by writing on large blank signs at the dig sites. Next, have students write minimum of one paragraph descriptions of the high risk and the low risk civilization in terms of health behaviors.
	 2. Student presentation of stories. Have artifacts displayed.
	 3. Instructor presents findings from research related to cardiovascular disease.
	 4. Class discussion comparing and fictional with actual civilization in the United States.
		1. Examination of sign at dig site to determine if student correctly identified collection of artifacts as belonging to low risk or high risk civilization for cardiovascular disease.
		 2. Examination of written paragraphs of fictional accounts of health behaviors of high risk and low risk civilizations.
		 3. In class written quiz asking students to list four major risk factors of cardiovascular disease as identified by the Framingham study or by Type A behavior research.
		 4. Teacher observation of student response of comparison and contrasting of their particular civilizations with present day American civilization.

generational deaths from heart disease. Traces of the low risk civilization include artifacts such as exercise artifacts (segments of racquet balls or parts of old tennis rackets), low fat food artifacts from wooden fruit containers such as apples and oranges, low fat chicken, tuna, etc. canned meat containers, a genealogical diary not showing family patterns of deaths due to cardiovascular disease, and a personal date book with a stressful, heavy schedule but with planned relaxation and scheduled exercise.

High risk and low risk artifacts are kept separate when buried in different areas at the dig site. Burying artifacts in this manner allows students to hypothesize whether artifacts represent health behaviors as a high risk or a low risk civilization in relation to cardiovascular disease. To evaluate this objective, blank signs are placed at different areas of the dig sites. After examining artifacts for their particular group, students are instructed to designate their particular site area by writing on the signs in large lettering either "High Risk Civilization for Cardiovascular Disease" or "Low Risk Civilization for Heart Disease."

Next, students are directed to write a minimum three paragraph fictional story describing the health behaviors of a low risk and a high risk civilization for cardiovascular disease. Students are urged to make stories creative, fun, and exciting while describing the health behaviors of a civilization. Each student is asked to complete this assignment as homework and asked to share the story at the follow-up session held indoors the next school day. Students are asked to bring their artifacts and visually present them as they read and discuss their stories with the class.

Second Class Period: Presentation of Student Fictional Stories Describing Low Risk and High Risk Civilizations for Cardiovascular Disease

The second class period is held indoors in the traditional classroom

format. Students are asked to read their fictional stories to the class, describing the particular civilization chosen.

Third Class Period: Instructor's Presentation of Research Findings of Risk Factors Related to Cardiovascular Disease

In the third and final class period, held inside in a traditional classroom format, the instructor presents background information on risk factors related to cardiovascular disease as identified in the Framingham, Massachusetts heart disease study and from Roseman and Friedman's (1971) research linking Type A behavior with coronary heart disease. After presentation of the risk factors is completed, the instructor, in a class discussion format, asks students to compare and contrast their fictional civilizations with our present American civilization in terms of health behaviors and cardiovascular disease.

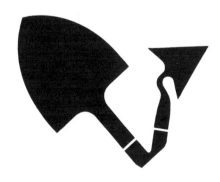

Student Reaction to Digging for Healthy Hearts

Various reactions from students in an introductory personal health course in a large midwestern university were positive. Examples of comments are: "It was a fun way to learn about heart disease, " "The dig was fun and I learned a lot about preventing heart disease," "I thought it was a crazy idea to start with, but it was fun and I learned a lot, " "I liked writing the stories about the civilizations, it was a fun way to learn, and I think I will

remember this stuff a lot better this way."

Summary

We would do well to reconsider the importance of inquiry as an educational technique for health education. As Goodlad, Stoephasius, and Klein (1966) noted two decades ago during a period of significant curriculum reform, "Many curriculum builders seek to organize their fields around the primary structural elements of each discipline: the concepts, key ideas, principles, and modes of inquiry. It is assumed that understanding these elements (rather than merely possessing the facts) gives the students the intellectual power to attack unfamiliar problems and enables them to grasp intuitively the relationship of new phenomena already experienced. Ability to think inductively becomes a built-in goal, and teachers are encouraged to let students discover meanings for themselves" (p. 15).

Inquiry techniques such as the Digging for Healthy Hearts teaching method are needed for students to discover the meaning of what effect their health behaviors can have in relationship to cardiovascular disease.

I would like to dedicate this article to my father, Eugene Hawkins, who died of cardiovascular disease on the day this article was submitted for publication. He was my teacher, my friend, and my mentor for life.

Goodlad, J., Steophasises, R., & Klein, M. (1966). *The changing school curriculum.* New York: Fund for the Advancement of Education.

Kime, R., Schlaadt, R., & Tritsch, L. (1977). *Health instruction: An action approach.* Englewood Cliffs, NJ: Prentice-Hall, Inc.

McCollum, J. & Davis, R. (1972). *Instructor's manual development of higher level thinking abilities.* Portland, OR: Northwest Regional Educational Laboratory.

Rosenman, R. & Friedman, M. (1971). The central nervous system and coronary heart disease. *Hospital Practice,* 6(10):87–97.

Cancer: A Mini-Documentary

Stephen C. Corey

From time to time, most health educators get the urge to deviate from standard methods of instruction and try something that might be out of the ordinary but profitable at the same time. For those broad topics such as cancer or heart disease, which tend to take days or weeks to cover, a mini-documentary might be just the thing to use. This program is meant to be set up like *60 Minutes* or *20/20* but involves each student as a specialist in his/her own field. The whole class can be given the opportunity to not only produce but be the "stars" of their own television show. The purpose of the documentary is to allow the students freedom to select an area that interests them while also enabling them to be creative in communicating their findings to others. Videotaping the show enables everyone to view the finished product and reinforces the material once again.

How the Mini-Documentary Works

Each student chooses a 3 x 5 card on a

particular area of cancer. On this card are several questions which he/she will research and discuss. They are also given a title for themselves and may choose their own name. As an example, a student chooses cancerous tumors. His card will read:

Dr. _____, leading oncologist from Harvard.

1. What are tumors?
2. What are two different types of tumors?
3. Any special tests for them?
4. Any special symptoms from them?

The rest is left up to him. He must find the correct answers and be able to report his findings on "TV." The following is a list which could be consulted for the remaining cancer topics.

1. Physiology of the cancer cells
2. Cancerous tumors
3. Most common causes of cancer
4. Carcinogens
5. Warning signals of cancer
6. Tests for cancer
7. Treatments for cancer
8. Most common cancers in women
9. Cancer of the uterus
10. Breast cancer
11. Most common cancers in males
12. Lung cancer
13. Cancer of the prostate gland
14. Cancer of the testes
15. Cancer of the larynx
16. Oral cancer

17. Skin cancer
18. Cancer of the esophagus
19. Cancer of the stomach
20. Colo-rectal cancer
21. Thyroid cancer
22. Hodgkin's disease
23. Leukemia
24. Cancer in children
25. The American Cancer Society

Two students must be chosen to fill the spots of commentator and interviewer. The commentator's job is to introduce the show and make some concluding statements at the end, while the interviewer is responsible for accepting the 3 x 5 cards from the specialists, introducing them, and asking the questions. (The students who have the most enthusiasm and originality seem to be best suited for these roles.) A small "set," consisting possibly of chairs, a table, and a lamp should be constructed so that the camerman can focus on both of the "stars" at once. To avoid confusion and allow continuity of the show while videotaping, a list should be posted so that everyone knows when his or her interview is coming up. The specialist takes his seat on the "set," gives his 3 x 5 card to the interviewer, and when all is quiet, the cameraman gives a "ready . . . action!"

As soon as the interview is finished, the next specialist comes up and gets ready to go. The interviewee may also wear a lab coat and a stethoscope to add

Stephen C. Corey is group health claim approver with the John Hancock Mutual Life Insurance Company. He can be reached at P.O. Box 682, Mansfield, MA 02048.

to the total effect. If each interview lasts one to two minutes, the whole show can be completed in a single class period.

The students may be evaluated on their degree of research and their ability to answer the questions correctly. With a little enthusiasm, originality, and even humor, a fairly monotonous topic can be developed into an exciting and refreshing educational tool.

Even though cancer is a prime example of the topics which could be used, the mini-documentary does not need to be limited to cancer only. Therefore, topic lists for drugs and infectious diseases are included for future mini-documentaries.

Drugs

1. Stimulants
2. Depressants
3. Hallucinogens
4. Drug abuse
5. Drug misuse
6. Antibiotics
7. Antiseptics
8. Analgesics
9. Tranquilizers
10. Narcotics
11. Cross tolerance
12. Reverse tolerance
13. Main effect
14. Side effect
15. Addiction
16. Withdrawal syndrome
17. Over-the-counter drugs
18. Medicine
19. Food and Drug Administration (FDA)
20. Tolerance
21. Synergism
22. Alcohol

Infectious Diseases

1. Virus
2. Bacteria
3. Fungi
4. Protozoa
5. Pathogen
6. Incubation period
7. Active immunity
8. Passive immunity
9. Diphtheria
10. Whooping cough
11. Tetanus
12. Poliomyelitis
13. Measles
14. German measles
15. Mumps
16. Chickenpox
17. Common cold
18. Influenza
19. Tuberculosis
20. Infectious mononucleosis
21. Infectious hepatitis

Consumer Health: Medical Quackery

Carolyn E. Cooper

An important aspect of consumerism is the evaluation of messages that are conveyed in advertisements for health care products or services. Only through educated analysis can consumers decide which purported health care products are quackery and which are legitimate. Since young adult consumers constitute a large target audience for advertisers, it is beneficial to teach analysis skills to students at the college level. Moreover, college students have indicated that they are interested in quackery and fraudulent health practices as a consumer health topic (Gaines, 1984).

Therefore, a lesson plan was developed to provide university students enrolled in a lower division general health education course with information about medical quackery and the opportunity in small group discussions to analyze health care advertisements. The lesson's objective was to equip students with the knowledge and analytic skills requisite to making decisions about whether or not advertisers are guilty of quackery. The following lesson plan may be implemented either during one or two class sessions (depending upon the quantity of content covered) as a component of a larger unit on consumer health.

Preparation for the Lesson

Prior to class, photocopy advertisements of suspect health care products, services, or programs. (The author selected advertisements from the two major newspapers in Los Angeles, the *Los AngelesTimes* and the *Herald Examiner*, in addition to the gossip tabloid, the *National Enquirer*. These newspapers advertised such products as diet pills, sunscreens, anti-balding ointments, and various programs for weight reduction, acupuncture, smoking cessation, foot surgery, and impotence.) The teacher

Carolyn E. Cooper is a graduate student in the Master of Public Health Program in the Department of Health Science at California State University, Northridge, CA.

should make enough copies of each ad to ensure that when students are placed in groups, each group will have two advertisements and each group member will have a copy of both advertisements. Also, if possible, have different advertisements for each group so that no two groups will have the same ad.

Content Material

Before students gather in groups to analyze the advertisements, it may be helpful to conduct a brief lecture on the following subject matter (Ensor, Means, & Henkel, 1985; Olsen, Redican, & Baffi, 1986).

I. Medical Quackery
   A. Definitions
      1. nostrum—unproven and generally unscientific, secret "remedies" for illnesses
      2. quacks—purveyors of misinformation about the treatment of disease, illness or a condition
   B. Common Characteristics of Quackery
      1. product or service being offered is a "secret" remedy that is not available from any other source
      2. sponsor claims to be battling the established medical profession because it does not accept his/her discovery
      3. remedy or product is sold door-to-door or by mail order advertisements
      4. treatment is valuable for a wide variety of illnesses
      5. anecdotes and testimonials are used to support claims
      6. overnight success is claimed
      7. scare tactics are utilized
      8. free trial packages of medicine or free first visit
   C. Characteristics of People Who Are Prey to Quacks
      1. want instant cure for painful, chronic, or incurable disease

2. want cure for ailment that medical practitioners have difficulty diagnosing and treating
3. believe they have had poor quality or unsympathetic medical care
4. believe they cannot afford a physician or a "high-priced" specialist
5. dissatisfied with their general appearance and do not think a physician will solve the problem.
6. cannot accept the inevitable process of aging, i.e., baldness, gray hair, or wrinkles

II. Propaganda Advertising Techniques Used to Persuade Consumers to Buy a Particular Health Product
   A. Bandwagon—everyone is doing or taking it
   B. Snob Appeal—only the privileged few use this product
   C. Testimony—it worked for me, so it will work for you
   D. False Image—you will be like someone else (possibly a movie star or athlete) if you use this product
   E. Rewards Appeal—free gift with product or upon signing up for service
   F. Humor appeal—use of jokes or catchy songs
   G. Just Plain Folks—ordinary people use this product, just like you
   H. Scientific Evidence—doctors recommend this product
   I. Non-verbal Appeal—extensive use of pictures
   J. Underdog Appeal—we're number two, but we try harder

Small Group Discussions

After advising students of their task to analyze these health care advertisements to determine if they are quackery, randomly assign students to groups so that each group consists of five to six students. Distribute the photocopies of advertisements, discussed above, to each group. (Each group should have two different advertisements to analyze.)

Distribute a 4x6 index card to each group. The cards contain the following questions, which will be answered collectively by the group members.

1. What is the product, remedy, or service being promoted?
2. Who do you believe is the intended audience?
3. What type(s) of propaganda advertising techniques are being utilized?
4. What is the promised outcome?
5. What characteristics does the ad have that may make you suspicious of quackery?
6. Do you believe this advertisement is quackery? Why or why not?

Write the names of propaganda techniques, outlined in Section II of the content material, on the chalk board for students to refer to when responding to question 3. The teacher may want to visit each group briefly to answer questions and to observe group members' interaction. Allow 20 to 30 minutes for this exercise.

Have students select a spokesperson to present each group's answers before the entire class. When discussing their groups' advertisements, spokespersons should also comment on dissenting opinions, if significant. For example, it may be interesting for the class to hear why three members strongly supported the opinion that an ad was quackery while three other members had the opposite opinion.

An unexpected issue that arose when the author implemented this lesson was the origin of the advertisements. Students were curious to learn which newspaper contained which advertisement. The class expressed the belief that most of the advertisements were obtained from the *National Enquirer*, when, in fact, the majority were selected from the *Los Angeles Times* and *Herald Examiner* (perceived by the students to be considerably more reputable newspapers than the *Enquirer*). Also, students found it interesting that advertisements pertaining to impotence were located in the business section, advertisements about baldness were in the sports section, and weight loss advertisements were in the women's feature section.

Ensor, P.G., Means, R.K., & Henkel, B.M. (1985). *Personal Health* (2nd ed.). New York: John Wiley and Sons, 286–289.

Gaines, J. (1984). A study of the consumer health interests of selected college students. *Journal of School Health, 54* (11), 437–438.

Olsen, L.K., Redican, K.J., & Baffi, C.R. (1986). *Health Today* (2nd ed.). New York: Macmillan Publishing Co., 554–560.

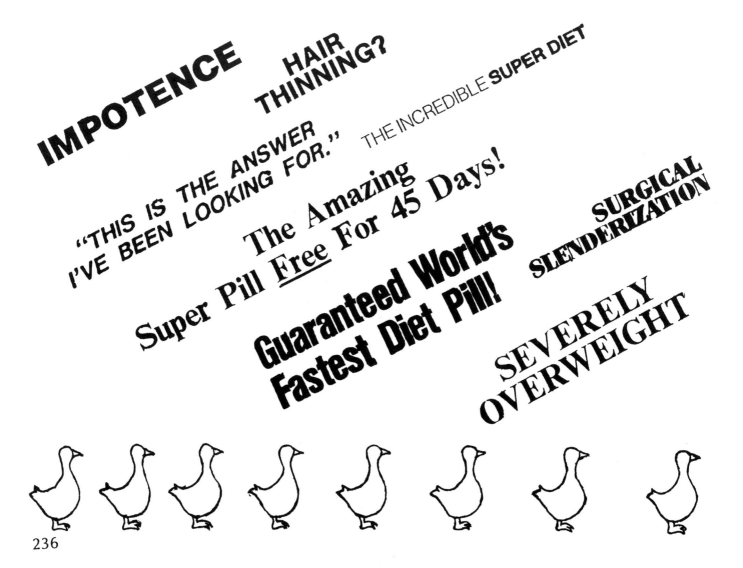

Environmental Health Simulations: Island City and Production

Glenn E. Richardson, Alan Burns, and Janet Falcone

Often it is difficult for students to enjoy concepts associated with environmental health because it is difficult to apply personally. Simulation activities are often beneficial and make a unit more interesting by helping students understand the complex issues associated with environmental control. The purpose of this paper is to give two examples of simulation activities that are fun, mimic or simulate environmental dilemmas, and allow for active participation by many students.

Island City

The purpose of the Island City simulation is to have students understand the environmental problems associated with growth and to sense some of the frustration of city planners who deal with the problems. The materials and what they represent in the story are as follows:

1. Poster paper (2' × 3') is the island.
2. Incense represents factories.
3. Cups, coffee filter, and water represent the water treatment plant.
4. Uncooked beans represent people.
5. Ash trays are used as incinerators.
6. Newspaper is solid waste.
7. Coffee and tea grounds are water pollutants.
8. Tape recorded city sounds represent noise pollution.
9. A non-aerosol spray or perfume spray represents air pollution.
10. Small toy cars represent the means of transportation.

Glenn E. Richardson is chair of the Department of Health Education at the University of Utah, Salt Lake City, UT 84112. Alan Burns is a health and physical education major in the Department of Health and Physical Education at Texas A&M University. Janet Falcone is in community education in the A&M Consolidated School District, College Station, TX.

Students are divided into groups of eight or more people (the number can vary based on the number of tasks) and each group is given the following setup: The piece of poster paper is placed in the middle of the group. Students are instructed that this is their island where they live and cannot leave. It is their responsibility to keep it clean and beautiful. Each group is given a bag of materials as described. Each student is given a bean to represent themselves on the island and may draw a small home and select his or her automobile. A factory (incense) where they work is also placed on the island and lighted. The water source (cup of water), and waste disposal site (ash tray) are also located where they deem appropriate. A commercial area of the island should be selected with stores, an area designated for parks, national forest, and wildlife preserve.

The activity begins with the following instructions:

1. Every 10 seconds a new bean is added to the island, which represents population growth.
2. Another car is added every minute.
3. Add another factory every two minutes.
4. Torn paper is added slowly, yet constantly.

Each student is given a task during the process. The following are representative of the tasks:

1. One person maintains the cleanliness of the water supply.
2. One person builds new homes for every set of three beans. Group consensus is necessary to determine placement or they go to a shelter which the home builder makes.
3. Two people help to coordinate the subdivision and roadways connecting the homes and factories (draw in roads with pencil).
4. One person adds people and cars.
5. Another person adds the factories. He or she needs to get group approval within 10 seconds before placing the factories.

6. One person should be responsible for maintaining parks and natural areas on the island.
7. Someone is responsible for removing and burning solid waste. (Note: Be sure it is permissable to burn bits of paper; if not conduct the activity where you are permitted to do so or delete this part of the activity.)

The instructor begins with the city sounds at very low volume and every 30 seconds or so turns up the volume slightly until it is quite loud by the end of the activity. Additionally, the instructor should drop coffee or tea grounds into the water source, causing the student responsible for the water source to go through the filtering process.

The activity continues until the chaos and confusion reach a breaking point. Discussions should revolve around questions related to frustration associated with controlling population growth, coordination of environmental control services, and cooperation among services when growth is so rapid.

Production

The purpose of this activity is to simulate developing, refining, using, and recycling of products. The student will experience some of the frustrations associated with reclaiming raw materials.

The materials necessary for this simulation are as follows:

1. Three 3" × 3" × ½" squares of playdough, each a different color (red, white, and blue) for each participating group.
2. A clear wrap and label for each group. Labels should have products such as car, airplane, milk carton, and book written on them.

Divide the class into four groups (depending on the size of the class) and give each group red, white, and blue squares of playdough wrapped in clear wrap labeled as a particular product, i.e. car or airplane. There will be five steps to this method, each step taking 5 to 7 minutes.

Step 1 (Raw Materials to Parts): The first step is for each group to take "raw materials'' (playdough squares) and construct the parts for the product indicated on the label. For example, if members of the group are constructing a car, then wheels, body, bumper, and lights should be manufactured but not assembled. *Note:* All or part of the playdough may be used for manufacturing parts but any that is not used will remain behind as waste.

Step 2 (Assembling): Moving clockwise between groups, the students pass their manufactured parts to the next group so that every group has parts made by a different group. The groups are to act as assembling factories and put the product together.

Step 3 (Consumer Use): Groups then pass their finished products clockwise again to the next group. This is the consumer stage. The ultimate outcome is that the product will be used and worn out. The car may get into a wreck or the milk carton smashed.

Step 4 (Recycling): The products are now passed to the next group to be salvaged and used for another purpose. The students are to take the worn out or wrecked product and make something else from it, utilizing the same materials and parts.

Step 5 (Restoring): The recycled products are passed back to the original groups. The groups should now try to restore the product to its original raw material state (three squares of red, white, and blue playdough). It will be virtually impossible to do this because the colors will be mixed due to the stickiness of the playdough.

Students will be asked to smell their hands following the activity. They will smell the distinct smell of the play-dough. This can represent the human exposure as the people work with some raw materials. The students will be so intent on making their products that they will forget that they are being exposed to the ''contaminants.'' The analogy is that many times people are so intent in making money that they forget the health consequences of exposure to their products.

Discussions will revolve around the issues of depletion of raw materials, factory hazards, assembly line stress, recycling, and economic issues.

Reducing Anxiety About Teaching a Human Sexuality Program

Louise Rowling

One of the problems for schools in the development of a human sexuality program is the inadequate preparation of teachers, many of whom feel anxious, embarrassed, and fearful of questions adolescents will ask. Preparation of teachers of human sexuality at a preservice or inservice level should aim to ease some of this discomfort (McCarthy, 1983).

Health educators have frequently used rehearsal behavior as a means of preparation for future events. McGuire's (1969) concept of psychological inoculation adds to the belief that examining a situation, and practicing ways to cope with it before it is experienced should help reduce anxiety and develop coping skills. These beliefs were combined with Finn's (1981) on how to deal with personal questions from students, to develop a cognitive behavioral technique that would enable teachers or trainee teachers to:

- anticipate controversial questions from adolescents relating to sexuality
- prepare responses that they would feel comfortable verbalizing
- gain experience in using "the language of sex."

The last aim attempted to fulfill Bruess and Greenberg's (1981) criteria for sex educators:

"The teacher of sex education needs to be able to use the language of sex easily and naturally, especially in the presence of the young."

Implementation of the Activity

1. Initiate a discussion focussing on the handling of controversial issues in the health curriculum. Often issues such as drugs and sexuality involve personal questions from adolescents to the teacher.

2. Present the three general ways of responding to personal questions proposed by Finn (1981): answer honestly, refuse to answer, equivocate or lie. Further exploration of these can then develop response guidelines: ensure educational value, be comfortable, be aboveboard (Finn, 1981).

3. Orient the discussion toward responding to questions in human sexuality lessons. Produce a question box and ask participants to write on a sheet of paper (anonymously) any questions they think that an adolescent may ask that they would feel uncomfortable or have difficulty responding to. The box is collected, the questions typed up, and a sheet of the questions handed out to the participants in the next session. (The session leader may also have added some questions.) Examples could include: "Do girls like it as much? Are you a virgin? Is it dangerous to masturbate?"

4. Participants then prepare responses to all the questions by discussing with friends and family and/or through reading.

5. At a subsequent session, participants are divided into small groups. (The session leader has prepared question boxes, one for each group, with the questions on individual sheets of paper.) Each group sits in a circle, one participant selects a piece of paper and asks the question of the person opposite. That person responds, preferably not reading a prepared answer, but giving the general idea of a planned response. The box is passed on around the circle until all questions have to be asked and responded to. (The length of this activity will depend on the number of questions.)

6. Small group discussion can occur after each question and answer and/or after the activity as a whole. Issues that may be considered are: the impact on adolescents of the responses, how participants felt, how difficult the research was. A general summary should focus on participants describing what they had gained from the exercise.

Feedback on the Activity

Participants have stated that the activity:

- forced them to personally confront many issues about sexuality education;
- under the guise of completing an assignment, opened up topics of discussion with friends and family, topics previously not broached;
- highlighted the need for the availability of simple straightforward information on sexuality for adolescents;
- made them feel more comfortable in dealing with questions from adolescents. This was based on the belief that it would be harder to deal with these questions among their "same age" group rather than with adolescents in the classroom.

The author has used this process successfully a number of times at the preservice level and believes it could be equally as effective in inservice programs.

Bruess, C. & Greenberg, J. (1981). *Sex education: Theory and practice.* Wadsworth: Belmont, CA.

Finn, P. (1981). Hey, Teach! Do you drink! *Journal of School Health,* 51(8), 538–542.

McCarthy, W. (ed). (1983). *Teaching about sex. The Australian experience.* George Allen & Unwin: Sydney.

McGuire, W. J. (1969). The nature of attitudes and attitude change. Lindzey, G. & Aronson, E. (eds). *Handbook of social psychology,* Vol. 3, Addison Wesley: Reading, MA.

Louise Rowling is a lecturer in the Health Education Department at Sydney Institute of Education, P.O. Box 63, Camperdown 2050 New South Wales, Australia.

Family Life Education

Are You Ready for Prime Time Birth Control?

Pamela Wild and Linda Berne

Grade Level: 9-12 (7-12 for high risk students)

Time: Two class periods, 50 minutes each

Materials: Questionnaire, paper, pencils, chalk board

Concepts: If a couple has sexual intercourse, they must perform many skills to use birth control effectively and avoid a pregnancy. It is harder for teenagers to be effective contraceptors than for older adults.

Teacher Background: "Why are these kids getting pregnant when clinics give away free birth control?" is a question commonly asked by those who are concerned with teen pregnancy. Perhaps the answer lies in the fact that of the annual abortions performed in the United States, less than a third are to teenagers. Adults, who should have the knowledge, maturity, resources, and life experiences that would enable them to prevent unintended pregnancies often don't do much better than teens.

For adults or teens to prevent pregnancies, a multitude of skills must be learned and used. Teenagers, however, must clear additional hurdles: denial of impending behavior, believing that nothing can happen to them, failing to see consequences of behavior, immobilizing fear or guilt of being "found out" or "planning it," lacking transportation

---

Pamela Wild is with the Children and Youth Services of Chattanooga, TN. Linda Berne is professor of health education at the University of North Carolina, Charlotte.

or money, inability to express concerns or emotions about sexuality, and ignorance of or misinformation about laws on confidentiality and age requirements for obtaining contraception.

Because life planning is so critical to opportunity in today's world, learning the skills to contracept and becoming motivated to use them are major needs of teens and adults who currently are or will be sexually active. Rather than asking "Why do teens become pregnant?" we should be asking "What prevents a teen from avoiding pregnancy?" Instruction to affect attitudes, knowledge, skills, and behaviors is necessary to help youths achieve positive relationships, sexual health, and maturity.

Objective: The student will identify skills needed to be an effective contraceptor, determine those in which he/she has competence, and develop the skills that would be difficult or impossible to perform.

Procedure: Say "We have already discussed how it takes skills to remain abstinent when there is so much pressure today to be sexually active. Let's review some of the skills you need to avoid unwanted sexual behavior" (see Berne & Wild, 1988). Write the skills students suggest on the chalkboard.

Session 1—Activity 1: Say "It takes <u>many</u> more skills for a person who is having sexual intercourse to avoid an unwanted pregnancy or STD. Divide yourselves into groups of four. Brainstorm and write down all the skills you can think of that a person must perform

to use birth control successfully." (The teacher should review the rules for brainstorming.) Tell students there are about 30 skills and challenge them to come up with 15 or more. Give 15 minutes for this activity and move among groups, prompting ideas.

Pull groups together and make a master list of skills. Have students write them on a sheet of paper with three columns to the right labeled "easy to do," "hard to do," and "impossible to do." Ask each student to make four copies of their sheet or make four photocopies.

Homework: Say "For homework, give your 'skills survey' to four people not in this class. Ask them how easy, hard, or impossible each skill would be for them to do now if they were sexually active. Try to have both sexes and adults as well as teens answer your questions. Record their age and sex, but not their name on the sheet. We will discuss your results on (day due — give three days)." During the interim days, teach about contraception.

Session 2—Activity 2: As students enter class, give each the questionnaire and have them rate their own comfort/skills and write why the skill is easy, hard, or difficult (20 minutes). Have students get out their homework surveys and review each skill one at a time, asking for reasons why they and other people they surveyed ranked the skill as they did. If you sense denial, play devil's advocate to bring the discussion to reality. If you sense embarrassment, move the discussion to "third person."

After going through the list, ask students to identify the most difficult skills and circle them. Have students break into groups and brainstorm suggestions and solutions to help a person overcome the difficulty in carrying out the skill. Share with the class afterwards and record ideas. Ask for "thumbs up" and "thumbs down" as to whether they think the solutions would work.

Processing Questions:

1. Can a person be sexually responsible without using contraception?

2. If you are too embarrassed or timid to do these skills, are you mature enough or in the right relationship to be having sex? Why? Why not?

3. Whose responsibility should contraception be? Why?

4. If two people equally share the pleasures of sex, how can the responsibilities be equally shared?

5. What could society do to assist sexually active teens in being better contraceptors without encouraging premarital sex?

Closure:
Ask students what they would like to do with the new information they learned. Some possible service projects are:

• Write a letter or send a student delegation to talk about findings with the health department, school, local newspaper, family planning council, or legislator.

• Tour local clinics and rate their services as being accessible or "user friendly" to teens.

• Develop an educational pamphlet or radio public service announcement directed toward sexually active teens.

• Participate in peer counselor training to help learn and teach skills that students have problems with.

• Write a creative skit for a teen audience and give performances. Allow the audience to interact in a discussion of the issues.

Evaluation:
1. Rate yourself:
   "1" - I probably would not become

involved in a pregnancy if I were sexually active.

"2" - I might become involved in a pregnancy if I were sexually active.

"3" - I would become involved in a pregnancy if I were sexually active.

Explain why you gave yourself the rating that you did.

2. Give detailed explanations of your strong and weak skills as well as other personal strengths and weaknesses as a possible contraceptive user.

3. What could you do to improve your birth control consumer skills?

Berne, L.A., & Wild, P.J. (1988). Teen sexual behavior: A leader's guide to practical strategies with youth. Reston, VA: AAHPERD.

ARE YOU READY FOR PRIME TIME BIRTH CONTROL?

Imagine you are a sexually active person but are not ready for a pregnancy. Rate your ability to do the following birth control skills:

(1) It would be <u>easy</u> for me to . . .
(2) It would be <u>hard</u> for me to . . .
(3) It would be <u>impossible</u> for me to . . .

___ 1. admit to myself that I'm going to have sexual intercourse.

___ 2. admit to myself that I could get pregnant or impregnate my partner.

___ 3. talk about my/my partner's past sexual experiences to see if one or both of us could be carrying STDs.

___ 4. talk with partner about needing birth control and which method is best for both of us.

___ 5. before having sex, deciding with partner what we would do if a pregnancy does occur.

___ 6. get transportation to clinic or doctor's office

___ 7. go alone (or with partner) to health department, public clinic, or private doctor's office.

___ 8. talk to strangers (doctor, nurse, counselor) honestly when they ask me questions about my sex life.

___ 9. have an internal pelvic exam, or go with my partner for a pelvic exam.

___ 10. ask questions when I don't understand the instructions.

___ 11. read and understand the instructions that come with birth control methods.

___ 12. buy birth control methods in a drug store or out in the public eye.

___ 13. pay for birth control methods

when I can not get them free at a clinic.

___ 14. store birth control in a cool, dark, and dry place.

___ 15. practice applying and removing birth control method prior to sexual intercourse.

___ 16. use a birth control method correctly <u>every time</u> I have sexual intercourse.

___ 17. use a backup method of birth control or abstain for the first four weeks taking the pill.

___ 18. remember to take pill at the same time each day, or remind partner.

___ 19. use more than one method (pill and condom) for more protection.

___ 20. touch my sex organs to apply and remove birth control method.

___ 21. touch partner's sex organs to help apply or remove birth control method.

___ 22. apply birth control in front of my partner.

___ 23. stop myself during sexual foreplay to apply birth control methods.

___ 24. stop sexual partner during foreplay to apply birth control methods.

___ 25. remember possible side effects of my birth control method and know what to do if they occur.

___ 26. carry birth control with me, or get it before sexual foreplay begins.

___ 27. return to clinic for regular medical check ups.

___ 28. remember to get more birth control items before they run out.

___ 29. continue to educate myself and learn new information on birth control methods.

Family Life Education

"Hey! How Did That Baby Live in That Test Tube?"

David A. Birch

Health education, like other academic areas, often relates directly to current issues and events extensively covered by various media. A current issue generating media coverage, invitro fertilization and embryo transfer or "test tube babies" has created curiosity among both adults and children.

However, even with extensive media coverage, not everyone understands the procedure involved with invitro fertilization. Part of this confusion can be traced to the commonly used term "test tube baby." The author, in his experience with junior high school students, became aware of many students whose perception of invitro fertilization included a live baby and a test tube. Thus, to some students, the question, "Hey! How did that baby live in that test tube?" is not as ludicrous as it may seem.

Another contributing factor to this misunderstanding is the tendency for both children and adults to look at or listen only to the headlines and not the details of a story. Thus if a child, or even an adult, hears only "test tube baby," it is easy to imagine misconceptions that could occur.

Because it is an important current health issue that could impact upon our society, these misunderstandings and misconceptions can and should be dealt with in health education classes. There are many areas in the health education curriculum which would relate directly to invitro fertilization and embryo transfer. The following information and teaching ideas should assist the health educator in covering this topic.

Background

Invitro fertilization and embryo trans-

fer is a procedure allowing women with blocked or missing Fallopian tubes to carry a baby in the uterus and subsequently give birth. Prior to institution of this procedure, these women were considered to be infertile.

Following births in England and Australia, the first American "test tube baby" was born in January, 1982. The term "test tube baby" is a misnomer since the procedure involves no actual test tube.

Using fertility inducing hormones to cause ovulation at a specified time, a long tube with a syringe is inserted at the time of ovulation through an incision in the abdomen and used to pull fluid containing the egg cell from the ovary. The egg cell is then deposited into a petri dish which has an environment similar to that inside the Fallopian tubes.

Sperm cells from the father are then deposited into the petri dish so that fertilization can occur. If fertilization occurs, the egg cell is inserted into the uterus through the vagina. If the fertilized egg implants itself into the wall of the uterus, prenatal development should continue.

While this procedure offers hope to some couples, there are objections to this procedure. Objections focus on issues such as the possible discarding of abnormal embryos, the potential risk to offspring from the procedure, the cost of the procedure, and the idea of physicians and scientists "playing God."

Vocabulary

To understand the procedure, students should become familiar with the following vocabulary words: uterus, Fallopian tubes, ovulation, egg cell, menstrual cycle, fertilization, infertile, sperm cell, and embryo.

Classroom Activities

The following activities should help

students understand cognitive aspects related to invitro fertilization and embryo transfer:

- *Using a drawing, chart, or model, demonstrate to students the path the egg cell normally follows through the Fallopian tube to the uterus, after ovulation.*
- *Using a drawing, chart, or model, explain to students the ramifications of blocked or missing Fallopian tubes on a woman's ability to have children.*
- *Using the same drawing, chart, or model, explain to students how an egg cell is removed from the body after ovulation, fertilized in a petri dish, and inserted into the uterus.*
- *Allow students to make their own audiovisual aids and to explain and review the situations listed above with their classmates.*

Students should also be given an opportunity to discuss related affective issues. A classroom discussion of the following questions will provide this opportunity:

- *Do you feel medical science has gone too far with invitro fertilization and that scientists are, in effect, "playing God"?*
- *Is it more appropriate for a couple that is infertile because of blocked Fallopian tubes to opt for invitro fertilization or to adopt one of the many children available for adoption?*
- *Should embryos that have developed deformities before implementation be discarded?*
- *Should private and public health insurance plans cover the cost of invitro fertilization and embryo transfer procedures?*

The issue of invitro fertilization and embryo transfer or the "test tube baby" issue stimulates interest in all age groups. Hopefully, the suggestions listed above will provide health educators with ideas for students at various levels. It is a current health issue with interest and implications for all segments of our society.

David A. Birch is with the Department of Educational and Cultural Services, State House Station 23, Augusta ME 04333.

Family Life Education

Actions Teach Better Than Words: Teen Life Theater and Role Play in Sex Education

Peggy Brick

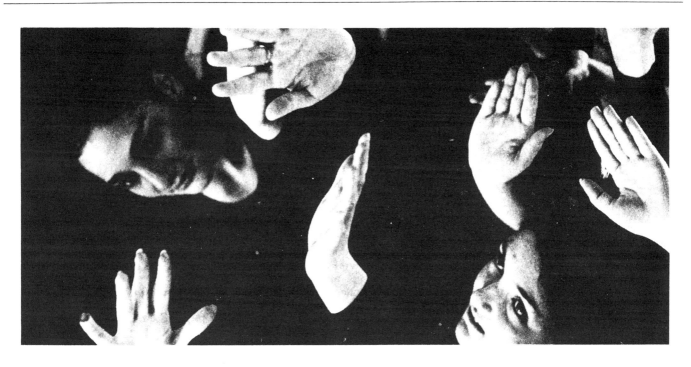

"Here comes the Teen Life Theater," I shout as 12 young actors dressed in logoed blue tee shirts run onto the stage and begin to introduce themselves. "I'm Margo and I wish my mother would try to understand me." "I'm Leo and I wish I didn't have VD." "I'm Marni and I wish my brother wasn't gay." "I'm Cal and I wish my friends wouldn't pressure me to smoke." When the introductions are over, the individual scenes depicting problems of adolescent life begin. The audience of students, parents, administrators, and board of education members is confronted with 12 unresolved dilemmas, such as the one

called "Sex Pressure" in which Robin and Tony arrive at the front door and discover a note saying that Robin's parents won't be home until late. Tony presses to come in, but Robin refuses: the family has a strict rule about boys in the house when Mom and Dad are not there. He insists; she resists. He gets angry and leaves, taunting, "Why don't you grow up?" At the end of the performances, the actors remain in their roles while the audience questions, challenges, and even joins them in trying alternative solutions. A few weeks later the board of education votes unanimously to fund this improvisational theater, thus adding a new dimension to the sexuality education program at Dwight Morrow High School in Englewood, N.J.

After fifteen years teaching sexuality education, I am convinced that this experiencing of adolescent dilemmas through life-like skits presented by the theater troupe, or in classroom role-

play, is a powerful method of educating for responsible sexuality. Many sex educators, busy "winning the battle" (Dickman, 1982), developing curriculum, and fielding questions, need to be reminded that improvisational theater may be the quintessential tool. Here the important ingredients of effective sex education coalesce. As students get into the act, they gain self-confidence, explore relationships, critique behavior, develop skills in communication and decision-making, learn to understand different points of view, and demystify sex. In our school, the Teen Life Theater now provides a model that encourages role-playing activities in the regular classrooms. In both formats students have a unique opportunity to practice confronting problems in their own lives. Our experience leads me to believe that improvisational theater should be a fundamental part of the family life education curriculum and basic in the preparation of sex educators.

Peggy Brick, recently retired from teaching Human Behavior, is Director of Affirmative Teaching Associates in Englewood, New Jersey and sexuality educator at Planned Parenthood of Bergen County, New Jersey.

Although family life theaters have become popular in a number of youth agencies during the past ten years (National Clearinghouse for Family Planning Information, 1982), few are supported by a board of education as part of the regular school program. Ours, initiated by a small grant from the county's Planned Parenthood, has been funded since 1981 by a board that values this direct method of confronting adolescent problems and appreciates the fact that in our multi-ethnic community, the Theater is unusual in its ability to attract students from a variety of groups. It is a living example of the intergroup cooperation and friendship that the board advocates.

During its first two years, the troupe performed at the state teachers' conventions, at institutes and workshops training teachers as family life education educators, and at a wide variety of schools, churches, community organizations, and youth groups. Within our own district they performed in health, behavioral science, English, and biology classes and in a number of mini-assemblies. Each performance is custom designed. During a session, following the performance of six to twelve skits, the audience may also get into the act.

Training the Theater Troupe

Teen Life Theater is an extracurricular activity, and 15 to 20 members train after school for two hours two days a week. The members also study the issues they are working on through reading, interviews with authorities, and films. Each receives a copy of R. Bell's *Changing Bodies, Changing Lives* (1980) as a basic resource. In addition, many of the actors are taking or have already taken the Human Behavior course taught by my co-advisor and me. The course and the Theater complement each other in many ways.

At the beginning of each rehearsal, theater warm-ups (Spolin, 1963) defuse anxiety, break-down self-consciousness, and build group spirit. We start by standing in a circle and one by one call out our names in a crazy way, the group echoing (a technique adapted from a workshop by *Playback Theater*). Next, a student moves to the center and creates a "sound and motion," an action using both voice and body. She moves in front of another member who imitates her, and, as she returns to her place in the circle, evolves her own action. The process is repeated as each invents, is imitated, laughed with, encouraged.

A final warm-up might be the machine exercise. One student begins a machine-like action with an appropriate sound. Others slowly add on, fitting into the building machine, which finally slows down and stops. Relaxed and energized, students are already practicing acting skills: perceiving, responding, imagining, creating (Siks, 1977).

During the early weeks, the director emphasizes the most fundamental skill, concentration, as students struggle to solve a variety of acting problems. Students must focus on each body sense, making "the object real" and trying to share their experience with their audience. They practice with half the troupe "on stage" while the other half observes. As the actors learn to focus, distractions are ignored and phoniness disappears; forgetting themselves, they "solve the problem" with increasing credibility. By being alternately actors and audience, students learn to evaluate when actions seem real and are communicated effectively.

Learning to Improvise

Soon the students are ready to solve larger problems by improvising a variety of scenes together. "You are on a boat. There's hardly room for all of you. It's beginning to sink. It goes under." "You are climbing a hill. It's very rocky. A strong wind comes from the summit. You reach the top and the view is beautiful." "You are all lifting a heavy box. You need more people. Gently now, up, up." Those observing are watching for concentration so complete they can feel the cold water, the strong wind, the heaviness of the box.

Next, students experiment with becoming different characters. The entire class mills slowly around the room: "You are 75 and going for your daily walk." The director gives actors time to become the character. Some will be healthy, striking with vigor; others will be crippled, plodding with difficulty. Each time, actors create their own character according to their own feelings. Later, actors will take much more time to develop the characters in skits for performance. For now, they are trying to experience themselves in another's body, imagining how that body reacts.

Gradually, these exercises change self-conscious posturers into persuasive actors. Actors will need considerable rehearsal in creating meaningful skits, but for most of them, their acting now will be natural and real as compared with most amateurs.

They are ready to begin "playmaking" (Siks, 1977), developing the skits about adolescent life that are the essence of Teen Life Theater. They brainstorm all the problems they might want to explore, select several, and divide into small groups to plan. They work on three areas: (1) *The scene.* Where and when is the incident occurring? What is beyond the scene in the present? in the past? in the future? (2) *The characters.* Who are they and what are their relationships? (3) *The Conflict.* After discussing these issues, they plan the basic actions and try them out.

When they feel some satisfaction, or if they are stuck at some point, they return to the whole group to work further with the director and present the germinating skits. Two boys are at urinals; one has a painful burning sensation, and they're off on a discussion of STDs. Three girls are in a locker room with one refusing to smoke and suffering the jeers of her friends. A girl tells her boyfriend that she is pregnant. Parents are upset with their son's interracial dating. A shy boy and girl struggle, merely to say "hello." A girl tries to get her alcoholic father to stop drinking. Each skit will have a fixed beginning and end, but no final resolution to the conflict. The aim of the Theater is to involve members of the audience in the crisis and leave them to work out their own solutions.

As students present rough skits, the director utilizes a number of techniques to help develop the drama being improvised. These methods facilitate the deeper exploration of character and situation and never instruct the actor in how to act. The director's job is to help students *discover* the right action in their character and situation in some of the following ways: (1) Act out an event that occurred before the present scene, to help "see" what caused this situation; or act out a future scene to understand the result of present actions. (2) Reverse roles. (3) Double: the director or another actor stands behind the character and while shadowing the actions, occasionally speaks a thought or feeling the character may not be expressing. (4) Contrapuntal argument: two actors in conflict, speaking simultaneously, assert their own argument without responding to each other. (5) Repeat the scene in pantomime. (6) Freeze the scene and ask the characters questions: "Did your mother treat you differently before she remarried?" "Do you get along better with other teachers?" "Have you ever had a long-term relationship with a boy?" (7) Freeze the scene and have each character assess

244

how the scene is "working" for them. (8) Change the pace if skit is serious, and make it into a comedy; if it's fast, "cool it." (9) "Physicalize" what's happening: for example, a child being "torn apart" by the parents' divorce. (10) Have a character monologue with the audience.

After eight weeks of this training, students are ready to perform before real audiences and to answer the challenging questions that will follow. We start off performing for classes within the school, but soon, we are out in the community and the responses reveal the impact. Parents report they had no idea that adolescents had so many problems. Teachers say the skits help them understand their students' attitudes toward school. An administrator writes that the skits made his students aware of their own disruptive and aggressive behaviors. A minister says it helps members of his congregation realize the need to develop a sex education program for the young people of the church. A professional whispers she wishes she had had the opportunity to see such a program when she was a child being sexually abused.

Role Play in the Classroom

There are, of course, significant differences between the Theater and classroom role play. Teen Life Theater is a voluntary, extracurricular activity directed to produce an entertaining as well as educational performance. In the classroom, however, I must be justified in taking time from other academic activities to have students play-act. Some teachers are uncomfortable with this idea, worrying, as one wrote at a recent workshop, that students will "goof off." And one administrator complained that he couldn't evaluate my lesson because the students were role playing and he couldn't "see me teach."

Both of these perceptions are mistaken. Yes, students do enjoy the acting, but through it they are dealing with problems of real life. I find students to be very serious about that. As for my teaching, I believe it is especially skilled and meaningful when I am facilitating role play. Here I am demonstrating that the information students are learning in my class is not just for knowing but for using. Role play, more than any other in-class pedagogical technique, forces students to apply learning to life. Although the same dilemmas can be examined in writing assignments and in discussions, the problems tend to remain cognitive, often subject to glib and

heady solutions. But when students act, emotions and complexities surface and the situation is experienced more fully. Acting allows students to experience themselves and others as whole persons in real-life contexts. With emotion-laden material such as sexuality, I find this approach indispensable. It is an effective prelude to honest discussion, serious writing, valid learning, and retention.

Although seeing a Teen Life Theater performance reduces student fears of acting and makes my task in the classroom easier, I still use a number of strategies to encourage the maximum possible participation in role play. I want everyone to experience themselves as someone else, to gain the empathy that comes from "being another." Here are three of the methods I use.

For the first, students take on a role, but do not act in front of the class. Desks are arranged in twos and, as students arrive, they divide into couples. Each pair will negotiate contracep-

tive decisions in imaginary situations listed on their assignment sheet: (1) You are both 14 and are considering having intercourse for the first time. (Students almost unanimously select abstinence for this one.) (2) You are both 23, living together, wanting to finish graduate school before you get married. (3) The man is 33 and the woman is 28; you are married; you do not want to have any children because a child would interfere with your career plans. In each case, the couple must record their decision, note why they selected the method they did and what steps they would need to take to implement their decision. After the couples complete their work, the class discusses the choices: explaining, arguing, revising as they hear each others' reasoning.

This exercise is valuable for several reasons. It normalizes talking to a partner about birth control. In enables students to apply their knowledge of contraception in specific situations. It demonstrates that people of different ages must communicate openly if they are to be sexually responsible. Finally, it makes clear the difference between making a decision and acting on that decision. This exercise is as close as I have come to breaking down the inhibitions that prevent contraceptive use among some sexually active adolescents.

A second method I use to facilitate student comfort in role play is placing students first in small groups. (Often they may select their own group with the stipulation that there is at least "one male, one female, one black, and one white" in each.) The group's first task is to reach agreement on what the main character should do in each of five situations. After the group has completed this assignment, it chooses one to act out for the entire class. This seems to be non-threatening and almost all students enjoy taking part in these skits.

After each group rehearses and acts out its skit, as in the Theater, members stay in role while the class questions and challenges. Since others have already come to their own conclusions about each scene, discussion is guaranteed to be lively and meaningful.

A third method demonstrated by Martha Roper at Syracuse University in 1981 involves all the students as part of a support system for the actors on stage. For example, for a scene in which John is telling his mother and dad that his girlfriend, Jenny, is pregnant, the class would divide into three groups: one supporting John, one supporting his dad, and one, his mother. Each group would receive a card describing its character; "Jenny's mom is 44 years old, and has two younger children: Brian, 10 and Sam, 13. She has been a computer programmer for five years and enjoys her work but worries that she leaves the children alone too much. Her salary is important for the family, especially since John plans to go to college next year. She frequently speaks with disapproval about teens who are sexually promiscuous. She has just come home from her aerobics class."

The card is read and the group selects a person to play the role. The group makes suggestions to its character and, during the enactment of the scene, can make recommendations in writing. The character can also leave the scene and ask another member to continue the action.

To begin, characters move to the front and, after introducing themselves, start the action which continues until there is a natural break. The actors are told to return to their groups for coaching or

for replacement. The scene then continues until a two-minute warning signals the end.

Following this drama, I might do a different kind of processing: (1) Have each player share reactions about the role and feelings toward the other players. (2) Have the class discuss the interpersonal dynamics that developed during the scene. (3) Discuss how the scene relates to the students' own lives. Careful processing is essential to successful role play. The teacher's questions help students understand the significance of what has happened so they gain insight into their own feelings and into human behavior.

Once students are accustomed to role play, our procedures become more informal. Anonymously, students submit on file cards problems they would like to see enacted. I'll read a card, ask for volunteers, and develop the scene on the spot. The school year is never long enough to explore all the problems students continue to submit.

Evaluating the Effects of Teen Theater and Classroom Role Play

At a time when everyone is searching for hard data on the effects of sex education, the evaluations of our programs, to date, are soft: responses, both written and oral, from audiences and sponsoring organizations, taped interviews with members of the Teen Life Theater troupe, both as individuals and together in a group; hundreds of student journals and essays that include discussion of theater performances and classroom role play. There are no statistics to document significant behavior change as a result of participation in improvisational theater. There are only the subjective reports of both participants and observers.

My interviews with Teen Life Theater members show that they believe the Theater has had a positive effect on their lives. Many report increased feelings of self-confidence.

Teen Life Theater also benefits its members through the strong bonding that develops between them. The Theater nurtures friendships and gives students a positive identity.

Student responses reinforce my own conclusions from teaching over 1,500 students: improvisational theater is an essential tool for the sex educator. It facilitates the implementation of four basic goals: to provide adequate knowledge of human sexuality in its physical, psychological, social and moral dimensions; to help students clarify and ap-

preciate their values and attitudes toward family and sexuality; to enhance student self esteem; and to increase skills in decision-making and communication. Only when students apply knowledge to life are these goals realized. Role play helps achieve this transition. In role play, students practice their new learnings in life-like situations. As they examine relationships between actors, as they defend their values in a particular scene, as they take pride in resolving a family crisis, as they communicate a strong belief, their knowledge is becoming personal and real. Through role play, sex education comes to life.

Bell, R. (1980). *Changing Bodies, Changing Lives: A Book for Teens on Sex and Relationships.* New York: Random House.

Dickman, I. R. (1982). *Winning the Battle for Sex Education.* New York: Sex Information and Education Council of the U.S.

National Clearinghouse for Family Planning Information. (August, 1982). Improvisational Theatre: An Effective Outreach and Education Medium. *Information Services Bulletin.*

Playback Theater, Innovative Studies. S.U.N.Y., New Paltz, New York, 12561.

Siks, G. B. (1977). *Drama With Children.* New York: Harper & Row.

Spolin, V. (1963). *Improvisation for the Theater.* Evanston, Illinois: Northwestern University Press.

photo: Greg Merhar

Family Life Education

Abortion Attitude Scale*

Linda A. Sloan

Perhaps the greatest crisis a contemporary teenager might face is having an untimely, unwanted pregnancy. Since more adolescents are sexually active and at younger ages than in past generations, the likelihood of its occurring has reached epidemic proportions in recent years. The pregnant teen has two major options: carrying the pregnancy to term or abortion.

Abortion, although legally available in the U.S. for almost a decade, has not ceased to be a highly volatile and hotly contested issue. Counseling the expectant mother on the abortion option is often inadequate because of three major intervening factors: (A) The counselor frequently has personal biases about the option; (B) It is difficult for the adolescent to identify her values about abortion; (C) Making the decision under the pressure of pregnancy may result in a different outcome than making a decision about abortion in a noncrisis setting.

Although health educators can have little impact on the personal biases of the counselor, they are in ideal positions to help students explore their values concerning abortion in nonthreatening circumstances. Chances of long term negative effects are reduced when one's behaviors are compatible with one's beliefs. Thus, helping students identify

Health educators are reminded of the highly sensitive, controversial nature of this topic. Though there is an urgent need to help teenagers, it is also imperative that the classroom teacher abide by district policies.

Linda A. Sloan is an assistant professor in the Department of Health and Physical Education, University of North Carolina at Charlotte, Charlotte, NC 28223.

Abortion Attitude Scale

Directions: This is not a test. There are no wrong or right answers to any of the statements, so just answer as honestly as you can. The statements ask you to tell how you feel about legal abortion (the voluntary removal of a human fetus from the mother during the first three months of pregnancy by a qualified medical person). Tell how you feel about each statement by circling one of the choices beside each sentence. Here is a practice statement:

SA   A   S1A   S1D   D   SD   *Abortion should be legalized*.

(SA = Strongly Agree; A = Agree; S1A = Slightly Agree; S1D = Slightly Disagree; D = Disagree; SD = Strongly Disagree)

Please respond to each statement and circle only one response. No one else will see your responses without your permission.

SA	A	S1A	S1D	D	SD	
5	4	3	2	1	0	1. The supreme court should strike down legal abortions in the United States.
5	4	3	2	1	0	2. Abortion is a good way of solving an unwanted pregnancy.
5	4	3	2	1	0	3. A mother should feel obligated to bear a child she has conceived.
5	4	3	2	1	0	4. Abortion is wrong no matter what the circumstances are.
5	4	3	2	1	0	5. A fetus is not a person until it can live outside its mother's body.
5	4	3	2	1	0	6. The decision to have an abortion should be the pregnant mother's.
5	4	3	2	1	0	7. Every conceived child has the right to be born.
5	4	3	2	1	0	8. A pregnant female not wanting to have a child should be encouraged to have an abortion.
5	4	3	2	1	0	9. Abortion should be considered killing a person.
5	4	3	2	1	0	10. People should not look down on those who choose to have abortions.
5	4	3	2	1	0	11. Abortion should be an available alternative for unmarried, pregnant teenagers.
5	4	3	2	1	0	12. Persons should not have the power over the life or death of a fetus.
5	4	3	2	1	0	13. Unwanted children should not be brought into the world.
5	4	3	2	1	0	14. A fetus should be considered a person at the moment of conception.

those beliefs without the pressure of extenuating circumstances may eventually aid them in making the best personal choice if they ever face the situation. The experiences provided in the classroom may also create such dissonance as to cause students to internalize the advantages of preventing pregnancy rather than having to cope with it once it occurs.

The health educator has little difficulty locating information on the history of abortion, the medical techniques, and groups to speak to its advantages and disadvantages. What may be more difficult to acquire is an instrument which somewhat objectively measures attitudes toward abortion. To meet this need, the author has developed and validated the following Abortion Attitude Scale for use with teenagers. The validation process involved interrater agreement, pilot testing, reliability estimates, factor analysis to determine unidimensionality and hypothesis testing. The scale was administered to populations including high school and college students, active Right to Life members, and abortion service associates. The test exhibited a high total test estimate of reliability (.92) and five hypotheses were supported on the construct validity assessment. Right to Life members' mean scores were 16.2 while abortion service associates' scores were 55.6. All other groups' mean scores fell in the middle range.

Classroom Uses:

Health teachers can use this instrument in several ways:

1. To generate discussion.

2. For pre-post testing on abortion unit.

3. For students to administer to parents and report.

4. For students to administer to friends and report.

5. For students to compare results from various groups.

6. To use as a background for debate.

7. To explore ranges of acceptance of abortion (in case of rape, incest, genetic defects, etc.).

8. To combine the scale with use of values clarification techniques such as a values continuum, popular song lyrics, etc.

Note to Teacher on Scoring:

Step 1—Reverse the point scale for items 1, 3, 4, 7, 9, 12, 14.

Step 2—Total point responses for all items.

Step 3—Provide students with scoring scale.

70–56 Strong pro abortion
55–44 Moderate pro abortion
43–27 Unsure
26–16 Moderate pro life
15–0   Strong pro life

248

Family Life Education

Marriage Yesterday and Today

Margaret J. Pope

In the Unites States today, more than 90 percent of the population will marry at least once. Statistics indicate that one half or more of these marriages end in divorce, a rate that has been rising steadily since World War II. The median length of marriages that end in divorce is seven years (Nass, Libby, & Fisher, 1984). Four out of five who divorce will remarry and many will marry more than twice. Why should so many marriages end within such a few years? Marriage experts cannot provide one clear answer (Payne & Hahn, 1986). There is, however, a general agreement among physicians, sociologists, mental health counselors, and ministers that many problems that confront people in marriage could be avoided if there were a more realistic approach to marriage.

People tend to marry those of similar background in age, race, education, intelligence, religion, economic status, and family. One of the keys to a successful marriage is communication. Effective communication involves being responsible for working out problems as they occur, being a good listener, and not being defensive as disagreements or differences arise (Hamrick, Anspaugh, & Ezell, 1987). The key to healthy disagreement is communication.

While teaching a unit on Marriage and Family Relationships in a health education class at the university undergraduate level, I decided to initiate a different approach to the marriage-

Margaret J. Pope is a professor of health education at Jacksonville State University, Jacksonville, AL 36265.

divorce syndrome of today's society. The objective was to discuss with four married couples how they resolve their marriage problems. This involved discussion of communication as well as other problems that arise when two people marry. Four couples were invited to visit the class on an appointed day.

Two had been married over 50 years and the two were college students who had married within the year. The class was to investigate, through discussion, some of the problems each couple had faced in adjustments to marriage. The same questions were asked of the young couples and those who had been married for over 50 years. The purpose was to draw comparisons between age groups and their approach to adjustment problems of marriage.

In preparation for the visit, the class was divided into groups, each with a student leader. The instructor suggested topics that could be used for discussion and asked the class for suggestions. Students were told they could not ask questions that were personal or offensive to the guests.

Broad topics chosen for discussion were:

Readiness for Marriage
Adjustment Problems
Age
Compatibility
Emotional
Maturity
Interests

Economic and Financial Security
Financial Goals
Occupation of Each Partner

Conflict in Marriage
Communication During Conflict
Resolving Disagreements

Structure of Family
Children

Each group of students developed questions pertinent to all broad topics. These were previewed in class the day before the couples visited.

On the day of the visit, desks and chairs were arranged in a circle and apple juice was served. This allowed guests and students to socialize before the discussion began. The topic both groups of couples discussed longest was "conflict in marriage." Student interest in resolving disagreements between married couples was high and guests were willing to discuss their solutions. One of the questions to the older couple was, "How have you held your marriage together for so long?" The two young couples were more involved with the "economic and financial security" topic.

There is no formula for a successful marriage; however, through preparation, recognition of potential problems, and opportunity for discussion with married couples, students can become more ready for this step in their lives. The four married couples' visits to the classroom facilitated opportunity for student growth through personal interaction.

Evaluations of the process were positive. Students indicated that this was a meaningful experience that caused them to begin to think more seriously about marriage and problems that might arise.

Family Life Education

Teaching Abstinence to Today's Teens

Dee Gibbs Smalley

Again, we confront a dilemma in the family life curriculum. Is it possible to take a positive stance on abstinence and still provide necessary information to those teens who are engaging in sexual activities? If it is possible, how do family life educators approach the issue of abstinence with their students in a manner to accommodate both groups - those electing to abstain and those who have chosen to become sexually active.

A vast majority of parents and teachers alike support abstinence as a curriculum topic. Forrest and Silverman report that one survey revealed about 25 percent of teachers cited abstinence as the most important message they have for their students. However, it, like most issues involving sexuality, is not an easy topic to discuss in a classroom filled with 30 fifteen-year-olds. To complicate matters even more, abstinence curricula and supplemental instructional programs are lacking in quantity as well as quality. Therefore, teachers frequently elect to develop their own teaching materials. This leads teach-

Dee Gibbs Smalley is the health and physical education curriculum development coordinator for Memphis City Schools, Memphis, TN 38104.

ers to question what should be discussed and how it should be presented to students. (Alan Guttmacher Institute, 1989).

In a 1986 poll, "American Teens Speak: Sex, Myths, TV, and Birth Control," conducted by Louis Harris and Associates, one thousand teens were asked their opinions on a number of issues. Two of the questions included: (1) Why do teens not wait to have sexual intercourse until they are older; and (2) What reasons are most useful in convincing peers to wait to have sex until they are older? (Peterson, 1988).

Peterson reports the top four reasons given by teenage girls for not wanting to have sexual intercourse revolved around dangers of diseases, such as AIDS and herpes - 65 percent, and the danger of pregnancy - 62 percent. Fifty percent of the teens worried about what their parents would do if they found out, and 29 percent felt that having sex would ruin their reputation (Peterson, 1988).

The 1986 Harris Poll reported that teens felt pressure by other teenagers to go further with sex than they wanted. Since both males and females felt this pressure, those curricula materials should be utilized which contain activities essential to helping teens learn how to resist this sexual pressure. It is so vitally important to empower youth to resist peer pressure. Such assertiveness skills have lifelong value. However, educators must be alert to teens' concerns where resisting peer pressure is involved. It is not always easy to say "no" even after learning the skill (Peterson, 1988).

Leo reports in *TIME* that studies are surfacing which present evidence

that most teens are looking for an excuse to abstain. In 1980, the teen services program at Atlanta's Grady Memorial Hospital found that of the thousand or so girls under age 16 in this program, many wanted to learn how to say no without hurting anyone's feelings. The key to the their final decision rests in their decision-making skills, their assertiveness, and their ability to communicate their values and feelings concerning abstinence.

In light of these critical facts, the following 55 minute lesson is a suggestion for those teachers who lack curricula materials but share the desire to teach abstinence. While the lesson is designed for middle school and junior high school students, it easily can be adapted for older students.

Instructional Objectives

The student will (1) recognize the importance of sexual abstinence and identify consequences of failure to abstain and (2) identify and practice techniques of assertiveness.

Set

Begin the instruction by writing the phrase "human sexuality" on the board. While this is visible to students, explain that although they are sexual beings, it is important not to act out on every sexual feeling until they are mature enough to accept responsibilities for their consequences. Inform students that the purpose of this lesson is to recognize the importance of sexual abstinence and identify consequences of failure to abstain, and to identify and practice techniques of assertiveness.

Instruction

Write three headings on the board for all students to see. The headings should read: (1) Reasons Frequently Given by Teens for Becoming Sexually Active, (2) Reasons Frequently Given by Teens for Postponing Sexual Activity, and (3) Possible Consequences of Becoming Sexually Active.

Begin with heading number 1. Allow students to brainstorm reasons that teens may become sexually active. As ideas are presented, list them on the board underneath the heading. Allow sufficient time for students to generate as many reasons as possible. Reasons may include pressure from peers, fun or pleasure, feel grown up, love, curiosity, hold onto girl/boyfriend, lonely, rebelling against parents as seen on TV or movies, or to escape problems at home. Allow for interaction between students.

Move to heading number 2. Have students brainstorm reasons that teens may postpone sexual activity. As before, list them on the board when generated. Reasons may include waiting until married, fear of pregnancy, fear of getting a sexually transmitted disease, AIDS, afraid parents will find out, may be painful, against religious beliefs, against value system, might interfere with future plans, not ready for responsibilities of a baby, not physically or emotionally ready, might ruin reputation, or simply didn't want to. Again, encourage discussion between students.

Finally, direct students' attention to heading number 3. Ask students to think of possible consequences of becoming sexually active. List them under the heading as students generate their ideas. Consequences may include, but are not limited to, unwanted pregnancy, sexually transmitted diseases, AIDS, dropping out of school because of pregnancy, damaged reputation, having to seek a job to support a child, changed relationship with boy/girlfriend, parents, and friends, losing self-respect, and feeling differently about oneself.

Ask students to compare mentally the reasons given for becoming sexually active with possible consequences of becoming sexually active. Ask them to identify the list of reasons which would have a greater impact on their lives both now and in the future and the plans, dreams, and goals they have set for themselves.

Explain to students that the decision to become sexually active or to remain abstinent is theirs - a decision only they can make. Unfortunately, pressures abound in society. Pressures from the media as well as peer pressure force many adolescents to become sexually active before they are physically, emotionally, and financially prepared to deal with the consequences.

Inform students that many adolescents are not prepared to deal with the pressure often exerted by a member of the opposite sex to become sexually active. Therefore, being able to say "no" assertively to a pressure situation may be very helpful. Explain that by knowing how to deal with these pressures, students will have more control over their lives and will be able to make wiser decisions.

Distribute a copy of the Handout - Lines (Figure 1) to each student. Have students write their response to each "line." After students have completed the assignment, provide volunteers with an opportunity to share their response. If sufficient time remains, have students select the most

Continued on page 253

Figure I. Handout-Lines

DIRECTIONS: Read each statement carefully. Write a response to each of the following.

1. Come on! Everyone is doing it!
   Response:_____

2. If you really love me, you'll do it!
   Response:_____

3. If you won't have sex with me, I won't see you again.
   Response:_____

4. Don't be afraid of what others will say.
   Response:_____

5. Having sex with me will make you a real man/woman.
   Response:_____

6. I promise we'll get married someday.
   Response:_____

7. Don't you want to try it to see what it's like?
   Response:_____

8. But I have to have it or I'll die.
   Response:_____

9. If you get pregnant, we'll get married.
   Response:_____

10. You know you want it as much as I do.
    Response:_____

11. If you love me, prove it.
    Response:_____

12. Come on, take a drink. It will get you in the mood.
    Response:_____

Family Life Education

Group Discussion on Contraceptive Issues

Barbara A. Rienzo

The problems and consequences of unplanned and unwanted pregnancy are well documented in the literature. Some of the costs to the mother, child, and society include high infant mortality rate, high rate of low birth weight or premature babies, higher risks of hypertension, toxemia, and other complications of pregnancy, interruption or ter-

Barbara A. Rienzo is an associate professor in the Department of Health Education, University of Florida, Gainesville, FL 32611.

mination of education, lower job/career possibilities, increased rates of child abuse, and birth defects, such as mental impairment and limb deformity. Most health and education professionals agree on the need for prevention of unwanted pregnancy.

Although we do not yet have a perfect contraceptive method many unwanted pregnancies could be prevented through consistent use of an effective contraceptive. There are a variety of reasons given for non-use of contraceptives among youth. These include ignorance, unavailability, lack of motivation, the desire to become pregnant.

The following exercise is an effective method of introducing the topic of birth control and facilitating discussion about motivational issues surrounding the use of birth control/contraceptives by sexually active young adults. It is appropriate for high school, college, and adult groups.

Initially the educator has the students take a half-page of paper and write whether they are male or female at the top. No names or distinguishing marks should be used to preserve anonymity. The class is then instructed to listen to the following situation. They will later be asked to write down their reaction.

The instructor tells the class: (The following may be modified to fit the specific audience)—

"You have been going out with this person for some length of time. You really care for him or her and have had a nice time this evening. You've been to a romantic dinner with candlelight and to a movie, and now you're back at your place. You are both feeling affectionate and things begin to get 'hot and heavy.' You realize that you'd really like to make love with this person (You had not had sex with him/her before)—but you don't have any contraceptive available. *What would you do?*"

The instructor tells the students to consider the situation silently and to write down on their papers as honestly as they can what they think they would do in that situation. The teacher should be sure to have students write down their answers without talking to others to ensure that individually considered responses are recorded. As the students finish writing (allow approximately five minutes), have the students fold their sheets of paper in half. The teacher should collect the sheets personally, shuffling them as they are handed in to preserve anonymity. When all the papers are collected, the instructor directs the class to form a circle of chairs (using about half of the chairs) in the center of room. Meanwhile, the students' papers should be separated into male and female responses. After this is accomplished, the teacher instructs all the males to sit in the inner circle. The class is told that this is a "fishbowl" exercise with the following rules:

1. All the persons in the inner circle are allowed to participate in the discussion. They are the *only* ones permitted to talk.
2. There should be enough chairs in the inner circle for all members of one sex *plus one empty chair.*
3. The persons in the outer circle must remain silent. They may only listen. If they wish to say something, they must take the empty chair in the inner circle.
4. The persons in the inner circle will be given the responses of the other sex by the instructor. The students are instructed to discuss the responses in terms of by answering the following:
   a. How do you *feel* about the response(s);

   b. Do you think the response is realistic?
   c. What are the implications or consequences of the response?
5. The instructor makes it clear that the discussion should be among the persons in the inner circle only and *no personal attacks* on other people are permitted. (Speak in "I" statements).

The instructor may need to initiate discussion by asking the persons in the inner circle to read the responses aloud to the group, and then use active listening skills to elicit their thoughts and feelings. The discussion time should be split evenly between the same-sex groups, and the instructor should allow a few minutes at the end of class time to summarize the session. Often, additional time must be spent during the next class period to summarize the discussion and allow students to express their feelings and thoughts about the exercise.

The major ideas generated through this exercise are:

1. Responsibility for birth control—
   a. Whose responsibility is it?
   b. How do you share the responsibility?
   c. How do you take responsibility?
   d. What obligation(s) does the male have in an unplanned pregnancy?
2. Communication—
   a. How do you talk about birth control with a partner?
   b. When is a good time to talk

about contraception?
3. Relationships—
   a. Does birth control responsibility vary with the type/intensity of the relationship?
4. Sex Roles—
   a. How do female sexuality stereotype influence birth control?
      1. Is a girl/woman bad/loose if she is prepared for sex?
      2. When a woman says "no" is she serious? Is she taken seriously?
   b. How do male sexuality stereotypes influence birth control?
      1. Is a guy always out for all he can get?
      2. Is it OK for a guy to say "no"?
5. Sexual behavior—
   a. Is sexual intercourse the only satisfying end/goal of lovemaking?
   b. Are there alternatives to sexual intercourse?
   c. Is "planned" sex less exciting?—Does sex have to be spontaneous to be good?

This exercise provides an opportunity for students to participate actively in class and to identify those issues which contribute in important ways to their decisions regarding contraceptive behavior. The teacher-facilitator has the responsibility to initiate (when necessary), summarize, and clarify issues from each group's responses. Both teacher and students can benefit greatly from the insight achieved through talking with and listening to other individuals.

Teaching Abstinence to Today's Teens

Continued from page 251

assertive response, the most clever response, and others.

Again, explain to students that the decision to become sexually active or to remain abstinent is theirs - a decision only they can make. Briefly review the possible consequences of becoming sexually active. Stress that a sexual relationship can be a most gratifying experience when a person is prepared physically, emotionally, and financially to deal with the consequences,

but it can be a terrifying experience under other conditions.

The Alan Guttmacher Institute. (1989). Risk and responsibility. New York: Author.

Forrest, J. D., & Silverman, J. (1989). What public school teachers teach about preventing pregnancy, AIDS, and sexually transmitted diseases. *Family Planning Perspectives, 21* (2), 65–72.

Leo, J. (1986, November 24). Sex and Schools. *Time,* 54–63.

Peterson, L. (1988). The issue- and controversy-surrounding adolescent sexuality and abstinence. *SIECUS Report, 17* (1), 1–8.

Family Life Education

Developing and Rejuvenating Relationships

Jane W. Lammers

For some people, developing personal relationships is very difficult. Equally as difficult for some is maintaining a continued interest in an old relationship. As Peck (1978) describes, relationships go through various stages, and hard work is necessary for relationships to flourish.

An ideal time to learn about relationships and their intricacies is during the developmental period of adolescence, when teenagers are very concerned about establishing ties with their peers and are testing their independence from the immediate family (Erickson, 1982). Yet, while the new relationships are being developed, old relationships need to be maintained and nurtured. By participating in the following activity, one is able to experience caring for several different types of relationships in his life.

The activity works well with teenagers but is applicable to anyone who desires renewal in a relationship. College students, whose ages range from 18 to elderly, have benefited from the experience. In health education classes, the activity integrates well into the human sexuality section, where a major emphasis is learning how to develop and appreciate a variety of relationships with family and friends (Educational Development Center, Inc., 1983).

The overall goal of the activity is to help an individual experience development and nurturing of a relationship. Specifically, the participant will renew a relationship with himself, a loved one, and one or more other people he does not know very well. The time allotted for the activity is

Jane W. Lammers is in the Department of Health Education at the University of Central Arkansas, Conway, AR 72032.

three weeks, with one week being devoted to each relationship. A helpful technique for insuring that the participant completes the activity is to provide an activity sheet for planning and recording the results (see Table 1 for an example of Week One).

In the first week, the participant is to renew a relationship with himself. He is asked to analyze how well he has been taking care of himself by writing down three things that he does to care for himself and listing in another column three things he does not do. Some examples that can be recorded in the "does not do" column might be general health habits that are recognized as beneficial for health: for example, exercising regularly, getting adequate sleep, eating well-balanced meals, managing stress, meditating, playing, and not using tobacco. He then chooses some specific thing that he will do everyday for himself for one week and records the planned activity on a particular day in a weekly log (each day's activity may be the same or all or some may be different). Examples might include meditation for 15 minutes, walking for 20 minutes, going to a movie, eating breakfast, not smoking cigarettes or chewing tobacco, or eating more fresh fruits and vegetables. At the end of each day, the participant records in the daily log what he did each day. At the end of the week, he writes a summary paragraph that describes the success or failure in being good to himself, feelings during the experience, plans for the future, and general comments about the activity, including how he might do it if he tried it again.

During the second week, the participant renews a relationship with a

loved one, either a family member or a close friend. To analyze the current status of the relationship with the person, the participant writes down three things that he does on a regular basis to nurture the relationship and three things that he could do. Examples might include 15 minutes of uninterrupted conversation with the other person without talking about himself, rubbing the person's back, washing the person's car, sending a card of appreciation to the individual for his contribution to the participant's life, taking the person out to eat, or keeping the person's house clean. For one week, the participant chooses something to do everyday for the other person without telling the person he is doing this for an assignment and records his planned activity in a daily log. At the end of each day, the participant records what he has done. At the end of the week, a summary paragraph is developed to describe successes, failures, feelings, and responses. The participant is asked to report what changes he might make if he were to do the activity again.

The final week is designed for the participant to establish a relationship with someone or several other people whom he does not know very well. Such an individual(s) might be someone in one of his classes, his employer, a fellow worker, a neighbor, or someone he has been wanting to meet. Each day for one week, the participant chooses something he will do to enhance a new relationship *without* letting anyone know about the project. Each day may be devoted to establishing a relationship with the same person or a different person. Some examples of ways to enhance the relationship might be to initiate a conversation, ask someone to go to a movie or party, offer to run an errand for someone, or just compliment someone. The participant lists the plan for each day in the daily log and then, after each day is completed, he will record what was done to enhance a new relationship. At the end of the week, the participant writes a summary paragraph reporting what happened, how the participant felt about the experience, how others responded, and how the experiment might be redone.

Generally, most students willingly participate in the activity; but, with encouragement, those who are initially apprehensive usually benefit most from the experience. Assignment of the activity may be all that is necessary to encourage the student to initiate the beginning or renewal of a desired relationship. Many students write in their reports that because of the activity they began a new relationship with someone they had wanted but had been too afraid to meet in the past. Some have used the activity as an opportunity to re-establish old ties with family and friends that previously had been severed by a disagreement. Some students even become philosophical. One student wrote after having completed the project:

> I have found the smallest of seeds sown sincerely will grow if cared for. Just like the seeds sown, a relationship needs to be nourished. A cared for relationship will grow and produce much beneficial fruit. An ignored one will wither. Relationships are active and can be directly influenced by the care given them. (Anonymous, 1988)

In summary, health educators can provide opportunities for students to develop skills that will enhance the quality of their lives. Caring for a relationship is an example of one skill that can be developed. The activity discussed provides a practical approach to learning how to care for oneself and others. With practice, individuals, whether in the home, workplace, or community, can begin to demonstrate their concern for themselves and others and thus become healthier people. In the final analysis, healthy relationships make for healthy people.

Figure 1. Discovering and Rejuvenating Relationships (Worksheet)

Week One: Renew a relationship with yourself.

A. Analyze how well you have been taking care of yourself. Write down three things that you do or do not do on a regular basis.

Things I do for myself

1._____

2._____

3._____

Things I do not do for myself

1._____

2._____

3._____

B. Choose something you will do everyday for yourself for one week. (Each day's activity may be different or all may be the same.) In the left hand column, write what you *plan to do* each day. In the right hand column, write what you *did* each day.

My daily plan

Day 1_____

Day 2_____

Day 3_____

Day 4_____

Day 5_____

Day 6_____

Day 7_____

What I did

_____

_____

_____

_____

_____

_____

_____

C. At the end of one week, write a summary paragraph that describes your success or failure in being good to yourself. Describe your feelings during the activity, plans for the future, and general analysis of the activity.

Note: Each week, the activity sheet would be modified.

Anonymous, (1988). Paper prepared for health education general education course.

Educational Development Center, Inc. (1983). *Having friends. The teenage health teaching modules.* Department of Health and Human Services (contract #200-79-0922).

Erickson, E. (1982). *The life cycle completed: A review.* New York: W .W. Norton & Co.

Peck, M. S. (1978). *The road less traveled.* New York: Simon & Schuster.

Family Life Education

Courtesies and Rights Within Relationships

Bethann Cinelli and Robert Nye

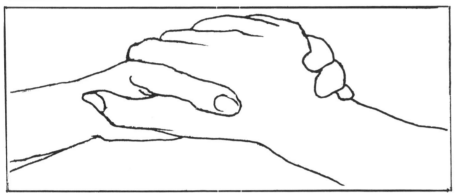

Courtesy, n., pl. -sies: 1. courteous behavior 2. a polite or considerate act (Gurlanik, 1984)

Right, n.: 1. what is right, just, etc. 2. a power, privilege, belonging to one by law, nature etc. (Gurlanik, 1984)

Human relationships present many challenges. For many people these include developing, building and maintaining of primary relationships and possible marriage. There are also many factors to a lasting love relationship. Rosenman has identified these as: self-acceptance, appreciation of one another, commitment, good communication, realistic expectations, shared interests and the ability to face conflict effectively (Rosenman, 1979).

As part of a Love and Marriage class, students are encouraged to develop their own definition of love, identify desirable traits they want in their potential mate, and then look at partner interactions which may be detrimental to or may enhance their

Bethann Cinelli is an assistant professor of health education, West Chester University, Department of Health, West Chester, PA 19383. Robert Nye is a professor of health education at West Chester University.

relationship. As the course progresses to discussing helping and doing things for each other, then to jealousy and honesty, many students become confused, frustrated and angry over expectations and what partners should and should not do for each other. This is most evident when discussing courtesies within a relationship. One can notice quickly that students have not yet defined for themselves the differences between courtesies and rights nor what to expect or demand within relationships.

Crooks and Baur (1987) refer to this as the "inclusion-response foundation." They describe this term as the "little things that count in a relationship." Often these behaviors may go unnoticed and, therefore, are taken for granted. These may include offering to help with a chore, opening doors, or being complimentary. Therefore the purpose of this activity is to help students distinguish between what they perceive to be courtesies within the relationship as well as what they perceive to be individual rights.

Activity

Instruct students to form small groups that are co-ed with approximately four or five students. For the next 15 to 20 minutes, each group will be asked to list the most important *courtesies* (there is no mention of *rights* at this time) that they would like

Table 1. Examples of a Courtesy List from Class Discussion
Not interrupting your partner when he or she is speaking
Opening doors
Being on time
Calling your partner if you are going to be late
Picking up after yourself
Being honest
Showing respect for partner
Not leaving hair in the sink
Telling your partner there is a change in plans
Remembering important dates (birthdays, anniversaries)
Allowing time for friends
Allowing your wife to work
Filling the gas tank when empty
Wife being given money for herself
Not drinking directly out of cartons in refrigerator
Not embarrassing your partner in public
Not smoking in bed
Putting toilet seat down after use
Paying attention or listening when your partner is talking
Being supportive of partner's career

extended to them by their partners. To record their responses, give each group a large (36" X 30") sheet of newsprint paper and a marker. Tell students that they may work within the classroom or may choose to work in the hallway or other available rooms.

When the lists have been completed, the instructor will attach them (an example of common responses can be found in Table 1) to walls around the room. Students then are asked to read over the lists while the instructor also reviews them. However, the instructor will place a check by the items which actually may be considered to be individual rights rather than courtesies. At this time, do not tell students why you are checking any particular item. Ask the groups to discuss each other's lists. As the questions and comments trail off, ask students why they think that you have checked certain items. If time is important, after these lists have been checked, go right to the question of "why" these items were highlighted.

After students offer their suggestions, the instructor can point out

that check marks actually may indicate "rights" rather than "courtesies" within a relationship. These "rights" are viewed as what is just, rather than as a courteous or considerate act. The instructor should note that confusion over courtesies and rights can be devastating to a relationship. What one partner may see as merely a courtesy, the other may believe is a right which must be observed.

The follow-up discussion will then address differences between courtesies and rights. Students will also be asked a key question about how they feel when an expected courtesy is not extended to them. Often they will express feelings of anger, disappointment or disillusionment. It then can be pointed out to them that perhaps this is an indication that they view the expected behavior as a *right* rather than as a *courtesy*. The denial of a courtesy should not generate the degree of anger some students exhibit. In differentiating between the two, students may discuss that there are universal rights which should be

extended to everyone at all times, and that there may be relationship rights which people define for themselves which may need to be identified early in the "getting to know each other" stage.

Conclusion

This activity is designed to offer the students an opportunity to show how, in actuality, (1) rights are often confused with courtesies, (2) communication between partners is essential in order to define courtesies and rights, (3) partner expectations need to be defined and (4) because of varying backgrounds, what one partner may consider to be a courtesy the other partner may consider to be a right.

Crooks, R. & Baur, K. (1987). *Our sexuality*. California: Benjamin Cummings, 226–228.

Gurlanik, D. B. (1984). *Webster's new world dictionary*. New York: Warner Books, 111, 144.

Rosenman, M. (1979). *Loving styles*. Englewood Cliffs, NJ: Prentice Hall.

CPR Drilling Revisited

Mark J. Kittleson

In 1980, this author published an article that discussed a possible alternative in teaching Cardiopulmonary Resuscitation (CPR). Entitled *CPR Drilling*, its main premise was that a great deal of CPR instruction is spent observing another person performing CPR. The author contended that much of this observing could be reduced by more efficient classroom management.

Over the past several years, the ideas suggested in the 1980 article have been refined and researched. This article will discuss four specific techniques that can be used in a CPR class to enhance the learning of this critically needed skill.

Bloom (1974) stated that on-task behavior is a critical component to learning any skill. Most of Bloom's research, as well as many of Bloom's followers, have only analyzed cognitive skills. Could such a theory be effective in a psychomotor skill such as CPR? Little, if any, research has been done to support this concept.

Kittleson's research (1986) showed that Bloom's time on task concept is relevant to psychomotor skills. He also went on to show how Cratty's theory of progressive part practice can also affect CPR instruction (Cratty, 1973).

Cratty believes that in order to learn a complex skill, one must first break the skill into several specific parts. Only after mastering these specific parts can one put the skill together.

The skills needed to learn single rescue CPR forms the basic of learning CPR. Once such skills are mastered, other techniques such as two person CPR can be taught. However, single rescue CPR is the major technique now

Mark J. Kittleson is an assistant professor in health education in the Department of Health and Physical Education at Youngstown State University, Youngstown, OH. He is also an instructor-trainer in advanced first aid for the American Red Cross as well as an instructor-trainer in CPR for the American Heart Association.

encouraged by the American Heart Association and the American Red Cross.

A critical part of single rescue CPR is the learning of various "parts" which include: mouth-to-mouth resuscitation, proper compression rate and depth, moving quickly from the chest to give two ventilations, combining chest compressions with two ventilations, as well as learning the steps to initiate CPR.

In Kittleson's study (1986), each of these skills were broken down and each skill is practiced by an individual until mastered. Once mastered, the individual can "combine" these parts. An individual is placed in a group of three, with each person responsible for a key component of the task. The *rescuer* is the person performing the actual skill; the *timer* is the individual who uses a stopwatch to detect speed; the *observer* carefully monitors the performance of the rescuer. Each of the three individuals rotate a role when the rescuer completes his/her task. Altogether, there are four specific tasks to complete.

This format will allow the instructor(s) to spend time with those individuals needing special assistance. It also sets the tone of the class that each person is not only responsible to learn CPR, but also is responsible to assist others in the learning of that task.

Task One: Initiating CPR

Rescuer's Role: Imagine you have walked into the room and you see "Annie" lying here. Although you do not know it at the time, Annie is in cardiac arrest. Go through the proper steps of determining unresponsiveness, calling for help, opening the airway and listening for breathing, giving two full breaths, and checking the pulse (while calling for somebody to get an ambulance).

After you have finished taking the pulse, position yourself to perform CPR. Once your hands are on the chest, you can sit back.

Timer's Role: Start the stopwatch once the person starts checking for unre-

sponsiveness. Keep track of how long each task takes. Be especially aware of the length of the pulse check. A rough idea for time should be as follows:

Task	Seconds	
	Min.	Max.
1. Determine Unresponsiveness (call for help)	4	8
2. Open Airway, listen for breathing	7	13
3. Give two full breaths	13	19
4. Check Pulse (tell somebody to call an ambulance)	17	29

Observer's Role: Your job is to make certain that the rescuer performed each specific criteria successfully. You are to make certain that proper position of the rescuer (as well as the victim) occur, at all times. Stop the rescuer if necessary to point out an error.

Have each person rotate after five complete performances.

Task Two: Proper Ventilation

This task is to get the rescuer comfortable with the idea that he/she is to move quickly from the chest when giving the two ventilations.

Rescuer's Role: Start in chest compression position. When you hear the timer say "go," leave the chest, give two full ventilations, go back to the chest position, and wait until the timer says "go" again. Make certain that you ventilate effectively and that you pinch the nostrils and open the airway sufficiently. If you get confused, or get behind in the sequence, stay on the chest until you hear the word "go" again.

Timer's Role: When the rescuer is ready, say the word "go." Keep your eyes on the stopwatch. Every six seconds say "go" loudly to the rescuer. Keep the watch running at all times; do not stop and reset each time. For example, say "go" at start, six, twelve, eighteen, twenty-four seconds, etc.

Go for thirty seconds, stop, and continue for another 75 seconds.

Observer's Role: Your job is to make certain that the mannikin is resuscitated completely. Make sure that the head tilt, chin lift is performed correctly, that the nostrils are being pinched, and that the rescuer's mouth completely covers the mouth of the mannikin. Finally, make certain that the rescuer finds the mannikin's xiphoid process before placing hands on the mannikin's chest.

Have each person rotate roles after completing one thirty second and one 75 second.

Task Three: CPR Compressions

The objective of this task is to make certain that the rescuer is able to perform proper chest compressions within the allotted time period.

Rescuer's Role: Position yourself on the chest, ready to do cardiac massage. Do 15 proper chest compressions within 8.5–9.0 seconds. Stop, receive your time, and repeat 10 times.

Timer's Role: When the rescuer starts compressing, start the stopwatch. When he/she completes the 15 compressions, stop the watch. Tell the rescuer his/her time. Reset the watch, and ready yourself to time the person once again.

Observer's Role: Make absolutely certain that the rescuer is compressing properly. Also, observe whether the rescuer has unnecessary movement (e. g., bobbing head).

Rotate after completion of 10 cycles.

Task Four: Combining Breathing and Compressions

This task has the objective to put together two of the previous tasks to form one fluid motion.

Rescuer's Role: Position yourself on the mannikin's chest. At your own discretion, start 15 chest compressions. After completing 15 compressions, move to the mannikin's head and give two full breaths. After giving two breaths, go back to the chest, and position yourself on the mannikin's chest (making sure you find the xiphoid process). After getting into this position, you may sit back.

Repeat after hearing your time eight times.

Timer's Role: When the rescuer starts compressions, start the watch. When the rescuer completes the two breaths and returns his/her hands to the chest, stop the watch. Do not stop the watch until the rescuer has placed his/her hands on the chest. Tell the rescuer the time that this particular cycle took.

Also note how long it took for the compressions, as well as the movement from chest to mouth (and back).

Observer's Role: Make certain the individual properly compresses, properly ventilates, as well as properly finds hand position. The time for each cycle should range between 13.5 to 15 seconds, although the time between leaving the chest, and returning to the chest (after breathing) should take no longer than six seconds.

Putting It into Practice

These progressive part practice sessions should only be utilized after seeing and practicing the general CPR sequence. How that practice is done is up to the individual instructor. This author pairs up each student, then directs the student in each CPR step (without actual ventilation and chest compressions). It is important that this general practice is done before the progressive part practice sessions to acquaint students with the overview of CPR. To use the progressive part practice without a general understanding of CPR would not allow total learning to occur.

Each task, with three individuals per group, can be accomplished within a 10–12 minute time period. Additional groups can be taken care of in one of the following ways:

1). Placed at additional manikins to practice critical tasks such as mouth-to-mouth breathing, and chest compressions.

2). Placed at a non-mannikin area to practice the entire CPR sequence on a member of the group. Obviously, chest compressions and ventilations are not permitted. The observer also serves as a timer.

Completion of each of the tasks usually provides a solid foundation of mastering the specific skills needed for CPR. Students also find this an acceptable method in that all students are involved at all times. By observing, assisting in individual performances, and in actual practice, CPR skills are enhanced.

Kittleson's research (1986) analyzed these specific tasks on effectiveness to teach single rescue CPR. The results of his study showed this approach to be more efficient at teaching CPR skills when compared to the traditional method of instruction endorsed by the American Heart Association.

Although not statistically tested, skills involving two person CPR and

infant resuscitation can also be broken down to increase teaching effectiveness. For example, the student who practices two person CPR can concentrate on "CPR Switching" only, or a student can practice ventilations on an infant. Once these specific skills are mastered, students can combine these skills to perform the entire sequence.

Bloom, B.S. (1974). Time and learning. *American Psychologist, 29,* 682–688.

Cratty, B.J. (1973). *Teaching Motor Skills.* Englewood Cliffs, NJ: Prentice Hall, Inc.

Kittleson, Mark J. (1986). Analysis and comparison of cardiopulmonary resuscitation methodology among college students. Unpublished Dissertation. The University of Akron, Akron, OH.

Kittleson, Mark J. (1980). CPR drilling, *Health Education, 11,* 22–23.

The Improvised Manikin—Homemade CPR Equipment

Mardie E. Burckes

"The Improvised Manikin" is an anatomic dummy which the Nebraska Department of Health-Emergency Medical Services designed to teach CPR in the Nebraska public schools. This manikin can be made by following the simple directions included in this article. The Nebraska Department of Health has given permission to reprint the directions for making the manikin, although the author has made some slight changes.

The manikin is made of the following materials: pillow, styrofoam head, rubber bands or tape, safety pins, t-shirt, handkerchief, Laerdal chest piece and steel chest band (optional).

Directions

1. Poke hole with a pencil or cut hole through the mouth to the hollow center core of the styrofoam head.
2. Tape or use an elastic band to hold a plastic bag to the neck. A small garbage bag (12" × 18") or grocery plastic bag both work well.
3. Place the plastic bag under chest piece if one is used, otherwise place the bag under the pillow. (The Nebraska Department of Health uses a pillow) If the bag is placed under the chest piece, the head can be tilted back to open the airway and the chest will rise when air is blown into the mouth.

Mardie E. Burckes is with the School of HPER, University of Nebraska at Omaha, Omaha, NE 68182.

4. Put a shirt on the pillow and a handkerchief on the manikin's neck; arrange the head, bag, and pillow as shown. Pin the bottom of the shirt snugly near the pillow.

The manikin could cost as little as $1.00 or as much as $50.00 depending on whether the Laerdal chest band and chest piece is used. If the chest piece and band is not used, a clorox plastic bottle cut into a 4 inch band could be placed over the pillow as a chest piece, but the edges should be taped or padded because they could be rough.

Why use an improvised manikin? Many times schools cannot get regular CPR manikins from various agencies or cannot afford the price tag of $600+ for a commercial CPR manikin. Also an improvised manikin works well in the public schools because it is lightweight and can be transported easily from one class to another.

A few safety rules should be followed when using the improvised manikins. Because styrofoam is porous and difficult to wash, each participant should use a four inch square of wax paper with a slit in the middle to cover the mouth of the manikin when ventilating. For sanitary reasons the styrofoam head and plastic bag should be removed and discarded after every few classes. The price of this is negligible—styrofoam head ($1.00), plastic bag (free) and could save a disease outbreak in the school.

To practice with "Improvised Manikin," place the dummy on its back and follow steps from the American Heart Association or the American Red Cross: Shake and shout, call for help, tilt the head back to open the air passage, look, listen, feel, 4 quick breaths, pulse, call for help, find proper hand position, cadence: 1 rescuer for an adult 15:2, 4 cycles of 15:2 in one minute, repeat or 2 rescuer, 5:1 following the instructed procedures.

Teaching the Four C's of First Aid

Mark J. Kittleson

First Aid, I now believe, can be an exciting and rewarding subject to teach: an opportunity to see students develop skills that can be of utmost service not only to themselves but to others suffering from illness or injury. Unfortunately, some instructors (including this author) have been guilty of terribly dry and unrewarding courses. I believe an exciting and practical approach to teaching first aid, which I call "The Four C's of First Aid," can provide the basis for an effective course. Each of the four C's is equally important, for without one, the other three cannot be maximized.

C Number One—Cognition

Cognition, or the knowledge of first aid, is an obvious essential. Without proper knowledge, a student could not make appropriate choices—choices which could place the life of the victim in jeopardy. Although cognition is the basis of first aid, it is not necessarily the sole goal of a first aid course, and it is not the sole responsibility of the instructor. Cognition is the prime responsibility of the student. If an instructor is forced to lecture on textbook material, what is the purpose of using a text? By requiring

Mark J. Kittleson is an instructor of Health Education in the HPE department at Youngstown State University, Youngstown, OH 44555. He is also certified as an Instructor-Trainer in First Aid with the American Red Cross and Instructor-Trainer in CPR with the American Heart Association.

students to read specific chapters (and to be responsible for this information), you, as the instructor, can devote more time to the other three C's.

To let your students realize the seriousness you attach to their readings, give daily quizzes on required readings. Any student who does poorly on one or two of these quizzes will quickly make it a point to study ahead of time.

A method this author uses to encourage cognition (besides lecture) is to provide all members of the first aid courses an old first aid final. This final, developed more than five years ago, does have some outdated material, but it is an excellent tool to promote study. These tests are for students to keep. They are to put down only answers they are sure of, and to look up the answers to questions of which they are unsure. They are allowed to work in pairs, groups, or alone, and can use any resource for answers or clarifications. This 235-item test is used throughout the quarter; every class meeting has some time devoted to its use. It is especially handy during a quiz or major tests. The students who finish their quiz early can work on this "final" while others are finishing. This prevents much idle time. Also, this provides an opportunity for one-on-one assistance to those students desiring such help.

C Number Two—Confidence

It seems rather foolhardy to provide a first aid course and not have students apply their skills. One of the main reasons people decide not to administer first aid is their lack of confidence. The in-

structor must go out of his or her way to provide encouragement. Although you must be cautious and not go overboard, try to find something good in even rather poor results. Encouraging and promoting confidence is part of your job as an instructor.

One trick found to be successful in promoting confidence is the continual reinforcement and practice of specific skills. For example, the first day of class, and each class thereafter, the author has a small portion of daily class time devoted to obstructed airway maneuvers and to bandaging. By the end of the course, the students have mastered a rather complicated procedure involving obstructed airway—for both conscious and unconscious victims. They are so sure of their ability to do the procedure properly that there is no doubt in their minds they can come to the aid of a choking victim.

The students are also proficient at bandaging—so much so that they can apply a sling, various head bandages, shoulder, chest, and hip bandages properly within thirty seconds.

C Number Three—Cooperation

The third C also falls under the responsibility of the instructor. Since accidents or illness have a tendency to bring many people together, a first aider is rarely alone. He or she must learn to cooperate and to deal with knowledgeable as well as uninformed people in the subject of first aid.

A classic example given by this author is a personal account of my initial opportunity to use first aid skills. As I came upon the scene immediately after an accident, two men were discussing (rather heatedly) what the proper steps should be to aid an older women with a scalp injury. While the heated discussion turned into a heated debate, I managed to sneak in to treat the victim. Soon thereafter, the two men started hitting each other. I am still amazed at that incident. While somebody was lying on the road bleeding profusely, two men were fighting over proper procedure. Students must be continuously reminded that they must learn to deal effectively with "know-it-alls." This author usually incorporates two to three simulations during the course, and often role-plays a "know-it-all" person (without letting the class realize what is happening).

Eventually the students develop effective skills in dealing with this type of person.

Cooperation is also encouraged by assigning specific tasks and grading on cooperation rather than procedure (without the students' knowledge that cooperation is what is looked for). Give tests and have two people work on them together (nothing provides more realistic pressure than assigning fifty true and false questions and giving the students ten minutes to answer them). Also, give certain accident situations for which students (as a group) must list appropriate first aid procedures. Students realize that not everybody interprets everything the same, and all have different perspectives regarding first aid treatment.

C Number Four—Creativeness

The chances of having an ambulance or a first aid station within easy access after an accident are rare. Chances are you will be twenty miles from nowhere when an accident occurs. Thus, it is ex-

tremely important that the instructor encourage creative thinking. We all learn to apply slings using the triangular bandage, but how many people carry triangular bandages with them? A person may have to use a shirt, jacket, or some other item.

The instructor needs to provide time for the student to improvise certain first aid equipment such as splints, bandages, litters, and other transporting devices.

Specific examples that can be utilized are to require of students that they obtain a triangular bandage and some other piece of clothing. They learn their bandage first with the triangular bandage, and later in the course they experiment with their extra clothing. I also encourage them to practice applying the bandage (sling, forehead, scalp, etc.) on themselves.

Conclusion

Murphy's Law ("If anything can go wrong, it will.") is a most appropriate quote to relay to your first aid class. As instructors of first aid, we must try to prepare students in all dimensions of first aid. This author has found the "Four C's" of first aid an effective attempt to meet these needs.

Mock Disaster: An Effective Lesson in Preparation for the Real Thing

Gary M. English and Cathie G. Stivers

The use of mock situations in first aid is not new, but effective uses of mocks are not easily found in the literature. Through trial and error a mock exercise has been developed that serves as a learning tool and is evaluated easily.

This exercise takes four class periods to complete.

First Class — Introduction

As an introduction to the upcoming major mock, a variety of "mini mock" situations are provided to encourage students to begin thinking about staging a mock situation. A series of 3x5 cards which identify specific injuries, signs and/or symptoms of victims of accident or illness are distributed among class members. Once cards are distributed, individuals form informal groups of three to four members and discuss their mock situation in terms of (1) identifying the situation, (2) listing props that could be used to enhance the scenario, (3) listing signs and symptoms associated with the injury

Gary M. English is a doctoral candidate and graduate teaching assistant in the Department of Health Promotion, Physical Education and Leisure Programs at the University of New Mexico, Albuquerque, NM 87131. Cathie G. Stivers is an assistant professor in the Department at The University of New Mexico.

and (4) listing proper treatments for the injury described in the mock situation. The goal of this exercise is to resolve the situation by correctly identifying these four criteria.

Once the exercise is completed and class members have gained an understanding of what is to be expected of them, students are divided into working groups to prepare for the major mock. Although it is not important that each group have an equal number of students, it is imperative that there is an even number of groups. Once groups are formed, the major mock forms are distributed (see Figure 1), and group planning begins. At this time, group members are encouraged to share phone numbers so that members can contact each other to arrange additional meetings outside class.

In concluding the first class period of this exercise, the instructor provides, via overhead projector and transparencies, an example of a completed mock situation form for students to view (see Figure 1*). When students see a completed form, many questions are answered and much confusion is resolved. Finally, half the groups are designated as victims and the other half as rescuers, for the third class period.

Second Class - Group Planning

Because of the time involved in developing the mock situation, the class does not formally meet during

this session. Instead, students are expected to gather to work with other members of their group in deciding what their group's mock will be, gathering props, and working out the logistics needed to complete the assignment. During this "open" class period, the instructor should be available to clarify any questions the students may have.

Third Class - Mock Disaster, Round One

During this class period, groups that were designated as victims during the first class period will enact their mock situations. Rescuers designated at that same time will demonstrate their first aid skills by rescuing the victim group.

Fourth Class - Mock Disaster, Round Two

The format for this class period is identical to that of the preceding class. However, groups will change roles, allowing everyone the opportunity to perform as a victim and as a rescuer.

Role of the Victim

The group's members selected to play the roles of victims must fill out their mock forms completely. It is important to stress to members of the victim group that they are to

Names: _____

_____

Major Mock Situation—Victim Report

I. Describe the situation you are going to display:
A bus on its way to the airport has overturned. You are among the first people to arrive at the accident scene. After surveying the situation, you find that two passengers have been injured.

List the injury(s) of each individual and the signs or symptoms for those injuries. List the most severely injured individual first, followed by the next serious to the least serious.

Victim 1

1. Injury:
Glass fragments in face.

Signs and symptoms:
Bleeding around the face and head.

2. Injury:
Vehicles antenna penetrated the victim's cheek.

Signs and symptoms:
Bleeding from the mouth, some teeth may be missing.

3. Injury:
Unsure??

Signs and symptoms:
Victim's pulse is weak and rapid, the skin is cold and clammy, and the victim appears to be pale.

Victim 2

1. Injury:
Fracture of the left forearm.

Signs and symptoms:
The arm is deformed between the wrist and the elbow.

2. Injury:
Unsure??

Signs and symptoms:
There is no pulse at the radial artery. However, there is extreme pain when the hand is held or touched.

3. Injury:
Unsure??

Signs and symptoms:
The victim is complaining of pain in the area where his chest came into contact with the seat in front of him.

II. What is the proper treatment for each victim? List treatments in the order in which they should be done. Assume that a good patient survey has been completed.

Victim 1

Treat for shock—maintain the ABC's; keep body temperature stable; elevate the lower extremities; reassure the victim; find and treat the source of the shock.
If there are teeth missing clear the mouth and remove any broken teeth.

Remove the antenna if it is still impaled in the cheek, unless this is too difficult: then stabilize and bandage around the object. Hold a gauze pad inside the cheek as well as outside. Do not leave gauze inside the mouth unless you're holding it.

Do not attempt to remove any large fragments of glass. Apply a sterile dressing to wounds and bandage. Do not apply pressure to wounds (doing so may cause further damage).

Transport immediately; stabilize the victim; keep the victim on his or her back.

Victim 2

While performing the secondary survey it was noticed that there was extreme pain when the left hand was touched. The pain was evident from the fingertips to the point of the suspected fracture. It was also noticed that there was no pulse at the radial artery. An occlusion should be suspected and corrected before splinting. The rescuer must move the arm to allow circulation to be restored to the hand *before splinting.*

Immobilize the arm by splinting above and below the suspected fracture sight. Once the arm has been immobilized, place it in a sling.

Examine the chest area for deformities that may indicate a fracture. Look for the signs and symptoms of a flail chest; place the victim in a lying or sitting position or whatever is most comfortable.

III. Explain why you put the victims in the order that you did.

From the signs and symptoms, it was apparent that victim 1 was going into shock. To prevent the shock from progressing, it was decided that this person would be treated first.

Victim 2 was treated second. The problems with this individual became more serious as time passed. The fracture was not a major concern; however, as time passed, the pain in the extremity became severe. The chest pains were attributed to the victim coming into contact with the front seat and did not appear to be very serious.

IV. What props will you use, or how will the rescuers find the information they need to figure out what happened?

Victim 1: Wire (for the antenna), broken glass around the accident sight, Chiclets (for the broken teeth).

Victim 2: A short round board to portray the fracture sight; a chair to suggest the front seat.

demonstrate, or act out, the victim scenario which they developed. All members of the group must be totally familiar with their own simulated injuries and treatment for those injuries, as they will assist in evaluating effectiveness of treatments rendered by rescuers.

To assist the rescuer, the victim may tell the rescuer of symptoms that can't be seen; however, the victim should only reveal the symptom when the rescuer assesses that particular body part.

Role of the Rescuer

While victims prepare for mock situations, rescuers should wait in a hallway or nearby classroom where they cannot see the victims in preparation. During the wait, the instructor reads the situation from the victims' major mock form. It may be necessary, at this time, for the instructor to remind rescuers to think carefully about the situation they are about to encounter. Rescuers may need to be reminded especially that there may be situations in which the best thing to offer, in terms of first aid to the victim, is reassurance.

Appropriate examples include an epileptic coming out of a seizure, or an accident victim with a suspected fracture of the thoracic vertebrae. The rescuers may choose to work as a group or as individuals, but communication among rescue group members is encouraged strongly. The mock is completed only when all victims have been attended and their conditions stabilized.

Evaluation

There are several ways to evaluate student performance during a mock situation. To assess cognitive aspects of first aid, the instructor must critically review each "treatment" section of the mock planning form. Since each victim identifies his/her treatment for each injury, the victim is in the best position to assess correctness of treatments rendered by the rescuer.

Because of this, victims are asked to complete an evaluation sheet as-sessing their rescuers' performances, once the mock situation has concluded. Criteria include questions such as "Did the rescuer find all the injuries without help?" "Were correct treatments given to those injuries?" "Were treatments done in correct order of priority?" "Did rescue team members work well together?" This assessment, along with the instructor's evaluation of how well rescuers performed, determines a grade for the affective learning component of the mock situation.

These two components comprise the majority of the evaluation process. A final component, then, is added to the mock to assure that individuals within the group contribute equally. Each individual is asked to list, on a separate sheet of paper, members of his/her group and to relate whether each member (1) contributed more than other group members, (2) contributed equally to the group effort or (3) contributed less than other group members.

Proven Success and Popularity

The use of the mock situation in final weeks of a semester of college-level first aid courses has proven to be successful in assessing students' comprehensive first aid knowledge and practical skills. An added feature of this procedure is its popularity with students.

Creativity elicited by this activity adds to the excitement. In one instance, members of a group of Native American Indians decided they would add to the confusion of the mock situation by speaking in their native language in order to see how rescuers would react. In another situation, a victim group displayed a spelunking accident and required rescuers to work in a darkened room under a long low table. Other situations have included skiing or camping accidents, motor vehicle accidents and gang fights. Possibilities are limited only by student imagination.

First Aid and Safety

The Importance of Child Safety Seat Education

Karen D. Liller

with their younger children or are using safety seats improperly. Students can serve as role models for their family and friends and, eventually, role models for their own children and future generations.

CSS education should include strategies shown effective through research and program implementation and evaluation. A CSS program should be comprehensive and address many reasons cited for low rates of compliance. An example of a two session high school CSS program follows. These sessions probably will take place over three or four class periods. However, instructors may shorten or lengthen the time and tailor the topics, depending on the particular setting and curriculum in use.

Student Participants

Male and female students should be randomly assigned to each other to serve as a parenting unit. If there is an unequal number of males and females, two females can be paired or two males, because there are many single parents today who bring a friend or acquaintance to parenting education sessions. Also, if there is an unequal number of students in the class, groups of threes can be used. Groups of "parents" should sit together in a large circle. Topics for teaching sessions are shown in the Session 1 and Session 2 boxes.

CSS education should be taking place in schools and other locations such as prenatal and postnatal classes (Kernish & London, 1986) and pediatricians' and obstetricians' offices. Other health settings such as pharmacies should have CSS material available. Community en-

Injuries are the leading cause of childhood death in the United States (Baker & Waller, 1989). Total motor vehicle injuries are the leading cause of death of children between the ages of 0 to 14 in every state (Baker & Waller, 1989). Based on these injury statistics, it is logical to assume that parents would comply with safety seat laws by always using a child safety seat (CSS) for infants and toddlers. Although all 50 states have now enacted CSS laws, less than 50 percent of three-year-old and four-year-old children, respectively, were restrained, in 1985 (Foss, 1989). Researchers have suggested that CSS expense,

Karen D. Liller is an assistant professor at the University of South Florida College of Public Health, Tampa, FL 33612.

difficulties in use, confrontations with toddlers, inaccurate beliefs and assessments of accident risks, and lack of role models contribute to parents' reluctance in using CSSs.

Because many of the parents of today's young parents did not use CSSs, this behavior has not been reinforced. Therefore, CSS education should be available to parents and young adults. High school students enrolled in health, life management, parenting, and other related courses also should receive this education. Although most of these students are not parents, they do participate in activities, such as baby-sitting infants and toddlers, which often require students to be responsible for children in a motor vehicle. Also, parents of students may not be using CSSs

vironments such as daycares or pre-schools also should have information to share with parents. Materials for instructors and community settings may include pamphlets, booklets, or videos available through local and state transportation safety groups, in addition to national sponsors such as the National Highway Traffic Safety Administration (NHTSA) or the American Academy of Pediatrics (AAP). This material may need to be revised so that it is targeted for the audience, reflecting age, cultural diversity, and socioeconomic status.

Although CSS legislation has been in effect for a decade, children continue to be injured and killed in motor vehicle accidents. Strict proponents of passive restraints such as air bags and automatic seat belts believe that passive devices are the answer to occupant protection. However, even if these restraints become standard in every motor vehicle, parents still will need to be educated about CSS use with these devices.

Individuals must be active in their own safety. For parents and others who care for young children, this also includes becoming active in children's safety.

Parenting and related classes in schools provide excellent opportunities for introducing and reinforcing use

of CSSs. This is a life-saving skill that has a definite place in our classrooms. The goal of CSS education is to make a significant impact on decline of the tragedy of childhood motor vehicle injuries and deaths. With education, legislation, and improved CSS technology in place, schools and communities can help make this a reality.

Baker, S. P., & Waller, A. E. (1989). *Childhood injury-state-by state mortality facts*. Baltimore: The Johns Hopkins Injury Prevention Center.

Foss, R. D. (1989). Evaluation of a community-wide incentive program to promote safety restraint use. *American Journal of Public Health, 79,* 304–306.

Kernish, R., & London, L. (1986). *Strategies to increase the use of child safety seats-An assessment of current knowledge.* (NHTSA Report No. DOT HS 807 116). Washington, DC: National Highway of Traffic Safety Administration (NTIS No. DTNH22-82-A-07197, Task 4).

Session 1

The instructor will:

1. Discuss laws, penalties, and safety features of approved infant and toddler CSSs. (A convertible infant/toddler seat may be used.)

2. Discuss availability of seats at a reduced cost through loaner/rental community programs.

3. Have available various models of child safety seats, with directions and names of vehicles in which they fit. These are available from manufacturers and loaner programs. Demonstrate proper use of an infant and toddler CSS with dolls.

4. Allow each parent to properly place a doll in both the infant and toddler seats. If time permits, have each parent place the doll and CSS in the instructor's vehicle or other available vehicles. Each student must do this properly!

5. Have each parent group discuss difficulties of using a CSS. Have them work with their partner/s to document questions or concerns that will be discussed at the next CSS session.

Session 2

The instructor will:

1. Have each group of parents read their questions and concerns to the rest of the class. The instructor will answer the questions and conduct a brief discussion session.

2. Review importance of using CSSs for both infants and toddlers.

3. Discuss and role-play parent/child interactions that will improve parental compliance. The instructor will need another teacher or student to assume the role of the toddler.

4. Recruit local parents who consistently comply with child safety seat laws to join the class. These parents can be located through various injury or safety groups in the community. Allow these parents to respond to questions and concerns from the class.

5. Have the class view videos of parent "testimonials" on importance of using CSSs. This should not be used for "shock value" but should emphasize that the health of the infant and toddler is dependent upon the parent, even when riding in a vehicle.

6. Have each class member write one or two paragraphs on benefits of CSS education and how each class member will implement this behavior now (if possible) and in the future.

7. Complete the session by providing each class member with a certificate for successful completion of the CSS education program.

AIDS "To Tell the Truth" Gaming Activity: A Teaching Method

Jon W. Hisgen

The AIDS epidemic has created a public outcry for effective and creative AIDS education at all grade levels. What has come out is a plethora of lectures, discussion materials, and talking-head audiovisual materials. The activity I have developed asks students to look at the billion dollar a year AIDS quackery business. The students make use of the technique from the old television game show "To Tell the Truth" to discover who are the charlatans and who is the reliable doctor. AIDS charlatans are very knowledgeable so some of the answers presented by each participant are accurate; students must sort out the false statements from the correct and appropriate responses.

The following are the objectives of this teaching method. The student will:

1. Differentiate between accurate and inaccurate AIDS information.
2. List the qualities of a health charlatan.
3. Analyze AIDS information so as to determine the accurate medical specialist.
4. Identify questionable practices.

The activity involves interviews of three contestants, all claiming to be a reliable AIDS specialist. Only one of them answers all questions accurately. The other two can respond with either correct or incorrect information.

Jon Hisgen is health coordinator for the Pewaukee Public Schools, Pewaukee, WI 53072.

Three contestants are given a set of answers a week before the activity; they review them carefully to learn accurate pronunciation of all words used. During the interview, a group of five panelists ask questions of any of the three contestants, for a two-minute period. After the questioning, the rest of the class decides who the real doctor is and why. All three contestants provide some accurate AIDS information, but only one will answer every question correctly. A discussion of each contestant's answers, beliefs, and philosophy should follow the identification of the real doctor.

The activity begins with the introduction of the three contestants. When asked by the announcer to "state your name and occupation," Contestants #1, #2, and #3 all respond: "My name is Dr. (Jane, James) Bluemner and I am a specialist working on treatments for AIDS patients."

The announcer then states: "Pond scum, exposing genitals to the sun at 4:00 o'clock, cell injunctions — these are some of the treatments offered for AIDS, a disease ripe for questionable cures. Dr. Bluemner has been a physician specializing in the study of the HIV virus for the past five years. The doctor has researched retroviruses at the Center for Disease Control since 1985 and is presently studying drugs that might prevent these viruses from entering the host nucleus. Dr. Bluemner recently won the American Medical Association research scholar award. We will begin the questioning with panelist #1."

The panelists, in turn, read the following 21 questions, asking any of the three contestants they chose.

Questions

1. Why is AIDS such a great problem in our world?
2. What is your opinion about self-treating an illness that is supposedly untreatable?
3. Who is at high risk for AIDS?
4. What is ARC?
5. Where did you get your MD degree?
6. If I wanted AIDS information from someone other than a doctor to whom should I turn?
7. What is the most dangerous AIDS treatment on the market today?
8. What is AZT?
9. Since the AIDS virus attacks the immune system what type of AIDS products do you think people are likely to sell to the unknowing AIDS patient?
10. What is the greatest problem teachers face educating about AIDS?
11. What is an AIDS guerrilla clinic?
12. What is L-721 and do you think it should be legalized?
13. Do you believe in AIDS testimonials?
14. What can Americans do to fight AIDS quackery?
15. Why does quackery thrive so much in our society?
16. What is DNCB and why do AIDS patients use it?
17. Is DNCB legal? If so, why?
18. What do you think should be done by people in a place where they are in contact with a known AIDS patient?
19. How is AIDS transmitted?
20. How could a person reduce his/her risk of exposure to the AIDS virus?
21. If you knew someone in your family with AIDS what would you do?

Answers for Contestant #1

1. Acquired immune deficiency syndrome is a worldwide concern because so many people are ignorant about the disease.

2. Self-treatment plays right into the hands of the money hungry charlatan. That is what they want.

3. Men who have had anal sex with other men since 1977 and people who share drug paraphernalia, specifically needles, are examples of persons exhibiting high risk behaviors.

4. AIDS related complex (ARC) is a pre-AIDS condition with such symptoms as severe weight loss.

5. I received my degree from Loma Linda Medical School in San Diego, California.

6. The Public Health Service and the Center for Disease Control have some up-to-date materials.

7. An $800 treatment for pills containing mice immune system substances after being given the AIDS virus. Instant death!

8. A drug that has been shown to stop AIDS symptoms in some patients.

9. Most of these treatments promise to strengthen immunity.

10. Developing guidelines for teaching about the disease within the values and concerns of every student's family.

11. A place where questionable AIDS treatments are sold or practiced.

12. It is a product made of a fat called lecithin that was purported to hinder the AIDS virus from attacking healthy cells. I think it should be approved for experimental use by willing patients.

13. Only if the testimonials say the disease is a killer.

14. Become knowledgeable of the at-risk behaviors and the seriousness of the infection once contracted.

15. People will grab at any claim when their life is at stake. They feel they have nothing to lose.

16. A chemical that diminishes the purplish lesions of Kaposi's sarcoma, a type of opportunistic, rare cancer that affects AIDS patients.

17. It is a chemical used by photographers in processing film.

18. Realize that if you do not engage in high-risk behaviors like anal, homosexual sex or sharing needles with this person you decrease your chance of having the infected person's blood or body fluids enter your body.

19. Mixing of blood or blood products with an infected person's blood or body fluids.

20. Abstinence, having only one sex partner, and use of condoms will definitely lower AIDS risks.

21. Show him/her the love and concern I felt for him/her before he/she contracted the disease.

Answers for Contestant #2

1. There is no ultimate AIDS cure in the foreseeable future.

2. Certain macrobiotic lifestyles like meditation and whole grain and vegetable diets are the only successful treatments that can be self-taught.

3. Anyone who gets the AIDS virus in their blood or body fluids.

4. It is a pre-AIDS condition with diarrhea, extreme weight loss, and depressed immunity.

5. I received my MD degree at the University of California and my nutritional consultant's degree from the Wholistic Health Clinic in Sacramento.

6. The HEAL group presents sound AIDS information.

7. Mail order bottles of T-cells to replace AIDS ravaged T-cells is an absolutely absurd treatment.

8. A drug shown to lessen AIDS symptoms.

9. They should buy Dr. Revici's herbal remedy but they end up purchasing blood serum contaminated with hepatitis B and AIDS. How utterly stupid!

10. Parents unwilling to allow sound health information for their kids.

11. Clinics that sell bogus health treatments.

12. A drug that can be made from health food store ingredients. Further research needs to be done before legalization.

13. I support solid research like Dr. Levy's that has shown many men became stronger after following a macrobiotic lifestyle.

14. Become educated as to the styles and techniques of the quack in our society. Be skeptical!

15. The government needs to make laws that will scare these charlatans off.

16. A drug that has FDA approval for warts.

17. Yes, but for warts, not AIDS.

18. Let doctors try promising new drugs with sound dietary practices on these people without FDA intervention.

19. Sex, transfusions, and crossing placental barriers to unborn children.

20. Develop a responsible macrobiotic lifestyle of diet, meditation, no intravenous drug use, and safe sex with condoms.

21. Get him/her to macrobiotic counseling.

Answers for Contestant #3

1. Acquired immune deficiency syndrome is a major problem because people are panic stricken whenever anyone says the word. We need to educate!

2. I think most people cannot self-treat and must be guided by competent, trained physicians.

3. Gays, needle sharers, prostitutes, hemophiliacs, and infants of infected mothers.

4. The beginning stages of the infection.

5. The State University of New York at Stony Brook with postgraduate work in the Bahamian AIDS research institute.

6. New York's HEAL group has many educational materials and many new treatments.

7. $10,000 treatment of thymus gland extract that is available in France.

8. A quack product that claims to alleviate AIDS symptoms.

9. I believe my life extension products like BHT are the only effective AIDS treatment on the market.

10. Our teachers' lack of knowledge of the most successful AIDS treatments.

11. Places that are forced to sell sound treatments because the FDA has harassed them into hiding.

12. An effective AIDS drug that U.S. and Israeli rsearchers have found successful in preventing AIDS.

13. If a person has been told he will die then I believe in personal accounts.

14. We must realize that our medical system has so little to offer that alternatives must be explored.

15. Because quacks are looking for a quick buck and people are always looking for a quick cure.

16. A drug that has been shown to help with Kaposi's sarcoma, an opportunistic cancer with purple splotches.

17. Yes, it is available in clinics like mine throughout the country.

18. Show care for the AIDS patient so he/she will feel better and live longer.

19. Anal intercourse, blood transfusions of infected blood, mixing of body fluids, sharing of needles, and sex with prostitutes.

20. Injections of bee pollen, garlic, or blue-green algae beefs up the immune system.

21. Have him/her become a part of my life extension program.

The first contestant is the person who gave all correct responses. Contestant #2 discussed health and nutritional treatments that, though they were harmless, involved claims that were loaded with half truths and outright false statements; one should encourage an AIDS patient to consume a sound, balanced diet but not the one promoted by macrobiologists. Contestant #3 exchanged many false and dangerous treatments and ideas with his/her patients.

This approach could be used for other areas of health education. Questions and answers are prepared by the teacher, but, depending on the interest and capabilities of the students, could be written by the students themselves.

AIDS/HIV Teaching Ideas

Barbara Beier, J. Leslie Oganowski, Richard A. Detert, and Kenneth Becker

AIDS/HIV education is essential for the understanding and prevention of the disease. AIDS/HIV is a complex issue and thus demands a multifaceted approach. The condition may be viewed as a disease issue, a decision-making issue, a sexuality issue, and a death and dying issue.

A series of four teaching ideas are presented as they address each of the AIDS/HIV issues. The teaching techniques are as follows:

1. "Understanding AIDS/HIV" — a disease issue
2. "Who Do You Trust?" — a decision-making issue
3. "A Safer Sex Continuum" — a sexuality issue
4. "The Living Years" — a death and dying issue

ACTIVITY #1:
"UNDERSTANDING AIDS/HIV"
Objective: After the bag demonstration, the student will be able to describe how HIV breaks down the immune system to allow the development of AIDS.

Preparation: Prepare envelopes for each student with the following shapes representing parts of the blood involved in the immune system. Place the HIV in only three of the envelopes.

Barbara Beier, J. Leslie Oganowski, Richard A. Detert, and Kenneth Becker are members of the faculty at the University of Wisconsin-LaCrosse.

| T-cells | white blood cells | B cells | HIV |

Necessary Materials:
1 lunch size paper bag for each student
2 lunch size bags for teacher demonstration
markers or crayons
prepared envelope for each student

Activity:
1. Instruct the students to color or decorate their bag to represent the skin.
2. Review the steps that take place when a germ enters the body by having each student put parts of the blood (from their envelope) in the bag. The teacher demonstrates by placing in the bag each cell type and explaining the action; i.e., white blood cells rush to the place where germs enter and attach to the germ to make it less dangerous to the person.
3. Introduce the functions of the immune system. A healthy immune system works to destroy nearly all types of germs, including many bacteria and viruses.
4. Write "immune" on the board. Have a student tell what is meant when someone says he/she is "immune" to something (protected/safe).
5. Conduct the following demonstration of the activities of the immune system in fighting germs.
a. Hold two bags to represent the skin as a barrier to keep germs out. As long as the skin remains uninjured, it holds what's inside the body in and keeps the rest safely out.
b. Reveal a break in the skin by tearing part of one bag. Have students name ways a break could occur (cuts, scratches, burns, scrapes, broken bones, surgery, intravenous drugs, ear piercing, tattoos, punctures).
c. Toss some objects into the bags representing foreign bacteria, viruses, or germs. Explain that our blood contains white blood cells that fight germs. One kind of white blood cell (macrophage) moves through the blood and tissues to surround and "eat" germs. Toss some macrophage cells into the bag.
d. T-cells are another type of white blood cell that help fight germs. T-cells attack and destroy viruses. Add T-cells to the bag. Stress that some T-cells serve as "command centers" for the body's battle against germs.
e. Another kind of white blood cell is called a B-cell. Add the B-cells to the bag. B-cells produce chemicals called antibodies. Explain that antibodies can destroy viruses and other germs.
f. Explain that some antibodies, even after destroying some germs, stay in the body to protect in case there is another exposure to the same type of germ. That is immunity.

g. Ask students "What happens when the `command center' in a real battle is destroyed?" Conclude that when germs attack the white blood cells (T-cells) that control the body's immune system, they can cripple the body's ability to fight off infection and disease.

h. Ask who has an "H" in his/her envelope. Toss the "H" into the bag. This represents an HIV condition. AIDS is caused by a virus called HIV (human immunodeficiency virus). HIV destroys the "command centers" (T-cells) of the immune system and the body cannot fight off certain infections.

i. The person with HIV does not usually die of HIV infection directly— the person with AIDS usually dies from other diseases that the body can no longer fight off.

Time Frame: The bag activity itself can be completed in a 30-40 minute class period. The preparatory information could take one class prior to the activity. Questions about symptoms of HIV, children with HIV, and feelings associated with having an "H" in his/her bag could take varying amounts of time.

Do discuss with the class the chances of "having an HIV in his/her bag" and the risks of infection. Include a discussion of caring for the feelings of people who are infected.

ACTIVITY #2:
"WHO DO YOU TRUST?"

Objective: At the completion of this activity, students will be able to discuss the benefits and consequences of taking risks.

Preparation: Before students enter the room, the teacher places objects inside each of four large brown paper bags: (bag #1 = one mouse trap that is not set; bag #2 = one small mouse trap that is set; bag #3 = one large rat trap that is set; bag #4 = one block of wood).

There is one block of wood on the corner of the table.

Necessary Materials:
   4 large brown paper bags numbered 1 to 4
   2 mouse traps
   1 large rat trap
   2 blocks of wood
   table

Activity:
1. Ask for three volunteers to come forward who are willing to take a risk. Describe the risk as selecting one of the paper bags. Volunteers will be asked to blindly reach to the bottom of the bag and grab whatever is in it. If it is the block of wood like the one on the corner of the table, they will receive a designated amount of money.

2. Ask for three volunteers who will assist the risk takers in their adventure. Instruct these volunteers to move to the other side of the room.

3. One at a time, ask each of the three assistants to open each of the bags and look at the contents. Ask them to be expressionless as they view each of the bags. Then ask each of the assistants if there is a block of wood in at least one of the bags. Once verified, ask (one at a time) if he/she would be willing to take the risk of reaching blindly into one of the bags. Some will say no; some, yes.

4. Ask each assistant to meet a risk taker and quietly whisper in his/her ear what was seen in the bags. Then instruct the risk taker to whisper the same message to one other person in the room. Once all three have additional information about the contents, ask each of the risk takers if he/she is still willing to take the risk. Those who say "no" can be seated; those who are still willing to continue remain standing.

5. Provide some more information to the risk takers (and the rest of the class) by revealing the contents of bag #1. Then reveal the contents of bag #2 by unsetting the mouse trap with a folded piece of paper. Ask again which risk takers would still be willing to blindly reach into one of the two remaining bags.

6. Ask the assistants to provide a bit more information to the risk takers and

the rest of the class by asking whether a consequence of reaching into one of the bags could result in a) pain, b) broken fingers, or c) the presence of blood? Then ask again who might be willing to take the risk.

7. Teacher places remaining risk takers in the front of the room and asks them one more time if they are willing to take the risk. If yes, mix the bags up and ask the risk takers to turn around. By now, most risk takers have quit!

8. Of course, the teacher stops the activity at this point as students could get injured if they actually reached into bag #3. The bag contents are now revealed.

9. Follow-up discussion:
a. Ask the risk takers to tell the group what their assistant whispered in their ear.

b. Did all the assistants see the same contents?

c. Discuss how the risk takers thought they could "beat the odds."

d. Discuss comments that encouraged/discouraged each from stopping or continuing with the activity.

e. Finally, discuss what risks each are willing to take; which would not be safe risks; what risks are involved with AIDS/HIV conditions.

Time Frame: This activity takes between 20-40 minutes to complete. The time frame may vary depending on grade level and the number of comments made or points raised during the discussion.

ACTIVITY #3:
"A SAFER SEX CONTINUUM"

Objective: At the completion of this activity the student will be able to identify means of transmission of AIDS/HIV on a safer to unsafe continuum.

Preparation: When discussing the issue of AIDS in the classroom, one way to introduce safe and unsafe sexual practices is by using the "Safer Sex Continuum." This activity would be part of a larger unit on sexuality or sexually transmitted diseases (STDs) and would be utilized once the students had developed a degree of comfort in discussing sexual topics.

Materials Necessary:
    chalkboard and chalk
    (or newsprint and marking pens)

Activity:

1. Introduce the topic by having students consider the methods of transmission of the HIV virus and sexual practices. Place the continuum shown at the bottom of the page on the chalkboard.

2. At this point, ask the students to "place" a sexual activity on this continuum on the appropriate position so as to indicate the "safeness" or "riskiness" of the behavior. As each behavior or sexual activity is suggested, the elements involved in ranking that behavior in that position should also be discussed. This method involves the students in analyzing each sexual activity based upon their knowledge of the transmission of the HIV virus. It is also a method that could be useful in introducing sensitive topics such as masturbation, condom use, and anal intercourse.

3. Clarification of certain activities is a productive outcome of this activity if students are allowed to engage in open discussion and ask questions. For instance, one popular misconception discovered with this approach was that some students considered a sexual monogamous relationship to mean having sex with "one person at a time.

Time Frame: This activity takes between 30 and 50 minutes to complete depending upon 1) the level of knowledge of the students, 2) the degree of comfort with discussing sexual topics, and 3) the amount of discussion time allowed.

ACTIVITY #4:
"THE LIVING YEARS"

Objective: At the completion of this activity, the student will be able to verbalize his/her reactions to AIDS as a death and dying issue.

Preparation: One effective way we found to address AIDS as a death and dying issue was to play a song that many students may have heard on popular hit radio stations. "The Living Years," recorded by Mike and the Mechanics, was played and students were encouraged to follow along with the printed words. Introductory statements may include: "Think about the words and what they say about death and dying," or, "As you listen to the words of this song, think about your thoughts on death, dying, and AIDS."

Materials Necessary:
    tape: "The Living Years," by Mike
      and the Mechanics
    printed words to the song
    tape player

The Living Years

Every generation
Blames the one before
And all of their frustrations
Come beating in your door.

I know that I'm a prisoner
To all my father held so dear
I know that I'm a hostage
To all his hopes and fears
I just wish I could have told him
In the living years.

Crumpled bits of paper
Filled with imperfect thought

Stilted conversations
I'm afraid that's all we've got.

You say you just don't see it
He says it's perfect sense
You just can't get agreement
In this present tense
We all talk a different language
Talking in defense.

Say it loud, say it clear
You can listen as well as you hear
It's too late when we die
To admit we don't see eye to eye.

So we open up in quarrel
Between the present and the past
We only sacrifice the future
It's the bitterness that lasts.

So don't yield to the fortunes
You sometimes see as fate
It may have a new perspective
On a different day
And if you don't give up,
And don't give in
You may just be OK.

Say it loud, say it clear
You can listen as well as you hear
It's too late when we die
To admit we don't see eye to eye.

I wasn't there that morning
When my father passed away
I did't get to tell him
All the things I had to say,
I think I caught his spirit
Later that same year
I'm sure I heard his echo
In my baby's new born tears
I just wish I could have told him
In the living years.

"The Living Years," Mike and the Mechanics (1988), Atlantic Record Corporation, 75 Rockefeller Plaza, New York, NY 10019.

Mental and Emotional Health

Stress Manifestations Among Adolescents: Actions, Situations, and Body Responses

Charles Regin

Grade Level: 7 - 12

Time Frame: 50 minutes

Materials: Gumby handouts, blank Gumby transparency, overhead projector, transparency marker. Note: any appropriate, genderless figure can be substituted for the Gumby figure illustrated.

Background Information: The impact of stress and stress related diseases is a major concern in American society. Either the mismanagement of stress or the use of maladaptive coping strategies among adolescents plays a significant role in the major health problem areas identified in the Surgeon General's report on health promotion and disease prevention. These problem areas include teen pregnancy, sexually transmitted diseases, mental illness, suicide, and homicide.

Preparation

In the first few classes of a stress management unit, it is important to establish similarities/common stress sources among students. This "we all have stress in our lives" sensitization allows for greater feelings of openness and a possible reduction of the feeling of "I am the only one who has these prob-

Charles Regin is an assistant professor of health eduction in the School of Health, Physical Education, and Recreation at the University of Nevada, Las Vegas, NV 89154.

lems." This activity is designed to address such issues. Specifically, the objectives of the activity are to:

1. Describe how the stress response can affect a person's physical well-being.
2. Demonstrate both similarities and differences in ways adolescents handle/mishandle stress.
3. Provide a supportive forum for a discussion regarding common ways adolescents respond to stressful situations.
4. Identify and describe how adolescents can reveal distress and eustress sources in their lives.

The teacher will need enough "Gumby" handouts (see next page) so there is one for each student. In addition, the instructor will need enough Gumby handouts reproduced on a second color so that there is one for each small group into which the class will be divided.

Implementation

Distribute a copy of Gumby to each student. Explain that the figure is a representation of themselves and that they will use it to explore how stress affects their lives in both a positive and negative manner.

The first step is designed to help students identify how stress affects the body. Direct the class to shade in the areas of Gumby that represent the parts of their bodies that are affected by too such stress. For example, some students will shade in the hands because their hands get cold when they experience too much stress. Other students will shade

in the head or stomach areas because they get headaches or upset stomachs. If appropriate, this can be shown using an overhead projector and a transparency of Gumby.

The second step is designed to help students identify current and past sources of stress. Tell the students that stress is both positive (eustress) and negative (distress). The line down the middle of the handout separates positive and negative stressors. Direct the class to fill in the circles with terms that represent current distressful and eustressful sources in their lives. Examples might include math class at school, a brother, or for older students, their boss at work. (Encourage them to be specific rather than writing general terms such as school, home, or work.) Also mention that some stressors can be placed on both sides of the line. The horizontal line near the bottom of the handout separates current from past stressors. Direct the students to reflect upon former stressors that they have "set aside" or have dealt with and label the circles below the line with those past situations or people.

The third step is designed to help students identify how they behave when they have or have had too much stress in their lives. Direct the students to write descriptions between the present stressors stating how they behave in both negative and positive stressful times. Positive behavior examples include singing, exercising, or feeling happy and smiling. Negative behavior examples include yelling, picking on people, or overeating. In the area of past stressors, ask students to identify the behavior that helped them deal with the stressor. Ex amples include talking with a friend or family member or seeing a counselor at school.

At the conclusion of this three-step process, form small groups of three to five students. Distribute the second Gumby handout and direct the students to fill out a composite that represents the group's eustress and distress situations. The teacher can conclude the activity with these small group discussions or can have one person from each group describe their Gumby composite.

Variations

There is a great deal of flexibility in this activity. Depending upon the age, readiness, and educational needs of the students, one, two, or all three steps can be completed. The number of examples can be varied at the beginning of each step, to help students fill in the circles or spaces between the circles.

It is also possible to use the Gumby figure so that the circles and spaces between focus on specific health education topics, such as smoking, teen pregnancy, or AIDS. The activity can easily be integrated into other classes that deal with these areas. This is accomplished by first describing a specific controversial situation (e.g., a teen pregnancy). The students then fill in the circles with positive and negative behaviors (e.g., tell parents, don't tell anyone) and the spaces in between with anticipated reactions by others (e.g., anger, fear, support).

Note: This activity is adapted from N.L. Tubesing and D.A. Tubesing, <u>Structured Exercises in Stress Management</u> (Duluth: Whole Person Press, 1983), pp. 21-27.

Drawing shown smaller than it should be for actual use by students.

275

An Introductory Activity for Adolescent Communication and Intimacy

G. Greg Wojtowicz

The purpose of this student activity is fourfold: 1) to provide students an opportunity to use intimacy as an effective communication tool, 2) to familiarize students with the concept of "behavioral scripts," 3) to aid student transitions into opposite sex age groupings, and 4) to use the concept of "scripting" as a classroom management technique in order to structure effective student groupings. This learning experience develops an awareness of individual behavior characteristics and supports the development of communication skills as they relate to intimacy, interpersonal behavior, and social cognition.

Adolescence and Intimacy

The ritualistic behaviors learned during childhood are given practical meaning during adolescence. Adolescent developmental issues such as autonomy, intimacy, and identity are critical as they relate to behavior. Schools serve to institutionalize peer relationships, thus teaching the adolescent how these issues are linked to emotions. The adolescent who establishes intimate relations with peers is challenged to socialize and communicate in both ideal and practical terms. Consequently, "peers play an extremely important role in socializing adolescents into roles of adulthood"

G. Greg Wojtowicz is an assistant professor of health education in the Department of Health Education and Physical Education, University of Alabama at Birmingham, Birmingham, AL 35294.

(Steinberg, 1985). In addition, the focus of psychosocial development shifts from same sex groupings to opposite sex interactions. This process supports the effective translation of real values into decision making skills and real behaviors into problem solving techniques. This exercise in communication allows the student to practice intimacy skills in a controlled environment.

Behavioral Scripts

"Behavioral scripts prescribe standard ways of behaving in given settings" (Jones, Shainberg, & Byer, 1985). These predetermined, unconscious ways of thinking and acting determine the who, what, why, when, and where of any specific behavior. Scripting helps to integrate personality. Failure to do so results in esteem fragmentation (Jones et al., 1985). This activity allows students to identify the varied components of their scripts and gives them an opportunity to match their script with peers who have similar interests.

The technique can be adapted to fit any classroom time frame at the junior and senior high school level. In addition, the activity can be effectively used to solve problems associated with the structuring of student groups. It requires students to use those communication skills essential to functioning as an effective member of an activity group.

Objectives

This technique is designed to achieve the following four behavioral objectives: The student will use inti-

macy, communication skills, and knowledge of behavioral scripts in order to:

1) identify five components of a behavioral script,

2) identify three issues related to adolescent development,

3) list two characteristics they appreciate in other people, and

4) begin to appreciate the unique elements of other personalities.

Methods

The activity begins with a discussion of important issues related to adolescent social development, communication, and behavioral scripts. Important terms such as autonomy, intimacy, and identity should be defined and discussed. A numbered "behavioral script" activity sheet (Figure 1) is used to allow students to identify components of their own behavioral script. Each activity sheet is identified by a number that corresponds with the numbers next to student names on the class attendance list. Students are told to put their number on their sheet and also write that number on a foam cup provided by the teacher. Students place the cups on a desk or chalk tray in numerical order and then are given sufficient time to complete the questions on their activity sheet.

When they have finished, scripts should be posted throughout the entire room, avoiding crowding in any one area. Students then circulate around the room and read each script. When they finish, they are instructed to choose three to five scripts that matched their interests by copying the numbers found on

YOUR BEHAVIORAL SCRIPT

Sharing information about your script can be a rewarding way to meet people and develop new friendships. Complete the following survey by placing information related to you and your script in the spaces provided. Thereafter, the scripts will be posted and you will be given an opportunity to meet those individuals who matched your script. Do not put your name on this sheet!

My favorite   color _____   food _____

             sport _____   music group _____

             video _____   TV programs_____

My height is _____feet _____inches

I am left/right handed _____

Clothes I like to wear

_____

_____

What I like to do on weekends

_____

_____

_____

My hobbies are

_____

_____

#_____

---

those sheets. Thereafter, students place a slip of paper that bears their own number in the cups that correspond with their choices.

The teacher should participate in the activity along with the students. Before the students are allowed to collect the slips in their cup, the teacher should check each container and place a slip in each empty cup. In this way, each student will be chosen at least once and will become part of at least one group.

When all are fininshed, students collect their containers and record the numbers found on the slips. They now have the numbers of the students who chose them and the numbers of the scripts they have chosen. The teacher then reads the names and numbers on the attendance sheet, so that the students can match names to numbers and generate a list of individuals they will meet.

Students are instructed to move about the room in order to meet each person on their list. A time limit should be placed on this in order to leave sufficient time for a summary of the activity. Students are told to ask peers for specific information as to why they were chosen and to record the appropriate information on their activity sheet. Before the end of the period, the teacher can summarize the activity by leading an open discussion about the experience. Teachers may choose to record the components of different scripts on the board.

The next class begins with grouping the students according to individual choice. All matches (students choosing each other) can become part of a group. Depending on the size of the class, this activity usually generates two to three large groups, a number of smaller groups, and a number of couples.

The teacher should divide these groups into smaller units using student input to maintain as many matches as possible. This class period can be used to identify unique personal characteristics of individual students, interests of groups, and hobbies shared by the entire class.

The groups formed can be used to:

1) support development of social skills within opposite sex groups,

2) facilitate student interactions involving decision making and problem solving,

3) structure role playing activities, and

4) group students in order to develop classroom simulation games.

Groupings consisting of matches made by the students can improve the effectiveness of group work by improving attention span, increasing motivation, and augmenting student interactions.

Materials needed for this activity are as follows: behavioral script activity sheets, a master sheet identifying each student, foam cups, small slips of paper, tape for posting the sheets, and an activity content outline used to record information associated with intimacy, scripting, and communication skills.

Conclusion

This activity provides students with the opportunity to develop communication skills essential to social cognition and psychosocial development. Adolescents who experience success in classroom activities and develop effective socialization techniques may develop positive skills that will carry over into adulthood. In addition, teachers can use this technique to structure effective activity groups.

This scripting methodology is successful for two reasons: 1) students are motivated to work together because they like one another and 2) task outcomes are easier to achieve because students exercise an autonomy or ownership of the experience after they choose members of the group.

This technique is most effective at the high school level (especially grades 11 and 12) because opposite sex relationships become the primary focus of psychosocial development. Junior high school students are more comfortable and more effective when allowed to participate in same sex groupings. However, repeated use of this activity can aid the transition into opposite sex groupings. Students who lack proactive social skills tend to be somewhat guarded at the beginning of the activity. However, after they warm to the task, they tend to approach the experience with enthusiasm.

References

Ford, M. (1982). Social cognition and social competence in adolescent developmental psychology. *Developmental psychology, 18,* 323-340.

Jones, K.L., Shainberg, L.W., & Byer, C.O. (1985). *Dimensions of human sexuality.* Dubuque, IA: Wm. C. Brown Publishers, College Division.

Katchadourian, H.H. (1989). *Fundamentals of human sexuality* (5th ed.). Orlando, FL: Dryden Press, Holt, Reinhart & Winston, Inc., p. 268.

Steinberg, L. (1985). *Adolescence.* New York: Alfred A. Knopf, Inc.

SHOW AND TELL
Developing an Appreciation of Diversity

Kathryn Katzman Rolland

This two-part lesson provides a vehicle for high school and college level students to examine the range of common needs and desires they share in terms of human fulfillment. In addition, the exercise works well as a trust-building experience.

Introduction

College students, majoring in education, gathered for the first class in a course that would deal with incorporating materials about AIDS/HIV in the elementary and secondary school curriculum. Like the students in the urban center in which most of them will eventually teach, the class encompassed a wide range of diversity. They were male and female, ranging in age from 20 through 50, African-American, European-American, and Latino, straight and gay, single, married, divorced and currently cohabiting, returning students, one pregnant female, single parents—and from a variety of economic strata.

At the first class meeting, they eyed me and each other somewhat warily. Their concern, though unspoken, was palpable. Would they be comfortable in this class? Would they feel out of place? Would they have anything to contribute? As educators, and particularly as health educators, we know these concerns well.

Kathryn Katzman Rolland is a faculty member in the Department of Health and Physical Education, Hunter College of the City University of New York, New York City.

Objectives

Realizing that the class would encompass subject matter that is controversial, emotional, and even frightening, I decided to begin with an exploration of a more "neutral" concept—the continuum of human values. (Obviously, these are the same values that transcend and impact upon our attitudes toward AIDS and people with AIDS.) I have found that discovering similarities facilitates a more honest and sensitive exploration of differences at a later time. My objective was to provide a forum where students could experience the similarities of their human needs in a way that was at once personal and yet offered adequate room for privacy, if needed.

Procedure

Because a homework assignment is an integral part of the lesson, a preliminary explanation of the teacher's expectations is required as part of a previous lesson.

Lesson One: As an assignment for the following class, each student was instructed to "bring to class something that has a special meaning for you—that makes you feel good." The only caveat was that living things had to be represented by photographs or drawings. Realizing that I was asking students to reveal a portion of themselves to "almost strangers," I included myself in the activity. Students were instructed to record their informal thoughts on the

process, especially such aspects of the exercise that related to how difficult it was to select something, what thoughts helped them to make the final decision, and what single feeling/emotion their special "thing" elicited. These notes would serve as personal reference material during the next meeting of the class. (How does it make you feel? What is it that you respond to? Did you have a difficult time making a decision? are helpful guidelines.) Students were instructed not to discuss the assignment with any other class members until the class met again.

Lesson Two: As I entered the classroom the following week, the anticipation and excitement were apparent. Students were talking animatedly with each other and their enthusiasm was infectious. I began the class by telling them that I would go first and that each person would go as he or she was ready. I would not call on them but everyone was expected to participate before the end of class. In this way, they could attend to each individual report instead of thinking, "three more people and it's my turn to go." A recorder kept track of key phrases as the discussion progressed.

Time Frame

The class required 60 minutes for all 20 students to complete their reports, but I have subsequently conducted the class in less time. It is important for students to know how long they will have to discuss their "show and tell" when the

Continued on page 281

Teaching Self-Awareness Through Idiosyncrasies

Patrick K. Tow, Beverly Johnson and Patricia N. Smith

Pet peeves, annoying habits, or eccentricities, whatever they may be called, are behavioral idiosyncrasies which everyone exhibits to some degree. These peculiarities develop over time as a result of convenience, laziness, or ignorance; however, most of us are more aware of others' idiosyncratic behavior than of our own. Self-awareness is an elusive quality.

By itself, a behavioral idiosyncrasy might not be considered a problem of great magnitude. At best, it may be a minor annoyance in an otherwise ideal character whose presence is appreciated and enjoyed. At worst, it may be considered an extreme annoyance requiring remediation. Whether major or minor, an annoying habit serves as a source of chronic irritation in a relationship.

Background

When people fail to recognize and put idiosyncrasies into proper perspective, continued growth and development of interpersonal relationships can be stunted. The crux of a critical interpersonal conflict can remain unaddressed while time and attention are consumed over minor points of antagonism. The continual masking

Patrick K. Tow is an associate professor in the Department of HPER at Old Dominion University, Norfolk, VA 23529-0196. Beverly Johnson is Chairperson of the Department of HPER at Old Dominion University. Patricia N. Smith is an English teacher at Norview High School, Norfolk, VA 23513.

of an underlying problem can only compound the gravity of a conflict and make it more difficult to resolve. The degree to which someone finds certain behaviors offensive varies according to one's relationship to the offending party. Pet peeves tend to be exaggerated when a person who is trusted or loved fails to line up to one's expectations. Nevertheless, a tendency toward idealization and infatuation should be tempered with a healthy dose of reality. People are not generally aware of their own idiosyncrasies, however obvious these may be to others. Behavioral habits may become an unconscious part of one's everyday repertoire. Thus, overall awareness of idiosyncrasies could bring a refreshing enlightenment to relationships.

Educational Merits of Strategy

This teaching strategy has real world application that may be rooted in a lesson plan dealing with family living or mental health. The strategy serves as a suitable vehicle to teach self-awareness as well as an awareness of others. It brings to a level of consciousness that which seldom is thought about until interpersonal conflicts surface. Even on these occasions, some people insist on denying their part in a disharmonious relationship.

This lesson is not designed to suggest specific solutions but reveals, instead, a perspective on the trials and tribulations of relationships in general. Anyone growing up with siblings will remember annoyances over which

family squabbles started. Married students, in particular, are able to compose a list of chronic irritations displayed by spouses. Students, who are also parents, will certainly have a list of pet peeves about their children. In short, every student will find some personal relevance in this lesson.

Classroom Procedure

Ideally, students should be asked to compile anonymously a personal list of pet peeves or annoying behaviors they note in others, allowing students freely to express personal thoughts without fear of social reprisal or a violation of personal privacy. After collecting the lists, the instructor should cite items from the lists openly to the class. The students should publicly vote on each pet peeve in the following manner: a raised fist with the thumb up means that the habit is perfectly tolerable by the voter's standard; a thumbs down vote reflects an intolerance for the habit. At the instructor's discretion, a third voting option may be crossed arms to indicate indecision on the part of the student.

Teachers are not obligated to make distinctions between major or minor behavioral problems, since the students will be value voting. This is part of the dilemma which they need to resolve during the voting process.

The following is a list of behavioral idiosyncrasies developed by students in classes on family life education and mental health:

Is inattentive during conversations
Leaves toilet seat up
Bites his/her fingernails
Flirts with others
Sleeps to an excess
Is preoccupied with television
Doesn't flush toilet
Interrupts conversation
Squeezes toothpaste tube in middle
Leaves cap off the toothpaste tube
Bathes or showers infrequently
Cuts fingernails or toenails in bed
Shows affection publicly
Changes underwear infrequently
Drinks directly out of milk container
Boasts about accomplishments
Doesn't rinse tub after use
Leaves clothing or shoes lying around
Nags
Dresses slovenly
Tells little "white" lies
Curses or swears
Is negligent about doing chores
Drives with a "lead foot" on gas pedal
Borrows without returning things
Borrows without asking permission
Stays out late without calling
Is negligent about keeping physically
   fit
Gossips or passes rumors
Is tardy or late frequently
Snores during sleep
Picks his/her nose
Eats too fast or too slow

Makes major purchases without
   consulting
Brings guests home with little or no
   warning
Doesn't wash hands after using toilet
Wastes water or electricity

As one can see, chronic habits found to be irritating range from the most commonplace to the preposterous. The instructor may elect to go through this listing selectively or to have students derive their own lists anonymously.

Conclusion

In the final analysis, what has been accomplished? First, students become more aware of their own behavioral idiosyncrasies and not only those of others. Second, they come to grips with the fact that their actions also can be a source of annoyance to others. Third, they are not alone in their perceptions of what constitutes irritating behaviors. Hopefully, some will come to realize that minor irritations often are blown out of proportion. Last, a humorously anecdotal discussion of past, present, and future living experiences with spouses parents, friends, or siblings is beneficial for those wanting to improve interpersonal relationships.

SHOW AND TELL
Continued from page 279

when the assignment is presented. (Three to five minutes is more than adequate.) Another 30 minutes was needed to adequately process the information and feelings presented. (In a high school class with 30 students, we broke up into six small groups and completed the assignment in 38 minutes.)

Reactions

The examples that students selected were diverse and included such items as an adopted son's birth certificate, crystals in a leather pouch, photos of pet cats and dogs, a nephew's photograph, several stuffed animals, a credit card, two portable cassette players, and a Bible. (Obviously, the choices will vary depending upon the age of the participants.) What was wonderfully exciting every time I have used this lesson was the ease with which students saw the connections and similarities among themselves. For example, a "walkman" reflected the importance of music in the students' lives, especially as a stress management technique. Pets gave unconditional love and did _not_ give advice.

The common threads that students identify are: security, self-worth and self-esteem, accomplishment, trust, intimacy, and desires. An assigned reading from Maslow's *Toward a Psychology of Being* (2nd ed., 1968, Van Nostrand) can be utilized at this point. A discussion of these basic human needs provides an avenue for discussion of ways in which society provides enabling opportunities as well as the kinds of barriers that exist. Students are asked to focus first on personal experiences and then to identify the similar ways they feel society has helped and hindered their development. Discussions about stereotyping, prejudice, and stigma can be an appropriate follow-up to this lesson.

Nutrition

Can You Name These Foods?

Eileen L. Daniel

Credit: Marshfilm

This learning activity can be used in a wide variety or ways in either a nutrition class or in a health education curriculum. Activities which are student-oriented are an interesting and exciting way to present a specific topic within a curriculum. A favorite activity of mine (and my students) is "can you name these foods?" Five or more foods are listed on an overhead projector or blackboard by ingredients only. Students are then asked to try and identify the food. Though most students fail to determine the food by ingredients only, the activity generates lively discussion and laughter!

Some examples of topics which can be addressed from this activity are:

● What information is on a food label?
● Order of ingredients indicates the order of their predominance in the food.
● Additives are listed by their chemical name.
● Food colors are listed as "natural or artificial color," not by their chemical name.
● The different forms of sugar used, i.e., dextrose, corn syrup, corn sweeteners.
● Risk versus benefit concept in using additives.
● The changing American diet which incorporates fabricated and convenience foods in increasing numbers.
● Nutritional implications when we change from foods like juices to sugar-based imitation products.

The activity can also be implemented by having the students bring in their own ingredient lists from foods found at home or in the supermarket. Taking turns, they can display their lists and have fellow students try to guess the food.

Whichever way the activity is presented, it has always generated much interest and discussion in nutrition, foods, and diet. Many students are very surprised at exactly what goes into the foods they eat, particularly sugars and additives.

Can you name these foods by seeing their ingredients only?

1. Water, hydrogenated coconut and palm kernel oils, sugar, corn syrup solids, sodium casseinate, dextrose, polysorbate 60, natural and artificial flavors, sorbitan monostearate, carrageenan, guar gum and artificial color.

2. Dehydrated tomato, corn sweeteners, modified food starch, sugar, nonfat dry milk, salt, monosodium glutamate, butterfat, partially hydrogenated coconut oil, dehydrated onion, artificial color, mono and diglycerides, silicon dioxide, sodium casseinate, dipotassium phosphate, natural and artificial flavor, citric acid, and BHA.

3. Corn syrup solids, partially hydrogenated vegetable oils, sodium casseinate, dipotassium phosphate, monoglycerides, sodium tripoly-phosphate, artificial flavors, beta carotene and riboflavin.

4. Sugar, dextrose, citric and malic acids, sodium citrate, natural and artificial flavors, tricalcium phosphate, vitamin C, cellulose gum and artificial color.

5. Sugar, gelatin, adinic acid, sodium citrate, fumaric acid, artificial flavor and color.

Answers:
1. Cool-Whip non-dairy whipped topping
2. Lipton Tomato Cup-A-Soup
3. Cremora non-dairy creamer
4. Tang
5. Jello gelatin (any flavor)

Eileen L. Daniel is an instructor in the Department of Health Science, State University of New York, Brockport, NY 14420.

"Digesting" Health Information

Richard A. Crosby

Ideally, health educators are in a state of neverending search for better methods. Sharing is bound to be the best contributor to this search.

In sharing, the author has found this play to be a highly motivating approach to the teaching of the digestive system. "What Happened to the Apple" is geared toward upper elementary aged students, but works quite well with "low achieving" junior high school students. Audience participation allows all class members to become involved and interested.

After the narrator closes the play, students may want to try different roles. The play takes no more than five minutes to perform and can easily be repeated. Hopefully, students will memorize the apple's path with enthusiasm.

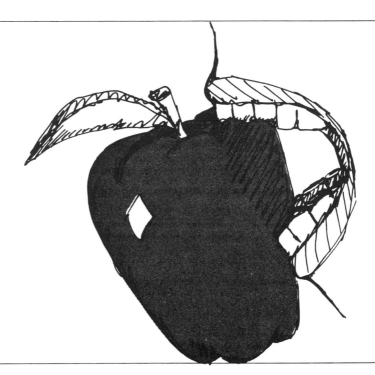

What Happened to the Apple?

Characters: Apple, Stomach, Small Intestine, Large Intestine, Mouth and Teeth, and the entire audience

Apple: That girl just picked me up. Oh No!

Mouth and Teeth: Let's grind this apple into small pieces so the stomach won't have to do it. Teeth, when you're finished, have the tongue move the smaller pieces back to the throat. Mouth, you turn on your hoses and wet this food down with saliva so that the throat won't complain when it swallows.

Apple: It sure is dark in here! Where am I anyway?

Audience: You, apple, are in the stomach! And you look more like applesauce after what the mouth and teeth did to you.

Apple: But how did I get here?

Audience: You came down the esophagus!

Stomach: Oops! Looks like my rest is over. I've got to get busy and digest more food. It sure is rough work breaking up carbohydrates and protein. But, at least there is no fat coming in this time. I hate breaking up fat!

Audience: Hey, stomach. Do you like your job?

Stomach: Most of the time my boss treats me pretty well, but every now and then he delivers the wrong kind of food and I go on strike!

Apple: Whoo! Where am I going now? What's happening to me?

Audience: Don't you know apple? Your time in the stomach is up now; you have to go to the small intestine.

Small Intestine: I can't wait to absorb you into my blood, apple!

Apple: But what will happen to me when I'm in your blood?

Small Intestine: Your carbohydrates will be burned for energy and your protein can be used for growth and repair of the body.

Audience: Hey small intestine! How are you going to absorb the apple?

Small Intestine: Well, I must admit, It won't be an easy task. I'll have to have help from my friends, Liver and Pancreas.

Apple: There's not much of me left! But I'm still here. The small intestine didn't use all of me. I still have my roughage and some of my water.

Audience: Here comes the large intestine.

Large Intestine: I'm gonna be glad to get that apple in me—I like roughage. I'll soak up that leftover water as well.

Narrator: The large intestine did soak up the apple's leftover water. Then the large intestine compacted and eliminated the roughage from the body. The body was grateful to the apple for providing so many good nutrients.

Richard A. Crosby is with the Department of Health Education at Central Michigan University, Mt. Pleasant, MI 48859.

Nutrition

Nutrition Is the Name of the Game

Paula R. Zaccone

Classroom approaches that preach the do's and don'ts of health practices have seen their day. The effect of television, video and audio recording devices, and the bombardment of advertising dictate that educational methods aiming to capture an audience must appeal as entertainment. Today it is not enough for health educators to appear before their students with scientific facts and a sincere interest in their delivery. Style and process of delivery are as important as the health message in determining the duration of effect.

Studies indicating why children and adults watch television (Lyle, 1972; Robinson, 1972; Schramm, Lyle, and Parker, 1961) give educators clues for planning class activities that are entertaining and informative. Teaching methods and learning activities that are amusing, relate to the interests of students, and that carry a health message are more likely to draw interest from both young and mature students.

What follows is an approach to nutrition education that can be appropriately employed by the health educator in a variety of educational settings. The *Nutrition Is the Name of the Game* approach may be useful to the health or physical educator who aims to teach that good

Paula R. Zaccone is an associate professor of Health Education at Seton Hall University, Department of Health, Physical Education, & Recreation, South Orange, NJ 07079.

eating habits complement habits of exercise for the maintenance of good health and in the prevention of disease. The coach whose responsibilities include guiding athletes toward proper physical conditioning may find that this teaching technique can be adapted to the specific sport interests of a particular team, e.g., wrestling, football, basketball, baseball, track and field, hockey, etc.

Tennis, a sport which has gained popularity in recent times because of its value for players of all ages, can aid in the development of coordination, speed, endurance, and accuracy. Introducing its techniques and terminology along with nutrition education further communicates that habits of eating and exercise are both determinants of health status.

For implementation of the tennis theme, 31 "tennis balls", 4-inch circles, need to be cut from paper or cardboard. Each ball bears a statement of nutrition information. In the statement, one or two terms are underlined that have significance for both the game of tennis and good eating habits.

The "tennis balls" are distributed to the students, and each in turn introduces the statement to the class. A discussion of the statement on the ball as it applies to the sport of tennis and to good habits of nutrition follows.

Teachers in search of means to integrate nutrition education into an already crowded academic schedule may find this approach useful. Classroom teachers and school nurses may elect to

mount the balls on a bulletin board in a calendar arrangement. For the purpose of integrating nutrition education into the daily curriculum, each day may begin with the disclosure of one statement which also bears the date. Weekend messages could be addressed on Mondays and Fridays. Brief nutrition and tennis discussions could precede other learning activities scheduled for the day.

The concepts that are to appear on each of the "tennis balls" are as follows:

1. A "tennis *nut*" is a protein.

T: Whereas "health nuts" have been described for their tendency "to spend inordinate amounts of time maintaining and promoting their health" (Bedworth, 1982), *tennis nut* refers to one who is frequently occupied by tennis play **(T:Tennis).**

N: Nutritionally speaking **(N:Nutrition),** "nuts of the edible kind are sources of protein, fats, the B vitamins, and some minerals.

2. The body is the *court* for the food we eat.

T: The tennis *court* is the place where the sport is played and the outcome is determined. For the doubles game, the court is 36 feet in width and 4½ feet narrower for the singles game.

N: The body is the place where the effects of eating habits are determined.

3. Eat within the *boundaries* of moderation.

T: The tennis court is marked by two

baselines, which are the end lines of the court, and two sidelines.

N: Eating, too, has its limitations which need to be regarded for the maintenance of good health. Excesses of even the most nutritious foods can become contributors to fat storage and the incidence of some diseases.

4. Eating a variety of foods is good *offense*.

T: *Offense* generally applies to being in control of the ball or having the ability to attack the opponent. The player who is about to serve is the offensive player.

N: Eating a variety of foods allows the body to produce antibodies to counteract harmful bacteria, assures an intake of essential nutrients, and protects the body from acquiring toxic levels of potentially harmful substances.

5. Eat green and yellow vegetables which *score* for good health.

T: The accumulation of points made in the game occur as love, 15, 30, 40, and game.

N: The accumulation of important nutrients such as vitamins A, C, and K, iron, potassium, and fiber is provided by green and yellow vegetables.

6. Vegetables without salt are a complete *set*.

T: The player/s who is/are first to win six games win(s) a *set*, providing there is a margin of at least two games over the opponent. A set is extended until this margin is achieved.

N: Vegetables derive minerals including sodium from the soil in which they grow. Processing may cause more sodium to be added. Thus, adding more salts to foods increase the blood volume and is risky to those who are susceptible to high blood pressure. Vegetables served without salt as an additive are nutritionally complete.

7. Carbohydrates are body *power*.

T: *Power* is the ability to provide sudden force to the ball.

N: Carbohydrates are excellent suppliers of suddenly needed energy for the body. In plants, sugars and starches are present along with vitamins and minerals, and thus provide excellent food sources of body energy.

8. Proteins from animal and plant sources make a good *match*.

T: Tennis competition generally con-

cludes when one side wins two out of three sets.

N: Amino acids provided by both dairy and plant sources combine to form complete proteins which will best serve the body's needs for proteins.

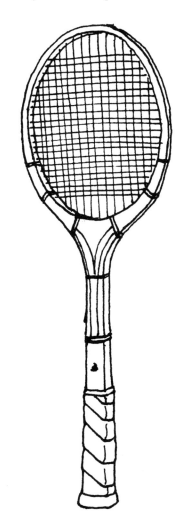

9. *Serve* fruits and vegetables for meals and snacks.

T: The method of putting the ball into play is called a *serve* and is done by a player who stands with both feet behind the base line and within an imaginery continuation of the center mark and the side line.

N: Furnishing the body with fruits and vegetables also provides the body with vitamins, minerals, water, and fiber in useful combinations. Sugar derived from fruits and vegetables supplies the body with the energy needed to metabolize these nutrients. Because of their high nutritive density, fruits and vegetables are superior to "empty calorie" foods as snacks.

10. *Pace* your eating or you'll suffer in the end.

T: *Pace*, the rate of movement or length of steps taken, is an important factor in executing tennis strokes.

N: Slower rates of eating will allow for efficient mastication and processing of food for digestion, absorption, and elimination. Furthermore, a controlled eating pace allows the stomach to send cues of satiety to the brain and the quanity of food eaten to be held in check. Problems related to eating too quickly (ingestion, nausea, diarrhea, and constipation) may be avoided by adopting slower-paced eating habits.

11. 1. Raisins, 2. apples, 3. bananas, and 4. nuts are *forehand* ("four hand") foods.

T: The basic drive which includes a backswing and a follow through using the whole arm is known as the *forehand*.

N: Each of the four foods listed can be eaten by hand, requires almost no preparation, and can also be convenient and nutritious as snacks.

12. Fats may be *backhanded* in their appearance.

T: A *backhand* drive is contacting the ball with the back of the hand turned in the direction of motion.

N: Whereas fats may add flavor, their presence in foods often times is invisible. The moisture in cakes and pastries may be attributable to fats which contribute to the high caloric value of these foods. Eating an excess of fatty foods has been associated with the accumulation of plaque on the walls of arteries, a condition that is not easily identified.

13. Dieting is often the need that follows an *over/swing*.

T: A common error in which the player uses too much backswing or follow-through frequently results in the ball landing too wide or too long.

N: Binge eating, periods when eating habits take on an "overswing," causes the body to store excess calories as body fat. Furthermore, some theorists maintain that overeating during periods of rapid cell division may permanently increase the propensity toward overfatness during inactivity and in adulthood.

14. Overeating is not your *foot's fault*.

T: A *foot fault* is a foul committed by the server who enters an area other than that behind the base line within the imaginery extension of the center mark and side line or who changes position by walking or running throughout the delivery of the service.

N: This statement suggests the need for overeaters to take control of their own eating habits. It serves no useful purpose to blame eating binges on others. They may have nothing to gain or lose by the overeater's gains (i.e., "My foot caused me to overeat"). Accepting responsibility for one's own eating habits and fitness status is a healthy approach toward coping with disappointments.

15. "If You Drink Alcohol, Do So in Moderation" (USDA, USDHHS, 1980) is a *slice* of good advice.
T: A *slice* is a short, choppy stroke in which the ball is hit downward with backspin and is aimed to bounce away from the opponent's reach.
N: A brief slice of nutritional advice is to avoid excessiveness in the drinking of alcohol. For healthy, non-pregnant adults who choose to drink alcohol, the recommendation made by the National Research Council (USDA, USDHHA) is to do so in moderation.

16. Let your mind, not your tummy, be the *judge*.
T: The official who makes the decisions regarding play tournaments may be the referee, umpire, or lines *judge*.
N: Sensations of thirst and hunger alone are not accurate indicators of the body's needs for liquids and food. Habits of meal planning to ensure adequate intake of all nutrients and regular replacements of water lost by perspiration and excretion are reliance on wisdom, rather than impulse, for good nutrition.

17. Avoid using food to *bounce back* from disappointments.
T: The term *bounce back* in tennis may refer to the ability of the ball or player to rebound after a hard hit.

N: Those who eat in search of psychological comfort would do better to find less self-defeating methods of coping. Try exercising or becoming involved in non-food related hobbies that expend rather than store surplus calories.

18. *Aim* to have meat, fish, poultry, or eggs at least twice daily.
T: To *aim* is to direct the ball to drop in a specific spot on the court.
N: These food items share the nutritive values of protein, fats, niacin, thiamin, iron, and other minerals. Efforts should be directed toward their consumption at least twice daily.

19. Milk products are needed for good *form*.
T: Players demonstrate good tennis *form* with efficient execution of tennis strokes and strategies.
N: Milk, cheese, yogurt, even puddings and ice cream made from milk contain nutrients important for building and maintaining strong bones and teeth. Found in milk products and specifically responsible for the strength of body structures, are vitamin D, calcium, phosphorus, and protein.

20. *Rush* the net, but pause through dinner.
T: Dashing to the front of the forecourt to play the ball as it crosses the net or drops over is known as *rushing the net*.
N: This statement points to the importance of controlled eating patterns. Reasonably paced ingestions of food that allow for pleasant conversation add to the enjoyment and longevity of the eating period. Habits that encourage awareness of quantity eaten and portion control enable the diner to acquire feelings of satiety that would escape the speed eater.

21. No *single* food is perfect.
T: *Single* play takes place when an individual player opposes one other player in competition.
N: No one food provides the body with all the substances needed to carry on its physiological processes and to maintain health. This statement invites a discussion of the need to eat a variety of foods (#4) and the relative values of foods. While milk is considered to be a highly nutritious food, it fails to meet the body's needs for iron and vitamin C. Fish, often said to be "brain food," is a worthy source of protein, but lacks the carbohydrates the brain requires for fuel.

22. *Doubles* of sweets can bring *doubles* of troubles.
T: The *doubles* game requires coopera-

tion and communication with a partner on a court that is wider than for singles play.
N: This statement addresses the hazards that are evident from eating an excess of sugar. Tooth decay and obestity are just two of the consequences related to excessive sugar in the diet. Other disorders of the cardiovascular and digestive systems have been associated with a surplus of calories derived from "empty calorie foods."

23. Milk is a good *partner* to many foods.
T: A tennis *partner* is a teammate in doubles play.
N: In addition to its vitamin and mineral constituents (vitamin A and D, riboflavin, calcium, phosphorus), milk contains protein ideally suited for use by the body when it combines with amino acids from grains and vegetables. The amino acids from milk and plant products are good protein partners.

24. Sugar is the *opponent* of good dental health.
T: The player/s on the other side of the net during play is/are an *opponent(s)*.
N: Sugar combines with acid in the mouth to produce decay-causing bacteria. Particularly when sugar lingers on the teeth of children, it opposes good dental health.

25. A well *strung* meal has dental floss as its *follow through*.
T: Tennis rackets may be *strung* with nylon, steel wire, or sheep gut. There is some concern that string tension that is too tight my contribute to painful "tennis elbows," an inflammation of the point where the tendons that straighten the

elbow attach. A *follow through* is the continuation of movement after contact with the ball is made.

N: Using dental floss after meals and before brushing will aid in removing cariogenic food particles and plaque from the teeth.

26. Eating should be neither torment, nor a *tournament*.

T: A *tournament* is a contest among players to determine a champion.

N: Discussion about many attitudes and food-related habits that result in unhealthy eating habits may evolve. Some examples are eating and drinking contests in which overindulging is encouraged, contests of rapid weight loss, using foods as rewards, and practices that encourage anxiety with eating such as force feeding and eating in stressful environments.

27. *Seeds* make the playing rough.

T: The playing of highly skilled players according to their ranked ability is a practice which has been designed to ensure challenge and competition among players.

N: *Seeds* and skins from various plant foods (fruits, vegetables, nuts) as as roughage in the digestive system and aid the body to rid itself of waste products.

28. For effective *elimination*, take in fiber, fats, and water.

T: An *elimination* tournament is one in which the loser is disqualified from further play.

N: Fiber functions to bind waste products for removal from the body. Fats and water lubricate the digestive tract so that processing of food for digestion and excretion is facilitated.

29. Water and sunshine make a dandy *deuce*.

T: *Deuce* in tennis refers to the score being tied at 40-all.

N: The need to replace body fluids lost during periods of exercise and heavy perspiration cannot be overemphasized. With higher temperatures, the body's need for water increases.

30. "The breakfast of champions" is daily.

T: *Champions* are those who acquire the greatest number of wins and are determined to be in first place at the end of the event.

N: Breakfast is considered to be in first place with regard to its importance for supplying the body with fuel and nutrients required for each day's activities. An additional consideration is the nutritional fact that the *breakfasts of champi-*ons need not come in a cardboard box bearing the picture of an athlete. Instead, breakfast foods should be a combination of those from the basic four food groups: grains, dairy, fruits and vegetables, and meat, fish, poultry, or nuts.

31. Calories *add (ad)* in.

T: *Ad in* refers to the point advantage to the server. This follows deuce. A point advantage to the receiving player would be called "ad-out."

N: Here, the concept of homonyms, words that sound alike but are different in meaning, would appropriately be integrated in a language arts and nutrition education lesson. Calories derived from second servings, snacks, and rich desserts add into the total caloric intake. No amount of will can erase the programming of an ingested calorie to carry out its fuel-serving function.

32. *Winning* is easy to digest.

T: To earn success or to achieve progress is *winning* for some players of tennis.

N: Taking responsibility for one's patterns of ingestion to restrict certain foods and drinks, and putting sound nutritional habits into practice is *winning*, whether it be in the battle of the unsightly bulge or in the fight against risk factors.

In the process it is important to realize that what you eat is as important as whether you lose or gain. Harm to health may occur as a result of excesses of fats, salt sugar, or calories. Moreover, nutrient imbalances promoted by fad diets and willfully induced starvation with hopes of achieving quick fat loss may be losing pounds without winning the benefits of good nutritional status.

Bedworth, A. The health educator as health nut. *Health Education*, 1982, 13 (2): 27–28.

Lyle, J. Television in daily life: patterns of use overview. In Rubenstein, E. A., Comstock, A., & Murray, J. P. (eds.). *Television and Social Behavior*, Vol. 4. Washington, DC: U.S. Dept. of Health, Education, & Welfare, 1972, pp. 1–32.

Robinson, J. P. Toward defining the functions of television. In E. A. Rubenstein, Comstock, A., & Murray, J. P. (eds). *Television and Social Behavior*, Vol. 4. Washington, DC: U.S. Dept. of Health, Education, and Welfare, 1972, pp. 568–601.

Schramm, W., Lyle, J., & Parker, E. B. *Television in the lives of our children*. Stanford: Stanford University Press, 1961.

United States Depts. of Agriculture and Health and Human Services. *Nutrition and your health: Dietary guidelines for Americans*, 1980.

Personal Health

Sun Smart: A Peer-Led Lesson on the Effects of Tanning and Sunning on the Skin

Mary Elesha-Adams and David M. White

Many adolescents and young adults spend a great deal of time sunning. Some university students even schedule classes and jobs around prime sunning time. It has been our experience in teaching personal health courses that not only do students typically have a number of misconceptions about sun exposure and skin cancer, but the information we provide often has little or no influence on their behavior. Because almost all of the more than 500,000 cases of non-melanoma skin cancer developed each year in the United States are considered to be sun-related, and recent studies show that sun exposure is a primary factory in the development of melanoma (American Cancer Society, 1988), we clearly needed to find more effective ways of delivering health education. To address this need, we developed a peer-led lesson on the effects of tanning and sunning. By designing the course to be led by peers, we also addressed another need at the university level. Peer teaching can provide valuable, practical experience for health education majors before their formal student teaching or internships.

The goals of the SUN SMART sessions are to:

1. Enable participants to make informed decisions regarding sunning and encourage safer sunning behavior, and

Mary Elesha-Adams is a health educator in the Student Health Service at East Carolina University Greenville, NC 27858-4353. David M. White is an assistant professor of health education in the Department of Health, Physical Education, Recreation, and Safety at East Carolina University, Greenville, NC 27858-4353.

2. Provide opportunities for undergraduate health education majors to gain practice experience.

Development and Implementation

Sessions are coordinated by the health educator at the University Health Service in cooperation with the Department of Health, Physical Education, Recreation and Safety. The peer educators may register for the experience as an independent study project and receive from one to three semester hours of academic credit, depending on the scope of involvement.

Peer health educators are trained in a preservice workshop. They develop teaching materials, role play instructional sessions, and work on group facilitation skills, then are assigned in terms to lead SUN SMART sessions. SUN SMART sessions have been requested most frequently during spring semester when students prepare for spring vacation and summer activities.

Objectives

The SUN SMART session has the following objectives.

1. Students should be able to describe complications caused by sunning including premature wrinkling, cataracts, and skin cancer.

2. Students should be able to identify medications that increase the likelihood of sensitivity to the sun, such as birth control pills, certain antibiotics, antihistamines, and Accutane.

3. Students should be able to determine their own skin type and define sun protection factor (SPF).

4. Students should be able to list two recommended methods to relieve sunburn.

5. Students should be able to identify the harmful effects of tanning beds and other indoor tanning devices, including skin rashes and eye injuries, and complications from overexposure, such as wrinkles and skin cancer.

6. Students should be able to describe safer sunning techniques, such as use of sunscreens, protective clothing and sunglasses, hats and visors, and avoiding tanning between 11:00 am–2:00 pm when the sun's rays are strongest.

7. Students should be able to describe self-examination procedures for skin cancer.

Materials and Resources

The one-hour SUN SMART sessions are informal, and comments and questions are encouraged throughout the presentation. A colorful handout developed by the peer health educator is given to each participant and referred to often during the presentation. The handout describes safer sunning tips, defines SPF, lists common suntan preparations and their SPF, and identifies medications that increase sun sensitivity. Free sunscreen and t-shirts reinforce safer sunning behavior and encourage attendance. We also used the following commercially produced materials, as reinforcements:

1. "Sun Sense," a brochure developed by Johnson & Johnson that emphasizes the use of SPF and sensible sun protection.

2. "Skin Cancer. Early Prevention, Early Detection," a brochure developed by the North Carolina Department of Human Resources that illustrates a 10-step procedure for checking for skin cancer.

3. "Progress Against Cancer of the Skin," published by the National Institutes of Health, a resource for peer health educators.

Applications

In addition to presentation at residence halls, peer health educators have provided SUN SMART demonstrations at two university health fairs. Instructors of university personal health and wellness courses can incorporate SUN SMART into the existing curriculum. The program can also be presented to high school students in classes or organization and club meetings.

Typical Misconceptions About Sunning

We developed a pretest for use during the SUN SMART sessions that focuses on high-risk groups and behaviors, detection and treatment of skin cancer, and perceived level of knowledge about safer sunning. Thus far, participants have been almost exclusively white, female, and aged 18 to 23. Although almost all (98 percent) knew that people with excessive exposure to the sun were at high risk for skin cancer, 17 percent did not know that redheads and blondes were at high risk, 13 percent did not believe that fair-skinned people were at high risk, and 12 percent did not realize that people who sunburn often were at high risk. Thirteen percent of the students inaccurately believed that the chances of developing skin cancer were reduced each time the skin darkens through tanning. One-fourth (25 percent)did not realize that the majority of the average person's total lifetime sun exposure is in the first 20 years of life. In terms of screening and detection, 22 percent did not think that the skin should be examined at least once yearly and 23 percent believed that it is not necessary to check areas of the body unexposed to the sun when checking for skin cancer.

Conclusion

The SUN SMART program has proven to be effective in increasing knowledge and awareness of safer sunning and has provided an opportunity for health education majors to gain valuable practical experience. Preliminary results indicate that this teaching idea can be beneficial to students, faculty, and staff. An evaluation of the effectiveness of this approach in changing sunning behavior is currently underway.

This project was funded, in part, by the North Carolina Division, American Cancer Society, Inc.

The authors would like to thank Jerri Harris for her expert editorial assistance.

American Cancer Society. (1988). *Cancer facts and figures–1988*. New York: Author.

A Quick and Easy Check for Foot Problems

Dianne Boswell O'Brien

The Foot Powder Test

Did you ever wonder why your pants or skirt move slightly to the left or to the right after you have been walking? If your slacks appear to be turning to the left after you have been walking, then you are probably taking a longer stride with the right foot than you are with the left foot. One way to check to see if your stride length is the same with both legs is to measure the distance between footprints. A simple powder test will tell you how long your stride length is with each leg.

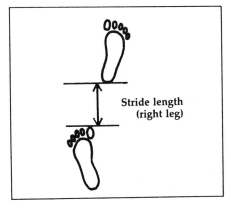

(Illustration 1)

To perform the test, just cover a dark floor with a sprinkle of foot powder. Then walk barefooted in a straight line through the powder. Your footprints should be clearly visible. The powdered surface should be large enough to accommodate

Dianne O'Brien is an assistant professor of health education in the Department of Health, Physical Education, Recreation and Dance at Murray State University, Murray, KY 42001. In 1980, she was named the outstanding young professional and given the Mabel Lee Award by AAHPERD.

about three steps; for example, a right-left-right or left-right-left. This is a distance of about ten feet.

Before walking onto the newly powdered surface, take about six natural steps so that your normal walking cadence and pattern are established before you strike the powdered surface.

Stride length

Once you have walked through the powdered surface take a tape measure and measure your right stride length by measuring the distance from your left big toeprint to the heel of your right footprint. Measure your left stride length in the same way.

Everyone needs a footprint test

Good foot health results from intelligent decisions about exercise habits, foot care and shoe selection. Much can be learned from just interpreting footprints. The simple footprint test given in the following paragraphs will indicate some individualized foot care needs.

To the Teacher: *This article is suitable for students and adults who may be in a health or fitness class. To perform the test with large groups, purchase a roll of butcher paper from a restaurant supply house. The cost will be approximately fifteen dollars. Purchase stamp pads from a book or stationery supply shop at a cost of about five dollars.*

Divide the paper into fifteen-foot sections and give each person a section of the paper. Have each person ink their feet with the stamp pads. Perform the test as directed, but omit the part of the test which directs the person to take several strides before stepping onto the paper. When ink is used, the person will step directly onto the paper. When checking the footprints, consider the first few steps as a gaining momentum. The last two steps should be investigated as the person's more natural stride.

The test assists a teacher in recognizing potential problems of students who will be asked to participate in endurance or sports activities. It is especially helpful in recognizing problems in adult populations.

A person who has a dominate right foot may take a longer stride with the right leg. People who are right-handed often have a dominate right foot.

If your right foot is dominate it may also be larger. You can also see size by comparing your right and left footprints. If your right footprint is larger you should make certain to try on the right shoe first when fitting new shoes. If the right shoe is large enough for your right foot then the left shoe should also be large enough for your smaller left foot.

Toeing Out or Pronation

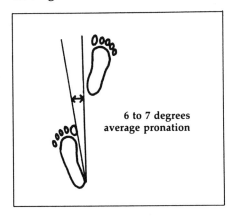

(Illustration 2)

The average toe-out position or pronation is 6 to 7 degrees (See Illustration 2). Toeing out increases with age and weight increases. Toeing out decreases as walking speed increases. (Cailliet, 1978) People who have extremely pronated feet tire easily and often experience leg pain.

The following exercises when done repeatedly (15 times once a day) for several weeks will strengthen muscles in the feet and legs which help to control pronation. Recommended activities are: (1) Strengthen muscles in the calf of the leg by holding on to a chair and rising on the toes, (2) Strengthen muscles of the feet by picking up pencils with the toes, (3) Strengthen feet and legs by standing with weight on the outer borders of the feet and curl toes inward and upward.

Foot Strain

Foot strain may occur in the under-exercised foot and pronated foot. The person who exercises infrequently and then decides to walk a long distance or engage in a Saturday ball game is a likely candidate for foot strain. Since 85% of the foot problems are caused by ill-chosen footwear, the lack of proper shoes is also a culprit in creating foot strain. Poor body mechanics and abuse through overuse or improperly fitting shoes can create excessive stress on the muscles and ligaments of the feet, thus causing chronic foot strain. Foot strain produces aching legs and feet. For brief bouts (acute) of foot strain, rest and proper foot wear are recommended. For long-term (chronic) foot strain, professional help should be sought.

When foot strain persists over long periods of time, pronation and a flattened transverse arch often accompany the condition (Cailliet, 1978).

Flat Feet

When the transverse arch (arch going across the foot) is flattened, a footprint will be noticably lacking the "normal" curve on the inside border of the foot (See Illustration 3).

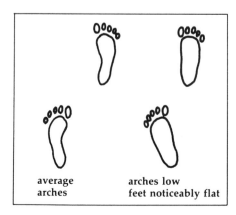

average
arches

arches low
feet noticeably flat

(Illustration 3)

Reading a footprint will give a person an indication of a flattened transverse arch.

Some people have inherited naturally flat feet. However, the older or heavier person's transverse arches may be abnormally depressed. This flattening of the transverse arch may cause calluses on the metatarsal heads (ball of foot). (See Illustration 4). These calluses may be padded with commercially available felt pads which are designed to relieve the pressure on the calluses.

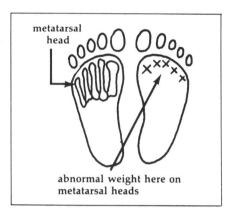

metatarsal
head

abnormal weight here on
metatarsal heads

(Illustration 4)

Metatarsal pads and heel pads will help relieve the pressure on the transverse arch. Metatarsal pads should be placed behind the metatarsal heads. Strengthening the arches of the foot, practicing good walking mechanics and correct footwear will help the problem. When there is persistent pain, a person should see a podiatrist.

Exercises for strengthening the foot were listed previously. They should be accompanied by exercises which stretch the achilles tendon (Cailliet, 1978). For example stand about two feet away from the wall and lean toward the wall. Place both hands on the wall and lean toward the wall keeping both feet flat on the floor. Feel the stretch on the back of the calf of the leg. Hold the position at least 20 seconds.

Pigeon Toed Walk

In adults a pigeon-toed walk (Illustration 5) may be a result of improper mechanics of the joints which are not located in the foot. For example, improper alignment of the knee joint and other multiple causes will cause the feet to turn inward.

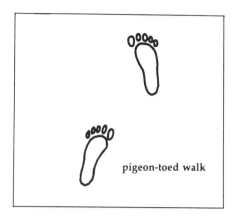

pigeon-toed walk

(Illustration 5)

In order to adequately diagnose the problem, assistance of professional help is recommended. For children, early treatment is of utmost importance.

Distance Between Footprints

To measure the distance between footprints, draw an extended line from the edge of the big toe through the most indented part of the arch. Do this for both feet. Then measure the distance between the lines (See Illustration 6).

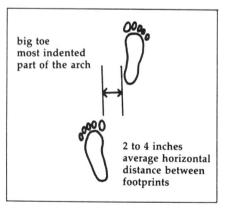

big toe
most indented
part of the arch

2 to 4 inches
average horizontal
distance between
footprints

(Illustration 6)

The average horizontal distance between footprints is 2 to 4 inches. The horizontal distance between footprints will be influenced by width of pelvic girdle and overall body size. A larger frame needs a wider base of support.

Shortened Big Toe

In some footprints the great toe appears to be shorter than the second toe (Illustration 7). This condition is often called Morton's toe and is usually inherited. In the average foot, metatarsal I should bear twice as much weight as metatarsal II. However, because metatarsal I is short, metatarsal II must bear additional weight. Therefore, calluses may form under the metatarsals (Cailliet, 1978).

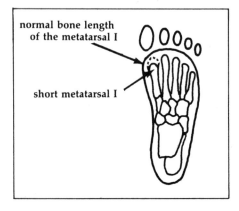

(Illustration 7)

A pad under metatarsal I will relieve some of the pressure from metatarsal II. Foot exercises listed above will also help to strengthen muscles which are often strained by this condition.

Big Toe Turns Inward

If the big toe turns toward the second toe (Illustration 8) there may be source of pain between the big toe and the second toe. This condition may be caused by wearing improperly designed shoes. A person with this condition should check to see if the toes of shoes allow adequate spread of toes when feet are bearing the weight of walking. Shoes which force toes into a pointed position should be discarded.

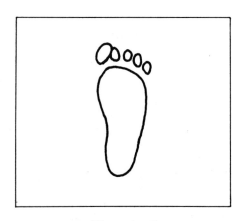

(Illustration 8)

Overlapping Fourth and Fifth Toes

A footprint that shows toes overlapping or together may indicate improper footwear that squeezes toes (Illustration 9). When shoes press the toes together soft corns between toes may result.

If soft corns between toes occur, separate toes with sponge rubber or lambs wool to prevent further pressure (Cailliet, 1978). Check shoes which may not allow toes to spread during walking. Sometimes a shoe repair shop may mechanically stretch a shoe in order to provide more toe room.

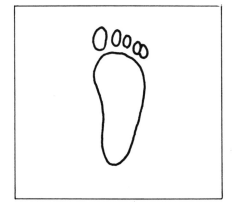

(Illustration 9)

Score Card

Good foot health results from intelligent decisions about exercise habits, foot care, and shoe selection. Good decisions can be seen in a person's footprints. Take the foot powder test and see how you score.

Cailliet, R. (1978) *Foot and Ankle Pain*. Philadelphia: F. A. Davis Company.